·Bartholomew·

MINI ATLAS
WORLD

· Bartholomew ·

MINI ATLAS
WORLD

Bartholomew
A Division of HarperCollins*Publishers*

Bartholomew
A Division of HarperCollins Publishers
Duncan Street, Edinburgh EH9 1TA

©HarperCollins Publishers 1993

First published by Bartholomew 1991
Revised editions 1992, 1993

ISBN 0 7028 2376 7 (paperback)
ISBN 0 7028 2375 9 (de luxe hardback)

Printed in Great Britain by Bartholomew, The Edinburgh Press Limited.

Details included in this atlas are subject to change without notice. Whilst every
effort is made to keep information up to date Bartholomew will not be
responsible for any loss, damage or inconvenience caused by inaccuracies in this
atlas. The publishers are always pleased to acknowledge any corrections brought
to their notice, and record their appreciation of the valuable services rendered in
the past by map users in assisting to maintain the accuracy of their publications

F/B6328

CONTENTS

viii-ix World Physical
x-xi World Political
xii-xiii World Time Zones
xiv-xv World Environment
xvi Key to Symbols

1 Arctic Ocean
2-3 North America
4-5 Canada, West
6-7 Canada, East
8-9 USA, West
10-11 USA, East
12 USA, Alaska
13 Canada Pacific
14-15 Lower Canada, USA North-East
16 Washington – New York – Boston
17 USA, South-East
18-19 USA, South-Central
20 USA, Pacific NW
21 USA, Pacific S
22 San Francisco & Los Angeles
23 Central Mexico
24-25 Mexico & Central America
26-27 Caribbean
28 South America
29 South America, South
30 South America, Central
31 South America, NE

32–33	South America, North
34	Central Argentina
35	South-East Brazil
36–37	Europe
38–39	Scandinavia
40–41	British Isles
42–43	England & Wales
44	Scotland, North
45	Ireland
46	Paris – Brussels – Ruhr
47	Alps
48–49	France
50–51	Spain & Portugal
52–53	Italy
54–55	The Balkans
56–57	Germany & Austria
58–59	East-Central Europe
60–61	European Russia, Ukraine & Baltic States
62	North Asia
63	Russian Federation, East
64–65	Russian Federation, West
66–67	South Asia
68–69	East Asia
70–71	South-East Asia
72–73	Central China
74	Japan & Korea
75	Central Japan
76–77	Indo-China & Singapore

Index

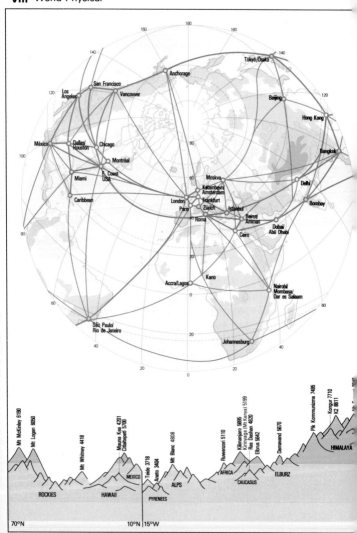

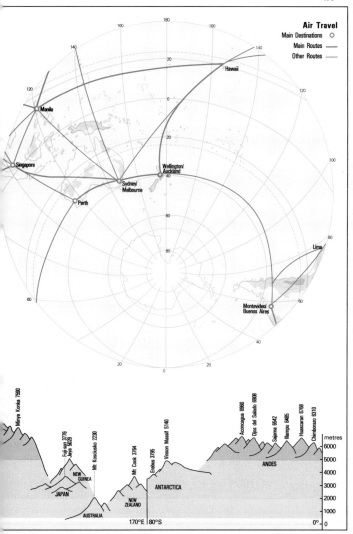

Air Travel

Main Destinations ○
Main Routes ——
Other Routes ——

180
160
160
140
140
120
120
100
80
60
40
20
0

Hawaii

Manila

Singapore

Sydney/
Melbourne

Wellington/
Auckland

Perth

Lima

Montevideo/
Buenos Aires

Minya Konka 7590
Fuji-san 3776
Jaya 5029
Mt Kosciusko 2230
Mt Cook 3764
Erebus 3795
Vinson Massif 5140
Aconcagua 6960
Ojos del Salado 6908
Sajama 6542
Illampu 6485
Huascarán 6768
Chimborazo 6310

metres
6000
5000
4000
3000
2000
1000
0

JAPAN
NEW GUINEA
AUSTRALIA
NEW ZEALAND
ANTARCTICA
ANDES

170°E
80°S
0°

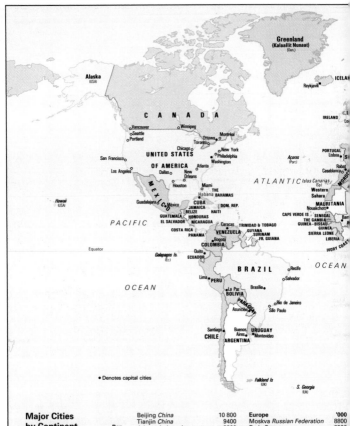

• Denotes capital cities

North and Central America	'000	South America	'000	Africa	'000
México *Mexico*	20 200	São Paulo *Brazil*	17 400	Cairo *Egypt*	9000
New York *USA*	16 200	Buenos Aires *Argentina*	11 500	Lagos *Nigeria*	7700
Los Angeles *USA*	11 900	Rio de Janeiro *Brazil*	10 700	Alexandria *Egypt*	3700
Chicago *USA*	7000	Lima *Peru*	6200	Kinshasa *Zaire*	3500
Philadelphia *USA*	4300	Santiago *Chile*	5000	Casablanca *Morocco*	3200
Detroit *USA*	3700	Bogotá *Colombia*	4900	Alger *Algeria*	3000
San Francisco *USA*	3700	Caracas *Venezuela*	4100	Cape Town *South Africa*	2300
Toronto *Canada*	3500	Belo Horizonte *Brazil*	3600	Abidjan *Ivory Coast*	2200
Dallas *USA*	3400	Pôrto Alegre *Brazil*	3100	Tarābulus *Libya*	2100
Guadalajara *Mexico*	3200	Recife *Brazil*	2500	Adis Abeba *Ethiopia*	1900
Houston *USA*	3000	Brasília *Brazil*	2400	Khartoum *Sudan*	1900
Monterrey *Mexico*	3000	Salvador *Brazil*	2400	Dar es Salaam *Tanzania*	1700
Montréal *Canada*	3000	Fortaleza *Brazil*	2100	Johannesburg *South Africa*	1700
Washington *USA*	2900	Curitiba *Brazil*	2000	Luanda *Angola*	1700
Boston *USA*	2800	Guayaquil *Ecuador*	1700	Maputo *Mozambique*	1600

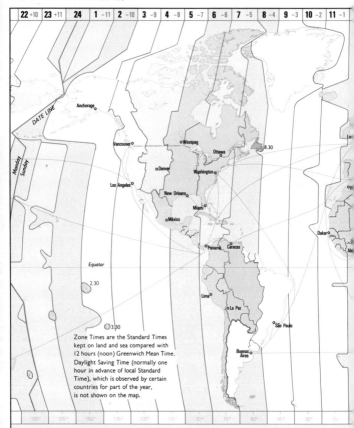

| 22 +10 | 23 +11 | 24 | 1 −11 | 2 −10 | 3 −9 | 4 −8 | 5 −7 | 6 −6 | 7 −5 | 8 −4 | 9 −3 | 10 −2 | 11 −1 |

DATE LINE

Monday
Sunday

Anchorage

Vancouver
Winnipeg
Ottawa
8.30

Denver
Washington

Los Angeles
New Orleans

Miami

México

Dakar

Panama
Caracas

Equator

2.30

Lima

3.30

La Paz

São Paulo

Zone Times are the Standard Times
kept on land and sea compared with
12 hours (noon) Greenwich Mean Time.
Daylight Saving Time (normally one
hour in advance of local Standard
Time), which is observed by certain
countries for part of the year,
is not shown on the map.

Buenos
Aires

180° 165° 150° 135° 120° 105° 90° 75° 60° 45° 30° 15°

Journey Times

Sail (via Cape)	**Steam** (via Cape)	**Steam** (via Suez)	**Supertanker**
164 days	43 days	30 days	(via Cape)
			28 days

Singapore ←

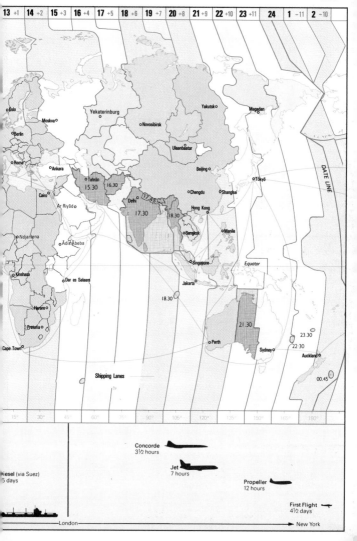

| 13 +1 | 14 +2 | 15 +3 | 16 +4 | 17 +5 | 18 +6 | 19 +7 | 20 +8 | 21 +9 | 22 +10 | 23 +11 | 24 | 1 −11 | 2 −10 |

Oslo
Moskva
Berlin
Roma
Ankara
Cairo
Ar Riyāḍ
Ndjamena
Ādīs Ābeba
Kinshasa
Dar es Salaam
Harare
Pretoria
Cape Town

Yekaterinburg
Novosibirsk
Ulaanbaatar
Yakutsk
Magadan
Beijing
Tōkyō
Tehrān 15.30
16.30
Delhi 17.45
Chengdu
Shanghai
17.30
18.30
Hong Kong
Bangkok
Manila
Singapore
Jakarta
18.30
21.30
Perth
Sydney
23.30
22.30
Auckland
00.45

DATE LINE

Equator

Shipping Lanes

15°   30°   45°   60°   75°   90°   105°   120°   135°   150°   165°   180°

Concorde
3½ hours

Jet
7 hours

Propeller
12 hours

First Flight
4½ days

Diesel (via Suez)
5 days

London

New York

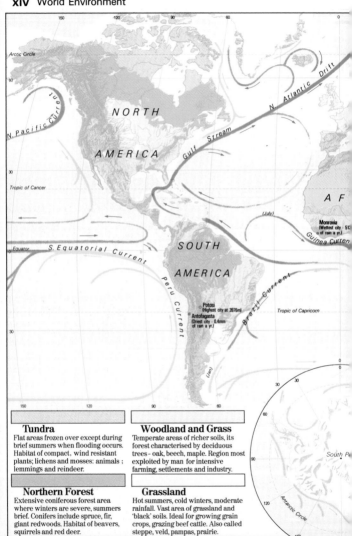

Tundra
Flat areas frozen over except during brief summers when flooding occurs. Habitat of compact, wind resistant plants; lichens and mosses: animals ; lemmings and reindeer.

Northern Forest
Extensive coniferous forest area where winters are severe, summers brief. Conifers include spruce, fir, giant redwoods. Habitat of beavers, squirrels and red deer.

Woodland and Grass
Temperate areas of richer soils, its forest characterised by deciduous trees- oak, beech, maple. Region most exploited by man for intensive farming, settlements and industry.

Grassland
Hot summers, cold winters, moderate rainfall. Vast area of grassland and 'black' soils. Ideal for growing grain crops, grazing beef cattle. Also called steppe, veld, pampas, prairie.

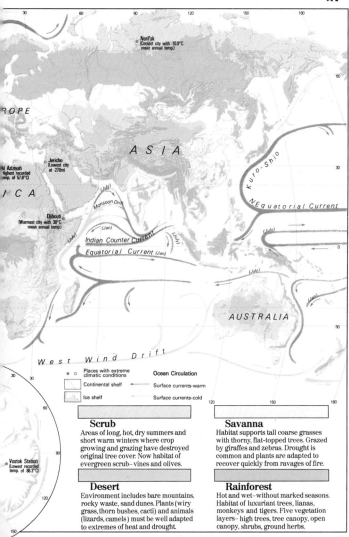

Scrub
Areas of long, hot, dry summers and short warm winters where crop growing and grazing have destroyed original tree cover. Now habitat of evergreen scrub–vines and olives.

Desert
Environment includes bare mountains, rocky waste, sand dunes. Plants (wiry grass, thorn bushes, cacti) and animals (lizards, camels) must be well adapted to extremes of heat and drought.

Savanna
Habitat supports tall coarse grasses with thorny, flat-topped trees. Grazed by giraffes and zebras. Drought is common and plants are adapted to recover quickly from ravages of fire.

Rainforest
Hot and wet–without marked seasons. Habitat of luxuriant trees, lianas, monkeys and tigers. Five vegetation layers– high trees, tree canopy, open canopy, shrubs, ground herbs.

BOUNDARIES

	International
	International under Dispute
	Cease Fire Line
	Autonomous or State
	Administrative
	Maritime (National)

LETTERING STYLES

CANADA	Independent Nation
FLORIDA	State, Province or Autonomous Region
Gibraltar (U.K.)	Sovereignty of Dependent Territory
Lothian	Administrative Area
LANGUEDOC	Historic Region
Lore **Vosges**	Physical Feature or Physical Region

TOWNS AND CITIES

Square Symbols denote capital cities. Each settlement is given a symbol according to its relative importance, with type size to match.

◘ ◉	**New York**	Major City
■ ●	**Montréal**	City
▫ ○	Ottawa	Small City
■ ●	**Québec**	Large Town
▫ ○	St John's	Town
▫ ○	Yorkton	Small Town
▫ ○	Jasper	Village
		Built-up-area

LAKE FEATURES

	Permanent
	Seasonal

OTHER FEATURES

	River
	Seasonal River
=	Pass, Gorge
	Dam, Barrage
	Waterfall, Rapid
	Aqueduct
	Reef
▲ 4231	Summit, Peak
. 217	Spot Height, Depth
	Well
◇	Oil Field
▲	Gas Field
Gas / Oil	Oil/Natural Gas Pipeline
Gemsbok Nat. Pk	National Park
.UR	Historic Site
	Main Railway
	Other Railway
	Under Construction
	Rail Tunnel
	Rail Ferry
	Canal
⊕	International Airport
✈	Other Airport

For pages 102-103, 104-105 only:

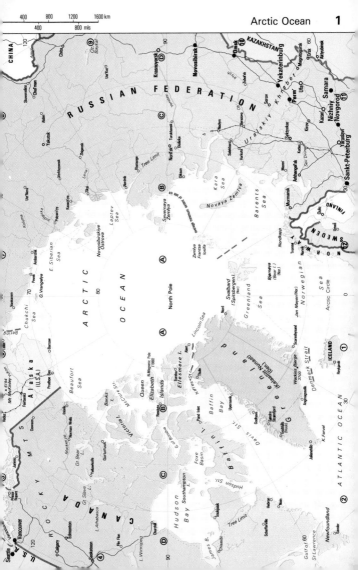

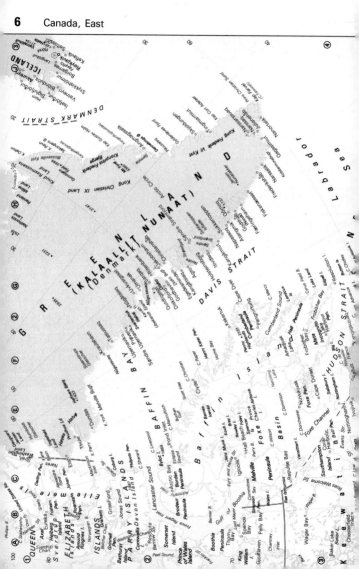

MANITOBA
ONTARIO
QUEBEC
NEW BRUNSWICK
MAINE
VERMONT
NEW HAMPSHIRE
NEW YORK
PENNSYLVANIA
OHIO
INDIANA
ILLINOIS
MICHIGAN
WISCONSIN
MINNESOTA
IOWA
James Bay
LAKE SUPERIOR
L. MICHIGAN
LAKE HURON
L. ONTARIO
LAKE ERIE
Georgian Bay
St Lawrence
Bay of Fundy
Delaware Bay
Winnipeg
Thunder Bay
Duluth
Minneapolis
St Paul
Milwaukee
Chicago
Detroit
Toronto
Buffalo
Cleveland
Pittsburgh
Columbus
Indianapolis
Philadelphia
New York
Boston
Providence
Hartford
Baltimore
Washington
Ottawa
Montréal
Québec
Sault Ste Marie
Sudbury
Fargo
Des Moines
Omaha
Lincoln
Madison
Lansing
Albany
Syracuse
Rochester
Saint John
Fredericton
Portland
Bangor
Augusta
Trois-Rivières
Sherbrooke
Hull
Kingston
Hamilton
London
Windsor
Toledo
Dayton
Akron
Harrisburg
Trenton
Newark
Wilmington
Dover
Annapolis
Gaspé
Sept-Îles
Anticosti Island
Chicoutimi
Baie-Comeau
Timmins
Kapuskasing
Kenora
Moosonee
Fort Albany
Attawapiskat
Chisasibi
Waskaganish
Big Trout Lake
Lansdowne House
Cat Lake
Red Lake
Bissett
Berens River
Norway House
Wabowden
Lake Nipigon
Peoria
Springfield
Cedar Rapids
Sioux Falls
Sioux City
Council Bluffs

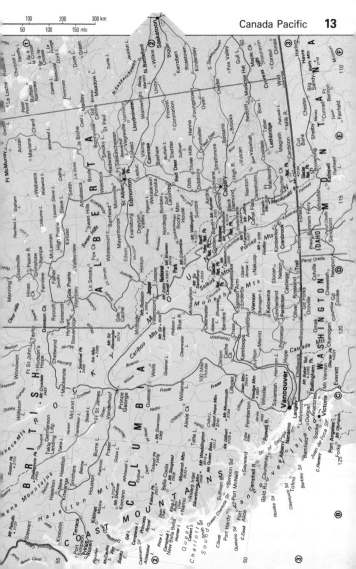

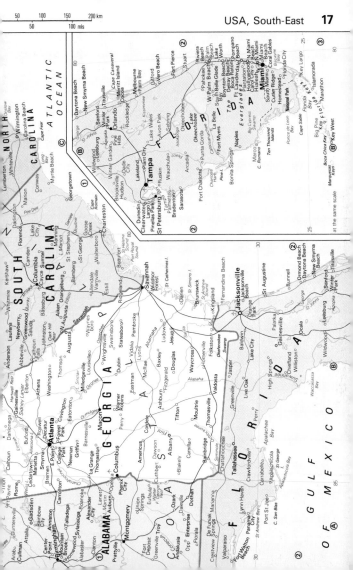

① ②

Wabash
Winamac
Logansport
Kentland
Lafayette
Attica
Frankfort
Kokomo
INDIANA
Indianapolis
Rockville
Crawfordsville
Spencer
Bloomfield
Bedford
Paoli
Jasper
Washington
Huntingburg
Owensboro

Danville
Terre Haute
Bloomington
Vincennes
Oakland City
Petersburg
Evansville
Henderson
KENTUCKY
Nashville
TENNESSEE

Gilman
Charleston
Marshall
Lawrenceville
Olney
Granville
Harrisburg
Madisonville
Hopkinsville
Clarksville
Dickson
Springfield
Gallatin

Kankakee
Bantoul
Urbana
Tuscola
Greenup
Flora
Salem
Fairfield
Carmi
West Frankfort
Benton
Marion
Eldorado
Carbondale
Vienna
Metropolis
Paducah
Murray
Mayfield
Martin
Dresden
Paris

Peru La Salle
Streator
Pontiac
Bloomington
Normal
El Paso
Champaign
Decatur
Pana
Vandalia
Centralia
Du Quoin
Chester
Perryville
Cape Girardeau
Chaffee
Charleston
Sikeston
Fulton
Dyersburg
Ripley

Kewanee
Galesburg
Monmouth
Peoria
Pekin
Lincoln
Springfield
Taylorville
Litchfield
Carlinville
Jerseyville
Alton
Collinsville
East St. Louis
St. Louis
Festus
Crystal City
Ste. Genevieve
Farmington
Frederick
Jackson
Dexter
Malden
Kennett
Blytheville
Osceola

ILLINOIS
ROCK RIVER
Monroe City
Hannibal

Rock Island
East Moline
Muscatine
Iowa City
Kalona
Washington
Mt. Pleasant
Burlington
Fort Madison
Keokuk
Kahoka
Quincy
Pittsfield
Rushville
Macomb
Jacksonville

Davenport
Des Moines
Oskaloosa
Ottumwa
Bloomfield
Centerville
Lancaster
Canton
Palmyra
New London

MISSOURI
St. Charles
Kirkwood
Washington
Union
St. James
Rolla
Waynesville
Lebanon
Marshfield
Mountain Grove
Willow Springs
West Plains
Mountain Home
Norfork L.
Batesville
Greers Ferry

Mexico
Columbia
Franklin
New Franklin
Fulton
Jefferson City
Tipton
Sedalia
California

Boston Mts
Ozark Plateau
L. of the Ozarks
Buffalo
Springfield
Ozark
Forsyth
Table Rock Res.
Branson
Harrison
Jasper

Des Moines
Indianola
Knoxville
Albia
Chariton
Osceola
Leon
Princeton
Trenton
Chillicothe
Brookfield
Marceline
Moberly

IOWA
Creston
Mount Ayr
Lamoni
Bethany
Cameron
Carrollton
Marshall
Warrensburg
Clinton

Thompson
Grand
Gallatin
Excelsior Springs
Liberty
Independence
Kansas City
Pleasant Hill
Harrisonville
Nevada
Stockton
Lamar
Carthage
Mount Vernon
Aurora
Monett
Springdale
Beaver L.
Rogers
Springdale
Fayetteville
The Cherokees

NEBRASKA
Columbus
Wahoo
Fremont
Omaha
Council Bluffs
Missouri Valley
Red Oak
Atlantic
Shenandoah
Clarinda
Hamburg
Tarkio
Maryville
Mound City
St. Joseph
Atchison
Leavenworth

Seward
Ashland
Lincoln
Big Blue
Crete
Beatrice
Auburn
Tecumseh
Falls City
Hiawatha
Holton
Turtle Creek Res.
Valley Falls
Topeka
Lawrence

Milford
Stromsburg
Geneva
Fairbury
Marysville
Manhattan
Junction City
Abilene
Salina

KANSAS
Belleville
Concordia
Clay Center
Emporia
Ottawa
Paola
Olathe
Osawatomie
Pomona Res.
Garnett
Iola
Chanute
Parsons
Pittsburg
Frontenac
Fort Scott
Columbus
Miami
Baxter Springs
Pryor
Claremore

McPherson
Florence
John Redmond Res.
Yates Center
Neodesha
Caney
Independence
Coffeyville
Nowata
Oologah
Collinsville
Owasso
Sapulpa
Tulsa

OKLAHOMA
Newton
El Dorado
Augusta
Wichita
Wellington
Winfield
Arkansas City
Caldwell
Blackwell
Ponca City
Tonkawa
Perry
Guthrie
Pawhuska
Bartlesville
Pawnee
Stillwater
Cushing

① ②

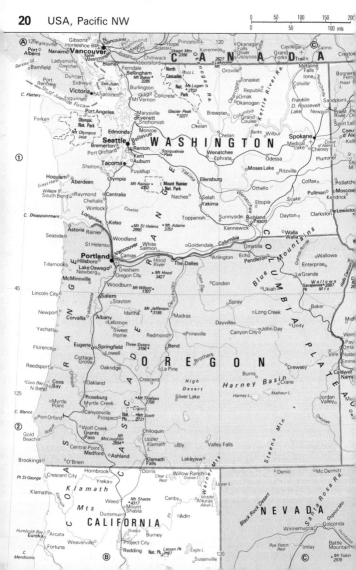

50 100 150 200 km
50 100 mls

PACIFIC OCEAN

NEVADA

CALIFORNIA

Dunsmuir Pt Adin
Arcata Shasta Burney
Eureka Weaverville Project City Lassen Pk.
Fortuna Redding Nat. Pk. 3187 Eagle L.
  Chester Susanville Winnemucca Golconda
Red Bluff Almanor Rye Patch Emigrant
  Resr Imlay Battle Pass
Paradise Quincy Lovelock Mountain Mt Tobin
Chico Feather Mid. Fork 2979
Oroville Humboldt 40
Grass L.
Williams Valley Reno Stillwater Ra. Shoshone Mtns
Yuba Colfax Sparks Fernley Eastgate Austin
City Auburn Donner Pass Fallon Summit Mtn
Roseville Virginia City Schurz 3188
Woodland Placerville Carson City Gabbs Wildcat Pk
Davis Tahoe Stewart Yerington Monitor Ra.
Sacramento Lake Walker Mt Jefferson
Carmichael Tahoe Hawthorne 3642
Vacaville S.Lake Tahoe Warm
Fairfield Sutter Creek Mono Coaldale Springs
Napa Galt Bridgeport Boundary
Vallejo Lodi San Andreas Peak 4005 Piper Pk Tonopah
San Rafael Antioch Sonora 2680 Goldfield
Berkeley Concord Stockton Yosemite White Mtn
Oakland Oakdale Nat. Park Peak 4342
San Francisco Alameda El Mono
Daly City Hayward Portola Beatty
San Mateo Livermore Modesto Bishop ②
Redwood City Turlock Mariposa Big Pine
Sunnyvale San Jose Gustine Merced Pine Flat Kings
Santa Clara Los Banos Madera Resr Canyon Independence
Los Gatos Los Banos Pinedale Nat. Park Lone Pine
Santa Cruz Gilroy Fresno Sequoia Mt Whitney Keeler
Watsonville Salinas Hanford Nat. Park 4418 Death
Pt Pinos King City Visalia Exeter Telescope Peak Valley
Monterey Gonzales Tulare Porterville 3368
  Coalinga Earlimart Inyokern
  Paso Robles Wasco Delano Johannesburg
Morro Bay Oildale Kern
San Luis Bakersfield Arvin
Obispo Mojave
Grover City Tehachapi Mts Barstow
Santa Tehachapi Pass Mojave Desert
Maria Lancaster Victorville Yermo
Lompoc Fillmore Mt San Bernardino
Santa Barbara Santa Paula San Antonio 3068 Redlands
Pt Conception Ventura Beverly Hills Burbank Pomona Beaumont
Santa Barbara Chan. Glendale Pasadena
San Miguel Santa Cruz Los Angeles Riverside San Jacinto
Channel Islands Santa Monica Palm Springs
  Torrance Anaheim Peak 3301
  Long Beach Santa Ana Palm
  Huntington Beach Laguna Beach Palomar Mtn
Santa Catalina San 1871 Vista
San Clemente Clemente Oceanside Escondido
Gulf of Carlsbad Ramona
Santa Catalina San Diego El
  Chula Vista National Cajon
  City Descanso
  Tijuana Tecate

Sacramento Valley
COAST RANGES
San Joaquin Valley
Diablo Range
Santa Lucia Range
SIERRA NEVADA
Panamint Range
Monterey Bay

USA, Hawaii

PACIFIC OCEAN

Ⓐ
Hanalei Kauai 1548 Kapaa
Mana Lihue
Kekaha Kaena Pt Kahuku Pt
Wahiawa Kailua
Oahu Kailua Kaneohe
  Waianae Honolulu
Kaunakakai Molokai Maui 3055
Lanai Lanai City Nat. Pk.
  Kahoolawe Kapaau
  Waimea Kealakekua Kailua
  Kailua Hawaii 4169 Kilauea
  Mauna Kea 4201 Crater
  Mauna Loa Pahala Pahoa
  Hawaii Volcanoes Nat. Park 1243
  Naalehu
  Ka Lae (South Cape)

Kauai Channel
Kaiwi Channel
Kalohi Chan.
Pailolo Chan.
Kealaikahiki Chan.
Alenuihaha Channel

USA, Hawaii
100 200 km
50 100 mls Ⓒ

20 N
160 155 Ⓑ

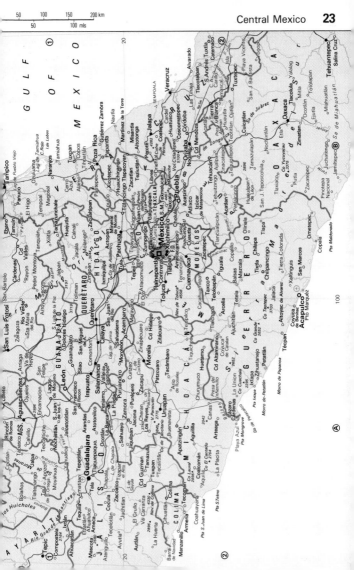

85

① Belle o Glade o Palm Beach *Grand* Ⓑ Marsh Harbour 75 Ⓖ
Naples o L.Worth *Great* S. Negril
F L O R I D A o Delray Beach o Freeport *Bahama* *Abaco* ① *Point*
Hollywood o Pompano Beach *Dunmore*
o Ft Lauderdale *Town* A Se
● **Miami** Nicholl's New o T
Town Providence Eleuthera L
Florida Bay □ Nassau A
25 Cat N
Key West *Florida Keys* o New Bight San Salvador T C
Marquesas Keys Kemps o Rum Cay I
Straits Bay *Great Exuma* C
of *Andros* Long Deadman's

Tropic of Cancer *Cay Sal* *Florida* Anguilla Cays *Bahama* *Island* Cay Acklins
Guanabacoa *Bank* *Bank* Ma
● **Habana** o Matanzas Ⓐ Ⓑ
② S.Antonio o o Güines Segua la Grande *Arch. de Camagüey* *Great Inagua*
de los Baños Santa L
Pinar del Rio o G.de Clara Morón Esmeralda Matthew Ma
Batabano o Cienfuegos C o Ciego o Nuevitas Town
de Ávila U Banes Sagua de Tánamo H
o Nueva Gerona B Camagüey Holguín o A
I.de la Juventud A Victoria ● Holguín o Baracoa I
(*I. de Pinos*) G *Jardines de* de las Tunas o Palma Soriano T
R *la Reina* Sta Cruz G.de Turquino ● Guantánamo Port-
20 del Sur Guacanayabo 2005 Santiago Cap-Haitien
U 'C.Cruz o Manzanillo T de Cuba H A I T I
Cayman Islands (U.K.) Little Cayman o R U *Windward Passage* Port-
Grand Cayman Cayman Brac E Anse au-Pr
C N d'Hainault o o La Massif de la Hotte Ja
A C H Gonâve
Y E o Les Cayes
③ M Montego Blue Mtn Pk Port
A Bay o 2256 c Antonio N
Swan I. N Savanna la Mar o Mandeville □ Kingston
(Hond.) **JAMAICA** Spanish ●
C Town

A *Pedro Cays*
R (*Jam.*)

I
B Brus Laguna B
Lag. de
o Caratasca *Caratasca*
H O N D U R A S E
④ Cabo Gracias B
Waspán o á Dios *Cayos Miskitos*
o Bonanza E
o La o Puerto Cabezas
Luz *I.de Providencia*
o Prinzapolca (*Col.*)
N o Rio Grande
I L.de A
C Perlas *I. del Maíz (Nic. & U.S.A.)*
A *I. de San Andrés (Col.)*
R o Bluefields
A
G San Juan
U *Sa Juan* del Norte Sta Riohacha
A *del* Marta o o
Viejo o *Marta* Ciénaga
C O S T A Alajuela Barranquilla ● o 5775
10 o Heredia o Limón Soledad o *Sa Nevada* Valledup
o San *de Sta Marta*
José Cartagena ● o Sabanalarga
R I C A *Volcán Barú* Colón S. Onofore o o Plato
Chiriquí 3477 *Golfo del* o Sincelejo El Banco
⑤ B. de o 80 *Darién* Ⓒ
Coronado o Palmar Sur P A N A M A Ⓑ C O L O M B I A
o La Chorrera Panamá

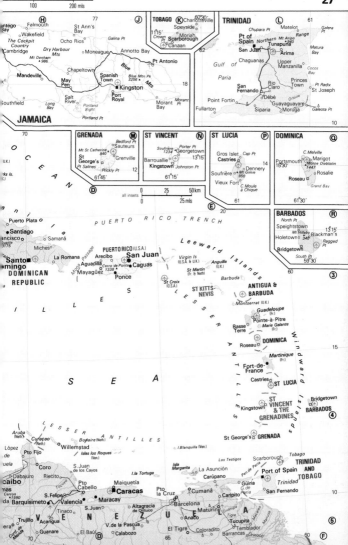

Scale

200 400 600 km
100 200 300 mls

Map Labels

ARGENTINA

BRAZIL

URUGUAY

ATLANTIC OCEAN

Co. del Toro 6380
Grl Manuel Belgrano 6250
Grl. La Rioja
La Serena
Coquimbo
Rivadavia
Jáchal
Sumampa
Reconquista
Goya
Mercedes
Paso de los Libres
Cruz Alta
Sta Maria
Cachoeira do Sul

La Rioja
S. Agustín
Cruz del Eje
L. Mar Chiquita
Vera
Santa
Fe
Ibicuí
Uruguaiana
Alegrete
Artigas
do Livramento
Bagé

Punitaqui
Ovalle
Illapel
Los Vilos
6282
Olivares 4960
S. Juan
Mercedario
5410
Córdoba
Va Dolores
Rafaela
S.Francisco
Concordia
Rivera
Durazno
Melo

Viña del Mar
Valparaíso
Quillota
S.Antonio
Aconcagua 6960
Mendoza
Alta Gracia
Santa Fe
Paraná
La Paz
Concepción
Salto
Tacuarembó
Treinta y Tres
Minas

S.Bernardo
Rancagua
Pichilemu
Santiago
Tupungato 6800
Vol.Maipo 5290
S.Luis
Villa María
Cda de Gómez
Rosario
San Nicolás
Pergamino
MERCEDES
Canelones
Florida
Trinidad
Chuí

Curicó
Constitución
Talca
S. Rafael
Vol.Peteroa 4090
Mendoza
Mercedes
Luis
Río Cuarto
Venado Tuerto
Rufino
Junín
Buenos
Aires
Avellaneda
La Plata
Maldonado
Punta del Este
Rocha
Montevideo

Linares
S.Carlos
Cauquenes
Vol.Domuyo 4800
Bardas Blancas
Telén
Grl Alvear
Lincoln
Chivilcoy
Buenos
Chascomús

Tomé
ahuano
cepción
Coronel
Chillán
Los
Angeles
La Pampa
Grl Pico
Sta Rosa
Trenque
Lauquén
Pehuajó
Las Flores
Dolores
Rio de la Plata

Lebu
Carahue
Temuco
Angol
Vol.Lonquimay
Vol.Llaima 3124
Zapala
Neuquén
Guamini
Carhué
Olavarría
Azul
Ayacucho
Va Gesell

Valdivia
La Unión
Osorno
Villarrica
Loncoche
Toltén
Vol.Lanín 3740
Grl Roca
El Chocón
Choele
Choel
Bahía Blanca
Tres Arroyos
Tandil
Balcarce
Necochea
Miramar
Mar del Plata

Pto Varas
uerto Montt
Ancud
Chiloé
Castro
Achao
Nahuel Huapi
S.Carlos de
Bariloche
El Bolsón
Paso Limay
Maquinchao
RÍO
NEGRO
S.Antonio
Oeste
Valcheta
Viedma
Punta Alta
Claromecó
Carmen de Patagones
Bahía Blanca
40

G.de
Corcovado
Esquel
Melimoyú 2400
Chubut
Las Plumas
Trelew
Gaimán
Rawson
Golfo
San Matías
Pto Pirámides
Pto Madryn

piélago
de las
ones
Pto Aisén
Coihaique
L. Musters
L.C Huapi
Sarmiento
Golfo
San Jorge
Camarones
C.Dos Bahías
Comodoro Rivadavia
Caleta Olivia
ATLANTIC
OCEAN
45

San Valentín 4058
L. Buenos
Aires
L. Carrera
L. Cochrane
Colonia
Las Heras
C.Tres Puntas
Deseado
Pta Médanosa

O'Higgins
S. Martín
S. Julián
Santa Cruz
5

G. de Penas
campana
meralda
re de Dios
Hanover
Lautaro 3380
Vol.
Murallón
L. Viedma
Sta Cruz
Calafate
Río
Turbio
Bahía Grande
Río Gallegos
FALKLAND ISLANDS
(ISLAS MALVINAS)
(U.K.)
Jason Is
West Falkland
C. Dolphin
Weddell
East Falkland
Stanley
Falkland Sd
50

Arch. de la
Reina Adelaida
Pto Natales
Pen de
Muñoz Gamero
Pen. de
Brunswick
Punta Arenas
Río Grande
Isla Grande
de Tierra
del Fuego
Tierra del Fuego
Beauchene Is
at the same scale
Shag Rocks
South Georgia
(U.K.)
C. Alexandra
Grytviken

Desolación
Santa Inés
Londonderry
Hoste
Navarino
Ushuaia
I. de los Estados
Is Wollaston
C. de Hornos
(C.Horn)
C. Disappointment

S.Diego Ramírez

70 75 65 60 55 50 45 40 35

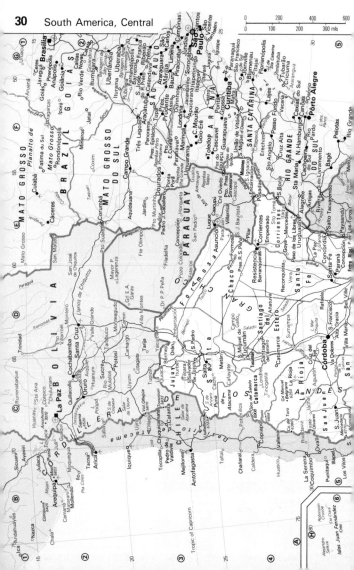

200 400 600 km
100 200 300 mls
Equator
Tropic of Capricorn
ATLANTIC
OCEAN
BRAZIL
PARÁ
MARANHÃO
CEARÁ
PIAUÍ
RIO GRANDE DO NORTE
PARAÍBA
PERNAMBUCO
ALAGOAS
SERGIPE
BAHIA
TOCANTINS
GOIÁS
MINAS GERAIS
ESPÍRITO SANTO
SÃO PAULO
Rio de Janeiro
Belém
São Luís
Fortaleza (Ceará)
Teresina
Natal
João Pessoa
Recife (Pernambuco)
Olinda
Maceió
Aracajú
Salvador (Bahia)
Brasília
Goiânia
Belo Horizonte
Vitória
São Paulo
Curitiba
Niterói
Santos
São Vicente
Campinas
Salinópolis
Bragança
Capanema
Abaetetuba
Cametá
Tucuruí
Marabá
Imperatriz
Alcântara
Pinheiro
Rosário
Parnaíba
Camocim
Acaraú
Itapipoca
Caucaia
Sobral
Sta Quitéria
Piripiri
Canindé
Aracati
Nova Russas
Quixadá
Morada N.
Crateús
Castelo
Campo Maior
Caxias
Codó
Coroatá
Chapadinha
Bacabal
Monção
Grajaú
Pto Franco
Carolina
Araguaína
Balsas
Floriano
Oeiras
Picos
Mombaça
Tauá
Acopiara
Iguatu
J.do Norte
Crato
Areia Branca
Macaú
Mossoró
Caicó
Patu
Sousa
Patos
Cabedelo
Campina Grande
Sa Talhada
Salgueiro
Ouricurí
Limoeiro
Caruaru
Palmares
Jaboatão
Barreiros
Garanhuns
Palmeira dos Ind.
Paulistana
Petrolina
Juàzeiro
S.Raimundo Nonato
Cach. de P. Afonso
Arapiraca
Penedo
Propriá
Sen.do Bonfim
Lagarto
Estância
Barra
Jacobina
Serrinha
R.deJacuipe
Alagoinhas
Feira de S.
Cachoeira
Castro Alves
Iaçu
Ibotirama
Barreiras
Bom Jesus da Lapa
Chapada Diamantina
Valença
Jequié
Ipiaú
Caetité
Vitória da Conquista
Itabuna
Ilhéus
Itapetinga
Canavieiras
Belmonte
Pôrto Seguro
Itamaraju
Nanuque
São Mateus
Linhares
Colatina
Vila Velha
Cachoeiro de Itapemirim
Januária
Porteirinha
Salinas
Montes Claros
Araçuaí
Sa do Chifre
Serra do Espinhaço
Teófilo Otôni
Diamantina
Gov. Valadares
Cnl Fabriciano
Itabira
Caratinga
Manhuaçu
Cariacica
Ponte Nova
Con. Lafaiete
Carangola
Barbacena
Itaperuna
Juiz de Fora
S.João da Barra
Campos
Nova Friburgo
Petrópolis
Magé
Volta Redonda
Barra Mansa
Sa de Mantiqueira
Lavras
S.João del Rei
Divinópolis
Sete Lagoas
Curvelo
Corinto
Pirapora
Paracatu
João Pinheiro
Patos de Minas
Araxá
Uberaba
Uberlândia
Araguari
Catalão
Goiandira
Itumbiara
Caldas Novas
Rio Verde
Anápolis
Pirenópolis
Jaraguá
Ceres
Formosa
Uruaçu
Aruanã
Goiás
São Francisco
Iturama
Barragem Agua Vermelha
Barragem de São Simão
Rubinéia
Ferandópolis
S.José do R.Prêto
Barretos
Franca
Passos
Ribeirão Prêto
Poços de Caldas
Catanduva
Araraquara
São Carlos
Marília
Bauru
Limeira
Piracicaba
Jundiaí
Sorocaba
Itapetininga
Itapeva
Jacarezinho
Itararé
Juquiá
Itanhaém
Iguape
Castro
Guarapuava
Paranaguá
Mafra
São Francisco do Sul
I. de Marajó
B. de Marajó
C. Maguarinho
B. de São Marcos
Rocas
I. Fernando de Noronha
Pta do Calcanhar
B. de T. os Santos
Ilha do Bananal
Tocantins
Araguaia
Parnaíba
São Francisco
Grande
Paranã
Contas
Jequitinhonha
Doce
Velhas
Paranaíba
Gurupi
Pindaré
Capim
Pará
Plat. do Borborema

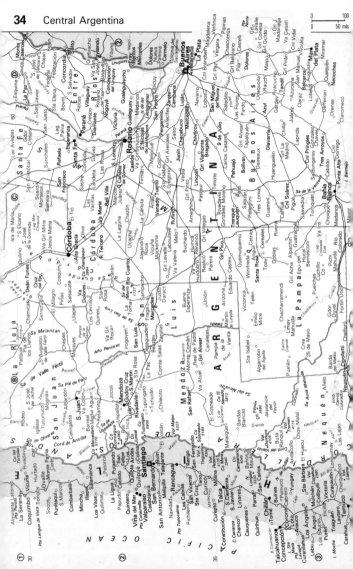

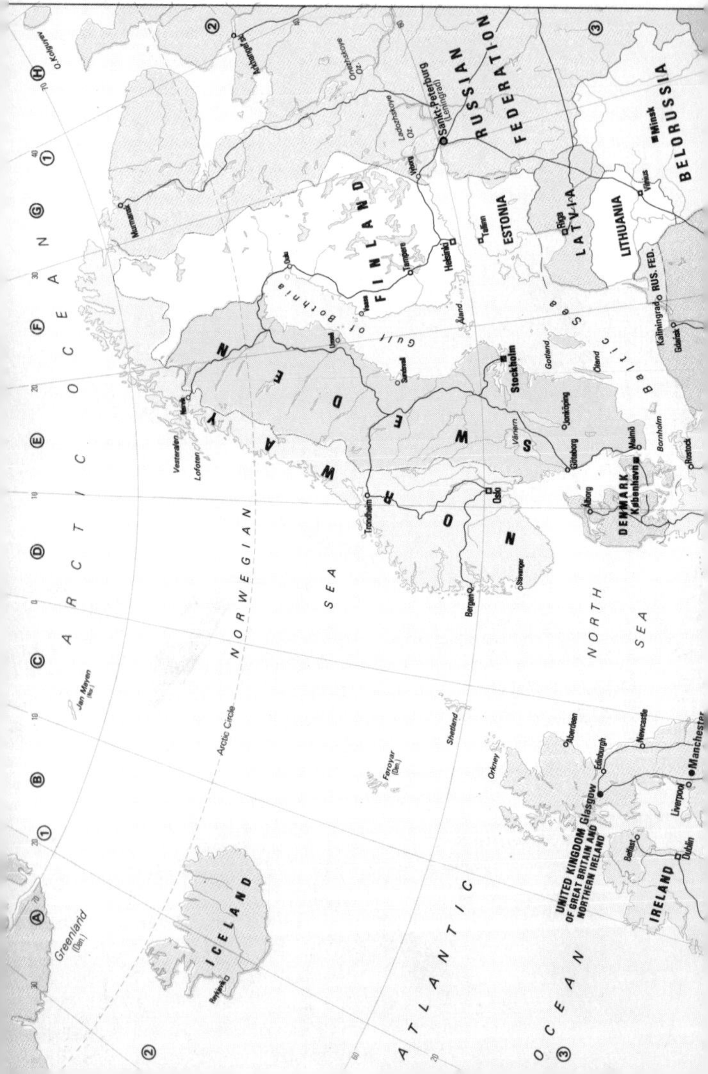

ARCTIC OCEAN

Greenland (Dan.)

ICELAND

Jan Mayen (Nor.)

Arctic Circle

NORWEGIAN SEA

Faeroyar (Dan.)

ATLANTIC OCEAN

Shetland

Orkney

Vesteralen
Lofoten

N O R W A Y

S V E R I G E
S W E D E N

Trondheim

Bergen

Oslo

Stavanger

Kristiansand

NORTH SEA

Stockholm

Göteborg

Öland
Gotland

Vänern

Norrköping

Malmö

Bornholm

DENMARK
København
Ålborg

UNITED KINGDOM
OF GREAT BRITAIN AND
NORTHERN IRELAND

Glasgow
Edinburgh
Newcastle
Manchester
Liverpool
Leeds
Aberdeen

IRELAND
Dublin
Belfast

FINLAND
Helsinki
Tampere

Gulf of Bothnia

Åland

Murmansk

Sankt-Peterburg
(Leningrad)

RUSSIAN FEDERATION

ESTONIA
Tallinn

LATVIA
Riga

LITHUANIA
Vilnius

Kaliningrad RUS. FED.

BELORUSSIA
Minsk

BALTIC SEA

Gdańsk

O. Kolguyev

O. Kildin

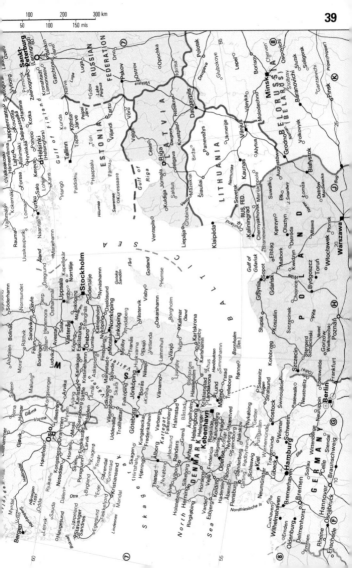

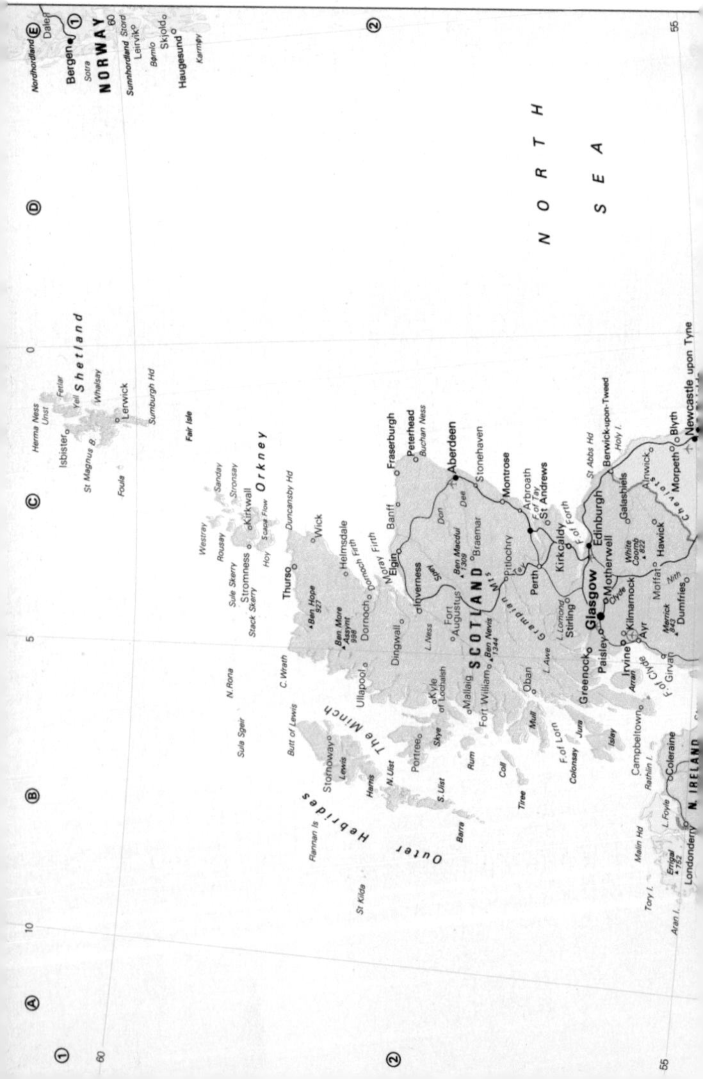

NORWAY

Nordlandshol o Dalen
Bergen o
Sogne
Sunnhordland Stord
Leirvik o
Siento
Skjold o
Haugesund
Karmøy

Herma Ness
Unst
Yell Shetland
Isbister o
St Magnus B.
Whalsay
Foula
Lerwick
Sumburgh Hd

Fair Isle

N O R T H   S E A

Westray
Sanday
Stronsay
Rousay
Stromness o Kirkwall
Sule Skerry
Hoy Scapa Flow
Stack Skerry Duncansby Hd

Orkney

N. Rona
C. Wrath
Thurso
Wick
o Helmsdale

Sula Sgeir
Blunt of Lewis
Stornoway o
Lewis
Ullapool
Dingwall o
Inverness
Ben More
917
Ben Wyvis
988
L. Ness
Fort Augustus
S C O T L A N D

Flannan Is
Harris
N. Uist
Portree o
Skye
Kyle of Lochalsh
Ben Macdui
4300
Ben Nevis
1344
Grampian
Braemar
Pitlochry
Perth
Dee
Don
Banff
Fraserburgh
Peterhead
Buchan Ness
Aberdeen
Stonehaven
Montrose
Arbroath
Ft of Tay
St. Andrews

St Kilda
S. Uist
Barra
Mallaig o
Fort William
Rum
Eigg
Coll
Tiree
Mull
Oban
L. Lomond
Stirling o
Kirkcaldy
F. of Forth
Edinburgh
St Abbs Hd
Galashiels
Berwick-upon-Tweed
Holy I.

Outer Hebrides

The Minch

Jura
Colonsay
Islay
Campbeltown o
Rathlin I.
Greenock o
Paisley o
Glasgow
Motherwell
Kilmarnock
Irvine o
Ayr
Girvan o
Merrick
843
Dumfries
White
Cheviot Hills
Morpeth o
Blyth
Newcastle upon Tyne
Hawick
Moffat
Nith
Cheviot
823

N. IRELAND

Tory I.
Errigal
752
Aran I.
Main Hd
L. Foyle
Londonderry o
Coleraine
Malin Hd

50   100   150   200 km
50   100 mls

③

NETHERLANDS
's-Gravenhage (Den Haag) Rotterdam
Antwerpen Mechelen
Brugge Gent Bruxelles/Brussel
Oostende Kortrijk Aalst
Vlissingen Zeebrugge
BELGIE/BELGIQUE
Dunkerque Lille Tournai Mons
Calais St-Omer Roubaix
Boulogne Béthune Valenciennes
Montreuil Arras Cambrai
PICARDIE
Abbeville Amiens St-Quentin Laon
Neufchâtel Beauvais Soissons
Dieppe Compiègne Château-Thierry
Le Tréport Rouen Senlis Meaux
Fécamp Bolbec Pontoise Paris
Le Havre Elbeuf Versailles
Deauville Louviers Rambouillet Provins
Honfleur Évreux Dreux Étampes Melun
Lisieux Fontainebleau
Bayeux Caen Chartres
Cherbourg NORMANDIE
St-Lô Argentan Alençon
Valognes Coutances
pte de Barfleur
C. de la Hague Granville Domfront
Alderney Guernsey St-Hélier Jersey Mont-St-Michel
Channel Is. Golfe de St-Malo St-Malo Fougères
Sark Dinan Dinard
St-Brieuc
Roscoff Morlaix Lannion Guingamp
Brest Châteaulin Carhaix

Harwich Felixstowe
Lowestoft
Great Yarmouth
Norwich Newmarket
King's Lynn Cambridge
Peterborough Ipswich Colchester
Boston Chelmsford
Grimsby Lincoln Bedford Southend
London
Doncaster Nottingham Luton Windsor
Sheffield Leicester Northampton Maidstone
Derby Coventry Oxford Reading Canterbury
Stoke-on-Trent Gloucester Guildford Crawley Dover
Manchester Birmingham Swindon Winchester Folkestone
Warrington Wolverhampton Worcester Bristol Southampton Brighton Hastings
Chester Shrewsbury Bath Salisbury Portsmouth Eastbourne
Crewe Hereford Weston-super-Mare Bournemouth Isle of Wight
ENGLAND
WALES Cardiff Newport Taunton Weymouth
Aberystwyth Brecon Swansea Barnstaple Exeter
Bangor Carmarthen Torquay
Holyhead Pwllheli Pembroke Plymouth
Anglesey St David's Hd Dartmoor
Cardigan Bay Bristol Chan. Newquay Truro
Fishguard Lundy Falmouth
Penzance Land's End Lizard Pt
Isles of Scilly

English Channel

Liverpool Birkenhead
Blackpool Preston Bolton Bradford Leeds York Hull
Southport Bury Huddersfield Harrogate Scarborough Flamborough Hd
Lancaster Kendal Morecambe
Barrow-in-Furness
Douglas Isle of Man
IRISH SEA

Newry Dundalk Drogheda
Dublin Baile Átha Cliath
Dún Laoghaire Bray Wicklow
Navan Monaghan Cavan Longford Mullingar Arklow
Roscommon Athlone Tullamore Portlaoise Carlow
REP. OF IRELAND Gorey Rosslare
Galway Ennis Nenagh Thurles Kilkenny Wexford
Tipperary Clonmel Waterford
Limerick Mallow Dungarvan Youghal
Tralee Killarney Cork Old Hd of Kinsale
Dingle B. Bantry C. Clear

St George's Chan.

Bangor Conwy Llandudno Snowdon
Wrexham

Ballina Castlebar Boyle L. Corrib L. Ree
Westport Claremorris L. Mask Shannon
Achill I. Clew B. Aran Is. Galway B.
Slyne Hd Kilrush Kenmare R.
Carnsore Pt
Start Pt
Prawle Pt

Trent Ouse Wash The
Severn Wye Avon

N O R T H   S E A

① 56
② 54
Ⓔ
Ⓓ 0
Ⓒ 2
Ⓑ
Ⓐ 6

West Side
Cleeton
Ravenspurn
Rough
Yar. Sta.
Ns. Sta.

Mablethorpe
Louth
Grimsby
Humber
Spurn Hd
Hornsea
Withernsea
Hull
Bridlington
Flamborough Hd
Humberside
Gt Driffield
Goole
Scarborough
Doncaster
East Retford
Gainsborough
Rotherham
Sheffield
Whitby
Yorkshire Moors Nat Park
Pickering
Malton
York
Selby
Wakefield
Leeds
Barnsley
S. Yorks
Huddersfield
W. Yorks
Harrogate
Ripon
Northallerton
Thirsk
N. Yorkshire
Bradford
Halifax
Rochdale
Oldham
C
Manchester
Gt Man.
Stockport
Salford
Warrington
St Helens
Merseyside
Birkenhead
Liverpool
Southport
Blackpool
Fleetwood
Preston
Blackburn
Burnley
Bolton
Wigan
Lancashire
Lancaster
Morecambe
Nat Park
Settle
P e n n i n e s
Skipton
The Dales
Ure
Ouse
Richmond
Darlington
Barnard Castle
Bishop Auckland
Durham
Gateshead
Newcastle upon Tyne
Sunderland
Tyne and Wear
Sth. Shields
Tynemouth
Blyth
Morpeth
Hartlepool
Redcar
Middlesbrough
Cleveland
Stockton
Nat Park
North York Moors

Alnwick
Northumberland Nat Park
Hexham
Alston
Haltwhistle
Longtown
Carlisle
Eden
Penrith
Appleby
Ullswater
Nat Park
Lake District
Keswick
Cumbria
Derwent W.
Scafell Pike 977
Windermere
Kendal
Ulverston
Barrow-in-Furness
St Bees Hd
Whitehaven
Workington
Maryport
Solway Firth

Dumfries and Galloway
Langholm
Lockerbie
Annan
Dumfries
Castle Douglas
Kirkcudbright
Wigtown B.
Newton Stewart
Galloway
Merrick 2764
Wigtown
Whithorn
Pt of Ayre
Isle of Man
Ramsey
Snaefell 2034
Douglas
Castletown
Port Erin
Calf of Man
Peel

B o r d e r s
Selkirk
Hawick
Jedburgh
Kelso
Teviot
Galashiels
Duns
Eyemouth
St Abb's Hd
Coldstream
Tweed
Berwick-upon-Tweed
Holy I.
Farne Is.
Farne Deep
Belford
Wooler
Tweed
Moorfoot Hills
Peebles
Moffat
Thornhill
Sanquhar
Cumnock
Lanark
Motherwell
Hamilton
Coatbridge
Glasgow
Paisley
Kilmarnock
Prestwick
Troon
Ayr
Maybole
Girvan
Ballantrae
Stranraer
Loch Ryan
Luce B.
Corsewall Pt

S t r a t h c l y d e
C l y d e
Firth of Clyde
Irvine
Ardrossan
Saltcoats
Largs
Brodick
Arran
Bute
Rothesay
Dunoon
Helensburgh
Dumbarton
Greenock
Port Glasgow

C e n t r a l
Stirling
Falkirk
L o t h i a n
Livingston
Edinburgh
Firth of Forth
Bathgate
F i f e
Kirkcaldy
Dunfermline
Kinross
Glenrothes
Cupar
Fife Ness
North Berwick
Haddington
Dunbar

Callander
L.Katrine
L.Lomond
Arrochar
Inveraray
Tarbert
Loch Fyne
J u r a
Islay
Colonsay
Gigha
Kintyre
Campbeltown
Mull of Kintyre
Ailsa Craig
Fair Hd

I R I S H   S E A
North Channel
Belfast
Lisburn
Bangor
Newtownards
D o w n
Downpatrick
Strangford L.
Dundrum B.
Newcastle
Larne
Carrickfergus
Holywood
Donaghadee

Holyhead
Anglesey
Llandudno
Gt Ormes Hd
Liverpool Bay

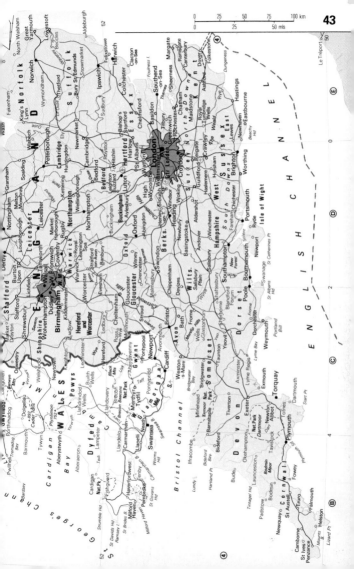

0 25 50 75 100
0 25 50 mls

Shetland

Unst
Hermaness Hd
Fetlar
Yell
Whalsay
Brae
Hillswick
St. Magnus Bay
Papa Stour
Scalloway
Foula
Fitful Hd
Sumburgh Hd
Fair Isle
Bressay
Noss
Lerwick
Gruthess
Isbister
The Faither

NORTH SEA

Long Forties

Buchan Deep

Orkney

N. Ronaldsay
Sanday
Stronsay
Shapinsay
Westray
Rousay
Eday
Kirkwall
Birsay
Mainland
Stromness
Scapa Flow
Hoy
S. Ronaldsay
Pentland Firth

Scotland North

Burray
Hoy
S. Ronaldsay
Pentland Firth
Duncansby Hd
John o' Groats
Dunnet Hd
Wick
Lybster
Thurso
Helmsdale
Brora
Golspie
Dornoch
Tain
Dingwall
Alness
Cromarty
Inverness
Nairn
Forres
Elgin
Lossiemouth
Keith
Huntly
Banff
Fraserburgh
Peterhead
Buchan Ness
Girdle Ness
Aberdeen
Stonehaven
Montrose
Arbroath
Dundee
St Andrews
North Berwick
Edinburgh
Haddington
Dunbar
St Abb's Hd
Eyemouth

Grampian
Don
Dee
Braemar
Ballater
Banchory
Brechin
Forfar
Blairgowrie
Perth
Crieff
Callander
Stirling
Falkirk
Glasgow
Paisley
Greenock
Dumbarton
Helensburgh

Western Isles
Lewis
Stornoway
Harris
Tarbert
North Uist
Benbecula
South Uist
Barra
Castlebay
Isle of Skye
Portree
Raasay
Rum
Eigg
Muck
Canna
Coll
Tiree
Tobermory
Mull
Staffa
Iona
Colonsay
Jura
Islay
Port Ellen

Ben Hope
Ben More Assynt
Ben Dearg
Ben Wyvis
Ben Attow
Ben Nevis
Monadhliath Mts
Cairngorms
Ben Macdui
Grampian Mts
Ben Lawers
Loch Ness
Loch Lomond

HIGHLAND
SCOTLAND
TAYSIDE
CENTRAL
FIFE
LOTHIAN

C. Wrath
Durness
Tongue
Loch Laxford
Lochinver
Ullapool
Gairloch
Mallaig
Fort William
Oban

25 50 75 100 km
25   50 mils

Ⓐ 10 Ⓑ 8 Ⓒ 6 Ⓓ

Mull of
Oa
Campbeltown
Rathlin I.
Main
Hd
Carndonagh
Portrush Fair
Ballycastle Hd Mull of
Tory I. Sheep Haven Coleraine Ballymoney Kintyre
L. Swilly Inishowen L. Foyle Limavady Antrim North Channel
Bloody Foreland Buncrana Londonderry Ballymena Larne
Errigal Ballymena
Aran I. +752 Strabane Magherafelt Belfast L.
Donegal Londonderry Sperrin Mts Bangor
Gweebarra B. Lifford Antrim Belfast Newtownards
Glenties Blue Stack Newton NORTHERN IRELAND Comber
Rossan Pt Donegal Mts +676 Stewart Omagh Tyrone Neagh L. Lisburn Strangford
Killybegs U L S T E R Lurgan Lough
Donegal Portadown Down
Donegal Bay Bundoran Ballyshannon Fintona Armagh Banbridge Downpatrick
Melvin Erne Enniskillen Armagh Newcastle Mourne
Inishmurray Fermanagh Monaghan Newry Mts Dundrum B.
Sligo B. Upper Clones Monaghan Warrenpoint
Bertrace Hd Sligo Leitrim Lower Erne Cootehill Dundalk
Erris Hd Ballycastle Ballina Mts Allen Oughter Carrickmacross Dundalk Bay
Belmullet of Sligo Cavan Louth Dunany Hd
Inishkea Blacksod B. Mts of Nephin 807 L. Conn Swinford Cavan Sheelin Ardee Drogheda
Achill Clare Mayo Castlebar Ballaghaderreen Carrick on Shannon Kells Balbriggan
Clew Boyle Boderg Longford Bowna U. Anaim Swords
Bay Westport M A Y O Claremorris Roscommon Meath Trim
Inishturk Mask Castlerea Derravaragh Dublin
Inishbofin C O N N A U G H T Ballinrobe Roscommon Longford Mullingar Royal Canal (Baile Atha Cliath)
Inishshark Mts of L. Corrib Tuam Athlone Westmeath L. Ennell Dún Laoghaire
Slyne Hd Connemara Clifden Galway Ballinasloe Clara Kildare Bray
Berraghboy B. Kilkieran B. Galway Loughrea R E P U B L I C Offaly Portarlington Naas Kippure Greystones
Inishmore Aran Is Gort O F Banagher Birr Port Athy Wicklow +754 Wicklow
Hags Hd Ennistimon Clare Ballyvaghan Roscrea Laoise Carlow Mts Arklow
Liscannor B. Inishmaan L E I N S T E R
Miltown Scariff Lough Templemore Carlow Gorey
Malbay Milltown Ennis Killaloe Derg I R E L A N D Muine Bheag
Kilkee Malbay Nenagh Thurles Kilkenny Enniscorthy Cahore Pt
Loop Hd Kilrush Limerick Tipperary Kilkenny Thomastown Wexford
Mouth of the Shannon Foynes Rathkeale Cashel Carrick- New Wexford
Listowel Limerick Tipperary Cahir on-Suir Ross Rosslare
Tralee Bay Abbeyfeale Newcastle W. Rath Luirc Clonmel Waterford Carnsore Pt
Tralee Castleisland Newmarket Mitchelstown M U N S T E R Comeragh Waterford
Dingle Kerry Fermoy Mts Dungarvan Tramore Hook
Blasket Killarney Boggeragh Mallow Blackwater Waterford Harb. Hd
MacGillycuddys 1041 Mts Mine Hd
Reeks Macroom Cork Youghal Harb.
Cahersiveen Kenmare Passage Cobh
Sneem River Bandon West
Caha Mts Kinsale
Dursey Bantry Dunmanway Old Head
Clonakilty of Kinsale
Mizen Hd Bantry Bay Skibbereen
Roaringwater B. Baltimore
C. Clear
Fastnet Kinsale
Rock

St George's Channel

54

Ⓐ 10 Ⓑ 8 Ⓒ 6 Ⓓ
①
②
③

Ⓐ 5 Barnstaple
Taunton Ⓑ ENGLAND
Bude Salisbury Guildford Maidstone
Newquay Winchester Crawley Canterbury
① Exeter Bournemouth Southampton Brighton Dover Folkestone
Dartmoor Weymouth Portsmouth Hastings
Penzance Truro Plymouth Torquay Isle of Wight Eastbourne Cal St-Or
50 Falmouth Prawle Pt Boulogne
Isles of Scilly Land's End
Lizard Pt English Channel Montreuil Abt

Le Tréport
C. de la Hague Pte de Barfleur Dieppe Amien
Alderney Cherbourg Le Havre Fécamp Neufchâtel
Guernsey Sark Valognes Bolbec Mont
Channel Is St-Lô Deauville Rouen B
(To U.K.) St Helier Bayeux Seine Elbeuf
Jersey Caen Lisieux Louviers
Golfe de St-Malo Coutances Evreux Mantes
Roscoff St-Malo N O R M A N D E Versailles
Brest Morlaix Dinan Granville Mont- Argentan Dreux Rambouillet
I. d'Ouessant St-Brieuc St-Michel Domfront Chartres Etampes
Châteaulin Carhaix Fougères Alençon Fontain
Plouguer Loudéac Mayenne A
Quimper Pontivy Rennes Vitré M A I N E R
Concarneau Quimperlé Laval Le Mans Châteaudun Orléans
② Lorient Ploërmel M A I N E Vendôme O R L É A
Vannes Redon Châteaubriant La Flèche Loir
Quiberon Nozay Angers Tours Romorantin
Belle-Ile St-Nazaire Rezé Saumur Loches Bourg
Île de Montaigu Cholet Thouars Châtellerault Issoudun
Noirmoutier La Roche- Bressuire Poitiers Châteauroux St Am
I. d'Yeu s.-Yon Fontenay- Parthenay P O I T O U Argenton Mont
Les Sables- le-Comte Bellac s. Creuse La Cr
d'Olonne Île de Ré Niort Guéret
La Rochelle Ruffec L I M O U S I
Rochefort St Jean- Charente St-Junien Fratous
B A Y O F B I S C A Y d'Angely Limoges
(GOLFE DE GASCOGNE) Royan Saintes Cognac Pons Angoulême Thiviers Uzerche Tulle
45 Barbezieux Périgueux Brive Auri
Blaye Isle Mussidan Souillac
Libourne Bergerac Figea Dec
Arcachon Bordeaux G U Y E Cahors
Langon Marmande N
Bazas Villeneuve Moissac Montauban Al
s.-Lot
Capbreton Agen Castelsarrasin Agout
Mont-de- Toulouse
Dax Marsan Auch Carcas
Biarritz Adour G A S Q.G.
Aviles C. de Peñas Santander Bayonne Orthez Pau St-Gaudens Pamiers
Gijón C. de Ajo San Sébastian Oloron- Lourdes Tarbes P Y R É N É E S Foix ROUS
Oviedo Torrelavega Bilbao (Donostia) Irún Ste-Marie Vignemale Viella ANDORRA
A S T U R I A S Picos de Europa Durango Eibar Vidangoz 3298 Monte Bou
Mieres 2615 Baracaldo Tolosa Jaca Pic d'Aneto Andorra
Cord Cantabric (Bilbo) VASCONGADAS Pamplona 3283 la-V Puigcerdà
La Robla Reinosa Vitoria N A V A R R A Aragón Se
León Osorno Miranda S P A I N
Astorga Sahagún de Ebro Logroño Tafalla
Benavente Burgos Ⓑ Calahorra
Ebro

50 100 150 200 km
50 100 mls

Albi ©
Toulouse
Nîmes
Montpellier
Arles
Salon-d.-P. ©
Aix-en-Provence

Mont-de-Marsan
Auch
Castres-s.T
Béziers
Sète
Martigues
Aubagne
Marseille

Dax
Adour
Pau
St-Gaudens
Pamiers
Narbonne
Golfe du Lion
Toulon Hyères

FRANCE
GASCOGNE

abreton
Bayonne Orthez
Pau
Tarbes
Lourdes
Foix
Quillan
ROUSSILLON
Perpignan

Irun
Oloron-Ste-Marie
Pic du Midi
PYRÉNÉES
Vignemale 3298
Monteny 2883
ANDORRA
Andorra-La Vella
Bourg-Madame
C. de Creus

amplona
Jaca
Sa de Guara
Puigcerdà
Sa del Codi
Figueras
(Figueres)

NAVARRA
Tafalla
Huesca
Barbastro
Segre
Vich
(Vic)
Gerona
(Girona)
San Feliu de G.
Costa Brava

Tudela
Alagón
Zaragoza
Emb. de
Mequinenza
Lérida
(Lleida)
Sabadell
Tarrasa
Granollers
Mataró
Badalona
Barcelona

yud
Daroca
Jiloca
ARAGON
Alcañiz
Caspe
CATALUÑA
Valls
Reus
Villanueva-y-G.
(Vilanova i la Geltrú)

Monreal
del C
Sa de Gudar
Tortosa
Golfo
de
San Jorge
C. de Tortosa

Albarracín
2019
Peñarroya
Teruel
Sarrion
Vinaroz
Benicarló
Torreblanca

N
Segorbe
Villarreal
Castellón de la P.
Is Columbretes
40

Utiel
Turia
Sagunto
Golfo de
Valencia
Mallorca
1445
Mayor
C. Formentor
C. de Caballeria
Menorca
C. de Ferrutx
Alcudia
Ciudadela
Mahón
C. Binibeca

Valencia
VALENCIA
Palma
de Mallorca
Capdepera
Manacor

Albacete
Almansa
Alcira
Játiva
Onteniente
Gandia
Denia
C. de la Nao
Ibiza
S. Antonio
Abad
Ibiza
C. de Salinas
Cabrera
Santañy

ISLAS BALEARES
(BALEARIC ISLANDS)
(Sp.)

RCIA
Hellin
Villena
Alcoy
Benidorm
Formentera

Elda
Alicante
Costa Blanca

Cieza
Elche
Orihuela

Caravaca
Murcia
Totana
Lorca
C. de Palos
Cartagena
2

Aguilas
G. de
Mazarrón

Vera
C. Gata

Alger
(Algiers)
Harrach
Dellys
Bejaïa
(Bougie)

Cherchell
Boufarik
Tizi Ouzou
Kherrata

Ténès
Blida
Bir
Bouira
Beni
Mansour
Sétif

Dahra
Miliana
Médéa
Rabalou
Djurdjura
Soummam

Bosquet
C. Ferrat
Ech Cheliff
Khemis
Ksar El
Boukhari
Isser
Bj bou
Arréridj
Mts du Hodna

Mers el Kebir
Arzew
Mostaganem
Massif de l'Ouarsenis
Ouassa
Aïn
Oussera
Aïn el
Hadjel
M'Sila
Barikaa

Oran
Relizane
Ksar El
Boukhari
Stisseba
Chott
el Hodna

Beni-Saf
O. Tlélat
Mohammadia
Mascara
Mina
Tiareto
Plat. du Sersou
Z. Chergui
Bou Saâda
A L G E R I A

Aïn
Témouchent
Sidi-bel-Abbès
Frenda
© Z. Gharbi
Monts des
Ouled Nail
36

MEDITERRANEAN SEA

5
3

Costa Blanca

BLACK SEA

UKRAINE
MOLDAVIA
ROMANIA
HUNGARY
YUGOSLAVIA
SERBIA
BULGARIA
BOSNIA-HERZEGOVINA
CROATIA
MONTENEGRO
KOSOVO
VOJVODINA

Odessa
Razdelnaja
Belgorod-Dnestrovskiy
Tiraspol
Dubossary
Bendery
Kishinev / Chişinău
Kotovsk
Kalarash
Husi
Kagul
Reni
Izmail
Vilkovo
Sulina
L. Razim
Constanta
Mangalia
Babadag
Medgidia
Tulcea
Braila
Galati
Tecuci
Focşani
Buzau
Ploiesti
Bucuresti / Bucharest
Giurgiu
Ruse
Turtukan
Silistra
Calarasi
Fetesti
Slobozia
Urziceni
Ramnicu Sarat
Bacau
Roman
Pascani
Suceava
Iaşi
Botosani
Birlad
Adjud
Onesti
Gheorghieni
Miercurea-Ciuc
Piatra-Neamt
Bistrita
Borşa
Baia Mare
Satu Mare
Carei
Marghita
Oradea
Salonta
Arad
Lipova
Timişoara
Lugoj
Caransebeş
Resita
Oravita
Vršac
Pančevo
Belgrade / Beograd
Smederevo
Požarevac
Zrenjanin
Novi Sad
Sombor
Subotica
Senta
Baja
Szeged
Hódmezővásárhely
Orosháza
Békéscsaba
Gyula
Debrecen
Nyiregyháza
Mátészalka
Budapest
Szolnok
Kecskemét
Kiskunhalas
Kiskunfélegyháza
Cegléd
Székesfehérvár
Dunaújváros
Paks
Szekszárd
Pécs
Siofok
Osijek
Vinkovci
Vukovar
Brčko
Tuzla
Zenica
Sarajevo
Mostar
Konjic
Goražde
Višegrad
Užice
Čačak
Kraljevo
Kragujevac
Jagodina
Paraćin
Ćuprija
Svetozarevo
Kruševac
Niš
Leskovac
Vranje
Kumanovo
Priština
Mitrovica
Uroševac
Prizren
Peć
Djakovica
Novi Pazar
Podgorica
Nikšić
Cetinje
Budva
Plevlja

Carpatii Meridionali (Transylvanian Alps)
Mtii Rodnei
Mtii Apuseni
Mtii Zarandului
Mtii Banatului
Stara Planina
Ludogorie
Yildiz Dag

Sofiya / Sofija
Pernik
Pleven
Lovech
Gabrovo
Troyan
Veliko Tarnovo
Sevlievo
Svishtov
Ruse
Razgrad
Šumen
Novi Pazar
Dobrich
Varna
Burgas
Aytos
Karnobat
Sliven
Yambol
Stara Zagora
Nova Zagora
Kazanlak
Plovdiv
Pazardzhik
Panagyurishte
Ihtiman
Samokov
Kyustendil
Blagoevgrad
Asenovgrad
Haskovo
Kŭrdzhali
Dimitrovgrad
Svilengrad
Edirne
Kirklareli
Dimitrovo

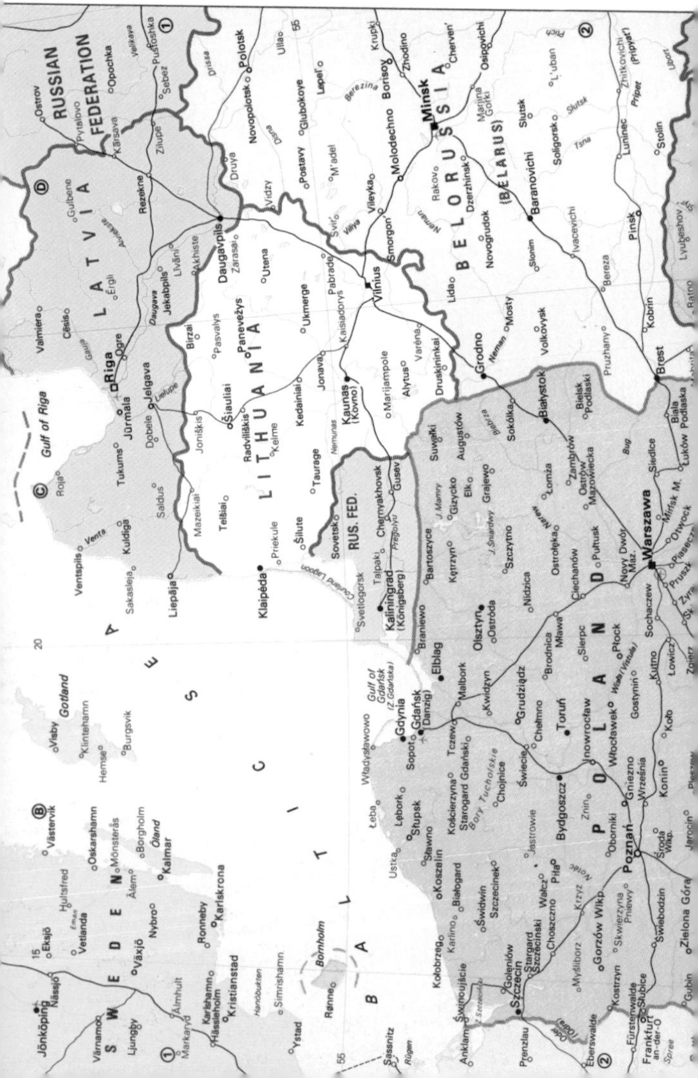

RUSSIAN FEDERATION

LATVIA

Riga
Jūrmala
Gulf of Riga

LITHUANIA
Vilnius
Kaunas (Kovno)
Klaipėda
Šiauliai
Panevėžys

BELORUSSIA (BELARUS)
Minsk
Baranovichi
Pinsk
Brest
Grodno

RUS. FED.
Kaliningrad (Königsberg)

SWEDEN
Gotland
Öland
Kalmar
Karlskrona

BALTIC SEA

Bornholm

POLAND
Warszawa
Gdańsk (Danzig)
Gdynia
Sopot
Elbląg
Malbork
Olsztyn
Toruń
Bydgoszcz
Poznań
Szczecin
Gorzów Wlkp.
Zielona Góra
Frankfurt an-der-Oder

50 100 150 200 km
50 100 mls

UKRAINE

HUNGARY

ROMANIA

AUSTRIA

SLOVENIA

CROATIA

C Z E C H   R E P.

S L O V A K I A

Carpații Meridionali (Transylvanian Alps)

Beskidy Zachodnie

Podolskaya Vozv.

Novograd V.
Polonnye
Starokonstantinov
Khmel'nitskiy
Letichev
Vinnitsa

Rovno
Dubno
Kremenets
Shepetovka
Dunayevtsy
Kamenets-Podol'skiy
Khotin
Yedintsy
Ryshkany

Lutsk
Brody
Ternopil'
Chortkov
Gorodok
Mogilev-Podol'skiy
Dorohoi
Botoşani

Vladimir-Volynskiy
Sokal'
L'vov
Zolochev
Chernovtsy
Storozhinets
Rădăuți
Suceava
Fălticeni
Pascani
Roman

Novovolynsk
Rava-Russkaya
Gorodok
Drogobych
Stryy
Kalush
Ivano-Frankovsk
Kolomyya
Nadvornaya
Yasinya
Rakhov
Siret
Bacău
Onești
Adjud
Focşani

Zamość
Tomaszów Lubelski
Jarosław
Sambor
Borislav
Uzhgorod
Mukachevo
Khust
Sighetu Marmaţiei
Vatra Dornei
Bistriţa
Reghin
Piatra-Neamţ
Sfîntu Gheorghe
Buzău
Ploieşti

Kraśnik
Stalowa Wola
Przemyśl
Sanok
Bardejov
Michalovce
Satu Mare
Baia Mare
Dej
Cluj-Napoca
Tîrgu Mureş
Sighişoara
Braşov
Tîrgovişte
Piteşti

Stalowa Wola
Rzeszów
Jasło
Preśov
Košice
Nyíregyháza
Carei
Oradea
Zalău
Turda
Sebeş
Sibiu
Mediaş
Făgăraş
Rîmnicu Vîlcea

Ostrowiec Świętokrzyski
Tarnobrzeg
Dębica
Krosno
Humenné
Satu Mare
Mátészalka
Debrecen
Hódmezővásárhely
Salonta
Arad
Deva
Hunedoara
Reşiţa
Caransebeş

Radom
Świętochłowice
Starachowice
Jędrzejów
Busko-Zdrój
Tarnów
Nowy Sącz
Bardejov
Rožňava
Miskolc
Eger
Hajdúszoboszló
Békéscsaba
Timişoara
Lugoj

Kielce
Dąbrowa Górn.
Kraków
Bochnia
Zakopane
Ružomberok
Banská Bystrica
Lučenec
Salgótarján
Karcag
Szolnok
Orosháza
Makó
Sînnicolau
Lipova

Częstochowa
Sosnowiec
Myślenice
Żywiec
Martin
Zvolen
Levice
Vác
Budapest
Cegléd
Kecskemét
Szeged
Subotica
Kikinda
Zrenjanin
Novi Sad

Radomsko
Zawiercie
Bytom
Gliwice
Żylina
Čadca
Trenčín
Nové Zámky
Esztergom
Székesfehérvár
Siófok
Kiskunhalas
Szekszárd
Sombor
Apatin
Osijek

Opole
Tychy
Bielsko-Biała
Karviná
Ostrava
Piešťany
Nitra
Komárno
Tatabánya
Dunaújváros
Baja
Subotica
Senta
Vukovar
Vinkovci

Wrocław
Opava
Hranice
Olomouc
Vyškov
Zilina
Trnava
Bratislava
Győr
Pápa
Veszprém
Kaposvár
Pécs
Mohács
Bosanski Brod

Kłodzko
Jeseník
Šumperk
Prostějov
Brno
Břeclav
Wien
Sopron
Szombathely
Zalaegerszeg
Nagykanizsa
Virovitica
Slavonski Brod

Dzierżoniów
Świdnica
Zábřeh
Svitavy
Jihlava
Třebíč
Znojmo
Hollabrunn
Mödling
Wiener Neustadt
Mór
Kaposvár
Varaždin
Zagreb
Bjelovar

Wałbrzych
Kłodzko
Hradec Králové
Pardubice
Havlíčkův Brod
Třebíč
Gmünd
Horn
St. Pölten
Neunkirchen
Graz
Maribor
Sisak

Jelenia Góra
Liberec
Mladá Boleslav
Kolín
Kutná Hora
Benešov
Tábor
České Budějovice
Freistadt
Linz
Leibnitz
Celje
Karlovac
Rijeka (Fiume)

Trutnov
Náchod
Praha (Prague)
Beroun
Třeboň
Gmünd
Klosterneuburg
Klagenfurt
Ljubljana
Novo Mesto

Kladno
Kralupy
Znaim
Stockerau
Melk
Mariazell
Bruck
Judenburg
Wolfsberg
Kranj

VÁH
SÁVA
DRÁVA
Odra
Labe
San
Wisła
Dunajec
Siret
Prut
Mureş
Tisa
Someş
Sava
Drava

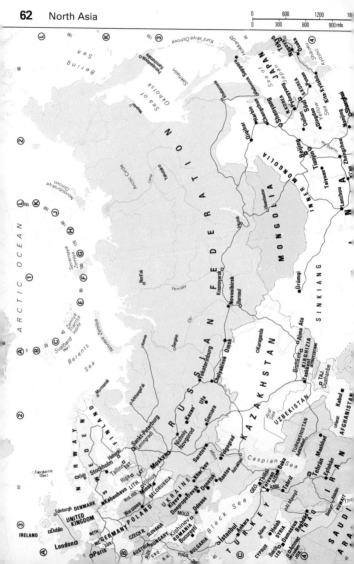

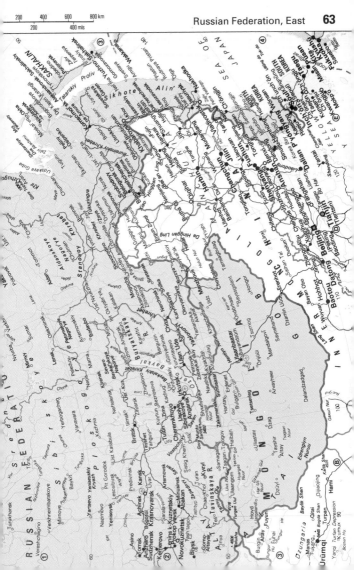

200   400   600   800 km
200   400 mils

RUSSIAN FEDERATION
1 Chuvashskaya R.
2 Checheno-Ingushskaya R.
3 Severo-Osetinskaya R.
4 Kabardino-Balkarskaya R.
GEORGIA
5 Abkhazskaya R.
6 Adzharskaya R.
AZERBAIJAN
7 Nakhichevanskaya R.

GREECE
Athínai
Sicilia
BULGARIA
Bucaresti
ROMANIA
Black Sea
Kharkov
Saratov
Dnepropetrovsk
Odessa
UKRAINE
Donetsk
Rostov
Volgograd
Volga
Astrakhan
RUSSIA
Ufa
Yekaterinburg
Chelyabinsk
Omsk
Nov

İstanbul
Ankara
TURKEY
GEORGIA
Tbilisi
CRIM
AZER.
Yerevan
Baku
Caspian Sea
KAZAKHSTAN
Karaganda

CYPRUS
Adana
Halab
SYRIA
Beirut
LEB.
Damascus
ISRAEL
Jerusalem
JOR.
Ammán
Baghdad
IRAQ
Tabriz
Al Mawsil
Tehrān
Mashhad
TURKMENISTAN
Ashkhabad
Aral Sea
UZBEKISTAN
Bishkek
Alma Ata
KIRGHIZIA
(KYRGYZSTAN)
Tashkent

LIBYA
Alexandria
Cairo
EGYPT
Aswân
RED SEA
SAUDI ARABIA
Makkah
Madina
Ar Riyâd
KUWAIT
The Gulf
BAHRAIN
QATAR
Abū Dhabi
U.A.E.
Esfahān
IRAN
Abādān
Kermân
Herat
Kabul
AFGHANISTAN
Islamabad
Kashmir
TAJIKISTAN
Dushanbe
PAKISTAN
Lahore
Delhi
NE

SUDAN
Khartoum
Asmara
YEMEN
San'ā
Aden
DJIBOUTI
G. of Aden
Masqat
OMAN
Karachi
Hyderābād
Jodh
ARABIAN SEA
Ahmadābād
Jabalpur
Bombay
Godavari
Nāgpur
Hyderābād
Krishna
INDIA
Kānpur
Lucknow
Pa

ETHIOPIA
Adīs Abeba
SOMALIA
Muqdisho
KENYA
Mombasa
Dar es Salaam
TANZANIA
Socotra (Yemen)
Equator
Lakshadweep (Ind.)
MALDIVES
Bangalore
Madras
Madurai
Colombo
Kandy
SRI LANKA

MOZAMBIQUE
COMOROS
SEYCHELLES
Aldabra Is. (Sey.)
INDIAN OCEAN
Chagos Arch. (U.K.)

MADAGASCAR
Antananarivo

200   400   600   800 km
200   400 mls

TAIWAN (FORMOSA) **D**
tung (China Nat. Rep.)
tung

P A **C** I **F** I **C**

Farallon de Pajaros
Maug Is   20

Batan Is

n Strait

C.Engaño
Aparri
Tuguegarao

Northern
Marianas

Parece Vela

Pagan
Alamagan
Guguan
Sarigan
Anatahan
Farallon
de Medinilla

M

A

R

I

A

N

Asuncion
Agrihan

Ilagan
LUZON
on
anatuan
azon City
Polillo Is
Manila

Saipan
Tinian **2**
Rota

Daet Catanduanes
Naga
Boac Legazpi
Bulan
Catarman
Masbate Oras
Masbate Guiuan
Roxas
Tacloban Leyte
acolod Dinagat -10265
Cebu Dinagat -10497
Bohol Surigao
Siaton Butuan

O

C

E

A

N

I

Guam
(U.S.A.)
Nero Deep
9637

Mantsyu Deep
9818
Challenger Deep
11033

10

Cagayan de Oro
Ozamiz Marawi
L. Lanao
Malanbang
Cotabato
Davao
General Digos
Santos Tinaca Pt.
Moro
Gulf

MINDANAO

Ulethi
Fais
Gafer Jt

Yap

Faraulep

Ngulu
Sorol
Woleai Ifalik
Lamotrek

Fed.States of Micronesia

Eauripik

Palau
Islands Koror
(U.S.A)

C A R O L I N E   I S L A N D S   3

Kepulauan
Talaud Karakelong
Tahuna
Sangihe

Sonsorol
Pulo Anna
Merir

BES

SEA

Kepulauan
Sangihe
Tobelo
Ternate Halmahera

T.Tobi
Helen Reef

Equator   0

Ninigo Group

Manado
Kuandang
Belang
Gorontalo
Luwuk Kep. Togian

Bacan
Teluk
Weda
Waigeo
Sorong Cendrawasih
Misool

Waigeo
Kwoka
3000+
Pk. Arfak
2939

Manokwari Supiori
Biak
Numfoor Yapen
Tg d'Urville
Sarmi

Mapia

Wuvulu

Aitape Schouten Is
Wewak

4

M O L U C C A S

Jayapura

Teluk
Cendrawasih

PAPUA

Peleng Taliabu Mangole
Kep. Obi
Banggai

Sula

Teluk Berau
Fakfak

Dom
1340
Pegunungan Maoke
Angemuk
3741
Pk. Jaya
5029
Pk. Mandala
4702

IRIAN

Sepik

NEW GUINEA

Mt
Hagen
Goroka

Central
Mendi
Kubor
4355
Lae

Namlea
Piru 3019 Bula
Seram
Ambon

Kaimana

JAYA

Wagu

Buru
Wowoni

Kep.Banda
Adi
Kokonau

Tanahmerah

GUINEA

PAPUA

Bulolo
Wau

Kolaka
pone Butung
Muna

Nila
Damar Teun

Kep.Kai Dobo
Wokam
Kep.
Aru
Kobroör
Trangan

Tk Flamingo

Keema

Kikori
Murray

Baubau Kep.
Tukangbesi

Port Moresby

SIA

B A N D A

S E A

P.Kolepom

Tg Vals

Merauke

Komoran

Gulf of
Papua

Lomblen Alor
Wetar Romang
Selat Damar
Dili Kep.Leti Babar
Atambua Sermata

Yamdena
Tanimbar
Saumlaki
Selaru

Kepulauan

Saibai
Daru

Mulgrave I. Banks I.
Torres Strait
Thursday I. C. York
Pr.of Wales I. Somerset

5

Endeh
avu Sea
Kupang

Roti

TIMOR

A R A F U R A   S E A

CORAL

C.Grenville

Ikon
Range

C.V.Diemen
Bathurst I. Melville Dundas St
Croker I.

D

TIMOR

SEA

Wessel Is
C. Arnhem

Saibai

Weipa

Barrier Rf

SEA

Clarence Str
Darwin
Arnhem Land
Nhulunbuy

AUSTRALIA

Albatross B.

140

E

F

Colbury Bay

Great

Torres Strait

Changchun · Jilin
Shenyang · Anshan · Dalian
Liaoning
KOREA BAY
Qinhuangdao · Tangshan
Tianjin (Tientsin)
BO HAI
Beijing (Peking)
Qingdao (Tsingtao)
YELLOW SEA (HUANG HAI)
Shandong
Jinan · Zibo
Hebei
Baoding
Shijiazhuang
Datong · Taiyuan
Hohhot · Baotou
Shanxi
Zhengzhou · Luoyang
Henan
Xuzhou
Jiangsu
Bengbu
Shaanxi
Xian (Sian) · Xianyang
Baoji
Qin Ling
Ningxia
Yinchuan
Lanzhou
Linxia
Xining
Qinghai
Gansu
Tianshui
MONGOLIA

YELLOW SEA
Lianyungang

C H I N A

Maoming · Wuchuan · Lianjiang · Zhanjiang

Beihai · Hepu · Lingshan · Hengxian · Leizhou Bandao · Xuwen · Haikou · Tongguo · Qionghai · Wanning

HAINAN · Yulin · Ya Xian

Nanning · Qinzhou · Fangcheng · Dongxing · Changjiang · Huangliu

Pingxiang · Lang Son · Ninh Binh · Thai Binh · Hon Gai · Haiphong

Gulf of Tongkin

Cao Bang · Bac Can · Thai Nguyen · Bac Ninh · Hanoi · Hoa Binh · Nam Dinh · Ninh Binh · Thanh Hoa · Quynh Luu · Vinh · Ha Tinh · Dong Hoi · Quang Tri · Hue · Da Nang

Ha Giang · Lao Cai · Yen Bai · Phu Tho · Viet Tri · Son La · Dien Bien Phu · Moc Chau

V I E T N A M

I N D O

Muong Sai · Saravane · Champassak · Pakse · Khong

Phong Saly · Dien Bien Phu · Luang Prabang · Xieng Khouang · Pak Sane · Nape · Khe Bo · Thakhek · Sepone

L A O S

Vientiane · Vang Vieng · Nong Khai · Udon Thani · Nakhon Phanom · M. Sakon Nakhon · Savannakhet

Luang Nam Tha · B. Houei Sai · Muong Sing · Chiang Rai · Fang

Kengtung · Mong Ping · Chiang Mai · Lamphun · M. Lampang · M. Phrae · Uttaradit

B U R M A (M Y A N M A R)

Mandalay · Meiktila · Taunggyi · Loikaw

T H A I L A N D

M. Phitsanulok · M. Phetchabun · M. Phichit · Chaiyaphum · Nakhon Ratchasima · Buriram · Surin · Sisaket · Ubon Ratchathani

Tak · Kamphaeng Phet · Nakhon Sawan · M. Chainat · M. Uthai Thani · Lop Buri · Saraburi · Prachin Buri

Bangkok · Nakhon Pathom · M. Samut Prakan · Chon Buri · Rayong · Chanthaburi

C A M B O D I A

Siem Reap · Battambang · Pursat · Kompong Thom · Kompong Cham · Phnom Penh · Prey Veng · Svay Rieng · Takeo · Kampot · Kompong Som · Kompong Speu

Stung Treng · Kratie · Tabeng · Kompong Chhnang

Kontum · Pleiku · An Nhon · Qui Nhon · Tuy Hoa · Nha Trang · Da Lat · Ban Me Thuot · Bao Loc · Phan Rang · Phan Thiet

Saigon · Bien Hoa · Vung Tau

Moulmein (Mawlamyine) · Thaton · Pegu (Bago) · Yangon (Rangoon) · Prome (Pye) · Henzada · Bassein (Pathein)

Tavoy (Dawei) · Mergui (Myeik) · Tenasserim (Tanintharyi)

A N D A M A N   S E A

Bay of Bengal

Gulf of Martaban

Irrawaddy · Mouths of the Irrawaddy

100   200   300   400 km
100   200 mils

④   ⑤   A   ⑥

S O U T H   SARAWAK (Malaysia)   B O R N E O

C H I N A   Kuching   Kalimantan

S E A   Singkawang

Phu Vinh
Rach Gia Can Mouths of   Pontianak   I N D O N E S I A
Tho   the Mekong
Khanh Hung   Kep.   Pangkalpinang   D
Quan Long   Vinh Loi   Anambas
Ca Mau   Nam Can
Mui Bai Bung   Belitung
Hon Khoai   Kep.
Lingga   Bangka

Ko Way   PENINSULAR
Ko Kut   Kuala   M Kuala
Dungun   Kuantan   A   L   JOHOR   SINGAPORE
Trengganu   A   Baharu
MALAYSIA   Y
Redang   S   Mersing
Kota Bharu   I   Kep. Riau
Narathiwat Tumpat   Keluang   A
Pattani Yala Gua Musang   Segamat

George
Town Butterworth Taiping Ipoh Kuala Lumpur

Alor Setar   Port Dickson
Melaka

THAILAND   Medan Pematangsiantar

I N D O N E S I A

Padang

Siberut

Banda Aceh

Equator   95

A

⑤   ⑥

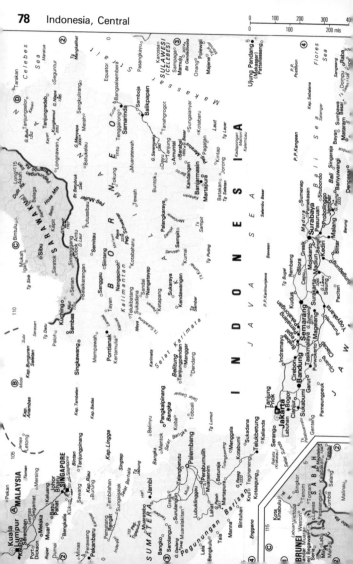

100   200   300   400 km
100   200 mls

PACIFIC

①

Luzon Batan
Strait Islands
Basco

OCEAN

20

Balintang Channel

Dongsha
Quindao

Babuyan Islands

Cape Bojeador   Babuyan Channel   Cape Engaño

Laoag   Claveria   Aparri

Bangued   Tuguegarao   Ilagan

②

Vigan   Santiago
Solano
San Fernando   Mt Pulog 2929   *LUZON*
La Trinidad   Bayombong
Baguio   San Jose   Baler
Lingayen   Dagupan   San
Angeles   Cabanatuan
San Carlos   Gapan   Polillo
Camiling   San Fernando   Islands
Cordillera Central 2934

SOUTH   Tarlac   Malolos   Calagua Islands
San Antonio   Quezon City   Jose Pañganiban
Olongapo   Manila   Laguna   Lamon   Daet
CHINA   Cavite   Santa Cruz   Bay   Catanduanes
Lubang   San Pablo   Lucban   15
Islands   Lipao   Lucena   Sipocot   Virac
SEA   Batangas   Naga   Mayon
Boac   Iriga   2417
Calapan   Marinduque   Sorsogon   Legazpi
MINDORO   Mt Halcon   Bulan   Gubat
Sablayan   2585   Bural
Mt Baco   *Sibuyan*   Masbate   Catarman
2488   Romblon   *Sea*   Calbayog   *SAMAR*
San Jose   Sibuyan
Tablas   Masbate   Catbalogan   ③

Busuanga   *Visayan*   San
Calmian   Kalibo   Bairan   Isidro   Carigara   Tacloban
Group   Roxas   Sea   Bogo   Ormoc   Guiuan
Culion   Escalante   *Leyte*
Linapacan Str   Pandan   Cadiz   *Gulf*
El Nido   *PANAY*   Silay   Baybay   Dinagat
Taytay   Dalanganem   Iloilo   Danao
Islands   Cuyo   Bacolod   Cebu   Lapu-Lapu
Cleopatra   Islands   La Carlota   Maasin
Needle 1593   Binalbagan   *Bohol*   Surigao   Siargao
Roxas   Dumaran   *Sea*
Bais   Tagbilaran   Butuan
Puerto   Cagayan   Sipalay   Tanjay   *Sea*
Princesa   Islands   Dumaguete   Camiguin   Gingoog   10
1798   Siaton   Dapitan   Oroquieta   Cagayan   Lianga
Aborlan   Dipolog   de Oro
Palawan Passage   Tubbataha   Mambajao   Mt Ozamiz   Iligan
Reefs   Manukan   2250   Bislig
PALAWAN   Liloy   Dapitan   Malaybalay
Mt   Tangub   *Lanao*   Marawi
Mantalingajan   Pagadian   *MINDANAO*   Tagum
SULU   SEA   Zamboanga   *Illanan*   Malabang   Davao   Mati
Pen.   *Bay*   Cotabato   Mt Apo 2954
Balabac   Mapin   Illana   Piang   Digos
Zamboanga   *Gulf*   Cape San Agustin
Balabac Strait   Isabela
Banggi   Jolo   General   Lais
Kudat   Pangutaran   Santos
Bandau   Group   Sarrales   ④
1216 Mt Palu   Telok   Jolo   *Group*   Tinaca Point
Ranau   Labuk   Parang   *Tawitawi*   Sarangani
SABAH   Sandakan   *Group*   Islands
Bingkor Kinabatangan   Tawitawi   Kepulauan
Kuamuto   Lahad   Group   *CELEBES*   Kawio
Datu   1606   Bum Bum   Kepulauan
Mt Maodalena   *Sulu Archipelago*   *SEA*   Nenusa
1138   Semporna   120   125   Karakelong
Kalabakan   ⑤

SOUTH CHINA SEA

PHILIPPINE SEA

PHILIPPINES

200 400 600 800 km
200 400 mls

⑤ ⑥

Banda Aceh
Lhokseumawe
Calang Takengon
Meulaboh Lègon
Balangpidié

Mentawai
Trench

Simeulue

D

Chang Mai ④
Taunggyi
Toungoo
Prome
Pegu
Yangon
(Rangoon)
Bassein
Henzada
Myanaung
Moulmein

B Sal Thanbyuzayat Ba
Tavoy Ye
Mergui
Lanbi

Amherst

G. of
Martaban

C Negrais

A N D A M A N

S E A

O F

ANDAMAN
ISLANDS
(India)

NICOBAR
ISLANDS
(India)

Ten Degree Channel

C a r p e n t e r   R i d g e

90

B E N G A L

B A Y

Cuttack
Sambalpur
Chilka Lake

I N D I A

Raipur
Chandrapur
Warangal
Vijayawada
Rajahmundry
Eluru
Vishakhapatnam
Kakinada
Anakapalle
Vizianagaram
Srikakulam

Madras
Kanchipuram
Pondicherry
Cuddalore
Nellore

SRI LANKA
Jaffna
Trincomalee
Batticaloa
Kandy
Badulla
Colombo
Galle
Matara   Dondra Head

Nizamabad
Hyderabad
Bijapur
Raichur
Bellary
Kurnool
Anantapur
Chitradurga
Bangalore
Mysore
Salem
Coimbatore
Tiruchirapalli
Cochin (Kochi)
Madurai
Tuticorin
Quilon (Kollam)
Trivandrum
(Thiruvananthapuram)
C Comorin

G. of Mannar

Akola
Amravati
Aurangabad
Ahmadnagar
Pune
Solapur
Kolhapur
Hubli
Shimoga
Mangalore
Calicut (Kozhikode)

W e s t e r n   G h a t s

Bombay
(Mumbai)

A R A B I A N

S E A

Surat
Vadodara
Bharuch
Nandurbar
Dhule
Jalgaon
Rajkot
Jamnagar
Junagadh
Diu
Bhavnagar
Khambhat

G. of
Khambhat

Nine Degree Channel
Eight Degree Channel

LACCADIVE
ISLANDS
(India)

MALDIVES

One and Half Degree Channel

M

I N D I A N   O C E A N

C

B

A

20

10

0

④ ⑤

70 80

100 200 300 km
50 100 150 mls
Kānpur
Āgra
Gwalior
Jhānsi
Mainpuri
Etāwah
Bhind
Morena
Datia
Auraiya
Kālpi
Orai
Hamīrpur
Rath
Charkhāri
Mahoba
Panna
Chhatarpur
Tikamgarh
Lalitpur
Damoh
Sihora
Jabalpur
Narsimhapur
Nainpur
Seoni
Tirodi
Tumsar
Bhandāra
Nāgpur
Kāmthi
Umred
Hinganghāt
Chandrapur
Mancherāl
Belampalli
Jagtial
Karimnagar
Nizāmābād
Ādilābād
Rājur
Wardha
Yavatmāl
Amrāvati
Chhindwāra
Betūl
Mahadeo Hills
Sāgar
Garhakota
Bina-Etawa
Tropic of Cancer
Sironj
Vidisha
Bhopāl
Hoshangābād
Harda
Khandwa
Achalpur
Akot
Akola
Kāranja
Wāshim
Pusad
Nānded
Nirmal
Bodhan
Udgir
Pūrna
Parbhani
Hingoli
Mehekar
Khāmgaon
Buldāna
Malkāpur
Bhusāwal
Burhānpur
Jalgaon
Jālna
Aurangābād
Bīr
Parli
Ahmadnagar
Godāvari
Chālisgaon
Manmād
Kopargaon
Dhule
Malegaon
Amalner
Tāpi
Sendhwa
Khargon
Barwāni
Narmada
Sanāwad
Barwāh
Mhow
Indore
Dewās
Ujjain
Dhār
Jhābua
Ratlām
Jaora
Mandsaur
Nīmach
Rāmpura
Gāndhi Sāgar
Shājāpur
Shujālpur
Rājgarh
Agar
Mālwa Plateau
Guna
Shivpuri
Sheopur
Sawai Mādhopur
Hindaun
Dausa
Jaipur
Tonk
Toda
Devli
Būndi
Kota
Bārān
Jhālāwār
Mālpura
Kishangarh
Ajmer
Kekri
Bhīlwāra
Chittaurgarh
Bari Sādri
Beāwar
Merta
Makrāna
Nāgaur
Bilāra
Sojat
Mārwār
Pāli
Jodhpur
Phalodi
Pokaran
Bālotra
Shergarh
Jaisalmer
Devikot
Barmer
Jālor
Sirohi
Sādri
Udaipur
Dūngarpur
Bānswāra
Dāhod
Godhra
Ahmadābād
Gāndhinagar
Himatnagar
Khed Brahma
Siddhapur
Pālanpur
Pātan
Mahesāna
Kādi
Nadiād
Petlād
Vadodara
Dabhoi
Rājpipla
Nandurbār
Sūrat
Bharūch
Jambusar
Navsāri
Valsād
Silvassa
Damān (G.D. & D.)
Nāsik
Deolāli
Sangamner
Kalyān
Lonāvale
Pune (Poona)
Thāne
Bombay (Mumbai)
Alībāg
Gulf of Khambhāt
Bhāvnagar
Pālitāna
Botād
Dhrāngadhra
Surendranagar
Jasdan
Rājkot
Morbi
Rādhanpur
Kundla
Mahuva
Amreli
Gir Hills
Diu
(Goa, Damān & Diu)
Gondal
Dhorāji
Jūnāgadh
Verāval
Māngrol
Porbandar
Jāmnagar
Navlakhi
Gāndhidhām
Bhuj
Māndvi
G. of Kachchh
Okha
Dwārka
Rann of Kachchh
Kāvda
Lakhpat
Kori Ck
Nagar Parkar
Chachro
Umarkot
Naokot
Sanghar
Sartanahu
Mirpur Khas
Tando Ādam
Nawabshah
Hyderabad
Tando Muhammad Khan
Badin
Kotri
Moro
Dadu
Sehwan
Tatta
Keti Bandar
Mouths of the Indus
Karachi
Korangi
Sonmiani
Sonmiani Bay
Uthal
Bela
Kalat
Central Makran Ra.
Makran Coast Range
Hingol
Kirthar Range
KHAIRPUR
SIND
RĀJASTHĀN
MADHYA PRADESH
MAHĀRĀSHTRA
GUJARĀT
Kāthiāwār
Vindhya Range
Sātpura Range
Arāvalli Range
ARABIAN SEA
25
20
70
75

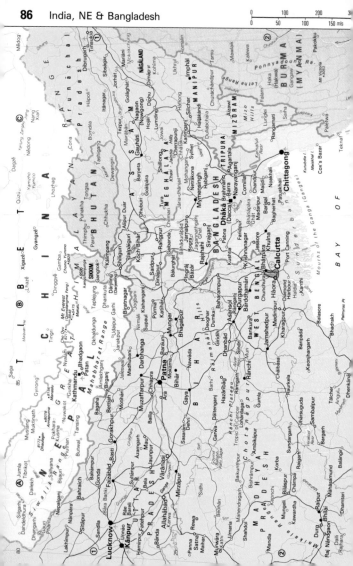

NORTH ATLANTIC OCEAN
Açores (Port.)
Madeira (Port.)
Islas Canarias (Sp.)
Bay of Biscay
North Sea
Baltic Sea
Adriatic Sea
Black Sea
Caspian Sea
Aral Sea
Mediterranean Sea
Red Sea
The Gulf
Gulf of Aden
UNITED KINGDOM
IRELAND
Dublin
London
Edinburgh
NORWAY
Oslo
SWEDEN
Stockholm
Göteborg
FINLAND
Helsinki
DENMARK
København
EST.
Tallinn
LAT.
Riga
LITH.
Vilnius
RUS. FED.
BELORUSSIA
Minsk
NETH.
's-Gravenhage
BELG.
Bruxelles
LUX.
GERMANY
Hamburg
Berlin
Bonn
München
POLAND
Warszawa
Gdańsk
Kraków
CZECH REPUBLIC
Praha
SLOVAKIA
AUSTRIA
Wien
HUNGARY
Budapest
SWITZ.
Bern
FRANCE
Paris
Bordeaux
Marseille
Seine
Rhône
Corse
Sardegna
Sicilia
ITALY
Milano
Roma
Napoli
SLOV.
CROATIA
B.-H.
Sarajevo
YUGO.
Beograd
ALB.
Tiranë
MAC.
ROMANIA
București
MOLDAVIA
Kishinev
BULGARIA
Sofiya
GREECE
Athinai
Kriti
UKRAINE
Kiyev
Odessa
Khar'kov
Dnieper
Danube
RUSSIAN FEDERATION
Sankt-Peterburg (Leningrad)
Moskva
Nizhniy Novgorod
Samara
Volgograd
Rostov
Magnitogorsk
Volga
Don
Ural
KAZAKHSTAN
UZBEKISTAN
TURKMENISTAN
Ashkhabad
Syr-Darya
Amu-Darya
GEORGIA
Tbilisi
ARM.
Yerevan
AZE.
Baku
TURKEY
Istanbul
Ankara
CYPRUS
Nicosia
SYRIA
Damascus
LEB.
Beirut
ISR.
Jerusalem
JORDAN
Amman
IRAQ
Baghdad
Tigris
Euphrates
Basra
KUWAIT
Kuwait
IRAN
Tehrān
Tabrīz
Mashhad
Shīraz
AFGHANISTAN
BAHRAIN
QATAR
Doha
UNITED ARAB EMIRATES
Abu Dhabi
Masqat
OMAN
Kuria Muria Is
SAUDI ARABIA
Ar Riyād
Makkah
YEMEN
San'ā
PORTUGAL
Porto
Lisboa
SPAIN
Madrid
Barcelona
Islas Baleares
Ebro
Tajo
MOROCCO
Tanger
Rabat
Casablanca
Fès
Marrakech
ALGERIA
Alger
Oran
Annaba
Constantine
Béchar
Tindouf
In Salah
Tamanrasset
TUNISIA
Tunis
Sfax
Ghadamis
LIBYA
Tripoli
Benghāzi
Sabhā
Ghāt
EGYPT
Alexandria
Cairo
Port Said
Suez
Asyūt
Aswān
Nile
L. Nasser
SUDAN
Port Sudan
Wadi Halfa
Atbara
Kassala
Omdurman
Khartoum
Asmara
Western Sahara
La'youn
MAURITANIA
Nouakchott
Nouâdhibou
F'dérik
SAHARA
MALI
Tombouctou
Niger
NIGER
Agadez
Niamey
CHAD
SENEGAL
Dakar
St-Louis
Sénégal
THE GAMBIA
Banjul
GUINEA-BISSAU
Bissau
Tropic of Cancer
A
B
C
D
E
F
G
H
J
K
L
M
2
3
4
5
6

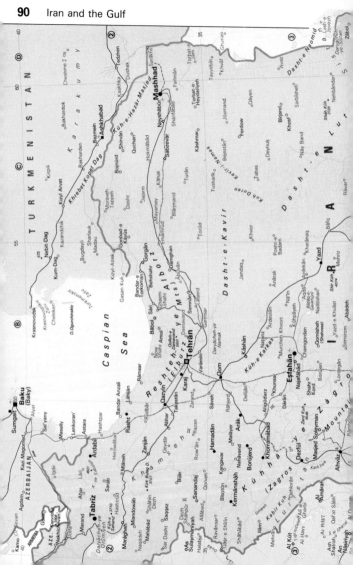

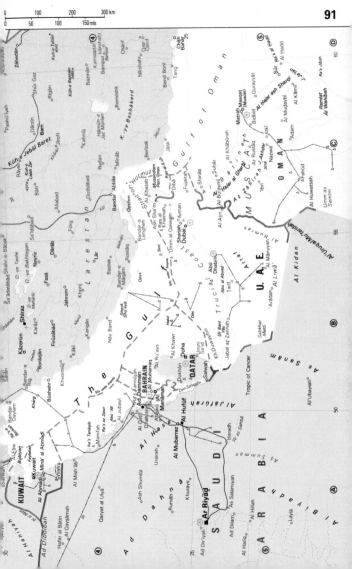

0 | 100 | 200 | 300 km
0 | 50 | 100 | 150 mls

Gulf of Oman

O M A N

Marsá Masqaţ (Muscat)
Maţraḥ
Al Ḩadd
Ra's al Ḩadd
Şūr
Quray̌yāt
Al Kāmil
Ramlat
Al Waḩībah
Adam
Al Muḑaybī
Nizwá
Izki
Bidbid
Al Ḩuwatah
Umm as
Samīm

Ṣuḩār
Al Khābūrah
Ar Rustāq
Al Buraymī
'Ibrī
Afahūd
'Ayn

Al Jabal al Akhḑar
Ḩajar ash Sharqī

Ḩajar al Gharbī

Kūh-ye Basshākerd

Band Boni
Chāh
Bahār

Khasab
Ra's al Khaimah
Dibā
Fujairah
Shināş
Al Khaşab
Ru'ūs al Jibāl
Masandam Pen. (Oman)
Madḥā
Strait of Hormuz
Bandar-e Lengheh
Qeshm
Berīzak
Jāsk

Ash Shāriqah
Sharjah Ajman
Umm al Qaywayn
Dubai

Trucial Coast

Abu Dhabi
Abū al Abyaḑ
U. A. E.
Al Maḩwah
'Arādah
Al Liwā'
Al Kidan
Sabkhat Maṭṭi

Dās
Ṣīr Banī
Yās
Abū al
Abyaḑ
Ḩalūl
Ţarīf

Shaykh Shu'ayb

The Gulf

Bandar-e Maqām
Rostāq
Qeys
Nāy Band
Khorramīj

Khārg
Būshehr
Bandar-e Daylam
Bandar-e Rīg
Genāveh
Deyr

L a r e s t a n

Fasā
Jahrom
Lār
Khonj
Bastak
Mīnāb
Abūdā
Ruḑān
Kahnūj

Shīrāz
Kāzerūn
Fīrūzābād
Kāzī
Khvormūj
Borāzjān

Kūh-e Jebāl Barez
Ravār
Laleh Zar
Baft
Jīroft
Kāshānī
Qotbābād
Aliābād
Fūrg
Darāb
Neyrīz
Khqīr
Māqūl
Gāvbandī

Rūdan
Bandar-e Maqām

Zāhedān
Kūh-e Taftān 4042
Khāsh
Bampūr
Bazmān
Kūh-e Bazmān 3489
Kamaşaptar
Īranshahr
Bāhū Kalāt

Pashō'īyeh
Dālgān
Shūr Gaz
Rīgān
Bān
Māhān

Kerman
Sa'īdābād Shahr-e Bābak
D.-ye Tashk
Sa'ādatābād
Māshīz

Chāh
Bahār

Gulf of Oman

Chābahār
Tang
Nīkshahr
Jāgīn

Ras Koh

QATAR
Doha
Ar Rayyān
Umm Sa'īd
Dukhān
Salwah
Al Khawr
Kh Duwayhin
Ṣ̌ir Banī

BAHRAIN
Al Manāmah
Al Muḩarraq

Ra's Tanāqib
Al Jubayl
Jabal 'Alī
Ad Dammām
Al Khubar
Qaţīf
Ra's az Zawr

S A U D I   A R A B I A
Al Ḩufūf
Al Hasa
Al Mubarraz
Ḩaraḑh
Yabrīn
As Sulb
Haradh
Al Jāfūrah
As Sahbā'

As Summān

Ad Dahnā'

Tropic of Cancer
Al 'Ubayiah

As Samman

Al Riyāḑ
Ad Dir'īyah
Layla
Al Kharj
Khurays
Al Ḩillah
Ad Dilam
As Salamīyah
Rumāḩ
Qaryat al 'Ulyā
Ash Shumlūl
Urairah
Al Ḩariq

A r a b i y a h

KUWAIT
Al Ḩmadī
Al Wafrah
Al Mish'āb
Mīnā' al Aḩmadī
Būbiyan
Faylakah
Al Jahrah
Ḩafar al Bāţin
Al Qayşūmah

Ad Dibdībah
Al Baţin

Wādī al Bāţin
Al Ḩsā'
Shatt al 'Arab
Ad Dibdibah

Al Ḩmadī
Al Ḩasā

30
25
60
55
50
25

BLACK SEA

100 200 300 km
50 100 150 mls

Batumi
Trabzon
Çayeli
Rize
Giresun
Tirebolu
Artvin
Ardahan
Akhalsikhe
Akhalkalaki
GEORGIA
Kumayri
Rustavi
Kazakh
Kuba
Mingechaurskoye Vokhr
Geokchay
Shemakha
Sumgait
Gümüşhane
Bayburt
Mescit D.
3236
Sarıkamış
Kars
Aragats
6090
Kirovakan
Kamo
Oz. Sevan
Gyandzha
AZERBAIJAN
Agdam
Yevlakh
Kazi Magomed
Alyat
Refahiye
2160
Erzincan
Aşkale
Erzurum
Horasan
Kağızman
Yerevan
ARMENIA
Aragats
Büyük
5165
Goris
AZE.
Kapydzhik
3906
Nakhichevan
Igdir
Saľyany
Aras
Masally
Lenkoran
Astara
Tunceli
Elazığ
Palu
Bingöl
Muş
Malazgirt
Patnos
Erciş
Süphan D.
4058
Doğubayazıt
Makü
Jülfa
Marand
Ahar
Lâri
Ları
Ardabil
4621
-ye Sabalan
Hashtpar
Herowabad
Malatya
Ergani
Diyarbakır
Silvan
Bitlis
Van Gölü
Tatvan
Van
2715
Gevaş
Khvoy
Salmas
Daryachen-ye
Orümiyeh
Tabriz
Sarab
Hashtrud
Hilvan
Siverek
Dicle
Batman
Siirt
Pervari
Midyat
Mor D.
3810
Hakkâri
Orümiyeh
Marãgheh
Kūh-e
Sahand
3710
Hashtrud
Miandowāb
Mianeh
Zanjan
Şanlıurfa
Ceylanpınar
Akçakale
Mardin
Nusaybin
Cizre
Zakho
Amãdiyah
Ra's al 'Ayn
J.'Abd al 'Aziz 920
Rawãndiz
Naqadeh
Mahãbãd
Shãhin
Dezh
Kirk Bulag D.
3707
Qeydãr
Razan
Oghlu
 Khãbur
Al Qãmishli
Al Hasakah
'Ayn
Zãlah
Al Mawşil (Mosul)
Dükãn
Sar Dasht
Saqqez
Bijãr
Bãlikh
Dijla/Tigris
Sinjãr
Tall 'Afar
Arbil
Shãhrũd
Sanandaj
Qorveh
Row'ãn
35
As Sabkhah
Al Hadr
Ash Sharqãt
As Sulaymãniyah
Halabja
Allãbãd
Al Badi
Hamadãn
Kangãvar
As Sukhnah
Mayãdin
Ba'iji
Kirkük
Tuz Khurmãtü
Ravãnsar
Qaşr-e Shirin
Kermãnshãh
Malãyer
Nahãvand
Tikrit
Khãnaqin
Borüjerd
Tudmur
Al Bu Kamãl
'Anãh
Al Qã'im
Sãmarrã
Al Miqdãdiyah
Shãhãbãd
Ilãm
Simareh
Khorramãbãd
Mileh Thartharh
Ba'qübah
Kabir Kuh
Dayr az Zawr
Al Hadithah
Hit
Ar Ramãdi
Baghdãd
Mehrãn
Dehlorãn
Dezfül
Muşayyib
Hawr al Habbãniyah
Al Fallüjah
Aş Şuwayrah
Ar Rutbah
Bahr al Milh
Al Musayyib
Al Kat
Al Hayy
Ali al Gharbi
Karbalã'
Al Hillah
An Najaf
Ad Diwãniyah
Ar Rifã'i
Qal'at Sãlih
Al 'Amãrah
Ahvãz
Khorramshahr
Abãdãn
Tukul ash Shamiyah
Abü Sukhayr
Nukhayb
As Samãwah
An Nãşiriyah
Süq ash Shuyükh
Al Qurnah
Az Zubayr
Basra
Safwãn
Badiyat ash Shãm
Ash Shabakh
Al Ma'niyah
As Salman
Ar Rihãb
Al Buşayyah
Hawr al Hammãr
Al Faw
Bübiyãn
Turayf
Al Jãlamid
Badanah
Ad Duwayd
Aş Şahrã
al Hijãrah
Al Haniyah
KUWAIT
Kuwait
Al Isawiyah
Sakãkah
Al Jawf
Raffã'
Al Jumaymah
Nişãb
Ad Dibdibah
Al Ahmadi
Mïnã' al Ahmadi
Wafra
Al Hawjã
ayra
SAUDI ARABIA
Al 'Uruq
An Nafüd
At Taysiyah
Hafar al Bãtin
Al Qayşamah
Al Mish'ãb
Qaryat al Ulyã
Qallbah
Jubbah
40
45

0   25   50   75   10
0   25   50 mls

Paleokhorio
Larnaca   Larnaca   34   C. Greco
Lefkara   Bay
Zyyi
Limassol   **CYPRUS**
Akrotiri Bay
C. Gata

B

Tartûs   Duraykish   Kafrûn Bashûr
Arwad   An   Nabrah   Tall B
Şamâ   Qal'at al   (KRAK-DES
Hamîdîyah   Tall Kalakh   CHEVALIERS)
Kleiat   Qoûbayat   Shi
El Mina   Al Qûsayr
Tripoli   Zghorta   Halba   Qornet es
(Tarâbulus esh Sham)   El Hermel   Saouda
Batroun   Amioune   3086
Jubail   Kartaba   Deir el   Laboue
BYBLOS   Ahmal   Day
LEBANON   Bhazîr   An
Jounie   Ba'albek   Yabrûc
Bikfaya   2628
Beirut   Bave de St Georges
(Beyrouth)   Ba'abda   Zahle   Rayak
Damour   Aley   Az   Outaylah
Beit ed Dîne   Zabdânî   'Ayn al Fîjah   1910
Machgharab   Dûma   Adi
Saida   Jezzine   Barâd   Tall
(Sidon)   Rachaya   Qatana   **Damas**
Hâsbaiya   A'waj (Mt Hermon)   Dimâsh
Marjaayoun   Al Kiswah
Tyr   Q. Shemona   Baniyas   Dayr 'Ali
(Tyre, Sour)   Jouai'ya   Mas'adah   CEASE FIRE   Ghabaghib   Bure
Enn Nâqoûra   Bennt   Al Qunaytirah   LINES 1974
Jbail   Aş Şanamayn   Mismly
Nahariya   Yesud   1208   Al Lâjâh   Khabab
Ma'alot   Har Meron   Hamadala   863   Izra'   Shahl
'Akko   Tarshîha   Khushnîyah   Nawâ
(Acre)   Zefat   Nâwa   Shaykh
Haifa   Q. Yam   (Safad)   Tiberias   Miskîn   As Suwaydâ
(Hefa)   Shefar'am   Yam Kinneret   Tasîl
'Atlit   Ata   Sea of Galilee   A'z Zaydî Buş
Carmel   Nazareth   Ma'agan   Irbid   Dar'a   ash
Zikhron Ya'aqov   Afula   Deir Abu   Husn   Ramtha
CAESAREA   MEGIDDO   Beyt S   Ajlûn   Mafraq
Pardes Hanna   ARMAGEDDON   Shean   Um el   Es Samra
Hadera   Jenin   Jarash   Daraj   Sabha
Qabatiya   Tubas   1247   Zarqa   Er Rumman
Netanya   Sabastîva   Nablus   Salt   Suweilih   Marka   **Amman**
Herzliyya   Kefar Sava   Bal'a   Karama   Sahâb
Ramat Gan   Petah Tiqwa   Naur   W. el
Tel Aviv   Yam   Zarqa   Jiza   Qasr el Kharane
Yafo (Jaffa)   Holon   Ramallah   Wadi es Sir   Da'ba   Jebel
Rishon le Zion   Lod   Jericho   Mudeisisat
Rehovot   Ramla   (Arîha)   Mâdabâ   Khan ez Zabib
Ashdod   Latrun   Jerusalem (El Quds)
Beit Jala   (Yerushalayim)   Dhîbân
Ashqelon   Giryat   Bethlehem   Jiza
Gat   Bet   (Bayt Lahm)   Qasr el
Guvrin   Dura   Hebron   Qatrâna
Gaza   Sederot   (El Khalil)   En Gedi
Gaza Strip   Edh   Yatta   MEZADA   El Lîsân
Khan Yunis   Dhahiriya   Mazra   Qal'a Hafra
Rafah   Ofaqim   Gerar   Arad
Zeelim   Sedom   K. el Meise   Manzil
El 'Arîsh   Revivim   Dimona   MAMSHIT   Mazâr   **JORDA**
Sabkhet   Bîr Lahfan   Yeroham   Sde   Hâşâ
el Bardawil   Abu 'Aweigila   NIZANA   Sedom   1305   Qa'el Jinz
SHIVTA   Boqer   El Ed Dabâb   Jurf ed Darawish   Jebel H
Qeziot   AVEDAT   N e g e v   Tafila
G. Maghâra   735   El Quseima   Rashâdîya   Qa'el Hafra
463   892   Mizpe   1356   Danâ   1641   Jebal
Bîr Gifgâfa   G. Libni   G. Halâl   Ramon   Ein   Jâbal   1082
E G Y P T   1305   Har Ramon   Shaubâk   Uneisa
1615   Har Saggi   Har Hakippa   PETRA
1006   467

A   C
34   36

① ② ③
34
34
32

200   400   600 km
100   200   300 mls

①
②
③

Tropic of Cancer

Al Jawf
Taymā'
Al 'Ulā
Al 'Aqaba
Ma'ān
Tabūk
Al 'Qā
Nakhl
Mar'īn
Yarū
Jerusalem
Gaza
El 'Arish

Mitts'iwa
(Massawa)
Adi Ugri
Keren
Asmera
Adwa
Adigrat
Om
Hager
Qala'en Nahl
Nak'fa
Bārentu

Port Sudan
Ras Abu
Shagara
Suakin
Haiya
Tokar
Karora

Marsā 'Alam
Muhammad Qawl
'Būr Safāga
'Qusēir

Berber
Ed Damer
Atbara
Karīma
Shendi
Kassala
El Gīrba
Khashm
el Girba
Khartoum North
Omdurman Khartoum
Wad Medani

Halāīb
Ras Banas
Yanbu'
al Bahr

Hurghada
Suez
Port Said
Dumyāt
El Mansūra
Tanta
Zagazig
Cairo
El Oāhira
El Giza
El Faiyūm
Beni Suef
El Minya
Mallawi
Asyūt
Akhmīm
Sohag
Qena
Luxor
Idfu
Aswān

Aswan
High Dam
Lake Nasser

Alexandria
Marsā
Matrūh
Shibīn el Kōm
Damanhur
Beni Mazār
Bahariya
Oasis
El Wāsta
Baharīya
Oasis

Sīdi
Barrānī

Wādī Halfa
Abri
Selīma
Oasis
Abu Hamed
Dongola
Merowe
Karīma
Abu 'Uruq
Bara
El Obeid
Ed Dueim
El Geteina
Sinnar
Singa

Nubian Desert

SUDAN

Farāfra
Oasis
Qasr Farāfra
Dakhla
Oasis
Mūt
Qasr
Farāfra
Khārga
Oasis

Kharga

Gilf Kebir
Plateau

Selīma
Oasis
Laqiya
Arba'īn

Jebel
Abyad

Wādī Howa

El 'Atrun
Oasis

Bīr Tarfāwi
Bir Misāha

Aīn
Zuwayyah
Al Jawf
Oasis
Ma'tan
as Sarra

Kutum
El Fasher
Umm
Keddada
Sodiri

LIBYA

Al Kufrah
Oasis
Rebiana
Sand Sea
Tāzirbu
Rebiana
Sarīr
Calanscio
Sand Sea
Great Sand Sea
Serir
Calanscio
A Serir

Al Burdī
Tobruk
Banghāzi
Al 'Aqaylah
Ajdābiyā
As Sidrah
Marādah
Az Zahra
Az Rāqūbah
Zaltan
Bel-Ah Wāhah
Jalū
Awjilah
Jaghbub
Al
Jaghbūb
Marsā
Sand Sea
Kufra
Nalūt

Surt
Gulf of Sirte
Misrātah
Tarhūnah
Al Khums
Al Qaryah
ash Sharqīyah
Ghar-yān
Tripoli
Tarābulus
Zuwārah
Zuwaylah
Wāw al Kabīr

Sirte Desert

Jabal as Sawdā'
Waddān
Hūn
Zillah

Sūknah
Adiri
Sabhā
Marzūq
Ubārī
Brach
Awbārī
Ghāt
Al Qatrūn

Hammādah al Hamra'
Jadu
Nālūt
Mizdah

Idehan
Marzūg
Idehan
Ubārī

Ghadāmis

S A H A R A

Tibesti

Aozou
Pic
Toussidé
3315
Emi Koussi
3415
Bardai
Zouar
Trou au
Natron
Aïn Galakka
Koro
Toro
Faya
(Largeau)
Fada
Ounianga
Kebir
Gouro
Oum
Chalouba
Erdi
Mourdi
Dépression du
Mourdi
Ennedi
Iriba
'Arada
Biltine
Abéché
Adré
Ouaddaï

CHAD

Borkou

Moussoro
Mao
Salal
Bol
Lake
Chad
Mousgoy
Kanem
Ati
Djouab
Bokoro
Massaguet
Guéréda

NIGER

Tanéré
Fachi
Agadem
Bilma
Dirkou
Madama
Plateau du
Manguéni
Plateau du
Djado
Plateau
Tchigaï
Séguédine
Chirfa

Ténéré
du
Tafassasset

Djanet
in Alakkas
Tin Ezzane

Tazóle
Termit
Tanout
Goudoumaria
Gouré
N'Guigmi
Maïné-Soroa
Diffa
Grand Erg de Bilma

①
②
③

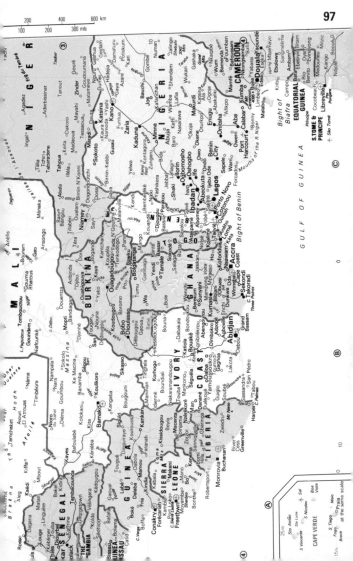

200   400   600 km
100   200   300 mls

SUDAN

Keren Mts'iwa Massawa
Kassala Adi Ugai Asmera
Khashm Barentu Om Mersa Fatma
el Girba Hajer Adwa Adigrat
Wad El Geteina Gedaref Qala'en Nahl Mek'ele Ed Ta'izz Al Shaykh 'Uthman
Medani El Gezira Adwa Aseb Mukha Adan
El Obeid Ed Ed Dueim Singa Dabat Sek'ot'a (Mocha) (Aden)
Bara Kosti El Hawata Gonder Debre Str. of Gulf of Aden
Er Rahad Umm El Jebelein Roseires Tabor Weldiya Bab el Mandeb
Dilling Ruwaba Dangila Bahir Abobe DJIBOUTI Obock
Rashad Kaka Belfodiyo Dar Guar Dese Tadjoura Djibouti
Kadugli Paloich Debre Fiche Abuye Dikhil Zeila Ras Karin
Nuba Markos Meda Al Abbe Khanzira Berbera
Mts Asosa Nejo Dire Dawa Biyo Kaboba Ceerigaabo
Kodok ETHIOPIA Harer Guban Burao
Malakal Dembi Dolo Nek'emte Awash Anwar Mts HARGEYSA Laascaanood
Fangak Nasir Sodo Adis Nazret Caynabo
Abwong Akobo Goba Abeba Asela Golocha Degeh Bur Damot
Mesha Ayod Tor Gore Jima Shashemene Ginir Aware Haud Gelad Warder
Er Req Duk Koma Yirga Goba Hara Imi Danan Ogaden Gaalkacyo
Shambe Faiwil Abera Alem Mendebo Fanna Shebele Sina Dhaqa
Rumbek Pibor Mizan Omo Mts Imi Dolo El Goran Ceelbuur
Yirol Post Teferi Arba Minch Negeli Odo Beled Teglow Dirri
Tali Bor Maji Bako Gidole Mega Mandera Luuq Weyne Buulo Mereg
Amadi Mongalla Juba Melka Abayo Moyale Xuddur Barde
Laylo Torit Kenamuke Guba Baydhabo Wanle Jowhar
Yei Swamp Lokichokio Buna Baardheere Buur Weyne Uarsciek
Faradje Moyo Nimule Kitgum Lokitaung Lake Marsabit Hakaba
Arua Kangetan Turkana Wajir Afgooye Muqdisho
Pakwach Gulu Lira Moroto Mt Kulal Afmadu Marka (Mugadishu)
Bunia Masindi Kyoga Mt Nyiru Mado Jilib Baraawe
Soroti Kateboke Mt Elgon Maralal Gashi
UGANDA Mbale Kitale Isiolo Nanyuki Giamame Equator Caluula
KENYA Eldoret Nyahururu Garissa Kismaayo Raas Boosaaso
Kampala Kapenguria Kericho Nyeri Kinangap Laasqoray Laz Hordiyo
Jinja Tororo Kisumu Nakuru Embu Ceerigaabo Daua Ras
Masaka Kisii Naivasha Carcar Mts Kaafuun
Lake Farime Nairobi Thika Qardho Bandarbeyla
Victoria Musoma Ushashi Kajiado Machakos Nugaal
Bukoba Nansio Makindu Patta I. Laascaanood Damot
RWANDA Muyinga Mwanza Loolmalasin Meru Tsavo Lamu SOMALIA Eyl
Butare Biharamulo Nyakabindi Ngorongoro Mt Malindi Jirriban
BURUNDI Geita Shinyanga Crater Moshi Voi Kilifi Dabaro
Gitega Kibondo Nzega Babati Lushoto Mombasa Gaalkacyo Hobyo
Kahama Sekenke Kondoa Kwale
Kigoma Kaliua Singida Kibaya Korogwe Tanga Wete
Ujiji Uvinza Tabora Dodoma Handeni Pangani Pemba I. at the same scale
TANZANIA Myonyi Mpwapwa Zanzibar
Mpanda Kitunda Rungwa Kilosa Morogoro Bagamoyo Moroni Grande COMOROS Is Glorieuses
Kipili Rungwa Mikumi Dar es Salaam Comore Anjouan
Sumbawanga Kasanga Iringa Kisiju Mutsamudu
Mbeya Njombe Sao Ifakara Mafia Maheli
Tunduma Hill Mahenge Mohoro Anjouan
Kyela Kilwa Kivinje Aldabra
Karonga Manda Liwale Kilwa Kisiwani Assumption SEYCHELLES
Isoka Chilumba Nachingwea Lindi Mtwara
Chinsali Rumphi Masasi C. Delgado
Mbamba Songea Newala Palma
Bay Tunduru Nkhata Bay Mueda Mocimboa da Praia
Mzuzu Mzimba Lupilichi Macomia Ibo
Lundazi Macaloge Quissanga
Metangula

200   400   600 km
100   200   300 mls

SEYCHELLES

Providence

Aldabra Is   Cosmoledo Is

Assumption   Farquhar Is

Is Glorieuses

Ruaha Nat.Pk.   Mikumi   Kisiju

Iringa   Ifakara   Kilindoni   Mafia

Chunya   Sao Hill   Mahenge   Mohoro

Mbeya   Rungwe   Njombe   Kilwa Kivinje

Kyuyu   Lwegu   Kilwa Kisiwani

Karonga   Liwale   Lindi

Manda   Nachingwea   Mtwara

Songea   Masasi   C. Delgado

Rumphi   Mbamba Bay   Tunduru   Newala   Palma

Mzuzu   Nkhata Bay   Lupilichi   Mecula   Mocimboa da Praia

Lundazi   Macaloge   Macomia   Ilbo

Metangula   Marrupa   Montepuez   Quissanga   B. de Pemba

Kasungu   Lichinga   Maúa   Namuno   Namapa   Pemba

Salima   Mandimba   Mecuburi   Meconta   Mecufi

Lilongwe   Dedza   Cuamba   Memba   Nacala

Furancungo   Malema   Ribáue   Moçambique

Cabora Bassa   Zomba   Chiuta   Molócuè   Nampula

Blantyre   Limbe   Errego   Gilé   Mogincual

Chikwawa   Milange   Angoche

Teto   Lugela   Moma

Changara   Mocuba   Pebane

Chemba   Murrumbala   Vila da Magaiza

Mutarara   Caia   Mopeia   Quelimane

Catandica   Marromeu   Chinde

Gorongosa   Dondo   Maintirano   Nosy Barren

Mutare   Chimoio   Sofala (Beira)

Chipinga   Vila Machado

Binga   Espungabera   MADAGASCAR

Machaze   Save   (MALAGASY REP.)

Nova Mambone   Morondava

Bartolomeu Dias   Bassas da India (Fr.)

Maboteo   Vilanculos   Morombe   Tanjona Ankaboa

Machaila   Pta de Barre Falsa   Europa (Fr.)   Ankazoabo

Funhalouro   Massinga   Sakaraha   Betroka

Massinger   Homoine   Morrumbene   Tôliara   Vangaindrano

Mabalane   Inhambane   Betioky   Midongy   Tropic of Capricorn

Chibuto   Quissico   Isoanala

Macia   Inharrime   Bekily

Manhica   Ampanihy   Amboasary   Tôlañaro

Xai Xai   Beloha   Ambovombe

Maputo   Tsihombe   Tanjona Vohimena

(Lourenço Marques)

Bela Vista

COMOROS

Moroni   Grande Comore   Tj. Babaomby

Mutsamudu   Anjouan   Antseranana

Mahéli   Mayotte (Fr.)   C. St Sébastien   Mgne. d'Ambre

Dzaoudzi   Ambilobe   Vohimarina

Nosy Bé   Massif du Tsaratanana

Ambanja   Sambava

Analalava   Antsohihy   Antalaha

B. de Mahajamba   Befandriana   Maroantsetra

Mahajanga   Marovoay   Mandritsara   C. Masoala

(Majunga)   Ambato-Boeny   Mampikony   Mananara   Nosy Boraha

Tsaratanana   Ivongo   I. Antongila

Besalampy   Maevatanana   Soanierana   Ambodifototra

Morafenobe   Ambatondrazaka   Atsinanana

Tsiroanomandidy   Moramanga   Toamasina (Tamatave)

Ambatolampy   Vohibinany

Miandrivazo   Antananarivo (Tananarive)

Betafo   Antsirabe   Mahanoro

Manabo   Atofinandrahana

Malaimbandy   Nosy Varika

Ambohimahasoa   Ambositra

Manja   Fianarantsoa   Ifanadiana   Mananjary

Ambalavao   Manakara

Ihosy   Ivohibe   Farafangana

Betroka   Vangaindrano

ORANGE FREE STATE   NATAL   LESOTHO

Swartruggens   Rustenburg   Brits   Middelburg   Waterval   Marracuene

Pretoria   Belfast   Boven   Barberton   Maputo

Swartruggens   Mafikeng   Koster   Randburg   Carolina   Kamati   Namacha   Matola

Krugersdorp   Randfontein   Breyton   Mbabane

Lichtenburg   Soweto   Johannesburg   SWAZILAND   Bela Vista

Coligny   Germiston   Springs   Leslie   Ermelo   Usutu   Stegi

Carletonville   Evaton   Bethal   Amsterdam

Potchefstroom   Sasolburg   Heidelberg   Morgenzon   Piet Retief

Ottosdal   Parys   Standerton   Vumisa

Klerksdorp   Vereeniging   Villiers   Sibayi L.

Schweizer Reneke   Viljoenskroon   Vaal Dam   Volksrust   Vryheid

Delareyville   Bothaville   Frankfort   Utrecht   Mkuzi

Vryburg   Wolmaransstad   Heilbron   Mooirivier   Pongola   Nongoma

B'tswana   Taung   Bloemhof   Vals   Petrus   Steyn   Newcastle   L. St Lucia

Christiana   Bultfontein   Lindley   Dundee   Mtubatuba

Warrenton   Boshof   Theunissen   Reitz   Bethlehem   Glencoe

Hoopstad   Virginia   Warden   Ladysmith   Melmoth

Kimberley   Dealesville   Winburg   Senekal   Colenso   Eshowe   Empangeni

Brandfort   Ficksburg   Weenen   Greytown   Richard's Bay

Bloemfontein   Maseru   Mokhotlong   Thabana Ntlenyana   Howick   New Hanover   Stanger   Gingindlovu

Kroonstad   Odendaalsrus   Welkom

Petrusburg   Modder   Ladybrand   Champagne Castle   Mooi River   Tongaat   Verulam

Hopetown   Kroonstad   Thaba Putsoa   Pietermaritzburg   Durban

Luckhoff   Fauresmith   Edenburg   Wepener   Mafeteng   Richmond   Donnybrook

Aliwal   Maseru   LESOTHO   Pietermaritzburg

0   100 km

0   50mls

600 1200 1800 2400 km
600 1200 mls

⑤ ⑥ ⑦ Ⓜ ⑧ Ⓛ Ⓚ Ⓙ Ⓘ Ⓗ Ⓖ Ⓕ Ⓔ Ⓓ Ⓒ Ⓑ Ⓐ

Tropic of Capricorn

Crozet Plateau

Agulhas Plateau

C. Agulhas

Prince Edward Is.

Atlantic-Indian Ridge

Atlantic-Indian Antarctic Basin

Angola Basin

Walvis Ridge

Cape Basin

St Helena

Discovery Tablemount 4111

Bouvet I.

Maud 1799

Mid-Atlantic Ridge

Ascension

Tristan da Cunha

Gough I.

ANTARCTICA

Brazil Basin

Martin Vaz

Trindade

Rio Grande Rise 637

Argentine Basin

S. Sandwich Tr. 8264

S. Georgia

S. Sandwich Is.

Scotia Sea

Weddell Sea

N. Scotia Ridge

S. Orkney Is.

Falkland Is.

Cabo de Hornos

Drake Passage

Antarctic Penin.

SOUTH AMERICA

Peru-Chile Trench

8065 7635

I. San Ambrosio
I. San Felix

7687

Is. Juan Fernandez

S.W. Peru or Nazca Ridge

Peter I.

Antarctic Circle

South East Pacific Basin

Pacific-Antarctic Ridge

A S I A

Sea of Japan

Huang He

Chang Jiang

Ganga

TAIWAN

Hainan

Bay of Bengal

Andaman Is

SRI LANKA (CEYLON)

Nicobar Is

MALDIVES

Maldives Ridge

Mekong

Sumatera

PHILIPPINES

South China Sea

C. Johnson Depth 10497

Philippine Trench

Ryukyu-Palau Ridge

S. Honshu Ridge

Japan Trench

Mariana Is (U.S.A.)

Guam

Challenger Depth

Mariana Trench

MICR

Palau (Belau) (USA)

FEDERATED STATES

Caroline Is OF MICRONES

M E

Celebes Sea

Borneo

Sulawesi

·Vityaz E 10542

·6920

Chagos Arch.

Mid Indian Basin

Ninety-East Ridge

INDONESIA

New Guinea

Planet Deep 9140

·1102

Great Barrier Reef

Coral Sea Basin

Mid-Indian Ridge

I N D I A N

O C E A N

Java Trench

·7450

·1737

Cocos Is

West Australian Basin

Jawa

Christmas I.

Timor

Arafura Sea

·1924

Tropic of Capricorn

AUSTRALIA

W. Australian Ridge

·2067

I.Amsterdam I.St Paul

·7102

South Australia Basin

Crozet Basin

Ta

Tasmani S

Ìs Crozet

Indian-Antarctic Ridge

Kerguelen Ridge

Ìs Kerguelen

Heard I.

·1922

Maco

| 600 | 1200 | 1800 | 2400 km |
| 600 | | 1200 mls | |

G 180 H 160 J 140 K 120 L 100 ① 40

NORTH AMERICA

Emperor Seamount Chain

Mendocino Seascarp 2926

②

18·

Murray Seascarp

104· Midway Is

C.Falso

Hawaiian Islands

Tropic of Cancer

20

d- Pacific Mountains

1477.

Is Revilla Gigedo

Clarion Fracture Zone

③

MARSHALL ISLANDS

P O L Y N E S I A

P A C I F I C   O C E A N

Line Is

Equator 0

NAURU

KIRIBATI

Phoenix Is

TUVALU

Tokelau (N.Z.)

Is Marquises

④

SOLOMON ISLANDS

6150·

American Samoa

French Polynesia

Wallis & (Fr.) Futuna WRN. SAMOA

Samoa Is de la Société

NUATU **FIJI** **TONGA**

Cook Is. (N.Z.)

Tahiti Is Tuamotu

20

Niue Cook Is

Nouvelle Calédonie (Fr.)

Is Tubuai

Is Gambier

Horizon Depth 10882

Pitcairn (U.K.)

Sala y Gómez 1344

I.de Pascua

S. Fiji Basin

Norfolk I.

10047

N.Cape

Norfolk I. Ridge

Kermadec Trench

INTERNATIONAL DATE LINE

South West Pacific Basin

⑤

40

NEW ZEALAND

Chatham Is

New Zealand Plateau

ckland Is

Campbell I.

732

Pacific-Antarctic Ridge

⑥

G 180 H 160 J 140 K 120 L 100 M

East Pacific Ridge

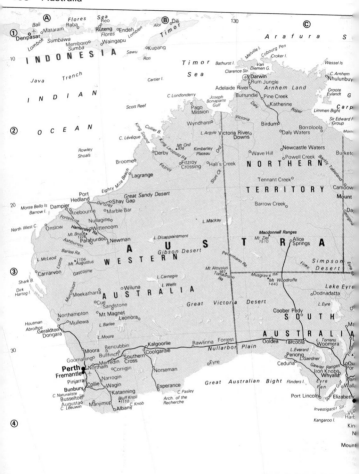

Map labels:

130

Ⓐ   Ⓑ   Ⓒ

Flores Sea
Bali   Reo
Lombok   Mataram   Ruteng   Endeh   Alor   Dili
Denpasar   Raba   Flores   Lomboto   *Timor*
Sumbawa   Waingapu
Memboro   Sumba
10   Kupang

I N D O N E S I A
Java   Trench
Sawu
Roti

A r a f u r a   S

Timor Sea
Bathurst I.   Melville I.   Cobourg Pen.
Cartier I.   Clarence Str.   Van Diemen G.   Croker I.
Darwin   Wessel Is
Rum Jungle   Nhulunbuy

I N D I A N

O C E A N

C. Londonderry
Scott Reef
Joseph Bonaparte Gulf   Adelaide River   Arnhem Land
Pago Mission   Burrundie   Pine Creek   Groote Eylandt
King Sound   Wyndham   Katherine   Roper   Limmen Bight   *Carp*
C. Lévêque   L. Argyle   Victoria   Victoria River Downs   Birdum   Daly Waters   Borroloola   Sir Edward
②   Collier B.   King Leopold Ra.   Kimberley Plateau   Wave Hill   Newcastle Waters   Mom Group
Rowley Shoals   Mt Ord   Derby   Hall's Creek   Powell Creek   Burket
Broome   Fitzroy   Fitzroy Crossing   Sturt Plat.   **N O R T H E R N**
Lagrange   Tennant Creek   Camow
Eighty Mile Beach   Great Sandy Desert   **T E R R I T O R Y**   Mount
Port Hedland   Shay Gap   Barrow Creek   Da
20   Marble Bar
Monte Bello Is   Dampier   Pilbara   Nullagine
Barrow I.   Roebourne
North West C.   Onslow   Fortescue   Wittenoom   L. Mackay
Mt Bruce   Hamersley Ra.   *Macdonnell Ranges*
Ashburton   Paraburdoo   Newman   L. Disappointment   Mt Ziel   Alice Springs
Barlee Ra.   1510   **A U S T R A**
L. McLeod   **A U S T R A**   Petermann Ra.   Finke   *Simpson Desert*
Carnarvon   Lyons   L.106 Augustus   Gibson Desert   Mt Aloysius   Musgrave Ra.   Mt Woodroffe
Shark B.   Gascoyne   **W E S T E R N**   Tomkinson Ra.   1440   Lake Eyre
③   Dirk Hartog I.   L. Carnegie   Oodnadatta
Meekatharra   Wiluna   L. Wells   L. Eyre
Cue   **A U S T R A L I A**   Great Victoria Desert   Coober Pedy   **S O U T H**
Houtman   Sandstone   Mt Magnet   Leonora   **A U S T R A L I A**
Abrolhos   Northampton   L. Barlee   L. Everard
Geraldton   Mullewa   L. Moore   Kalgoorlie   Rawlinna   Forrest   Ooldea   Tarcoola   Woomera
Dongara   Moora   Bencubbin   Coolgardie   *Nullarbor Plain*   L. Torrens   Gawler Ranges
30   Goomalling   Bullfinch   Ceduna   Penong   L. Gairdner   Iron Knob
Perth   Northam   Merredin   Southern Cross   Eyre   Whyalla
Fremantle   Corrigin   Norseman   Eyre Pen.   Port
Pinjarra   Narrogin   *Great Australian Bight*   Elizabeth
Bunbury   Wagin   Esperance   Port Lincoln   Spencer Gulf
Collie   Katanning   Flinders I.   Investigator Str.
C. Naturaliste   Bluff Knoll   Arch. of the Recherche   Harb.
Busselton   1110   C. Pasley   Kangaroo I.   Kin
Augusta   Manjimup   Albany   Ne
④   C. Leeuwin   Knob   Mount

40

⑤

110   Ⓐ   120   Ⓑ   130   Ⓒ

200 400 600 800 km
200 400 mls

PAPUA
Gulf of Papua Popondetta
Daru Port Moresby Kokoda D'Entrecasteaux Woodlark
Saibai Torres Strait C. York Somerset **NEW GUINEA** Kupiano Samarai Rossel
Cape of Wales C. Grenville Misima Louisiade Arch. Tagula
Weipa Cape York Iron Range
Coen Princess Charlotte B. C o r a l
Peninsula
Mitchell River Cooktown **Coral Sea**
Laura Willis Group **Island Territories**
Gilbert Mt Bartle Frere Cairns Coringa Is
Normanton Ravenshoe Innisfail 1812
Croydon Forsayth Palm Is S
Ingham
Mt Townsville Ayr E
Charters Towers Bowen Proserpine Marion Reef
Richmond Collinsville A
Hughenden Mackay
Selwyn Northumberland Is
QUEENSLAND Sarina Swain Reefs
Winton Clermont Cato
Longreach Barcaldine Mount Morgan
Blackall Emerald Rockhampton
Gladstone
Windorah Theodore Bundaberg Fraser or Gt Sandy I
Charleville Taroom Maryborough
Quilpie Roma Miles Dalby Gympie
St George Toowoomba **Brisbane**
Cunnamulla Goondiwindi Warwick Ipswich
Bourke Moree Stanthorpe Lismore
Milparinka Walgett Glen Innes Casino
Narrabri Armidale Grafton
Broken Hill Cobar Nyngan Tamworth Round Mtn
Menindee Dubbo Barrington Port Macquarie
Ivanhoe Gunnedah Taree
NEW SOUTH WALES Orange Maitland
Condobolin Bathurst Newcastle
Hay Griffith Lithgow **Sydney**
Mildura Cootamundra **Wollongong**
Balranald Wagga Wagga Yass Goulburn
Deniliquin Junee **Canberra** A.C.T.
Shepparton Albury Mt Kosciusko
Swan Hill 2230 Bombala
VICTORIA Bendigo Australian Alps C. Howe
Ararat Ballarat
Melbourne Orbost
Geelong Colac Morwell Bairnsdale
Hamilton Wonthaggi
Warrnambool Wilson's Prom.
King I. **Bass Strait** Furneaux Group Flinders
C. Barren
C. Grim Smithton Burnie
Devonport Launceston
Queenstown Mt Ossa St Mary's
1617
Hobart
Geeveston **TASMANIA**
South West C. South East C.

SOLOMON ISLANDS
New Georgia Santa Isabel
Florida Is Malaita Maramasike
Guadalcanal Honiara Stewart Is
San Cristobal
Rennell

Récifs d'Entrecasteaux
Îles Chesterfield (Fr.)
Iles Bélep
Bellona Reefs Muéo Uvéa Lifu
Nouvelle Calédonie (Fr.) Bourail Nouméa Île des Pins
Tropic of Capricorn

P A C I F I C

O C E A N

Norfolk I. (Aust.)

Lord Howe I. (Aust.)

T A S M A N

S E A

NEW ZEALAND C. Farewell Westport Nelson
South Island Greymouth

(E) (F)
(1)
(2)
(3)
(4)

QUEEN

SOUTH

AUSTRALIA

NEW

VICTOR

Great Australian Bight

Simpson
Desert

L a k e s   E y r e   B a s i n

Lake
Eyre
(North)

Lake
Eyre
(South)

Lake Torrens

Lake Gairdner

Lake
Frome

Flinders Range

Eyre
Peninsula

Yorke
Peninsula

Spencer Gulf

Gulf St Vincent

Investigator Strait

Kangaroo I.

Oodnadatta
Mt Dutton
Peake
Warrina
Edwards Ck
Conway

Alberga
Pedirka
Macumba

Frome Road Flats
Peera Peera
Poolanna L.

Pandie Pandie
L. Ulpawaranie

Dutrie
Betoota
Moonda L.
Birdsville
Haddon
Corner

Cordillo Downs

Clifton Hills

Durham Downs
Haddon Downs
Yamma Yamma

Eromanga

Thylungra
Adavale

Quilpie
Cheepie

Toompine

Humeburro
Dundoo

L. Etamunbanie

L. Umaroona
Warrandirinna
Kallakoopah
Warburton

Cooper Creek

Cooper
Basin
Innamincka

Wilson

Thargomindah
Cunnamulla
Eulo

Dynevor
Downs

Bulloo

Warri

Alton
Ⓐ
Narico

Bulloo Downs

Hungerford

Gray R.

Paroo R.

Caiwarro

Anna Ck
William Ck

Beresford
Coward
Springs

Etadunna

Marree

L. Gregory

Callanna

Moomba
Orientos
Sturt

L. Blanche
Ft Grey
Narylico

Desert

Lake Stewart
Callabonna
Tibooburra

Yandama
Milparinka

Yantabulla

Wanaaring
Fords Bridge

Goombalie

Darling R.

Millers Creek

Mount Eba
Parakylia
Bon Bon
Andamooka

Lyndhurst
Leigh Creek

Blinman

Mt Hack

L. Callabonna

White Cliffs

Wilcannia

L. Poopelloe

Coobowie

Kingoonya
Coondambo
L. Everard

Island
Lagoon

Woomera

Parachilna

St Mary Pk

Curnamona
Baratta

Silverton
Cockburn
Mingary

Broken Hill

Stephens Ck
Darling R.

Ivanhoe
Mount
Manara

Gil

L. Acraman
Gawler
Ranges

Paratoo
Pindari

Hawker

Mt Hope
Poochera

Buckleboo
Kyancutta
Kimba

Iron Knob
Iron Baron
Mt Giles

Port Augusta
Quorn
Carrieton
Wilmington
Orroroo
Peterborough

Mannahill
Olary

Yunta

Menindee L.
Menindee

Tandou L.

Darnick

Conoble

Ivanhoe

Tride

Mt Remarkable

Coonbah
Popilta L.

Pooncarie

Mossgiel

Willandra

Elliston
Lock
Cleve
Cowell

Whyalla

Port Pirie
Crystal
Brook
Gladstone

Jamestown

Oakbank

Canopus

Mindona L.
Traveller's L.

Hatfield

Booligal

Goolgowi

Mt Bryan

Snowtown
Wallaroo
Moonta

Kadina

Burra

Renmark

Burtundy

L. Victoria

Wentworth

Maude

Lachlan R.

Gr

Port
Kenny

Kyancutta

Yeelanna
Cummins

Maitland
Minlaton

Balaklava
Kapunda
Nuriootpa
Gawler

Eudunda

Waikerie

Barmera
Berri
Loxton

Mildura
Cal

Red Cliffs

Robinvale

Murrumbidgee R.

Balranald

Darlington Pt

Wanganella

Mt Hope
Tumby
Bay

Hardwicke B.

Stirling
Strathalbyn

Adelaide

Mannum

Cowangie

Alawoona

Hattah

Kulwin

Ouyen
Nyah West

Swan Hill
Sea Lake

Moulamein

Deniliquin
Finley

Port Lincoln
C. Carnot

C. Spence
Yorketown

Goolwa
Victor
Harbour

Murray Bridge

Tailem Bend
Meningie

Pinnaroo

Peebinga

Patchewollock

Hopetoun

Kerang
Cohuna

Pyramid Hill

Echuca
Rochester

Numurkah
Nathalia
Kyabram

Shep

Finley
Lowes

C. Catastrophe
C. Borda

Kingscote
C. Willoughby

Tintinara

Keith

Yanac
Jeparit
Nhill

Rainbow

Birchip
Charlton

Inglewood

Bendigo

Benai

C. du Couedic

C. Gantheaume

Bordertown
Padthaway

Naracoorte

Lacepede B.
Kingston S.E.
C. Jaffa

Wolseley

Warracknabeal
Murtoa

Maryborough

Castlemaine

Seymour

Rocklands
Resr
Stawell

Ararat

Creswick
Ballarat

Bacchus Marsh

Dandeno

Millicent

Penola

Balmoral

Casterton
Mt William

Horsham

Hamilton
Branxholme

Mortlake

Camperdown

Maryborough

Colac

Queenscliff

Melbourne

Geelong
Port Phillip Bay

Mount Gambier
Port MacDonnell

Discovery Bay
Portland

Koroit
Pt Fairy

Warrnambool

Port Campbell

Lorne

Apollo Bay

Healesville

Wonthagg

C. Nelson

C. Otway

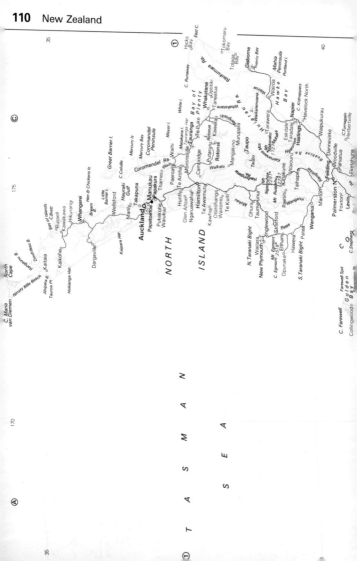

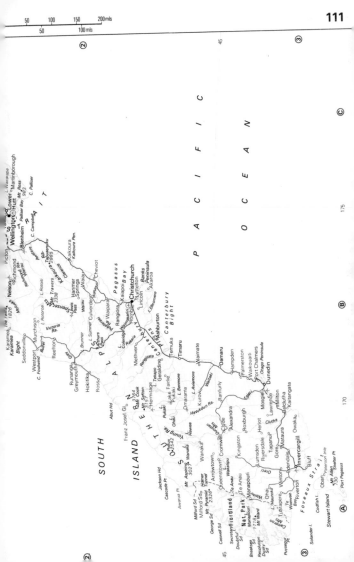

A map of Antarctica showing:

Scale: 0 — 400 — 800 — 1200 — 1600 k
0 — 400 — 800 mls

Oceans and Seas:
- INDIAN OCEAN
- ATLANTIC OCEAN
- PACIFIC OCEAN
- Weddell Sea
- Scotia Sea
- Bellingshausen Sea
- Amundsen Sea
- Ross Sea
- Drake Passage

Land regions:
- Enderby Land
- Dronning Maud Land (Nor. Claim)
- Coats Land
- Mac. Robertson Land
- American Highland
- Queen Mary Land
- Wilkes Land (Fr. Claim) (Aust. Claim)
- Victoria Land
- GREATER ANTARCTICA
- LESSER ANTARCTICA
- Palmer Land
- Ellsworth Land
- Marie Byrd Land
- Graham Land
- Coats Land
- Pensacola Mts
- Transantarctic Mts
- Trans Antarctic Mts

Ice shelves:
- Shackleton Ice Shelf
- Amery Ice Shelf
- Ronne Ice Shelf
- Ross Ice Shelf

Features:
- Howard I. (Aust.)
- Heard I. (Aust.)
- Antarctic Circle
- South Pole Amundsen-Scott (U.S.A.)
- S. Magnetic Pole (1990)
- Knox Coast
- Walgreen Coast
- Mawson
- C. Darnley
- C. Poinsett
- C. Adare
- C. Norvegia
- C. Colbeck
- Alexander I.
- Charcot I.
- Thurston I.
- Spike I.
- Roosevelt I.
- Scott I.
- Balleny Is
- Oates Land
- Sturge I.
- Antarctic Peninsula
- Palmer Arch.
- S. Shetland Is
- S. Orkney Is
- Falkland Is (U.K.)
- Tierra del Fuego
- ARGENTINA
- CHILE
- Vinson Massif 5140
- Mt Sidley 4181
- Mt Markham 4351
- Mt Kirkpatrick
- Mt Erebus
- Berkner I.
- Grf. Belgrano
- Lambert Gl.
- Prince Charles Mts — 3355

Antarctic Research Stations
1. Artigas (Uruguay)
2. Eminente Rodolfo Marsh Martin (Chile)
3. Bellingshausen (Rus. Fed.)
4. Chang Cheng (Great Wall) (China)
5. Comandante Ferraz (Brazil)
6. Henryk Arctowski (Poland)
7. Teniente Jubany (Arg.)
8. King Sejong (Korea)
9. Capitán Arturo Prat (Chile)
10. General Bernardo O'Higgins (Chile)
11. Esperanza (Arg.)
12. Vicecomodoro Marambio (Arg.)
13. Palmer (USA)
14. Faraday (UK)
15. Rothera (UK)
16. General San Martín (Arg.)
17. Mendel Vojtěch (Czech Rep.)

Index

In the index, the first number refers to the page, and the following letter and number to the section of the map in which the index entry can be found. For example, 48C2 **Paris** means that Paris can be found on page 48 where column C and row 2 meet.

Abbreviations used in the index

fghan	Afghanistan	Hung	Hungary	Pol	Poland	Arch	Archipelago
lb	Albania	Ind	Indonesia	Port	Portugal	B	Bay
lg	Algeria	Irish Rep	Ireland	Rom	Romania	C	Cape
nt	Antarctica	Leb	Lebanon	Russian Fed	Russian	Chan	Channel
rg	Argentina	Lib	Liberia		Federation	Gl	Glacier
ust	Australia	Liech	Liechtenstein	S Arabia	Saudi Arabia	I(s)	Island(s)
ang	Bangladesh	Lux	Luxembourg	Scot	Scotland	Lg	Lagoon
elg	Belgium	Madag	Madagascar	Sen	Senegal	L	Lake
ol	Bolivia	Malay	Malaysia	S Africa	South Africa	Mt(s)	Mountain(s)
ulg	Bulgaria	Maur	Mauritania	Switz	Switzerland	O	Ocean
urk	Burkina	Mor	Morocco	Tanz	Tanzania	P	Pass
amb	Cambodia	Mozam	Mozambique	Thai	Thailand	Pen	Peninsula
an	Canada	Neth	Netherlands	Turk	Turkey	Plat	Plateau
AR	Central African Republic	NZ	New Zealand	USA	United States	Pt	Point
		Nic	Nicaragua		of America	Res	Reservoir
en	Denmark	N Ire	Northern Ireland	Urug	Uruguay	R	River
om Rep	Dominican Republic	Nig	Nigeria	Ven	Venezuela	S	Sea
l Sal	El Salvador	Nor	Norway	Viet	Vietnam	Sd	Sound
ng	England	Pak	Pakistan	Yugos	Yugoslavia	Str	Strait
q Guinea	Equatorial Guinea	PNG	Papua New Guinea	Zim	Zimbabwe	V	Valley
th	Ethiopia	Paar	Paraguay				
in	Finland	Phil	Philippines				
erm	Germany						

A

57B2 Aachen Germany
46C1 Aalst Belg
38K6 Äänekoski Fin
47C1 Aarau Switz
47B1 Aare R Switz
72A3 Aba China
97C4 Aba Nig
99D2 Aba Zaire
91A3 Ābādān Iran
90B3 Ābādeh Iran
96B1 Abadla Alg
35B1 Abaeté Brazil
35B1 Abaeté R Brazil
31B2 Abaetetuba Brazil
72D1 Abagnar Qi China
43D4 Abingdon Eng
47C1 Abala Nig
63B2 Abakan Russian Fed
97C3 Abala Niger
96C2 Abalessa Alg
32C6 Abancay Peru
90B3 Abarqu Iran
74E2 Abashiri Japan
74E2 Abashiri-wan B
  Japan
71F4 Abau PNG
99D2 Abaya L Eth
99D1 Abbai R Eth
99E1 Abbe L Eth
48C1 Abbeville France
19B4 Abbeville Louisiana,
  USA
17B1 Abbeville S Carolina,
  USA
45B2 Abbeyfeale Irish Rep
47C2 Abbiategrasso Italy
20B1 Abbotsford Can
84C2 Abbottabad Pak
61H3 Abdulino
  Russian Fed
98C1 Abéché Chad
39F7 Abenrå Den
97C4 Abeokuta Nig
99D2 Abera Eth
43B3 Aberaeron Wales
15C3 Aberdeen Maryland,
  USA

100B4 Aberdeen S Africa
44C3 Aberdeen Scot
8D2 Aberdeen S Dakota,
  USA
8A2 Aberdeen
  Washington, USA
4J3 Aberdeen L Can
44C3 Aberfeldy Scot
43C4 Abergavenny Wales
43B3 Aberystwyth Wales
81C4 Abhā S Arabia
90A2 Abhar Iran
97B4 Abidjan Ivory Coast
18A2 Abilene Kansas, USA
9D3 Abilene Texas, USA
43D4 Abingdon Eng
7B4 Abitibi R Can
7C5 Abitibi,L Can
61F5 Abkhazskaya
  Respublika, Georgia
84C2 Abohar India
97C4 Abomey Benin
98B2 Abong Mbang Cam
79A4 Aborlan Phil
90A2 Abou Deia Chad
91A4 Abqaiq S Arabia
50A2 Abrantes Port
106A3 Abrolhos Is Aust
8B2 Absaroka Range Mts
  USA
91A4 Abū al Abyad I UAE
91A4 Abū 'Alī I S Arabia
91B5 Abu Dhabi UAE
95C3 Abu Hamed Sudan
97C4 Abuja Nig
33D5 Abunã Brazil
32D6 Abuná R Bol
93D3 Abū Sukhayr Iraq
111B2 Abut Head C NZ
95C3 Abu 'Urug Well
  Sudan
99D1 Abuye Meda Mt Eth
99C1 Abu Zabad Sudan
99D2 Abwong Sudan
56B1 Åby Den
94B3 Aby 'Aweigila Well
  Egypt

99C2 Abyei Sudan
24B2 Acámbaro Mexico
24B2 Acaponeta Mexico
24B3 Acapulco Mexico
31D2 Acaraú Brazil
31D2 Acaraú R Brazil
32B2 Acarigua Ven
24C3 Acatlán Mexico
23B2 Acatzingo Mexico
97B4 Accra Ghana
85D4 Achalpur India
29B4 Achao Chile
47D1 Achensee L Austria
46E2 Achern Germany
41A3 Achill I Irish Rep
63B2 Achinsk Russian Fed
53C3 Acireale Italy
26C2 Acklins I,
  Caribbean S
32C6 Acobamba Peru
29B2 Aconcagua Mt Chile
31D3 Acopiara Brazil
88B4 Açores Is Atlantic O
  A Coruña = La Coruña
47C2 Acqui Italy
108A2 Acraman,L Aust
  Acre = 'Akko
32C5 Acre State, Brazil
23B1 Actopan Mexico
23B1 Actopan Mexico
24B3 Actopan Mexico
19A3 Ada USA
50B1 Adaja R Spain
91C5 Adam Oman
35A2 Adamantina Brazil
98B2 Adamaoua Region,
  Nig/Cam
47D1 Adamello Mt Italy
16C1 Adams USA
87B3 Adam's Bridge India/
  Sri Lanka
13D2 Adams L Can
8A2 Adams,Mt USA
87C3 Adam's Peak Mt
  Sri Lanka
81C4 'Adan Yemen
22D3 Adana Turk
60D5 Adapazari Turk
11287 Adare,C Ant
108B1 Adavale Aust

47C2 Adda R Italy
91A4 Ad Dahna' Region,
  S Arabia
96A2 Ad Dakhla Mor
81C4 Ad Dali' Yemen
91B4 Ad Damman
  S Arabia
91A4 Ad Dibdibah Region,
  S Arabia
91A5 Ad Dilam S Arabia
91A5 Ad Dir'iyah S Arabia
93D3 Ad Diwaniyah Iraq
93D3 Ad Duwayd S Arabia
106C4 Adelaide Aust
4J3 Adelaide Pen Can
22D3 Adelanto USA
  Aden = 'Adan
81C4 Aden,G of Yemen/
  Somalia
97C3 Aderbissinat Niger
94C2 Adhra Syria
71E4 Adi I Indon
52B1 Adige R Italy
99D1 Adigrat Eth
85D5 Adilabad India
20B2 Adin USA
15D2 Adirondack Mts USA
99D2 Adis Abeba Eth
95C3 Adi Ugai Eth
93C2 Adiyaman Turk
54C1 Adjud Rom
6B2 Admiralty I USA
6B2 Admiralty Inlet B
  Can
87B1 Adoni India
48B3 Adour R France
96A2 Adrar Region, Maur
96C2 Adrar Alg
96A2 Adrar Soutouf
  Region, Mor
98C1 Adré Chad
95A2 Adri Libya
47E2 Adria Italy
14B2 Adrian Michigan,
  USA
52B2 Adriatic S S Europe
99D1 Adwa Eth
97B4 Adzopé Ivory Coast

55B3 **Aegean** S Greece
80E2 **Afghanistan**
 Republic, Asia
99E2 **Afgooye** Somalia
97C4 **Aflou** Alg
38G6 **Afjord** Nor
96C1 **Afmadu** Kenya
99E2 **Afmadu** Somalia
97A3 **Afolle** Region, Maur
94B2 **Afula** Israel
92B2 **Afyon** Turk
94A3 **Agadem** Niger
97C3 **Agadez** Niger
96B1 **Agadir** Mor
85D4 **Agar** India
86C2 **Agartala** India
20B1 **Agassiz** Can
97B4 **Agboville** Ivory Coast
93E1 **Agdam** Azerbaijan
75B1 **Agematsu** Japan
48C3 **Agen** France
90A3 **Agha Jāri** Iran
96A2 **Aghwinit** Well Mor
47D2 **Agno** R Italy
47E1 **Agordo** Italy
48C3 **Agout** R France
85D3 **Agra** India
93D2 **Ağri** Turk
53C2 **Agri** R Italy
53B3 **Agrigento** Italy
55B3 **Agrinion** Greece
34A3 **Agrio** R Chile
53B2 **Agropoli** Italy
61H2 **Agryz** Russian Fed
6E3 **Agto** Greenland
27D3 **Aguadilla** Puerto
 Rico
24B1 **Agua Prieta** Mexico
24B2 **Aguascalientes**
 Mexico
23A1 **Aguascalientes**
 State, Mexico
35C1 **Aguas Formosas**
 Brazil
50A1 **Agueda** Port
96C3 **Aguelhok** Mali
50A2 **Aguilas** Spain
23A2 **Aguililla** Mexico
100B4 **Agulhas,C** S Africa
79C4 **Agusan** R Phil
 Ahaggar = Hoggar
93E2 **Ahar** Iran
110B1 **Ahipara B** NZ
85C4 **Ahmadabad** India
87A1 **Ahmadnagar** India
99E2 **Ahmar** Mts Eth
46D1 **Ahr** R Germany
46D1 **Ahrgebirge** Region,
 Germany
23A1 **Ahuacatlán** Mexico
23A1 **Ahualulco** Mexico
39G7 **Åhus** Sweden
90B2 **Ahuvān** Iran
90A3 **Ahvāz** Iran
26A4 **Aiajuela** Costa Rica
47B1 **Aigle** Switz
47B2 **Aiguille d'Arves** Mt
 France
47B2 **Aiguille de la Grand
 Sassière** Mt France
75B1 **Aikawa** Japan
17B1 **Aiken** USA
73A5 **Ailao Shan** Upland
 China
35C1 **Aimorés** Brazil
96B1 **Ain Beni Mathar** Mor
95B2 **Ain Dalla** Well Egypt
51C2 **Ain el Hadjel** Alg
95A3 **Ain Galakka** Chad
96B1 **Ain Sefra** Alg
92B4 **'Ain Sukhna** Egypt
75A2 **Aioi** Japan
96B2 **Aioun Abd el Malek**
 Well Maur
97B3 **Aioun El Atrouss**
 Maur
30C2 **Aiquile** Bol
97C3 **Air** Desert Region
 Niger
13E2 **Airdrie** Can
46B1 **Aire** France
42D3 **Aire** R Eng
46C2 **Aire** R France
47C1 **Airforce I** Can
47C1 **Airolo** Switz

4E3 **Aishihik** Can
12G2 **Aishihik L** Can
46B2 **Aisne** Department,
 France
49C2 **Aisne** R France
71F4 **Aitape** PNG
58D1 **Aiviekste** R Latvia
72B2 **Aixa Zuogi** China
49D3 **Aix-en-Provence**
 France
47A2 **Aix-les-Bains** France
86B2 **Aiyar Res** India
55B3 **Aiyion** Greece
55B3 **Aíyna** R Greece
86C2 **Aizawl** India
100A3 **Aizeb** R Namibia
74E3 **Aizu-Wakamatsu**
 Japan
52A2 **Ajaccio** Corse
23B2 **Ajalpan** Mexico
95B1 **Ajdābiyā** Libya
74E2 **Ajigasawa** Japan
94B2 **Ajlun** Jordan
91C4 **Ajman** UAE
85C3 **Ajmer** India
9B3 **Ajo** USA
23A2 **Ajuchitan** Mexico
55C3 **Ak** R Turk
75B1 **Akaishi-sanchi** Mts
 Japan
87B1 **Akalkot** India
111B2 **Akaroa** NZ
75A2 **Akashi** Japan
61J3 **Akbulak** Russian Fed
93C2 **Akçakale** Turk
96A2 **Akchar** Watercourse
 Maur
55C3 **Akdağ** Mt Turk
98C2 **Aketi** Zaïre
93D1 **Akhalkalaki** Georgia
93D1 **Akhalsikhe** Georgia
55B3 **Akharnái** Greece
12D3 **Akhiok** USA
58D1 **Akhiste** Latvia
55C2 **Akhmîm** Egypt
61G4 **Akhtubinsk**
 Russian Fed
60D4 **Akhtyrka** Ukraine
75A2 **Aki** Japan
7B4 **Akimiski I** Can
74E3 **Akita** Japan
96A3 **Akjoujt** Maur
94B2 **'Akko** Israel
4E3 **Aklavik** USA
97B3 **Aklé Aouana** Desert
 Region Maur
99D2 **Akobo** Sudan
99D2 **Akobo** R Sudan
84B1 **Akoha** Afghan
85D4 **Akola** India
85D4 **Akot** India
6D3 **Akpatok I** Can
55B3 **Akra Kafirévs** C
 Greece
55B3 **Akra Maléa** C Greece
38A2 **Akranes** Iceland
55C3 **Akra Sídheros** C
 Greece
55B3 **Akra Spátha** C
 Greece
55C3 **Akra Taínaron** C
 Greece
10B2 **Akron** USA
94A1 **Akrotiri B** Cyprus
84D1 **Aksai Chin** Mts
 China
92B2 **Aksaray** Turk
61H3 **Aksay** Russian Fed
84D1 **Aksayqin Hu** L
 China
92B2 **Akşehir** Turk
92B2 **Akseki** Turk
63D2 **Aksenovo Zilovskoye**
 Russian Fed
68D1 **Aksha** Russian Fed
82C1 **Aksu** China
61H5 **Aktau** Kazakhstan
65J5 **Aktogay** Kazakhstan
61J4 **Aktumsyk**
 Kazakhstan
65G4 **Aktyubinsk**
 Kazakhstan
38I1 **Akureyri** Iceland
 Akyab = Sittwe

65K5 **Akzhal** Kazakhstan
11B3 **Alabama** State, USA
11B3 **Alabama** R USA
17A1 **Alabaster** USA
92C2 **Ala Dağlari** Mts Turk
61F5 **Alagir** Russian Fed
47B2 **Alagna** Italy
31D3 **Alagoas** State, Brazil
31D4 **Alagoinhas** Brazil
51B1 **Alagón** Spain
93E4 **Al Ahmadi** Kuwait
25D3 **Alajuela** Costa Rica
12B2 **Alakanuk** USA
38L5 **Alakurtti** Russian Fed
93E3 **Al Amārah** Iraq
21A2 **Alameda** USA
23B1 **Alamo** Mexico
9C3 **Alamogordo** USA
9C3 **Alamosa** USA
39H6 **Åland** I Fin
92B2 **Alanya** Turk
17B1 **Alapaha** R USA
65H4 **Alapayevsk**
 Russian Fed
92A2 **Alaşehir** Turk
68C3 **Ala Shan** Mts China
4C3 **Alaska** State, USA
4D3 **Alaska,G of** USA
12C3 **Alaska Pen** USA
4C3 **Alaska Range** Mts
 USA
52A2 **Alassio** Italy
12D1 **Alatna** R USA
61G3 **Alatyr'** Russian Fed
108B2 **Alawoona** Aust
91C5 **Al'Ayn** UAE
82B2 **Alayskiy Khrebet** Mts
 Tajikistan
49D3 **Alba** Italy
92C2 **Al Bāb** Syria
51B2 **Albacete** Spain
50A1 **Alba de Tormes**
 Spain
93D2 **Al Badī** Iraq
54B1 **Alba Iulia** Rom
54A2 **Albania** Republic,
 Europe
106A4 **Albany** Aust
17B1 **Albany** Georgia, USA
15D2 **Albany** New York,
 USA
8A2 **Albany** Oregon, USA
7B4 **Albany** R Can
34B2 **Albardón** Arg
91C5 **Al Batinah** Region,
 Oman
71F5 **Albatross B** Aust
91B5 **Al Baydā** Libya
11C3 **Albemarle Sd** USA
50B1 **Alberche** R Spain
108A1 **Alberga** Aust
46B1 **Albert** France
5G4 **Alberta** Province,
 Can
99D2 **Albert,L** Uganda/
 Zaïre
10A2 **Albert Lea** USA
99D2 **Albert Nile** R
 Uganda
49D2 **Albertville** France
48C3 **Albi** France
18B1 **Albia** USA
33G2 **Albina** Suriname
14B2 **Albion** Michigan,
 USA
15C2 **Albion** New York,
 USA
92C4 **Al Bi'r** S Arabia
91A5 **Al Biyadh** Region,
 S Arabia
50B2 **Alborán** I Spain
39G7 **Ålborg** Den
93D3 **Al Bū Kamāl** Syria
47C1 **Albula** R Switz
9C3 **Albuquerque** USA
91C5 **Al Buraymi** Oman
91A5 **Al Burayqah** Libya
95B1 **Al Burdi** Libya
107D4 **Albury** Aust
93E3 **Al Buşayyah** Iraq
50B1 **Alcalá de Henares**
 Spain
53B3 **Alcamo** Italy
51B1 **Alcañiz** Spain
31C2 **Alcântara** Brazil

50B2 **Alcaraz** Spain
50B2 **Alcázar de San Juan**
 Spain
51B2 **Alcira** Spain
35D1 **Alcobaça** Brazil
50B1 **Alcolea de Pinar**
 Spain
51B2 **Alcoy** Spain
51C2 **Alcudia** Spain
89J8 **Aldabra** Is Indian O
63E2 **Aldan** Russian Fed
63E2 **Aldanskoye Nagor'y**
 Upland Russian Fed
43E3 **Aldeburgh** Eng
48B2 **Alderney** I UK
43D4 **Aldershot** Eng
97A3 **Aleg** Maur
30E4 **Alegrete** Brazil
34C2 **Alejandro Roca** Arg
30H6 **Alejandro Selkirk** I
 Chile
63G2 **Aleksandrovsk
 Sakhalinskiy**
 Russian Fed
65J4 **Alekseyevka**
 Kazakhstan
60E3 **Aleksin** Russian Fed
58B1 **Alem** Sweden
35C2 **Além Paraíba** Brazil
49C2 **Alençon** France
21C4 **Alenuihaha Chan**
 Hawaiian Is
 Aleppo = Ḥalab
6D1 **Alert** Can
49C3 **Alès** France
52A2 **Alessandria** Italy
64B3 **Ålesund** Nor
12C3 **Aleutian Range** Mts
 USA
4E4 **Alexander Arch**
 USA
100A3 **Alexander Bay**
 S Africa
17A1 **Alexander City** USA
112C3 **Alexander I** Ant
111A3 **Alexandra** NZ
29G8 **Alexandra,C** South
 Georgia
6C2 **Alexandra Fjord** Can
95B1 **Alexandria** Egypt
11A3 **Alexandria**
 Louisiana, USA
10A2 **Alexandria**
 Minnesota, USA
10C3 **Alexandria** Virginia,
 USA
55C2 **Alexandroúpolis**
 Greece
13C2 **Alexis Creek** Can
94B2 **Aley** Leb
65K4 **Aleysk** Russian Fed
93D3 **Al Fallūjah** Iraq
51B1 **Alfaro** Spain
54C2 **Alfatar** Bulg
93E3 **Al Fāw** Iraq
35B2 **Alfenas** Brazil
55B3 **Alfiós** R Greece
47D2 **Alfonsine** Italy
35C2 **Alfonzo Cláudio**
 Brazil
35C2 **Alfredo Chaves** Brazil
61J4 **Alga** Kazakhstan
34B3 **Algarrobo del Aguila**
 Arg
50A2 **Algeciras** Spain
96C1 **Alger** Alg
96B2 **Algeria** Republic,
 Africa
53A2 **Alghero** Sardegna
 Algiers = Alger
15C1 **Algonquin Park** Can
91C5 **Al Hadd** Oman
93D3 **Al Hadīthah** Iraq
92C3 **Al Hadīthah** S Arabia
93D2 **Al Hadr** Iraq
91C5 **Al Hajar al Gharbi**
 Mts Oman
91C5 **Al Hajar ash Sharqi**
 Mts Oman
93C3 **Al Hamad** Desert
 Region Jordan/
 S Arabia
93E4 **Al Haniyah** Desert
 Region Iraq
91A5 **Al Hariq** S Arabia

93C3 Al Harrah *Desert Region* S Arabia
95A2 Al Haruj al Aswad *Upland* Libya
91A4 Al Hasa *R* Arabia
93D2 Al Hasakah Syria
93C4 Al Hawjā' S Arabia
93B1 Al Hayy Iraq
94C2 Al Hijanah Syria
93D3 Al Hillah Iraq
91A5 Al Hinnah S Arabia
96B1 Al Hoceima Mor
91A4 Al Hufūf S Arabia
91B5 Al Humrah *Region,* UAE
90A2 Al Huwatsam Oman
90A2 Aliābad Iran
93E3 Aliákmon *R* Greece
93E3 Ali al Gharbi Iraq
87A1 Alibāg India
51B2 Alicante Spain
9D4 Alice USA
06C3 Alice Springs Aust
53B3 Alicudi *I* Italy
84D3 Aligarh India
84B3 Aligūdarz Iran
84D2 Alīābād Iran
55C3 Alimnía *I* Greece
86B1 Alīpur Duār India
14B2 Aliquippa USA
22B2 Alīvāl USA
93C3 Al' Isawiyah S Arabia
95B2 Al Jaghbūb Libya
93D3 Al Jalamid S Arabia
93C4 Al Jawf Libya
93C4 Al Jawf S Arabia
93D2 Al Jazirah *Desert Region* Syria/Iraq
50A2 Aljezur Port
91A4 Al Jubayl S Arabia
91C5 Al Kāmil Oman
93D2 Al Khābūr *R* Syria
91C5 Al Khāburah Oman
93D3 Al Khālis Iraq
91C4 Al Khasab Oman
91B4 Al Khawr Qatar
91B5 Al Khums Libya
91A5 Al Kidan *Region,* S Arabia
56A2 Alkmaar Neth
92C3 Al Kufrah Oasis Libya
93E3 Al Kūt Iraq
93C3 Al Lādhiqīyah Syria
86A1 Allahābād India
84C1 Al Lajāh *Mt* Syria
12D1 Allakaket USA
108D1 Allanmyo Burma
95C2 'Allaqi *Watercourse* Egypt
17B1 Allatoona L USA
15C2 Allegheny *R* USA
10C3 Allegheny Mts USA
17B1 Allendale USA
11A3 Allen,Mt NZ
15C2 Allentown USA
83B3 Alleppey India
49C2 Aller *R* France
47D1 Allgäu *Mts* Germany
81C3 Al Lith S Arabia
91B5 Al Liwā *Region,* UAE
109D1 Allora Aust
14B2 Alma Michigan, USA
82B1 Alma Ata Kazakhstan
50A2 Almada Port
Al Madinah = Medina
71F2 Almagan *I* Pacific O
91B4 Al Manamah Bahrain
93D3 Al Ma'niyah Iraq
51A1 Almanor,L USA
21A1 Almansa Spain
13B1 Alma Peak *Mt* Can
91B5 Al Māriyah UAE
81 Al Marj Libya
Almaty = Alma Ata
93D2 Al Mawsil Iraq
50B1 Almazán Spain
35C1 Almenara Brazil
50B2 Almería Spain
61H3 Al'met'yevsk Russian Fed

56C1 Älmhult Sweden
93E3 Al Miqdādīyah Iraq
112C3 Almirante Brown *Base* Ant
34A1 Almirante Latorre Chile
55B3 Almirós Greece
91A4 Al Mish'ab S Arabia
50A2 Almodôvar Port
84D3 Almora India
91A4 Al Mubarraz S Arabia
92C4 Al Mudawwara Jordan
91C5 Al Mudaybi Oman
91B4 Al Muharraq Bahrain
81C4 Al Mukallā Yemen
81C4 Al Mukha Yemen
93D3 Al Musayyib Iraq
93C3 Al Nu'māniyah Iraq
42D2 Alnwick Eng
71D4 Alor *I* Indon
77C4 Alor Setar Malay
Alost = Aalst
107E2 Alotau PNG
106B3 Aloysius,Mt Aust
34C3 Alpachiri Arg
14B1 Alpena USA
47B2 Alpes du Valais *Mts* Switz
52B1 Alpi Dolomitiche *Mts* Italy
47B2 Alpi Graie *Mts* Italy
9C3 Alpine Texas, USA
47C1 Alpi Orobie *Mts* Italy
47B2 Alpi Pennine *Mts* Italy
47C1 Alpi Retiche *Mts* Switz
47D1 Alpi Venoste *Mts* Italy
52A1 Alps *Mts* Europe
95A1 Al Qaddāhīyah Libya
94C1 Al Qadmūs Syria
93D3 Al Qā'im Iraq
93C4 Al Qalībah S Arabia
93D2 Al Qāmishli Syria
95A1 Al Qaryah ash Sharqīyah Libya
92C3 Al Qaryatayn Syria
91A4 Al Qatīf S Arabia
95A2 Al Qatrūn Libya
91A4 Al Qaysūmah S Arabia
94C2 Al Quatayfah Syria
50A2 Alqueva *R* Port
92C3 Al Qunaytirah Syria
81C4 Al Qunfidhah S Arabia
93E3 Al Qurnah Iraq
94C2 Al Quşayr Syria
92C3 Al Qutayfah Syria
56B1 Als *I* Den
49D2 Alsace *Region,* France
57B2 Alsfeld Germany
42C2 Alston Eng
29D2 Alta Gracia Arg
27D5 Altagracia de Orituco Ven
68D2 Altai *Mts* Mongolia
17B1 Altamaha *R* USA
33G4 Altamira Brazil
23B1 Altamira Mexico
53C2 Altamura Italy
68C1 Altanbulag Mongolia
71F4 Altape PNG
24B2 Altata Mexico
63A3 Altay China
63B3 Altay Mongolia
63A2 Altay *Mts* Russian Fed
47C1 Altdorf Switz
46D1 Altenkirchen Germany
34B3 Altiplanicie del Payún *Plat* Arg
47B1 Altkirch France
101C2 Alto Molócue Mozam
10A3 Alton USA
34B2 Alto Pencoso *Mts* Arg
35A1 Alto Sucuriú Brazil

23B2 Altotonga Mexico
23A2 Altoyac de Alvarez Mexico
82C2 Altun Shan *Mts* China
20B2 Alturas USA
9D2 Altus USA
91B5 Al'Ubaylah S Arabia
93C4 Al Urayq *Desert Region* Arab/S Arabia
91B5 Al'Uruq al Mu'taridah *Region,* S Arabia
9D2 Alva USA
23B2 Alvarado Mexico
19A3 Alvarado USA
39G6 Älvdalen Sweden
19A4 Alvin USA
38J5 Alvsbyn Sweden
80B3 Al Wajh S Arabia
84D3 Alwar India
93D3 Al Widyān *Desert Region* Iraq/S Arabia
72A2 Alxa Youqi China
93E2 Alyat Azerbaijan
39J8 Alytus Lithuania
46E2 Alzey Germany
23B2 Amacuzac *R* Mexico
99D2 Amadi Sudan
93D3 Amādīyah Iraq
6C3 Amadjuak L Can
39J7 Åmål Sweden
63D2 Amalat *R* Russian Fed
55B3 Amaliás Greece
85D4 Amalner India
69E4 Amami *I* Japan
69E4 Amami gunto *Arch* Japan
100C4 Amanzimtoti S Africa
33G3 Amapá Brazil
33G3 Amapá *State,* Brazil
9C3 Amarillo USA
60E5 Amasya Turk
23A1 Amatitan Mexico
Amazonas = Solimões
32D4 Amazonas *State,* Brazil
28C3 Amazonas *R* Brazil
84D2 Ambāla India
87C3 Ambalangoda Sri Lanka
98B2 Ambam Cam
101D2 Ambanja Madag
1C7 Ambarchik Russian Fed
32B4 Ambato Ecuador
101D2 Ambato-Boeny Madag
101D2 Ambatolampy Madag
101D2 Ambatondrazaka Madag
57C3 Amberg Germany
25D3 Ambergris Cay *I* Belize
86A2 Ambikāpur India
101D2 Ambilobe Madag
101D2 Amboasary Madag
101D2 Ambodifototra Madag
101D2 Ambohimahasoa Madag
71D4 Ambon Indon
101D2 Ambositra Madag
101D2 Ambovombe Madag
98B3 Ambriz Angola
98C1 Am Dam Chad
64H3 Amderma Russian Fed
24B2 Ameca Mexico
23B2 Amecameca Mexico
34C2 Ameghino Arg
56B2 Ameland *I* Neth
16C2 Amenia USA
112B10 American Highland *Upland* Ant
105H4 American Samoa *Is* Pacific O
17B1 Americus USA

101G1 Amersfoort S Africa
112C10 Amery Ice Shelf Ant
55B3 Amfilokhía Greece
55B3 Ámfissa Greece
63F1 Amga Russian Fed
63F1 Amga *R* Russian Fed
69F2 Amgu Russian Fed
69F2 Amgun' *R* Russian Fed
99D1 Amhara *Region* Eth
7D5 Amherst Can
16C1 Amherst Massachusetts, USA
Amherst = Kyaikkami
87B2 Amhür India
48C2 Amiens France
75B1 Amino Japan
14B2 Amisk L Can
89K8 Amirante *Is* Indian O
86B1 Amlekhgan Nepal
92C3 Amman Jordan
38K6 Ammassalik Greenland
56B2 Ammersfoort Neth
84M2 Amol Iran
55C3 Amorgós *I* Greece
7C5 Amos Can
Amoy = Xiamen
101D3 Ampanihy Madag
35B2 Amparo Brazil
51C1 Amposta Spain
85D4 Amravati India
85C4 Amreli India
84C2 Amritsar India
56A2 Amsterdam Neth
101H1 Amsterdam S Africa
15D2 Amsterdam USA
98C1 Am Timan Chad
88L3 Amu Darya *R* Uzbekistan
6A2 Amund Ringes *I* Can
4F2 Amundsen *G* Can
112B4 Amundsen-Scott *Base* Ant
80E Amundsen-Scott *Base* Ant
78D3 Amuntai Indon
63E2 Amur *R* Russian Fed
33E2 Anaco Ven
8B2 Anaconda USA
20B1 Anacortes USA
55C3 Anáfi *I* Greece
93D3 'Anah Iraq
22C3 Anaheim USA
87B2 Anaimalai Hills India
83C4 Anakapalle India
12E1 Anaktuvuk P USA
101D2 Analalava Madag
92B2 Anamur Turk
75A2 Anan Japan
87B2 Anantapur India
84D2 Anantnag India
90C3 Anār Iran
90B3 Anārak Iran
71F2 Anatahan *I* Pacific O
30D4 Añatuya Arg
74B3 Anbyŏn N Korea
22C4 Anacpa *Is* USA
4D3 Anchorage USA
30C2 Ancohuma *Mt* Bol
32B6 Ancón Peru
52B2 Ancona Italy
16C1 Ancram USA
29B4 Ancud Chile
34A3 Andacollo Arg
108A1 Andado Aust
32C6 Andahuaylas Peru
38F6 Andalsnes Nor
50A2 Andalucia *Region,* Spain
17A1 Andalusia USA
83D4 Andaman *Is* Burma
83D4 Andaman *S* Burma
108A2 Andamooka Aust
38H5 Andenes Nor
47C1 Andermatt Switz
57B2 Andernach Germany
14A2 Anderson Indiana, USA
18B2 Anderson Missouri, USA
17B1 Anderson S Carolina, USA
4F3 Anderson *R* Can

Andhra Pradesh

87B1 Andhra Pradesh
State, India
55B3 Andikíthira I Greece
65J5 Andizhan Uzbekistan
65H6 Andkhui Afghan
74B3 Andong S Korea
51C1 Andorra Principality,
SW Europe
51C1 Andorra-La-Vella
Andorra
43D4 Andover Eng
35A2 Andradina Brazil
12B2 Andreafsky USA
92B2 Andreas,C Cyprus
53C2 Andria Italy
11C4 Andros / The
Bahamas
55B3 Andros I Greece
87A2 Andrott I India
50B2 Andújar Spain
97A4 Andulo Angola
97C4 Andoho Togo
97C3 Anéfis Mali
34B3 Añelo Arg
63C2 Angarsk Russian Fed
38H6 Ange Sweden
24A2 Angel de la Guarda I
Mexico
79B2 Angeles Phil
39G7 Angelholm Sweden
109C1 Angellala Creek R
Aust
22B1 Angels Camp USA
71E4 Angemuk Mt Indon
48B2 Angers France
76C3 Angkor Hist Site
Camb
41C3 Anglesey I Wales
19A4 Angleton USA
6G3 Angmagssalik
Greenland
101D2 Angoche Mozam
29B3 Angol Chile
14B2 Angola Indiana, USA
15C1 Angola State, Africa
103H6 Angola Basin
Atlantic O
12H3 Angoon USA
48C2 Angoulême France
96A1 Angra do Heroismo
Açores
35C2 Angra dos Reis Brazil
34C3 Anguil Arg
27E3 Anguilla I
Caribbean S
26B2 Anguilla Cays Is
Caribbean S
86B2 Angul India
99C3 Angumu Zaire
56C1 Anholt I Den
73C4 Anhua China
72D3 Anhui Province,
China
12C2 Aniak USA
35B1 Anicuns Brazil
46B2 Anizy-le-Château
France
4C3 Anjak USA
48B2 Anjou Region, France
101D2 Anjouan I Comoros
101D2 Anjozorobe Madag
74B3 Anju N Korea
72B3 Ankang China
92B2 Ankara Turk
101D2 Ankaratra Mt Madag
101D3 Ankazoabo Madag
101D2 Ankazobe Madag
56C2 Anklam Germany
76D3 An Loc Viet
73B4 Anlong China
73C3 Anlu China
18C2 Anna USA
16C1 'Annaba Alg
92C3 An Nabk S Arabia
92C3 An Nabk Syria
108A1 Anna Creek Aust
80C3 An Nafud Desert
S Arabia
93D3 An Najaf Iraq
42C2 Annan Scot
15C3 Annapolis USA
86A1 Annapurna Mt Nepal
14B2 Ann Arbor USA
94C1 An Näsirah Syria

93E3 An Nāsiriyah Iraq
47B2 Annecy France
47B1 Annemasse France
76D3 An Nhon Viet
73A5 Anning China
17A1 Anniston USA
89E8 Annobon I Eq
Guinea
49C2 Annonay France
27J1 Annotto Bay
Jamaica
73D3 Anqing China
72B2 Ansai China
57C3 Ansbach Germany
26C3 Anse d'Hainault Haiti
72E1 Anshan China
73B4 Anshun China
97C3 Ansongo Mali
14B3 Ansted USA
92C2 Antakya Turk
101E2 Antalaha Madag
92B2 Antalya Turk
92B2 Antalya Körfezi B
Turk
101D2 Antananarivo
Madag
112C1 Antarctic Circle Ant
112C3 Antarctic Pen Ant
50B2 Antequera Spain
96B2 Anti-Atlas Mts
7D5 Anticosti, I. d' Can
27E3 Antigua I
Caribbean S
Anti Lebanon = Jebel
esh Sharqi
21A2 Antioch USA
19A3 Antlers USA
30B3 Antofagasta Chile
45C1 Antrim County, N Ire
45C1 Antrim N Ire
45C1 Antrim Hills N Ire
101D2 Antseranana Madag
101D2 Antsiabe Madag
16D2 An Tuc Viet
46C1 Antwerpen Belg
45C2 An Uaimh Irish Rep
84C3 Anupgarh India
87C3 Anuradhapura
Sri Lanka
Anvers = Antwerpen
4B3 Anvik USA
63B3 Anxi China
72C2 Anyang China
72A3 A'nyêmaqên Shan
Upland China
47C2 Anza R Italy
13E1 Anzac Can
65K4 Anzhero-Sudzhensk
Russian Fed
53B2 Anzio Italy
52A1 Aosta Italy
97B3 Aoukar Desert
Region Maur
96C2 Aoulef Alg
96A2 Aozou Chad
30E3 Apa R Brazil/Par
11B4 Apalachee B USA
17B2 Apalachicola USA
17B2 Apalachicola B USA
23B2 Apan Mexico
64E3 Apatity Russian Fed
32C3 Apaporis R
Colombia
35A2 Aparecida do
Taboado Brazil
79B2 Aparri Phil
54A1 Apatin Croatia
64E3 Apatity Russian Fed
24B3 Apatzingán Mexico
56B2 Apeldoorn Neth
35B2 Apiaí Brazil
33F2 Apoera Surinam
108B3 Apollo Bay Aust
79C4 Apo,Mt Mt Phil
17B2 Apopka,L USA
30F2 Aporé R Brazil
10A2 Apostle Is USA
10A2 Apostle I, USA
23A1 Apozol Mexico
11B3 Appalachian Mts
USA
52B2 Appenino Abruzzese
Mts Italy

52A2 Appennino Ligure
Mts Italy
53C2 Appennino Lucano
Mts Italy
53B2 Appennino
Napoletano Mts Italy
52B2 Appennino Tosco-
Emiliano Mts Italy
52B2 Appennino Umbro-
Marchigiano Mts
Italy
47C1 Appenzell Switz
42C2 Appleby Eng
14A2 Appleton Wisconsin,
USA
30F3 Apucarana Brazil
23B1 Apulco Mexico
32D2 Apure R Ven
32C6 Apurimac R Peru
92C4 'Aqaba Jordan
92B4 'Aqaba,G of Egypt/
S Arabia
90B3 'Aqda Iran
30E3 Aquidauana Brazil
23A2 Aquila Italy
86A1 Ara India
17A1 Arab USA
81D4 Arabian S Asia/
Arabian Pen
31D4 Aracaju Brazil
30E3 Aracanguy, Mts de
Par
31D2 Aracati Brazil
30F3 Araçatuba Brazil
50A2 Aracena Spain
31C5 Araçuai Brazil
94B3 Arad Israel
60B4 Arad Rom
98C1 Arada Chad
91B5 'Arādah UAE
106C1 Arafura S Indon/Aust
30F2 Aragarças Brazil
51B1 Aragón Region,
Spain
50B1 Aragón R Spain
33G6 Araguacia R Brazil
31B3 Araguaina Brazil
35B1 Araguari Brazil
35B1 Araguari R Brazil
84B1 Arak Iran
96C2 Arak Alg
90A3 Arāk Iran
76A2 Arakan Yoma Mts
Burma
87B2 Arakkonam India
65G5 Aral Sea Kazakhstan/
Uzbekistan
80E1 Aral'sk Kazakhstan
Aral'skoye More =
Aral S
40B2 Aran I Irish Rep
50B1 Aranda de Duero
Spain
24A1 Arandas Mexico
50B1 Aranjuez Spain
75A2 Arao Japan
97B3 Araouane Mali
29E2 Arapey R Urug
31D4 Arapiraca Brazil
35A2 Araporgas Brazil
30G4 Arapongas Brazil
31B6 Araraquara Brazil
35B2 Araras Brazil
31B3 Araras Brazil
107D4 Ararat Aust
93D2 Ararat Armenia
93E2 Aras R Azerbaijan
75C1 Arato Japan
32D2 Arauca R Ven
34A3 Arauco Chile
32C2 Arauea Colombia
84C4 Aravalli Range Mts
India
31B5 Araxá Brazil
99D2 Arba Minch Eth
53A3 Arbatax Sardegna
93D2 Arbil Iraq
47A1 Arbois France
39H6 Arbrä Sweden
44C3 Arbroath Scot
47A1 Arc France
47B2 Arc R France
48B3 Arcachon France
17B2 Arcadia USA
20B2 Arcata USA
23A2 Arcelia Mexico

26B2 Archipiélago de
Camaguey Arch
Cuba
29B6 Archipiélago de la
Reina Adelaida Ar
Chile
29B4 Archipiélago de las
Chones Arch Chile
32B2 Archipiélago de las
Perlas Arch Panar
35B2 Arcos Brazil
50A2 Arcos de la Fronter
Spain
4E3 Arctic Bay Can
1C1 Arctic Circle
4E3 Arctic Red Can
4E3 Arctic Red R Can
4D3 Arctic Village USA
54C2 Arda R Bulg
65F6 Ardabil Iran
93D1 Ardahan Turk
39F6 Ardal Nor
76C2 Ardar des Iforas
Upland Alg/Mali
45C2 Ardee Irish Rep
90B3 Ardekän Iran
46C2 Ardennes
Department, France
46C2 Ardennes Region,
Belg
90B3 Ardestan Iran
92C3 Ardh es Suwwan
Desert Region
Jordan
50A2 Ardila R Port
109C2 Ardlethan Aust
9D3 Ardmore USA
44A3 Ardnamurchan Pt
Scot
44B5 Ardres France
44B3 Ardrishaig Scot
42B2 Ardrossan Scot
27D3 Arecibo Puerto Ric
31D2 Areia Branca Brazil
21A2 Arena,Pt USA
39F7 Arendal Nor
30B2 Arequipa Peru
52B2 Arezzo Italy
49C2 Argentan France
49C2 Argenteuil France
48B2 Argenteuil France
28C7 Argentina Republic
S America
103F7 Argentine Basin
Atlantic O
48C2 Argenton-sur-Creus
France
54C2 Argeş R Rom
84B2 Arghardab R Afgha
55B3 Argolikós Kólpos G
Greece
46C2 Argonne Region,
France
53A3 Argos Greece
55B3 Argostólion Greece
22B3 Arguello,Pt USA
106B2 Argyle,L Aust
56C1 Arhus Den
100A3 Ariamsvlei Namibi
50B1 Arién zón R Spain
34C2 Arias Arg
97B3 Aribinda Burkina
30B2 Arica Chile
84B3 Arifwala Pak
Arihā = Jericho
27L1 Arima Trinidad
35B1 Arinos Brazil
33F6 Arinos R Brazil
23A2 Ario de Rosales
Mexico
27L1 Aripo,Mt Trinidad
33E5 Aripuana Brazil
33E5 Aripuaná R Brazil
48A3 Arisaig Scot
87B2 Ariskere India
12B2 Aristazabal I Can
34B3 Arizona Arg
9B3 Arizona State, USA
39G7 Arjang Sweden
61F3 Arkadak Russian Fe
19B3 Arkadelphia USA
65H4 Arkaly Kazakhstan
11A3 Arkansas State, USA
11A3 Arkansas R USA
18A2 Arkansas City USA

64F3 Arkhangel'sk Russian Fed
41B3 Arklow Irish Rep
47D1 Arlberg P Austria
49C3 Arles France
19A3 Arlington Texas, USA
15C3 Arlington Virginia, USA
20B1 Arlington Washington, USA
97C3 Arlit Niger
57B3 Arlon Belg
Armageddon = Megiddo
45C1 Armagh County, N Ire
45C1 Armagh N Ire
61F5 Armavir Russian Fed
22A2 Armenia Colombia
63F3 Armenia Republic, Europe
107E4 Armidale Aust
13D2 Armstrong Can
7C3 Arnaud R Can
92B2 Arnauti C Cyprus
56B2 Arnhem Neth
106C2 Arnhem,C Aust
106C2 Arnhem Land Aust
22B1 Arnold USA
15C1 Arnprior Can
46E1 Arnsberg Germany
63F3 Aroab Namibia
47C2 Arona Switz
12B2 Aropuk L USA
52A1 Arosa Switz
97A3 Arquipélago dos Bijagós Arch Guinea-Bissau
93D3 Ar Ramādī Iraq
42B2 Arran I Scot
93C2 Ar Raqqah Syria
95A2 Ar Rāqūbah Libya
49C1 Arras France
96A2 Arrecife Canary Is
34C2 Arrecifes Arg
23A1 Arriaga Mexico
93E3 Ar Rifa't Iraq
93E3 Ar Rihāb Desert Region Iraq
91A5 Ar Riyād S Arabia
44B3 Arrochar Scot
111A2 Arrowtown NZ
23B1 Arroyo Seco Mexico
91B4 Ar Ru'ays Qatar
91C5 Ar Rustaq Oman
93D3 Ar Rutbah Iraq
47D2 Arsiero Italy
49D2 Arsizio Italy
61G2 Arsk Russian Fed
57B3 Árta Greece
23A2 Arteaga Mexico
63B2 Artemovsk Russian Fed
63D2 Artemovskiy Russian Fed
9C3 Artesia USA
111B2 Arthurs P NZ
112C2 Arthurs Pass NZ
29E2 Artigas Urug
4H3 Artillery L Can
47C1 Artois Region, France
112C2 Arturo Prat Base Ant
93D1 Artvin Turk
99D2 Aru Zaire
33G6 Aruanã Brazil
27C4 Aruba I Caribbean S
86B1 Arun R Nepal
86C1 Arunāchal Pradesh Union Territory, India
87B3 Aruppukkottai India
99D3 Arusha Tanz
98C2 Aruwimi R Zaire
68C2 Arvayheer Mongolia
47B2 Arve R France
7C5 Arvida Can
38H5 Arvidsjaur Sweden
39G7 Arvika Sweden
21B2 Arvin USA
94B1 Arwad I Syria
61F2 Arzamas Russian Fed
84C2 Asadabad Afghan
75A2 Asahi R Japan

74E2 Asahi dake Mt Japan
74E2 Asahikawa Japan
86B2 Asansol India
95A2 Asawanwah Well Libya
61K2 Asbest Russian Fed
15D2 Asbury Park USA
103H5 Ascension I Atlantic O
57B3 Aschaffenburg Germany
56C2 Aschersleben Germany
52C2 Ascoli Piceno Italy
47C1 Ascona Switz
99E1 Aseb Eth
96C2 Asedjirad Upland Alg
99D2 Asela Eth
38H6 Åsele Sweden
54B2 Asenovgrad Bulg
46C2 Asfeld France
61J2 Asha Russian Fed
17B1 Ashburn USA
111B2 Ashburton NZ
106A3 Ashburton R Aust
92B3 Ashdod Israel
19B3 Ashdown USA
11B3 Asheville USA
109D1 Ashford Aust
43E4 Ashford Eng
74D3 Ashikaga Japan
75A2 Ashizuri-misaki Pt Japan
65G6 Ashkhabad Turkmenistan
10B3 Ashland Kentucky, USA
14B2 Ashland Nebraska, USA
14B2 Ashland Ohio, USA
8A2 Ashland Oregon, USA
109C1 Ashley Aust
16B2 Ashokan Res USA
94B3 Ashqelon Israel
91C4 Ash Sha'm UAE
93D2 Ash Sharqāt Iraq
93E3 Ash Shatrah Iraq
81C4 Ash Shihr Yemen
91A4 Ash Shumlul S Arabia
95C3 Ashtabula USA
7D4 Ashuanipi L Can
72A2 'Aşī R Syria
47D2 Asiago Italy
53A2 Asinara I Medit S
65K4 Asino Russian Fed
93D2 Aşkale Turk
39G7 Askersund Sweden
84C1 Asmar Afghan
95C3 Asmera Eth
75A2 Aso Japan
99D1 Asosa Eth
111A2 Aspiring,Mt NZ
93C2 As Sabkhah Syria
91A5 As Salamiyah S Arabia
91A5 As Salamīyah S Arabia
92C2 As Salamīyah Syria
93D3 As Salmān Iraq
86C1 Assam State, India
93E3 As Samāwah Iraq
91B5 As Şanām Region, S Arabia
94C2 As Sanamayn Syria
56B2 Assen Neth
56B1 Assens Den
95A2 As Sīdrah Libya
5H5 Assiniboia Can
5G4 Assiniboine,Mt Can
30F3 Assis Brazil
93C3 As Sukhnah Syria
93E2 As Sulaymānīyah Iraq
91A5 As Summan Region, S Arabia
99E3 Assumption I Seychelles
93C2 As Suwaydā' Syria
93D3 As Suwayrah Iraq
93E2 Astara Azerbaijan

52A2 Asti Italy
55C3 Astipálaia I Greece
50A1 Astorga Spain
8A2 Astoria USA
61G4 Astrakhan' Russian Fed
50A1 Asturias Region, Spain
30E4 Asunción Par
99D2 Aswa R Uganda
80B3 Aswân Egypt
80B3 Aswân High Dam Egypt
95C2 Asyût Egypt
92C3 Az Zilaf Syria
97C4 Atakpamé Togo
71D4 Atambua Indon
6E3 Atangmik Greenland
96A2 Atar Maur
65J5 Atasu Kazakhstan
95C3 Atatisk Baraji Res Turkmenistan
8B3 Atbara Sudan
65H4 Atbasar Kazakhstan
11A3 Atchafalaya B USA
10A3 Atchison USA
23A1 Atenguillo Mexico
52B2 Atessa Italy
46B1 Ath Belg
13E2 Athabasca R Can
5G4 Athabasca L Can
5H4 Athabasca L Can
45B2 Athenry Irish Rep
Athens = Athínai
11B3 Athens Georgia, USA
14B3 Athens Ohio, USA
19A3 Athens Texas, USA
55B3 Athínai Greece
41B3 Athlone Irish Rep
16C1 Athol USA
55B2 Áthos Mt Greece
45C2 Athy Irish Rep
98B1 Ati Chad
7A5 Atikoken Can
61F3 Atkarsk Russian Fed
18B2 Atkins USA
23B2 Atlacomulco Mexico
11B3 Atlanta Georgia, USA
14B2 Atlanta Michigan, USA
18A1 Atlantic USA
10C3 Atlantic City USA
16B2 Atlantic Highlands USA
103H8 Atlantic Indian Basin Atlantic O
103H7 Atlantic Indian Ridge Atlantic O
96C1 Atlas Saharien Mts Alg
4E4 Atlin Can
4E4 Atlin L Can
94B2 'Atlit Israel
23B2 Atlixco Mexico
11B3 Atmore USA
101D3 Atofinandrahana Madag
12D3 Atognak I USA
19A3 Atoka USA
23A1 Atotonilco Mexico
23B2 Atoyac R Mexico
32B2 Atrato R Colombia
91B5 Attaf Region, UAE
81C3 At Tā'if S Arabia
94C2 At Tall Syria
17A1 Attalla USA
7B4 Attauapiskat Can
7B4 Attauapiskat R Can
93D3 At Taysīyah Desert Region S Arabia
16A3 Attica India, USA
46C2 Attigny France
15D2 Attleboro Massachusetts, USA
76D3 Attopeu Laos
92C4 At Tubayq Upland S Arabia
34B3 Atuel R Arg
39H7 Åtvidaberg Sweden
22B2 Atwater USA
49D3 Aubagne France
46C2 Aube Department, France

49C3 Aubenas France
17A1 Auburn Alabama, USA
21A2 Auburn California, USA
14A2 Auburn Indiana, USA
18A1 Auburn Nebraska, USA
15C2 Auburn New York, USA
20B1 Auburn Washington, USA
48C3 Auch France
110B1 Auckland NZ
110G6 Auckland Is NZ
48C3 Aude R France
47B1 Audincourt France
109C1 Augathella Aust
57C3 Augsburg Germany
106A4 Augusta Aust
11B3 Augusta Georgia, USA
18A2 Augusta Kansas, USA
10D2 Augusta Maine, USA
12D3 Augustine I USA
58C2 Augustów Pol
106A3 Augustus,Mt Aust
46A2 Aumale France
85D3 Aurangābād India
96C1 Aurès Mts Alg
48C2 Aurillac France
8C3 Aurora Colorado, USA
10B2 Aurora Illinois, USA
14B3 Aurora Indiana, USA
18B2 Aurora Mississippi, USA
100A3 Aus Namibia
14B2 Au Sable USA
10A2 Austin Minnesota, USA
21B2 Austin Nevada, USA
9D3 Austin Texas, USA
106C3 Australia Fed. State/Monarchy
107D4 Australian Alps Mts Aust
37E4 Austria Federal Republic, Europe
46A1 Authie R France
24B3 Autlán Mexico
49C2 Autun France
49C2 Auvergne Region, France
49C2 Auxerre France
46B1 Auxi-le-Châteaux France
22C4 Avalon USA
7C5 Avalon Pen Can
35B2 Avaré Brazil
90D3 Avaz Iran
94B3 Avedat Hist Site Israel
33F4 Aveiro Brazil
50A1 Aveiro Port
29E2 Avellaneda Arg
53B2 Avellino Italy
46B1 Avesnes-sur-Helpe France
39H6 Avesta Sweden
53B2 Avezzano Italy
44C3 Aviemore Scot
111B2 Aviemore,L NZ
47B2 Avigliana Italy
49C3 Avignon France
50B1 Avila Spain
50A1 Aviles Spain
47D1 Avisio R Italy
108B3 Avoca R Aust
43C4 Avon County, Eng
43D4 Avon R Dorset, Eng
43D3 Avon R Warwick, Eng
43C4 Avonmouth Wales
17B2 Avon Park USA
46B2 Avre R France
54A2 Avtovac Bosnia-Herzegovina
94C2 A'waj R Syria
74D4 Awaji-shima I Japan

99E2 Awarē Eth
111A2 Awarua Pt NZ
99E2 Awash R Eth
99E2 Awash R Eth
75B1 Awa-shima I Japan
111B2 Awatere R NZ
95A2 Awbārī Libya
99D2 Aweil Sudan
95B2 Awjilah Libya
96A2 Awarē Well Mor
6A2 Axel Heiburg I Can
43C4 Axminster Eng
75B1 Ayabe Japan
29E3 Ayacucho Arg
32C6 Ayacucho Peru
65K5 Ayaguz Kazakhstan
82C2 Ayakkum Hu L
China
50A2 Ayamonte Spain
63F2 Ayan Russian Fed
32C6 Ayauiri Peru
92A2 Aydin Turk
55C3 Áyios Evstrátios I
Greece
43D4 Aylesbury Eng
13D2 Aylmer,Mt Can
94C2 'Ayn al Fijah Syria
93D2 Ayn Zālah Iraq
95B2 Ayn Zuwayyah Well
Libya
99D2 Ayod Sudan
107D2 Ayr Aust
42B2 Ayr Scot
42B2 Ayr R Scot
54C2 Ayr,Pt of Eng
76C3 Aytthaya Thai
23A1 Ayutla Mexico
55C3 Ayvacik Turk
55C3 Ayvalik Turk
86A1 Azamgarh India
97B3 Azaouad Desert
Region Mali
97D3 Azare Nig
92C2 A'Zāz Syria
65F5 Azerbaijan Republic,
Russian Fed
32B4 Azogues Ecuador
Azores = Açores
98C1 Azoum R Chad
60E4 Azov, Sea of
Russian Fed/Ukraine
Azovskoye More =
Azov, Sea of
96B1 Azrou Mor
34D3 Azucena Arg
32A2 Azuero,Pen de
Panama
29E3 Azúl Arg
94C2 Az-Zabdānī Syria
91C5 Az Zāhirah Mts
Oman
95A2 Az Zahra Iraq
96A2 Azzeffal R Maur
93E3 Az Zubayr Iraq

B

94B2 Ba'abda Leb
92C3 Ba'albek Leb
94B3 Ba'al Hazor Mt
Israel
99E2 Baardheere Somalia
54C2 Babadag Rom
92A1 Babaeski Turk
32B4 Babahoyo Ecuador
81C4 Bāb el Mandab Str
Djibouti/Yemen
71D4 Babar I Indon
99D3 Babati Tanz
60E2 Babayevo
Russian Fed
14B2 Baberton USA
13B1 Babine R Can
5F4 Babine L Can
90B2 Bābol Iran
79B2 Babuyan Chan Phil
79B2 Babuyan Is Phil
21C2 Bacabal Rom
71D4 Bacan I Indon
60C4 Bacău Rom
76D1 Bac Can Viet
108B3 Bacchus Marsh Aust
82B2 Bachu China
4J3 Back R Can

12J2 Backbone Ranges
Mts Can
76D1 Bac Ninh Viet
79B3 Bacolod Phil
79B3 Baco,Mt Phil
87B2 Badagara India
72A1 Badain Jaran Shamo
Desert China
50A2 Badajoz Spain
51C1 Badalona Spain
93D3 Badanah S Arabia
46D2 Bad Bergzabern
Germany
46D1 Bad Ems Germany
47C1 Baden Switz
57B3 Baden-Baden
Germany
57B3 Baden-Württemberg
State, Germany
57C3 Badgastein Austria
22C2 Badger USA
57B2 Bad-Godesberg
Germany
57B2 Bad Hersfeld
Germany
46D1 Bad Honnef
Germany
85B4 Badin Pak
52B1 Bad Ischl Austria
93C3 Badiyat ash Sham
Desert Region
Jordan/Iraq
57B3 Bad-Kreuznach
Germany
46D1 Bad Nevenahr-
Ahrweiler Germany
47C1 Bad Ragaz Switz
57C3 Bad Tolz Germany
87C3 Badulla Sri Lanka
50C3 Baena Spain
97A3 Bafatá Guinea-Bissau
4H2 Baffin B Greenland/
Can
6C2 Baffin I Can
6C2 Baffin I Can
98B2 Bafia Cam
97A3 Bafing R Mali
97A3 Bafoulabé Mali
98B2 Bafoussam Cam
90C3 Bāfq Iran
60E5 Bafra Burun Pt Turk
91C4 Bāft Iran
98C2 Bafwasende Zaire
86A1 Bagaha India
87B1 Bāgalkot India
99D3 Bagamoyo Tanz
29F2 Bagé Brazil
93D3 Baghdad Iraq
86B2 Bāgherhat Bang
91C3 Bāghin Iran
84B1 Baghlan Afghan
49C3 Bagnols-sur-Cèze
France
97B3 Bagoé R Mali
Bagu = Pegu
79B2 Baguio Phil
86B1 Bāhadurābād India
11C4 Bahamas,The Is
Caribbean S
86B2 Baharampur India
92A4 Bahariya Oasis Egypt
84C3 Bahawalpur Pak
84C3 Bahawalpur
Province, Pak
85C3 Bahawathagar Pak
31C4 Bahia State, Brazil
29D3 Bahía Blanca Arg
29D3 Bahía Blanca R Arg
34A3 Bahía Concepción
Chile
35C2 Bahia da Ilha Grande
B Brazil
24B2 Bahía de Banderas B
Mexico
24C2 Bahía de Campeche B
Mexico
25D3 Bahía de la Ascensión
B Mexico
24B3 Bahía de Petacalco B
Mexico
96A2 Bahia de Rio de Oro
B Mor
35C2 Bahia de Sepetiba B
Brazil

29C6 Bahía Grande B Arg
9B4 Bahía Kino Mexico
24A2 Bahía Magdalena B
Mexico
24A2 Bahía Sebastia
Vizcaino B Mexico
99D1 Bahar Dar Eth
86A1 Bahraich India
80D3 Bahrain Sheikdom,
Arabian Pen
93D3 Bahr al Milh L Iraq
98C2 Bahr Aouk R Chad/
CAR
Bahrat Lut = Dead S
98C2 Bahr el Arab
Watercourse Sudan
99D2 Bahr el Ghazal R
Sudan
98B1 Bahr el Ghazal
Watercourse Chad
101H1 Baia de Maputo B
Mozam
31B2 Baia de Marajó B
Brazil
31C2 Baia de Pemba B
Mozam
31C2 Baia de São Marcos
B Brazil
50A2 Baia de Setúbal B
Port
31D4 Baia de Todos os
Santos B Brazil
100A2 Baia dos Tigres
Angola
60A4 Baia Mare Rom
98B2 Baïbokoum Chad
69E2 Baicheng China
101E2 Baie Antongila R
Madag
7D5 Baie-Comeau Can
101D2 Baie de Bombetoka
B Madag
101D2 Baie de Mahajamba
B Madag
101D3 Baie de St Augustin
B Madag
94B2 Baie de St Georges B
Leb
10D2 Baie des Chaleurs B
Can
7C4 Baie-du-Poste Can
72B3 Baihe China
72C3 Bai He R China
93D3 Ba'iji China
86A2 Baikunthpur India
Baile Atha Cliath =
Dublin
54B2 Băilesti Rom
46B1 Bailleul France
72A3 Baima China
17B1 Bainbridge USA
12B2 Baird Inlet USA
4B3 Baird Mts USA
72D1 Bairin Youqi China
72D1 Bairin Zuoqi China
107D4 Bairnsdale Aust
79B4 Bais Phil
54A1 Baja Hung
9B3 Baja California State,
Mexico
24A1 Baja California Pen
Mexico
61J2 Bakal Russian Fed
98C2 Bakala CAR
97A3 Bakel Sen
8C2 Baker Montana, USA
8B2 Baker Oregon, USA
6A3 Baker Foreland Pt
Can
4J3 Baker L Can
4J3 Baker Lake Can
9B3 Bakersfield USA
90C2 Bakharden
Turkmenistan
90C2 Bakhardok
Turkmenistan
60D3 Bakhmach Ukraine
38C1 Bakkaflói B Iceland
99D2 Bako Eth
98C2 Bakouma CAR
65F5 Baku Azerbaijan
Baky = Baku
92B2 Balā Syria
79A4 Balabac I Phil

70C3 Balabac Str Malay
79C2 Balaikarangan Indo
108A2 Balaklava Aust
61J3 Balakovo
Russian Fed
86A2 Balāngir India
61F3 Balashov
Russian Fed
86B2 Balasore India
80A3 Balāt Egypt
52C1 Balaton L Hung
45C2 Balbriggan Irish Re
29E3 Balcarce Arg
54C2 Balchik Bulg
111B3 Balclutha NZ
18B2 Bald Knob USA
17B1 Baldwin USA
9C3 Baldy Peak Mt USA
Balearic Is = Islas
Baleares
78C2 Balem R Malay
79B2 Baler Phil
61H2 Balezino Russian Fe
106A1 Bali I Indon
92A2 Balikesir Turk
78D3 Balikpapan Indon
79B2 Balintang Chan Phi
78C4 Bali S Indon
35A1 Baliza Brazil
84B1 Balkh Afghan
65J5 Balkhash Kazakhstan
44B3 Ballachulish Scot
45B2 Ballaghaderreen
Irish Rep
42B2 Ballantrae Scot
4G2 Ballantyne Str Can
87B2 Ballapur India
107D4 Ballarat Aust
44C3 Ballater Scot
112C7 Balleny Is Ant
86A1 Ballia India
109D1 Ballina Aust
41B3 Ballina Irish Rep
45B2 Ballinasloe Irish Rep
45B2 Ballinrobe Irish Rep
45B1 Ballycastle Irish Rep
45C1 Ballycastle N Ire
45C1 Ballymena N Ire
45C1 Ballymoney N Ire
45C1 Ballyshannon
Irish Rep
45B2 Ballyvaghan
Irish Rep
108B3 Balmoral Aust
34C2 Balnearia Arg
84B3 Balochistan Region,
Pak
100A2 Balombo Angola
109C1 Balonn R Aust
85C3 Balotra India
86A1 Balrāmpur India
107D4 Balranald Aust
31B3 Balsas Brazil
23B2 Balsas Mexico
24B3 Balsas R Mexico
60C4 Balta Ukraine
39H7 Baltic S N Europe
92B3 Baltim Egypt
45B3 Baltimore Irish Rep
10C3 Baltimore USA
88I1 Bālurghāt India
61H4 Balykshi Kazakhstan
91C4 Bam Iran
98B1 Bama Nig
97B3 Bamako Mali
98C2 Bambari CAR
17B1 Bamberg USA
57C3 Bamberg Germany
98C2 Bambili CAR
35B2 Bambui Brazil
98B2 Bamenda Cam
13C3 Bamfield Can
98B2 Bamingui R CAR
98B2 Bamingui Bangoran
National Park CAR
84B2 Bamiyan Afghan
91D4 Bampur Iran
98C2 Banalia Zaire
97B3 Banamba Mali
76C3 Ban Aranyaprathet
Thai
76C2 Ban Ban Laos

77C4 **Ban Betong** Thai	

Ban Betong — Baunt index:

77C4 **Ban Betong** Thai
45C1 **Banbridge** N Ire
44C3 **Banbury** Eng
25D3 **Banco Chinchorro** *Is* Mexico
11C5 **Bancroft** Can
86A1 **Banda** India
70A3 **Banda Aceh** Indon
97B4 **Bandama** *R* Ivory Coast
91C4 **Bandar Abbās** Iran
90A2 **Bandar Anzali** Iran
99F2 **Bandarbeyla** Somalia
91B4 **Bandar-e Daylam** Iran
91B4 **Bandar-e Lengheh** Iran
91B4 **Bandar-e Māqām** Iran
91B4 **Bandar-e Rīg** Iran
90B2 **Bandar-e Torkoman** Iran
91A3 **Bandar Khomeyni** Iran
78C2 **Bandar Seri Begawan** Brunei
71D4 **Banda S** Indon
91C4 **Band Bonī** Iran
86C2 **Bandeira** *Mt* Brazil
97B3 **Bandiagara** Mali
71C4 **Bandirma** Turk
45B3 **Bandon** Irish Rep
70A4 **Bandundu** Zaire
78B4 **Bandung** Indon
25E2 **Banes** Cuba
13D2 **Banff** Can
44C3 **Banff** Scot
56 **Banff** *R* Can
13D2 **Banff Nat Pk** Can
87B2 **Bangalore** India
98C2 **Bangassou** CAR
70C3 **Bangaī** *R* Indon
96B1 **Banghāzī** Libya
78B3 **Bang Hieng** *R* Laos
78B3 **Bangka** *I* Indon
78A3 **Bangko** Indon
76C3 **Bangkok** Thai
72 **Bangladesh** Republic, Asia
84D2 **Bangong Co** *L* China
10D2 **Bangor** Maine, USA
45C1 **Bangor** N Ire
16B2 **Bangor** Pennsylvania, USA
42B3 **Bangor** Wales
78D3 **Bangsalsembera** Indon
76B3 **Bang Saphan Yai** Thai
98D2 **Bangued** Phil
98B2 **Bangui** CAR
100C2 **Bangweulu** *L* Zambia
77C4 **Ban Hat Yai** Thai
71F5 **Banks I** Aust
76C1 **Ban Houei Sai** Laos
76C1 **Ban Hua Hin** Thai
97B3 **Bani** *R* Mali
98A2 **Bani Bangou** Niger
95A1 **Bani Walid** Libya
54B2 **Bāniyās** Syria
54B2 **Bāniyās** Syria
52C2 **Banja Luka** Bosnia-Herzegovina
78C3 **Banjarmasin** Indon
97A3 **Banjul** The Gambia
77B4 **Ban Kantang** Thai
76D2 **Ban Khemmarat** Laos
77B4 **Ban Khok Kloi** Thai
71F5 **Banks I** Aust
5E4 **Banks I** British Columbia, Can
4F2 **Banks I** Northwest Territories, Can
20C1 **Banks L** USA
111B2 **Banks Pen** NZ
20C1 **Banks Str** Aust
86B2 **Bankura** India
76B2 **Ban Mae Sariang** Thai
76B2 **Ban Mae Sot** Thai
76D3 **Ban Me Thuot** Viet
45C1 **Bann** *R* N Ire

77B4 **Ban Na San** Thai
84C2 **Bannu** Pak
34A3 **Baños Maule** Chile
77C4 **Ban Pak Neun** Laos
77C4 **Ban Pak Phanang** Thai
76D3 **Ban Ru Kroy** Camb
76B3 **Ban Sai Yok** Thai
76C3 **Ban Sattahip** Thai
59B3 **Banská Bystrica** Slovakia
85C4 **Bānswāra** India
77B4 **Ban Tha Kham** Thai
76C2 **Ban Thateng** Laos
76C2 **Ban Tha Tum** Thai
41A3 **Bantry** Irish Rep
41A3 **Bantry B** Irish Rep
76D3 **Ban Ya Soup** Viet
78C4 **Banyuwangi** Indon
72C3 **Baofeng** China
76C1 **Bao Ha** Viet
72B3 **Baoji** China
76D3 **Bao Loc** Viet
68B4 **Baoshan** China
72C1 **Baotou** China
87C1 **Bāpatla** India
46B1 **Bapaume** France
93D3 **Ba'Qūbah** Iraq
32J7 **Baquerizo Morena** Ecuador
54A2 **Bar** Montenegro, Yugos
99D1 **Bara** Sudan
99E2 **Baraawe** Somalia
78D3 **Barabai** Indon
86A1 **Bāra Banki** India
50B1 **Barabinsk** Russian Fed
65J4 **Barabinskaya Step** *Steppe* Kazakhstan/Russian Fed
50B1 **Baracaldo** Spain
26C2 **Baracoa** Cuba
94C2 **Baradā** *R* Syria
109C2 **Baradine** Aust
87A1 **Bārāmati** India
85D3 **Bārān** India
79B3 **Barangas** Phil
4E4 **Baranof I** USA
60C3 **Baranovichi** Belorussia
108A2 **Baratta** Aust
86B1 **Barauni** India
31C6 **Barbacena** Brazil
27F4 **Barbados** *I* Caribbean S
51C1 **Barbastro** Spain
101H1 **Barberton** S Africa
48B2 **Barbezieux** France
32C2 **Barbosa** Colombia
27E3 **Barbuda** *I* Caribbean S
107D3 **Barcaldine** Aust
Barce = Al Marj
53C2 **Barcellona** Italy
51C1 **Barcelona** Spain
33E1 **Barcelona** Ven
107D3 **Barcoo** *R* Aust
34B3 **Barda del Medio** Arg
95A2 **Bardaī** Chad
86B2 **Barddhamān** India
59C3 **Bardejov** Slovakia
47C2 **Bardi** Italy
47B2 **Bardonecchia** Italy
43B3 **Bardsey** *I* Wales
84D3 **Bareilly** India
64D2 **Barentsøya** *I* Barents S
4C2 **Barents S**
45C2 **Barents B**
95D3 **Barentu** Eritrea
86A2 **Bargarh** India
47B2 **Barge** Italy
63D2 **Barguzin** *R* Russian Fed
63D2 **Barguzin** *R* Russian Fed
86B2 **Barhi** India
54C2 **Bari** Italy
31C2 **Barima** *R* Ven
86B2 **Baripāda** India
86B2 **Bari Sādri** India

86C2 **Barisal** Bang
78C3 **Barito** *R* Indon
95A2 **Barjuj** *Watercourse* Libya
73A3 **Barkam** China
18C2 **Barkley,L** USA
13B3 **Barkley Sd** Can
100B4 **Barkly East** S Africa
106C2 **Barkly Tableland** *Mts* Aust
46C2 **Bar-le-Duc** France
106A3 **Barlee,L** Aust
106A3 **Barlee Range** *Mts* Aust
53C2 **Barletta** Italy
85C3 **Barmer** India
108B2 **Barmera** Aust
43B3 **Barmouth** Wales
23D4 **Barnard Castle** Eng
65K4 **Barnaul** Russian Fed
16B3 **Barnegat** USA
16B3 **Barnegat B** USA
6C2 **Barnes Icecap** Can
17B1 **Barnesville** Georgia, USA
14B3 **Barnesville** Ohio, USA
43D3 **Barnsley** Eng
43B4 **Barnstaple** Eng
97C4 **Baro** Nig
86C1 **Barpeta** India
32D1 **Barquisimeto** Ven
31C4 **Barra** Brazil
44A3 **Barra** *I* Scot
109D2 **Barraba** Aust
23A2 **Barra de Navidad** Mexico
35C2 **Barra de Pirai** Brazil
35A1 **Barragem de São Simão** *Res* Brazil
35A1 **Barra do Garças** Brazil
35B1 **Barragem Agua Vermelha** *Res* Brazil
50A2 **Barragem do Castelo do Bode** *Res* Port
50A2 **Barragem do Maranhão** *Res* Port
35A2 **Barragem Três Irmãos** *Res* Brazil
44A3 **Barra Head** *Pt* Scot
31C6 **Barra Mansa** Brazil
32B6 **Barranca** Peru
32C2 **Barrancabermeja** Colombia
33E2 **Barrancas** Ven
30E4 **Barranqueras** Arg
32C1 **Barranquilla** Colombia
44A3 **Barra,Sound of** *Chan* Scot
16C1 **Barre** USA
34B2 **Barreal** Arg
50A2 **Barreiro** Port
31D3 **Barreiros** Brazil
107D5 **Barren,C** Aust
12D3 **Barren Is** USA
31B6 **Barretos** Brazil
13E2 **Barrhead** Can
14C2 **Barrie** Can
13C2 **Barrière** Can
108B2 **Barrier Range** *Mts* Aust
107E4 **Barrington,Mt** Aust
27N2 **Barrouaillie** St Vincent and the Grenadines
4C2 **Barrow** USA
45C2 **Barrow** *R* Irish Rep
106C3 **Barrow Creek** Aust
106A3 **Barrow I** Aust
42C2 **Barrow-in-Furness** Eng
4C2 **Barrow,Pt** USA
6A2 **Barrow Str** Can
15C1 **Barry's Bay** Can
87B1 **Barsi** India
19B3 **Barstow** USA
49C2 **Bar-sur-Aube** France
93F1 **Bartica** Guyana
92B1 **Bartın** Turk
107D2 **Bartle Frere,Mt** Aust
9D3 **Bartlesville** USA

101C3 **Bartolomeu Dias** Mozam
58C2 **Bartoszyce** Pol
7D4 **Barung** *I* Indon
85D4 **Barwah** India
85C4 **Barwāni** India
109C1 **Barwon** *R* Aust
61G3 **Barysh** Russian Fed
98B2 **Basankusa** Zaire
34D2 **Basavilbas** Arg
79B1 **Basco** Phil
52A1 **Basel** Switz
53C2 **Basento** *R* Italy
13E2 **Bashaw** Can
79B1 **Bashi Chan** Phil
61H3 **Bashkortostan** Russian Fed
79B4 **Basilan** Phil
79B4 **Basilan** *I* Phil
43E4 **Basildon** Eng
43D4 **Basingstoke** Eng
8B2 **Basin Region** USA
93E3 **Basra** Iraq
46D2 **Bas-Rhin** *Department*, France
76D3 **Bassac** *R* Camb
13E2 **Bassano** Italy
52B1 **Bassano** Italy
47D2 **Bassano del Grappa** Italy
97C4 **Bassari** Togo
101C3 **Bassas da India** *I* Mozam Chan
76A2 **Bassein** Burma
27E3 **Basse Terre** Guadeloupe
97C4 **Bassila** Benin
22C2 **Bass Lake** USA
107D4 **Bass Str** Aust
39G7 **Båstad** Sweden
91B4 **Bastak** Iran
86A1 **Bastī** India
52A2 **Bastia** Corse
57B3 **Bastogne** Belg
19B3 **Bastrop** Louisiana, USA
19A3 **Bastrop** Texas, USA
98A2 **Bata** Eq Guinea
78C3 **Batakan** Indon
84D2 **Batala** India
72B3 **Batang** China
98B2 **Batangafo** CAR
79B3 **Batan Is** Phil
35B2 **Batatais** Brazil
15C2 **Batavia** USA
109C3 **Batemans Bay** Aust
17B1 **Batesburg** USA
19C3 **Batesville** Arkansas, USA
19C3 **Batesville** Mississippi, USA
43C4 **Bath** Eng
15C2 **Bath** New York, USA
98B1 **Batha** *R* Chad
107D4 **Bathurst** Aust
7D5 **Bathurst** Can
106C2 **Bathurst,C** Aust
4H2 **Bathurst I** Can
4H3 **Bathurst Inlet** *B* Can
97B3 **Batié** Burkina
90B3 **Bātlāq-e-Gavkhūni** *Salt Flat* Iran
109C3 **Batlow** Aust
93D2 **Batman** Turk
96C1 **Batna** Alg
11B3 **Baton Rouge** USA
94B1 **Batroun** Leb
76C3 **Battambang** Camb
87C3 **Batticaloa** Sri Lanka
13F2 **Battle** *R* Can
10B2 **Battle Creek** USA
7E4 **Battle Harbour** Can
20C2 **Battle Mountain** USA
78D2 **Batukelau** Indon
65F5 **Batumi** Georgia
77C5 **Batu Pahat** Malay
78A3 **Baturaja** Indon
94B2 **Bat Yam** Israel
78D4 **Baubau** Indon
97C3 **Bauchi** Nig
47B2 **Bauges** *Mts* France
7E4 **Bauld,C** Can
47B1 **Baumes-les-Dames** France
63D2 **Baunt** Russian Fed

31B6 **Bauru** Brazil
35A1 **Baus** Brazil
57C2 **Bautzen** Germany
78C4 **Baween** I Indon
95B2 **Bawiti** Egypt
87B3 **Bawku** Ghana
82B3 **Bawlake** Burma
108A2 **Bawlen** Aust
17B1 **Baxley** USA
25E2 **Bayamo** Cuba
78D4 **Bayan** Indon
68C2 **Bayandzürh** Mongolia
68B3 **Bayan Har Shan** Mts China
72A1 **Bayan Mod** China
72B1 **Bayan Obo** China
47A2 **Bayard** P France
12J3 **Bayard,Mt** Can
63D3 **Bayasgalant** Mongolia
79B3 **Baybay** Phil
93D1 **Bayburt** Turk
14A2 **Bay City** Michigan, USA
19A4 **Bay City** Texas, USA
92B2 **Bay Dağ** Turk
64H3 **Baydaratskaya Guba** B Russian Fed
99E2 **Baydhabo** Somalia
48B2 **Bayeux** France
47D1 **Bayerische Alpen** Mts Germany
57C3 **Bayern** State, Germany
92C3 **Bäyir** Jordan
63C2 **Baykalskiy Khrebet** Mts Russian Fed
63B1 **Baykit** Russian Fed
63B3 **Baylik Shan** Mts China/Mongolia
61J3 **Baymak** Russian Fed
79B2 **Bayombang** Phil
48A2 **Bayonne** France
57C3 **Bayreuth** Germany
19C3 **Bay St Louis** USA
15D2 **Bay Shore** USA
15C1 **Bays,L of** Can
68A2 **Baytik Shan** Mts China
Bayt Lahm =
Bethlehem
19B4 **Baytown** USA
50B2 **Baza** Spain
59D3 **Bazaliya** Ukraine
48B3 **Bazas** France
73B3 **Bazhong** China
91D4 **Bazmän** Iran
94C1 **Bcharre** Leb
16B3 **Beach Haven** USA
43E4 **Beachy Head** Eng
16C2 **Beacon** USA
101D2 **Bealanana** Madag
18B1 **Beardstown** USA
Bear I = Bjørnøya
22B1 **Bear Valley** USA
8D2 **Beatrice** USA
44C2 **Beatrice** Oilfield N Sea
13C1 **Beatton** R Can
5F4 **Beatton River** Can
29E6 **Beauchene Is** Falkland Is
109D1 **Beaudesert** Aust
1B5 **Beaufort S** Can
100B4 **Beaufort West** S Africa
15D1 **Beauharnois** Can
44B3 **Beauly** Scot
21B3 **Beaumont** California, USA
11A3 **Beaumont** Texas, USA
49C2 **Beaune** France
48C2 **Beauvais** France
5H4 **Beauval** Can
12E1 **Beaver** Alaska, USA
13F2 **Beaver** R Saskatchewan, Can
4D3 **Beaver Creek** Can
12E1 **Beaver Creek** USA
12C1 **Beaver Dam** Kentucky, USA
13E2 **Beaverhill L** Can
14A1 **Beaver I** USA

18B2 **Beaver L** USA
13D1 **Beaverlodge** Can
85C3 **Beawar** India
35B2 **Bebedouro** Brazil
43E3 **Beccles** Eng
54B1 **Bečej** Serbia, Yugos
96B1 **Béchar** Alg
12C3 **Becharof L** USA
11B3 **Beckley** USA
43D3 **Bedford** County, Eng
43D3 **Bedford** Eng
14A3 **Bedford** Indiana, USA
27M2 **Bedford Pt** Grenada
4D2 **Beechey Pt** USA
109C3 **Beechworth** Aust
109D1 **Beenleigh** Aust
92B3 **Beersheba** Israel
Beér Sheva =
Beersheba
94B3 **Beér Sheva** R Israel
9D4 **Beeville** USA
98C2 **Befale** Zaire
101D2 **Befandriana** Madag
109C3 **Bega** Aust
91B3 **Behbehan** Iran
12H3 **Behm Canal** Sd USA
90B2 **Behshahr** Iran
84B2 **Behsud** Afghan
69E2 **Bei'an** China
73B5 **Beihai** China
72D2 **Beijing** China
76E1 **Beiliu** China
73B4 **Beipan Jiang** R China
72E1 **Beipiao** China
Beira = Sofala
92C3 **Beirut** Leb
84B2 **Bei Shan** Mts China
94B2 **Beit ed Dine** Leb
94B3 **Beit Jala** Israel
50A2 **Beja** Port
96C1 **Beja** Tunisia
96C1 **Bejaia** Alg
50A1 **Béjar** Spain
90C3 **Bejestan** Iran
59C3 **Békéscsaba** Hung
101D3 **Bekily** Madag
86A1 **Bela** India
85B3 **Bela** Pak
78C2 **Belaga** Malay
16A3 **Bel Air** USA
87B1 **Belamoalli** India
71D3 **Belang** Indon
70A3 **Belangpidie** Indon
Belarus = Belorussia
Belau = Palau Is.
101C3 **Bela Vista** Mozam
70A3 **Belawan** Indon
61J2 **Belaya** R Ukraine
6A2 **Belcher Chan** Can
7C4 **Belcher Is** Can
84B1 **Belchiragh** Afghan
61J3 **Beleburg** Russian Fed
99E2 **Beled Weyne** Somalia
31B2 **Belém** Brazil
32B3 **Belén** Colombia
34D2 **Belén** Urug
9C3 **Belen** USA
45D1 **Belfast** N Ire
101H1 **Belfast** S Africa
45D1 **Belfast Lough** Estuary N Ire
99D1 **Bélfodiyo** Eth
42D2 **Belford** Eng
49D2 **Belfort** France
87A1 **Belgaum** India
56A2 **Belgium** Kingdom, N W Europe
60E3 **Belgorod** Russian Fed
60D4 **Belgorod Dnestrovskiy** Ukraine
Belgrade = Beograd
95A2 **Bel Hedan** Libya
78B3 **Belinyu** Indon
78B3 **Belitung** I Indon
25D3 **Belize** Belize
25D3 **Belize** Republic, Cent America
48C2 **Bellac** France
5F4 **Bella Coola** Can
47C2 **Bellagio** Italy

19A4 **Bellaire** USA
47C1 **Bellano** Italy
87B1 **Bellary** India
109C1 **Bellata** Aust
47B2 **Belledonne** Mts France
8C2 **Belle Fourche** USA
49D2 **Bellegarde** France
17B2 **Belle Glade** USA
7E4 **Belle I** Can
48B2 **Belle-Ile** I France
7E4 **Belle Isle,Str of** Can
7C5 **Belleville** Can
18A2 **Belleville** USA
20B1 **Bellevue** Washington, USA
109D2 **Bellingen** Aust
8A2 **Bellingham** USA
112C2 **Bellingshausen** Base Ant
112C3 **Bellingshausen S** Ant
52A1 **Bellinzona** Switz
32B3 **Bello** Colombia
107E3 **Bellona Reefs** Nouvelle Calédonie
22B1 **Bellota** USA
15D2 **Bellows Falls** USA
6B3 **Bell Pen** Can
52B1 **Belluno** Italy
29D2 **Bell Ville** Arg
31D5 **Belmonte** Brazil
25D3 **Belmopan** Belize
45B1 **Belmullet** Irish Rep
69E1 **Belogorsk** Russian Fed
101D3 **Beloha** Madag
31C5 **Belo Horizonte** Brazil
10B2 **Beloit** Wisconsin, USA
64E3 **Belomorsk** Russian Fed
61J3 **Beloretsk** Russian Fed
Belorussia = Belorussia
60C3 **Belorussia** Republic, Europe
101D2 **Belo-Tsiribihina** Madag
64E3 **Beloye More** S Russian Fed
60E1 **Beloye Ozero** L Russian Fed
60E1 **Belozersk** Russian Fed
14B3 **Belpre** USA
108A2 **Beltana** Aust
19A3 **Belton** USA
59D3 **Bel'tsy** Moldavia
16B2 **Belvidere** New Jersey, USA
98B3 **Bembe** Angola
97C3 **Bembérèke** Benin
10A2 **Bemidji** USA
39G6 **Bena** Nor
98C3 **Bena Dibele** Zaire
108C3 **Benalla** Aust
44B3 **Ben Attow** Mt Scot
50A1 **Benavente** Spain
44A3 **Benbecula** I Scot
106A4 **Bencubbin** Aust
8A2 **Bend** USA
44B3 **Ben Dearg** Mt Scot
60C4 **Bendery** Moldavia
107D4 **Bendigo** Aust
53C2 **Benešov** Czech Republic
53B2 **Benevento** Italy
83C4 **Bengal,B of** Asia
96D1 **Ben Gardane** Tunisia
72D3 **Bengbu** China
78A2 **Bengkalis** Indon
78A3 **Bengkulu** Indon
100A2 **Benguela** Angola
92B3 **Benha** Egypt
44B2 **Ben Hope** Mt Scot
99C2 **Beni** Zaire
32D6 **Beni** R Bol
96B1 **Beni Abbes** Alg
51C1 **Benicarló** Spain
7A5 **Benidji** USA
51B2 **Benidorm** Spain
51C2 **Beni Mansour** Alg
95C2 **Beni Mazar** Egypt
96B1 **Beni Mellal** Mor

97C4 **Benin** Republic, Africa
97C4 **Benin City** Nig
95C2 **Beni Suef** Egypt
44B2 **Ben Kilbreck** Mt S-
44B3 **Ben Lawers** Mt Uki
109C4 **Ben Lomond** Mt Aust
44C3 **Ben Macdui** Mt Sco
44B2 **Ben More Assynt** M Scot
111B2 **Benmore,L** NZ
44B3 **Ben Nevis** Mt Scot
15D2 **Bennington** USA
94B3 **Bennt Jbail** Leb
98B2 **Bénoué** R Cam
9B3 **Benson** Arizona, U'
99C2 **Bentiu** Sudan
19B3 **Benton** Arkansas, USA
18C2 **Benton** Kentucky, USA
14A2 **Benton Harbor** US.
97C4 **Benue** R Nig
44B1 **Benwee Hd** C
44B3 **Ben Wyvis** Mt Sco
72C1 **Benxi** China
54B2 **Beograd** Serbia, Yugos
86A2 **Beohári** India
74C4 **Beppu** Japan
55A2 **Berat** Alb
99E1 **Berber** Sudan
99E1 **Berbera** Somalia
98B2 **Berbérati** CAR
46A1 **Berck** France
60C4 **Berdichev** Ukraine
60E4 **Berdyansk** Ukraine
97B4 **Bereekum** Ghana
22B2 **Berenda** USA
5J4 **Berens** R Can
5J4 **Berens River** Can
108A1 **Beresford** Aust
58D2 **Berestovd-Hur**
59C3 **Berezhany** Ukraine
62C3 **Bereza** Belorussia
60D4 **Berezina** R Russian Fed
60D4 **Berezovka** Ukraine
64H3 **Berezovo** Russian Fed
92A2 **Bergama** Turk
52A1 **Bergamo** Italy
39F6 **Bergen** Nor
46C1 **Bergen op Zoom** Neth
48B2 **Bergerac** France
46D3 **Bergisch-Gladbach** Germany
12F2 **Bering Gl** USA
1C6 **Bering Str** USA/ Russian Fed
91C4 **Berizak** Iran
50B2 **Berja** Spain
8A3 **Berkeley** USA
112B2 **Berkner I** Ant
54B2 **Berkovitsa** Bulg
43D4 **Berkshire** County, Eng
16C1 **Berkshire Hills** USA
13D2 **Berland** R Can
56C2 **Berlin** Germany
56C2 **Berlin** State, German
15D2 **Berlin** New Hampshire, USA
30D4 **Bermejo** Bol
30D4 **Bermejo** R Arg
3M5 **Bermuda** I Atlantic
52A1 **Bern** Switz
16B2 **Bernardsville** USA
34C3 **Bernasconi** Arg
56C2 **Bernburg** Germany
47B1 **Berner Oberland** M Switz
6B2 **Bernier Is** Can
57C3 **Berounka** R Czech Republic
108B2 **Berri** Aust
46C1 **Berriane** Alg
48C2 **Berry** Region, France
22A1 **Berryessa,L** USA
11C4 **Berry Is** The Bahamas
98B2 **Bertoua** Cam

45B2 Bertraghboy B Irish Rep
15C2 Berwick USA
42C2 Berwick-upon-Tweed Eng
43C3 Berwyn Mts Wales
01D2 Besalampy Madag
49D2 Besançon France
59C2 Beskidy Zachodnie Mts Pol
93C2 Besni Turk
94B3 Besor R Israel
11B3 Bessemer USA
01D2 Betafo Madag
50A1 Betanzos Spain
01G1 Bet Guvrin Israel
01G1 Bethal S Africa
00A3 Bethanie Namibia
18B1 Bethany Missouri, USA
18A2 Bethany Oklahoma, USA
4B3 Bethel Alaska, USA
16C2 Bethel Connecticut, USA
14B2 Bethel Park USA
15C2 Bethesda USA
94B3 Bethlehem Israel
01E1 Bethlehem S Africa
13E3 Bethlehem USA
48C1 Bethune France
01D3 Betioky Madag
08B1 Betoota Aust
01D3 Betou Congo
82A1 Betpak Dala Steppe Kazakhstan
01D3 Betroka Madag
7D5 Betsiamites Can
86A1 Bettiah India
12C1 Bettles USA
47C2 Béttola Italy
85D3 Betwa R India
46D1 Betzdorf Germany
12C3 Beverley,L USA
11B3 Beverly USA
97B4 Beverly Hills USA
97B4 Beyla Guinea
     Beyrouth = Beirut
92B2 Beyşehir Turk
92B2 Beyşehir Gölü L Turk
94B2 Bey't Shean Israel
47C1 Bezau Austria
60E2 Bezhetsk Russian Fed
49C3 Béziers France
90C2 Bezmein Turkmenistan
63C2 Beznosova Russian Fed
86B1 Bhadgaon Nepal
87C1 Bhadrachalam India
86B1 Bhadrakh India
87B2 Bhadra Res India
87B2 Bhadrāvati India
84B3 Bhag Pak
86B1 Bhāgalpur India
86C2 Bhakkar Pak
87D3 Bhamo Burma
85D4 Bhandāra India
85D3 Bharatpur India
85C4 Bharūch India
86B1 Bhātiāpāra Ghat Bang
84C2 Bhatinda India
87A2 Bhatkal India
86B2 Bhātpāra India
84C2 Bhāvnagar India
86A1 Bheri R Nepal
86A2 Bhilai India
85C4 Bhilwāra India
87C1 Bhīmavaram India
85D3 Bhind India
84D3 Bhiwāni India
87B1 Bhongir India
85D4 Bhopal India
86B2 Bhubaneshwar India
85B4 Bhuj India
85D4 Bhusāwal India
82C3 Bhutan Kingdom, Asia
71E4 Biak I Indon
58C2 Biala Podlaska Pol

58B2 Bialogard Pol
58C2 Bialystok Pol
38A1 Biargtangar C Iceland
90C2 Biarjmand Iran
48B3 Biarritz France
47C1 Biasca Switz
92B4 Biba Egypt
74E2 Bibai Japan
100A2 Bibala Angola
57B3 Biberach Germany
97B4 Bibiani Ghana
54C1 Bicaz Rom
97C4 Bida Nig
87B1 Bidar India
91C5 Bidbid Oman
43B4 Bideford Eng
43B4 Bideford B Eng
96C2 Bidon 5 Alg
52A1 Biel Switz
59B2 Bielawa Pol
56B2 Bielefeld Germany
52A1 Bieler See L Switz
52A1 Biella Italy
58C2 Bielsk Podlaski Pol
76D3 Bien Hoa Viet
53B2 Biferno R Italy
92A1 Biga Turk
55C3 Bigadiç Turk
13B3 Big Black R USA
18A1 Big Blue R USA
17B2 Big Cypress Swamp USA
4D3 Big Delta USA
49D2 Bigent Germany
13F2 Biggar Can
5H4 Biggar Kindersley Can
01D1 Biggenden Aust
12G3 Bigger,Mt USA
6C2 Bighorn R USA
76C3 Bight of Bangkok B Thai
97C4 Bight of Benin B W Africa
97C4 Bight of Biafra B Cam
6C3 Big I Can
44D3 Bignasco Switz
91A3 Bignona Sen
21B2 Big Pine USA
17B2 Big Pine Key USA
22C3 Big Pine Mt USA
14A2 Big Rapids USA
5H4 Big River Can
9C3 Big Spring USA
7A4 Big Trout L Can
7B4 Big Trout Lake Can
52C2 Bihać Bosnia-Herzegovina
86B1 Bihār India
86B2 Bihar State, India
99D3 Biharamulo Tanz
64A6 Bihor Mt Rom
87B1 Bijāpur India
87C1 Bijapur India
90A2 Bījār Iran
86A1 Bijauri Nepal
54A2 Bijeljina Bosnia-Herzegovina
73B4 Bijie China
84D3 Bijnor India
84C3 Bijnot Pak
84C3 Bīkaner India
94B2 Bikfaya Leb
69F2 Bikin Russian Fed
98B3 Bikoro Zaire
85C3 Bilara India
84D2 Bilāspur India
86A2 Bilāspur India
76B3 Bilauktaung Range Mts Thai
50B1 Bilbao Spain
     Bilbo = Bilbao
52C2 Bilé Czech Republic
54A2 Bileća Bosnia-Herzegovina
92B1 Bilecik Turk
98C2 Bili R Zaire
79B3 Biliran I Phil
8C2 Billings USA
95A3 Bilma Niger
11B3 Biloxi USA

98C1 Biltine Chad
85D4 Bina-Etawa India
79B3 Binalbagan Phil
101C2 Bindura Zim
100B2 Binga Zim
101C2 Binga Mt Zim
100D1 Bingara Aust
57B3 Bingen Germany
10C2 Binghamton USA
78D1 Bingkor Malay
93D2 Bingol Turk
72D3 Binhai China
78A2 Bintan I Indon
78A3 Bintulu Indon
78C2 Bintulu Malay
29B3 Bío Bío R Chile
102J4 Bioko I Atlantic O
87B1 Bir India
95B2 Bir Abu Husein Well Egypt
95B2 Bi'r al Harash Well Libya
98C1 Birao CAR
86B1 Biratnagar Nepal
12E1 Birch Creek USA
108B3 Birch Hills Can
5G4 Birch Mts Can
7A4 Bird Can
106C3 Birdsville Aust
106C2 Birdum Aust
86A1 Birganj Nepal
94A3 Bir Gifgâfa Well Egypt
94A3 Bir Hasana Well Egypt
35C2 Birigui Brazil
90C3 Birjand Iran
92B4 Birkat Qarun L Egypt
46D2 Birkenfeld Germany
42C3 Birkenhead Eng
60C4 Birlad Rom
94A3 Bir Lahfân Well Egypt
43C3 Birmingham Eng
11B3 Birmingham USA
95B2 Bir Misâha Well Egypt
96A2 Bir Moghrein Maur
97C3 Birnin Kebbi Nig
97C3 Birni N'Konni Nig
69F2 Birobidzhan Russian Fed
45C2 Birr Irish Rep
51C2 Bir Rabalou Alg
109C1 Birrie R Aust
44C2 Birsay Scot
61J2 Birsk Russian Fed
95B2 Bîr Tarfâwi Well Egypt
63B2 Biryusa Russian Fed
39J7 Biržai Lithuania
96B2 Bir Zreigat Well Egypt
48A2 Biscay,B of France/Spain
17B2 Biscayne,B USA
46D2 Bischwiller France
73B4 Bishan China
82B1 Bishkek Kirghizia
8B3 Bishop USA
82D2 Bishop Auckland Eng
43E4 Bishop's Stortford Eng
86A2 Bishrāmpur India
96C1 Biskra Alg
79C4 Bislig Phil
8C2 Bismarck USA
90A3 Bīsotūn Iran
10A1 Bissett Can
5G4 Bistcho L Can
54C1 Bistrita R Rom
98B2 Bitam Gabon
57B3 Bitburg Germany
48D2 Bitche France
93D2 Bitlis Turk
55B2 Bitola Macedonia
56C2 Bitterfeld Germany
100A4 Bitterfontein S Africa
92B3 Bitter Lakes Egypt
8B2 Bitterroot Range Mts USA
74D3 Biwa-ko L Japan
99E1 Biyo Kaboba Eth

65K4 Biysk Russian Fed
96C1 Bizerte Tunisia
51C2 Bj bou Arrèridj Alg
52C1 Bjelovar Croatia
96B2 Bj Five Ste Marie Alg
64C2 Bjørneya I Barents S
12F1 Black R USA
18B2 Black R USA
107D3 Blackall Aust
42C3 Blackburn Eng
4D3 Blackburn,Mt USA
13E2 Black Diamond Can
5H5 Black Hills USA
44B3 Black Isle Pen Scot
27H1 Black River Jamaica
8B2 Black Rock Desert USA
65E5 Black S Asia/Europe
45A1 Blacksod B Irish Rep
109D2 Black Sugarloaf Mt Aust
97B3 Black Volta R Ghana
41B3 Blackwater R Irish Rep
18A2 Blackwell USA
54B2 Blagoevgrad Bulg
63E2 Blagoveshchensk Russian Fed
20B1 Blaine USA
44C3 Blair Atholl Scot
44C3 Blairgowrie Scot
17B1 Blakely USA
108A1 Blanche,L Aust
34A2 Blanco R Arg
34A2 Blanco R Arg
8B2 Blanco,C USA
7E4 Blanc Sablon Can
43C4 Blandford Forum Eng
     Blangy-sur-Bresle France
46B1 Blankenberge Belg
101C2 Blantyre Malawi
48C2 Blaye France
109C2 Blayney Aust
111B2 Blenheim NZ
96C1 Blida Alg
14B1 Blind River Can
108A2 Blinman Aust
78B4 Blitar Indon
15D2 Block I USA
16D2 Block Island Sd USA
101G1 Bloemfontein S Africa
101G1 Bloemhof S Africa
101G1 Bloemhof Dam Res S Africa
33F3 Blommesteinmeer L Suriname
38A1 Blonduos Iceland
45B1 Bloody Foreland C Irish Rep
14A3 Bloomfield Indiana, USA
18B1 Bloomfield Iowa, USA
10B2 Bloomington Illinois, USA
14A3 Bloomington Indiana, USA
14A2 Bloomsburg USA
78C4 Blora Indon
6H3 Blosseville Kyst Mts Greenland
57B3 Bludenz Austria
11B3 Bluefield USA
32A1 Bluefields Nic
26B3 Blue Mountain Peak Mt Jamaica
109D2 Blue Mts Aust
27J1 Blue Mts Jamaica
8A2 Blue Mts USA
     Blue Nile = Bahr el Azraq
99D1 Blue Nile R Sudan
4G3 Bluenose L Can
11B3 Blue Ridge Mts USA
13D2 Blue River Can
45B1 Blue Stack Mt Irish Rep
111A2 Bluff NZ

106A4 Bluff Knoll Mt Aust
30G4 Blumenau Brazil
49D2 Blundez Austria
20B2 Bly USA
12E3 Blying Sd USA
42D2 Blyth Eng
9B3 Blythe USA
11B3 Blytheville USA
97A4 Bo Sierra Leone
79B3 Boac Phil
72D2 Boading China
14B2 Boardman USA
63C3 Boatou China
33E3 Boa Vista Brazil
97A4 Boa Vista I Cape Verde
76E1 Bobai China
47B2 Bóbbio Italy
97B3 Bobo Dioulasso Burkina
60C3 Bobruysk Belorussia
17B2 Boca Chica Key I USA
32D5 Bôca do Acre Brazil
35C1 Bocaiúva Brazil
97B3 Bocaranga CAR
17B2 Boca Raton USA
59C3 Bochnia Pol
56B2 Bocholt Germany
46D1 Bochum Germany
100A2 Bocoio Angola
98B2 Bodo CAR
63D2 Bodaybo Russian Fed
21A2 Bodega Head Pt USA
95A3 Bodélé Region Chad
38J5 Boden Sweden
47C1 Bodensee L Switz/Germany
87B1 Bodhan India
87B2 Bodináyakkanúr India
43B4 Bodmin Eng
43B4 Bodmin Moor Upland Eng
38G5 Bodø Nor
55C3 Bodrum Turk
55C3 Boende Zaire
97A3 Boffa Guinea
76B2 Bogale Burma
19C3 Bogalusa USA
109C2 Bogan R Aust
26B2 Bogandé Burkina
6H3 Bogarnes Iceland
92C2 Bogazlıyan Turk
61K2 Bogdanovich Russian Fed
68A2 Bogda Shan Mt China
100A3 Bogenfels Namibia
109D1 Boggabilla Aust
109C2 Boggabri Aust
97A3 Boggeragh Mts Irish Rep
79B3 Bogo Phil
109C3 Bogong,Mt Aust
78B4 Bogor Indon
61H2 Bogorodskoye Russian Fed
32C3 Bogotá Colombia
63A2 Bogotol Russian Fed
86B2 Bogra Bang
72D2 Bo Hai B China
46B2 Bohain-en-Vermandois France
72D2 Bohai Wan B China
57C3 Böhmer-Wald Upland Germany
79B4 Bohol I Phil
79B4 Bohol S Phil
35A1 Bois R Brazil
14B1 Bois Blanc I USA
8A2 Boise USA
96A2 Bojador,C Mor
79B2 Bojeador,C Phil
90C2 Bojnúrd Iran
97A3 Boké Guinea
109C1 Bokhara R Aust
39F7 Boknafjord Inlet Nor
98B3 Boko Congo
76C3 Bokor Camb
98C3 Bokungu Zaire
98B1 Bol Chad
23A1 Bolaños Mexico

97A3 Bolama Guinea-Bissau
23A1 Bolanos R Mexico
48C2 Bolene France
97B4 Bole Ghana
59B2 Bolesławiec Pol
97B3 Bolgatanga Ghana
60C4 Bolgrad Ukraine
34C3 Bolívar R Arg
18B2 Bolivar Missouri, USA
18C2 Bolivar Tennessee, USA
30C2 Bolivia Republic, S America
38H6 Bollnäs Sweden
109C1 Bollon Aust
32C2 Bolívar Mt Ven
52B2 Bologna Italy
60D2 Bologoye Russian Fed
69F2 Bolon' Russian Fed
61G3 Bol'shoy Irgiz R Russian Fed
74C2 Bol'shoy Kamen Russian Fed
Bol'shoy Kavkaz = Caucasus
61G4 Bol'shoy Uzen R Kazakhstan
9C4 Bolson de Mapimi Desert Mexico
43C3 Bolton Eng
92B1 Bolu Turk
38A1 Bolungarvik Iceland
52B1 Bolvadin Turk
52B1 Bolzano Italy
98B3 Boma Zaire
107D4 Bombala Aust
87A1 Bombay India
99D2 Bombo Uganda
35B1 Bom Despacho Brazil
86C1 Bomdila India
97A4 Bom Hills Lib
31C4 Bom Jesus da Lapa Brazil
63E2 Bomnak Russian Fed
99C2 Bomokandi R Zaire
98C2 Bomu R CAR/Zaire
27D4 Bonaire I Caribbean S
12F2 Bona,Mt USA
25D3 Bonanza Nic
7E5 Bonavista Can
108A2 Bon Bon Aust
98C2 Bondo Zaire
97B4 Bondoukou Ivory Coast
Bône = 'Annaba
98C2 Bongandanga Zaire
98B1 Bongor Chad
19A3 Bonham USA
53A2 Bonifacio Corse
52A2 Bonifacio,Str of Chan Medit S
Bonin Is = Ogasawara Gunto
17B2 Bonita Springs USA
57B2 Bonn Germany
20C1 Bonners Ferry USA
12H1 Bonnet Plume R Can
13E2 Bonnyville Can
97A4 Bonthe Sierra Leone
99E1 Booaaso Somalia
108B2 Booligal Aust
15C2 Boonville USA
109C2 Boorowa Aust
6A2 Boothia,G of Can
6A2 Boothia Pen Can
98B3 Booué Gabon
108A1 Bopeechee Aust
99D2 Bor Sudan
92B2 Bor Turk
54B2 Bor Serbia, Yugos
8B2 Borah Peak Mt USA
39G7 Borås Sweden
91B4 Borázjan Iran
108A3 Borda,C Aust
48B3 Bordeaux France
42C2 Borden Pen Can
6B2 Borden Pen Can
16B2 Bordentown USA
42C2 Borders Region, Scot

108B3 Bordertown Aust
96C2 Bordj Omar Dris Alg
8D1 Borens River Can
38A2 Borgarnes Iceland
9C3 Borger USA
19B3 Borgholm Sweden
47C2 Borgosia Italy
47D1 Borgo Valsugana Italy
59C3 Borislav Ukraine
61F3 Borisoglebsk Russian Fed
60D3 Borisov Belorussia
60E3 Borisovka Russian Fed
95A3 Borkou Region Chad
39H6 Borlänge Sweden
47C2 Bormida Italy
47D1 Bormio Italy
67F5 Borneo I Malay/Indon
39H7 Bornholm I Den
55C3 Bornova Turk
98C2 Boro R Sudan
97B3 Boromo Burkina
60D2 Borovichi Russian Fed
107D2 Borroloola Aust
54B1 Borsa Rom
90A3 Borújed Iran
90B3 Borüjen Iran
58B2 Boryslav Pol
63D2 Borzya Russian Fed
73B5 Bose China
101G1 Boshof S Africa
54A2 Bosna R Bosnia-Herzegovina
37E4 Bosnia-Herzegovina Republic, Europe
75C1 Bōsō-hantō B Japan
Bosporus = Karadeniz Boğazi
51C2 Bosquet Alg
98B2 Bossangoa CAR
98B2 Bossèmbélé CAR
19B3 Bossier City USA
65K5 Bosten Hu L China
43D3 Boston Eng
10C2 Boston USA
11A3 Boston Mts USA
85C4 Botād India
54B2 Botevgrad Bulg
101G1 Bothaville S Africa
64C3 Bothnia,G of Sweden/Fin
100B3 Botletli R Botswana
60C4 Botosani Rom
100B3 Botswana Republic, Africa
53C3 Botte Donato Mt Italy
46D1 Bottrop Germany
35B2 Botucatu Brazil
7E5 Botwood Can
97B4 Bouaké Ivory Coast
98B2 Bouar CAR
96B1 Bouārfa Mor
98B2 Bouca CAR
51C2 Boufarik Alg
Bougie = Bejaia
97B3 Bougouni Mali
46C2 Bouillon France
96B2 Bou Izakarn Mor
46D2 Boulay-Moselle France
8C2 Boulder Colorado, USA
9B3 Boulder City USA
22A2 Boulder Creek USA
48C1 Boulogne France
98B2 Boumba R CAR
97B4 Bouna Ivory Coast
8B3 Boundary Peak Mt USA
97B4 Boundiali Ivory Coast
107F3 Bourail Nouvelle Calédonie
97B3 Bourem Mali
49D2 Bourg France
49D2 Bourg de Péage France
48C2 Bourges France
48C3 Bourg-Madame France

49C2 Bourgogne Region France
47B2 Bourg-St-Maurice France
108C2 Bourke Aust
43D4 Bournemouth Eng
96C1 Bou Saâda Alg
98B1 Bousso Chad
103J7 Bouvet I Atlantic O
34D2 Bovril Arg
13E2 Bow R Can
107D2 Bowen Aust
19A3 Bowie Texas, USA
13A2 Bow Island Can
11B3 Bowling Green Kentucky, USA
18B2 Bowling Green Missouri, USA
14B2 Bowling Green Ohio, USA
15C3 Bowling Green Virginia, USA
109D2 Bowmanville Can
109D2 Bowral Aust
13C2 Bowron R Can
72D3 Bo Xian China
72D2 Boxing China
92B1 Boyabat Turk
98B2 Boyali CAR
5J4 Boyd Can
16B2 Boyertown USA
13E2 Boyle Can
41B3 Boyle Irish Rep
45C2 Boyne R Irish Rep
17B2 Boynton Beach USA
98C2 Boyoma Falls Zaire
55C3 Boz Dağları Mts Turk
8B2 Bozeman USA
Bozen = Bolzano
98B2 Bozene Zaire
98B2 Bozoum CAR
47B2 Bra Italy
52C2 Brač I Croatia
15C1 Bracebridge Can
95A2 Brach Libya
38H6 Bräcke Sweden
17B2 Bradenton USA
42D3 Bradford Eng
44E1 Brae Scot
44C3 Braemar Scot
50A1 Braga Port
34C3 Bragado Arg
50A1 Bragança Port
31B2 Bragança Brazil
35B2 Bragança Paulista Brazil
86B2 Brahman-Baria Bang
86B2 Brahmani R India
86C1 Brahmaputra R India
7E5 Braie Verte Can
6O4 Brăila Rom
10A2 Brainerd USA
97A3 Brakna Region, Maur
5F4 Bralorne Can
14C2 Brampton Can
33E3 Branco R Brazil
100A3 Brandberg Mt Namibia
56C2 Brandenburg Germany
56C2 Brandenburg State, Germany
101G1 Brandfort S Africa
8D2 Brandon Can
100B4 Brandvlei S Africa
57C2 Brandys nad Labem Czech Republic
58B2 Braniewo Pol
10B2 Brantford Can
100B3 Branxholme Aust
7D5 Bras D'Or L Can
35C1 Brasila de Minas Brazil
32D6 Brasiléia Brazil
31B5 Brasilia Brazil
54C1 Brasov Rom
78D1 Brassay Range Mts Malay
59B3 Bratislava Slovakia
63C2 Bratsk Russian Fed
15D2 Brattleboro USA

56C2 Braunschweig Germany
97A4 Brava r Cape Verde
9B3 Brawley USA
45C2 Bray Irish Rep
6C3 Bray I Can
13D2 Brazeau r Can
13D2 Brazeau,Mt Can
28G4 Brazil Republic, S America
03G8 Brazil Basin Atlantic O
9D3 Brazos r USA
98B3 Brazzaville Congo
57C3 Brčy Upland Russian Fed
11A3 Breaksea Sd NZ
10B1 Bream B NZ
78B4 Brebes Indon
44C3 Brechin Scot
46C1 Brecht Belg
59B3 Břeclav Czech Republic
43C4 Brecon Wales
59B3 Brecon Wales
43C4 Brecon Beacons Mts Wales
43B4 Brecon Beacons Nat Pk Wales
56A2 Breda Neth
100B4 Bredasdorp S Africa
38H6 Bredbyn Sweden
61J3 Bredy Russian Fed
16C2 Breezewood USA
47C1 Bregenz Austria
47C1 Bregenzer Ache r Austria
38A1 Breiðafjörður B Iceland
47C2 Brembo r Italy
47T1 Bremen USA
56B2 Bremen Germany
56B2 Bremerhaven Germany
20B1 Bremerton USA
19A3 Brenham USA
57C3 Brenner P Austria/Italy
47D2 Brenta r Italy
52B1 Brescia Italy
Breslau = Wrocław
44E1 Bressay I Scot
48B2 Bressuire France
48B2 Brest Belorussia
48B2 Brest France
48B2 Bretagne Region, France
46B2 Breteuil France
16B2 Breton Woods USA
110B1 Brett,C NZ
16C2 Brewarrina Aust
16C2 Brewster New York, USA
20C1 Brewster Washington, USA
101G1 Breyten S Africa
52C2 Brežice Slovenia
98C2 Bria CAR
49D3 Briançon France
49C2 Briare France
21B2 Bridgeport California, USA
16B3 Bridgeport Connecticut, USA
19A3 Bridgeport Texas, USA
22C1 Bridgeport Res USA
16B3 Bridgeton USA
27F4 Bridgetown Barbados
7D5 Bridgewater Can
16D2 Bridgewater USA
43C4 Bridgwater Eng
43C4 Bridgwater B Eng
42D2 Bridlington Eng
109C4 Bridport Aust
47B1 Brienzer See L Switz
46C2 Briey France
52A1 Brig Switz
8B2 Brigham City USA
109C3 Bright Aust
43D4 Brighton Eng
46E1 Brilon Germany

55A2 Brindisi Italy
19B3 Brinkley USA
107E3 Brisbane Aust
15D2 Bristol Connecticut, USA
43C4 Bristol Eng
15D2 Bristol Pennsylvania, USA
16D2 Bristol Rhode Island, USA
11B3 Bristol Tennessee, USA
12B3 Bristol B USA
43B4 Bristol Chan Eng/Wales
4D3 British Mts Can
5F4 British Columbia Province, Can
6B1 British Empire Range Mts Can
101G1 Brits S Africa
100B4 Britstown S Africa
42C2 Brive France
59B3 Brno Czech Republic
17B1 Broad r USA
7C4 Broadback r Can
44A2 Broad Bay Inlet Scot
44B3 Broadford Scot
5H4 Brochet Can
44C2 Brock I Can
15C2 Brockport USA
16D1 Brockton USA
15C2 Brockville Can
6B2 Brodeur Pen Can
42B2 Brodick Scot
58B2 Brodnica Pol
60C3 Brody Ukraine
19B3 Broken Bow Oklahoma, USA
19B3 Broken Bow L USA
107D4 Broken Hill Aust
47C2 Broni Italy
38G5 Brønnøysund Nor
16C2 Bronx Borough, New York, USA
79A4 Brooke's Point Phil
18B2 Brookfield Missouri, USA
11A3 Brookhaven USA
20B2 Brookings Oregon, USA
8D2 Brookings South Dakota, USA
16D1 Brookline USA
16C2 Brooklyn Borough, New York, USA
5G4 Brooks Can
12C3 Brooks,L USA
12A1 Brooks Mt USA
4C3 Brooks Range Mts USA
17B2 Brooksville USA
109D1 Brooloo Aust
100B2 Broome Aust
44C2 Brora Scot
20B2 Brothers USA
95A3 Broulkou Chad
9D4 Browning USA
9D3 Brownsville USA
9D3 Brownwood USA
46B1 Bruay-en-Artois France
106A3 Bruce,Mt Aust
14B1 Bruce Pen Can
59B3 Brück an der Mur Austria
Bruges = Brugge
46B1 Brugge Belg
46D1 Brühl Germany
78C2 Brunei Sultanate, S E Asia
52B1 Brunico Italy
111B2 Brunner,L NZ
11B3 Brunswick Georgia, USA
11B3 Brunswick Mississippi, USA
29B6 Brunswick,Pen de Chile
109C4 Bruny I Aust
61F1 Brusenets Russian Fed
26A3 Brus Laguna Honduras
Brüssel = Bruxelles

56A2 Bruxelles Belg
9D3 Bryan USA
108A2 Bryan,Mt Aust
60D3 Bryansk Russian Fed
19B3 Bryant USA
59B2 Brzeg Pol
93E4 Būbiyan I Kuwait/Iraq
99D3 Bubu r Tanz
32C2 Bucaramanga Colombia
44D3 Buchan Oilfield N Sea
97A4 Buchanan Lib
44D3 Buchan Deep N Sea
6C2 Buchan G Can
40C2 Buchan Ness Pen Scot
7E5 Buchans Can
54C2 BucharArg
Bucharest = Bucureşti
47C1 Buchs Switz
43D3 Buckingham Eng
12B1 Buckland USA
12B1 Buckland r USA
108A2 Buckleboo Aust
98B3 Buco Zau Congo
54C2 Bucureşti Rom
59B3 Budapest Hung
86A1 Budaun India
43B4 Bude Eng
19B3 Bude USA
61F5 Budennovsk Russian Fed
54A2 Budva Montenegro, Yugos
98A2 Buéa Cam
22B3 Buellton USA
34B2 Buena Esperanza Arg
32B3 Buenaventura Colombia
23A2 Buenavista Mexico
29E2 Buenos Aires Arg
29D3 Buenos Aires State, Arg
18B2 Buffalo Mississipi, USA
10C2 Buffalo New York, USA
8C2 Buffalo South Dakota, USA
19A3 Buffalo Texas, USA
8C2 Buffalo Wyoming, USA
101H1 Buffalo r S Africa
13E2 Buffalo L Alberta, Can
5G3 Buffalo L Northwest Territories, Can
5H4 Buffalo Narrows Can
17B1 Buford USA
54C2 Buftea Rom
32B3 Buga r Pol/Ukraine
32B3 Buga Colombia
90B2 Bugdayli Turkmenistan
61H3 Bugulma Russian Fed
61H3 Buguruslan Russian Fed
92B2 Buhayrat al Asad Res Syria
41C3 Builth Wells Wales
34A2 Buin Chile
99C3 Bujumbura Burundi
99C3 Bukama Zaïre
99C3 Bukavu Zaïre
80E2 Bukhara Uzbekistan
78C2 Bukit Batubrok Mt Indon
70B4 Bukittinggi Indon
99D3 Bukoba Tanz
79B3 Buku Gandadiwata Mt Indon
71E4 Bula Indon
79B3 Bulan Phil
85D3 Bulandshahr India
100B3 Bulawayo Zim
55C3 Buldan Turk
85D4 Buldāna India
68C2 Bulgan Mongolia
54B2 Bulgaria Republic, Europe
47B1 Bulle Switz
111B2 Buller r NZ

109C3 Buller,Mt Aust
106A4 Bullfinch Aust
108B1 Bulloo r Aust
108B1 Bulloo Downs Aust
108B1 Bulloo L Aust
18B2 Bull Shoals Res USA
34A3 Bulnes Chile
71F4 Bulolo PNG
101G1 Bultfontein S Africa
98C2 Bumba Zaïre
76B2 Bumphal Dam Thai
99D2 Buna Kenya
106A4 Bunbury Aust
45C1 Buncrana Irish Rep
107E3 Bundaberg Aust
109D2 Bundarra Aust
85D3 Bundi India
45B1 Bundoran Irish Rep
109C1 Bungil r Aust
98B3 Bungo Angola
75A2 Bungo-suidō Str Japan
70B3 Bunguran r Ind
99D2 Bunia Zaïre
18B2 Bunker USA
19B3 Bunkie USA
17B2 Bunnell USA
78C3 Buntok Indon
71D3 Buol Indon
98D1 Buram Sudan
99E2 Burao Somalia
80C3 Buraydah S Arabia
21B3 Burbank USA
109C2 Burcher Aust
92B2 Burdur Turk
81H3 Bureinskiy Khrebet Mts Russian Fed
56C2 Burg Germany
54C2 Burgas Bulg
17C1 Burgaw USA
47B1 Burgdorf Switz
100B4 Burgersdorp S Africa
50B1 Burgos Spain
38H6 Burgsvik Sweden
55C3 Burhaniye Turk
85D4 Burhanpur India
79B3 Burias r Phil
76C2 Buriram Thai
35B1 Buritis Brazil
13B2 Burke Chan Can
106C2 Burketown Aust
99D3 Burkina Republic, Africa
15C1 Burks Falls Can
8B2 Burley USA
10A2 Burlington Iowa, USA
18B2 Burlington New Jersey, USA
10C2 Burlington Vermont, USA
20B1 Burlington Washington, USA
83D3 Burma Republic, Asia
9B2 Burney USA
16A2 Burnham USA
107D5 Burnie Aust
42C3 Burnley Eng
20C2 Burns USA
5F4 Burns Lake Can
82C1 Burqin China
108A2 Burra Aust
109C2 Burragorang,L Aust
44C2 Burray r Scot
109C2 Burren Junction Aust
109C2 Burrinjuck Res Aust
60C5 Burrs Turk
80B3 Bur Safaga Egypt
Bür Sa'id = Port Said
43D3 Burton upon Trent Eng
38J6 Burträsk Sweden
108B2 Burtundy Aust
71D4 Buru Indon
99C3 Burundi Republic, Africa
78A3 Burung Indon
63D2 Buryatskaya Respublika, Russian Fed
99D1 Burye Eth

61H4 Burynshik
  Kazakhstan
43E3 Bury St Edmunds
  Eng
9J84 Büshehr Iran
98B3 Busira R Zaire
58C2 Buskozdroj Pol
94C2 Busrá ash Shām
  Syria
106A4 Busselton Aust
49D2 Busto Italy
52A1 Busto Arsizio Italy
79A3 Busuanga I Phil
98C2 Buta Zaire
34B3 Buta Ranquil Arg
99C3 Butare Rwanda
42B2 Bute I Scot
69E2 Butha Qi China
14C2 Butler USA
8B2 Butte USA
77C4 Butterworth Malay
40B2 Butt of Lewis I
  Scot
6D3 Button Is Can
79C4 Butuan Phil
71D4 Butung I Indon
61F3 Buturlinovka
  Russian Fed
86A1 Butwal Nepal
99E2 Buulo Barde Somalia
99E2 Buur Hakaba
  Somalia
61F2 Buy Russian Fed
72B1 Buyant Ovvo
  Mongolia
61G5 Buynaksk
  Russian Fed
63D3 Buyr Nuur L
  Mongolia
93D2 Büyük Ağri Mt Turk
92A2 Büyük Menderes R
  Turk
54C1 Buzău Rom
54C1 Buzau R Rom
61H3 Buzuluk Russian Fed
16D2 Buzzards B USA
54C2 Byala Bulg
54B2 Byala Slatina Bulg
4H2 Byam Martin Chan
  Can
4H2 Byam Martin I Can
94B1 Byblos = Jubail
58B2 Byblos Hist Site, Leb
39F7 Bygland Nor
6C2 Bylot I Can
109C2 Byrock Aust
22B2 Byron USA
109D1 Byron,C Aust
59B2 Bytom Pol

C

30E4 Caacupé Par
100A2 Caála Angola
13B2 Caamano Sd Can
30E4 Caazapá Par
79B2 Cabanatuan Phil
31E3 Cabedelo Brazil
50A2 Cabeza del Buey
  Spain
34C3 Cabildo Arg
34A2 Cabildo Chile
32C1 Cabimas Ven
98B3 Cabinda Angola
98B3 Cabinda Province,
  Angola
27C3 Cabo Beata Dom Rep
51C2 Cabo Binibeca C
  Spain
53A3 Cabo Carbonara C
  Sardegna
34A3 Cabo Carranza C
  Chile
50A2 Cabo Carvoeiro C
  Port
9B3 Cabo Colnett C
  Mexico
32B2 Cabo Corrientes C
  Colombia
24B2 Cabo Corrientes C
  Mexico
26B3 Cabo Cruz C Cuba
50B1 Cabo de Ajo C Spain
51C1 Cabo de Caballeria C
  Spain
51C1 Cabo de Creus C
  Spain
50B2 Cabo de Gata C
  Spain
29C7 Cabo de Hornos C
  Chile
51C2 Cabo de la Nao C
  Spain
50A1 Cabo de Peñas C
  Spain
50A2 Cabo de Roca C Port
51C2 Cabo de Salinas C
  Spain
35C2 Cabo de São Tomé C
  Brazil
50A2 Cabo de São Vicente
  C Port
50A2 Cabo de Sines C
  Port
51C1 Cabo de Tortosa C
  Spain
29C4 Cabo Dos Bahias C
  Arg
50A2 Cabo Espichel C Port
9B4 Cabo Falso C Mexico
51B2 Cabo Ferrat C Alg
50A1 Cabo Finisterre C
  Spain
51C1 Cabo Formentor C
  Spain
35C2 Cabo Frio Brazil
35C2 Cabo Frio C Brazil
26A4 Cabo Gracias à Dios
  Honduras
31B2 Cabo Maguarinho C
  Brazil
50A2 Cabo Negro C Mor
10D1 Caboolture Aust
33G3 Cabo Orange C
  Brazil
21B3 Cabo Punta Banda C
  Mexico
101C2 Cabora Bassa Dam
  Mozam
24A1 Caborca Mexico
24C2 Cabo Rojo C Mexico
23B1 Cabos Mexico
29C6 Cabo San Diego C
  Arg
32A4 Cabo San Lorenzo C
  Ecuador
53A3 Cabo Teulada C
  Sardegna
50A2 Cabo Trafalgar C
  Spain
50B2 Cabo Tres Forcas C
  Mor
29C5 Cabo Tres Puntas C
  Arg
7D5 Cabot Str Can
50B2 Cabra Spain
50A1 Cabreira Mt Port
51C2 Cabrera I Spain
34A3 Cabrero Chile
51B2 Cabriel R Spain
23B2 Cacahuatepla
  Mexico
54B2 Čačak Serbia, Yugos
23B2 C A Carillo Mexico
30E2 Cáceres Brazil
50A2 Cáceres Spain
13C2 Cache R USA
13C2 Cache Creek Can
30C4 Cachi Arg
33G5 Cachimbo Brazil
31D4 Cachoeira Brazil
35A1 Cachoeira Alta Brazil
31D3 Cachoeira de Paulo
  Alfonso Waterfall
  Brazil
29F2 Cachoeira do Sul
  Brazil
31C6 Cachoeiro de
  Itapemirim Brazil
22C3 Cachuma,L USA
100A2 Cacolo Angola
100A2 Caconda Angola
35A1 Caçu Brazil
100A2 Cacula R Angola
59B3 Cadca Slovakia
43C3 Cader Idris Mts
  Wales
10B2 Cadillac USA
79B3 Cadiz Phil
50A2 Cadiz Spain

48B2 Caen France
42B3 Caernarfon Wales
43B3 Caernarfon B Wales
94B2 Caesarea Hist Site
  Israel
31C4 Caetité Brazil
30C4 Cafayate Arg
92B2 Caga Tepe Turk
79B2 Cagayan R Phil
79B3 Cagayan de Oro Phil
79B4 Cagayan Is Phil
53A3 Cagliari Sardegna
27D3 Caguas Puerto Rico
45B3 Caha Mts Irish Rep
45A3 Cahersiveen
  Irish Rep
45C2 Cahir Irish Rep
45C2 Cahone Pt Irish Rep
48C3 Cahors France
101C2 Caia Mozam
100B2 Caianda Angola
35A1 Caiapó R Brazil
35A1 Caiapônia Brazil
26D3 Caicó Brazil
26C2 Caicos Is
  Caribbean S
11C4 Caicos Pass The
  Bahamas
12C2 Cairn Mt USA
44C3 Cairngorms Mts
  Scot
107D2 Cairns Aust
92B3 Cairo Egypt
11B3 Cairo USA
10B1 Caiwarro Aust
32B5 Cajabamba Peru
32B5 Cajamarca Peru
27D5 Calabozo Ven
54B2 Calafat Rom
29B6 Calafate Arg
79B3 Calagua Is Phil
51B1 Calahorra Spain
48C1 Calais France
30C3 Calama Chile
32C3 Calamar Colombia
79A3 Calamian Group Is
  Phil
98B3 Calandula Angola
70A3 Calang Indon
95B2 Calanscio Sand Sea
  Libya
79B3 Calapan Phil
54C2 Calarasi Rom
51B1 Calatayud Spain
22A1 Calaveras Res USA
79B3 Calbayog Phil
19B4 Calcasieu L USA
86B2 Calcutta India
50A2 Caldas da Rainha
  Port
31B5 Caldas Novas Brazil
30B4 Caldera Chile
8B2 Caldwell USA
29C5 Caleta Olivia Arg
9B3 Calexico USA
7B4 Calgary Can
19B3 Calhoun USA
17B1 Calhoun Falls USA
32B3 Cali Colombia
87B2 Calicut India
8A3 Caliente Nevada,
  USA
8A3 California State, USA
22C3 California Aqueduct
  USA
87B2 Calimera,Pt India
22A1 Calingasta Arg
22A1 Calistoga USA
108B1 Callabonna R Aust
108A1 Callabonna,L Aust
44B3 Callander Scot
32B6 Callao Peru
13E1 Calling L Can
23B1 Calnali Mexico
17B2 Caloosahatchee R
  USA
109D1 Caloundra Aust
23B2 Calpulalpan Mexico
53B3 Caltanissetta Italy
98B3 Caluango Angola
100A2 Calulo Angola
100A2 Caluquembe Angola
99F1 Caluula Somalia

13B2 Calvert I Can
52A2 Calvi Corse
23A1 Calvillo Mexico
100A4 Calvinia S Africa
25E2 Camagüey Cuba
25E2 Camaguey,Arch de
  Cuba
32B6 Camaná Peru
30C3 Camargo Bol
22C3 Camarillo USA
29C4 Camarones Arg
20B1 Camas USA
98B3 Camaxilo Angola
98B3 Cambatela Angola
76C3 Cambodia Republic
  S E Asia
43B4 Camborne Eng
49C1 Cambrai France
43C3 Cambrian Mts Wall
14B2 Cambridge Can
43D3 Cambridge County
  Eng
27H1 Cambridge Jamaic
15C3 Cambridge
  Maryland, USA .
15D2 Cambridge
  Massachusetts, US
110C1 Cambridge NZ
14B2 Cambridge Ohio,
  USA
4H3 Cambridge Bay Ca
60E5 Cam Burun Pt Turk
11A3 Camden Arkansas,
  USA
109D2 Camden Aust
15D3 Camden New Jerse
17B1 Camden South
  Carolina, USA
18B2 Cameron Missouri,
  USA
19A3 Cameron Texas,
  USA
4H2 Cameron I Can
111A3 Cameron Mts NZ
98A2 Cameroon Federal
  Republic, Africa
98A2 Cameroun Mt Cam
31B2 Cametá Brazil
79B1 Camiguin I Phil
79B2 Camiling Phil
17B1 Camilla USA
22B1 Camino USA
30D3 Camiri Bol
31C2 Camocim Brazil
98C3 Camissombo Ango
106C2 Camoowead Aust
34D2 Campana Arg
29A5 Campana I Chile
13B2 Campania I Can
111B2 Campbell,C NZ
13B2 Campbell I Can
105G6 Campbell I NZ
4E3 Campbell,Mt Can
84C2 Campbellpore Pak
5F5 Campbell River Can
7D5 Campbellton Can
109D2 Campbelltown Aust
42B2 Campbeltown Scot
25C3 Campeche Mexico
108B3 Camperdown Aust
31D3 Campina Grande
  Brazil
31B6 Campinas Brazil
35B1 Campina Verde
  Brazil
98A2 Campo Cam
53B2 Campobasso Italy
35B2 Campo Belo Brazil
35B1 Campo Florido Braz
30D4 Campo Gallo Arg
30F3 Campo Grande Braz
31C2 Campo Maior Braz
30F3 Campo Mourão
  Brazil
35C2 Campos Brazil
35B1 Campos Altos Brazil
47D1 Campo Tures Italy
76D3 Cam Ranh Viet
5G4 Camrose Can
98A2 Camucuio Angola
27K1 Canaan Tobago
16C1 Canaan USA
100A2 Canacupa Angola

Caucasia

2F3 **Canada** Dominion, N America
29D2 **Cañada de Gomez** Arg
9C3 **Canadian** R USA
60C5 **Çanakkale** Turk
13D2 **Canalejas** Arg
13D2 **Canal Flats** Can
24A1 **Cananea** Mexico
02G3 **Canary Basin** Atlantic O
Canary Is = Islas Canarias
23A2 **Canas** Mexico
24B2 **Canatlan** Mexico
11B4 **Canaveral,C** USA
11D5 **Canavieiras** Brazil
07D4 **Canberra** Aust
22B2 **Canby** California, USA
55C3 **Çandarli Körfezi** B Turk
16C2 **Candlewood,L** USA
29E2 **Canelones** Urug
24A2 **Caney** USA
00A2 **Cangamba** Angola
02B2 **Cangombe** Angola
72D2 **Cangzhou** China
70D4 **Caniapiscau** R Can
53B3 **Canicatti** Italy
31D2 **Canindé** Brazil
92B1 **Çankırı** Turk
13D2 **Canmore** Can
44A3 **Canna** I Scot
87B2 **Cannanore** India
49D2 **Cannes** France
29C3 **Cann River** Aust
30F4 **Canôas** Brazil
13F1 **Canoe L** Can
9C3 **Canon City** USA
08B2 **Canopus** Aust
5H4 **Canora** Can
29C2 **Canowindra** Aust
45C2 **Cansore Pt** Irish Rep
11B2 **Canterbury** Eng
11B2 **Canterbury Bight** B NZ
43E4 **Canterbury** Eng
11B2 **Canterbury Plains** NZ
77D4 **Can Tho** Viet
Canton = Guangzhou
19C3 **Canton** Mississippi, USA
18B1 **Canton** Missouri, USA
12E2 **Canton** Ohio, USA
20C2 **Cantwell** USA
12J2 **Canyon City** USA
20B2 **Canyon Range** Mts Can
2082 **Canyonville** USA
98C2 **Canzar** Angola
76D1 **Cao Bang** Viet
31B2 **Capanema** Brazil
35B2 **Capão Bonito** Brazil
48B3 **Capbreton** France
24B2 **Cap Corrientes** C Mexico
52A2 **Cap Corse** C Corse
48B2 **Cap de la Hague** C France
15D1 **Cap-de-la-Madeleine** Can
6C3 **Cap de Nouvelle-France** C Can
51C2 **Capdepera** Spain
24B2 **Cap de Tancitario** C Mexico
09C4 **Cape Barren I** Aust
03J6 **Cape Basin** Atlantic O
7E5 **Cape Breton I** Can
97A4 **Cape Coast** Ghana
15D2 **Cape Cod B** USA
6C3 **Cape Dorset** Can
17C1 **Cape Fear** R USA
6B3 **Cape Girardeau** USA
6B3 **Cape Henrietta Maria** C Can
Cape Horn = Cabo de Hornos
04E3 **Cape Johnston Depth** Pacific O
31B3 **Capelinha** Brazil
48B3 **Cape Lisburne** USA
00A2 **Capelongo** Angola
15D3 **Cape May** USA

5F5 **Cape Mendocino** USA
98B3 **Capenda Camulemba** Angola
4F2 **Cape Perry** Can
100B4 **Cape Province** S Africa
7A4 **Cape Tatnam** Can
100A4 **Cape Town** S Africa
102G4 **Cape Verde** Is Atlantic O
102G4 **Cape Verde Basin** Atlantic O
12F3 **Cape Yakataga** USA
107D2 **Cape York Pen** Aust
46A1 **Cap Gris Nez** C France
26C3 **Cap-Haïtien** Haiti
31B2 **Capim** R Brazil
112C2 **Capitán Arturo Prat** Base Ant
27P2 **Cap Moule à Chique** C St Lucia
53C3 **Capo Isola de Correnti** C Italy
53C3 **Capo Rizzuto** C Italy
55A3 **Capo Santa Maria di Leuca** C Italy
53B3 **Capo San Vito** Italy
53C3 **Capo Spartivento** C Italy
27P2 **Cap Pt** St Lucia
53B2 **Capri** I Italy
100B2 **Caprivi Strip** Region, Namibia
52A2 **Cap Rosso** C Corse
102H4 **Cap Vert** C Sen
32C4 **Caquetá** R Colombia
54B2 **Caracal** Rom
33A3 **Caracaraí** Brazil
32D1 **Caracas** Ven
35B2 **Caraguatatuba** Brazil
29B3 **Carahue** Chile
35C1 **Caraí** Brazil
31C6 **Carangola** Brazil
54B1 **Caransebes** Rom
108A2 **Carappee Hill** Mt Aust
26A3 **Caratasca** Honduras
35C1 **Caratinga** Brazil
51B2 **Caravaca** Spain
35D1 **Caravelas** Brazil
18C2 **Carbondale** Illinois, USA
53A3 **Carbonia** Sardegna
7E5 **Carbonear** Can
5C4 **Carcaión** Can
99E1 **Carcar Mts** Somalia
48C3 **Carcassonne** France
4E3 **Carcross** Can
23B2 **Cardel** Mexico
25D2 **Cárdenas** Cuba
23B1 **Cárdenas** Mexico
43C4 **Cardiff** Wales
43B3 **Cardigan** Wales
43B3 **Cardigan B** Wales
13E2 **Cardston** Can
54B1 **Carei** Rom
33F4 **Careiro** Can
34A2 **Carén** Chile
14B2 **Carey** USA
48B2 **Carhaix-Plouguer** France
29D3 **Carhué** Arg
31C6 **Cariacica** Brazil
32C4 **Caribou** R Can
5G4 **Caribou** Can
5G4 **Caribou Mts** Alberta, Can
5F4 **Caribou Mts** British Columbia, Can
79B3 **Carigara** Phil
46C2 **Carignan** France
33E1 **Caripito** Ven
15C1 **Carleton Place** Can
101G1 **Carletonville** S Africa
18C2 **Carlinville** USA
42C2 **Carlisle** Eng
15C2 **Carlisle** USA
34C3 **Carlos Arg**
35C1 **Carlos Chagas** Brazil
45C2 **Carlow** County, Irish Rep
45C2 **Carlow** Irish Rep

21B3 **Carlsbad** California, USA
9C3 **Carlsbad** New Mexico, USA
5H5 **Carlyle** Can
12G2 **Carmacks** Can
47B2 **Carmagnola** Italy
43B4 **Carmarthen** Wales
43B4 **Carmarthen B** Wales
22B2 **Carmel** California, USA
16C2 **Carmel** New York, USA
94B2 **Carmel,Mt** Israel
34D2 **Carmelo** Urug
22B2 **Carmel Valley** USA
4M **Carmen** I Mexico
29D4 **Carmen de Patagones** Arg
18C2 **Carmi** USA
21A2 **Carmichael** USA
35B1 **Carmo do Paranaíba** Brazil
50A2 **Carmona** Spain
106A3 **Carnarvon** Aust
100B4 **Carnarvon** S Africa
35D1 **Carncacá** Brazil
45C1 **Carndonagh** Irish Rep
106B3 **Carnegie,L** Aust
98B2 **Carnot** CAR
108A2 **Carnot,C** Aust
17B2 **Carol City** USA
31B3 **Carolina** Brazil
101H1 **Carolina** S Africa
17C1 **Carolina Beach** USA
16B4 **Carolina Is** Pacific O
60B4 **Carpathians** Mts E Europe
59D3 **Carpatii Orientali** Mts Rom
106C2 **Carpentaria,G of** Aust
83C5 **Carpenter Ridge** Indian O
49D3 **Carpentras** France
52B2 **Carpi** Italy
22C3 **Carpinteria** USA
17B2 **Carrabelle** USA
52B2 **Carrara** Italy
41B3 **Carrauntoohil** Mt Irish Rep
45C2 **Carrickmacross** Irish Rep
45B2 **Carrick on Shannon** Irish Rep
45C2 **Carrick-on-Suir** Irish Rep
108A2 **Carrieton** Aust
8D2 **Carrington** USA
50B1 **Carrión** R Spain
10A2 **Carroll** USA
17A1 **Carrollton** Georgia, USA
14A3 **Carrollton** Kentucky, USA
18B1 **Carrollton** Missouri, USA
1882 **Carruthersville** USA
60E5 **Carsamba** Turk
92B2 **Carsamba** R Turk
14B3 **Carson City** USA
14B2 **Carsonville** USA
26B4 **Cartagena** Colombia
51B2 **Cartagena** Spain
32B3 **Cartago** Colombia
25D4 **Cartago** Costa Rica
111C2 **Carterton** NZ
18B2 **Carthage** Missouri, USA
15C2 **Carthage** New York, USA
19B3 **Carthage** Texas, USA
106B2 **Cartier I** Timor S
7E4 **Cartwright** Can
31D3 **Caruaru** Brazil
33E1 **Carúpano** Ven
46B1 **Carvin** France
34A2 **Casablanca** Chile
9681 **Casablanca** Mor
9B3 **Casa Grande** USA
52A1 **Casale Monferrato** Italy
47D2 **Casalmaggiore** Italy

34C3 **Casares** Arg
13C3 **Cascade** Can/USA
111A2 **Cascade Pt** NZ
8A2 **Cascade Range** Mts USA
30F3 **Cascavel** Brazil
53B2 **Caserta** Italy
112C9 **Casey** Base Ant
45C2 **Cashel** Irish Rep
34C2 **Casilda** Arg
16C1 **Casino** Aust
32B5 **Casma** Peru
51B1 **Casper** USA
8C2 **Casper** USA
61G4 **Caspian Depression** Region Kazakhstan
65G6 **Caspian S** Asia/Europe
14C3 **Cass** USA
100B2 **Cassamba** Angola
46B1 **Cassel** France
12J3 **Cassiar** Can
4E3 **Cassiar Mts** Can
3A1 **Cassilândia** Brazil
53B2 **Cassino** Italy
22C3 **Castaic** USA
38B2 **Castaño** R Arg
47D2 **Castelfranco** Italy
49D3 **Castellane** France
34D3 **Castelli** Arg
51B2 **Castellón de la Plana** Spain
31C3 **Castelo** Brazil
50A2 **Castelo Branco** Port
48C3 **Castelsarrasin** France
50A2 **Castelvetrano** Italy
108B3 **Casterton** Aust
50B2 **Castilla La Nueva** Region, Spain
50B1 **Castilla la Vieja** Region, Spain
45B1 **Castlebar** Irish Rep
44A3 **Castlebay** Scot
22C1 **Castle Douglas** Scot
20C1 **Castlegar** Can
45B2 **Castleisland** Irish Rep
8B3 **Castlemain** Aust
45B2 **Castlerea** Irish Rep
109C2 **Castlereagh** Aust
48C3 **Castres-sur-l'Agout** France
27E4 **Castries** St Lucia
29B4 **Castro** Arg
30F3 **Castro** Brazil
53C3 **Castro Alves** Brazil
53C3 **Castrovillari** Italy
22B2 **Castroville** USA
25E2 **Cat** I The Bahamas
79B3 **Catabalogan** Phil
32A5 **Catacaos** Peru
35B2 **Cataguases** Brazil
19B3 **Catahoula L** USA
35B1 **Catalão** Brazil
51C1 **Cataluña** Region, Spain
30C4 **Catamarca** Arg
30C4 **Catamarca** State, Arg
101C2 **Catandica** Mozam
79B3 **Catanduanes** I Phil
35B2 **Catanduva** Brazil
53C3 **Catania** Italy
79B3 **Catanzaro** Italy
108A2 **Catastrophe,C** Aust
26C5 **Catatumbo** R Ven
16A2 **Catawissa** USA
23B2 **Catemaco** Mexico
49D3 **Cater** Corse
52A2 **Cateraggio** Corse
98B3 **Catete** Angola
97A3 **Catio** Guinea-Bissau
10E3 **Cato** I Aust
23C2 **Catlegar** Can
16A3 **Catoche,C** Mexico
15C3 **Catoctin Mt** USA
15C3 **Catonsville** USA
32B2 **Catrilo** Arg
15D2 **Catskill** USA
15D2 **Catskill Mts** USA
32C2 **Cauca** R Colombia
31D2 **Caucaia** Brazil
32B2 **Caucasia** Colombia

65F5 Caucasus Mts Georgia
46B1 Caudry France
98B3 Caungula Angola
87B2 Cauquenes Chile
49D3 Cauvery R India
47D1 Cavalese Italy
97B4 Cavally R Lib
45C2 Cavan County, Irish Rep
45C2 Cavan Irish Rep
79B3 Cavite Phil
32C4 Caxias Brazil
30F4 Caxias do Sul Brazil
98B3 Caxito Angola
17B1 Cayce USA
93D1 Çayeli Turk
33G3 Cayenne French Guiana
46A1 Cayeux-sur-Mer France
25E3 Cayman Brac I / Caribbean S
26A3 Cayman Is Caribbean S
26A3 Cayman Trench Caribbean S
99E2 Caynabo Somalia
25E2 Cayo Romana I / Cuba
25D3 Cayos Miskitos Is Nic
26A2 Cay Sal I / Caribbean S
100B2 Cazombo Angola
Ceará = Fortaleza
31C3 Ceara State, Brazil
79B3 Cebu Phil
79B3 Cebu I Phil
16B3 Cecilton USA
52B2 Cecina Italy
68J3 Cedar City USA
19A3 Cedar Creek Res USA
5J4 Cedar L Can
10A2 Cedar Rapids USA
17A1 Cedartown USA
24A2 Cedros I Mexico
106C4 Ceduna Aust
99E2 Ceelbuur Somalia
99E1 Ceerigaabo Somalia
53B3 Cefalù Italy
59B3 Cegléd Hung
100A2 Cela Angola
24B2 Celaya Mexico
Celebes = Sulawesi
70C3 Celebes S S E Asia
14B2 Celina USA
52C1 Celje Slovenia
56C2 Celle Germany
71E4 Cendrawasih Pen Indon
47C2 Ceno R Italy
19B3 Center USA
16C2 Center Moriches USA
17A1 Center Point USA
47D2 Cento Italy
44B3 Central Region, Scot
98B2 Central African Republic Africa
16D2 Central Falls USA
18C2 Centralia Illinois, USA
8A2 Centralia Washington, USA
20B2 Central Point USA
71F4 Central Range Mts PNG
16A3 Centreville Maryland, USA
78C4 Cepu Indon
Ceram = Seram
71D4 Ceram Sea Indon
34C2 Cereales Arg
31B5 Ceres Brazil
100A4 Ceres S Africa
22B2 Ceres USA
48C2 Cergy-Pontoise France
53C2 Cerignola Italy
60C5 Cernavodă Rom
9C4 Cerralvo I Mexico
23A1 Cerritos Mexico

34B2 Cerro Aconcagua Mt Arg
23B1 Cerro Azul Mexico
34A3 Cerro Campanario Mt Chile
34C2 Cerro Champaqui Mt Arg
23A2 Cerro Cuachaia Mt Mexico
23B1 Cerro de Astillero Mexico
34B2 Cerro de Olivares Mt Arg
32B6 Cerro de Pasco Peru
27D3 Cerro de Punta Mt Puerto Rico
23A2 Cerro El Cantado Mt Arg
34B3 Cerro El Nevado Mt Arg
23A2 Cerro Grande Mts Mexico
34A2 Cerro Juncal Mt Arg/Chile
23A1 Cerro la Ardilla Mts Mexico
34B1 Cerro las Tortolas Mt Chile
23A2 Cerro Laurel Mt Mexico
34A2 Cerro Mercedario Mt Arg
34A3 Cerro Mora Mt Chile
27C4 Cerron Mt Ven
34B3 Cerro Payún Mt Arg
23B2 Cerro Penón del Rosario Mt Mexico
34B2 Cerro Sosneado Mt Arg
23A2 Cerro Teotepec Mt Mexico
34B2 Cerro Tupungato Mt Arg
23B2 Cerro Yucuyacau Mt Mexico
47C2 Cervo R Italy
52B2 Cesena Italy
60B2 Cēsis Latvia
57C3 České Budějovice Czech Republic
59B3 Českomoravská Vysocina Mts Czech Republic
55C3 Çeşme Turk
107E4 Cessnock Aust
52C2 Cetina R Croatia
96B1 Ceuta N W Africa
92C2 Ceyhan Turk
92C2 Ceyhan R Turk
92C2 Ceylanpinar Turk
Ceylon = Sri Lanka
63B2 Chaa-Khol Russian Fed
48C2 Châteaudun France
47B1 Chablais Region, France
34C2 Chacabuco Arg
32B5 Chachapoyas Peru
34B3 Chacharramendi Arg
84C3 Chachran Pak
30D4 Chaco State, Arg
98B1 Chad Republic, Africa
98B1 Chad L C Africa
8C2 Chadron USA
85A3 Chagai Pak
63F2 Chagda Russian Fed
84B2 Chaghcharan Afghan
104B4 Chagos Arch Indian O
27L1 Chaguanas Trinidad
91D4 Chāh Bahār Iran
76C2 Chai Badan Thai
76C3 Chaîne des Cardamomes Mts Camb
98C4 Chaine des Mitumba Mts Zaire
76C2 Chaiyaphum Thai
34D2 Chajari Arg
84C2 Chakwal Pak
30B2 Chala Peru
100C2 Chalabesa Zambia

84A2 Chalap Dalam Mts Afghan
73C4 Chaling China
85C4 Chālisgaon India
12F1 Chalkyitsik USA
46C2 Challerange France
46C2 Châlons sur Marne France
49C2 Chalon sur Saône France
57C3 Cham Germany
84D2 Chaman Pak
84B2 Chamba India
85D3 Chambal R India
15C3 Chambersburg USA
49D2 Chambéry France
46B2 Chambly France
85A3 Chambor Kalat Pak
90B3 Chamgordan Iran
34B2 Chamical Arg
47B2 Chamonix France
86C2 Champa India
49C2 Champagne Region, France
101G1 Champagne Castle Mt Lesotho
47A1 Champagnole France
10B2 Champaign USA
76D3 Champassak Laos
10C2 Champlain,L USA
87B2 Chāmrājnagar India
30B4 Chañaral Chile
34A3 Chanco Chile
4D3 Chandalar USA
4D3 Chandalar R USA
84D2 Chandigarh India
86C2 Chandpur Bangla
85D5 Chandrapur India
91D4 Chānf Iran
101C2 Changara Mozam
74B2 Changbai China
69E2 Changchun China
73C4 Changde China
68E4 Chang-hua Taiwan
76D2 Chang,Kaw I Thai
73D3 Chang Jiang R China
74B2 Changjin N Korea
73C4 Changsha China
72E3 Changshu China
74A2 Changtu China
74B3 Changyon N Korea
72C2 Changzhi China
73E3 Changzhou China
76C3 Chanthaburi Thai
46B2 Chantilly France
18A2 Chanute USA
63B2 Chany,Ozero L Russian Fed
73D5 Chao'an China
73D4 Chao Hu L China
76C3 Chao Phraya R Thai
72E1 Chaoyang China
31C4 Chapada Diamantina Mts Brazil
31C2 Chapadinha Brazil
23A1 Chapala Brazil
23A1 Chapala,Lac de L Mexico
61H3 Chapayevo Kazakhstan
30F4 Chapecó Brazil
27H1 Chapeltown Jamaica
7B5 Chapleau Can
63F2 Chaplygin Russian Fed
112C3 Charcot I Ant
80E2 Chardzhou Turkmenistan
48C2 Charente R France
98B1 Chari R Chad
98B1 Chari Baguirmi Region, Chad
84B1 Charikar Afghan
18B1 Chariton R USA
33F2 Charity Guyana
85D3 Charkhāri India
46C1 Charleroi Belg
18C2 Charleston Illinois, USA
18C2 Charleston Missouri, USA

11C3 Charleston S Carolina, USA
10B3 Charleston W Virginia, USA
98C3 Charlesville Zaïre
107D3 Charleville Aust
49C2 Charleville-Mézières France
14A1 Charlevoix USA
14B2 Charlotte Michigan, USA
11B3 Charlotte N Carolina USA
17B2 Charlotte Harbor USA
10C3 Charlottesville USA
7D5 Charlottetown Can
27K1 Charlotteville Tobago
108B3 Charlton Aust
10C1 Charlton I Can
84C2 Charsadda Pak
107D3 Charters Towers Aust
48C2 Chartres France
29E3 Chascomús Arg
13D2 Chase Can
48C2 Châteaubriant France
48C2 Châteaulin France
48C2 Châteauneuf France
48C2 Châteauroux France
46D2 Château-Salins France
48C2 Château-Thierry France
46C1 Châtelet Belg
48C2 Châtellerault France
43E4 Chatham Eng
7D5 Chatham New Brunswick, Can
16C1 Chatham New York, USA
15C1 Chatham Ontario, Can
13B3 Chatham Sd Can
12H3 Chatham Str USA
49C2 Châtillon France
47B2 Châtillon Italy
16B3 Chatsworth USA
17B1 Chattahoochee USA
17A1 Chattahoochee R USA
11B3 Chattanooga USA
76A1 Chauk Burma
49D2 Chaumont France
77D3 Chau Phu Viet
50A1 Chaves Port
61H2 Chaykovskiy Russian Fed
50B2 Chazaouet Alg
34C2 Chazón Arg
32C2 Chcontá Colombia
57C2 Cheb Czech Republic
65F4 Cheboksary Russian Fed
10B2 Cheboygan USA
74B3 Chech'ŏn S Korea
18A2 Checotah USA
76A2 Cheduba I Burma
108B1 Cheepie Aust
86B2 Chegga Maur
100C2 Chegutu Zim
20B1 Chehalis USA
74B4 Cheju S Korea
74B4 Cheju do I S Korea
74B4 Cheju-haehyŏp St Korea
63F2 Chekunda Russian Fed
20B1 Chelan,L USA
90B2 Cheleken Turkmenistan
34B3 Chelforo Arg
80D1 Chelkar Kazakhstan
59C2 Chełm Pol
58B2 Chełmno Pol
43E4 Chelmsford Eng
43C4 Cheltenham Eng
65H4 Chelyabinsk Russian Fed
101C2 Chemba Mozam
57C2 Chemnitz German

84D2 Chenab R India/Pak
96B2 Chenachame Alg
20C1 Cheney USA
18A2 Cheney Res USA
72D1 Chengda China
73A3 Chengdu China
72E2 Chengshan Jiao Pt China
73C4 Chenxi China
73C4 Chen Xian China
73D3 Cheo Xian China
32B5 Chepén Peru
34B2 Chepes Arg
48C2 Cher R France
23A2 Cheran Mexico
17C1 Cheraw USA
48B2 Cherbourg France
96C1 Cherchell Alg
63C2 Cheremkhovo Russian Fed
60E2 Cherepovets Russian Fed
60D4 Cherkassy Ukraine
61F5 Cherkessk Russian Fed
60D3 Chernigov Ukraine
60C3 Chernobyl Ukraine
60C4 Chernovtsy Ukraine
61J2 Chernushka Russian Fed
60B3 Chernyakhovsk Russian Fed
61G4 Chernyye Zemli Region, Russian Fed
18A2 Cherokees,L o'the USA
34A3 Cherquenco Chile
86C1 Cherrapunji India
60C3 Cherven' Belorussia
59C2 Chervonograd Ukraine
10C3 Chesapeake B USA
42C3 Chesapeake USA
16C1 Cheshire Eng
64F3 Chëshskaya Guba B Russian Fed
21A1 Chester California, USA
42C3 Chester Eng
42C3 Chester Illinois, USA
15C1 Chester Massachusets, USA
17B1 Chester Pennsylvania, USA
17B1 Chester S Carolina, USA
16A3 Chester R USA
42D3 Chesterfield Eng
6A3 Chesterfield Inlet Can
16A3 Chestertown USA
25D3 Chetumal Mexico
13C1 Chetwynd Can
12A2 Chevak USA
4C2 Cheviot NZ
40C2 Cheviots Hills Eng/Scot
13D3 Chewelah USA
8C2 Cheyenne USA
86A1 Chhapra India
86C1 Chhatak Bang
85D4 Chhatarpur India
85D4 Chhindwāra India
78E5 Chho'l Taiwan
100A2 Chiange Angola
76C2 Chiang Kham Thai
76B2 Chiang Mai Thai
47C1 Chiavenna Italy
74E3 Chiba Japan
86B2 Chibāsa India
100A2 Chibia Angola
7C4 Chibougamau Can
75A1 Chiburi-jima I Japan
101C3 Chibuto Mozam
10B2 Chicago USA
14A2 Chicago Heights USA
12G3 Chichagof I USA
43D4 Chichester Eng
75B1 Chichibu Japan
69G4 Chichi-jima I Japan
11B3 Chickamauga L USA
19C3 Chickasawhay R USA

9D3 Chickasha USA
12F2 Chicken USA
32A5 Chiclayo Peru
8A3 Chico USA
29C4 Chico R Arg
10C2 Chicoa Mozam
15D2 Chicopee USA
7C5 Chicoutimi Can
101C3 Chicualacuala Mozam
87B2 Chidambaram India
6D3 Chidley,C Can
17B2 Chiefland USA
99C3 Chiengi Zambia
52A2 Chieri Italy
46C2 Chiers R France
47C1 Chiesa Italy
47D2 Chiese R Italy
52B2 Chieti Italy
72D1 Chifeng China
12C3 Chiginagak Mt USA
4C3 Chigmit Mts USA
23B2 Chignahuapán Arg
12C3 Chignik USA
24B2 Chihuahua Mexico
87B2 Chik Ballapur India
87B2 Chikmagalūr India
12C2 Chikuminuk L USA
101C2 Chikwawa Malawi
76A1 Chi-kyaw Burma
87B2 Chilakalūrupet India
23C2 Chilapa Mexico
87B3 Chilaw Sri Lanka
28B6 Chile Republic
34B2 Chilecito Mendoza, Arg
100B2 Chililabombwe Zambia
86B2 Chilka L India
13C2 Chilko R Can
5F4 Chilko L Can
13C2 Chilkotin R Can
34A3 Chillán Chile
34D3 Chillar Arg
18B2 Chillicothe Missouri, USA
14B3 Chillicothe Ohio, USA
13C3 Chilliwack Can
86B1 Chilmari India
101C2 Chilongozi Zambia
20B2 Chiloquin USA
23B2 Chilpancingo Mexico
43D4 Chiltern Hills Upland Eng
14A2 Chilton USA
101C2 Chilumba Malawi
69E4 Chi-lung Taiwan
101C2 Chilwa L Malawi
100C2 Chimanimani Zim
46C1 Chimay Belg
65G5 Chimbay Uzbekistan
32B4 Chimborazo Mt Ecuador
32B5 Chimbote Peru
65H5 Chimkent Kazakhstan
101C2 Chimoio Mozam
67E3 China Republic, Asia
China National Republic = Taiwan
25D3 Chinandega Nic
32B6 Chincha Alta Peru
109D1 Chinchilla Aust
101C2 Chinde Mozam
86C2 Chindwin R Burma
100B2 Chingola Zambia
100A2 Chinguar Angola
96A2 Chinguetti Maur
74B3 Chinhae S Korea
100C2 Chinhoyi Zim
120B3 Chiniak,C USA
84C2 Chiniot Pak
74B3 Chinju S Korea
98C2 Chinko R CAR
75B1 Chino Japan
76C3 Chinon France
87A1 Chintamani India
43C4 Chippenham Eng
10A2 Chippewa Falls USA
32A4 Chira R Peru

87C1 Chīrāla India
101C3 Chiredzi Zim
95A2 Chirfa Niger
32A2 Chiriqui Mt Panama
54C2 Chirpan Bulg
32A2 Chirripo Grande Mt Costa Rica
100B2 Chirundu Zim
100B2 Chisamba Zambia
7C4 Chisasibi Can
73B4 Chishui He R China
Chişinău = Kishinev
47B2 Chisone R Italy
61H2 Chistopol Russian Fed
68D1 Chita Russian Fed
100A2 Chitado Angola
100A2 Chitembo Angola
12F2 Chitina USA
12F2 Chitina R USA
87B2 Chitradurga India
84C1 Chitral Pak
32A2 Chitré Panama
86C2 Chittagong Bang
85C4 Chittaurgarh India
87B2 Chittoor India
100B2 Chiume Angola
47D1 Chiusa Italy
47B2 Chivasso Italy
100C2 Chivhu Zim
29D2 Chivilcoy Arg
100C2 Chivu Zim
75A1 Chizu Japan
29C3 Choele Choel Arg
34C3 Choique Arg
24B2 Choix Mexico
58B2 Chojnice Pol
99D1 Choke Mts Eth
48B2 Cholet France
23B2 Cholula Mexico
100B2 Choma Zambia
77C2 Chomo Yummo Mt China/India
57C2 Chomutov Czech Republic
63C1 Chona R Russian Fed
74B3 Ch'onan S Korea
76C3 Chon Buri Thai
32A4 Chone Ecuador
74B2 Ch'ongjin N Korea
74B3 Chongju N Korea
74B3 Ch'ongju S Korea
100A2 Chongoroi Angola
73B4 Chongqing China
74B3 Chŏngŭp S Korea
74B3 Chŏnju S Korea
77D3 Chooyu Mt China/Nepal
59D3 Chortkov Ukraine
74B3 Ch'ŏrwŏn N Korea
59B2 Chorzow Pol
34A3 Chos-Malal Arg
58B2 Choszczno Pol
86A2 Chotanagpur Region, India
96C1 Chott Melrhir Alg
22B2 Chowchilla USA
22B2 Chowchilla USA
6A3 Chrantrey Inlet B Can
111B2 Christchurch NZ
101G1 Christiana S Africa
6D2 Christian,C Can
12H3 Christian Sd USA
6B3 Christianshab Greenland
104D4 Christmas I Indian O
Chu Kazakhstan
65J5 Chu R Kazakhstan
29C4 Chubut State, Arg
29C4 Chubut R Arg
60D2 Chudovo Russian Fed
Chudskoye Ozero = Peipus, Lake
4D3 Chugach Mts USA
12E2 Chugiak USA
75A1 Chūgoku-sanchi Mts Japan
7C2 Chui Brazil
29B3 Chuillán Chile
77C5 Chukai Malay

76D2 Chu Lai Viet
21B3 Chula Vista USA
12E2 Chulitna USA
63E2 Chulman Russian Fed
32A5 Chulucanas Peru
30C2 Chulumani Bol
65K4 Chulym Russian Fed
63A2 Chulym R Russian Fed
63B2 Chuma R Russian Fed
84D2 Chumar India
63C2 Chumikan Russian Fed
77B3 Chumphon Thai
74B3 Ch'unch'ŏn S Korea
86B2 Chunchura India
74B3 Ch'ungju S Korea
Chungking = Chongqing
99D3 Chunya Tanz
63C1 Chunya R Russian Fed
27L1 Chupara Pt Trinidad
30A3 Chuquicamata Chile
52A1 Chur Switz
86C2 Churāchāndpur India
7A4 Churchill Can
7D4 Churchill R Labrador, Can
7A4 Churchill R Manitoba, Can
7A4 Churchill,C Can
5H4 Churchill Falls Can
84C3 Chūru India
23A2 Churumuco Mexico
61J2 Chusovoy Russian Fed
61G2 Chuvashskaya Respublika, Russian Fed
68B4 Chuxiong China
76D3 Chu Yang Sin Mt Viet
78B4 Cianjur Indon
47D2 Ciano d'Enza Italy
35A2 Cianorte Brazil
58C2 Ciechanów Pol
25E2 Ciego de Avila Cuba
32C1 Ciénaga Colombia
25D2 Cienfuegos Cuba
59B3 Cieszyn Pol
51B2 Cieza Spain
92B2 Cihanbeyli Turk
23A2 Cihuatlán Mexico
78B4 Cijulang Indon
54C1 Cimpina Rom
51C1 Cinca R Spain
52C2 Cinçer Mt Bosnia-Herzegovina
10B3 Cincinnati USA
54B1 Cindrelu Mt Rom
55B2 Cine R Turk
46C1 Ciney Belg
34B3 Cipolletti Arg
4D3 Circle Alaska, USA
14B3 Circleville USA
78B4 Cirebon Indon
43D4 Cirencester Eng
47D2 Citadella Italy
24C3 Citlaltepetl Mt Mexico
100A4 Citrusdal S Africa
52B2 Citta del Vaticano Italy
52B2 Citta di Castello Italy
23A2 Ciudad Acuña Mexico
23A2 Ciudad Altamirano Mexico
33E2 Ciudad Bolivar Ven
24B2 Ciudad Camargo Mexico
25C3 Ciudad del Carmen Mexico
23B1 Ciudad del Maiz Mexico
51C1 Ciudadela Spain
33E2 Ciudad Guayana Ven
24B3 Ciudad Guzman Mexico

23A2 Ciudad Hidalgo
 Mexico
24B1 Ciudad Juárez
 Mexico
9C4 Ciudad Lerdo Mexico
24C2 Ciudad Madero
 Mexico
23B2 Ciudad Mendoza
 Mexico
24B2 Ciudad Obregon
 Mexico
27C4 Ciudad Ojeda Ven
33E2 Ciudad Piar Ven
50B2 Ciudad Real Spain
50A1 Ciudad Rodrigo
 Spain
24C2 Ciudad Valles
 Mexico
24C2 Ciudad Victoria
 Mexico
52B2 Civitavecchia Italy
93D2 Cizre Turk
43E4 Clacton-on-Sea Eng
5G4 Claire,L Can
14C2 Clairton USA
47A1 Clairvaux France
17A1 Clanton USA
100A4 Clanwilliam S Africa
45C2 Clara Irish Rep
34D3 Claraz Arg
45B2 Clare County,
 Irish Rep
14B2 Clare USA
45A2 Clare I Irish Rep
15D2 Claremont USA
18A2 Claremore USA
45B2 Claremorris Irish Rep
109D1 Clarence R Aust
111B2 Clarence R NZ
106C2 Clarence Str Aust
12H3 Clarence Str USA
19B3 Clarendon USA
7E5 Clarenville Can
5G4 Claresholm Can
18A1 Clarinda USA
15C2 Clarion
 Pennsylvania, USA
24A3 Clarión I Mexico
15C2 Clarion R USA
105J3 Clarion Fracture Zone
 Pacific O
11B3 Clark Hill Res USA
14B2 Clark,Pt Can
11A3 Clarksburg USA
12C3 Clarks Point USA
20C1 Clarkston USA
18B2 Clarksville Arkansas,
 USA
35A1 Claro R Brazil
29D3 Claromecó Arg
18A2 Clay Center USA
44D2 Claymore Oilfield
 N Sea
13B3 Clayoquot Sd Can
9C3 Clayton New Mexico,
 USA
15C2 Clayton New York,
 USA
41B3 Clear C Irish Rep
12E3 Cleare,C USA
13D1 Clear Hills Mts Can
21A2 Clear L USA
20B2 Clear Lake Res USA
13D2 Clearwater Can
11B4 Clearwater USA
13E1 Clearwater R Can
13C2 Clearwater L Can
9D3 Cleburne USA
42E2 Cleeton Oilfield
 North Sea
22B1 Clements USA
79A3 Cleopatra Needle Mt
 Phil
107D3 Clermont Aust
46B2 Clermont France
46C2 Clermont-en-Argonne
 France
49C2 Clermont-Ferrand
 France
46D1 Clervaux Germany
47D1 Cles Italy
108A2 Cleve Aust
42D2 Cleveland County,
 Eng

19B3 Cleveland
 Mississippi, USA
10B2 Cleveland Ohio, USA
11B3 Cleveland
 Tennessee, USA
19A3 Cleveland Texas,
 USA
41B3 Clew B Irish Rep
45A2 Clifden Irish Rep
109D1 Clifton Aust
16B2 Clifton New Jersey,
 USA
108A1 Clifton Hills Aust
13F3 Climax USA
18B2 Clinton Arkansas,
 USA
5F4 Clinton Can
16C2 Clinton Connecticut,
 USA
16D1 Clinton
 Massachusetts, USA
11B3 Clinton Mississippi,
 USA
18B2 Clinton Missouri,
 USA
16B2 Clinton New Jersey,
 USA
4H3 Clinton-Colden L Can
24B3 Clipperton I Pacific O
30C2 Cliza Bol
45B3 Clonakilty Irish Rep
107D3 Cloncurry Aust
45C1 Clones Irish Rep
45C2 Clonmel Irish Rep
10A2 Cloquet USA
12C2 Cloudy Mt USA
22C2 Clovis California,
 USA
9C3 Clovis New Mexico,
 USA
60B4 Cluj Rom
54B1 Cluj-Napoca Rom
47B1 Cluses France
47C2 Clusone Italy
11A3 Clutha R NZ
43C3 Clwyd County, Wales
6D2 Clyde Can
111A3 Clyde NZ
42B2 Clyde R Scot
42B2 Clyde,Firth of R Scot
23A2 Coahuayana Mexico
23A2 Coalcomán Mexico
13E2 Coaldale Can
21B2 Coaldale USA
21A2 Coalinga USA
33E5 Coari R Brazil
17A1 Coastal Plain USA
4E4 Coast Mts Can
8A2 Coast Ranges Mts
 USA
42B2 Coatbridge Scot
23B2 Coatepec Mexico
16B3 Coatesville USA
15D1 Coaticook Can
6B3 Coats I Can
112B1 Coats Land Region,
 Ant
25C3 Coatzacoalcos
 Mexico
7C5 Cobalt Can
25C3 Cobán Guatemala
107D4 Cobar Aust
109C3 Cobargo Aust
45B3 Cobh Irish Rep
32D6 Cobija Bol
16B1 Cobleskill USA
51B2 Cobo de Palos C
 Spain
7C5 Cobourg Can
106C2 Cobourg Pen Aust
57C2 Coburg Germany
32B4 Coca Ecuador
17B2 Coca USA
30C2 Cochabamba Bol
46D1 Cochem Germany
87B3 Cochin India
13E2 Cochrane Alberta,
 Can
7B5 Cochrane Ontario,
 Can
108B2 Cockburn Aust
16A3 Cockeysville USA
27H1 Cockpit Country,The
 Jamaica
25D3 Coco R Honduras/
 Nic

98A2 Cocobeach Gabon
27L1 Cocos B Trinidad
104C4 Cocos Is Indian O
23A1 Cocula Mexico
10C2 Cod,C USA
111A3 Codfish I NZ
7D4 Cod I Can
47E2 Codigoro Italy
31C2 Codó Brazil
47C2 Codogno Italy
52C2 Cody USA
56B2 Coesfeld Germany
8B2 Coeur d'Alene USA
9D3 Coffeyville USA
108A2 Coffin B Aust
109D2 Coff's Harbour Aust
23B2 Cofre de Perote Mt
 Mexico
48B2 Cognac France
15D2 Cohoes USA
108B3 Cohuna Aust
29B5 Coihaique Chile
87B2 Coimbatore India
50A1 Coimbra Port
32A3 Cojimies Ecuador
107D4 Colac Aust
31C5 Colatina Brazil
112B6 Colbeck,C Ant
43E4 Colchester Eng
16C2 Colchester USA
47B1 Col de la Faucille
 France
13E2 Cold L USA
52A1 Col du Grand St
 Bernard P Italy/Switz
47B2 Col du Lautaret P
 France
52A1 Col du Mont Cenis P
 France/Italy
14B2 Coldwater USA
12F1 Coleen R USA
14B2 Coleman Michigan,
 USA
101G1 Colenso S Africa
45C1 Coleraine N Ire
111B2 Coleridge,L NZ
100B4 Colesberg S Africa
22C1 Coleville USA
21A2 Colfax California,
 USA
19B3 Colfax Louisiana,
 USA
20C1 Colfax Washington,
 USA
24B3 Colima Mexico
23A2 Colima State, Mexico
34A2 Colina Chile
44A3 Coll I Scot
109C1 Collarenebri Aust
52A2 Colle de Tende P
 France/Italy
12E2 College USA
17B1 College Park
 Georgia, USA
16A3 College Park
 Washington, USA
19A3 College Station
 USA
106A4 Collie Aust
106B2 Collier B Aust
46A1 Collines de L'Artois
 Mts France
46B2 Collines de Thiérache
 France
14B2 Collingwood Can
110B2 Collingwood NZ
19C3 Collins Mississippi,
 USA
4H2 Collinson Pen Can
107D3 Collinsville Aust
18C2 Collinsville Illinois,
 USA
18A2 Collinsville
 Oklahoma, USA
34A3 Collipulli Chile
49D2 Colmar France
 Cologne = Köln
35B2 Colômbia Brazil
32B3 Colombia Republic,
 S America
15C3 Colombia USA
87B3 Colombo Sri Lanka
25D2 Colón Cuba
32B2 Colón Panama
29E2 Colonia Urug

34D2 Colonia del
 Sacramento Urug
34B3 Colonia 25 de Mayo
 Arg
29C5 Colonia Las Heras
 Arg
44A3 Colonsay I Scot
23A1 Colontlán Mexico
27E5 Coloradro Ven
8C3 Colorado State, USA
9B3 Colorado R Arizon,
 USA
29D3 Colorado R
 Buenos Aires, Arg
9D3 Colorado R Texas,
 USA
9B3 Colorado Plat USA
8C3 Colorado Springs
 USA
22D3 Colton USA
16A3 Columbia Marylan,
 USA
19C3 Columbia
 Mississippi, USA
10A3 Columbia Missouri,
 USA
15C2 Columbia
 Pennsylvania, USA
11B3 Columbia S Caroli-
 USA
11B3 Columbia Tenness,
 USA
13D2 Columbia R Can
8A2 Columbia R USA
5G4 Columbia,Mt Can
20C1 Columbia Plat USA
11B3 Columbia Georgia,
 USA
14A3 Columbus Indiana,
 USA
11B3 Columbus
 Mississippi, USA
8D2 Columbus Nebrask,
 USA
10B2 Columbus Ohio,
 USA
19A4 Columbus Texas,
 USA
20C1 Colville USA
4C3 Colville R USA
110C1 Colville,C NZ
4F3 Colville L Can
42C3 Colwyn Bay Wales,
 47E2 Comacchio Italy
22B1 Comanche Res USA
112C2 Comandante Ferraz
 Base Ant
25D3 Comayagua
 Honduras
34A2 Combarbalá Chile
45C2 Comeragh Mts
 Irish Rep
86C2 Comilla Bang
25C3 Comitán Mexico
46C2 Commercy France
6B3 Committees B Can
52A1 Como Italy
29C5 Comodoro Rivadav,
 Arg
23A1 Cornonfort Mexico,
87B3 Comorin,C India
101D2 Comoros Is Indian,
49C2 Compiègne France
23A1 Compostela Mexico
34B2 Comte Salas Arg
86C1 Cona China
79A4 Conakry Guinea
34B2 Concarán Arg
48B2 Concarneau France
31B6 Conceição da Barra
 Brazil
31B3 Conceição do
 Araguaia Brazil
35C1 Conceição do Mato
 Dentro Brazil
29B3 Concepción Chile
30E3 Concepción Par
29E2 Concepción R Arg
24B2 Concepción del Oro
 Mexico
34D2 Concepcion del
 Uruguay Arg
9A3 Conception,Pt USA
35B2 Conchas Brazil
9C4 Conchos R Mexico

21A2 Concord California, USA
10C2 Concord New Hampshire, USA
29E2 Concordia Arg
80B3 Concordia USA
20B1 Concrete USA
9D1 Condamine Aust
46C1 Condé Mts Belg
20B1 Condon USA
47E2 Conegliano Italy
89F8 Congo R Congo
Congo,R = Zaire
14B1 Coniston Eng
14B2 Connaught Region, Irish Rep
14B2 Conneaut USA
10C2 Connecticut State, USA
15D2 Connecticut R USA
15B2 Connellsville USA
14B2 Connemara,Mts of Irish Rep
44A3 Connerville USA
08B2 Conoble Aust
19A3 Conobre Aust
35C2 Conselheiro Lafaiete Brazil
77D4 Con Son R Viet
Constance,L = Bodensee
60C5 Constanta Rom
96C1 Constantine Alg
12C3 Constantine,C USA
29B3 Constitución Chile
13F3 Consul Can
25C2 Contarina Italy
31C4 Contas R Brazil
23D2 Contreras Mexico
4H3 Contuoyto L Can
77D4 Conway Arkansas, USA
15D2 Conway New Hampshire, USA
17C1 Conway South Carolina, USA
08A1 Conway,L Aust
42C3 Conwy Wales
10B2 Cook Pedy Aust
10B2 Cook Str NZ
43C2 Cook,C Can
4C3 Cook Inlet B USA
05H4 Cook Is Pacific O
35A2 Cook,Mt NZ
77D2 Cooktown Aust
09C2 Coolabah Aust
08C1 Cooladdi Aust
7C5 Coolah Aust
09C2 Coolamon Aust
06B4 Coolgardie Aust
09C3 Cooma Aust
09C2 Coonabarabran Aust
09C2 Coonamble Aust
08C1 Coonbah Aust
08C1 Coondambo Aust
08C1 Coongoola Aust
87B2 Coonoor India
06C3 Cooper Basin Aust
06C3 Cooper Creek Aust
88A3 Cooper Creek R Aust
08A3 Coorong,The Aust
09C1 Cooroy Aust
20B2 Coos Bay USA
09D3 Cootamundra Aust
45C1 Cootehill Irish Rep
23B2 Copala Mexico
4G3 Coronation G Can
29B3 Coronel Chile
Copenhagen = København
30B4 Copiapó Chile
47D2 Copparo Italy
12F2 Copper R USA
4D3 Copper Centre USA
14B1 Copper Cliff Can
Coppermine = Qurlurtuq
4G3 Coppermine R Can
Coquilhatville = Mbandaka
30B4 Coquimbo Chile

54B2 Corabia Rom
17B2 Coral Gables USA
6B3 Coral Harbour Can
107D2 Coral S Aust/PNG
104F4 Coral Sea Basin Pacific O
107E2 Coral Sea Island Territories
108B3 Corangamite,L Aust
33F3 Corantijn R Surinam/Guyana
46B2 Corbeil-Essonnes France
50A1 Corcubion Spain
11B3 Cordele USA
50A1 Cordillera Cantabrica Mts Spain
26C3 Cordillera Central Mts Dom Rep
79B2 Cordillera Central Mts Phil
34B2 Cordillera de Ansita Mts Arg
32B5 Cordillera de los Andes Mts Peru
30C4 Cordillera del Toro Mt Arg
32C2 Cordillera de Mérida Ven
34A3 Cordillera de Viento Mts Arg
25D3 Cordillera Isabelia Mts Nic
32B3 Cordillera Occidental Mts Colombia
32B3 Cordillera Oriental Mts Colombia
108B1 Cordillo Downs Aust
29D2 Córdoba Arg
24C3 Córdoba Mexico
50B2 Córdoba Spain
29D2 Córdoba State, Arg
4D3 Cordova USA
Corfu = Kérkira
109D2 Coricudgy,Mt Aust
53C3 Corigliano Calabro Italy
11B3 Corinth USA
31C5 Corinto Brazil
45B2 Cork County, Irish Rep
41B3 Cork Irish Rep
92A1 Çorlu Turk
31C5 Cornel Fabriciano Brazil
35A2 Cornelio Procópio Brazil
7E5 Corner Brook Can
109C3 Corner Inlet B Aust
15C2 Corning USA
7C5 Cornwall Can
43B4 Cornwall County, Eng
43B4 Cornwall,C Eng
4H2 Cornwall I Can
6A2 Cornwallis I Can
32D1 Coro Ven
31C2 Coroatá Brazil
30C2 Coroico Bol
35B1 Coromandel Brazil
87C2 Coromandel Coast India
110C1 Coromandel Pen NZ
110C1 Coromandel Range Mts NZ
22D4 Corona California, USA
13E2 Coronation USA
34D3 Coronel Brandsen Arg
35C1 Coronel Dorrego Arg
34C3 Coronel Fabriciano Brazil
30E4 Coronel Oviedo Par
29D3 Coronel Pringles Arg
34C3 Coronel Suárez Arg
34D3 Coronel Vidal Arg
30B2 Coropuna Mt Peru
109C3 Corowa Aust
49D3 Corps France
9D4 Corpus Christi USA

9D4 Corpus Christi,L USA
79B3 Corregidor I Phil
35A1 Corrente R Mato Grosso, Brazil
30E4 Corrientes Arg
30E4 Corrientes State, Arg
19B3 Corrigan USA
106A4 Corrigin Aust
12G2 Corringe Is Aust
109C3 Corryong Aust
52A2 Corse I Medit S
42B2 Corsewall Pt Scot
Corsica = Corse
52A2 Corte Corse
9C3 Cortez USA
52B1 Cortina d'Ampezzo Italy
15C2 Cortland USA
23A2 Coruca de Catalan Mexico
93D1 Çoruh R Turk
60E5 Çorum Turk
30E2 Corumbá Brazil
35B1 Corumba R Brazil
35B1 Corumbaiba Brazil
20B2 Corvallis USA
96A1 Corvo I Açores
43C3 Corwen Wales
23B2 Coscomatopec Mexico
53C3 Cosenza Italy
101D1 Cosmoledo Is Seychelles
34C2 Cosquin Arg
51B2 Costa Blanca Region, Spain
51C1 Costa Brava Region, Spain
50B2 Costa de la Luz Region, Spain
50B2 Costa del Sol Region, Spain
22D4 Costa Mesa USA
25D3 Costa Rica Republic, Cent America
79B4 Cotabato Phil
30C3 Cotagaita Bol
49D3 Côte d'Azur Region, France
46C2 Côtes de Meuse Mts France
97C4 Cotonou Benin
32B4 Cotopaxi Mt Ecuador
43C4 Cotswold Hills Upland Eng
20B2 Cottage Grove USA
56C2 Cottbus Germany
108A3 Couedic,C du Aust
20C1 Couer d'Alene L USA
46B2 Coulommiers France
7C5 Coulonge R Can
22B2 Coulterville USA
4B3 Council USA
8D2 Council Bluffs USA
58C1 Courland Lagoon Lg Lithuania/Russian Fed
47B2 Courmayeur Italy
13B3 Courtenay Can
Courtrai = Kortrijk
48B2 Coutances France
43D3 Coventry Eng
50A1 Covilhã Spain
17B1 Covington Georgia, USA
19B3 Covington Louisiana, USA
109C2 Cowal,L Aust
108B3 Cowangie Aust
15D1 Cowansville Can
108A1 Coward Springs Aust
108B3 Cowell Aust
108C3 Cowes Aust
110B2 Cowichan L Can
20B1 Cowlitz R USA
109C2 Cowra Aust
30F2 Coxim Brazil
16C1 Coxsackie USA
86C2 Cox's Bazar Bang
22B2 Coyote USA
23A2 Coyuca de Benitez Mexico
59B2 Cracow Pol
100B4 Cradock S Africa

8C2 Craig USA
57C3 Crailsheim Germany
54B2 Craiova Rom
15D2 Cranberry L USA
5G5 Cranbrook Can
20C2 Crane Oregon, USA
16D2 Cranston USA
11D2 Crater L USA
20B2 Crater Lake Nat Pk USA
31C3 Crateus Brazil
31D3 Crato Brazil
14A2 Crawfordsville USA
17B1 Crawfordville USA
43D4 Crawley Eng
5H4 Cree L Can
46B2 Creil France
52B1 Crema Italy
47D2 Cremona Italy
46B2 Crépy-en-Valois France
52B2 Cres I Yugos
20B2 Crescent City USA
34C2 Crespo Arg
13D3 Creston Can
18B1 Creston USA
17A1 Crestview USA
108B3 Creswick Aust
47A1 Crêt de la Neige Mt France
Crete = Kríti
18A1 Crete USA
55B3 Crete,S of Greece
48C2 Creuse R France
43C3 Crewe Eng
44B3 Crianlarich Scot
30G4 Criciuma Brazil
44C3 Crieff Scot
12G3 Crillon,Mt USA
35B1 Cristalina Brazil
52C1 Croatia Republic, Europe
78D1 Crocker Range Mts Malay
19A3 Crockett USA
106C2 Croker I Aust
44C3 Cromarty Scot
43E3 Cromer Eng
111A3 Cromwell NZ
11C4 Crooked I The Bahamas
13C2 Crooked R Can
8D2 Crookston USA
106A4 Crosswell Aust
109D1 Croppa Creek Aust
11A3 Crossett USA
12G3 Cross Sd USA
53C3 Crotone Italy
19B3 Crowley USA
27K1 Crown Pt Tobago
109D1 Crows Nest Aust
107D2 Croydon Aust
43D4 Croydon Eng
104B5 Crozet Basin Indian O
4F2 Crozier Chan Can
30H4 Cruz Alta Brazil
25E3 Cruz,C Cuba
29D2 Cruz del Eje Arg
35C2 Cruzeiro Brazil
32C5 Cruzeiro do Sul Brazil
13C1 Crysdale,Mt Can
108A2 Crystal Brook Aust
18B2 Crystal City Missouri, USA
14A1 Crystal Falls USA
101C2 Cuamba Mozam
100B2 Cuando R Angola
100A2 Cuangar Angola
100A2 Cuango,R = Kwango,R
34C2 Cuarto R Arg
24B2 Cuauhtémoc Mexico
23B2 Cuautla Mexico
25D2 Cuba Republic, Caribbean S
100A2 Cubango R Angola
100A2 Cuchi R Angola
34C3 Cuchillo Có Arg
32D3 Cucui Brazil
32C2 Cúcuta Colombia
87B2 Cuddalore India
87B2 Cuddapah India
106A3 Cue Aust

Cuenca

18

32B4 Cuenca Ecuador
51B1 Cuenca Spain
24C3 Cuernavaca Mexico
19A4 Cuero USA
30E2 Cuiabá Brazil
30E2 Cuiabá R Brazil
23B2 Cuicatlan Mexico
35C1 Cuieté Brazil
44A3 Cuillin Hills Mts Scot
88B3 Cuilo R Angola
100A2 Cuito R Angola
100A2 Cuito Cunavale Angola
23A2 Cuitzeo Mexico
77D3 Cu Lao Hon I Viet
109C3 Culcairn Aust
109C1 Culgoa R Aust
24B2 Culiacán Mexico
79A3 Culion I Phil
17A1 Cullman USA
47A2 Culoz France
15C3 Culpeper USA
32J7 Culpepper I Ecuador
17B2 Culter Ridge USA
111B2 Culverden NZ
33E1 Cumaná Ven
31C5 Cumberland Maryland, USA
11B3 Cumberland R USA
6D3 Cumberland Pen Can
6D3 Cumbernauld Sd Can
42C2 Cumbria Eng
21A2 Cummings USA
108A2 Cummins Aust
42B2 Cumnock Scot
34A3 Cunco Chile
100A2 Cunene R Angola/Namibia
52A2 Cuneo Italy
107D3 Cunnamulla Aust
44C3 Cupar Scot
54B2 Čuprija Serbia, Yugos
27D4 Curaçao I Caribbean
34A3 Curacautín Chile
34B3 Curaco R Arg
34A3 Curanilahue Chile
34A3 Curepto Chile
29B2 Curicó Chile
30G4 Curitiba Brazil
108A2 Curnamona Aust
100A2 Curoca R Angola
10C5 Curvelo Brazil
18A2 Cushing USA
13D2 Cutbank R Can
17B1 Cuthbert USA
34A3 Cutral-Có Arg
86B2 Cuttack India
100A2 Cuvelai Angola
56B2 Cuxhaven Germany
14B2 Cuyahoga Falls USA
79B3 Cuyo Is Phil
32C6 Cuzco Peru
99C3 Cyangugu Zaire
    Cyclades = Kikládhes
13F3 Cypress Hills Mts Can
92B3 Cyprus Republic, Medit S
6D3 Cyrus Field B Can
59B3 Czech Republic Republic, Europe
59B2 Częstochowa Pol

D

76C1 Da R Viet
69E2 Da'an China
94C3 Dab'a Jordan
27C4 Dabajuro Ven
99E2 Dabaro Somalia
73B3 Daba Shan Mts China
99D1 Dabat Eth
85C4 Dabhoi India
73C3 Dabie Shan Mts China
97A3 Dabola Guinea
97B4 Dabou Ivory Coast
59B2 Dabrowa Gorn Pol
57C3 Dachau Germany
52B1 Dachstein Mt Austria
73A3 Dachu He R China
17B2 Dade City USA
84B3 Dadhar Pak

85B3 Dadu Pak
68C3 Dadu He R China
79B3 Daet Phil
73B4 Dafang China
76B2 Daga R Burma
99E2 Dagabur Eth
97A3 Dagana Sen
65F5 Dagestanskaya Respublic, Russian Fed
79B2 Dagupan Phil
92B4 Dahab Egypt
63E3 Da Hinggan Ling Mts China
17B1 Dahlonega USA
85C4 Dāhod India
86A1 Dailekh Nepal
34C3 Daireaux Arg
69F4 Daitō Is Pacific O
106C3 Dajarra Aust
97A3 Dakar Sen
95B2 Dakhla Oasis Egypt
97C3 Dakoro Niger
54B2 Dakovica Serbia, Yugos
54A1 Đakovo Croatia
100B2 Dala Angola
97A3 Dalaba Guinea
72D1 Dalai Nur L China
68C2 Dalandzadgad Mongolia
79B3 Dalanganem Is Phil
76D3 Da Lat Viet
72A1 Dalay Mongolia
107E3 Dalby Aust
39F7 Dalen Nor
42C2 Dales,The Upland Eng
17A1 Daleville USA
9C3 Dalhart USA
4E2 Dalhousie,C Can
72E2 Dalian China
9D3 Dallas USA
20B1 Dalles,The USA
5C4 Dall I USA
86A2 Dalli Rajhara India
97C3 Dallol R Niger
97C3 Dallol Bosso R Niger
52C2 Dalmatia Region Bosnia-Herzegovina
69F2 Dal'nerechensk Russian Fed
97B4 Daloa Ivory Coast
73B4 Dalou Shan Mts China
86A2 Dāltenganj India
17B1 Dalton Georgia, USA
16C1 Dalton Massachusetts, USA
106C2 Daly R Aust
21A2 Daly City USA
106C2 Daly Waters Aust
79B3 Damaguete Phil
85C4 Damān India
92B3 Damanhūr Egypt
71D4 Damar I Indon
98B2 Damara CAR
92C3 Damascus Syria
16A3 Damascus USA
97D3 Damaturu Nig
90B2 Damävand Iran
98B3 Damba Angola
97C3 Dambulla Sri Lanka
90B2 Damghan Iran
85D4 Damoh India
94B2 Damot Leb
106A3 Dampier Aust
94B3 Danā Jordan
24A2 Dana,Mt USA
97B4 Danane Ivory Coast
76D2 Da Nang Viet
79B3 Danao Phil
70A3 Danau Tobu L Indon
71D4 Danau Tuwuti L Indon
73A3 Danbu China
15D2 Danbury USA
87A1 Dandeldhura Nepal
108C3 Dandenong Aust
74A2 Dandong China
100A4 Danger Pt S Africa
99D1 Dangila Eth

6D1 Danguard Jenson Land Region Can
7E4 Daniels Harbour Can
6J3 Dannebrogs Øy I Greenland
110C2 Dannevirke NZ
87C1 Dantewära India
    Danube = Donau
10B2 Danville Illinois, USA
11B3 Danville Kentucky, USA
16A2 Danville Pennsylvania, USA
11C3 Danville Virginia, USA
    Danzig = Gdańsk
73C4 Dao Xian China
73B4 Daozhen China
79B4 Dapiak,Mt Phil
79B4 Dapitan Phil
68B3 Da Qaidam China
69E2 Daqing China
94C2 Dar'a Syria
54B2 Daravica Mt
91A4 Dārāb Iran
91A4 Daraj Libya
90B3 Dārān Iran
92C3 Dar'ā Salkhad Syria
86B1 Darbhanga India
22C1 Dardanelle USA
11C3 Dardanelle,L USA
    Dar-el-Beida = Casablanca
99D3 Dar es Salaam Tanz
111A3 Dargaville NZ
17B1 Darien USA
    Darjeeling = Därjiling
86B1 Därjiling India
107D4 Darling R Aust
109C1 Darling Downs Aust
18C2 Darling Pen Can
108B2 Darlington Aust
42D2 Darlington Eng
17C1 Darlington USA
57B3 Darmstadt Germany
95B1 Darnah Libya
108B2 Darnick Aust
4F3 Darnley B Can
112C10 Darnley,C Ant
51B1 Daroca Spain
98C2 Dar Rounga Region CAR
43C4 Dart R Eng
43C4 Dartmoor Moorland Eng
43C4 Dartmoor Nat Pk Eng
7D5 Dartmouth Can
43C4 Dartmouth Eng
107D1 Daru PNG
52C1 Daruvar Croatia
91B4 Darwin Aust
90B3 Daryacheh-ye Bakhtegan L Iran
90B3 Daryacheh-ye Mahārlū L Iran
90B3 Daryacheh-ye Namak Salt Flat Iran
90D3 Daryacheh-ye Sistan Salt L Iran/Afghan
91B4 Daryacheh-ye Tashk L Iran
90B2 Daryācheh-ye Orümiyeh L Iran
91C4 Darzin Iran
91C4 Das I UAE
73C3 Dashennonglia Mt China
90C2 Dasht Iran
90B3 Dasht-e-Kavir Salt Desert Iran
90C3 Dasht-e Lut Salt Desert Iran
90D3 Dasht-e Naomid Desert Region Iran
85D3 Datia India
72A2 Datong China
72C1 Datong China
72A2 Datong He R China
79B4 Datu Piang Phil
39K7 Daugava R Latvia
60C2 Daugavpils Latvia
6D1 Dauguard Jensen Land Greenland
84A1 Daulatabad Afghan
85D3 Daulpur India
46D1 Daun Germany

87A1 Daund India
5H4 Dauphin Can
16A2 Dauphin USA
49D2 Dauphiné Region France
97C3 Daura India
85D3 Dausa India
87B2 Dāvangere India
79C4 Davao Phil
79C4 Davao G Phil
22A2 Davenport Califo USA
10A2 Davenport Iowa, USA
32A2 David Panama
4D3 Davidson Mts US
21A2 Davis USA
112C10 Davis Base Ant
7D4 Davis Inlet Can
6E3 Davis Str Greenla
61J3 Davlekanovo Russian Fed
47C1 Davos Switz
99E2 Dawa R Eth
73A4 Dawan China
84B2 Dawat Yar Afghan
    Dawei = Tavoy
91B4 Dawhat Salwah B Qatar/S Arabia
76B2 Dawna Range Mts Burma
4E3 Dawson Can
107D3 Dawson R Aust
5F4 Dawson Creek Ca
13D2 Dawson,Mt Ca
109C2 Dawson Range Mt Can
73A3 Dawu China
73C3 Dawu China
48B3 Dax France
73B3 Daxian China
73B5 Daxin China
73A3 Daxue Shan Mts China
73C4 Dayong China
94C1 Dayr 'Ali Syria
94C1 Dayr 'Atiyah Syria
93D2 Dayr az Zawr Syria
10B3 Dayton Ohio, USA
19B4 Dayton Texas, USA
20C1 Dayton Washingto USA
11B4 Daytona Beach US USA
20C2 Dayville USA
78D3 Dayu Indon
72D2 Da Yunhe R China
73B3 Dazhu China
73B3 Dazu China
100B4 De Aar S Africa
25E2 Deadman's Cay Th Bahamas
93C3 Dead S Israel/Jord
44A3 Deal Eng
101G1 Dealesville S Afric
13B2 Dean R Can
13B2 Dean Chan Can
34C2 Deán Funes Arg
14B2 Dearborn USA
4F3 Dease Arm B Can
4E4 Dease Lake Can
983 Death V USA
97B4 Deauville France
97B4 Debakala Ivory Coast
12B2 Debauch Mt USA
27L1 Debe Trinidad
58C2 Debica Pol
58C2 Deblin Pol
97B3 Débo,L Mali
59C3 Debrecen Hung
99D2 Debre Birhan Eth
99D1 Debre Markos Eth
99D1 Debre Tabor Eth
11B3 Decatur Alabama, USA
17B1 Decatur Georgia, USA
10B3 Decatur Illinois, US USA
14B2 Decatur Indiana, USA
48C3 Decazeville France
73A4 Dechang China
97B3 Dédougou Burkina

01C2 Dedza Malawi
42B2 Dee R Dumfries and
 Galloway, Scot
44C3 Dee R Eng/Wales
 Dee R Grampian,
 Scot
15C1 Deep River Can
16C2 Deep River USA
00D1 Deepwater Aust
7E5 Deer Lake Can
8B2 Deer Lodge USA
34D3 Defferrari Arg
17A1 De Funiak Springs
 USA
68B3 Dêgê China
99E1 Degeh Bur Eth
06A3 De Grey R Aust
91B3 Deh Bid Iran
98D1 Dehi Afghan
96D1 Dehibat Tunisia
87B3 Dehiwala-Mt Lavinia
 Sri Lanka
90A3 Dehloran Iran
84D2 Dehra Dün India
86A2 Dehri India
98C2 Deim Zubeir Sudan
 Deir Abu Sa'id
 Jordan
94C1 Deir el Ahmar Leb
60B4 Dej Rom
19B3 De Kalb Texas, USA
63G2 De Kastri
 Russian Fed
98C3 Dekese Zaire
98C2 Dekoa CAR
106B1 Dekusi Indon
9B3 Delano USA
10C3 Delaware State,
 USA
14B2 Delaware USA
15C2 Delaware R USA
10C3 Delaware B USA
109C3 Delegate Aust
47B1 Delemont Switz
01D2 Delgado R Mozam
84D3 Delhi India
 Delhi New York, USA
15C2 Delice Turk
24B2 Delicias Mexico
90B3 Delijän Iran
47B1 Delle France
22D4 Del Mar USA
39F8 Delmenhorst
 Germany
4B3 De Long Mts USA
109C4 Deloraine Aust
5H5 Deloraine Can
17B2 Delray Beach USA
9C4 Del Rio USA
8B3 Delta USA
12E1 Delta USA
12E2 Delta Junction USA
99D2 Dembi Dolo Eth
46C1 Demer R Belg
9C2 Deming USA
15C2 Demirköy Turk
49C1 Demain France
82A2 Denau Uzbekistan
42C3 Denbigh Wales
12C2 Denbigh,C USA
78B3 Dendang Indon
46C1 Dendermond Belg
99D2 Dendi Mt Eth
46B1 Dendre R Belg
72B1 Dengkou China
72C3 Deng Xian China
 Den Haag = 's-
 Gravenhage
27H1 Denham,Mt Jamaica
56A2 Den Helder Neth
51C2 Denia Spain
107D4 Deniliquin Aust
20C2 Denio USA
9D3 Denison Texas, USA
12D3 Denison,Mt USA
92A2 Denizli Turk
39F7 Denmark
 Kingdom, Europe
1C1 Denmark Str
 Greenland/Iceland
27P2 Dennery St Lucia
78D4 Denpasar Indon
16B3 Denton Maryland,
 USA
9D3 Denton Texas, USA

107E1 D'Entrecasteaux Is
 PNG
47B1 Dents du Midi Mt
 Switz
8C3 Denver USA
98B2 Déo R Cam
86B2 Deoghar India
85C5 Deolali India
84D1 Deosai Plain India
95B3 Dépression du
 Mourdi Chad
19B3 De Queen USA
84C3 Dera Pak
84B3 Dera Bugti Pak
84D3 Dera Ismail Khan Pak
108B2 Derby Aust
16C2 Derby Connecticut,
 USA
43D3 Derby Eng
18A2 Derby Kansas, USA
60E3 Dergachi Ukraine
19B3 De Ridder USA
95C3 Derudeb Sudan
109C4 Derwent Bridge Aust
34B2 Desaguadero Arg
30C2 Desaguadero R Bol
2183 Descanso Mexico
20B2 Deschutes R USA
99D1 Desê Eth
29C5 Deseado Arg
29C5 Deseado R Arg
47D2 Desenzano Italy
96A1 Deserta Grande I
 Medeira
30C4 Desierto de Atacama
 Desert Chile
42A3 Desloge USA
10A2 Des Moines Iowa,
 USA
60D3 Desna R Russian Fed
29B6 Desolación I Chile
14A2 Des Plaines I
56C2 Dessau Germany
15C2 Destruction Bay Can
46A1 Desvres France
54B1 Deta Rom
100B2 Dete Zim
56B2 Detmold Germany
18C2 Detroit USA
16D3 Det Udom Thai
54B1 Deva Rom
56B2 Deventer Neth
44C3 Deveron R Scot
99C1 Devikot India
22C2 Devil Postpile Nat
 Mon USA
22C1 Devils Gate P USA
 Devil's Island = Isla
 du Diable
8D2 Devils Lake USA
12H3 Devils Paw Mt Can
43D4 Devizes Eng
85D3 Devoll R Alb
43B4 Devon County, Eng
6A2 Devon I Can
107D5 Devonport Aust
86C1 Dewangiri Bhutan
85D4 Dewãs India
101G1 Dewetsdorp S Africa
11B3 Dewey Res USA
19B3 De Witt USA
18C2 Dexter Missouri,
 USA
73A3 Deyang China
90C3 Deyhuk Iran
90A3 Dezful Iran
72D2 Dezhou China
90A2 Dezh Shãhpur Iran
91B4 Dhahran S Arabia
86C2 Dhãka Bang
87B2 Dhamavaram India
86A2 Dhamtari India
86B2 Dhanbad India
86A1 Dhangarhi Nepal
86B1 Dhankuta Nepal
85C4 Dhãr India
85D5 Dharmapuri India
84D2 Dharmshala India
 Dhar Oualata Desert
 Region Maur
86A1 Dhaulagiri Mt Nepal
86B2 Dhenkanãi India

94B3 Dhibah Jordan
55C3 Dhíkti Óri Mt
 Greece
55C3 Dhodhekánisos Is
 Greece
55B3 Dhomokós Greece
87B1 Dhone India
85C4 Dhoraji India
85C4 Dhrãngadhra India
85C4 Dhule India
22B2 Diablo,Mt USA
21A2 Diablo Range Mts
 USA
34C2 Diamante Arg
34B2 Diamante R Arg
31C5 Diamantina Brazil
107D3 Diamantina R Aust
86B2 Diamond Harbours
 India
22B1 Diamond Springs
 USA
91C4 Dibã UAE
98C3 Dibaya Zaire
86C1 Dibrugarh India
8C2 Dickinson USA
93D2 Dickson City USA
93D2 Dicle R Turk
13E2 Didsbury Can
85C3 Didwãna India
97B3 Diebougou Burkina
46D2 Diekirch Lux
97B3 Diéma Mali
76C1 Dien Bien Phu Viet
56B2 Diepholz Germany
48C2 Dieppe France
46C1 Diest Belg
46D2 Dieuze France
73D2 Digby Can
49D3 Digne-les-Bains
 France
49C2 Digoin France
71E4 Digul R Indon
86C1 Dihang R India
 Dijlah = Tigris
49C2 Dijon France
98B2 Dik Chad
99E1 Dikhil Djibouti
46B1 Diksmuide Belg
1I0 Dikson Russian Fed
82A2 Dilaram Afghan
106B1 Dili Indon
76D3 Di Linh Viet
54B1 Dilingen Germany
99C1 Dilling Sudan
12C3 Dillingham USA
8B2 Dillon USA
16A2 Dillsburg USA
100B2 Dilolo Zaire
 Dimashq = Damascus
98C3 Dimbelenge Zaire
97B4 Dimbokro Ivory
 Coast
54C2 Dimitrovgrad Bulg
61G3 Dimitrovgrad
 Russian Fed
92B3 Dimona Israel
86C1 Dimãpur India
79C3 Dinagat I Phil
86B1 Dinajpur India
48B2 Dinan France
46C1 Dinant Belg
92B2 Dinar Turk
99D1 Dinder R Sudan
87B2 Dindigul India
72B2 Dingbian China
86B1 Dinggyê China
41A3 Dingle Irish Rep
41A3 Dingle B Irish Rep
97A3 Dinguiraye Guinea
44B3 Dingwall Scot
72A2 Dingxi China
72D2 Ding Xian China
76D1 Dinh Lap Viet
22C2 Dinuba USA
97A3 Diouloulou Sen
85D3 Diphu India
99E2 Dire Dawa Eth
106A3 Dirk Hartog I Aust
95A3 Dirkou Niger
109C1 Dirranbandi Aust
99E2 Dirri Somalia
29G8 Disappointment,C
 South Georgia

20B1 Disappointment,C
 USA
106B3 Disappointment,L
 Aust
108B3 Discovery B Aust
103J7 Discovery
 Tablemount
 Atlantic O
47C1 Disentis Muster
 Switz
6E3 Disko Greenland
6E3 Disko Bugt P
 Greenland
6E3 Diskorjord Greenland
58D1 Disna R Belorussia
35B1 Distrito Federal
 Federal District, Brazil
85C4 Diu India
71C4 Diuat Mts Phil
31C6 Divinópolis Brazil
61F4 Divnoye Russian Fed
93C2 Divriği Turk
85C2 Dixon California,
 USA
5E4 Dixon Entrance Sd
 Can/USA
13D1 Dixonville Can
93E3 Diyãlã R Iraq
65F6 Diyarbakir Turk
90B3 Diz R Iran
98B2 Dja R Cam
96C1 Djadi R Alg
95A2 Djado,Plat du Niger
98B3 Djambala Congo
96C2 Djanet Alg
96A2 Djebel Bouhalla Mt
 Mor
51C2 Djelfa Alg
98C2 Djéma CAR
97B3 Djenné Mali
97B3 Djibo Burkina
99E1 Djibouti Djibouti
99E1 Djibouti Republic, E
 Africa
98C2 Djougou Zaire
97C4 Djougou Benin
99D2 Djugu Zaire
38B2 Djúpivogur Iceland
51C2 Djurdjura Mts Alg
60E2 Dmitrov Russian Fed
60D4 Dnepr = Dnieper
60D4 Dneprodzerzhinsk
 Ukraine
60E4 Dnepropetrovsk
 Ukraine
60C3 Dneprovskaya
 Nizmennost' Region,
 Belorussia
60D4 Dnestr = Dniester
60D4 Dnieper R Ukraine
60D4 Dniester R Ukraine
60D2 Dno Russian Fed
98B2 Doba Chad
58C1 Dobele Latvia
34C3 Doblas Arg
71E4 Dobo Indon
54B2 Doboj Bosnia-
 Herzegovina
54B2 Dobreta-Turnu-
 Severin Rom
54C2 Dobrich Bulg
60D3 Dobrush Belorussia
31C5 Doce R Brazil
30D3 Doctor R P Peña Arg
06D3 Dod India
87B2 Doda Betta Mt India
 Dodecanese =
 Sporadhes
9C3 Dodge City USA
99D3 Dodoma Tanz
75A1 Dögo I Japan
97C3 Dogondoutchi Niger
93D2 Dogubayazit Turk
91B4 Doha Qatar
7C5 Dolbeau Can
49D2 Dôle France
43C3 Dolgellau Wales
52B2 Dolomitche Mts Italy
98E2 Dolo Odo Eth
29E3 Dolores Arg
34D2 Dolores Urug
23A1 Dolores Hidalgo
 Mexico
4G3 Dolphin and Union
 Str Can

29E6 Dolphin,C Falkland Is
71E4 Dom Mt Indon
65G4 Dombarovskiy Russian Fed
38F6 Dombas Nor
46D2 Dombasle-sur-Meurthe France
54A1 Dombóvár Hung
48B2 Domfront France
27E3 Dominica I Caribbean S
27C3 Dominican Republic Caribbean S
6C3 Dominion,C Can
7E4 Domino Can
68D1 Domna Russian Fed
52A1 Domodossola Italy
78D4 Dompu Indon
29B3 Domuyo Mt Arg
109D1 Domville,Mt Aust
44C3 Don R Scot
61F4 Don R Russian Fed
45C1 Donaghadee N Ire
57C3 Donau R Germany
57C3 Donauwörth Germany
50A2 Don Benito Spain
42D3 Doncaster Eng
101C2 Dondo Mozam
87C3 Dondra Head C Sri Lanka
45B1 Donegal County, Irish Rep
40B3 Donegal Irish Rep
40B3 Donegal B Irish Rep
45B1 Donegal Mts Irish Rep
60E4 Donetsk Ukraine
73C4 Dong'an China
106A3 Dongara Aust
73C4 Dongchuan China
76D2 Dongfang China
74B2 Dongfeng China
70C4 Donggala Indon
68B3 Dongqi Cona L China
74A3 Donggou China
73C5 Donghai Dao I China
72A1 Dong He R China
76D2 Dong Hoi Viet
73C5 Dong Jiang R China
95C3 Dongola Sudan
73D5 Dongshan China
68D4 Dongsha Qundao I China
72C2 Dongsheng China
72E3 Dongtai China
73C4 Dongting Hu L China
73B5 Dongxing China
73D3 Dongzhi China
18B2 Doniphan USA
52C2 Donji Vakuf Bosnia-Herzegovina
38G5 Dønna I Nor
21A2 Donner P USA
46D2 Donnersberg Mt Germany
101G1 Donnybrook S Africa
Donostia = San Sebastian
22B2 Don Pedro Res USA
12D1 Doonerak,Mt USA
19B4 Dopolong Phil
73A3 Do Qu R China
47B2 Dora Baltea R Italy
49D2 Dorbirn Austria
43C4 Dorchester Eng
6C3 Dorchester,C Can
48C2 Dordogne R France
56A2 Dordrecht Neth
13F2 Dore L Can
13F2 Dore Lake Can
97B3 Dori Burkina
46B2 Dormans France
57B3 Dornbirn Austria
44B3 Dornoch Scot
44B3 Dornoch Firth Estuary Scot
38H6 Dorotea Sweden
109D2 Dorrigo Aust
20B2 Dorris USA
43C4 Dorset County, Eng
46D1 Dorsten Germany
56B2 Dortmund Germany

98C2 Doruma Zaïre
63D2 Dosatuy Russian Fed
84B1 Doshi Afghan
22B2 Dos Palos USA
97C3 Dosso Niger
65G5 Dossor Kazakhstan
11B3 Dothan USA
49C1 Douai France
98A2 Douala Cam
109D1 Double Island Pt Aust
49D2 Doubs R France
111A3 Doubtful Sd NZ
97B3 Douentza Mali
9C3 Douglas Arizona, USA
42B2 Douglas Eng
17B1 Douglas Georgia, USA
8C2 Douglas Wyoming, USA
12A1 Douglas,C USA
13B2 Douglas Chan Can
12D3 Douglas,Mt USA
46B1 Doullens France
45C1 Doun County, N Ire
30F3 Dourados Brazil
50A1 Douro R Port
15C3 Dover Delaware, USA
43E4 Dover Eng
15D2 Dover New Hampshire, USA
16B2 Dover New Jersey, USA
14B2 Dover Ohio, USA
43D3 Dover R Eng
41D3 Dover,Str of UK/France
16B3 Downington USA
42B2 Downpatrick N Ire
13C2 Downton,Mt Can
16B2 Doylestown USA
75A1 Dōzen I Japan
96A2 Dr'aa R Mor
35A2 Dracena Brazil
16D1 Dracut USA
49D3 Draguignan France
101C3 Drakensberg Mts S Africa
101G1 Drakensberg Mt S Africa
103E7 Drake Pass Pacific/Atlantic O
55B2 Dráma Greece
39G7 Drammen Nor
38A1 Drangajökull Iceland
52C1 Drava R Slovenia
13D2 Drayton Valley Can
49C2 Dreaux France
57C2 Dresden Germany
48C2 Dreux France
20C2 Drewsey USA
54B2 Drin R Alb
54A2 Drina R Bosnia-Herzegovina/Serbia
58D1 Drissa R Belorussia
45C2 Drogheda Irish Rep
59C3 Drogobych Ukraine
112B12 Dronning Maud Land Region, Ant
30D3 Dr P.P. Pená Par
5G4 Drumheller Can
14B1 Drummond I USA
15D1 Drummondville Can
58C2 Druskininksi Lithuania
12G3 Dry B USA
7A5 Dryden Can
27H1 Dry Harbour Mts Jamaica
76B3 Duang I Burma
91C4 Dubai UAE
5H3 Dubawnt R Can
4H3 Dubawnt L Can
107D4 Dubbo Aust
45C2 Dublin County, Irish Rep
45C2 Dublin Irish Rep
17B1 Dublin USA
20A2 Dubois Russian Fed
60C3 Dubno Ukraine
15C2 Du Bois USA
13B2 Dubose,Mt Can
15C2 Dubrovica Ukraine

54A2 Dubrovnik Croatia
10A2 Dubuque USA
46D2 Dudelange Lux
1C10 Dudinka Russian Fed
43C3 Dudley Eng
97B4 Duekoué Ivory Coast
50B1 Duero R Spain
44C3 Dufftown Scot
52B2 Dugi Otok I Croatia
56B2 Duisburg Germany
93E3 Dükan Iraq
99D2 Duk Faiwil Sudan
91B4 Dukhan Qatar
73A4 Dukou China
68B3 Dulan China
34C2 Dulce R Arg
78C2 Dulit Range Mts Malay
86C2 Dullabchara India
10A2 Duluth USA
94C2 Dūmā Syria
78A2 Dumai Indon
79A3 Dumaran I Phil
9C3 Dumas USA
94C2 Dumayr Syria
42B2 Dumbarton Scot
42C2 Dumfries Scot
42B2 Dumfries and Galloway Region, Scot
86B2 Dumka India
15C1 Dumoine,L Can
112C8 Dumont d'Urville Base Ant
94C1 Dumyat Egypt
54C2 Dunărea R Rom
45C2 Dunary Head Pt Irish Rep
54B2 Dunav R Bulg
59D3 Dunayevtsy Ukraine
13C3 Duncan Can
16A2 Duncannon USA
44C2 Duncansby Head Pt Scot
45C1 Dundalk Irish Rep
16A3 Dundalk USA
45C2 Dundalk B Irish Rep
6D2 Dundas Greenland
4G2 Dundas Pen Can
71E5 Dundas Str Aust
101H1 Dundee S Africa
44C3 Dundee Scot
108B1 Dundoo Aust
42B2 Dundrum B N Ire
11B3 Dunedin NZ
109C2 Dunedoo Aust
44C3 Dunfermline Scot
85C4 Dungarpur India
45C2 Dungarvan Irish Rep
43E4 Dungeness Eng
109D2 Dungog Aust
99C2 Dungu Zaïre
99D1 Dungunab Sudan
68B2 Dunhuang China
46B1 Dunkerque France
10C2 Dunkirk USA
99D1 Dunkur Eth
97B4 Dunkwa Ghana
41B3 Dun Laoghaire Irish Rep
45B3 Dunmanway Irish Rep
26B1 Dunmore Town The Bahamas
44C2 Dunnet Head Pt Scot
42C2 Duns Scot
20B2 Dunsmuir USA
111A2 Dunstan Mts NZ
46C2 Dun-sur-Meuse France
72D1 Duolun China
18C2 Du Quoin USA
94B3 Dura Israel
49D3 Durance R France
24B2 Durango Mexico
50B1 Durango Spain
9C3 Durango USA
29E2 Durano Urug
9D3 Durant USA
94C1 Duraykīsh Syria
101H1 Durban S Africa
46D1 Düren Germany
86A2 Durg India
86B2 Durgapur India

42D2 Durham County, E[ng]
42D2 Durham Eng
11C3 Durham N Carolin[a] USA
16D1 Durham New Hampshire, USA
108B1 Durham Downs A[ust]
54A2 Durmitor Mt Montenegro, Yugo[slavia]
44B2 Durness Scot
55A2 Durrës Alb
108B1 Durrie Aust
45A3 Dursey I Irish Rep
55C3 Dursunbey Turk
110B2 D'Urville I NZ
90D2 Dušak Turkmenistan
73B4 Dushan China
82A2 Dushanbe Tajikista[n]
111A3 Dusky Sd NZ
56B2 Düsseldorf German[y]
73B4 Duyun China
92B1 Düzce Turk
60C2 Dvina R Latvia
85B4 Dwárka India
8D3 Dyer,C Can
11B3 Dyersburg USA
43B3 Dyfed County, Wal[es]
61F5 Dykh Tau Mt Russian Fed
108B1 Dynevor Downs A[ust]
68B2 Dzag Mongolia
63C3 Dzamin Uüd Mongolia
101D2 Dzaoudzi Mayotte
68C2 Dzamin Uüd Mongolia
68B2 Dzavhan Gol R Mongolia
80E1 Dzhezkazgan Kazakhstan
61F2 Dzerzhinsk Russian Fed
63E2 Dzhalinda Russian Fed
65J5 Dzhambul Kazakhstan
60D4 Dzhankoy Ukraine
Dzharkent = Panfilo[v]
65H4 Dzhezkazgan Kazakhstan
84B1 Dzhilikul' Tajikistan
65J5 Dzhungarskiy Alata[u] Mts Kazakhstan
59B2 Dzierzoniow Pol
63B3 Dzüyl Mongolia
82C1 Dzungaria Basin, China

E

7B4 Eabamet L Can
12F2 Eagle Alaska, USA
20B2 Eagle L California, USA
19A3 Eagle Mountain L USA
9C4 Eagle Pass USA
4E3 Eagle Plain Can
12E2 Eagle River USA
21B2 Earlimart USA
17B1 Easley USA
15C2 East Aurora USA
43D4 Eastbourne Eng
14A2 East Chicago USA
69E3 East China Sea China/Japan
83B4 Eastern Ghats Mts India
19A3 East Fork R USA
21B2 Eastgate USA
16C1 Easthampton USA
16C2 East Hampton USA
14A2 East Lake USA
14B2 East Liverpool USA
100B4 East London S Africa
7C4 Eastmain Can
7C4 Eastmain R Can
17B1 Eastman USA
15C3 Easton Maryland, USA
15C2 Easton Pennsylvania, USA
16B2 East Orange USA

105L4 East Pacific Ridge Pacific O
17B1 East Point USA
42D3 East Retford USA
11A3 East St Louis USA
1B7 East Siberian S Russian Fed
43E4 East Sussex County, Eng
17B1 Eatonton USA
10A2 Eau Claire USA
23B1 Ebano USA
98B2 Ebebiyin Eq Guinea
56C2 Eberswalde Germany
73A4 Eblan China
65K5 Ebinur L China
53C2 Eboli Italy
98B2 Ebolowa Cam
51B1 Ebro R Spain
92A1 Eceabat Turk
96C1 Ech Cheliff Alg
72D2 Eching China
20C1 Echo USA
44C3 Echo Bay Can
46D2 Echternach Lux
108B3 Echuca Aust
50A2 Ecija Spain
6B2 Eclipse Sd Can
32B4 Ecuador Republic, S America
99E1 Ed Eth
44C2 Eday I Scot
98C1 Ed Da'ein Sudan
95C3 Ed Damer Sudan
95C3 Ed Debba Sudan
44B2 Eddrachillis B Scot
95D3 Ed Dueim Sudan
109C4 Eddystone Pt Aust
98A2 Edea Cam
109C3 Eden Aust
42C2 Eden R Eng
101G1 Edenburg S Africa
11A3 Edendale NZ
46E2 Edenkoben Germany
46E1 Eder R Germany
65D1 Edgell I Can
6D2 Edgeoya I Barents S
16A3 Edgewood USA
94B3 Edh Dhahiriya Israel
55B2 Edhessa Greece
11C3 Edinburgh Scot
60C5 Edirne Turk
17B1 Edisto R USA
13D2 Edith Cavell,Mt Can
20B1 Edmonds USA
5G4 Edmonton Can
7D5 Edmundston Can
19A4 Edna USA
12H3 Edna Bay USA
52B1 Edolo Italy
94B3 Edom Region, Jordan
92A2 Edremit Turk
55C3 Edremit Körfezi B Turk
92B1 Edrengiyn Nuruu Mts Mongolia
5G4 Edson Can
34C3 Eduardo Castex Arg
12J2 Eduni,Mt Can
108B3 Edward R Aust
99C3 Edward,L Uganda/ Zaire
18C2 Edwardesville USA
9C3 Edwards Creek Aust
9C3 Edwards Plat USA
18C2 Edwardsville USA
12H3 Edziza,Mt Can
12B2 Eek USA
46B1 Eeklo Belg
10B3 Effingham USA
6E3 Egedesminde Greenland
12C3 Egegik USA
59C3 Eger Hung
39F7 Egersund Nor
12B1 Egg Harbor City USA
4G2 Eglinton I Can
110B1 Egmont,C NZ
110B1 Egmont,Mt NZ
92B2 Eğridir Gölü L Turk
95B2 Egypt Republic, Africa
50B1 Eibar Spain

49C2 Eibeuf France
46D1 Eifel Region, Germany
44B3 Eigg I Scot
83B5 Eight Degree Chan Indian O
106B2 Eighty Mile Beach Aust
108C3 Eildon,L Aust
56B2 Eindhoven Neth
47C1 Einsiedeln Switz
94B3 Ein Yahav Israel
57C2 Eisenach Germany
57C3 Eisenerz Austria
72A1 Ejin qi China
23B2 Ejutla Mexico
110C2 Eketahuna NZ
65J4 Ekibastuz Kazakhstan
63F2 Ekimchan Russian Fed
92B3 Ek Mahalla el Kubra Egypt
39H7 Eksjo Sweden
10B1 Ekwen R Can
92A3 El'Alamein Egypt
92B3 El'Arish Egypt
92B4 Eilat Israel
92B3 El Atrun Oasis Sudan
92A2 Elazig Turk
52B2 Elba I Italy
95C2 El Balyana Egypt
32C2 El Banco Colombia
55B2 El Baul Ven
57C2 Elbe R Germany
94C1 El Bega'a R Leb
14A2 Elberta USA
45C3 Elbert,Mt USA
17B1 Elberton USA
92C2 Elbistan Turk
58B2 Elblag Pol
29B4 El Bolson Arg
61F5 Elbrus Mt Russian Fed
Elburz Mts = Reshteh-ye Alborz
21B3 El Cajon USA
19A4 El Campo USA
51B2 Elche Spain
51B2 Elda Spain
32B3 El Diviso Colombia
96B2 El Djouf Desert Region Maur
18B2 Eldon USA
11A3 El Dorado Arkansas, USA
35B2 Eldorado Brazil
9D3 El Dorado Kansas, USA
24B2 El Dorado Mexico
33E2 El Dorado Ven
99D2 Eldoret Kenya
22C1 Eleanor,L USA
96B2 El Eglab Region, Alg
51B1 El Escorial Spain
92D3 Eleşkirt Turk
11C4 Eleuthera I The Bahamas
92B4 El Faiyûm Egypt
96B2 El Farsia Well Mor
98C1 El Fasher Sudan
92B4 El Fashn Egypt
50A1 El Ferrol del Caudillo Spain
99C1 El Fula Sudan
96C1 El Gassi Alg
99D1 El Geteina Sudan
99D1 El Gezira Region, Sudan
94B3 El Ghor V Israel/ Jordan
10B2 Elgin Illinois, USA
44C3 Elgin Scot
92B3 El Giza Egypt
96C1 El Golea Alg
99D2 Elgon,Mt Uganda/ Kenya
99E2 El Goran Eth
23A2 El Grullo Mexico
96B2 El Guettara Well Mali

96B2 El Haricha Desert Region Mali
92A4 El Harra Egypt
51C2 El Harrach Alg
91A4 El Hawata Sudan
23B1 El Higo Mexico
34A3 El Huecu Arg
92B4 El'Igma Desert Region Egypt
12B2 Elim USA
4H2 Elira,C Can
Elisabethville = Lubumbashi
39K6 Elisenvaara Fin
El Iskandariya = Alexandria
61F4 Elista Russian Fed
106C4 Elizabeth Aust
15D2 Elizabeth USA
11C3 Elizabeth City USA
17C1 Elizabethtown N Carolina, USA
16A2 Elizabethtown Pennsylvania, USA
96B1 El Jadida Mor
92C3 El Jafr Jordan
99D1 El Jebelein Sudan
96D1 El Jem Tunisia
58C2 Elk Pol
16B3 Elk R Maryland, USA
14B3 Elk R W Virginia, USA
95C3 El Kamlin Sudan
22B1 Elk Grove USA
El Khalil = Hebron
80B3 El Khârga Egypt
80B3 El Khârga Oasis Egypt
14A2 Elkhart USA
96B2 El Khenachich Desert Region Mali
54C2 Elkhovo Bulg
14C3 Elkins USA
8B2 Elko USA
16B3 Elkton USA
92B3 El Kuntilla Egypt
99C1 El Lagowa Sudan
4H2 Ellef Ringnes I Can
8A2 Ellensburg USA
16B2 Ellenville USA
6B2 Ellesmere I Can
110B2 Ellesmere,L NZ
16A3 Ellicott City USA
100B4 Elliot S Africa
7B5 Elliot Lake Can
94B3 El Lisan Pen Jordan
112B3 Ellsworth Land Region Ant
95B1 El Maghra L Egypt
92B3 El Mansûra Egypt
16B3 Elmer USA
96B3 El Merelé Desert Region Maur
34B2 El Milagro Arg
94B1 El Mina Leb
92B4 El Minya Egypt
22B1 Elmira California, USA
10C2 Elmira New York, USA
96B2 El Mreïti Well Maur
23B1 Elmshorn Germany
98C1 El Muglad Sudan
96B2 El Mzereb Well Mali
79A3 El Nido Phil
99D1 El Obeid Sudan
23A2 El Oro Mexico
96C1 El Oued Alg
21A2 El Porta USA
22C2 El Portal USA
50A2 El Puerto del Sta Maria Spain
El Qâhira = Cairo
El Quds = Jerusalem
94B3 El Quseima Egypt
9D3 El Reno USA
4E3 Elsa Can
25D3 El Salvador Republic, Cent America
22D4 Elsinore L USA
34B3 El Sosneade Arg
57C2 Elsterwerde Germany
El Suweis = Suez

50A1 El Teleno Mt Spain
110B1 Eltham NZ
33E2 El Tigre Ven
92B4 El Tih Desert Region Egypt
34C2 El Tio Arg
20C1 Eltopia USA
92B4 El Tur Egypt
87C1 Elūru India
50A2 Elvas Port
32C5 Elvira Brazil
34A2 El Volcán Chile
14A2 Elwood USA
10A2 Ely Minnesota, USA
8B3 Ely Nevada, USA
43E3 Ely Eng
14A2 Elyria USA
90B2 Emāmrūd Iran
84B1 Emām Sāheb Afghan
58B1 Eman R Sweden
61J4 Emba Kazakhstan
61J4 Emba R Kazakhstan
29C3 Embalse Cerros Colorados L Ven
51B2 Embalse de Alarcón Res Spain
50A2 Embalse de Alcántara Res Spain
50A1 Embalse de Almendra Res Spain
50A2 Embalse de Garcia de Sola Res Spain
33E2 Embalse de Guri L Ven
51B1 Embalse de Mequinenza Res Spain
51B1 Embalse de Ricobayo Res Spain
29E2 Embalse de Rio Negro Res Urug
29C3 Embalse El Chocón L Arg
29C4 Embalse Florentine Ameghino L Arg
50A1 Embalse Gabriel y Galan Res Spain
30D3 Embarcación Arg
5G4 Embarras Portage Can
47B2 Embrun France
59D3 Emca Kenya
73A4 Emei China
107D3 Emerald Aust
7D4 Emeri Can
5J5 Emerson Can
21B1 Emigrant P USA
95A3 Emi Koussi Mt Chad
34B3 Emilo Mitre Arg
92B2 Emirdağ Turk
16B2 Emmaus USA
56B2 Emmen Neth
20C2 Emmett USA
11A3 Emmitsburg USA
12B2 Emmonak USA
9C4 Emory Peak Mt USA
24A2 Empalme Mexico
101H1 Empangeni S Africa
30E4 Empedrado Arg
105G1 Emperor Seamount Chain Pacific O
18A2 Emporia Kansas, USA
56B2 Ems R Germany
44B2 Enard B Scot
23A1 Encarnacion Mexico
30E4 Encarnacion Par
97B4 Enchi Ghana
22D4 Encinitas USA
35C1 Encruzilhada Brazil
106B1 Endeh Indon
13D2 Enderby Can
112C11 Enderby Land Region, Ant
15C2 Endicott USA
12D1 Endicott Mts USA
47D1 Engadin Mts Switz
79B2 Engaño,C Phil
94B3 En Gedi Israel
47C1 Engelberg Switz
78A4 Engano I Indon
41C3 England Country, UK
7E4 Englee Can

English Channel

41C3 English Channel Eng/France
97B3 Enji Well Maur
39H7 Enkoping Sweden
53B3 Enna Italy
99C1 En Nahud Sudan
98B3 Ennedi Region Chad
109C1 Enngonia Aust
4J83 Ennis Irish Rep
19A3 Ennis Texas, USA
45C2 Enniscorthy Irish Rep
45C1 Enniskillen N Ire
45B2 Ennistimon Irish Rep
94B2 Enn Nâqoûra Leb
57C3 Enns R Austria
8B8 Enschede Neth
24A1 Ensenada Mexico
73B3 Enshi China
99D2 Entebbe Uganda
17A1 Enterprise Alabama, USA
20C1 Enterprise Oregon, USA
97C4 Enugu Nig
75B1 Enzan Japan
49C2 Epernay France
16A2 Ephrata Pennsylvania, USA
20C1 Ephrata Washington, USA
49D2 Epinal France
46A2 Epte R France
100A3 Epukiro Namibia
54C3 Epu pel Arg
90B3 Eqlid Iran
89D7 Equator
98A2 Equatorial Guinea Republic, Africa
47C2 Erba Italy
46D2 Erbeskopf Mt Germany
34A3 Ercilla Chile
93D2 Erciş Turk
92C2 Erciyas Daglari Mt Turk
74B2 Erdaobaihe China
67C1 Erdene Mongolia
68C2 Erdenet Mongolia
98B3 Erdi Region Chad
30F4 Erechim Brazil
92B1 Eregli Turk
92B2 Eregli Turk
68D2 Erenhot China
50B1 Eresma R Spain
46D1 Erft R Germany
57C2 Erfurt Germany
93C2 Ergani Turk
96B2 Erg Chech Desert Region Alg
95A3 Erg du Djourab Desert Chad
97D3 Erg Du Ténéré Desert Region Niger
92A1 Ergene R Turk
96B2 Erg Iguidi Region Alg
58D1 Ergli Latvia
98B1 Erguig R Chad
68D1 Ergun' R China/Russian Fed
63E2 Ergun Zuoqi China
95C3 Eriba Sudan
10C2 Erie USA
42B2 Erie,L Can/USA
44A3 Eriskay I Scot
46D1 Erkelenz Germany
57C3 Erlangen Germany
19B3 Erling,L USA
101G1 Ermelo S Africa
87B3 Ernakulam India
87B2 Erode India
22A2 Erromango Aust
96B1 Er Rachidia Mor
99D1 Er Rahad Sudan
101C2 Errego Mozam
40B2 Errigal Mt Irish Rep
41A3 Erris Head Pt Irish Rep
99D1 Er Roseires Sudan
94B2 Er Rummân Jordan
57C2 Erzgebirge Upland Germany
93C2 Erzincan Turk
65F6 Erzurum Turk

48C3 Esara R Spain
56B1 Esbjerg Den
9C4 Escalón Mexico
10B2 Escanaba USA
25C3 Escárcega Mexico
46C2 Esch Lux
21B3 Escondido USA
24B2 Escuinapa Mexico
25C3 Escuintla Guatemala
98B2 Eséka Cam
51C1 Esera R Spain
52B1 Esfahan Iran
90B3 Esfahan Iran
10H1 Eshowe S Africa
10C1 Eskdale NZ
38C1 Eskifjörður Iceland
39H7 Eskilstuna Sweden
4E3 Eskimo L Can
7A3 Eskimo Point Can
92B2 Eskişehir Turk
50A1 Esla R Spain
29A5 Esmeralda I Chile
32B3 Esmeraldas Ecuador
26B2 Esmerelda Cuba
49C3 Espalion France
14B1 Espanola USA
72E1 Espanola I Ecuador
106B4 Esperance Aust
34C2 Esperanza Arg
112C2 Esperanza Base Ant
35C1 Espírito Santo State, Brazil
101C3 Espungabera Mozam
29B4 Esquel Arg
20B1 Esquimalt Can
34D2 Esquina Arg
96B1 Essaouira Mor
96A2 Es Semara Mor
56B2 Essen Germany
33F3 Essequibo R Guyana
43E4 Essex County, Eng
14B2 Essexville USA
57B3 Esslingen Germany
49C2 Essonne France
31D4 Estância Brazil
101G1 Estcourt S Africa
47D2 Este Italy
46B2 Esternay France
30D3 Esteros Par
5H5 Estevan Can
17B1 Estill USA
60B2 Estonia Republic, Europe
29B6 Estrecho de Magallanes Str Chile
50A2 Estremoz Port
59B3 Esztergom Hung
14B1 Etadunna Aust
46C2 Etain France
48C2 Etampes France
108A1 Etamunbanie,L Aust
46B1 Etaples France
85D3 Etāwah India
99D2 Ethiopia Republic, Africa
23B2 Etla Mexico
53B3 Etna Mt Italy
12H3 Etolin I USA
12A2 Etolin Str USA
6C2 Eton Can
100A2 Etosha Nat Pk Namibia
100A2 Etosha Pan Salt L Namibia
17B1 Etowah USA
46D1 Ettelbruck Lux
109C2 Euabalong Aust
14B2 Euclid USA
109C3 Eucumbene,L Aust
14B2 Eudunda Aust
19A2 Eufala L USA
17A1 Eufaula USA
8A2 Eugene USA
108C1 Eulo Aust
19B3 Eunice Louisiana, USA
46D1 Eupen Germany
93D3 Euphrates R Iraq
19B3 Eupora USA
48C2 Eure R France
20A2 Eureka California, USA
6B1 Eureka Can
8B3 Eureka Nevada, USA
6B2 Eureka Sd Can

108C3 Euroa Aust
109C1 Eurombah R Aust
101D3 Europa I Mozam Chan
57B2 Euskirchen Germany
13B2 Eutsuk L Can
13D2 Evansburg Can
6B1 Evans,C Can
7C4 Evans,L Can
6B3 Evans Str Can
14A2 Evanston Illinois, USA
8B2 Evanston Wyoming, USA
11B3 Evansville Indiana, USA
101G1 Evaton S Africa
106C4 Everard,L Aust
82C3 Everest,Mt China/Nepal
8A2 Everett Washington, USA
16C1 Everett,Mt USA
11B4 Everglades,The Swamp USA
43D3 Evesham Eng
98B2 Evinayong Eq Guinea
39F7 Evje Nor
47B1 Evolène Switz
50A2 Évora Port
48C2 Evreux France
55B3 Évvoia I Greece
98B3 Ewo Congo
12C1 Excelsior Mt USA
18B2 Excelsior Springs USA
21B2 Exeter California, USA
43C4 Exeter Eng
15D2 Exeter New Hampshire, USA
18A1 Exmoor Nat Pk Eng
43C4 Exmouth Eng
50B2 Extremadura Region, Spain
25E2 Exuma Sd The Bahamas
99D3 Eyasi L Tanz
42C2 Eyemouth Scot
99E2 Eyl Somalia
106B4 Eyre Aust
106C3 Eyre Pen Aust
79B3 Eyre I Phil
55C3 Ezatlan Mexico
55C3 Ezine Turk

F

4G3 Faber L Can
39G7 Fåborg Den
52B2 Fabriano Italy
97A3 Fachi Niger
95B3 Fada Chad
97C3 Fada N'Gourma Burkina
52B2 Faenza Italy
6E3 Faeringehavn Greenland
98B2 Fafa R CAR
99E2 Fafan R Eth
46C1 Fagnes Region, Belg
97B3 Faguibine,L L Mali
95C2 Fahud Oman
96A1 Faiol I Açores
40D2 Fairbanks USA
14B3 Fairborn USA
8D2 Fairbury USA
16A3 Fairfax USA
21A2 Fairfield California, USA
16C2 Fairfield Connecticut, USA
14B3 Fairfield Ohio, USA
45C1 Fair Head Pt N Ire
40C2 Fair Isle I Scot
111B2 Fairlie NZ
14B3 Fairmont W Virginia, USA
13D1 Fairview USA
4E4 Fairweather,Mt Can/USA
71F3 Fais I Pacific O
84C2 Faisalabad Pak
8C2 Faith USA

44E1 Faither,The Pen Scot
86A1 Faizabad India
43E3 Fakenham Eng
39G7 Fåköping Sweden
86C2 Falam Burma
24C2 Falcon Res Mexico/USA
97A3 Falémé R Mali/Sen
31B3 Falkenberg Sweden
42C2 Falkirk Scot
29D6 Falkland Is Dependency, S Atlantic
29E6 Falkland Sd Falkland Is
22D4 Fallbrook USA
8B3 Fallon USA
15D2 Fall River USA
18A1 Falls City USA
43B4 Falmouth Eng
27H1 Falmouth Jamaica
16D2 Falmouth Massachusetts, USA
100A4 False B S Africa
24A2 Falso,C Mexico
56C2 Falster I Den
54C1 Fâlticeni Rom
39H6 Falun Sweden
92B2 Famagusta Cyprus
46C1 Famenne Region, Belg
76B2 Fang Thai
99D2 Fangak Sudan
73E5 Fang liao Taiwan
52B2 Fano Italy
112C3 Faraday Base Ant
99C2 Faradje Zaire
101D3 Farafangana Madag
95B2 Farafra Oasis Egypt
80E2 Farah Afghan
71F2 Farallon de Medinilla I Pacific O
97A3 Faranah Guinea
71F3 Faraulep I Pacific O
43D4 Fareham Eng
7C5 Farewell,C = Kap Farvel
107G5 Farewell,C NZ
110B2 Farewell Spit Pt NZ
8D2 Fargo USA
94B2 Fari'a R Israel
10A2 Faribault USA
86B2 Faridpur Bang
90C2 Fariman Iran
18B2 Farmington Missouri, USA
9C3 Farmington New Mexico, USA
22B2 Farmington Res USA
52A2 Farne Deep N Sea
13D2 Farnham,Mt Can
12H2 Faro Can
50A2 Faro Port
39H7 Faro I Sweden
89K9 Farquhar Is Indian O
44B3 Farrar R Scot
14B2 Farrell USA
55B3 Fársala Greece
91B4 Fasa Iran
45B3 Fastnet Rock Irish Rep
60C3 Fastov Ukraine
86A1 Fatehpur India
13D1 Father Can
30F2 Fatima do Sul Brazil
101G1 Fauresmith S Africa
48B2 Faverges France
78A4 Fawn R Can
38H6 Fax R Sweden
38A2 Faxaflói B Iceland
95A3 Faya Chad
11A3 Fayetteville Arkansas, USA
11B3 Fayetteville N Carolina, USA
93E4 Faylakah I Kuwait
84C2 Fazilka India
96A2 Fdérik Maur
11C3 Fear,C USA
21A2 Feather Middle Fork R USA
48C2 Fécamp France
34D2 Federación Arg
34D2 Federal Arg

71F3 Federated States of Micronesia *Is* Pacific O
56C2 Fehmarn *I* Germany
32C5 Feijó Brazil
73C5 Feilai Xai Bei Jiang *R* China
110C2 Feilding NZ
100C2 Feira Zambia
31D4 Feira de Santan Brazil
92C2 Feke Turk
57B3 Feldkirch Austria
34D2 Feliciano *R* Arg
41D3 Felixstowe Eng
47D1 Feltre Italy
58G6 Femund *L* Nor
74A2 Fengcheng China
73B4 Fengdu China
72D1 Fenging China
73B3 Fengjie China
72D3 Feng Xian China
72C1 Fengzhen China
72C2 Fen He *R* China
101D2 Fenoarivo Atsinanana Madag
6E3 Feodosiya Ukraine
90C3 Ferdow Iran
108G5 Fernando de Noronha *I* Atlantic O
35A2 Fernandópolis Brazil
20B1 Ferndale USA
21B2 Fernley USA
52B2 Ferrara Italy
32B5 Ferreñafe Peru
19B3 Ferriday USA
96B1 Fès Mor
96B1 Festus USA
54C2 Feteşti Rom
92A2 Fethiye Turk
61H5 Fetisovo Kazakhstan
84E1 Fetlar *I* Scot
84C1 Feyzabad Afghan
101D3 Fianarantsoa Madag
99D2 Fiché Eth
101G1 Ficksburg S Africa
47D2 Fidenza Italy
55A2 Fier Alb
47D1 Fiera Di Primeiro Italy
44C3 Fife Region, Scot
84E3 Fife Ness *Pen* Scot
48C3 Figeac France
50A1 Figueira da Foz Port
51C1 Figueras Spain
Figueres = Figueras
96B1 Figuig Mor
105G4 Fiji *Is* Pacific O
3D03 Filadelfia Par
54B2 Filiaşi Rom
55B3 Filiatrá Greece
53B3 Filicudi *I* Italy
21B3 Fillmore California, USA
44B3 Findhorn *R* Scot
13D2 Findlay,Mt Can
13D2 Findlay USA
15C2 Finger Lakes USA
101C2 Fingoè Mozam
32B2 Finike Turk
106C3 Finke *R* Aust
106C3 Finke Flood Flats Aust
64D3 Finland Republic, N Europe
39J7 Finland,G of N Europe
5F4 Finlay *R* Can
5F4 Finlay Forks Can
58H5 Finnsnes Nor
71F4 Finschhafen PNG
47C1 Finsteraarhorn *Mt* Switz

56C2 Finsterwalde Germany
45C1 Fintona N Ire
111A3 Fiordland Nat Pk NZ
94B2 Fiq Syria
93C2 Firat *R* Turk
52B2 Firebaugh USA
52B2 Firenze Italy
34C2 Firmat Arg
85D3 Firozabad India
84C2 Firozpur India
39H7 Firspang Sweden
42B2 Firth of Clyde *Estuary* Scot
44C3 Firth of Forth *Estuary* Scot
44A3 Firth of Lorn *Estuary* Scot
40C2 Firth of Tay *Estuary* Scot
91B4 Fīrūzābād Iran
100A3 Fish *R* Namibia
22C2 Fish Camp USA
16C2 Fishers L USA
6B3 Fishere Str Can
43B4 Fishguard Wales
6E3 Fiskenaesset Greenland
46B2 Fismes France
15D2 Fitchburg USA
44E2 Fitful Head *Pt* Scot
17B1 Fitzgerald USA
106B2 Fitzroy *R* Aust
106B2 Fitzroy Crossing Aust
14B1 Fitzwilliam I Can
Fiume = Rijeka
99C3 Fizi *R* Zaire
9B3 Flagstaff USA
42D2 Flamborough Head *C* Eng
8C2 Flaming Gorge Res USA
44A2 Flannan Isles *Is* Scot
12J2 Flat *R* Can
13E3 Flathead *R* USA
82B2 Flathead L USA
18B2 Flat River USA
82A2 Flattery,C USA
42C3 Fleetwood Eng
39F7 Flekkefjord Nor
69G4 Fleming Deep Pacific O
52B2 Flemington USA
56B2 Flensburg Germany
47B1 Fleurier Switz
106C4 Flinders *I* Aust
107D4 Flinders *R* Aust
107D2 Flinders *R* Aust
106C4 Flinders Range *Mts* Aust
5H4 Flin Flon Can
10B2 Flint Can
42C3 Flint Wales
11B3 Flint *R* USA
48B2 Flixecourt France
17A1 Florala USA
11B3 Florence Alabama, USA
18A2 Florence Kansas, USA
20B2 Florence Oregon, USA
11C3 Florence S Carolina, USA
32B3 Florencia Colombia
46C2 Florenville Belg
25D3 Flores Guatemala
96A1 Flores *I* Açores
106B1 Flores *I* Indon
34D3 Flores *R* Arg
70C4 Flores S Indon
31C3 Floriano Brazil
30G4 Florianópolis Brazil
25D2 Florida State, USA
29E2 Florida Urug
17B2 Florida B USA
17B2 Florida City USA
107E1 Florida Is Solomon Is
11B4 Florida Keys *Is* USA
11B4 Florida,Strs of USA
55B2 Flórina Greece
38F6 Florø Nor
47D1 Fluchthorn *Mt* Austria

54C1 Focsani Rom
53C2 Foggia Italy
97A4 Fogo *I* Cape Verde
48C3 Foix France
6C3 Foley I Can
52B2 Foligno Italy
43E4 Folkestone Eng
17B1 Folkston USA
52B2 Follonica Italy
22B1 Folsom USA
22B1 Folsom L L USA
5H4 Fond-du-Lac Can
10B2 Fond du Lac Can
48C2 Fontainebleau France
52C1 Fontenac USA
48B2 Fontenay-le-Comte France
52C1 Fonyód Hung
Foochow = Fuzhou
12D2 Foraker,Mt USA
46D2 Forbach France
109C2 Forbes Aust
97C4 Forcados Nig
38F6 Forde Nor
108C1 Fords Bridge Aust
19B3 Fordyce USA
97A4 Forécariah Guinea
6G3 Forel,Mt Greenland
14B2 Forest Can
17B1 Forest Park USA
22A1 Forestville USA
44C3 Forfar Scot
46A2 Forges-les-Eaux France
20B1 Forks USA
52B2 Forlì Italy
51C2 Formentera *I* Spain
53B2 Formia Italy
96A1 Formigas *I* Açores
Formosa = Taiwan
29B4 Formosa Arg
31B5 Formosa Brazil
30D3 Formosa State, Arg
73D5 Formosa Str Taiwan/China
47D2 Fornovo di Taro Italy
38D3 Føroyar *Is* N Atlantic O
44C3 Forres Scot
106B4 Forrest Aust
11A3 Forrest City USA
77D2 Forsayth Aust
32A6 Forssa Fin
109D2 Forster Aust
18B2 Forsyth Missouri, USA
84C3 Fort Abbas Pak
7B4 Fort Albany Can
31D2 Fortaleza Brazil
44B3 Fort Augustus Scot
100B4 Fort Beaufort S Africa
21A2 Fort Bragg USA
8C2 Fort Collins USA
15C1 Fort Coulogne Can
27E4 Fort de France Martinique
17A1 Fort Deposit USA
10A2 Fort Dodge USA
106A3 Fortescue *R* Aust
7A5 Fortress Lake Can
4F3 Fort Franklin Can
4F3 Fort Good Hope Can
108B1 Fort Grey Aust
44B3 Forth *R* Scot
7B4 Fort Hope Can
34B3 Fortin Uno Arg
4F3 Fort Laird Can
96C1 Fort Lallemand Alg
Fort Lamy = Ndjamena
11B4 Fort Lauderdale USA
4F3 Fort Liard Can
5G4 Fort Mackay Can
5G5 Fort Macleod Can
5G4 Fort McMurray Can
4E3 Fort McPherson Can
18B2 Fort Madison USA
8C2 Fort Morgan USA
11B4 Fort Myers USA
5F4 Fort Nelson Can
4F3 Fort Norman Can
17A1 Fort Payne USA
8C2 Fort Peck Res USA

11B4 Fort Pierce USA
4G3 Fort Providence Can
5G3 Fort Resolution Can
98B3 Fort Rousset Congo
5F4 Fort St James Can
13C1 Fort St John Can
13E2 Fort Saskatchewan Can
18B2 Fort Scott USA
4E3 Fort Selkirk Can
7B4 Fort Severn Can
61H5 Fort Shevchenko Kazakhstan
4F3 Fort Simpson Can
5G3 Fort Smith Can
4G3 Fort Smith Region, Can
11A3 Fort Smith USA
9C3 Fort Stockton USA
20B2 Fortuna California, USA
5G4 Fort Vermillion Can
17A1 Fort Walton Beach USA
10B2 Fort Wayne USA
44B3 Fort William Scot
9D3 Fort Worth USA
12F2 Fortymile *R* USA
12E1 Fort Yukon USA
73C5 Foshan China
47B2 Fossano Italy
12G3 Foster,Mt USA
98B3 Fougamou Gabon
48B2 Fougères France
44D1 Foula *I* Scot
43A4 Foulness I Eng
111B2 Foulwind,C NZ
98B2 Foumban Cam
49C1 Fourmies France
55C3 Foúrnoi *I* Greece
97A3 Fouta Djallon *Mts* Guinea
111B3 Foveaux *Str* NZ
43A4 Fowey Eng
13D2 Fox Creek Can
6B3 Foxe Basin *G* Can
6B3 Foxe Chan Can
6C3 Foxe Pen Can
110C2 Foxton NZ
13F2 Fox Valley Can
45B3 Foynes Irish Rep
100A2 Foz do Cuene Angola
30F4 Foz do Iguaçu Brazil
16A2 Frackville USA
34B2 Fraga Arg
31B6 Franca Brazil
49C2 France Republic, Europe
12J2 Frances Can
49D2 Franche Comté Region, France
100B3 Francistown Botswana
12J2 Francois L Can
14A2 Frankfort Indiana, USA
11B3 Frankfort Kentucky, USA
101G1 Frankfort S Africa
57B2 Frankfurt Germany
46E1 Frankfurt am Main Germany
56C2 Frankfurt-an-der-Oder Germany
57C3 Fränkischer Alb *Upland* Germany
14A3 Franklin Indiana, USA
19B4 Franklin Louisiana, USA
16D1 Franklin Massachusetts, USA
16B2 Franklin New Jersey, USA
14C2 Franklin Pennsylvania, USA
4F2 Franklin B Can
20C1 Franklin D Roosevelt *L* USA
4F3 Franklin Mts Can
4J2 Franklin Str Can
111B2 Franz Josef Glacier NZ

Franz-Joseph-Land =
Zemlya Frantsa Iosifa
5F5 Fraser R Can
4C3 Fraserburgh Scot
10E3 Fraser L Aust
13B2 Fraser L Can
47B1 France French
47C1 Frauenfeld Switz
24D2 Fray Bentos Urug
40C2 Fraserburgh Scot
16B3 Fredericia USA
56B1 Fredericia Den
15C3 Frederick Maryland,
USA
15C3 Fredericksburg
Virginia, USA
12H3 Frederick Sd USA
18B2 Fredericktown USA
7D5 Fredericton Can
6E3 Frederikshåb
Greenland
39G7 Frederikshavn Den
15C2 Fredonia USA
39G7 Frederikstad Nor
16B2 Freehold USA
26B1 Freeport The
Bahamas
19A4 Freeport Texas, USA
97A4 Freetown Sierra
Leone
57B3 Freiburg Germany
57C3 Freistadt Austria
106A4 Fremantle Aust
22B2 Fremont California,
USA
18A1 Fremont Nebraska,
USA
14B2 Fremont Ohio, USA
33G3 French Guiana
Dependency,
S America
109C4 Frenchmans Cap Mt
Aust
105J4 French Polynesia Is
Pacific O
24B2 Fresnillo Mexico
8B3 Fresno USA
22C2 Fresno R USA
47B1 Fretigney France
46B1 Frévent France
109C4 Freycinet Pen Aust
97A3 Fria Guinea
22C2 Friant USA
22C2 Friant Dam USA
52A1 Fribourg Switz
57B3 Friedrichshafen
Germany
6D3 Frobisher B Can
6D3 Frobisher Bay Can
5H4 Frobisher L Can
61F4 Frolovo Russian Fed
43C4 Frome Eng
108A1 Frome R Aust
43C4 Frome R Eng
106C4 Frome,L Aust
25C3 Frontera Mexico
15C2 Front Royal USA
53B2 Frosinone Italy
73C5 Fuchuan China
73E4 Fuding China
24B2 Fuerte R Mexico
30E3 Fuerte Olimpo Par
96A2 Fuerteventura I
Canary Is
72C2 Fugu China
68A2 Fuhai China
91C4 Fujairah UAE
75B1 Fuji Japan
73D4 Fujian Province,
China
69F2 Fujin China
75B1 Fujinomiya Japan
74D3 Fuji-san Mt Japan
75B1 Fujisawa Japan
75B1 Fuji-Yoshida Japan
63A3 Fukang China
74C3 Fukuchiyima Japan
74D3 Fukui Japan
74C4 Fukuoka Japan
74E3 Fukushima Japan
74C4 Fukuyama Japan
57B2 Fulda Germany
57B2 Fulda R Germany
73B4 Fuling China
27L1 Fullarton Trinidad

22D4 Fullerton USA
18C2 Fulton Kentucky,
USA
15C2 Fulton New York,
USA
46C1 Fumay France
75C1 Funabashi Japan
96A1 Funchal Medeira
35C1 Fundão Brazil
7D5 Fundy,B of Can
101C3 Funhalouro Mozam
72D3 Funing China
73B5 Funing China
101C2 Furancungo Mozam
91C4 Fürg Iran
47C1 Furka P Switz
107D5 Furneaux Group Is
Aust
56C2 Fürstenwalde
Germany
57C3 Fürth Germany
74D3 Furukawa Japan
6B3 Fury and Hecla St
Can
74A2 Fushun Liaoning,
China
73A4 Fushun Sichuan,
China
74B2 Fusong China
57C3 Füssen Germany
72E2 Fu Xian China
72E1 Fuxin China
72D3 Fuyang China
72E1 Fuyuan Liaoning,
China
73A4 Fuyuan Yunnan,
China
68A2 Fuyun China
73D4 Fuzhou China
56C1 Fyn I Den

G

99E2 Gaalkacyo Somalia
21B2 Gabbs USA
100A2 Gabela Angola
96D1 Gabe's Tunisia
22B2 Gabilan Range Mts
USA
98B3 Gabon Republic,
Africa
100B3 Gaborone Botswana
54B2 Gabrovo Bulg
91B3 Gach Sārān Iran
17A1 Gadsden Alabama,
USA
10A1 Gads L Can
53B2 Gaeta Italy
71F3 Gaferut I Pacific O
96C1 Gafsa Tunisia
60D2 Gagarin Russian Fed
97B4 Gagnoa Ivory Coast
7D4 Gagnon Can
61F5 Gagra Georgia
86B1 Gaibanda India
29C4 Gaimán Arg
17B2 Gainesville Florida,
USA
17B1 Gainesville Georgia,
USA
19A3 Gainesville Texas,
USA
42D3 Gainsborough Eng
108A2 Gairdner,L Aust
44B3 Gairloch Scot
16A3 Gaithersburg USA
87B1 Gajendragarh India
73D4 Ga Jiang R China
99D3 Galana R Kenya
103D5 Galapagos Is
Pacific O
42C2 Galashiels Scot
54C1 Galaţi Rom
63A2 Galena Alaska, USA
18B2 Galena Kansas, USA
27L1 Galeota Pt Trinidad
27L1 Galera Pt Trinidad
10A2 Galesburg USA
15C2 Galeton USA
61F2 Galich Russian Fed
50A1 Galicia Region, Spain
Galilee,S of =
Tiberias,L
27J1 Galina Pt Jamaica

99D1 Gallabat Sudan
47C2 Gallarate Italy
87C3 Galle Sri Lanka
51B1 Gállego R Spain
55A2 Gallípoli Italy
38J5 Gällivare Sweden
42B2 Galloway District
42B2 Galloway,Mull of C
Scot
8C3 Gallup USA
22B1 Galt USA
96A2 Galtat Zemmour Mor
25C2 Galveston USA
11A4 Galveston B USA
34C2 Gálvez Arg
49D3 Galvi Corse
45B2 Galway County,
Irish Rep
41B3 Galway Irish Rep
41B3 Galway B Irish Rep
86B1 Gamba China
97B3 Gambaga Ghana
97B3 Gambaga Ghana
100A2 Gamboma Congo
87C3 Gampola Sri Lanka
91C2 Ganale Dorya R Eth
15C2 Gananoque Can
Gand = Gent
100A2 Ganda Angola
98C3 Gandajika Zaire
84B3 Gandava Pak
7E5 Gander Can
85C4 Gāndhīdhām India
85C4 Gāndhīnagar India
85D4 Gāndhī Sāgar L
India
51B2 Gandia Spain
86B1 Ganga R India
85C3 Ganganar India
86C2 Gangaw Burma
72A2 Gangca China
82C2 Gangdise Shan Mts
China
Ganges = Ganga
86B1 Gangtok India
72B3 Gangu China
8C2 Gannett Peak Mt
USA
72B2 Ganquan China
108A3 Gantheaume C Aust
39K8 Gantsevichi
Belorussia
73D4 Ganzhou China
97C3 Gao Mali
72C2 Gaolan China
72C2 Gaoping China
97B3 Gaoua Burkina
97A3 Gaoual Guinea
72D3 Gaoyou Hu L China
73C5 Gaozhou China
49D3 Gap France
72C2 Gapan Phil
109C1 Garah Aust
31D3 Garanhuns Brazil
21A1 Garberville USA
35B2 Garça Brazil
35A2 Garcias Brazil
47D2 Garda Italy
9C3 Garden City USA
14A1 Garden Pen USA
34D3 Gardey Arg
84B2 Gardez Afghan
16C2 Gardiners I USA
16D1 Gardner USA
47D2 Gardone Italy
85D4 Garhākota India
61K2 Gari Russian Fed
94B2 Garies S Africa
99D3 Garissa Kenya
19A3 Garland USA
57C3 Garmisch-
Partenkirchen
90C2 Garmsar Iran
18A2 Garnett USA
8B2 Garnett Peak Mt
USA

48C3 Garonne R France
44B3 Garry R Scot
78B4 Garut Indon
86A2 Garwa India
14A2 Gary USA
82C2 Garyarsa China
4H3 Gary,L Can
19A3 Garza-Little Elm Res
USA
90B2 Gasan Kuli
Turkmenistan
44B3 Gascogne Region,
France
18B2 Gasconade R USA
46A3 Gascoyne R Aust
98B2 Gashaka Nig
97D3 Gashua Nig
10D2 Gaspé Can
10D2 Gaspé,C. de Can
94A1 Gata,C Cyprus
60D2 Gatchina
Russian Fed
42D2 Gateshead Eng
14A3 Gatesville USA
15C1 Gatineau Can
15C1 Gatineau R Can
109D1 Gatton Aust
86C1 Gauhāti India
58C1 Gauja R Latvia
86A1 Gauri Phanta India
22B3 Gaviota USA
39H6 Gävle Sweden
108A2 Gawler Ranges Mts
Aust
72A1 Gaxun Nur L China
86A2 Gaya India
97C3 Gaya Niger
14B1 Gaylord USA
109D1 Gayndah Aust
61H1 Gayny Russian Fed
60C4 Gaysin Ukraine
92C2 Gaza Israel
92C2 Gaziantep Turk
97B4 Gbaringa Lib
51B2 Gdańsk Pol
51B2 Gdańsk,G of Pol
39K7 Gdov Russian Fed
58B2 Gdynia Pol
94A3 Gebel Halâl Mt
Egypt
95C2 Gebel Hamata Mt
Egypt
92B4 Gebel Katherina Mt
Egypt
94A3 Gebel Libni Mt
Egypt
94A3 Gebel Maghâra Mt
Egypt
99D1 Gedaref Sudan
55C3 Gediz R Turk
56C2 Gedser Den
46D1 Geel Belg
108B3 Geelong Aust
97D3 Geeveston Aust
97D3 Geidam Nig
46D1 Geilenkirchen
Germany
99D3 Geita Tanz
73A5 Gejiu China
53B3 Gela Italy
99E2 Geladi Eth
46D1 Geldern Germany
55C2 Gelibolu Turk
92B2 Gelidonya Burun
Turk
46D1 Gelsenkirchen
Germany
39F8 Gelting Germany
77C5 Gemas Malay
46D1 Gembloux Belg
98B2 Gemena Zaire
92C2 Gemerek Turk
92A1 Gemlik Turk
52B1 Gemona Italy
100B3 Gemsbok Nat Pk
Botswana
98C1 Geneina Sudan
34C3 General Acha Arg
34C3 General Alvear
Buenos Aires, Arg
34B2 General Alvear
Mendoza, Arg
34D3 General Arenales Arg
34D3 General Belgrano
Arg

112B2 **General Belgrano** Base Ant
112C2 **General Bernardo O'Higgins** Base Ant
34D3 **General Conesa** Buenos Aires, Arg
30D3 **General Eugenio A Garay** Par
34D3 **General Guido** Arg
34C3 **General La Madrid** Arg
34D3 **General Levalle** Arg
30C4 **General Manuel Belgrano** Mt Arg
34D3 **General Paz** Buenos Aires, Arg
34D2 **General Pico** Arg
34D2 **General Piran** Arg
29C3 **General Roca** Arg
112C3 **General San Martin** Base Ant
79C4 **General Santos** Phil
34C3 **General Viamonte** Arg
34C3 **General Villegas** Arg
15C2 **Genesee** USA
15C2 **Geneseo** USA
Geneva = Genève
15C2 **Geneva** Nebraska, USA
15C2 **Geneva** New York, USA
Geneva,L of = LacLéman
52A1 **Genève** Switz
50B2 **Genil** R Spain
52A2 **Genoa** = Genova
10C3 **Genoa** Aust
52A2 **Genova** Italy
32J7 **Genovesa** I Ecuador
46B1 **Gent** Belg
78B4 **Genteng** Indon
56C2 **Genthin** Germany
93E1 **Geokchay** Azerbaijan
100B4 **George** S Africa
7D4 **George** R Can
109C2 **George,L** Aust
17B2 **George,L** Florida, USA
15D2 **George,L** New York, USA
111A2 **George Sd** NZ
109C4 **Georgetown** Aust
15C3 **Georgetown** Delaware, USA
33F2 **Georgetown** Guyana
14B3 **Georgetown** Kentucky, USA
77C4 **George Town** Malay
27N2 **Georgetown** St Vincent and the Grenadines
17C1 **Georgetown** S Carolina, USA
19A3 **Georgetown** Texas, USA
97A3 **Georgetown** The Gambia
112C8 **George V Land** Region, Ant
65F5 **Georgia** Republic, Europe
112C12 **Georg Forster** Base Ant
17B1 **Georgia** State, USA
14B1 **Georgian B** Can
13C3 **Georgia,Str of** Can
106C3 **Georgina** R Aust
61F5 **Georgiyevsk** Russian Fed
57C2 **Gera** Germany
46B1 **Geraardsbergen** Belg
111B2 **Geraldine** NZ
106A3 **Geraldton** Aust
10B2 **Geraldton** Can
94B3 **Gerar** R Israel
4C3 **Gerdine,Mt** USA
12E2 **Gerdova Peak** Mt USA
77C4 **Gerik** Malay
60B4 **Gerlachovsky** Mt Pol
13E1 **Germanson Lodge** Can

56C2 **Germany** Republic, Europe
101G1 **Germiston** S Africa
46D1 **Gerolstein** Germany
51C1 **Gerona** Spain
46E1 **Geseke** Germany
99E2 **Gestro** R Eth
50B1 **Getafe** Spain
16A3 **Gettysburg** Pennsylvania, USA
93D2 **Gevaş** Turk
55B2 **Gevgelija** Macedonia
47B1 **Gex** France
94C2 **Ghabaghib** Syria
96C1 **Ghadamis** Libya
90B2 **Ghaem Shahr** Iran
86A1 **Ghāghara** R India
97B4 **Ghana** Republic, Africa
100B3 **Ghanzi** Botswana
96C1 **Ghardaia** Alg
95A1 **Gharyan** Libya
96C2 **Ghāt** Libya
84D3 **Ghāziābād** India
84C3 **Ghazi Khan** Pak
84B2 **Ghazni** Afghan
54C1 **Gheorgheni** Rom
88E4 **Ghudamis** Alg
90D3 **Ghurian** Afghan
95B2 **Giälo** Libya
99E2 **Giamame** Somalia
53C3 **Giarre** Italy
50A2 **Gibeon** Namibia
50A2 **Gibraltar** Colony, SW Europe
50A2 **Gibraltar,Str of** Spain/Africa
106B3 **Gibson Desert** Aust
20B1 **Gibsons** Can
87B1 **Giddalür** India
99D2 **Gidole** Eth
57B2 **Giessen** Germany
17B2 **Gifford** USA
74D3 **Gifu** Japan
42B2 **Gigha** I Scot
52B2 **Giglio** I Italy
50A1 **Gijón** Spain
107D2 **Gilbert** R Aust
87B1 **Gilbert,Mt** Can
101C2 **Gîle** Mozam
94B2 **Gilead** Region, USA
95B2 **Gilf Kebir Plat** Egypt
109C2 **Gilgandra** Aust
84C1 **Gilgit** Pak
84C1 **Gilgit** R Pak
108C2 **Gilgunnia** Aust
108A2 **Gillam** Can
108A2 **Gilles L** Aust
13B2 **Gills I** USA
14A1 **Gills Rock** USA
14A2 **Gilman** USA
22B2 **Gilroy** USA
8D1 **Gimli** Can
101H1 **Gingindlovu** S Africa
79C4 **Gingoog** Phil
99E2 **Ginir** Eth
55B3 **Gióna** Mt Greece
109C3 **Gippsland** Mts Aust
14B2 **Girard** USA
32C3 **Girardot** Colombia
44C3 **Girdle Ness** Pen Scot
53J1 **Giresun** Turk
84C5 **Gir Hills** India
98B2 **Giri** R Zaire
88B2 **Giridih** India
Girona = Gerona
48B2 **Gironde** R France
98B1 **Girvan** Scot
111C2 **Gisborne** NZ
46A2 **Gisors** France
99E3 **Gitega** Burundi
Giuba,R = Juba,R
54C2 **Giurgiu** Rom
46C1 **Givet** Belg
58C2 **Gizycko** Pol
55B2 **Gjirokastër** Alb
4J3 **Gjoatlaven** Can
39C6 **Gjøvik** Nor
7D5 **Glace Bay** Can
12G3 **Glacier Bay Nat Mon** Can
13E3 **Glacier Nat Pk** USA/Can

20B1 **Glacier Peak** Mt USA
6B2 **Glacier Str** Can
107E3 **Gladstone** Queensland, Aust
108A2 **Gladstone** S Aust, Aust
109C4 **Gladstone** Tasmania, Aust
14A1 **Gladstone** USA
38A1 **Glåma** Mt Iceland
39G6 **Glåma** R Nor
56C2 **Glan** R Germany
47C1 **Glärner** Mts Switz
47C1 **Glarus** Switz
18A2 **Glasco** USA
8C2 **Glasgow** Montana, USA
42B2 **Glasgow** Scot
16B3 **Glassboro** USA
43C4 **Glastonbury** Eng
61H2 **Glazov** Russian Fed
59B3 **Gleisdorf** Austria
110C1 **Glen Afton** NZ
16A3 **Glen Burnie** USA
101H1 **Glencoe** S Africa
9B3 **Glendale** Arizona, USA
22C3 **Glendale** California, USA
109D1 **Glen Innes** Aust
109C1 **Glenmorgan** Aust
109D2 **Glenreagh** Aust
18B2 **Glen Rock** USA
16A3 **Glen Rose** USA
44C3 **Glenrothes** UK
15D2 **Glens Falls** USA
45B1 **Glenties** Irish Rep
19B3 **Glenwood** Arkansas, USA
8C3 **Glenwood Springs** USA
39F6 **Glittertind** Mt Nor
59B2 **Gliwice** Pol
9B3 **Globe** USA
58B2 **Głogów** Pol
38G5 **Glomfjord** Nor
109D2 **Gloucester** Aust
43C4 **Gloucester** Eng
16D1 **Gloucester** USA
58D1 **Glubokoye** Belorussia
60D3 **Glukhov** Russian Fed
59B3 **Gmünd** Austria
57C3 **Gmunden** Austria
58B2 **Gniezno** Pol
100A3 **Goabeg** Namibia
87A1 **Goa, Daman and Diu** Union Territory, India
86C1 **Goalpāra** India
76A2 **Goba** Eth
100A3 **Gobabis** Namibia
34C2 **Gobernador Crespo** Arg
34B3 **Gobernador Duval** Arg
72B1 **Gobi** Desert China/Mongolia
75B2 **Gobo** Japan
87B1 **Godāg** India
87C1 **Godāvari** R India
14B2 **Goderich** Can
6E3 **Godhavn** Greenland
85C4 **Godhra** India
34B2 **Godoy Cruz** Arg
7A4 **Gods L** Can
6E3 **Godthab** Greenland
Godwin Austen = K2
35B1 **Goiandira** Brazil
35B1 **Goianésia** Brazil
35B1 **Goiânia** Brazil
35A1 **Goiás** Brazil
31B4 **Goiás** State, Brazil
35A2 **Gio-Erê** Brazil
99D2 **Gojab** R Eth
55C2 **Gökçeada** I Turk
55C3 **Gökova Körfezi** B Turk
92C2 **Göksun** Turk
63C3 **Gol** R Mongolia
93C1 **Gölbaşi** Turk
99C2 **Golconda** USA
20B2 **Gold Beach** USA
109D1 **Gold Coast** Aust

13D2 **Golden** Can
110B2 **Golden B** NZ
20B1 **Goldendale** USA
22A2 **Golden Gate** Chan
19B4 **Golden Meadow** USA
21B2 **Goldfield** USA
13B3 **Gold River** Can
56C2 **Goleniów** Pol
22C3 **Goleta** USA
52A2 **Golfe d'Ajaccio** Corse
96D1 **Golfe de Gabes** Tunisia
Golfe de Gascogne = Biscay,Bay of
48B2 **Golfe de St Florent** B Corse
49C3 **Golfe du Lion** France
29B4 **Golfo Corcovado** G Chile
50B2 **Golfo de Almeria** G Spain
29B4 **Golfo de Ancud** G Chile
25D2 **Golfo de Batabanó** G Cuba
50A2 **Golfo de Cadiz** G Spain
53A3 **Golfo de Cagliari** G Sardegna
24A1 **Golfo de California** G Mexico
25D4 **Golfo de Chiriqui** G Panama
25D3 **Golfo de Fonseca** G Honduras
25D2 **Golfo de Guacanayabo** G Cuba
32A4 **Golfo de Guayaquil** G Ecuador
26B5 **Golfo del Darien** G Colombia/Panama
32A2 **Golfo de los Mosquitos** G Panama
25D3 **Golfo del Papagaya** G Nic
52B2 **Golfo de Mazarrón** G Spain
25D4 **Golfo de Nicoya** G Costa Rica
53A3 **Golfo de Oristano** G Sardegna
25E4 **Golfo de Panamá** G Panama
25D3 **Golfo de Papagayo** G Costa Rica
27E4 **Golfo de Paria** G Ven
29B5 **Golfo de Penas** G Chile
49D3 **Golfo de St Florent** Corse
51C1 **Golfo de San Jorge** G Spain
24C3 **Golfo de Tehuantepec** G Mexico
32B3 **Golfo de Torugas** G Colombia
32B2 **Golfo de Uraba** G Colombia
51C2 **Golfo de Valencia** G Spain
27C4 **Golfo de Venezuela** G Ven
52A2 **Golfo di Genova** G Italy
53C3 **Golfo di Policastro** G Italy
53C3 **Golfo di Squillace** G Italy
53C2 **Golfo di Taranto** G Italy
52B1 **Golfo di Venezia** G Italy
25D4 **Golfo Dulce** G Costa Rica
29C5 **Golfo San Jorge** G Arg

29D4 **Golfo San Matias** G Arg
68B3 **Golmud** China
99E2 **Golocha** Eth
12B2 **Golovin** S USA
74F2 **Golovnino** Russian Fed
99C3 **Goma** Zaire
97D3 **Gombe** Nig
60D3 **Gomel'** Belorussia
96A2 **Gomera** I Canary Is
24B2 **Gómez Palacio** Mexico
63E2 **Gonam** R Russian Fed
90C2 **Gonbad-e Kávús** Iran
86A1 **Gonda** India
85C4 **Gondal** India
99D1 **Gonder** Eth
92A1 **Gönen** Turk
55C3 **Gönen** R Turk
73A4 **Gongga Shan** Mt China
72A2 **Gonghe** China
97D3 **Gongola** R Nig
22B2 **Gonzales** California, USA
19A4 **Gonzales** Texas, USA
34C3 **Gonzalez Chaves** Arg
13C2 **Good Hope** Mt C
13C2 **Goodland** USA
12B3 **Goodnews Bay** USA
109C1 **Goodooga** R Aust
42D3 **Goole** Eng
108C2 **Goolgowi** Aust
108A3 **Goolwa** Aust
108A4 **Goomalling** Aust
108C2 **Goombalie** Aust
109D1 **Goomeri** Aust
109D1 **Goondiwindi** Aust
7E4 **Goose Bay** Can
17C1 **Goose Creek** USA
20B2 **Goose L** USA
87B1 **Gooty** India
63C2 **Gora Munku Sardyk** Mt Mongolia/ Russian Fed
64H3 **Gora Narodnaya** Mt Russian Fed
64G3 **Gora Tel'pos-iz** Russian Fed
54A2 **Goražde** Bosnia-Herzegovina
4D3 **Gordon** USA
13E1 **Gordon L** Can
15C3 **Gordonsville** USA
98B2 **Goré** Chad
99D2 **Gore** Eth
111A3 **Gore** NZ
63F2 **Gore Topko** Mt Russian Fed
45C2 **Gorey** Irish Rep
90B2 **Gorgán** Iran
93E2 **Goris** Armenia
52B1 **Gorizia** Italy
61F2 **Gor'kiy = Nizniy Novgorod**
61F2 **Gor'kovskoye Vodokhranilishche** Res Russian Fed
57C2 **Görlitz** Germany
60E4 **Gorlovka** Ukraine
22C3 **Gorman** USA
54C2 **Gorna Orjahovica** Bulg
68A1 **Gorno-Altaysk** Russian Fed
69G2 **Gornozavodsk** Russian Fed
61F2 **Gorodets** Russian Fed
59C3 **Gorodok** Ukraine
59D3 **Gorodok** Ukraine
71F4 **Goroka** PNG
86A1 **Gorokhpur** India
101C2 **Gorongosa** Mozam
71D3 **Gorontalo** Indon
61K2 **Goro Yurma** Mt Russian Fed
45B2 **Gort** Irish Rep
63C2 **Goryachinsk** Russian Fed
59D3 **Goryn'** R Ukraine

59C2 **Góry Świetokrzyskie** Upland Pol
64G3 **Gory Tel'pos-iz** Mt Russian Fed
39H8 **Gorzów Wielkopolski** Pol
74E2 **Goshogawara** Japan
52C2 **Gospić** Croatia
54B2 **Gostivar** Macedonia
58B2 **Gostynin** Pol
39G7 **Göteborg** Sweden
98B2 **Gotel** Mts Nig
39H7 **Gotland** I Sweden
74B4 **Gotō-retto** I Japan
39H7 **Gotska Sandön** I Sweden
74C3 **Gōtsu** Japan
98B1 **Goudoumaria** Niger
103H7 **Gough I** Atlantic O
109C2 **Goulburn** R Aust
97B3 **Goumbou** Mali
97B3 **Goundam** Mali
98B1 **Gouré** Niger
97B3 **Gourma Rharous** Mali
46A2 **Gournay-en-Bray** France
95A3 **Gouro** Chad
71E5 **Gove Pen** Aust
60B4 **Goverla** Mt Ukraine
35C1 **Governador Valadares** Brazil
86A2 **Govind Ballabh Paht Sāgar** L India
15C2 **Gowanda** USA
84B3 **Gowāran** Afghan
30E4 **Goya** Arg
98C1 **Goz-Beida** Chad
53B3 **Gozo** I Medit S
95C3 **Goz Regeb** Sudan
100B4 **Graaff-Reinet** S Africa
15C1 **Gracefield** Can
109D1 **Grafton** Aust
8D2 **Grafton** N Dakota, USA
14B3 **Grafton** W Virginia, USA
5E4 **Graham** I Can
13C1 **Graham** R Can
9C3 **Graham** Mt USA
100B4 **Grahamstown** S Africa
31B3 **Grajaú** Brazil
58B2 **Grajewo** Pol
55B2 **Grámmos** Mt Greece/Alb
44C3 **Grampian** Region, Scot
44B3 **Grampian** Mts Scot
32C3 **Granada** Colombia
25D3 **Granada** Nic
50B2 **Granada** Spain
15D1 **Granby** Can
96A2 **Gran Canaria** I Canary Is
30D4 **Gran Chaco** Region Arg
14A2 **Grand** R Michigan, USA
18B1 **Grand** R Missouri, USA
27Q2 **Grand** D Dominica
11C4 **Grand Bahama** I The Bahamas
7E5 **Grand Bank** Can
102F2 **Grand Banks** Atlantic O
97B4 **Grand Bassam** Ivory Coast
9B3 **Grand Canyon** USA
26A3 **Grand Cayman** I Caribbean S
13E2 **Grand Centre** Can
20C1 **Grand Coulee** USA
34B3 **Grande** R Arg
31C4 **Grande** R Bahia, Brazil
35B1 **Grande** R Minas Gerais/São Paulo, Brazil
13D2 **Grande Cache** Can
47A2 **Grande Chartreuse** Region, France

101D2 **Grande Comore** I Comoros
13D1 **Grande Prairie** Can
19A3 **Grande Prairie** USA
95A3 **Grand Erg de Bilma** Desert Niger
96B2 **Grand erg Occidental** Mts Alg
96C2 **Grand erg Oriental** Mts Alg
7C4 **Grande Rivière de la Baleine** R Can
20C1 **Grande Ronde** R USA
7D5 **Grand Falls** New Brunswick, Can
7E5 **Grand Falls** Newfoundland, Can
20C1 **Grand Forks** Can
8D2 **Grand Forks** USA
16B1 **Grand Gorge** USA
14A2 **Grand Haven** USA
19C3 **Grand Isle** USA
19B4 **Grand L** USA
15D1 **Grand Mère** Can
50A2 **Grândola** Port
5J4 **Grand Rapids** Can
14A2 **Grand Rapids** Michigan, USA
10A2 **Grand Rapids** Minnesota, USA
47B2 **Grand St Bernard** P Italy/Switz
8B2 **Grand Teton** Mt USA
8B2 **Grand Teton Nat Pk** USA
46A2 **Grandvilliers** France
25D1 **Grangeburg** USA
51C1 **Granollers** Spain
52A1 **Gran Paradiso** Mt Italy
47D1 **Gran Pilastro** Mt Austria/Italy
43D3 **Grantham** Eng
21B2 **Grant,Mt** USA
44C3 **Grantown-on-Spey** Scot
9C3 **Grants** USA
20B2 **Grants Pass** USA
48B2 **Granville** France
5H4 **Granville L** Can
35C1 **Grão Mogol** Brazil
49D3 **Grasse** France
21A2 **Grass Valley** USA
5H5 **Gravelbourg** Can
46B1 **Gravelines** France
100C3 **Gravelotte** S Africa
15C2 **Gravenhurst** Can
109D1 **Gravesend** Aust
12H3 **Gravina I** USA
12B2 **Grayling** USA
20B1 **Grays Harbor** B USA
14B3 **Grayson** USA
18C2 **Grayville** USA
59B3 **Graz** Austria
27H1 **Great** R Jamaica
11C4 **Great Abaco** I The Bahamas
106B4 **Great Australian Bight** G Aust
16B3 **Great B** New Jersey, USA
25E2 **Great Bahama Bank** The Bahamas
110C1 **Great Barrier I** NZ
107D2 **Great Barrier Reef** Is Aust
16C1 **Great Barrington** USA
4F3 **Great Bear L** Can
9D2 **Great Bend** USA
107D3 **Great Dividing Range** Mts Aust
42D2 **Great Driffield** Eng
16B3 **Great Egg Harbor** B USA
112B10 **Greater Antarctic** Region, Ant
26B2 **Greater Antilles** Is Caribbean S
43D4 **Greater London** Metropolitan County, Eng

43C3 **Greater Manchester** County, Eng
25E2 **Great Exuma** I The Bahamas
8B2 **Great Falls** USA
44B3 **Great Glen** V Scot
86B1 **Great Himalayan Range** Mts Asia
11C4 **Great Inagua** I The Bahamas
100B4 **Great Karroo** Mts S Africa
109C4 **Great L** Aust
100A3 **Great Namaland** Region, Namibia
42C3 **Great Ormes Head** C Wales
11C4 **Great Ragged** I The Bahamas
99D3 **Great Ruaha** R Tanz
15D2 **Great Sacandaga** L USA
8B2 **Great Salt L** USA
95B2 **Great Sand Sea** Libya/Egypt
106B3 **Great Sandy Desert** Aust
8A2 **Great Sandy Desert** USA
Great Sandy I = Fraser I
4G3 **Great Slave L** Can
16C2 **Great South** B USA
106B3 **Great Victoria Desert** Aust
112C2 **Great Wall** Base Ant
72B2 **Great Wall** China
43E3 **Great Yarmouth** Eng
94B1 **Greco,C** Cyprus
55B3 **Greece**
Greece Republic, Europe
8C2 **Greeley** USA
6B1 **Greely Fjord** Can
14A1 **Green** B USA
14A2 **Green Bay** USA
14A3 **Greencastle** Indiana, USA
16C1 **Greenfield** Massachusetts, USA
14A2 **Greenfield** Wisconsin, USA
13F2 **Green Lake** Can
6F2 **Greenland** Dependency, N Atlantic O
102H1 **Greenland Basin** Greenland S
1B1 **Greenland S** Greenland
42B2 **Greenock** Scot
16C2 **Greenport** USA
16B3 **Greensboro** Maryland, USA
11C3 **Greensboro** N Carolina, USA
15C2 **Greensburg** Pennsylvania, USA
44B3 **Greenstone** Pt Scot
18C2 **Greenup** USA
17A1 **Greenville** Alabama, USA
97B4 **Greenville** Lib
19B3 **Greenville** Mississippi, USA
16D1 **Greenville** N Hampshire, USA
14B2 **Greenville** Ohio, USA
17B1 **Greenville** S Carolina, USA
19A3 **Greenville** Texas, USA
43E4 **Greenwich** Eng
16C2 **Greenwich** USA
16B3 **Greenwood** Delaware, USA
19B3 **Greenwood** Mississippi, USA
17B1 **Greenwood** S Carolina, USA
18B2 **Greers Ferry L** USA
108A1 **Gregory,L** Aust
107D2 **Gregory Range** Mts Aust
56C2 **Greifswald** Germany

64F3 Gremikha Russian Fed	71F2 Guam / Pacific O	58D1 Gulbene Latvia	109C2 Gwabegar Aust
56C1 Grenå Den	34C3 Guaminí Arg	87B1 Guledagudda India	85D3 Gwalior India
19C3 Grenada USA	77C5 Gua Musang Malay	80D3 Gulf,The S W Asia	100B3 Gwanda Zim
27E4 Grenada / Caribbean S	23A1 Guanajuato Mexico	78C4 Gulgong Aust	98C2 Gwane Zaire
109C2 Grenfell Aust	23A1 Guanajuato State, Mexico	73B4 Gulin China	82A3 Gwardar Pak
49D2 Grenoble France	32D2 Guanare Ven	12E2 Gulkana USA	45B1 Gweebarra B Irish Rep
27M2 Grenville Grenada	25D2 Guane Cuba	12E2 Gulkana R USA	89G9 Gwelo Zim
107D2 Grenville,C Aust	73C5 Guangdong Province, China	13E2 Gull L Can	43C4 Gwent County, Wales
81B1 Gresham USA	73A3 Guanghan China	53C3 Güllük Körfezi B Turk	100B2 Gweru Zim
78C4 Gresik Jawa, Indon	72C3 Guanghua China	99D2 Gulu Uganda	100C2 Gwydir R Aust
78A3 Gresik Sumatera, Indon	73A4 Guangmao Shan Mt China	73C5 Guluguba Aust	43C3 Gwynedd Wales
19B4 Gretna USA	73B5 Guangnan China	97C3 Gumel Nig	65F5 Gyandzha Azerbaijan
111B2 Grey R NZ	72B3 Guangyuan China	46D1 Gummersbach Germany	86B1 Gyangze China
12G2 Grey Hunter Pk Mt Can	73D4 Guangze China	86A2 Gumpla India	68B3 Gyaring Hu L China
27E4 Grey Is Can	73C5 Guangzhou China	93C1 Gümüshane Turk	64J2 Gydanskiy Poluostrov Pen Russian Fed
16C1 Greylock,Mt USA	35C1 Guanhães Brazil	85D4 Guna India	86B1 Gyirong China
111B2 Greymouth NZ	32D3 Guania R Colombia	99D1 Guna R India	6F3 Gyldenlues Greenland
107D3 Grey Range Mts Aust	27E5 Guanipa R Ven	109C3 Gundagai Aust	109D1 Gympie Aust
45C2 Greystones Irish Rep	26B2 Guantánamo Cuba	98B3 Gungu Zaire	59B3 Gyöngyös Hung
101H1 Greytown S Africa	72D3 Guanting Shuiku Res China	6H3 Gunnbjørn Fjeld Mt Greenland	59B3 Györ Hung
101H1 Griekwastad S Africa	73B5 Guanxi Province, China	109D2 Gunnedah Aust	
17B1 Griffin USA	73A3 Guan Xian China	87B1 Guntakal India	**H**
108C2 Griffith Aust	33E2 Guapa Colombia	17A1 Guntersville USA	38K6 Haapajärvi Fin
107D5 Grim,C Aust	32E6 Guapore R Brazil/Bol	17A1 Guntersville L USA	60B2 Haapsalu Estonia
15C2 Grimsby Can	30C2 Guaqui Bol	87C1 Güntür India	56A2 Haarlem Neth
42D3 Grimsby Eng	32A4 Guaranda Ecuador	77C5 Gunung Batu Putch Mt Malay	46D1 Haarstrang Region, Germany
13D1 Grimshaw Can	30K4 Guarapuava Brazil	78D3 Gunung Besar Mt Indon	25D2 Habana Cuba
39F7 Grimstad Nor	35B2 Guaratinguetá Brazil	78D2 Gunung Bulu Mt Indon	86C2 Habiganj Bang
47C1 Grindelwald Switz	50A1 Guarda Port	78A3 Gunung Gedang Mt Indon	74D4 Hachijō-jima / Japan
6A2 Grinnell Pen Can	35B1 Guarda Mor Brazil	77C6 Gunung Lawit Mt Malay	75B1 Hachiman Japan
6B2 Grise Fjord Can	9C4 Guasave Mexico	78C4 Gunung Lawu Mt Indon	74E2 Hachinohe Japan
61H1 Griva Russian Fed	47D2 Guastalla Italy	78D2 Gunung Menyapa Mt Indon	75B1 Hachiōji Japan
39J7 Grobina Latvia	25C3 Guatemala Guatemala	78D2 Gunung Niapa Mt Indon	16B2 Hackettstown USA
58C2 Grodno Belorussia	25C3 Guatemala Republic, Cent America	78A3 Gunung Patah Mt Indon	108A2 Hack,Mt Mt Aust
86A1 Gromati R India	34C3 Guatraché Arg	78C4 Gunung Raung Mt Indon	42C2 Haddington Scot
56B2 Groningen Neth	32C3 Guaviare R Colombia	78D3 Gunung Resag Mt Indon	108B1 Haddon Corner Aust
106C2 Groote Eylandt / Aust	35B2 Guaxupé Brazil	78D3 Gunung Sarempaka Mt Indon	108B1 Haddon Downs Aust
100A2 Grootfontein Namibia	27L1 Guayaguayare Trinidad	78C4 Gunung Sumbing Mt Indon	97D3 Hadejia Nig
100B3 Grootvloer Salt L S Africa	32A4 Guayaquil Ecuador	77C5 Gunung Tahan Mt Malay	97C3 Hadejia R Nig
27P2 Gros Islet St Lucia	24A2 Guaymas Mexico	78A2 Gunung Talakmau Mt Indon	94B2 Hadera Israel
46E1 Grosser Feldberg Mt Germany	34D2 Guayquiraro R Arg	100A2 Gunza Angola	56B1 Haderslev Den
52B2 Grosseto Italy	100B2 Guba Zaire	72D3 Guoyang China	81D4 Hadiboh Socotra
46E2 Gross-Gerau Germany	99E2 Guban Region Somalia	84C2 Gurdaspur India	4H2 Hadley B Can
57C3 Grossglockner Mt Austria	79B3 Gubat Phil	84D3 Gurgaon India	73B5 Hadong Vietnam
47E1 Gross Venediger Mt Austria	56C2 Gubin Pol	86A1 Gurkha Nepal	81C4 Hadramawt Region, Yemen
12C3 Grosvenor,L USA	87B2 Güdür India	92C2 Gürün Turk	56C1 Hadsund Den
22B2 Groveland USA	14B2 Guelpho Can	31B2 Gurupi R Brazil	74B3 Haeju N Korea
21A2 Grover City USA	26A2 Guenabacoa Cuba	100C2 Guruve Zim	91A4 Hafar al Bātin S Arabia
15D2 Groveton USA	98C1 Guéréda Chad	71J1 Gurvan Sayhan Uul Upland Mongolia	6D2 Haffners Bjerg Mt Greenland
61G5 Groznyy Russian Fed	48C2 Guéret France	61H4 Gur'yev Kazakhstan	84C2 Hafizabad Pak
58B2 Grudziadz Pol	48B2 Guernsey / UK	97C3 Gusau Nig	86C1 Häflong India
100A3 Grünau Namibia	23A2 Guerrero State, Mexico	58C2 Gusev Russian Fed	38A2 Hafnafjörður Iceland
44E2 Grutness Scot	99D2 Gughe Mt Eth	61F2 Gus'khrustalnyy Russian Fed	12B3 Hagemeister / USA
61F3 Gryazi Russian Fed	63E2 Gugigu China	12G3 Gustavus USA	56B2 Hagen Germany
61E2 Gryazovets Russian Fed	71F2 Guguan / Pacific O	22B2 Gustine USA	15C3 Hagerstown USA
29G8 Grytviken South Georgia	109C2 Guiargambone Aust	11B3 Guston USA	75A2 Hagi Japan
45A2 Gt Blasket / Irish Rep	73C4 Guidong China	56B2 Gütersloh Germany	73A5 Ha Giang Vietnam
35C2 Guaçui Brazil	97B4 Guiglo Ivory Coast	18C2 Guthrie Kentucky, USA	46D2 Hagondange France
23A1 Guadalajara Mexico	73C5 Gui Jiang R China	18A2 Guthrie Oklahoma, USA	45B2 Hags Hd C Irish Rep
50B1 Guadalajara Spain	43D4 Guildford Eng	23B1 Gutierrez Zamora Mexico	46D2 Haguenau France
107E1 Guadalcanal / Solomon Is	73C4 Guilin China	33F3 Guyana Republic, S America	96A2 Hagunia Well Mor
50B2 Guadalimar R Spain	47B2 Guillestre France	102F4 Guyana Basin Atlantic O	69C4 Haha-jima / Japan
51B1 Guadalope R Spain	72A2 Guinan China	72C1 Guyang China	68B3 Hah Xil Hu L China
50B2 Guadalqivir R Spain	97A3 Guinea Republic, Africa	48B3 Guyenne Region, France	74A2 Haicheng China
24B2 Guadalupe Mexico	102H4 Guinea Basin Atlantic O	9C3 Guymon USA	76D1 Hai Duong Viet
3G6 Guadalupe / Mexico	97A3 Guinea-Bissau Republic, Africa	72A2 Guyra Aust	94B2 Haifa Israel
27E3 Guadeloupe / Caribbean S	97A4 Guinea,G of W Africa	72B2 Guyuan China	94B2 Haifa,B of Israel
50B2 Guadian R Spain	26A2 Güines Cuba		72C5 Haikang China
50A2 Guadiana R Port	97B3 Guir Well Mali		76E1 Haikou China
50B2 Guadix Spain	84C1 Guiranwala Pak		80C3 Ha'il S Arabia
32D6 Guajará Mirim Brazil	38E1 Güiria Ven		86C2 Hailākāndi India
32C1 Guajira,Pen de Colombia	46B2 Guise France		63D3 Hailar China
32B4 Gualaceo Ecuador	79C3 Guiuan Phil		74B2 Hailong China
34D2 Gualeguay Arg	73B5 Gui Xian China		69E2 Hailun China
34D2 Gualeguaychú Arg	73B4 Guiyang China		38J5 Hailuoto / Fin
	73B4 Guizhou Province, China		76D2 Hainan / China
	85C4 Gujarat State, India		12G3 Haines USA
	84C2 Gujrat Pak		12G2 Haines Junction Can
	87B1 Gulbarga India		59B3 Hainfeld Austria
			73B5 Haiphong Vietnam
			26C3 Haiti Republic, Caribbean S
			99C3 Haiya Sudan
			72A2 Haiyan China
			72B2 Haiyuan China

72D3 Haizhou Wan *B* China
59C3 Hajdúböszörmény Hung
75B1 Hajiki-saki *Pt* Japan
86C2 Haka Burma
27C4 Hakalau Hawaiian Is
93D2 Hakkâri Turk
74E2 Hakodate Japan
Hakwa = Haka
75B1 Hakui Japan
75B1 Haku-san *Mt* Japan
92C2 Halab Syria
93E3 Halabja Iraq
95C2 Halaib Sudan
94C1 Halba Leb
68B2 Halban Mongolia
56C2 Halberstadt Germany
79B3 Halcon,Mt Phil
39G7 Halden Nor
86B2 Haldia India
84D3 Haldwāni India
13C1 Halfway *R* Can
7D5 Halifax Can
42D3 Halifax Eng
6D1 Hall Basin *Sd* Can
6B3 Hall Beach Can
46C1 Halle Belg
56C2 Halle Germany
112B1 Halley *Base* Ant
39F6 Hallingdal *R* Nor
6D3 Hall Pen Can
106B2 Hall's Creek Aust
71D3 Halmahera *I* Indon
39G7 Halmstad Sweden
56B2 Haltern Germany
38J5 Halti *Mt* Nor
42C2 Haltwhistle Eng
91B4 Halul *I* Qatar
94B3 Haluza *Hist Site* Israel
75A2 Hamada Japan
96C2 Hamada de Tinrhert *Desert Region* Alg
96B2 Hamada du Dra *Upland* Alg
90A3 Hamadān Iran
96B2 Hamada Tounassine *Region,* Alg
92C2 Hamāh Syria
75B2 Hamamatsu Japan
39G6 Hamar Nor
87C3 Hambantota Sri Lanka
19B3 Hamburg Arkansas, USA
18A1 Hamburg Iowa, USA
16B2 Hamburg Pennsylvania, USA
56B2 Hamburg Germany
16C2 Hamden USA
39J6 Hämeenlinna Fin
106A3 Hamersley Range *Mts* Aust
74B2 Hamgyong Sanmaek *Mts* N Korea
74B2 Hamhŭng N Korea
68D2 Hami China
94B1 Hamīdīyah Syria
108B3 Hamilton Aust
14C2 Hamilton Can
11C1 Hamilton NZ
14B3 Hamilton Ohio, USA
42B2 Hamilton Scot
22B2 Hamilton,Mt USA
38K6 Hamina Fin
86A1 Hamīrpur India
56B2 Hamm Germany
95A2 Hammādah al Hamra *Upland* Libya
38H6 Hammerdal Sweden
38J4 Hammerfest Nor
14A2 Hammond Illinois, USA
19B3 Hammond Louisiana, USA
18B3 Hammonton USA
111B3 Hampden NZ
43D4 Hampshire *County,* Eng
19B3 Hampton Arkansas, USA
91C4 Hāmūn-e Jaz Mūriān *L* Iran

84B3 Hamun-i-Lora *Salt L* Pak
21C4 Hana Hawaiian Is
21C4 Hanalei Hawaiian Is
74E3 Hanamaki Japan
72C2 Hancheng China
73C3 Hanchuan China
15C3 Hancock Maryland, USA
10B2 Hancock Michigan, USA
75B2 Handa Japan
72C2 Handan China
99D3 Handeni Tanz
72B2 Hanggin Qi China
39J7 Hangö Fin
73D3 Hangzhou China
73E3 Hangzhou Wan *B* China
76D1 Hanoi Viet
16A3 Hanover USA
29B6 Hanover *I* Chile
72B3 Han Shui China
73C3 Han Shui *R* China
85D3 Hānsi India
68C2 Hantay Mongolia
72B3 Hanzhong China
86B2 Hāora India
38J5 Haparanda Sweden
86C1 Hāpoli India
92C4 Haql S Arabia
91A5 Haradh S Arabia
99E2 Hara Fanna Eth
75C1 Haranochi Japan
101C2 Harare Zim
98C1 Harazé Chad
14E2 Harbor Beach USA
85D4 Harda India
39F6 Hardangerfjord *Inlet* Nor
46D2 Hardt *Region,* Germany
108A2 Hardwicke B Aust
18B2 Hardy Aust
99E2 Harer Eth
99E2 Hargeysa Somalia
94B2 Har Hakippa *Mt* Israel
68B3 Harhu *L* China
78A3 Hari *R* Indon
75A2 Harima-nada *B* Japan
56B2 Harlingen Neth
9D4 Harlingen USA
43E4 Harlow Eng
94B2 Har Meron *Mt* Israel
20C2 Harney Basin USA
20C2 Harney L USA
38H6 Härnösand Sweden
63B3 Har Nuur *L* Mongolia
97B4 Harper Lib
12F2 Harper,Mt USA
15C3 Harpers Ferry USA
94B3 Har Ramon *Mt* Israel
7C4 Harricanaw *R* Can
16B3 Harrington USA
7E4 Harrington Harbour Can
44A3 Harris *District* Scot
18C2 Harrisburg Illinois, USA
16A2 Harrisburg Pennsylvania, USA
101G1 Harrismith S Africa
18B2 Harrison Arkansas, USA
15C3 Harrisonburg USA
13C3 Harrison L Can
18B2 Harrisonville USA
44A3 Harris,Sound of *Chan* Scot
14B2 Harrisville USA
42D3 Harrogate Eng
94B3 Har Saggi *Mt* Israel
38H5 Harstad Nor
12G2 Hart *R* Can
39F6 Hårteigen *Mt* Nor

16C2 Hartford Connecticut, USA
14A2 Hartford Michigan, USA
38G6 Hårteigen *Mt* Nor
108A2 Hart,L Aust
43B4 Hartland Pt Eng
42D2 Hartlepool Eng
19A3 Hartshorne USA
17B1 Hartwell Res USA
101F1 Hartz *R* S Africa
68B2 Har Us Nuur *L* Mongolia
43E4 Harwich Eng
84D3 Haryāna State, India
94B3 Hāsā Jordan
94B2 Hāsbaiya Leb
75B2 Haselmere Eng
90A2 Hashtpar Iran
90A2 Hashtrūd Iran
56B2 Hassan India
56B2 Hasselt Belg
96C2 Hassi Inifel Alg
96B2 Hassi Mdakane *Well* Alg
96C1 Hassi Messaoud Alg
72C2 Hebi China
43E4 Hastings Eng
8D2 Hastings Nebraska, USA
110C1 Hastings NZ
12B1 Hatfield Aust
76D2 Ha Tinh Viet
108B2 Hattah Aust
16C3 Hatteras,C USA
19C3 Hattiesburg USA
16C3 Hatton USA
76B3 Hau Bon Viet
99E2 Haud Region, Eth
110C1 Hauhungaroa Range *Mts* NZ
13F1 Haultain *R* Can
110B1 Hauraki G NZ
111A3 Hauroko,L NZ
47C1 Hausstock *Mt* Switz
96B1 Haut Atlas *Mts* Mor
98C2 Haute Kotto *Region,* CAR
46C1 Hautes Fagnes *Mts* Belg
46B1 Hautmont Belg
96B1 Hauts Plateaux *Mts* Alg
90D3 Hauzdar Iran
18B1 Havana USA
Havana = Habana
87B3 Havankulam Sri Lanka
110C1 Havelock North NZ
43B4 Haverfordwest Wales
16D1 Haverhill USA
87B2 Hāveri India
16C2 Haverstraw USA
59B3 Havlíčkův Brod Czech Republic
8C2 Havre USA
16A3 Havre de Grace USA
7D4 Havre-St-Pierre Can
54C2 Havsa Turk
21C4 Hawaii *I* Hawaiian Is
21C4 Hawaii Volcanoes *Nat Pk* Hawaiian Is
111A2 Hawea,L NZ
110B1 Hawera NZ
42C2 Hawick Scot
111A2 Hawkdun Range *Mts* NZ
110C1 Hawke B NZ
108A2 Hawke,C Aust
76B1 Hawng Luk Burma
93D3 Hawr al Habbānīyah *L* Iraq
93E3 Hawr al Hammār *L* Iraq
21B2 Hawthorne USA
108B2 Hay Aust
5G3 Hay *R* Can
46D2 Hayange France
4B3 Haycock USA

7A4 Hayes *R* Can
6D2 Hayes Halvø *Regic* Greenland
12E2 Hayes,Mt USA
5G3 Hay River Can
18A2 Haysville USA
9A2 Hayward California, USA
86B2 Hazārībāg India
19B3 Hazelhurst USA
19B3 Hazelhurst USA
4G2 Hazel Str Can
5F4 Hazelton Can
13B1 Hazelton Mts Can
6C1 Hazen L Can
94B3 Hazeva Israel
16B2 Hazleton USA
22A1 Healdsburg USA
109C1 Healesville Aust
12E2 Healy USA
104B6 Heard I Indian O
19A3 Hearne USA
10B2 Hearst Can
72D2 Hebei Province, China
109C1 Hebel Aust
72C2 Hebi China
72C2 Hebian China
7D4 Hebron Can
94B3 Hebron Israel
18A1 Hebron Nebraska, USA
5E4 Hecate Str Can
12H3 Heceta I USA
73B5 Hechi China
4G2 Hecla and Griper B Can
111C2 Hector,Mt NZ
58C3 Hede Sweden
39H6 Hedemora Sweden
20C1 He Devil Mt USA
46C1 Heerlen Neth
Hefa = Haifa
72D3 Hefei China
73B4 Hefeng China
69F2 Hegang China
75B1 Hegura-jima *I* Japan
94B3 Heidan *R* Jordan
56B2 Heide Germany
101G1 Heidelberg Transvaal, S Africa
57B3 Heidelberg Germany
62E2 Heihe China
101G1 Heilbron S Africa
57B3 Heilbronn Germany
56C2 Heiligenstadt Germany
38K6 Heinola Fin
73B4 Hejiang China
6J3 Hekla *Mt* Iceland
76D1 Hekou Viet
73A5 Hekou Yaozou Zizhixian China
72B2 Helan China
72B2 Helan Shan *Mt* China
19B3 Helena Arkansas, USA
8C2 Helena Montana, USA
71E3 Helen Reef *I* Pacific O
44B3 Helensburgh Scot
91B4 Helleh *R* Iran
5J2 Hellin Spain
20C1 Hells Canyon *R* USA
46D1 Hellweg *Region,* Germany
56B2 Helmand *R* Afghan
100A3 Helmeringhausen Namibia
46C1 Helmond Neth
44C2 Helmsdale Scot
74B2 Helong China
39G7 Helsingborg Sweden
Helsingfors = Helsinki
56C1 Helsingør Den
38J6 Helsinki Fin
43B4 Helston Eng
43C4 Helvellyn *Mt* Eng
19A3 Hempstead USA
39H7 Hemse Sweden

72A3 Henan China
72C3 Henan Province, China
110B1 Hen and Chicken Is NZ
14A3 Henderson Kentucky, USA
9B3 Henderson Nevada, USA
19B3 Henderson Texas, USA
73E5 Heng-ch'un Taiwan
68B4 Hengduan Shan Mts China
56B2 Hengelo Neth
72D2 Hengshan China
76D1 Heng Xian China
73C4 Hengyang China
77A4 Henhoaha Nicobar Is
43D4 Henley-on-Thames Eng
16B3 Henlopen,C USA
7B4 Henrietta Maria,C Can
18A2 Henryetta USA
112C2 Henryk Arctowski Base Ant
6D3 Henry Kater Pen Can
68C2 Henryin Nuruu Mts Mongolia
76B2 Henzada Burma
73B5 Hepu China
8E2 Herat Afghan
5H4 Herbert Can
110C2 Herbertville Aust
46E1 Herborn Germany
26A4 Heredia Costa Rica
43C3 Hereford Eng
46C1 Hereford & Worcester County, Eng
46C1 Herentals Belg
47B1 Herford France
18A2 Herington USA
111A3 Heriot NZ
47C1 Herisau Switz
15D2 Herkimer USA
44E1 Herma Ness Pen Scot
109C2 Hermidale Aust
111B2 Hermon,Mt NZ
Hermon,Mt = Jebel ash Shaykh
24A2 Hermosillo Mexico
16A2 Herndon Pennsylvania, USA
22C2 Herndon California, USA
46D1 Herne Germany
56B1 Herning Den
90A2 Herowābād Iran
50A2 Herrera del Duque Spain
16A2 Hershey USA
43D4 Hertford County, Eng
94B2 Herzliyya Israel
46C1 Hesbaye Region, Belg
46B1 Hesdin France
72B2 Heshui China
22D3 Hesperia USA
12H2 Hess R Can
57B2 Hessen State, Germany
22C2 Hetch Hetchy Res USA
42C2 Hexham Eng
73C5 He Xian China
73C5 Heyuan China
108B3 Heywood Aust
72D2 Heze China
17B2 Hialeah USA
110C1 Hicks Bay NZ
109C3 Hicks,Pt Aust
23B1 Hidalgo State, Mexico
24B2 Hidalgo del Parral Mexico
35B1 Hidrolândia Brazil
96A2 Hierro I Canary Is
74E1 Higashine Japan
75C1 Higashi-suidō Str Japan
20B2 High Desert USA

19B4 High Island USA
44B3 Highland Region, Scot
22D3 Highland USA
22C1 Highland Peak Mt USA
16B2 Highlands Falls USA
11B3 High Point USA
13D1 High Prairie Can
5G4 High River Can
17B2 High Springs USA
16B2 Highstown USA
43D4 High Wycombe Eng
39J7 Hiiumaa I Estonia
80B3 Hijaz Region, S Arabia
75B2 Hikigawa Japan
75B1 Hikone Japan
110B1 Hikurangi NZ
9C4 Hidalgo del Parral Mexico
56B2 Hildesheim Germany
27B3 Hillaby,Mt Barbados
56C1 Hillerød Den
14B3 Hillsboro Ohio, USA
20B1 Hillsboro Oregon, USA
19A3 Hillsboro Texas, USA
108C2 Hillston Aust
44E1 Hillswick Scot
21C4 Hilo Hawaiian Is
93C2 Hilvan Turk
56B2 Hilversum Neth
84D2 Himachal Pradesh State, India
82B3 Himalaya Mts Asia
85C4 Himatnagar India
74C4 Himeji Japan
74D3 Himi Japan
92C3 Hims Syria
12E2 Hinchinbrook Entrance USA
12E2 Hinchinbrook I USA
85D3 Hindaun India
84B1 Hindu Kush Mts Afghan
87B2 Hindupur India
13D1 Hines Creek Can
85D4 Hinganghāt India
69E2 Hinggan Ling Upland China
85B3 Hingol R Pak
85D5 Hingoli India
38H5 Hinneya I Nor
16C1 Hinsdale USA
13D2 Hinton Can
34B2 Hipolito Itrogoyen Arg
86A2 Hirakud Res India
92B2 Hirfanli Baraji Res Turk
87B2 Hirihar India
74E2 Hiroaki Japan
74C4 Hiroshima Japan
46C2 Hirson France
54C2 Hirşova Rom
56B1 Hirtshals Den
84D3 Hisar India
26C3 Hispaniola / Caribbean S
94C1 Hisyah Syria
93D3 Hit Iraq
74E3 Hitachi Japan
75C1 Hitachi-Ōta Japan
43D4 Hitchin Eng
38F6 Hitra / Nor
75A2 Hiuchi-nada B Japan
75A2 Hiwasa Japan
56B1 Hjørring Den
76B1 Hka R Burma
97C4 Ho Ghana
76D1 Hoa Binh Viet
76D3 Hoa Da Viet
109C4 Hobart Aust
56B1 Hobro Den
20C3 Hobson L Can
99E2 Hobyo Somalia
76D3 Ho Chi Minh Viet
57C3 Hochkönig Mt Austria
54B1 Hódmező'hely Hung
59B3 Hodonín Czech Republic

74B2 Hoeryong N Korea
57C2 Hof Germany
38B2 Hofsjökull Mts Iceland
74C4 Höfu Japan
96C2 Hoggar Upland Alg
46D1 Hohe Acht Mt Germany
72C1 Hohhot China
6J3 Höhn Iceland
68B3 Hoh Sai Hu L China
82C2 Hoh Xil Shan Mts China
99D2 Hoima Uganda
86C1 Hojāi India
75A2 Hojo Japan
110B1 Hokianga Harbour B NZ
112B2 Hokitika NZ
74E2 Hokkaidō Japan
90C2 Hokmābād Iran
98B3 Holbrook Aust
19A2 Holdenville USA
87B2 Hole Narsipur India
27B3 Holetown Barbados
26B2 Holguín Cuba
111B2 Holitika NZ
12C2 Holitna R USA
59B3 Hollabrunn Austria
14A2 Holland USA
22B2 Hollister USA
19C3 Holly Springs USA
22C3 Hollywood California, USA
17B2 Hollywood Florida, USA
4G2 Holman Island Can
38J6 Holmsund Sweden
94B2 Holon Israel
56B1 Holstebro Den
6E3 Holsteinborg Greenland
14B2 Holt USA
18A2 Holton USA
12C2 Holy Cross USA
42B3 Holyhead Wales
42D2 Holy I Eng
43B3 Holy I Wales
16C1 Holyoke Massachusetts, USA
82C2 Homalin Burma
6D3 Home B Can
12D3 Homer Alaska, USA
19B3 Homer Louisiana, USA
111A2 Homer Tunnel NZ
17B1 Homerville USA
17B2 Homestead USA
17A1 Homewood USA
87B1 Homnābād India
101C3 Homoine Mozam
25D3 Hondo R Mexico
25D3 Honduras Republic, Cent America
25D3 Honduras,G of Honduras
39G6 Hønefoss Nor
15C2 Honesdale USA
21A1 Honey L USA
76C1 Hong R Viet
76D1 Hon Gai Viet
73A4 Honggou China
73C4 Hong Hu L China
72B2 Honghui China
73C4 Hongjiang China
73C5 Hong Kong Colony, S E Asia
68D2 Hongor Mongolia
73B5 Hongshui He R China
72A3 Hongyuan China
72D3 Hongze Hu L China
107E1 Honiara Solomon Is
76C1 Hon Khoai / Camb
76D3 Hon Lan / Viet
38K4 Honnigsvåg Nor
21C4 Honolulu Hawaiian Is
77C4 Hon Panjang / Viet
74D3 Honshū I Japan
20B1 Hood,Mt USA
20B1 Hood River USA
45C2 Hook Head C Irish Rep
12G3 Hoonah USA

12A2 Hooper Bay USA
101G1 Hoopstad S Africa
56A2 Hoorn Neth
9B3 Hoover Dam USA
12E2 Hope Alaska, USA
19B3 Hope Arkansas, USA
13C3 Hope Can
7D4 Hopedale Can
64D2 Hopen / Barents S
6D3 Hopes Advance,C Can
108B3 Hopetoun Aust
100B3 Hopetown S Africa
18C2 Hopkinsville USA
20B1 Hoquiam USA
92C2 Horasan Turk
99F1 Hordiyo Somalia
47C1 Horgen Switz
105H5 Horizon Depth Pacific O
91C4 Hormuz,Str of Oman/ Iran
59B3 Horn Austria
6H3 Horn C Iceland
38H5 Hornavan L Sweden
19B3 Hornbeck USA
20B2 Hornbrook USA
111B2 Hornby NZ
7B5 Hornepayne Can
4F3 Horn Mts Can
42D3 Hornsea Eng
72B1 Horn Uul Mt Mongolia
30E3 Horqueta Par
15C2 Horseheads USA
56C1 Horsens Den
20B1 Horseshoe Bay Can
108B3 Horsham Aust
43D4 Horsham Eng
39G7 Horten Nor
4F3 Horton R Can
78C2 Hose Mts Malay
85D4 Hoshangābād India
84D2 Hoshiārpur India
87B1 Hospet India
29C7 Hoste / Chile
82B2 Hotan China
19B3 Hot Springs Arkansas, USA
4G3 Hot Springs S. Dakota, USA
4G3 Hottah L Can
72C2 Houdan France
72C2 Houma China
19B4 Houma USA
16C2 Housatonic R USA
13B2 Houston Can
18B2 Houston Mississippi, USA
19A4 Houston Texas, USA
106A3 Houtman Is Aust
68B2 Hövd Mongolia
68C1 Hövsgöl Nuur L Mongolia
14A2 Howard City USA
12C1 Howard P USA
109C3 Howe,C Aust
101H1 Howick S Africa
44C2 Hoy / Scot
39F6 Høyanger Nor
59B2 Hradec-Králové Czech Republic
59B3 Hranice Czech Republic
59B3 Hron R Slovakia
73E5 Hsin-chu Taiwan
73E5 Hsüeh Shan Mt Taiwan
72B2 Huachi China
32B6 Huacho Peru
72C1 Huade China
72D3 Huaibei China
72D3 Huai He R China
73C4 Huaihua China
72D3 Huainan China
69E4 Hua-lien Taiwan
32B5 Huallaga R Peru
32B5 Huallanca Peru
32B5 Huamachuco Peru
100A2 Huambo Angola
30C2 Huanay Bol
32B5 Huancabamba Peru
32B6 Huancavelica Peru

32B6 **Huancayo** Peru
73D3 **Huangchuan** China
 Huang Hai = Yellow S
72D2 **Huang He** R China
72B2 **Huangling** China
76D2 **Huangliu** China
72D2 **Huangni** China
73C3 **Huangshi** China
73D4 **Huangshan** China
73D3 **Huangshi** China
34C3 **Huanguelén** Arg
33E4 **Huangyan** China
74B2 **Huanren** China
32B5 **Huánuco** Peru
30C2 **Huanuni** Bol
73B4 **Huan Xian** China
32B5 **Huaráz** Peru
32B6 **Huarmey** Peru
32B5 **Huascarán** Mt Peru
30B4 **Huasco** Chile
23B2 **Huatusco** Mexico
23B1 **Huauchinango** Mexico

23B2 **Huautla** Mexico
72C2 **Hua Xian** China
24B2 **Huayapan** R Mexico
73C3 **Hubei** Province, China
87B1 **Hubli** India
34C3 **Hucal** Arg
74B2 **Huch'ang** N Korea
42D3 **Huddersfield** Eng
39H6 **Hudiksvall** Sweden
17B2 **Hudson** Florida, USA

14B2 **Hudson** Michigan, USA

16C1 **Hudson** New York, USA

16C1 **Hudson** R USA
7B4 **Hudson B** Can
5H4 **Hudson Bay** Can
13C1 **Hudson's Hope** Can
6C3 **Hudson Str** Can
76D2 **Hue** Viet
23B1 **Huejutla** Mexico
23A2 **Huelva** Spain
51B2 **Huércal Overa** Spain
51B1 **Huesca** Spain
23B2 **Huexotla** Hist Site Mexico
107D3 **Hughenden** Aust
12D1 **Hughes** USA
86B2 **Hugli** R India
53D4 **Hugo** USA
73D4 **Hui'an** China
110C1 **Huiarau Range** Mts NZ
74B2 **Huich'ŏn** N Korea
74B2 **Huifa He** R China
32B3 **Huila** Mt Colombia
73D5 **Huilai** China
73A4 **Huili** China
73A4 **Huinan** China
34C2 **Huinca Renancó** Arg
25C3 **Huixtla** Mexico
73A4 **Huize** China
73C5 **Huizhou** China
23B2 **Hujupapan de Léon** Mexico
69F2 **Hulin** China
15C1 **Hull** Can
42D3 **Hull** Eng
54B1 **Hultsfred** Sweden
63D3 **Hulun Nur** L China
69E1 **Huma** China
73B4 **Humaitá** Brazil
100B4 **Humansdorp** S Africa
42D3 **Humber** R Eng
42D3 **Humberside** County, Eng
5H4 **Humboldt** Can
20C2 **Humboldt** R USA
20B2 **Humboldt B** USA
6D2 **Humboldt Gletscher** Gl Greenland
21B2 **Humboldt L** USA
108C1 **Humeburn** Aust
109C3 **Hume,L** Aust
100A2 **Humpata** Angola
22C2 **Humphreys** USA
38A1 **Húnaflói** B Iceland
73C4 **Hunan** Province, China
74C2 **Hunchun** China

13C2 **Hundred Mile House** Can
54B1 **Hunedoara** Rom
59B3 **Hungary** Republic, Europe
108B1 **Hungerford** Aust
74B3 **Hüngnam** N Korea
74B2 **Hunjiang** China
46D2 **Hunsrück** Mts, Germany
109D2 **Hunter** R Aust
13B2 **Hunter I** Can
109C4 **Hunter Is** Aust
12D2 **Hunter,Mt** USA
14A3 **Huntingburg** USA
43D3 **Huntingdon** Eng
14A2 **Huntington** Indiana, USA
14B3 **Huntington** W Virginia, USA
22C4 **Huntington Beach** USA

22C2 **Huntington L** USA
110C1 **Huntly** NZ
44C3 **Huntly** Scot
12J2 **Hunt,Mt** Can
108A1 **Hunt Pen** Aust
17A1 **Huntsville** Alabama, USA

15C1 **Huntsville** Can
19A3 **Huntsville** Texas, USA

76D2 **Huong Khe** Viet
71F4 **Huon Peninsula** Pen PNG
109C4 **Huonville** Anst
14B1 **Hurd,C** Can
80B3 **Hurghada** Egypt
8D2 **Huron** S. Dakota, USA

14B1 **Huron,L** Can/USA
34A2 **Hurtado** Chile
111B2 **Hurunui** R NZ
54C1 **Huşi** Rom
39G7 **Huskvarna** Sweden
12C1 **Huslia** USA
94B2 **Huşn** Jordan
56B2 **Husum** Germany
109C1 **Hutton,Mt** Aust
72D2 **Hutuo He** R China
46C1 **Huy** Belg
72A2 **Huzhu** China
52C2 **Hvar** I Croatia
100B2 **Hwange** Zim
100B2 **Hwange Nat Pk** Zim
15D2 **Hyannis** USA
5E4 **Hydaburg** Can
16C2 **Hyde Park** USA
87B1 **Hyderābad** India
85B3 **Hyderābad** Pak
49D3 **Hyères** France
12J2 **Hyland** R Can
8B2 **Hyndman Peak** Mt USA
38K6 **Hyrynsalmi** Fin
13D1 **Hythe** Can
74C4 **Hyūga** Japan
39J6 **Hyvikää** Fin

I

31C4 **Iaçu** Brazil
54C2 **Ialomiţa** R Rom
54C1 **Iaşi** Rom
97C4 **Ibadan** Nig
32B3 **Ibagué** Colombia
54B2 **Ibar** R Montenegro/ Serbia, Yugos
32B3 **Ibarra** Ecuador
35B1 **Ibiá** Brazil
30E4 **Ibicuí** R Brazil
34D2 **Ibicuy** Arg
51C2 **Ibiza** Spain
51C2 **Ibiza** I Spain
100D2 **Ibo** Mozam
31C4 **Ibotirama** Brazil
91C5 **'Ibrī** Oman
32B6 **Ica** Peru
32D4 **Icá** R Brazil
32D3 **Içana** Brazil
38A1 **Iceland** Republic, N Atlantic O
13C2 **Ice Box** Can

87A1 **Ichalkaranji** India
74E3 **Ichihara** Japan
75B1 **Ichinomiya** Japan
74E3 **Ichinoseki** Japan
12F3 **Icy B** USA
4B2 **Icy C** USA
19B3 **Idabell** USA
8B2 **Idaho Falls** USA
20B2 **Idanha** USA
46D2 **Idar Oberstein** Germany
95A2 **Idehan Marzūg** Desert Libya
95A2 **Idehan Ubari** Desert Libya
96B2 **Idelès** Alg
68B2 **Iderlym Gol** R Mongolia
95C2 **Idfu** Egypt
55B3 **Idhi Oros** Mt Greece
55B3 **Idhra** I Greece
98B3 **Idiofa** Zaire
12C2 **Iditarod** R USA
92C2 **Idlib** Syria
39K7 **Idritsa** Russian Fed
100B4 **Idutywa** S Africa
55C3 **Ierápetra** Greece
46B1 **Ieper** Belg
63D2 **Iet Oktyobr'ya** Russian Fed
99D3 **Ifakara** Tanz
71F3 **Ifalik** I Pacific O
101D3 **Ifanadiana** Madag
97C4 **Ife** Nig
96C3 **Ifērouane** Niger
78C2 **Igan** Malay
35B2 **Igarapana** Brazil
93E2 **Igdir** Iran
39H6 **Iggesund** Sweden
34B2 **Iglesia** Arg
53A3 **Iglesias** Sardegna
6B3 **Igloolik** Can
10A2 **Ignace** Can
55B3 **Igoumenitsa** Greece
61H2 **Igra** Russian Fed
23B2 **Iguala** Mexico
35B2 **Iguape** Brazil
35B2 **Iguatama** Brazil
31D3 **Iguatu** Brazil
98A3 **Iguéla** Gabon
101D3 **Ihosy** Madag
74D3 **Iida** Japan
75B1 **Iide-san** Mt Japan
38K6 **Iisalmi** Fin
75A2 **Iizuka** Japan
97C4 **Ijebu Ode** Nig
56B2 **Ijsselmeer** S Neth
55C3 **Ikaria** I Greece
74E2 **Ikeda** Japan
98C3 **Ikela** Zaire
54B2 **Ikhtiman** Bulg
12D3 **Ikolik,C** USA
101D2 **Ikopa** R Madag
79B2 **Ilagan** Phil
90A3 **Īlām** Iran
47C1 **Ilanz** Switz
13F1 **Île a la Crosse** Can
13F1 **Île a la Crosse,L** Can
89G8 **Ilebo** Zaire
96D1 **Île de Jerba** I Tunisia
48B2 **Île de Noirmoutier** I France
48B2 **Île de Ré** I France
107F3 **Île des Pins** I Nouvelle Calédonie
48A2 **Île d'Ouessant** I France
48B2 **Île d'Yeu** I France
61J3 **Ilek** R Russian Fed
107F2 **Îles Bélep** Nouvelle Calédonie
107E2 **Îles Chesterfield** Nouvelle Calédonie
49D3 **Îles d'Hyères** Is France
43B4 **Ilfracombe** Eng
92B1 **Ilgaz Daglari** Mts Turk
101C3 **Ilha Bazaruto** I Mozam
33G3 **Ilha De Maracá** I Brazil
33G4 **Ilha de Marajó** I Brazil

35B2 **Ilha de São Sebastião** I Brazil
33G6 **Ilha do Bananal** Region Brazil
35C2 **Ilha Grande** I Brazil
35B2 **Ilha Santo Amaro** I Brazil
96A1 **Ilhas Selvagens** I Atlantic O
35A2 **Ilha Solteira Dam** Brazil
31D4 **Ilhéus** Brazil
12C3 **Iliamna L** USA
12C3 **Iliamna V** USA
79B4 **Iligan** Phil
63C2 **Ilim** R Russian Fed
63C2 **Ilim** Russian Fed
63G3 **Il'inskiy** Russian Fed
79B4 **Illana B** Phil
34A2 **Illapel** Chile
34A2 **Illapel** R Chile
97C3 **Illéla** Niger
47C1 **Iller** R Germany
4C4 **Illiamna L** USA
10A2 **Illinois** State, USA
18B2 **Illinois** R USA
96C2 **Illizi** Alg
30B2 **Ilo** Peru
79B3 **Iloilo** Phil
38L6 **Ilomantsi** Fin
97C4 **Ilorin** Nig
75A2 **Imabari** Japan
75B1 **Imaichi** Japan
60C1 **Imatra** Fin
30C4 **Imbituba** Brazil
99E2 **Imi** Eth
20C2 **Imlay** USA
47D1 **Immenstadt** Germany
52B2 **Imola** Italy
31B3 **Imperatriz** Brazil
52A2 **Imperia** Italy
98B2 **Impfondo** Congo
86C2 **Imphal** India
47D1 **Imst** Austria
12B1 **Imuruk L** USA
75B1 **Ina** Japan
96C2 **In Afahleleh** Well Alg
75B2 **Inamba-jima** I Japan
96C2 **In Amenas** Alg
38K5 **Inari** Fin
38K5 **Inarijärvi** L Fin
75C1 **Inawashiro-ko** L Japan
96C2 **In Belbel** Alg
60E5 **Ince Burun** Pt Turk
92B2 **Incekum Burun** Pt Turk
74B3 **Inch'ŏn** S Korea
96B2 **In Dagouber** Well Mali
35B1 **Indaia** R Brazil
38H6 **Indals** R Sweden
21B2 **Independence** California, USA
18A2 **Independence** Kansas, USA
18B2 **Independence** Missouri, USA
78A3 **Inderagiri** R Indon
61H4 **Inderborskiy** Kazakhstan
83B3 **India** Federal Republic, Asia
14D2 **Indiana** State, USA
15C2 **Indiana** USA
104C6 **Indian-Antarctic Ridge** Indian O
14A3 **Indianapolis** USA
 Indian Desert = Thar Desert
7E4 **Indian Harbour** Can
104B4 **Indian O**
18B1 **Indianola** Iowa, USA
19B3 **Indianola** Mississippi, USA
35B1 **Indianópolis** Brazil
76D2 **Indo China** Region, S E Asia
70C4 **Indonesia** Republic, S E Asia
85D4 **Indore** India
78B4 **Indramayu** Indon
48C2 **Indre** R France

85B3 Indus *R* Pak
60D5 Inebdu Turk
96C2 In Ebeggi *Well* Alg
96C2 In Ecker Alg
92A1 Inegöl Turk
96D2 In Ezzane Alg
97C3 Ingal Niger
14B2 Ingersoll Can
107D2 Ingham Aust
6D2 Inglefield Land *Region* Can
110B1 Inglewood NZ
109D1 Inglewood Queensland, Aust
22C4 Inglewood USA
108B3 Inglewood Victoria, Aust
38B2 Ingólfshöfbi *I* Iceland
57C3 Ingolstadt Germany
86B2 Ingrāj Bāzār India
96C3 In-Guezzam *Well* Alg
101C3 Inhambane Mozam
101C3 Inharrime Mozam
35B1 Inhumas Brazil
32D3 Inírida *R* Colombia
45A2 Inishbofin *I* Irish Rep
45A1 Inishkea *I* Irish Rep
45B2 Inishmaan *I* Irish Rep
45B2 Inishmore *I* Irish Rep
45B1 Inishmurray *I* Irish Rep
45C1 Inishowen District, Irish Rep
45A2 Inishshark *I* Irish Rep
45A2 Inishturk *I* Irish Rep
109C1 Injune Aust
12H3 Inklin Can
12H3 Inklin *R* Can
47D1 Inn *R* Austria
10881 Innamincka Aust
68C2 Inner Mongolia Autonomous Region, China
107D2 Innisfail Aust
12C2 Innoko *R* USA
57C3 Innsbruck Austria
33F3 Inongo Zaire
58B2 Inowrocław Pol
96C2 In Salah Alg
47B1 Interlaken Switz
24C3 Intexpec Mexico
47C2 Intra Italy
78D3 Intu Indon
75C1 Inubo-saki *C* Japan
7C4 Inukjuak Can
4E3 Inuvik Can
4F3 Inuvik *Region* Can
44B3 Inveraray Scot
111A3 Invercargill NZ
109D1 Inverell Aust
13D2 Invermere Can
44C3 Inverness Scot
44C3 Inverurie Scot
108A3 Investigator Str Aust
68A1 Inya Russian Fed
2182 Inyokern USA
9983 Inzia *R* Zaire
55B3 Ioánnina Greece
15A3 Iola USA
44A3 Iona *I* Scot
100A2 Iôna Nat Pk Angola
20C1 Ione USA
Ionian Is = Ionioi Nisoi
55A3 Ionian S Italy/Greece
55B3 Ionioi Nisoi *Is* Greece
55C3 Ios *I* Greece
10A2 Iowa *R* USA
10A2 Iowa City USA
35B1 Ipameri Brazil
35C1 Ipanema Brazil
81F4 Ipatovo Russian Fed
32B3 Ipiales Colombia
77C5 Ipoh Malay
30F2 Iporá Brazil
55C2 Ipsala Turk
109D1 Ipswich Aust
43E3 Ipswich Eng
16D1 Ipswich USA
32D4 Iquique Chile
32C4 Iquitos Peru
55C3 Iráklion Greece

80D2 Iran Republic, S W Asia
91D4 Iranshahr Iran
23A1 Irapuato Mexico
93D3 Iraq Republic, S W Asia
95A2 Ia Wan *Watercourse* Libya
94B2 Irbid Jordan
61K2 Irbit Russian Fed
36C3 Ireland Republic, NW Europe
33F3 Ireng *R* Guyana
74B3 Iri S Korea
71E4 Irian Jaya Province, Indon
95B3 Iriba Chad
79B3 Iriga Phil
99D3 Iringa Tanz
69E4 Iriomote *I* Japan
33G5 Iriri *R* Brazil
42B3 Irish S Eng/Irish Rep
12D1 Irkillik *R* USA
63C2 Irkutsk Russian Fed
65J4 Irtysh *R* Kazakhstan
108A2 Iron Knob Aust
14A1 Iron Mountain USA
107D2 Iron Range Aust
14A1 Iron River USA
14A1 Irontown USA
10A2 Ironwood USA
10B2 Iroquois Falls Can
75B2 Iro-zaki *C* Japan
76A2 Irrawaddy,Mouths of the Burma
65H4 Irtysh *R* Russian Fed
51B1 Irun Spain
42B2 Irvine Scot
19A3 Irving USA
79B4 Isabela Phil
32J7 Isabela *I* Ecuador
4H2 Isachsen Can
4H2 Isachsen,C Can
6H3 Isafjörður Iceland
74C4 Isahaya Japan
98C2 Isangi Zaire
47D1 Isar *R* Germany
44E1 Isbister Scot
47D1 Ischgl Austria
53B2 Ischia *I* Italy
75B2 Ise Japan
47D2 Iseo Italy
46D1 Iserlohn Germany
53B2 Isernia Italy
75C1 Ise-wan *B* Japan
69E4 Ishigaki *I* Japan
74E2 Ishikari *R* Japan
74E2 Ishikari-wan *B* Japan
65H4 Ishim Russian Fed
65H4 Ishim *R* Kazakhstan
74E3 Ishinomaki Japan
75C1 Ishioka Japan
84C1 Ishkashim Afghan
14A1 Ishpeming USA
65J4 Isil'kul' Russian Fed
99D2 Isiolo Kenya
98C2 Isiro Zaire
92C2 Iskenderun Turk
92C2 Iskenderun Körfezi *B* Turk
92B1 Iskilip Turk
65K4 Iskitim Russian Fed
54B2 Iskur *R* Bulg
12H3 Iskut *R* Can/USA
23B2 Isla Mexico
34C3 Isla Bermejo *I* Arg
27E4 Isla Blanquilla Ven
32A2 Isla Coiba *I* Panama
9B4 Isla de Cedros *I* Mexico
29B4 Isla de Chiloé *I* Chile
25D2 Isla de Cozumel *I* Mexico
26C3 Isla de la Gonâve Cuba
26A2 Isla de la Juventud *I* Cuba
34D2 Isla de las Lechiguanas *I* Arg
3K8 Isla del Coco *I* Costa Rica
25D3 Isla del Maíz *I* Caribbean S

23B1 Isla de Lobos *I* Mexico
29D6 Isla de los Estados *I* Arg
28E2 Isla de Marajó *I* Brazil
105L5 Isla de Pascua *I* Pacific O
26A4 Isla de Providencia *I* Caribbean S
26A4 Isla de San Andres *I* Caribbean S
30G4 Isla de Santa Catarina *I* Brazil
33G2 Isla du Diable *I* French Guiana
31E2 Isla Fernando de Noronha *I* Brazil
29C6 Isla Grande de Tierra del Fuego *I* Chile
27D4 Isla la Tortuga *I* Ven
84C2 Islamabad Pak
24A2 Isla Magdalena *I* Mexico
27E4 Isla Margarita Ven
34A3 Isla Mocha Chile
17B2 Islamorada USA
10A1 Island L Can
10A2 Island Lg Aust
110B1 Islands,B of NZ
32A4 Isla Puná *I* Ecuador
103D6 Isla San Ambrosia *I* Pacific O
105D6 Isla San Felix *I* Pacific O
24A2 Isla Santa Margarita *I* Mexico
34A3 Isla Santa Maria *I* Chile
51C2 Islas Baleares *Is* Spain
96A2 Islas Canarias *Is* Atlantic O
51C2 Islas Columbretes *Is* Spain
25D3 Islas de la Bahía *Is* Honduras
26A4 Islas del Maíz *Is* Caribbean S
33E1 Islas de Margarita *I* Ven
29C7 Islas Diego Ramirez *Is* Chile
32J7 Islas Galapagos *Is* Pacific O
30H6 Islas Juan Fernández *Is* Chile
32D1 Islas los Roques *Is* Ven
Islas Malvinas = Falkland Is
105L3 Islas Revilla Gigedo *Is* Pacific O
29C7 Islas Wollaston *Is* Chile
99B3 Isla Tidra *I* Maur
29B5 Isla Wellington *I* Chile
48C2 Isle *R* France
104B5 Isle Amsterdam *I*
43D4 Isle of Wight *I* Eng
10B2 Isle Royale *I* USA
104B5 Isle St Paul *I* Indian O
104A6 Isles Crozet *I* Indian O
105J4 Isles de la Société *Is* Pacific O
105K5 Isles Gambier *Is* Pacific O
101D2 Isles Glorieuses *Is* Madag
101D3 Isles Kerguelen *Is* Indian O
105K4 Isles Marquises *Is* Pacific O
105J4 Isles Tuamotu *Is* Pacific O
105J5 Isles Tubai *Is* Pacific O
22B1 Isleton USA
92B3 Ismâ'ilîya Egypt
101D3 Isoanala Madag
101C2 Isoka Zambia

53B3 Isola Egadi *I* Italy
52B2 Isola Ponziane *I* Italy
53B3 Isole Lipari *Is* Italy
52C2 Isoles Tremiti *Is* Italy
75B1 Isosaki Japan
92B2 Isparta Turk
94B2 Israel Republic, S W Asia
51C2 Isser *R* Alg
48C2 Issoire France
49C2 Issoudun France
92A1 Istanbul Turk
55B3 Istiáia Greece
25C3 Istmo de Tehuantepec *Isthmus* Mexico
17B2 Istokpoga,L USA
52B1 Istra *Pen* Croatia
35C1 Itaberai Brazil
35C2 Itabirito Brazil
31D4 Itabuna Brazil
33E4 Itacoatiara Brazil
32B2 Itagui Colombia
33F4 Itaituba Brazil
30G4 Itajaí Brazil
35C2 Itajuba Brazil
52 Italy Republic, Europe
35D1 Itamaraju Brazil
35D1 Itamarandiba Brazil
35C1 Itambacuri Brazil
35C1 Itambé *Mt* Brazil
86C1 Itánagar India
35B2 Itanhaém Brazil
35C1 Itanhém Brazil
35C1 Itanhém *R* Brazil
35B2 Itapecerica Brazil
35C2 Itaperuna Brazil
31C5 Itapetinga Brazil
35B2 Itapetininga Brazil
35B2 Itapeva Brazil
31D2 Itapipoca Brazil
35B1 Itapuranga Brazil
30E4 Itaqui Brazil
35C1 Itarantim Brazil
35C2 Itararé *R* Brazil
35C2 Itaúna Brazil
35B2 Itbayat *I* Brazil/Bol
15C2 Ithaca USA
98C2 Itimbiri *R* Zaire
35C1 Itinga Brazil
66E3 Itivdleq Greenland
75B2 Ito Japan
74D3 Itoigawa Japan
33G6 Itonomas *R* Bol
35B2 Itu Brazil
35A1 Iturama Brazil
30C3 Iturbe Arg
35B1 Iturutaba Brazil
56B2 Itzehoe Germany
58D2 Ivacevichi Belorussia
35A2 Ivai *R* Brazil
38K5 Ivalo Fin
54A2 Ivangrad Montenegro, Yugos
108B2 Ivanhoe Aust
59C3 Ivano-Frankovsk Ukraine
61F2 Ivanovo Russian Fed
65H3 Ivdel' Russian Fed
98B2 Ivindo *R* Gabon
101D3 Ivohibe Madag
101D2 Ivongo Soanierana Madag
97B4 Ivory Coast Republic, Africa
52A1 Ivrea Italy
6C3 Ivujivik Can
74E3 Iwaki Japan
74C4 Iwakuni Japan
74E2 Iwanai Japan
97C4 Iwo Nig
69G4 Iwo Jima *I* Japan
23B1 Ixmiguilpa Mexico
23A2 Ixtapa Mexico
23A1 Ixtlán Mexico
75A2 Iyo-nada *B* Japan
65G4 Izhevsk Russian Fed
64G3 Izhma Russian Fed
91C5 Izki Oman
60C4 Izmail Ukraine

92A2	İzmir Turk
55C3	İzmir Körfezi *B* Turk
92A1	İzmit Turk
92A1	İznik Turk
55C2	İznik Gölü *L* Turk
94C2	Izra' Syria
23B2	Izúcar de Matamoros Mexico
75B2	Izumi-sano Japan
75A1	Izumo Japan
74D4	Izu-shotō *Is* Japan

J

95B1	Jabal al Akhdar *Mts* Libya
94C2	Jabal al 'Arab Syria
95A2	Jabal as Sawdā *Mts* Libya
91B5	Jabal az Zannah UAE
94C1	Jabal Halimah *Mt* Leb/Syria
83B3	Jabalpur India
59B2	Jablonec nad Nisou Czech Republic
31D3	Jaboatão Brazil
35B2	Jaboticabal Brazil
51B1	Jaca Spain
23B1	Jacala Mexico
33F5	Jacareacanga Brazil
35B2	Jacareí Brazil
30F3	Jacarezinho Brazil
29C2	Jáchal Arg
35C1	Jacinto Brazil
13F2	Jackfish *L* Can
109C1	Jackson Aust
22B1	Jackson California, USA
14B2	Jackson Michigan, USA
19B3	Jackson Mississippi, USA
18C2	Jackson Missouri, USA
14B3	Jackson Ohio, USA
11B3	Jackson Tennessee, USA
111B2	Jackson,C NZ
111A2	Jackson Head *Pt* NZ
19B3	Jacksonville Arkansas, USA
17B1	Jacksonville Florida, USA
18B2	Jacksonville Illinois, USA
17C1	Jacksonville N Carolina, USA
19A3	Jacksonville Texas, USA
17B1	Jacksonville Beach USA
26C3	Jacmel Haiti
84B3	Jacobabad Pak
31C4	Jacobina Brazil
23A2	Jacona Mexico
	Jadotville = Likasi
32B5	Jaén Peru
50B2	Jaén Spain
	Jaffa = Tel Aviv Yafo
108A3	Jaffa,C Aust
87B3	Jaffna Sri Lanka
86B2	Jagannathganj Ghat Bang
87C1	Jagdalpur India
91C4	Jagin *R* Iran
87B1	Jagtial India
29F2	Jaguarão Brazil
35B2	Jaguariaíva Brazil
91B4	Jahrom Iran
85D5	Jāina India
72A2	Jainca China
83D3	Jaipur India
85C3	Jaisalmer India
90C2	Jajarm Iran
52C2	Jajce Bosnia- Herzegovina
78B4	Jakarta Indon
6E3	Jakobshavn Greenland
38J6	Jakobstad Fin
23B2	Jalaca Mexico
84B2	Jalai-Kut Afghan
84D2	Jalandhar India
23B2	Jalapa Mexico
35A2	Jales Brazil
86B1	Jaleswar Nepal

85D4	Jalgaon India
97D4	Jalingo Nig
51B1	Jalón *R* Spain
85C3	Jālor India
23A1	Jalostotitlan Mexico
86B1	Jalpaiguri India
23B1	Jalpan Mexico
95B2	Jalu Oasis Libya
32A4	Jama Ecuador
26B3	Jamaica *I* Caribbean S
26B3	Jamaica Chan Caribbean S
86B2	Jamalpur Bang
78A3	Jambi Indon
85C4	Jambussar India
7B4	James *B* Can
5J5	Jameston USA
108A2	Jamestown Aust
8D2	Jamestown N. Dakota, USA
15C2	Jamestown New York, USA
16D2	Jamestown Rhode Island, USA
23B2	Jamiltepec Mexico
87B1	Jamkhandi India
84C2	Jammu India
84D2	Jammu and Kashmir State, India
85B4	Jamnagar India
84C3	Jampur Pak
38K6	Jämsä Fin
86B2	Jamshedpur India
86B1	Janakpur Nepal
35C1	Janaúba Brazil
90B3	Jandaq Iran
109D1	Jandowae Aust
1B1	Jan Mayen *I* Norwegian S
35C1	Januária Brazil
85D4	Jaora India
51	Japan Empire, E Asia
74C3	Japan,S of *S* E Asia
104F2	Japan Trench Pacific O
32D4	Japurá *R* Brazil
93C2	Jarābulus Syria
33B3	Jaraguá Brazil
50B1	Jarama *R* Spain
94B2	Jarash Jordan
30E3	Jardim Brazil
51B2	Jardín *R* Spain
26B2	Jardines de la Reina *Is* Cuba
	Jargalant = Hovd
33G3	Jari *R* Brazil
86C1	Jaria Jhānjail Bang
46C2	Jarny France
58B2	Jarocin Pol
59C2	Jarosław Pol
38G6	Järpen Sweden
72B2	Jartai China
85C4	Jasdan India
97C4	Jasikan Ghana
91C4	Jāsk Iran
59C3	Jasło Pol
29D6	Jason Is Falkland Is
18B2	Jasper Arkansas, USA
13D2	Jasper Can
17B1	Jasper Florida, USA
14A3	Jasper Indiana, USA
19B3	Jasper Texas, USA
13D2	Jasper Nat Pk Can
53B2	Jastrowie Pol
35A1	Jataí Brazil
51B2	Játiva Spain
34C2	Jaú Brazil
32B6	Jauja Peru
86A1	Jaunpur India
	Java = Jawa
87B2	Javadi Hills India
	Javari = Yavari
70B4	Java Trench Indon
71F4	Jayapura Indon
94C2	Jayrūd Syria
96B2	Jbel Ouarkziz *Mts* Mor
96B1	Jbel Sarhro *Mt* Mor
19B4	Jeanerette USA
97C4	Jebba Nig

93D2	Jebel 'Abd al 'Aziz *Mt* Syria
95B3	Jebel Abyad Sudan
91C5	Jebel Akhdar *Mt* Oman
92C4	Jebel al Lawz *Mt* S Arabia
94B2	Jebel ash Shaykh *Mt* Syria
95C2	Jebel Asoteriba *Mt* Sudan
94B3	Jebel Ed Dabab *Mt* Jordan
94B3	Jebel el Ata'ita *Mt* Jordan
92C3	Jebel esh Sharqi *Mt* Leb/Syria
94C3	Jebel Ithriyat *Mt* Jordan
91C5	Jebel Ja'lan *Mt* Oman
94B2	Jebel Liban *Mts* Leb
94C2	Jebel Ma'lūlā *Mt* Syria
98C1	Jebel Marra *Mt* Sudan
94B3	Jebel Mudeisisat *Mt* Jordan
95C2	Jebel Oda *Mt* Sudan
94B3	Jebel Qasr ed Deir *Mt* Jordan
94B2	Jebel Um ed Daraj *Mt* Jordan
95B2	Jebel Uweinat *Mt* Sudan
42C2	Jedburgh Scot
	Jedda = Jiddah
59C2	Jedrzejów Pol
19B3	Jefferson Texas, USA
11A3	Jefferson City USA
8B3	Jefferson,Mt USA
14A3	Jeffersonville USA
60C2	Jekabpils Latvia
59B2	Jelena Gora Pol
60B2	Jelgava Latvia
78C4	Jember Indon
57C2	Jena Germany
78B2	Jenaja *I* Indon
47D1	Jenbach Austria
94B2	Jenin Israel
19B3	Jennings USA
59B2	Jesenicky Upland Czech Republic
6F3	Jensen Nunatakker Mt Greenland
6B3	Jens Munk *I* Can
108B3	Jeparit Aust
31D4	Jequié Brazil
35C1	Jequitaí *R* Brazil
31C5	Jequitinhonha Brazil
	Jequitinhonha *R* Brazil
50A2	Jerez de la Frontera Spain
50A2	Jerez de los Caballeros Spain
94B3	Jericho Israel
108C3	Jerilderie Aust
48B2	Jersey *I* UK
10C2	Jersey City USA
15C2	Jersey Shore USA
18B2	Jerseyville USA
92C3	Jerusalem Israel
109D3	Jervis B Aust
13B3	Jervis Inlet *Sd* Can
52B1	Jesenice Slovenia
86B2	Jessore Bang
11B3	Jesup USA
34C2	Jesus Maria Arg
16D2	Jewett City USA
54A2	Jezerce *Mt* Alb
58C2	Jezioro Mamry *L* Pol
58C2	Jezioro Sniardwy *L* Pol
94B2	Jezzine Leb
85D4	Jhabua India
85D4	Jhālāwār India
85C3	Jhang Maghiana Pak
85D3	Jhānsi India
86A2	Jharsuguda India
84C2	Jhelum Pak
84C2	Jhelum *R* Pak
11C3	J H Kerr L USA
84D3	Jhunjhunūn India

69F2	Jiamusi China
73C4	Ji'an Jiangxi, China
73B4	Ji'an Jilin, China
73A4	Jiande China
73B4	Jiang'an China
73D4	Jiangbiancun China
73A5	Jiangcheng China
73B3	Jiang Jiang *R* China
73C5	Jiangmen China
72D3	Jiangsu Province, China
73C4	Jiangxi Province, China
73A3	Jiangyou China
72D1	Jianping China
73A5	Jianshui China
73A4	Jian Xi *R* China
73D4	Jianyang China
72E2	Jiaonan China
72E2	Jiao Xian China
72E2	Jiaozhou Wan *B* China
72C2	Jiaozuo China
73E3	Jiaxiang China
68B3	Jiayuguan China
81B3	Jiddah S Arabia
72D3	Jieshou China
72C2	Jiexiu China
72A3	Jigzhi China
59B3	Jihlava Czech Republic
99E2	Jilib Somalia
69E2	Jilin China
51B1	Jiloca *R* Spain
9C4	Jiménez Coahuila, Mexico
72D2	Jinan China
84D3	Jind India
72B2	Jingbian China
73D4	Jingdezhen China
76C1	Jinghong China
73C3	Jingmen China
72B2	Jingning China
73B4	Jing Xiang China
73D4	Jinhua China
72C1	Jining Nei Monggol, China
72D2	Jining Shandong, China
99D2	Jinja Uganda
76C1	Jinping China
73A4	Jinsha Jiang *R* China
73C4	Jinshi China
72E1	Jinxi China
72E2	Jin Xian China
72E1	Jinzhou China
33E5	Jiparaná *R* Brazil
32A4	Jipijapa Ecuador
23A2	Jiquilpan Mexico
91C4	Jiroft Iran
99E2	Jirriban Somalia
73B4	Jishou China
92C2	Jisr ash Shughūr Syria
54B2	Jiu *R* Rom
73D4	Jiujiang China
73A4	Jiulong China
73D4	Jiulong Jiang *R* China
69F2	Jixi China
94B3	Jiza Jordan
81C4	Jīzan S Arabia
97A3	Joal Sen
35C1	João Monlevade Brazil
31E8	João Pessoa Brazil
35B1	João Pirheiro Brazil
34B2	Jocoli Arg
85C3	Jodhpur India
38K6	Joensuu Fin
46C2	Joeuf France
47B1	Joffre,Mt Can
86B1	Jogbani India
87A2	Jog Falls India
101G1	Johannesburg S Africa
21B2	Johannesburg USA
6C2	Johan Pen Can
12D1	John *R* USA
20C2	John Day USA
20B1	John Day *R* USA
44C2	John O'Groats Scot
18A2	John Redmond Res USA

11B3 Johnson City Tennessee, USA
17B1 Johnston USA
27N2 Johnston Pt St Vincent and the Grenadines
15C2 Johnstown Pennsylvania, USA
77C5 Johor Bharu Malay
49C2 Joigny France
30G4 Joinville Brazil
61H3 Jok R Russian Fed
38H5 Jokkmokk Sweden
93E2 Jolfa Iran
10B2 Joliet USA
7C5 Joliette Can
79B4 Jolo Phil
79B4 Jolo I Phil
8D2 Joma Mt China
58C1 Jonava Lithuania
72A3 Jonё China
11A3 Jonesboro Arkansas, USA
19B3 Jonesboro Louisiana, USA
26C5 Jones Sd Can
58C1 Joniskis Lithuania
39G7 Jönköping Sweden
11A3 Joplin USA
92C3 Jordan Kingdom, S W Asia
94B2 Jordan R Israel
20C2 Jordan Valley USA
86C1 Jorhat India
43L5 Jörn Sweden
78C3 Jorong Indon
39J7 Jerpeland Nor
79B3 Jose Pañganiban Phil
10682 Joseph Bonaparte G Aust
64B3 Jotunheimen Mt Nor
94B2 Jouai'ya Leb
94B2 Jounie Leb
81C2 Joval India
99E2 Jowhar Somalia
12H2 Joy,Mt Can
5F5 Juan de Fuca,Str of Can/USA
101D2 Juan de Nova I Mozam Chan
34D3 Juárez Arg
31C3 Juàzeiro Brazil
31D3 Juazeiro do Norte Brazil
99D2 Juba Sudan
99E2 Juba R Somalia
94B1 Jubail Leb
93D3 Jubbah S Arabia
96A2 Juby,C Mor
51B2 Jucar R Spain
23B2 Juchatengo Mexico
23A1 Juchipila R Mexico
23A1 Juchitlan Mexico
57C3 Judenburg Austria
30B2 Juilaca Peru
73C4 Juiling Shan Hills China
31C6 Juiz de Fora Brazil
30C3 Jujuy State, Arg
30C2 Juli Peru
33F3 Julianatop Mt Suriname
6F3 Julianehab Greenland
46D1 Jülich Germany
84A1 Jumla Nepal
94B3 Jum Suwwana Mt Jordan
85C4 Junagadh India
72D2 Junan China
9D3 Junction City USA
31B6 Jundiai Brazil
4E4 Juneau USA
107D4 Junee Aust
22C2 June Lake USA
52A1 Jungfrau Mt Switz
16A2 Juniata R USA
29D2 Junin Arg
73A4 Junlian China
31B6 Juquiá Brazil
99C2 Jur R Sudan
42B2 Jura I Scot
49D2 Jura Mts France
44B3 Jura,Sound of Chan Scot

94B3 Jurf ed Darāwīsh Jordan
65K4 Jurga Russian Fed
60B2 Jürmala Latvia
32D4 Juruá R Brazil
33F6 Juruena R Brazil
94C1 Jūsiyah Syria
32E4 Justo Daract Arg
32D4 Jutai R Brazil
25D3 Juticalpa Honduras
　Jutland = Jylland
90C3 Juymand Iran
56B1 Jylland Pen Den
38K6 Jyväskyla Fin

K

82B2 K2 Mt China/India
90C2 Kaakhka Turkmenistan
101H1 Kaapmuiden S Africa
71D4 Kabaena I Indon
97A4 Kabala Sierra Leone
99D3 Kabale Rwanda
98C3 Kabalo Zaire
98C3 Kabambare Zaire
90A3 Kabir Kuh Mts Iran
100B2 Kabompo Zambia
100B2 Kabompo R Zambia
98C3 Kabongo Zaire
84B2 Kabul Afghan
85B4 Kachchh,G of India
61J2 Kachkanar Russian Fed
63C2 Kachug Russian Fed
76B3 Kadan Burma
78B3 Kadapongan I Indon
85C4 Kadi India
108A2 Kadina Aust
92B2 Kadinhani Turk
87B2 Kadiri India
60E4 Kadiyevka Ukraine
100B2 Kadoma Jim
99C1 Kadugli Sudan
97C3 Kaduna R Nig
87B2 Kadur India
97A3 Kaédi Maur
21C4 Kaena Pt Hawaiian Is
74B3 Kaesŏng N Korea
97C4 Kafanchan Nig
97A3 Kaffrine Sen
94C2 Kafr Behnd Syria
94B2 Kafr Behar Syria
100B2 Kafue Zambia
100B2 Kafue R Zambia
100B2 Kafue Nat Pk Zambia
74D3 Kaga Japan
65H6 Kagan Kazakhstan
93D1 Kagizman Turk
74C4 Kagoshima Japan
90C2 Kähak Iran
99D3 Kahama Tanz
84B3 Kahan Pak
74C4 Kahayan R Indon
98B3 Kahemba Zaire
46E1 Kahler Asten Mt Germany
91C4 Kahnuj Iran
18B1 Kahoka USA
21C4 Kahoolawe I Hawaiian Is
92C2 Kahramanmaraş Turk
21C4 Kahuku Pt Hawaiian Is
111B2 Kaiapoi NZ
33F2 Kaieteur Fall Guyana
72C3 Kaifeng China
110B1 Kaikohe NZ
111B2 Kaikoura NZ
111B2 Kaikoura Pen NZ
111B2 Kaikoura Range Mts NZ
73B4 Kaili China
21C4 Kailua Hawaiian Is
71C4 Kaimana Indon
75B2 Kainan Japan
97C3 Kainji Res Nig
110B1 Kaipara Harbour B NZ
73C5 Kaiping China
96D1 Kairouan Tunisia
22C2 Kaiser Peak Mt USA

57B3 Kaiserslautern Germany
74B2 Kaishantun China
58D2 Kaisiadorys Lithuania
110B1 Kaitaia NZ
111A3 Kaitangata NZ
84D3 Kaithal India
21C4 Kaiwi Chan Hawaiian Is
73B3 Kai Xian China
73A5 Kaiyuan Liaoning, China
74A2 Kaiyuan Yunnan, China
12C2 Kaiyuh Mts USA
38K6 Kajaani Fin
84B2 Kajaki Afghan
99D3 Kajiado Kenya
84B2 Kajrān Afghan
99D1 Kaka Sudan
99D2 Kakamega Kenya
75A2 Kake Japan
12H3 Kake USA
12D3 Kakhonak USA
65E5 Kakhovskoye Vodokhranilishche Res Ukraine
91B4 Kākī Iran
87B1 Kākināda India
75A2 Kakogawa Japan
4D2 Kaktovik USA
75C1 Kakuda Japan
　Kalaallit Nunaat = Greenland
55B3 Kalábaka Greece
78D1 Kalabakan Malay
100B2 Kalabo Zambia
61F3 Kalach Russian Fed
61F3 Kalach-na-Donu Russian Fed
86C2 Kaladan R Burma
21C4 Ka Lae C Hawaiian Is
100B3 Kalahari Desert Botswana
38J6 Kalajoki Fin
63D2 Kalakan Russian Fed
70A3 Kalakepen Indon
84C2 Kalam Pak
55B3 Kalámai Greece
10B2 Kalamazoo USA
84B3 Kalat Pak
92B1 Kalecik Turk
78D3 Kalembau I Indon
99C3 Kalémié Zaire
38L5 Kalevala Russian Fed
86C2 Kalewa Burma
12D2 Kalgin I USA
108A3 Kalgoorlie Aust
78B4 Kalianda Indon
79B3 Kalibo Phil
78C3 Kalima Zaire
78C3 Kalimantan Province, Indon
55C3 Kálimnos I Greece
86B1 Kalimpang India
60D3 Kaliningrad Russian Fed
60C3 Kalinkovichi Belorussia
8B2 Kalispell USA
58D2 Kalisz Pol
99D3 Kaliua Tanz
38J5 Kālix R Sweden
100A3 Kalkfeld Namibia
100A3 Kalkrand Namibia
108A1 Kallakoopah R Aust
38K6 Kallávesi L Fin
55C3 Kallonis Kólpos B Greece
39H7 Kalmar Sweden
61G4 Kalmytskaya Respublika, Russian Fed
100B2 Kalomo Zambia
18B1 Kalona USA
13B2 Kalone Peak Mt Can
87A2 Kalpeni I India
85D3 Kalpi India
53A3 Kalsat Khasba Tunisia
12B2 Kalskag USA
12C2 Kaltag USA
60E3 Kaluga Russian Fed
39G7 Kalundborg Den
59C3 Kalush Ukraine

87B2 Kalyandurg India
60E2 Kalyazin Russian Fed
61H1 Kama R Russian Fed
74E3 Kamaishi Japan
84C2 Kamalia Pak
110C1 Kamanawa Mts NZ
100A2 Kamanjab Namibia
84D2 Kamat Mt India
87B3 Kamban India
61H2 Kambarka Russian Fed
97A4 Kambia Sierra Leone
59D3 Kamenets Podolskiy Ukraine
61F3 Kamenka Russian Fed
65K4 Kamen-na-Obi Russian Fed
61K2 Kamensk-Ural'skiy Russian Fed
5H3 Kamilukuak L Can
98C3 Kamina Zaire
7A3 Kaminak L Can
75C1 Kaminoyama Japan
5F4 Kamloops Can
93E1 Kamo Armenia
75A2 Kamogawa Japan
99D2 Kampala Uganda
77C5 Kampar Malay
78A2 Kampar R Indon
56B2 Kampen Neth
　Kamphaeng Phet Thai
77C3 Kampot Camb
91D4 Kamsaptar Iran
61J2 Kamskoye Vodokhranilishche Res Russian Fed
85D4 Kāmthi India
61G3 Kamyshin Russian Fed
61K2 Kamyshlov Russian Fed
7C4 Kanaaupscow R Can
32B4 Kananga Zaire
61G2 Kanash Russian Fed
75B1 Kanayama Japan
74D3 Kanazawa Japan
4C3 Kanbisha USA
87B2 Kanchipuram India
84B2 Kandahar Afghan
64E3 Kandalaksha Russian Fed
38L5 Kandalakshskaya Guba B Russian Fed
97C3 Kandi Benin
109C2 Kandos Aust
87C3 Kandy Sri Lanka
15C2 Kane USA
6C1 Kane Basin B Can
91B4 Kanem Desert Region Chad
97B3 Kangaba Mali
92C2 Kangal Turk
6E3 Kangâmiut Greenland
91B4 Kangān Iran
77C4 Kangar Malay
106C4 Kangaroo I Aust
6E3 Kangâtsiaq Greenland
90A3 Kangavar Iran
72C1 Kangbao China
82C3 Kangchenjunga Mt Nepal
73A4 Kangding China
6G3 Kangerdlugssuaq B Greenland
6G3 Kangerdlugssvatsiaq B Greenland
99D2 Kangetet Kenya
74B2 Kanggye N Korea
7D4 Kangiqsualujjuaq Can
6C3 Kangiqsujuaq Can
7C3 Kangirsuk Can
74B3 Kangnŭng S Korea
98B2 Kango Gabon
68B4 Kangto Mt China
72B3 Kang Xian China
71D4 Kanh Hung Viet
38J6 Kaniama India
39J6 Kankaanpää Fin
14A2 Kankakee USA

14A2 Kankakee R USA	74B4 Karatsu Japan	Kaspiyskiy = Lagan'	93C2 Keban Baraji Res Turk
97B3 Kankan Guinea	91B4 Karäz Iran	95C3 Kassala Sudan	97A3 Kébémer Sen
86A2 Kanker India	93D3 Karbalä' Iraq	56B2 Kassel Germany	96C1 Kebili Turk
87B3 Känniyäkumän India	59C3 Karcag Hung	96C1 Kasserine Tunisia	94C1 Kebir R Leb/Syria
97C3 Kano Nig	55B3 Kardhitsa Greece	100A2 Kassinga Angola	38H5 Kebrekaise Mt Sweden
74C4 Kanoya Japan	64E3 Karel'skaya Respublika, Russian Fed	92B1 Kastamonou Turk	59B3 Kecskemét Hung
86A1 Känpur India		55B3 Kastélli Greece	56C1 Kedainiai Lithuania
9D3 Kansas State, USA	38J5 Karesvando Sweden	92A2 Kastéllorizon I Greece	97A3 Kédougou Sen
18A2 Kansas R USA	96B2 Karet Desert Region Maur	55C3 Kastoria Greece	12J2 Keele R Can
10A3 Kansas City USA	65K4 Kargasok Russian Fed	55C3 Kástron Greece	12H2 Keele Pk Mt Can
73D5 Kanshi China	97D3 Kari Nig	74D3 Kasugai Japan	21B2 Keeler USA
63B2 Kansk Russian Fed	100B2 Kariba Zim	75A1 Kasumi Japan	15D2 Keene New Hampshire, USA
97C3 Kantchari Burkina	100B2 Kariba L Zim/Zambia	101C2 Kasungu Malawi	100A3 Keetmanshoop Namibia
86B2 Kanthi India	100B2 Kariba Dam Zim/ Zambia	84C2 Kasur Pak	18C1 Keewanee USA
12D2 Kantishna USA	95C3 Karima Sudan	100B2 Kataba Zambia	6A3 Keewatin Region Can
12D2 Kantishna R USA	78B3 Karimata I Indon	98C3 Katako-kombe Zaire	55B3 Kefallínia I Greece
100B3 Kanye Botswana	86C2 Karimganj Bang	4D3 Katalla USA	94B2 Kefar Sava Israel
68D4 Kao-hsiung Taiwan	87B1 Karimnagar India	63G2 Katangli Russian Fed	97C4 Keffi Nig
100A2 Kaoka Veld Plain Namibia	99E1 Karin Somalia	106A4 Katanning Aust	38A2 Keflavík Iceland
74A3 Kaolack Sen	39J6 Karis Fin	55B2 Katerini Greece	5G4 Keg River Can
100B2 Kaoma Zambia	99C3 Karishimbe Mt Zaire	5E4 Kates Needle Mt Can/USA	76B1 Kehsi Mansam Burma
21C4 Kapaau Hawaiian Is	55C3 Káristos Greece	82D3 Katha Burma	100B3 Keith Aust
98C3 Kapanga Zaire	87A2 Kärkal India	106C2 Katherine Aust	44C3 Keith Scot
6F3 Kap Cort Adelaer C Greenland	71F4 Karkar I PNG	85C4 Käthiäwär Pen India	4F3 Keith Arm B Can
6H3 Kap Dalton C Greenland	90A3 Karkheh R Iran	86B1 Käthmandu Nepal	6G3 Kekertuk Can
39H7 Kapellskär Sweden	60D4 Karkinitskiy Zaliv B Ukraine	84D2 Kathua India	85D3 Kekri India
6F3 Kap Farvel C Greenland	63B3 Karlik Shan Mt China	86B1 Katihär India	77C5 Kelang Malay
6G3 Kap Gustav Holm C Greenland	58B2 Karlino Pol	100B2 Katima Mulilo Namibia	77C4 Kelantan R Malay
100B2 Kapiri Zambia	52C2 Karlobag Croatia	4C4 Katmai,Mt USA	92C1 Kelkit R Turk
78C2 Kapit Malay	52C1 Karlovac Croatia	12D3 Katmai Nat Mon USA	98B3 Kellé Congo
19B3 Kaplan USA	54B2 Karlovo Bulg	86A2 Katni India	4F2 Kellet,C Can
57C3 Kaplice Czech Republic	57C2 Karlovy Vary Czech Republic	109D2 Katoomba Aust	20C1 Kellogg USA
77B4 Kapoe Thai	39G7 Karlshamn Sweden	59B2 Katowice Pol	64D3 Kelloselka Fin
99C3 Kapona Zaire	39G7 Karlskoga Sweden	39H7 Katrineholm Sweden	45C2 Kells Irish Rep
52C1 Kaposvár Hung	39G7 Karlskrona Sweden	72C2 Katsina Nig	42B2 Kells Range Hills Scot
6C2 Kap Parry C Can	57B3 Karlsruhe Germany	97C4 Katsina Ala Nig	58C1 Kelme Lithuania
6H3 Kap Ravn C Greenland	39G7 Karlstad Sweden	75C1 Katsuta Japan	5G5 Kelowna Can
78B3 Kapuas R Indon	12D3 Karluk USA	75C1 Katsuura Japan	5F4 Kelsey Bay Can
108A2 Kapunda Aust	86C2 Karnafuli Res Bang	75B1 Katsuy Japan	42C2 Kelso Scot
84D2 Kapurthala India	84D3 Karnal India	65H6 Kattakurgan Uzbekistan	20C1 Kelso USA
7B5 Kapuskasing Can	87A1 Karnataka State, India	39G7 Kattegat Str Den/ Sweden	64E3 Kem' Russian Fed
109D2 Kaputar Mt Aust	54C2 Karnobat Bulg	21C4 Kauai I Hawaiian Is	38L6 Kem' R Russian Fed
93E2 Kapydzhik Mt Armenia	100B2 Karo Zim	21C4 Kauai Chan Hawaiian Is	97B3 Ke Macina Mali
6D2 Kap York C	99C3 Karonga Malawi	21C4 Kaulakahi Chan Hawaiian Is	13B2 Kemano Can
92B1 Karabük Turk	95C3 Karora Sudan	21C4 Kaunakaki Hawaiian Is	65K4 Kemerovo Russian Fed
55C2 Karacabey Turk	78D3 Karossa Indon	60B3 Kaunas Lithuania	38J5 Kemi Fin
85B4 Karachi Pak	55C3 Karpathos I Greece	97C3 Kaura Namoda Nig	38K5 Kemi R Fin
87A1 Karäd India	6E2 Karrats Fjord Greenland	38J5 Kautokeino Nor	38K5 Kemijärvi Fin
60E5 Kara Dağ Mt Turk	93D1 Kars Turk	55B2 Kavadarci Macedonia	46C1 Kempen Region, Belg
54C5 Kardeniz Boğazi Sd Turk	65H4 Karsakpay Kazakhstan	55A2 Kavajë Alb	26B2 Kemps Bay The Bahamas
68D1 Karaftit Russian Fed	58D1 Kärsava Latvia	87B2 Kävali India	109D2 Kempsey Aust
65J5 Karaganda Kazakhstan	80E2 Karshi Uzbekistan	55B2 Kaválla Greece	57C3 Kempten Germany
65J5 Karagayly Kazakhstan	38J6 Karstula Fin	85B4 Kävda India	12D2 Kenai USA
87B2 Käraikäl India	94B1 Kartaba Leb	75B1 Kawagoe Japan	12D3 Kenai Mts USA
90B2 Karaj Iran	54C2 Kartal Turk	75B1 Kawaguchi Japan	12D2 Kenai Pen USA
92C3 Karak Jordan	61K3 Kartaly Russian Fed	110B1 Kawakawa NZ	99D2 Kenamuke Swamp Sudan
65G5 Kara-Kalpakskaya Respublika, Uzbekistan	90A3 Kärün R Iran	99C3 Kawambwa Zambia	42C2 Kendal Eng
	86A1 Karwa India	86A2 Kawardha India	109D2 Kendall Aust
84D1 Karakax He R China	87A2 Kärwär India	15C2 Kawartha Lakes Can	71D4 Kendari Indon
71D3 Karakelong I Indon	68D1 Karymskoye Russian Fed	74D3 Kawasaki Japan	78C3 Kendawangan Indon
84D1 Karakoram Mts India	98C3 Kasai Zaire	110B1 Kawerau NZ	86B2 Kendrapära India
84D1 Karakoram P India/ China	100B2 Kasaji Zaire	110B1 Kawhia NZ	20C1 Kendrick USA
97A3 Karakoro R Maur/ Sen	101C2 Kasama Zambia	97B3 Kaya Burkina	97A4 Kenema Sierra Leone
65G6 Karakumy Desert Russian Fed	99D3 Kasanga Tanz	12F3 Kayak I USA	98B3 Kenge Zaire
94B3 Karama Jordan	87A2 Käsaragod India	78D2 Kayan R Indon	76B1 Kengtung Burma
92B2 Karaman Turk	5H3 Kasba L Can	87B3 Kayankulam India	100B3 Kenhardt S Africa
65K5 Karamay China	100B2 Kasempa Zambia	97A3 Kayes Mali	97A3 Kéniéba Mali
111B2 Karamea NZ	100B2 Kasenga Zaire	92C2 Kayseri Turk	96B1 Kenitra Mor
111B2 Karamea Bight B NZ	99D2 Kasese Uganda	1B8 Kazach'ye Russian Fed	45B3 Kenmare Irish Rep
84D3 Karanja India	90B3 Käshän Iran	93E1 Kazakh Azerbaijan	45B3 Kenmare R Irish Rep
92B2 Karapinar Turk	12C2 Kashegelok USA	65G5 Kazakhstan Republic, Asia	19B4 Kenner USA
64H2 Kara S Russian Fed	82B2 Kashi China	61G2 Kazan' Russian Fed	18C2 Kennett USA
100A3 Karasburg Namibia	84D3 Kashipur India	54C2 Kazanlük Bulg	16B3 Kennett Square USA
38K5 Karasjok Nor	74D3 Kashiwazaki Japan	69G4 Kazan Retto Is Japan	20C1 Kennewick USA
65J4 Karasuk Russian Fed	90C2 Käshmar Iran	91B4 Käzerün Iran	5F4 Kenny Dam Can
92C2 Karataş Turk	66D3 Kashmir State, India	61H1 Kazhim Russian Fed	7A5 Kenora Canada
65H5 Kara Tau Mts Kazakhstan	61F3 Kasimov Russian Fed	93E1 Kazi Magomed Azerbaijan	10B2 Kenosha USA
76B3 Karathuri Burma	18C2 Kaskaskia R USA	59C3 Kazincbarcika Hung	43E4 Kent County, Eng
	38J6 Kaskinen Fin	55B3 Kéa I Greece	20B1 Kent Washington, USA
	61K2 Kasli Russian Fed	21C4 Kealaikahiki Chan Hawaiian Is	14A2 Kentland USA
	5G5 Kaslo Can	8D2 Kearney USA	14B2 Kenton USA
	98C3 Kasongo Zaire		4H3 Kent Pen Can
	98B3 Kasongo-Lunda Zaire		
	55C3 Kásos I Greece		

11B3 Kentucky State, USA
11B3 Kentucky L USA
19B3 Kentwood Louisiana, USA
14A2 Kentwood Michigan, USA
99D2 Kenya Republic, Africa
Kenya,Mt = Kirinyaga
18B1 Keokuk USA
86A2 Keonchi India
86B2 Keonjhargarh India
71E4 Kepaluan Tanimbar Arch Indon
6H3 Keplavik Iceland
59B2 Kepno Pol
78B2 Kepulauan Anambas Arch Indon
71E4 Kepulauan Aru Arch Indon
78B2 Kepulauan Badas Is Indon
71E4 Kepulauan Leti I Indon
78A3 Kepulauan Lingga Is Indon
70A4 Kepulauan Mentawi Arch Indon
78A2 Kepulauan Riau Arch Indon
78D4 Kepulauan Sabalana Arch Indon
71D3 Kepulauan Sangihe Is Indon
71D4 Kepulauan Sula I Indon
71D3 Kepulauan Talaud Arch Indon
78B2 Kepulauan Tambelan Is Indon
71E4 Kepulauan Tanimbar I Indon
71D4 Kepulauan Togian I Indon
71D4 Kepulauan Tukambesi Is Indon
87B2 Kerala State, India
108B3 Kerang Aust
39K6 Kerava Fin
60E4 Kerch' Ukraine
71E4 Kerema PNG
20C1 Keremeps Can
95C3 Keren Eth
104B6 Kerguelen Ridge Indian O
99D3 Kericho Kenya
70B4 Kerinci Mt Indon
99D2 Kerio R Kenya
80E2 Kerki Turkmenistan
55A3 Kerkira Greece
55A3 Kérkira I Greece
91C3 Kerman Iran
22B2 Kerman USA
90A3 Kermānshāh Iran
21B2 Kern R USA
13F2 Kerrobert Can
45B2 Kerry County, Irish Rep
17B1 Kershaw USA
78B3 Kertamulia Indon
63D3 Kerulen R Mongolia
96B2 Kerzaz Alg
55C2 Keşan Turk
74E3 Kesennuma Japan
38L5 Kesten 'ga Russian Fed
42C2 Keswick Eng
65K4 Ket R Russian Fed
97C4 Keta Ghana
78C3 Ketapang Indon
5E4 Ketchikan USA
55C3 Ketia Niger
85B4 Keti Bandar Pak
58C2 Ketrzyn Pol
11E4 Kettering Eng
14B3 Kettering USA
20C1 Kettle R Can

20C1 Kettle River Range Mts USA
7C3 Kettlestone B Can
90C3 Kevir-i Namak Salt Flat Iran
14A2 Kewaunee USA
14B1 Key Harbour Can
17B2 Key Largo USA
11B4 Key West USA
63C2 Kezhma Russian Fed
54A1 K'felegyháza Hung
12B2 Kgun L USA
94C2 Khabab Syria
62H3 Khabarovsk Russian Fed
85B3 Khairpur Pak
85B3 Khairpur Region, Pak
100B3 Khakhea Botswana
91C4 Khalīj-e Fārs G
55B2 Khalkidhikí Pen Greece
55B3 Khalkis Greece
61G2 Khalturin Russian Fed
85C4 Khambhát,G of India
85D4 Khāmgaon India
76C2 Kham Keut Laos
87C1 Khammam India
90A2 Khamseh Mts Iran
76C2 Khan R Laos
85C4 Khanabad Afghan
93E3 Khanaqin Iraq
85D4 Khandwa India
84C2 Khanewal Pak
94C3 Khan ez Zabib Jordan
77D4 Khanh Hung Viet
55B3 Khaniá Greece
84C3 Khanpur Pak
65H3 Khanty-Mansiysk Russian Fed
94B3 Khan Yunis Egypt
84D1 Khapalu India
68C2 Khapcheranga Russian Fed
61G4 Kharabali Russian Fed
86B2 Kharagpur India
91C4 Khārān Iran
84B3 Kharan Pak
90B3 Kharanaq Iran
91B4 Khārg Is Iran
95C2 Khārga Oasis Egypt
85D4 Khargon India
60E4 Khar'kov Ukraine
54C2 Kharmanli Bulg
61F2 Kharovsk Russian Fed
95C3 Khartoum Sudan
95C3 Khartoum North Sudan
74C2 Khasan Russian Fed
95C3 Khashm el Girba Sudan
86C1 Khasi-Jaintia Hills India
54C2 Khaskovo Bulg
1B9 Khatanga Russian Fed
76B3 Khawsa Burma
76C2 Khe Bo Viet
85D4 Khed Brahma India
51C2 Khemis Alg
96B1 Khenifra Mor
51D2 Kherrata Alg
60D4 Kherson Ukraine
63D2 Khilok Russian Fed
55C3 Khíos Greece
55C3 Khíos I Greece
60C4 Khmel'nitskiy Ukraine
59C3 Khodorov Ukraine
84B1 Kholm Afghan
76D3 Khong Laos
91B4 Khonj Iran
69F2 Khor Russian Fed
91A3 Khoramshahr Iran
91B5 Khor Duwayhin B UAE
84C1 Khorog Tajikistan
90A3 Khorrāmābād Iran
90C3 Khosf Iran
84B2 Khost Pak
60C4 Khotin Ukraine
12C2 Khotol Mt USA

60C3 Khoyniki Belorussia
63F2 Khrebet Dzhugdzhur Mts Russian Fed
90C2 Khrebet Kopet Dag Mts Turkmenistan
64H3 Khrebet Pay-khoy Mts Russian Fed
82C1 Khrebet Tarbagatay Mts Kazakhstan
63E2 Khrebet Tukuringra Mts Russian Fed
82A1 Khudzhand Tajikistan
86B2 Khulna Bang
84D1 Khunjerab P China/India
90B3 Khunsar Iran
91A4 Khurays S Arabia
86B2 Khurda India
84D3 Khurja India
84C2 Khushab Pak
94B2 Khushniyah Syria
59C3 Khust Ukraine
99C1 Khuwei Sudan
85B3 Khuzdar Pak
90D3 Khvāf Iran
61G3 Khvalynsk Russian Fed
90C3 Khvor Iran
91B4 Khvormūj Iran
93D2 Khvoy Iran
84C1 Khwaja Muhammad Mts Afghan
84C2 Khyber P Afghan/Pak
99C3 Kiambi Zaire
74C3 Kiamichi R USA
12B1 Kiana USA
98B3 Kibangou Congo
99D3 Kibaya Tanz
98C3 Kibombo Zaire
99D3 Kibondo Tanz
99D3 Kibungu Rwanda
55B2 Kičevo Macedonia
5G4 Kicking Horse P Can
97C3 Kidal Mali
43C3 Kidderminster Eng
97A3 Kidira Sen
110C1 Kidnappers,C NZ
56C2 Kiel Germany
59C2 Kielce Pol
56C2 Kieler Bucht B Germany
Kiev = Kiyev
80E2 Kifab Uzbekistan
97A3 Kiffa Maur
89H8 Kigali Rwanda
12A2 Kigluaik Mts USA
99D3 Kigoma Tanz
75B2 Kii-sanchi Mts Japan
74C4 Kii-suido B Japan
54B1 Kikinda Serbia, Yugos
55B3 Kikládhes Is Greece
71F4 Kikori PNG
98B3 Kikwit Zaire
98C3 Kilauea Crater Mt Hawaiian Is
4C3 Kilbuck Mts USA
74B2 Kilchu N Korea
109D1 Kilcoy Aust
45C2 Kildare County, Irish Rep
45C2 Kildare Irish Rep
19B3 Kilgore USA
99D3 Kilifi Kenya
99D3 Kilimanjaro Mt Tanz
99D3 Kilindoni Tanz
92C2 Kilis Turk
45B3 Kilkee Irish Rep
45C2 Kilkenny County, Irish Rep
45C2 Kilkenny Irish Rep
45B2 Kilkieran B Irish Rep
55B2 Kilkis Greece
45B1 Killala B Irish Rep
45B2 Killaloe Irish Rep
109D1 Killarney Aust
41B3 Killarney Irish Rep
19A3 Killeen USA
12D1 Killik R USA
44B3 Killin Scot
55B3 Killíni Mt Greece
45B1 Killybegs Irish Rep
42B2 Kilmarnock Scot
61H2 Kil'mez Russian Fed
99D3 Kilosa Tanz

41B3 Kilrush Irish Rep
99C3 Kilwa Zaire
99D3 Kilwa Kisiwani Tanz
99D3 Kilwa Kivinje Tanz
108A2 Kimba Aust
12F2 Kimball,Mt USA
13D2 Kimberley Can
10F1 Kimberley S Africa
106B2 Kimberley Plat Aust
74B2 Kimch'aek N Korea
74B3 Kimch'ŏn S Korea
55B3 Kími Greece
60E2 Kimry Russian Fed
70C3 Kinabalu Mt Malay
78D1 Kinabatangan R Malay
14A2 Kincardine Can
13B1 Kincolith Can
19B3 Kinder USA
13F2 Kindersley Can
97A3 Kindia Guinea
98C3 Kindu Zaire
61H3 Kinel' Russian Fed
61F2 Kineshma Russian Fed
109D1 Kingaroy Aust
21A2 King City USA
5F4 Kingcome Inlet Can
7C4 King George Is Can
107D4 King I Aust
13B2 King I Can
106B2 King Leopold Range Mts Aust
9B3 Kingman USA
98C3 Kingombe Zaire
108A2 Kingoonya Aust
22C2 Kingsburg USA
21B2 Kings Canyon Nat Pk USA
108A3 Kingscote Aust
106B2 King Sd Aust
112C2 King Sejong Base Ant
14A1 Kingsford USA
17B1 Kingsland USA
43E3 King's Lynn Eng
16C2 Kings Park USA
8B2 Kings Peak Mt USA
107C4 Kingston Aust
7C5 Kingston Can
25E3 Kingston Jamaica
15D2 Kingston New York, USA
111A3 Kingston NZ
27E4 Kingston St Vincent and the Grenadines
9D4 Kingsville USA
44B3 Kingussie Scot
4J3 King William I Can
100B4 King William's Town S Africa
99B3 Kinkala Congo
39G7 Kinna Sweden
44D3 Kinnairds Head Pt Scot
75B1 Kinomoto Japan
44C3 Kinross Scot
45B3 Kinsale Irish Rep
99C3 Kinshasa Zaire
78D3 Kintap Indon
42B2 Kintyre Pen Scot
13D1 Kinuso Can
99D2 Kinyeti Mt Sudan
55B3 Kiparissía Greece
55B3 Kiparissiakós Kólpos G Greece
15C1 Kipawa,L Can
99D3 Kipili Tanz
12B3 Kipnuk USA
45C2 Kippure Mt Irish Rep
100B2 Kipushi Zaire
63C2 Kirensk Russian Fed
65J5 Kirghizia Republic, Asia
82B1 Kirgizskiy Khrebet Mts Kirghizia
98B3 Kiri Zaire
105G4 Kiribati Is Pacific O
92B2 Kırıkkale Turk
99D3 Kirinyaga Mt Kenya
60D2 Kirishi Russian Fed
85B3 Kirithar Range Mts Pak
55C3 Kirkağaç Turk

Kirk Bulāg Dāgh

90A2 Kirk Bulāg Dāgh Mt Iran
42C2 Kirkby Eng
44C3 Kirkcaldy Scot
42B2 Kirkcudbright Scot
38K5 Kirkenes Nor
7B5 Kirkland Lake Can
112A Kirkpatrick,Mt Ant
10A2 Kirksville USA
93D2 Kirkūk Iraq
44C2 Kirkwall Scot
18B2 Kirkwood USA
60D3 Kirov Russian Fed
61G2 Kirov Russian Fed
93D1 Kirovakan Armenia
61J2 Kirovgrad Russian Fed
60D4 Kirovograd Ukraine
61H2 Kirs Russian Fed
92B2 Kirşehir Turk
56C2 Kiruna Sweden
75B1 Kiryū Japan
98C2 Kisangani Zaire
75B1 Kisarazu Japan
86B1 Kishanganj India
85C3 Kishangarh India
60C4 Kishinev Moldavia
75B2 Kishiwada Japan
99D3 Kisii Kenya
99D3 Kisiju Tanz
59B3 Kiskunhalas Hung
65F5 Kislovodsk Russian Fed
99E3 Kismaayo Somalia
75B1 Kiso-sammyaku Mts Japan
97A4 Kissidougou Guinea
17B2 Kissimmee,L USA
99D3 Kisumu Kenya
59C3 Kisvárda Hung
97B3 Kita Mali
65H6 Kitab Uzbekistan
75C1 Kitakata Japan
74C4 Kita-Kyūshū Japan
99D2 Kitale Kenya
69G4 Kitami Japan
74E2 Kitami Japan
7B5 Kitchener Can
99D2 Kitgum Uganda
55B3 Kíthira I Greece
55B3 Kíthnos I Greece
94A1 Kíti,C Cyprus
4H3 Kitikmeot Region Can
5F4 Kitimat Can
38K5 Kitnen R Fin
75A2 Kitsuki Japan
15C2 Kittanning USA
38J5 Kittilä Fin
99D3 Kitunda Tanz
13B1 Kitwanga Can
100B2 Kitwe Zambia
57C3 Kitzbühel Austria
47E1 Kitzbüheler Alpen Mts Austria
57C3 Kitzingen Germany
98C3 Kiumbi Zaire
12B1 Kivalina USA
59D2 Kivercy Ukraine
99C3 Kivu,L Zaire/Rwanda
4B3 Kiwalik USA
60D3 Kiyev Ukraine
61J2 Kizel Russian Fed
92C2 Kizil R Turk
80D2 Kizyl-Arvat Turkmenistan
90A2 Kizyl-Atrek Turkmenistan
57C2 Kladno Czech Republic
57C3 Klagenfurt Austria
60B3 Klaipėda Lithuania
8A2 Klamath USA
20B2 Klamath R USA
8A2 Klamath Falls USA
20B2 Klamath Mts USA
57C2 Klatovy Czech Republic
12H3 Klawak USA
94B1 Kleat Leb
101G1 Klerksdorp S Africa
60E2 Klin Russian Fed
58B1 Klintehamn Sweden
60D3 Klintsy Russian Fed

52C2 Ključ Bosnia-Herzegovina
59B2 Kłodzko Pol
12G2 Klondike R Can/USA
4D3 Klondike Plat Can/USA
59B3 Klosterneuburg Austria
12G2 Kluane R Can
12G2 Kluane L Can
12G2 Kluane Nat Pk Can
59B2 Kluczbork Pol
12G3 Klukwan USA
12E2 Klutina L USA
12E2 Knight I USA
12G3 Knighton Wales
52C2 Knin Croatia
106A4 Knob,C Aust
46B1 Knokke-Heist Belg
112C9 Knox Coast Ant
11B3 Knoxville USA
6H3 Knud Ramsussens Land Region Greenland
78B3 Koba Indon
6F3 Kobbermirebugt Greenland
74D4 Kobe Japan
56C1 København Den
57B2 Koblenz Germany
60B3 Kobrin Russian Fed
71E4 Kobroör I Indon
12C1 Kobuk R USA
54B2 Kočani Macedonia
76C3 Ko Chang I Thai
86B1 Koch Bihār India
47D1 Kochel Germany
6C3 Koch I Can
Kochi = Cochin
74C4 Kōchi Japan
12D3 Kodiak USA
12D3 Kodiak I USA
87B2 Kodiyakkari India
99D2 Kodok Sudan
100A3 Koes Namibia
101G1 Koffiefontein S Africa
97B4 Koforidua Ghana
74D3 Kōfu Japan
75B1 Koga Japan
39G7 Koge Den
84C2 Kohat Pak
84B2 Koh-i-Baba Mts Afghan
84B1 Koh-i-Hisar Mts Afghan
84B2 Koh-i-Khurd Mt Afghan
86C1 Kohima India
84B1 Koh-i-Mazar Mt Afghan
84B3 Kohlu Pak
60C2 Kohtla-Järve Estonia
75B1 Koide Japan
12F2 Koidern Can
77A4 Koihoa Is Nicobar Is
76B4 Köje-do I S Korea
65H4 Kokchetav Kazakhstan
39J6 Kokemaki L Fin
38J6 Kokkola Fin
107D1 Kokoda PNG
14A2 Kokomo USA
71E4 Kokonau Indon
65K5 Kokpekty Kazakhstan
7K4 Koksoak R Can
100B4 Kokstad S Africa
76C3 Ko Kut I Thai
38L5 Kola Russian Fed
71D4 Kolaka Indon
77B4 Ko Lanta I Thai
Kollam = Quilon
87B2 Kolār India
87B2 Kolār Gold Fields India
97A3 Kolda Sen
39F7 Kolding Den
87A1 Kolhāpur India
12C3 Koliganek USA
57C2 Kolín Czech Republic
58B2 Kolo Pol
58B2 Kolobrzeg Pol
97B3 Kolokani Mali

60E2 Kolomna Russian Fed
60C4 Kolomyya Ukraine
65K4 Kolpashevo Russian Fed
55C3 Kólpos Merabéllou B Greece
55B2 Kólpos Singitikós G Greece
55B2 Kólpos Strimonikós G Greece
55B2 Kólpos Toronaíos G Greece
38L5 Kol'skiy Poluostrov Pen Russian Fed
38G6 Kolvereid Nor
100B2 Kolwezi Zaire
1C7 Kolyma R Russian Fed
99D2 Koma Eth
97D3 Komaduga Gana R Nig
59B3 Komárno Slovakia
101H1 Komati R S Africa
74D3 Komatsu Japan
75A2 Komatsushima Japan
64G3 Komi Respublika, Russian Fed
70C4 Komodo I Indon
71E4 Komoran I Indon
75B1 Komoro Japan
55B2 Komotiní Greece
76D3 Kompong Cham Camb
76C3 Kompong Chhnang Mts Camb
77C3 Kompong Som Camb
76D3 Kompong Thom Camb
76D3 Kompong Trabek Camb
63F2 Komsomol'sk na Amure Russian Fed
65H4 Konda R Russian Fed
99D3 Kondoa Tanz
87B1 Kondukūr India
6G3 Kong Christian IX Land Region Greenland
6F3 Kong Frederik VI Kyst Mts Greenland
64C2 Kong Karls Land Is Barents S
78D2 Kongkemul Mt Indon
98C3 Kongolo Zaire
39F7 Kongsberg Den
39G6 Kongsvinger Nor
Königsberg = Kaliningrad
58B2 Konin Pol
54A2 Konjic Bosnia-Herzegovina
61F1 Konosha Russian Fed
75B1 Konosu Japan
60D3 Konotop Ukraine
59C2 Końskie Pol
49D2 Konstanz Germany
97C3 Kontagora Nig
76D3 Kontum Viet
92B2 Konya Turk
13D3 Kootenay R Can
85C5 Kopargaon India
6J3 Kópasker Iceland
38A2 Kópavogur Iceland
52B1 Koper Slovenia
80D2 Kopet Dag Mts Iran/Turkmenistan
61K2 Kopeysk Russian Fed
77C4 Ko Phangan I Thai
77B4 Ko Phuket I Thai
39H7 Köping Sweden
87B1 Koppal India
52C1 Koprivnica Croatia
85B4 Korangi Pak
87C1 Koraput India
86A2 Korba India
57B2 Korbach Germany
4B3 Korbuk R USA
55B2 Korçë Alb

52C2 Korčula I Croatia
72E2 Korea B China/Korea
74B4 Korea Str S Korea/Japan
59D2 Korec Ukraine
92B1 Körglu Tepesi Mt Turk
97B4 Korhogo Ivory Coast
85B4 Kori Creek India
55B3 Korinthiakós Kólpos G Greece
55B3 Kórinthos Greece
74E3 Kōriyama Japan
61K3 Korkino Russian Fed
92C2 Korkuteli Turk
82C1 Korla China
60D5 Köröglu Tepesi Mt Turk
99D3 Korogwe Tanz
108B3 Koroit Aust
7E3 Koror Palau Is, Pacific O
59C3 Korös R Hung
60C3 Korosten Ukraine
95A3 Koro Toro Chad
12B3 Korovin I USA
69G2 Korsakov Russian Fed
39G7 Korsør Den
46B1 Kortrijk Belg
55C3 Kós I Greece
77C4 Ko Samui I Thai
58B2 Kościerzyna Pol
107D4 Kosciusko Mt Aust
12H3 Kosciusko I USA
74B4 Koshikijima-retto I Japan
59C3 Košice Slovakia
74B3 Kosŏng N Korea
54B2 Kosovo Aut Republic, Serbia, Yugos
97B4 Kossou L Ivory Coast
101G1 Koster S Africa
99D1 Kosti Sudan
59D2 Kostopol' Ukraine
61F2 Kostroma Russian Fed
56C2 Kostrzyn Pol
39H8 Koszalin Pol
85D3 Kota India
78A4 Kotaagung Indon
78C3 Kotabaharu Indon
78D3 Kotabaru Indon
78A3 Kota Bharu Malay
78A3 Kotabumi Indon
84C2 Kot Addu Pak
78C1 Kota Kinabulu Malay
87C1 Kotapad India
61G2 Kotel'nich Russian Fed
61F4 Kotel'nikovo Russian Fed
39K6 Kotka Fin
64F3 Kotlas Russian Fed
12B2 Kotlik USA
54A2 Kotor Montenegro, Yugos
60C4 Kotovsk Ukraine
85B3 Kotri Pak
87C1 Kottagüdem India
87B3 Kottayam India
98C2 Kotto R CAR
87B2 Kottūru India
12B1 Kotzebue USA
12B1 Kotzebue Sd USA
97C3 Kouande Benin
98C2 Kouango CAR
97B3 Koudougou Burkina
97B3 Koulikoro Mali
97B3 Koupéla Burkina
33G2 Kourou French Guiana
97B3 Kouroussa Guinea
98B1 Kousséri Cam
39K6 Kouvola Fin
38L5 Kovdor Russian Fed
60B3 Kovel' Ukraine
Kovno = Kaunas
61F2 Kovrov Russian Fed
61F3 Kovylkino Russian Fed

60E1 Kovzha R
77C4 Ko Way I Thai
73C5 Kowloon Hong Kong
84B2 Kowt-e-Ashrow Afghan
92A2 Köyceggiz Turk
38L5 Koydor Russian Fed
87A1 Koyna Res India
12B2 Koyuk USA
12B1 Koyuk R USA
12C1 Koyukuk R USA
92C2 Kozan Turk
55B2 Kozani Greece
Kozhikode = Calicut
61G2 Koz'modemyansk Russian Fed
75B2 Kōzu-shima I Japan
39F7 Kragero Nor
54B2 Kragujevac Serbia, Yugos
77B3 Kra,Isthmus of Burma/Malay
Krakatau = Rakata
94C1 Krak des Chevaliers Hist Site Syria
Kraków = Cracow
54B2 Kraljevo Serbia, Yugos
60E4 Kramatorsk Ukraine
38H6 Kramfors Sweden
52B1 Kranj Slovenia
61G1 Krasavino Russian Fed
64G2 Krasino Russian Fed
59C2 Kraśnik Pol
61G3 Krasnoarmeysk Russian Fed
60E5 Krasnodar Russian Fed
61J2 Krasnokamsk Russian Fed
61K2 Krasnotur'insk Russian Fed
61J2 Krasnoufimsk Russian Fed
61J3 Krasnousol'skiy Russian Fed
65G3 Krasnovishersk Russian Fed
65G5 Krasnovodsk Turkmenistan
63B2 Krasnoyarsk Russian Fed
59C2 Krasnystaw Pol
61G3 Krasnyy Kut Russian Fed
60E4 Krasnyy Luch Ukraine
61G4 Krasnyy Yar Russian Fed
76D3 Kratie Camb
6E2 Kraulshavn Greenland
56B2 Krefeld Germany
60D4 Kremenchug Ukraine
60D4 Kremenchugskoye Vodokhranilische Res Ukraine
59D2 Kremenets Ukraine
98A2 Kribi Cam
60D3 Krichev Belorussia
47E1 Krimml Austria
87B1 Krishna R India
87B2 Krishnagiri India
86B2 Krishnanagar India
37G7 Kristiansand Nor
64B3 Kristiansund Nor
39G7 Kristinehamn Sweden
38J6 Kristiinankaupunki Fin
55B3 Kriti I Greece
60D4 Krivoy Rog Ukraine
52B1 Krk I Croatia
6G3 Kronpris Frederik Bjerge Mts Greenland
39K7 Kroonshtadt Russian Fed
101G1 Kroonstad S Africa
65F5 Kropotkin Russian Fed

101G1 Krugersdorp S Africa
78A4 Krui Indon
55A2 Kruje Alb
58D2 Krupki Belorussia
12B1 Krusenstern,C USA
54B2 Kruševac Serbia, Yugos
39K7 Krustpils Latvia
12G3 Kruzof I USA
60E5 Krym Pen Ukraine
60E5 Krymsk Russian Fed
55B2 Krzyz Pol
96C1 Ksar El Boukhari Alg
96B1 Ksar el Kebir Mor
70C3 Kuala Indon
77C5 Kuala Dungun Malay
77C4 Kuala Kerai Malay
77C5 Kuala Kubu Baharu Malay
77C5 Kuala Lipis Malay
77C5 Kuala Lumpur Malay
77C4 Kuala Trengganu Malay
78D1 Kuamut Malay
74A2 Kuandian China
77C5 Kuantan Malay
93E1 Kuba Azerbaijan
78C2 Kubar PNG
70C3 Kudat Malay
78C4 Kudus Indon
61H2 Kudymkar Russian Fed
57C3 Kufstein Austria
90C3 Kuh Duren Upland Iran
91C4 Küh e Bazmān Mt Iran
90B3 Küh-e-Dinar Mt Iran
90C2 Küh-e-Hazār Masjed Mts Iran
91C4 Küh-e Jebāl Barez Mts Iran
90B3 Küh-e Karkas Mts Iran
91C4 Küh-e Laleh Zar Mt Iran
90A2 Küh-e Sahand Mt Iran
91D4 Kūh e Taftān Mt Iran
90B3 Kūhhaye Sabalan Mt Iran
90A3 Kūhhā-ye Zāgros Mts Iran
38K6 Kuhmo Fin
90B3 Kūhpāyeh Iran
90C3 Kūhpāyeh Iran
91C4 Kūh ye Bashākerd Mts Iran
90A2 Küh ye Sabalan Mt Iran
100A3 Kuibis Namibia
4B4 Kuigillingok USA
100A2 Kuito Angola
12H3 Kuiu I USA
74E2 Kuji Japan
75A2 Kuju-san Mt Japan
12C3 Kukaklek L USA
54B2 Kukës Alb
77C5 Kukup Malay
91C4 Kūl R Iran
55C3 Kula Turk
61J4 Kulakshi Kazakhstan
99D2 Kulal,Mt Kenya
55B2 Kulata Bulg
60B2 Kuldiga Latvia
61H4 Kul'sary Kazakhstan
82B2 Kulu Turk
65J4 Kulunda Russian Fed
32D6 Kulwin Aust
75B1 Kumagaya Japan
78C3 Kumai Indon
74C4 Kumamoto Japan
75B2 Kumano Japan
54B2 Kumanovo Macedonia
63E2 Kumara China
97B4 Kumasi Ghana
93E1 Kumayri Armenia
98A2 Kumba Cam
87B2 Kumbakonam India
61J3 Kumertau Russian Fed

74B3 Kümhwa S Korea
39H7 Kumla Sweden
87A2 Kumta India
82C1 Kümüx China
91D4 Kunar R Afghan
39K7 Kunda Estonia
87A2 Kundāpura India
84B1 Kunduz Afghan
89F9 Kunene R Angola
39G7 Kungsbacka Sweden
61J2 Kungur Russian Fed
76B1 Kunhing Burma
82B2 Kunlun Shan Mts China
73A4 Kunming China
74B3 Kunsan S Korea
38K6 Kuopio Fin
52C1 Kupa R Croatia/Bosnia-Herzegovina
106B2 Kupang Indon
71E4 Kupiano PNG
12H3 Kupreanof I USA
60E4 Kupyansk Ukraine
82C1 Kuqa China
72E1 Kurabe Japan
74C4 Kurashiki Japan
75A1 Kurayoshi Japan
54C2 Kürdzhali Bulg
74C4 Kure Japan
60B2 Kuressaare Estonia
63A1 Kureyka R Russian Fed
65H4 Kurgan Russian Fed
88K6 Kuria Muria Is Oman
38J6 Kurikka Fin
Kuril Is = Kuril'skoye Osrova
69H2 Kuril'skiye Ostrova
87B1 Kurnool India
75C1 Kuroiso Japan
111B2 Kurow NZ
109D2 Kurri Kurri Aust
60E3 Kursk Russian Fed
Kurskiy Zaliv = Courland Lagoon
68A2 Kuruktag R China
100B3 Kuruman S Africa
74C4 Kurume Japan
87C3 Kurunegala Sri Lanka
65K5 Kurunktag R China
61J2 Kusa Russian Fed
55C3 Kuşadasi Körfezi B Turk
55C2 Kus Golü L Turk
74D4 Kushimoto Japan
74E2 Kushiro Japan
86B2 Kushtia Bang
61H3 Kushum R Russian Fed
80E2 Kushka Afghan
65G4 Kushva Russian Fed
12B2 Kuskokwim R USA
12B3 Kuskokwim B USA
12B3 Kuskokwim Mts USA
84B1 Kusma Nepal
74E2 Kussharo-ko L Japan
65H4 Kustanay Kazakhstan
92A2 Kütahya Turk
78D3 Kutai R Indon
59B3 Kutná Hora Czech Republic
58B2 Kutno Pol
98B3 Kutu Zaire
86C2 Kutubdia I Bang
14F1 Kutum Sudan
7D4 Kuujjuaq Can
7C4 Kuujjuarapik Can
38K5 Kuusamo Fin
61J3 Kuvandyk Russian Fed
93E4 Kuwait Kuwait
80C3 Kuwait Sheikhdom, S W Asia
75B1 Kuwana Japan
Kuybyshev = Samara
65J4 Kuybyshev
61G3 Kuybyshevskoye Vodokhranilishche Res Russian Fed

63C2 Kuytun Russian Fed
60E5 Kuzey Anadolu Daglari Mts Turk
61G3 Kuznetsk Russian Fed
38J4 Kvaenangen Sd Nor
12C3 Kvichak USA
12C3 Kvichak R USA
12C3 Kvichak B USA
38G5 Kvigtind Mt Nor
38H5 Kvikkjokk Sweden
99D3 Kwale Kenya
74B3 Kwangju S Korea
98B3 Kwango R Zaire
100B2 Kwekwe Zim
12B2 Kwethluk USA
12C3 Kwethluk R USA
58B2 Kwidzyn Pol
71E4 Kwoka Mt Indon
108C3 Kyabram Aust
76B1 Kyaikkami Burma
76B2 Kyaikto Burma
68C1 Kyakhta Russian Fed
108A2 Kyancutta Aust
76B1 Kyaukme Burma
76B1 Kyauk-padaung Burma
76A2 Kyaukpyu Burma
40B2 Kyle of Lochalsh Scot
46D1 Kyll R Germany
108B3 Kyneton Aust
99D2 Kyoga L Uganda
100D1 Kyoga L
74B3 Kyŏngju S Korea
75B2 Kyoto Japan
Kyrgyzstan = Kirghizia
65H4 Kyshtym Russian Fed
74C4 Kyūshū I Japan
104E3 Kyushu-Palau Ridge Pacific O
54B2 Kyustendil Bulg
68B1 Kyzyl Russian Fed
65H5 Kyzylkum Desert Uzbekistan
65H5 Kzyl Orda Kazakhstan

L

99E2 Laascaanood Somalia
46E1 Laasphe Germany
99E1 Laasqoray Somalia
33E1 La Asunción Ven
96A2 Laâyoune Mor
23A1 La Barca Mexico
97A3 Labé Guinea
59B2 Labe R Czech Republic
15D1 Labelle Can
17B2 La Belle USA
12G2 Laberge,L Can
78D1 Labi Brunei
13E2 la Biche,L Can
61F5 Labinsk Russian Fed
94C1 Laboué Leb
34C2 Laboulaye Arg
7D4 Labrador Region Can
7D4 Labrador City Can
7E3 Labrador S Greenland/Can
33E5 Lábrea Brazil
78D1 Labuan I Malay
78B2 Labuhan Indon
76A2 Labutta Burma
62C2 Labytnangi Russian Fed
7C4 Lac à l'eau Claire Can
46B2 La Capelle France
34C2 La Carlota Arg
79B3 La Carlota Phil
12J1 Lac Belot L Can
7C4 Lac Bienville L Can
81B4 Laccadive Is India
47B1 Lac d'Annecy L France
4G3 Lac de Gras L Can
47B1 Lac de Joux L Switz
47B1 Lac de Neuchâtel L Switz
23A2 Lac de Patzcuaro L Mexico

23A2 Lac de Sayula L Mexico
4F3 Lac des Bois L Can
47A2 Lac du Bourget L France
25D3 La Ceiba Honduras
108A3 Lacepede B Aust
48C2 La Châtre France
47B1 La-Chaux-de-Fonds Switz
94B3 Lachish Hist Site Israel
107D4 Lachlan R Aust
32B2 La Chorrera Panama
15D1 Lachute Can
14C1 Lackawanna USA
5G4 La Biche Can
4G3 Lac la Martre L Can
5H4 La Ronge L Can
52A1 Lac Léman L Switz/France
10C1 Lac Manouane L Can
15D1 Lac Megantic Can
7C4 Lac Mistassini L Can
13E2 Lacombe Can
15D2 Laconia USA
50A1 La Coruña Spain
10A2 La Crosse USA
9C3 La Cruces USA
7A4 Lac Seul L Can
18B2 La Cygne USA
84D2 Ladakh Range India
5G2 Ládnun India
73B5 Ladong China
60D1 Ladozhskoye Ozero L Ukraine
11A3 Lady Ann Str Can
109C4 Lady Barron Aust
101G1 Ladybrand S Africa
13C3 Ladysmith Can
101G1 Ladysmith S Africa
71F4 Lae PNG
76C3 Laem Ngop Thai
56C1 Laeso / Den
10B2 Lafayette Indiana, USA
11A3 Lafayette Louisiana, USA
46B2 La Fère France
46B2 La-Ferté-sous-Jouarre France
97C4 Lafia Nig
97C4 Lafiagi Nig
48B2 La Flèche France
96C1 La Galite / Tunisia
61G4 Lagan' Russian Fed
56C1 Lagan R Sweden
31D4 Lagarto Brazil
96C1 Laghouat Alg
35C2 Lagoa de Araruama Brazil
29F2 Lagoa dos Patos Lg Brazil
35C2 Lagoa Feia Brazil
32B4 Lago Agrio Ecuador
35C1 Lagoa Juparanã Brazil
29D2 Lagoa mar Chiguita L Arg
29F2 Lagoa Mirim L Brazil/Urug
29B6 Lago Argentino L Arg
29B5 Lago Buenos Aires L Arg
29B5 Lago Cochrane L Arg
29C5 Lago Colhué Huapi L Arg
24B2 Lago de Chapala L Mexico
32A2 Lago de Chiriqui L Panama
24C2 Lago de Cuitzeo L Mexico
Lago de la Laja L Chile
53A2 Lago del Coghinas L Sardegna
32C2 Lago de Maracaibo L Ven
25D3 Lago de Nicaragua L Nic
32A1 Lago de Perlas L Nic

52B2 Lago di Bolsena L Italy
52B2 Lago di Bracciano L Italy
52A1 Lago di Como L Italy
47D2 Lago d'Idro L Italy
52B1 Lago di Garda L Italy
47C2 Lago di Lecco L Italy
47C2 Lago di Lugano L Italy
47D2 Lago d'Iseo L Italy
47C2 Lago d'Orta L Italy
29B5 Lago General Carrera L Chile
52A1 Lago Maggiore L Italy
29C5 Lago Musters L Arg
48B3 Lagos France
29B4 Lago Nahuel Haupi L Arg
29B5 Lago O'Higgins L Chile
53A2 Lago Omodeo L Sardegna
29B4 Lago Ranco L Chile
32D6 Lago Rogaguado L Bol
97C4 Lagos Nig
50A2 Lagos Port
29B5 Lago San Martin L Arg/Chile
24B2 Lagos de Moreno Mexico
30C2 Lago Titicaca Bol/Peru
29B5 Lago Viedma L Arg
8B2 La Grande R Can
106B2 Lagrange Aust
11B3 La Grange Georgia, USA
14A3 La Grange Kentucky, USA
19A4 La Grange Texas, USA
33E2 La Gran Sabana Mts Ven
47B2 La Grave France
48B3 Logroño Spain
34A3 Laguna Aluminé L Arg
21B3 Laguna Beach USA
34C3 Laguna Colorada Grande L Arg
79B3 Laguna de Bay Lg Phil
25D3 Laguna de Caratasca Lg Honduras
25D4 Laguna de Chiriqui L Panama
25D3 Laguna de Managua L Nic
25D3 Laguna de Nicaragua L Nic
26A4 Laguna de Perlas Lg Nic
23B1 Laguna de Pueblo Viejo L Mexico
24C2 Laguna de Tamiahua Lg Mexico
25C3 Laguna de Términos Lg Mexico
23A1 Laguna de Yuriria L Mexico
23B1 Laguna le Altamira Mexico
24C2 Laguna Madre Lg USA
34C2 Laguna Mar Chiquita L Arg
29B4 Laguna Nahuel Huapi L Arg
34C2 Laguna Paiva Arg
29B4 Laguna Ranco Chile
9C4 Laguna Seca Mexico
23B1 Laguna Tortugas L Mexico
70C3 Lahad Datu Malay
78A3 Lahat Indon
38J6 Lahia Fin
90B2 Lähijän Iran
46D1 Lahn R Germany
46D1 Lahnstein Germany
84C2 Lahore Pak
39K6 Lahti Fin

23A2 La Huerta Mexico
98B2 Lai Chad
73B5 Laibin China
76C1 Lai Chau Viet
100B4 Laingsburg S Africa
44B2 Lairg Scot
79C4 Lais Indon
79C4 Lais Phil
72E2 Laiyang China
72D2 Laizhou Wan B China
34A3 Laja R Chile
30F4 Lajes Brazil
9C3 La Junta USA
109C2 Lake Cargelligo Aust
11A3 Lake Charles USA
17B1 Lake City Florida, USA
17C1 Lake City S Carolina, USA
42C2 Lake District Region, Eng
22D4 Lake Elsinore USA
106C3 Lake Eyre Basin Aust
15C2 Lakefield Can
6D3 Lake Harbour Can
22C3 Lake Hughes USA
16B2 Lakehurst USA
19A4 Lake Jackson USA
5G4 Lake la Biche Can
17B2 Lakeland USA
7A5 Lake of the Woods Can
20B1 Lake Oswego USA
21A2 Lakeport USA
19B3 Lake Providence USA
111B2 Lake Pukaki NZ
109C3 Lakes Entrance Aust
22C2 Lakeshore USA
108B1 Lake Stewart Aust
15C1 Lake Traverse Can
8A2 Lakeview USA
20B1 Lakeview Mt Can
19B3 Lake Village USA
17B2 Lake Wales USA
22C4 Lakewood California, USA
16B2 Lakewood New Jersey, USA
14B2 Lakewood Ohio, USA
17B2 Lake Worth USA
87B2 Lakhimpur India
85B4 Lakhpat India
84C2 Lakki Pak
55B3 Lakonikós Kólpos G Greece
97B4 Lakota Ivory Coast
38K4 Laksefjord Inlet Nor
38K4 Lakselv Nor
32A4 La Laguna Arg
32A4 La Libertad Ecuador
34A2 La Ligua Chile
50A2 La Linea Spain
85D4 Lalitpur India
5H4 La Loche Can
46C1 La Louvière Belg
26A4 La Luz Nic
7C5 La Malbaie Can
23B2 La Malinche Mt Mexico
50B2 La Mancha Region, Spain
9C3 Lamar Colorado, USA
18B2 Lamar Missouri, USA
14A2 La Marque USA
98B3 Lambaréné Gabon
32A5 Lambayeque Peru
112B10 Lambert Gl Ant
16B2 Lambertville USA
47C2 Lambro R Italy
76C2 Lam Chi R Thai
50A1 Lamego Port
47B2 La Meije Mt France
32B6 La Merced Peru
21B3 La Mesa USA
55B3 Lamia Greece
42C2 Lammermuir Hills Scot
39G7 Lammhult Sweden

79B3 Lamon B Phil
18B1 Lamoni USA
71F3 Lamotrek I Pacific O
43B3 Lampeter Wales
99E3 Lamu Kenya
47D1 Lana Italy
21C4 Lanai I Hawaiian Is
21C4 Lanai City Hawaiian Is
42C2 Lanark Scot
76C1 Lanbi I Burma
14A2 Lancang R China
42C3 Lancashire County, Eng
21B3 Lancaster California, USA
42C2 Lancaster Eng
18B1 Lancaster Mississippi, USA
15D2 Lancaster New Hampshire, USA
14B3 Lancaster Ohio, USA
10C3 Lancaster Pennsylvania, USA
17B1 Lancaster S Carolina, USA
6B2 Lancaster Sd Can
78B3 Landak R Indon
14B1 Landen Germany
57C3 Landeck Austria
8C2 Lander USA
34C2 Landeta Arg
35B2 Landsberg Germany
4F2 Lands End C Can
43B4 Land's End Pt Eng
57C3 Landshut Germany
39G7 Landskrona Sweden
17A1 Lanett USA
38A2 Langanfljót Mts Iceland
77B4 Langkawi I Malay
13C3 Langley Can
108C1 Langlo R Aust
47B1 Langnau Switz
49D2 Langres France
70A3 langsa Indon
68C2 Lang Shan Mts China
76D1 Lang Son Viet
48C3 Languedoc Region, France
29B3 Lanin Mt Arg
79B4 Lanoa,L L Phil
16B2 Lansdale USA
7B4 Lansdowne House Can
16B2 Lansford USA
10B2 Lansing USA
47B2 Lanslebourg France
96A2 Lanzarote I Canary Is
72A2 Lanzhou China
47B2 Lanzo Torinese Italy
79B2 Laoag Phil
76D1 Lao Cai Viet
72D1 Laoha He R China
45C2 Laois County, Irish Rep
46B2 Laon France
32B6 La Oroya Peru
76C2 Laos Republic, S E Asia
49C2 Lapalisse France
32B2 la Palma Panama
96A2 La Palma I Canary Is
34B3 La Pampa State, Arg
33E2 La Paragua Ven
29E2 La Paz Arg
34B2 La Paz Arg
30C2 La Paz Bol
24A2 La Paz Mexico
69G2 La Perouse Str Japan/Russian Fed
23A1 La Piedad Mexico
20B2 La Pine USA
19B3 Laplace USA
23A1 la Placita Mexico
29E2 La Plata Arg
13F1 La Plonge,L Can
14A2 La Porte USA
39K6 Lappeenranta Fin

38H5 Lappland *Region* Sweden/Fin
34C3 Laprida Arg
18B Laptev S Russian Fed
38J6 Lapua Fin
79B3 Lapu-Lapu Phil
9A La Purisma Mexico
95B2 Laqiya Arba'in *Well* Sudan
30C3 La Quiaca Arg
52B2 L'Aquila Italy
91B4 Lär Iran
96B1 Larache Mor
9C2 Laramie USA
8C2 Laramie Range *Mts* USA
50B2 Larca Spain
9D4 Laredo USA
9184 Larestan *Region,* Iran
Largeau = Faya
47B2 L'Argentière France
17B2 Largo USA
42A Largs Scot
90A2 Lär Iran
30C4 La Rioja Arg
50B1 La Rioja *State,* Arg
53B2 Lárisa Greece
85B3 Larkana Pak
92B3 Larnaca Cyprus
45D1 Larne N Ire
50A1 La Robla Spain
46C1 La Roche-en-Ardenne Belg
48B2 La Rochelle France
47B1 La Roche-sur-Foron France
48B2 La Roche-sur-Yon France
51B2 La Roda Spain
27D3 La Romana Dom Rep
5H4 La Ronge Can
5H4 La Ronge,L Can
39F7 Larvik Nor
65J3 Laryak Russian Fed
50B2 La Sagra *Mt* Spain
15D1 La Salle USA
18C1 La Salle USA
7C5 La Sarre Can
34C1 Las Avispas Arg
34C2 Las Cabras Chile
5G4 Lascombe Can
9C2 Las Cruces USA
26C3 La Selle *Mt* Haiti
72B2 Lasengning China
30B4 La Serena Chile
29E3 Las Flores Arg
53C3 La Sila *Mts* Italy
90B2 Läsjerd Iran
34A3 Las Lajas Chile
50A2 Las Marismas *Marshland* Spain
96A2 Las Palmas de Gran Canaria Canary Is
52A La Spezia Italy
29C4 Las Plumas Arg
34C2 Las Rosas Arg
20B2 Lassen Peak *Mt* USA
13E2 Lassen Volcanic Nat Pk USA
23B2 las Tinaja Mexico
98B3 Lastoursville Gabon
52C3 Lastovo *I* Croatia
24B2 Las Tres Marias *Is* Mexico
34C2 Las Varillas Arg
3D2 Las Vegas USA
Latakia = Al Lädhiqiyah
53B2 Latina Italy
34B2 La Toma Arg
32D1 La Tortuga *I* Ven
79B2 La Trinidad Phil
109C4 Latrobe Aust
94B3 Latrun Israel
7C5 La Tuque Can
87B1 Lätür India
60B2 Latvia Republic, Europe
107D5 Launceston Aust
43B4 Launceston Eng
29B4 La Unión Chile
25D3 La Unión El Salvador
23B2 La Unión Mexico

32B5 La Unión Peru
107D2 Laura Aust
15C3 Laurel Delaware, USA
16A3 Laurel Maryland, USA
11B3 Laurel Mississippi, USA
17B1 Laurens USA
17C1 Laurinburg USA
52A1 Lausanne Switz
78D3 Laut *I* Indon
29B5 Lautaro *Mt* Chile
46D2 Lauterecken Germany
15D1 Laval Can
48B2 Laval France
22B2 Laveaga Peak *Mt* USA
47C2 Laveno Italy
31B6 Lavras Brazil
4A3 Lavrentiya Russian Fed
101H1 Lavumisa Swaziland
78D1 Lawas Malay
76B1 Lawksawk Burma
18A2 Lawrence Kansas, USA
15D2 Lawrence Massachusetts, USA
111A3 Lawrence NZ
14A3 Lawrenceville Illinois, USA
9A Lawton USA
91A5 Layla S Arabia
99D2 Laylo Sudan
23A2 Lázaro Cárdenas Mexico
99E1 Laz Daua Somalia
79B4 Lazi Phil
8C2 Lead USA
13F2 Leader Can
18A2 Leavenworth USA
58B2 Leba Pol
18B2 Lebanon Missouri, USA
20B2 Lebanon Oregon, USA
15C2 Lebanon Pennsylvania, USA
92C3 Lebanon Republic, S W Asia
101C3 Lebombo *Mts* Mozam/S Africa/ Swaziland
58B2 Lebork Pol
47A2 Le Bourg-d'Oisans France
47B1 Le Brassus Switz
29B3 Lebu Chile
47B1 Le Buet *Mt* France
46B1 Le Cateau France
55A2 Lecce Italy
52A1 Lecco Italy
47D1 Lech *R* Austria
47D1 Lechtaler Alpen *Mts* Austria
49C2 Le Creusot France
43C3 Ledbury Eng
13E2 Leduc Can
16C1 Lee USA
45B3 Lee *R* Irish Rep
41C3 Leeds Eng
43C3 Leek Eng
56B2 Leer Germany
17B2 Leesburg Florida, USA
16A3 Leesburg Virginia, USA
19B3 Leesville USA
109C2 Leeton Aust
56B2 Leeuwarden Neth
106A4 Leeuwin,C Aust
22C2 Lee Vining USA
27E3 Leeward Is Caribbean S
94A1 Lefkara Cyprus
79B3 Legazpi Phil
47D2 Legnago Italy
59B2 Legnica Pol
33F2 Leguan Inlet Guyana
32C4 Leguizamo Colombia
84D2 Leh India
48C2 Le Havre France
16B2 Lehigh *R* USA

16B2 Lehighton USA
84C2 Leiah Pak
59B3 Leibnitz Austria
43D3 Leicester County, Eng
43D3 Leicester Eng
107C2 Leichhardt *R* Aust
56A2 Leiden Neth
57B2 Leie *R* Belg
106C4 Leigh Creek Aust
43D4 Leighton Buzzard Eng
56B2 Leine *R* Germany
45C2 Leinster Region, Irish Rep
57C2 Leipzig Germany
50A2 Leiria Port
39F7 Leirvik Nor
45B1 Leitrim County, Irish Rep
73C4 Leiyang China
73B5 Leizhou Bandao *Pen* China
73C5 Leizhou Wan *B* China
44C2 Lek *R* Neth
96C1 Le Kef Tunisia
19B3 Leland USA
54A2 Lelija *Mt* Bosnia-Herzegovina
47B1 Le Locle France
48C2 Le Mans France
6D3 Lemieux Is Can
8C2 Lemmon USA
21B2 Lemoore USA
49C2 Lempdes France
86C2 Lemro *R* Burma
52C2 Le Murge Region, Italy
63C2 Lena *R* Russian Fed
38L6 Lendery Russian Fed
73C4 Lengshujiang China
Leningrad = Sankt-Peterburg
112B7 Leningradskaya *Base* Ant
61H3 Leninogorsk Tatarskaya Respublika, Russian Fed
68A1 Leninogorsk Kazakhstan
65K4 Lenin-Kuznetskiy Russian Fed
69F2 Leninskoye Russian Fed
65F6 Lenkoran' Azerbaijan
46E1 Lenne *R* Germany
16C1 Lenox USA
46B1 Lens France
63D1 Lensk Russian Fed
53B3 Lentini Italy
87B2 Lenya *R* Burma
52B1 Leoben Austria
43C3 Leominster Eng
16D1 Leominster USA
24B2 León Mexico
25D3 León Nic
50A1 León Region, Spain
50A1 León Spain
100A3 Leonardville Namibia
106B3 Leonora Aust
35C2 Leopoldina Brazil
Léopoldville = Kinshasa
60C3 Lepel Belorussia
73D4 Leping China
49C2 Le Puy-en-Velay France
98B2 Léré Chad
101G1 Leribe Lesotho
53C2 Lerici Italy
51C1 Lérida Spain
23A1 Lerma *R* Mexico
57C3 Lermoos Austria
55C3 Léros *I* Greece
44E1 Lerwick Scot
46A2 Les Andelys France
26C3 Les Cayes Haiti
47B2 Les Ecrins *Mt* France
73A4 Leshan China
54B2 Leskovac Serbia, Yugos
48B3 Les Landes Region, France

101G1 Leslie S Africa
61H2 Lesnoy Russian Fed
63B2 Lesosibirsk Russian Fed
101G1 Lesotho Kingdom, S Africa
69F2 Lesozavodsk Russian Fed
48B2 Les Sables-d'Olonne France
112A Lesser Antarctica Region, Ant
27D4 Lesser Antilles *Is* Caribbean S
65F5 Lesser Caucasus *Mts* Azerbaijan/Georgia
13E1 Lesser Slave L Can
55C3 Lésvos *I* Greece
58B2 Leszno Pol
86C2 Letha Range *Mts* Burma
5G5 Lethbridge Can
33F3 Lethem Guyana
59D3 Letichev Ukraine
63D2 Let Oktyobr'ya Russian Fed
78B2 Letong Indon
46A1 Le Touquet-Paris-Plage France
76B2 Letpadan Burma
48C1 Le Tréport France
47B1 Leuk Switz
57A2 Leuven Belg
55B3 Levádhia Greece
38G6 Levanger Nor
47B2 Levanna *Mt* Italy
71D5 Léveque,C Aust
46D1 Leverkusen Germany
59B3 Levice Slovakia
47D1 Levico Italy
110C2 Levin NZ
7C5 Lévis Can
15D2 Levittown USA
55B3 Levka el *Mt* Greece
55B3 Levkás Greece
55B3 Levkás *I* Greece
106B2 Lévêque,C Aust
54C1 Levski Bulg
43E4 Lewes Eng
40B2 Lewis *I* Scot
16A2 Lewisburg USA
111B2 Lewis P NZ
8B2 Lewis Range *Mts* USA
13E1 Lewiston Idaho, USA
10C2 Lewiston Maine, USA
8C2 Lewistown Montana, USA
15C2 Lewistown Pennsylvania, USA
19B3 Lewisville USA
11B3 Lexington Kentucky, USA
18B2 Lexington Missouri, USA
15C3 Lexington Park USA
79C3 Leyte G Phil
54A2 Lezhe Alb
82D3 Lhasa China
86B1 Lhazê China
70A3 Lhokseumawe Indon
86C2 Lhozhag China
68B4 Lhünzê China
Liancourt Rocks = Tok-do
79C4 Lianga Phil
73C5 Liangdang China
73C5 Lianjiang China
73C5 Lianping China
73C5 Lian Xian China
73D4 Lianyuan China
72E1 Liaodong Bandao *Pen* China
72E1 Liaodong Wan *B* China
72E1 Liao He *R* China
72E1 Liaoning Province, China
72E1 Liaoyang China
72E1 Liaoyuan China
4F3 Liard *R* Can
4F4 Liard River Can
46C2 Liart France

98B2 **Libenge** Zaire
9C3 **Liberal** USA
57C2 **Liberec** Czech Republic
97A4 **Liberia** Republic, Africa
18B2 **Liberty** Missouri, USA
15D2 **Liberty** New York, USA
19B3 **Liberty** Texas, USA
48B3 **Libourne** France
23B2 **Libres** Mexico
98A2 **Libreville** Gabon
95A2 **Libya** Republic, Africa
95B2 **Libyan Desert** Libya
95B1 **Libyan Plat** Egypt
53B3 **Licata** Italy
43D3 **Lichfield** Eng
101C2 **Lichinga** Mozam
101C1 **Lichtenburg** S Africa
14B3 **Licking** R USA
22B2 **Lick Observatory** USA
60C3 **Lida** Belorussia
39G7 **Lidköping** Sweden
53B2 **Lido di Ostia** Italy
52A1 **Liechtenstein** Principality, Europe
57B2 **Liège** Belg
58C1 **Lielupe** R Latvia
98C2 **Lienart** Zaire
57C3 **Lienz** Austria
60B2 **Liepaja** Latvia
46C1 **Lier** Belg
47B1 **Liestal** Switz
15C1 **Liévre** R Can
57C3 **Liezen** Austria
45C2 **Liffey** R Irish Rep
45C1 **Lifford** Irish Rep
107F3 **Lifu** I Nouvelle Calédonie
109C1 **Lightning Ridge** Aust
46C2 **Ligny-en-Barrois** France
101C2 **Ligonha** R Mozam
47C2 **Liguria** Region, Italy
52A2 **Ligurian** S Italy
21C4 **Lihue** Hawaiian Is
100B2 **Likasi** Zaire
49C1 **Lille** France
39G6 **Lillehammer** Nor
46B1 **Lillers** France
39G7 **Lillestøm** Nor
13C2 **Lillooet** Can
13C2 **Lillooet** R Can
101C2 **Lilongwe** Malawi
79B4 **Liloy** Phil
54A2 **Lim** R Montenegro/ Serbia, Yugos
32B6 **Lima** Peru
50A1 **Lima** USA
10B2 **Lima** USA
92B3 **Limassol** Cyprus
45C1 **Limavady** N Ire
34B3 **Limay** R Arg
34B3 **Limay Mahuida** Arg
98A2 **Limbe** Cam
101C2 **Limbe** Malawi
57B2 **Limburg** W Gem
31B6 **Limeira** Brazil
45B2 **Limerick** County, Irish Rep
41B3 **Limerick** Irish Rep
56B1 **Limfjorden** L Den
106C2 **Limmen Bight** B Aust
55C3 **Limnos** I Greece
31D3 **Limoeiro** Brazil
48C2 **Limoges** France
25D4 **Limón** Costa Rica
8C3 **Limon** USA
48C2 **Limousin** Region, France
79A3 **Linapacan Str** Phil
29B3 **Linares** Brazil
9D4 **Linares** Mexico
50B2 **Linares** Spain
68B4 **Lincang** China
29D2 **Lincoln** Arg
18A1 **Lincoln** California, USA
42D3 **Lincoln** County, Eng
42D3 **Lincoln** Eng
18C1 **Lincoln** Illinois, USA
8D2 **Lincoln** Nebraska, USA
15D2 **Lincoln** New Hampshire, USA
111B2 **Lincoln** NZ
80A **Lincoln** S Greenland
20B2 **Lincoln City** USA
14B2 **Lincoln Park** USA
52A2 **L'Incudina** Mt Corse
57B3 **Lindau** Germany
33F2 **Linden** Guyana
39F7 **Lindesnes** C Nor
99D3 **Lindi** Tanz
98C2 **Lindi** R Zaire
101G1 **Lindley** S Africa
55C3 **Lindos** Greece
15C2 **Lindsay** Can
105J3 **Line Is** Pacific O
72C2 **Linfen** China
76D2 **Lingao** China
79B2 **Lingayen** Phil
56B2 **Lingen** Germany
73C4 **Lingling** China
73B5 **Lingshan** China
72C2 **Lingshi** China
97A3 **Linguère** Sen
73E4 **Linhai** Rhejiang, China
31D5 **Linhares** Brazil
72B1 **Linhe** China
74B2 **Linjiang** China
39H7 **Linköping** Sweden
72D2 **Linqing** China
35B2 **Lins** Brazil
72A2 **Lintao** China
47C1 **Linthal** Switz
68D2 **Linxi** China
72A2 **Linxia** China
57C3 **Linz** Austria
79B3 **Lipa** Phil
53B3 **Lipari** I Italy
61E3 **Lipetsk** Russian Fed
54B1 **Lipova** Rom
57B2 **Lippe** R Germany
46E1 **Lippstadt** Germany
99D2 **Lira** Uganda
98B3 **Liranga** Congo
98C2 **Lisala** Zaire
50A2 **Lisboa** Port **Lisbon = Lisboa**
45C1 **Lisburn** N Ire
45B2 **Liscannor B** Irish Rep
73C4 **Lishui** China
73C4 **Li Shui** R China
60E4 **Lisichansk** Ukraine
48C2 **Lisieux** France
60E3 **Liski** Russian Fed
46B2 **L'Isle-Adam** France
47B1 **L'Isle-sur-la-Doubs** France
109F3 **Lismore** Aust
45B2 **Listowel** Irish Rep
73B5 **Litang** China
94B2 **Litani** R Leb
33G3 **Litani** R Surinam
18C2 **Litchfield** USA
107E4 **Lithgow** Aust
60B2 **Lithuania** Republic, Europe
16A2 **Lititz** USA
69F2 **Litovko** Russian Fed
19A3 **Little** R USA
11C4 **Little Abaco** I The Bahamas
11A3 **Little Falls** USA
22D3 **Littlerock** USA
13D2 **Little Smoky** Can
13D2 **Little Smoky** R Can
16A3 **Littlestown** USA
15D2 **Littleton** New Hampshire, USA
74B2 **Liuhe** China
73B5 **Liuzhou** China
55B3 **Livanátais** Greece
58D1 **Livani** Latvia
12E1 **Livengood** USA
17B1 **Live Oak** USA
21A2 **Livermore** USA
7D5 **Liverpool** Can
42C3 **Liverpool** Eng
4E2 **Liverpool B** Can
42C3 **Liverpool B** Eng
6C2 **Liverpool,C** Can
109D2 **Liverpool Range** Mts Aust
8B2 **Livingston** Montana, USA
19B3 **Livingston** Texas, USA
44C4 **Livingston** UK **Livingstone = Maramba**
19A3 **Livingston,L** USA
52A2 **Livorno** Italy
99D3 **Liwale** Tanz
52B1 **Ljubljana** Slovenia
38G6 **Ljungan** R Sweden
39G7 **Ljungby** Sweden
39H6 **Ljusdal** Sweden
38H6 **Ljusnan** R Sweden
43C4 **Llandeilo** Wales
43C4 **Llandovery** Wales
43C3 **Llandrindod Wells** Wales
43C3 **Llandudno** Wales
43C4 **Llanelli** Wales
43C3 **Llangollen** Wales
9C3 **Llano Estacado** Plat USA
32C2 **Llanos** Region, Colombia/Ven
30D2 **Llanos de Chiquitos** Region, Bol **Lleida = Lérida**
50A2 **Llerena** Spain
43B3 **Lleyn** Pen Wales
89E7 **Llorin** NG
5H4 **Lloydminster** Can
30C3 **Llullaillaco** Mt Arg/Chil
30C3 **Loa** R Chile
49C2 **Loan** France
98B3 **Loange** R Zaire
98B2 **Lobatse** Botswana
98B2 **Lobaye** R CAR
34D3 **Loberia** Arg
100A2 **Lobito** Angola
34D3 **Lobos** Arg
47B2 **Locano** Italy
47C1 **Locarno** Switz
44B3 **Loch Broom** Estuary Scot
42B2 **Loch Doon** L Scot
44B3 **Loch Earn** L Scot
44B3 **Loch Eriboll** Inlet Scot
44B3 **Loch Etive** Inlet Scot
48C2 **Loches** France
44B3 **Loch Ewe** Inlet Scot
44B3 **Loch Fyne** Inlet Scot
44B3 **Loch Hourn** Inlet Scot
44B2 **Lochinver** Scot
44B3 **Loch Katrine** L Scot
44C3 **Loch Leven** L Scot
44B3 **Loch Linnhe** Inlet Scot
44B3 **Loch Lochy** L Scot
44B3 **Loch Lomond** L Scot
44B3 **Loch Long** Inlet Scot
44A3 **Lochmaddy** Scot
44B3 **Loch Maree** L Scot
44B3 **Loch Morar** L Scot
44B3 **Lochnagar** Mt Scot
44B3 **Loch Ness** L Scot
44B3 **Loch Rannoch** L Scot
44A2 **Loch Roag** Inlet Scot
44B2 **Loch Sheil** L Scot
44B2 **Loch Shin** L Scot
44A3 **Loch Snizort** Inlet Scot
44B3 **Loch Sunart** Inlet Scot
44B3 **Loch Tay** L Scot
44B3 **Loch Torridon** Inlet Scot
108A2 **Lock** Aust
42C2 **Lockerbie** Scot
15C2 **Lock Haven** USA
15C2 **Lockport** USA
76D3 **Loc Ninh** Viet
53C3 **Locri** Italy
94B3 **Lod** Israel
108B3 **Loddon** R Aust
60D1 **Lodeynoye Pole** Russian Fed
84C3 **Lodhran** Pak
52A1 **Lodi** Italy
21A2 **Lodi** USA
98C3 **Lodja** Zaire
47B1 **Lods** France
99D2 **Lodwar** Kenya
58B2 **Łódź** Pol
38G5 **Lofoten** Is Nor
9B2 **Logan** Utah, USA
4D3 **Logan,Mt** Can
14A2 **Logansport** Indiana, USA
19B3 **Logansport** Louisiana, USA
50B1 **Logroño** Spain
86A2 **Lohārdaga** India
39J6 **Lohja** Fin
76B2 **Loikaw** Burma
39J6 **Loimaa** Fin
48C2 **Loir** R France
48C2 **Loire** R France
48C2 **Loire** R France
32B4 **Loja** Ecuador
50B2 **Loja** Spain
38K5 **Lokan Tekojärvi** Res Fin
46B1 **Lokeren** Belg
99D2 **Lokitaung** Kenya
58D1 **Loknya** Russian Fed
98C3 **Lokolo** R Zaire
98C3 **Lokoro** R Zaire
6D3 **Loks Land** I Can
56C2 **Lolland** I Den
54B2 **Lom** Bulg
98C3 **Lomami** R Zaire
97A4 **Loma Mts** Sierra Leone/Guinea
47C2 **Lombardia** Region, Italy
71D4 **Lomblen** I Indon
78D4 **Lombok** I Indon
97C4 **Lomé** Togo
98C3 **Lomela** Zaire
98C3 **Lomela** R Zaire
60C2 **Lomonosov** Russian Fed
49C1 **Lomont** Region, France
21A3 **Lompoc** USA
58C2 **Łomza** Pol
87A1 **Lonāvale** India
29B3 **Loncoche** Chile
7B5 **London** Can
6D3 **London** Eng
45C1 **Londonderry** Coun N Ire
45C1 **Londonderry** N Ire
29B7 **Londonderry** I Chil
108B2 **Londonderry,C** Aus
30C4 **Londres** Arg
30F3 **Londrina** Brazil
21B2 **Lone Pine** USA
11C4 **Long** I The Bahama
71F4 **Long** I PNG
78C2 **Long Akah** Malay
47E1 **Longarone** Italy
34A3 **Longaví** Mt Chile
27H2 **Long B** Jamaica
17C1 **Long B** USA
9B3 **Long Beach** California, USA
15D2 **Long Beach** New York, USA
13D5 **Long Branch** USA
73D5 **Longchuan** China
20C2 **Long Creek** USA
109C4 **Longford** Aust
45C2 **Longford** County, Irish Rep

45C2 Longford Irish Rep
44D3 Long Forties Region N Sea
72D1 Longhua China
7C4 Long I Can
10C2 Long I USA
16C2 Long Island Sd USA
7B4 Longlac Can
73B5 Longlin China
8C2 Longmont USA
78D2 Longnawan Indon
29B3 Longquimay Chile
107D3 Longreach Aust
72A2 Longshou Shan Upland China
42C2 Longtown Eng
15D1 Longueuil Can
34A3 Longuimay Chile
46C2 Longuyon France
11A3 Longview Texas, USA
8A2 Longview Washington, USA
46C2 Longwy France
72A3 Longxi China
77D3 Long Xuyen Viet
73D4 Longyan China
73B5 Longzhou China
47D2 Lonigo Italy
49D2 Lons-le-Saunier France
11C3 Lookout,C USA
99D3 Loolmalasin Mt Tanz
13D1 Loon R Can
45B2 Loop Hd C Irish Rep
76C3 Lop Buri Thai
98A3 Lopez C Gabon
68B2 Lop Nor L China
50A2 Lora del Rio Spain
10B2 Lorain USA
84B2 Loralai Pak
90B3 Lordegan Iran
107E4 Lord Howe I Aust
105G5 Lord Howe Rise Pacific O
6A3 Lord Mayor B Can
9C3 Lordsburg USA
35B2 Lorena Brazil
47E2 Loreo Italy
23A1 Loreto Mexico
48B2 Lorient France
108B3 Lorne Aust
57B3 Lörrach Germany
49D2 Lorraine Region France
9C3 Los Alamos USA
34A2 Los Andes Chile
29B3 Los Angeles Chile
9B3 Los Angeles USA
21A2 Los Banos USA
34B2 Los Cerrillos Arg
21A2 Los Gatos USA
52B2 Lošinj I Croatia
29B3 Los Lagos Chile
24B2 Los Mochis Mexico
22B3 Los Olivos USA
34A3 Los Sauces Chile
44C3 Lossiemouth Scot
27E4 Los Testigos Is Ven
29B2 Los Vilos Chile
48C3 Lot R France
34A3 Lota Chile
42C2 Lothian Region, Scot
99D2 Lotikipi Plain Sudan/Kenya
98C3 Loto Zaire
47B1 Lötschberg Tunnel Switz
38K5 Lotta R Fin/Russian Fed
48B2 Loudéac France
97A3 Louga Sen
41B3 Lough Allen L Irish Rep
41B3 Lough Boderg L Irish Rep
43D3 Loughborough Eng
45C2 Lough Bowna L Irish Rep
45C1 Lough Carlingford L N Ire
41B3 Lough Conn L Irish Rep
41B3 Lough Corrib L Irish Rep

41B3 Lough Derg L Irish Rep
45C2 Lough Derravaragh L Irish Rep
4H2 Loughead I Can
45C2 Lough Ennell L Irish Rep
41B3 Lough Erne L N Ire
40B2 Lough Foyle Estuary N Ire/Irish Rep
40B3 Lough Neagh L N Ire
45C1 Lough Oughter L Irish Rep
45B2 Loughrea Irish Rep
45C2 Lough Ree L Irish Rep
45C2 Lough Sheelin L Irish Rep
42B2 Lough Strangford L Irish Rep
45C1 Lough Swilly Estuary Irish Rep
14B3 Louisa USA
70C3 Louisa Reef I S E Asia
12E2 Louise,L USA
107E2 Louisiade Arch Solomon Is
11A3 Louisiana State, USA
17B1 Louisville Georgia, USA
11B3 Louisville Kentucky, USA
38L5 Loukhi Russian Fed
48B3 Lourdes France
108C2 Louth Aust
45C2 Louth County, Irish Rep
42D3 Louth Eng
Louvain = Leuven
46C1 Louviers France
60D2 Lovat R Russian Fed
54B2 Lovech Bulg
21B1 Lovelock USA
52B1 Lóvere Italy
9C3 Lovington USA
38L5 Lovozero Russian Fed
6B3 Low,C Can
10C2 Lowell Massachusetts, USA
20B2 Lowell Oregon, USA
16D1 Lowell USA
111B2 Lower Hutt NZ
43E3 Lowestoft Eng
58B2 Łowicz Pol
108B2 Loxton Aust
5F4 Loyd George,Mt Can
54A2 Loznica Serbia, Yugos
23A2 Loz Reyes Mexico
65H3 Lozva R Russian Fed
100B2 Luacano Angola
98C3 Luachimo Angola
98C3 Lualaba R Zaire
100B2 Luampa Angola
98B3 Luân Angola
98B3 Lu'an China
100A2 Luanda Angola
100B2 Luanginga R Angola
76C1 Luang Namtha Laos
76C2 Luang Prabang Laos
98B3 Luangue R Angola
100C2 Luangwa R Zambia
72D1 Luan He R China
72D1 Luanping China
100B2 Luanshya Zambia
100B2 Luapula R Zaire
50A1 Luarca Spain
98B3 Lubalo Angola
58D2 L'uban Belorussia
79B3 Lubang Is Phil
100A2 Lubango Angola
9C3 Lubbock USA
57C2 Lübeck Germany
98C3 Lubefu Zaire
98C3 Lubefu R Zaire
99C3 Lubero Zaire
58B2 Lublin Pol
59C2 Lubny Ukraine
60D3 Lubny Ukraine
78C2 Lubok Antu Malay
98C3 Lubudi Zaire

98C3 Lubudi R Zaire
78A3 Lubuklinggau Indon
100B2 Lubumbashi Zaire
98C3 Lubutu Zaire
79B3 Lucban Phil
52B2 Lucca Italy
42B2 Luce B Scot
19C3 Lucedale USA
79B3 Lucena Phil
59B3 Lucenec Slovakia
52B2 Lucern = Luzern
73C5 Luchuan China
56C2 Luckenwalde Germany
101F1 Luckhoff S Africa
86A1 Lucknow India
100B2 Lucusse Angola
46D1 Lüdenscheid Germany
100A3 Lüderitz Namibia
84D2 Ludhiana India
43C3 Ludlow Eng
54C2 Ludogorie Upland Bulg
17B1 Ludowici USA
54B1 Luduş Rom
39H6 Ludvika Sweden
57B3 Ludwigsburg Germany
57B3 Ludwigshafen Germany
56C2 Ludwigslust Germany
98C3 Luebo Zaire
98C3 Luema R Zaire
98C3 Luembe R Angola
100A2 Luena R Angola
100B2 Luene R Angola
72B3 Lüeyang China
73D5 Lufeng China
11A3 Lufkin USA
60C2 Luga Russian Fed
60C2 Luga R Russian Fed
52A1 Lugano Switz
60E4 Lugansk Ukraine
101C2 Lugela Mozam
101C2 Lugenda R Mozam
50A1 Lugo Spain
54B1 Lugoj Rom
72A3 Luhuo China
98B3 Lui R Angola
100B2 Luiana Angola
100B2 Luiana R Angola
Luichow Peninsula = Leizhou Bandao
47C2 Luino Italy
98B2 Luionga R Angola
72B2 Luipan Shan Upland China
100B2 Luishia Zaire
68B4 Luixi China
98C3 Luiza Zaire
34B2 Luján Arg
73D3 Lujiang China
99B3 Lukenie R Zaire
64E4 Luki Russian Fed
98B3 Lukolela Zaire
58C2 Luków Pol
99C3 Lukuga R Zaire
100B2 Lukulu Zambia
38J5 Lule R Sweden
38J5 Luleå Sweden
54C2 Lüleburgaz Turk
72C2 Lüliang Shan Mts China
19A4 Luling USA
98C2 Lulonga R Zaire
Luluabourg = Kananga
100B2 Lumbala Kaquengue Angola
11C3 Lumberton USA
78D1 Lumbis Indon
86C1 Lumding India
100B2 Lumeje Angola
111A3 Lumsden NZ
39G7 Lund Sweden
101C2 Lundazi Zambia
38J5 Lundi R Zim
43B4 Lundy I Eng
56C2 Lüneburg Germany
46D2 Lunéville France
100B2 Lunga R Zambia
86C2 Lunglei India

100A2 Lungue Bungo R Angola
58D2 Luninec Belorussia
98B3 Luobomo Congo
73B5 Luocheng China
73C5 Luoding China
72C3 Luohe China
72C3 Luo He R Henan, China
72B2 Luo He R Shaanxi, China
73C4 Luoxiao Shan Hills China
72C3 Luoyang China
98B3 Luozi Zaire
100B2 Lupane Zim
101C2 Lupilichi Mozam
Lu Qu = Tao He
30E4 Luque Par
101C2 Lurio R Mozam
90A3 Luristan Region, Iran
100B2 Lusaka Zambia
98C3 Lusambo Zaire
55A2 Lushnjë Alb
99D3 Lushoto Tanz
68B4 Lushui China
72E2 Lushun China
43D4 Luton Eng
60C3 Lutsk Ukraine
99C3 Luuq Somalia
99C3 Luvua R Zaire
99D3 Luwegu R Tanz
100C2 Luwingu Zambia
71D4 Luwuk Indon
46D2 Luxembourg Grand Duchy, N W Europe
46D2 Luxembourg Lux
73A5 Luxi China
95C2 Luxor Egypt
61G1 Luza Russian Fed
61G1 Luza R Russian Fed
52A1 Luzern Switz
73B5 Luzhai China
73B4 Luzhou China
35B1 Luziânia Brazil
79B2 Luzon I Phil
79B1 Luzon Str Phil
59C3 L'vov Ukraine
44C2 Lybster Scot
38H6 Lycksele Sweden
100B3 Lydenburg S Africa
8B3 Lyell,Mt USA
16A2 Lykens USA
43C4 Lyme B Eng
43C4 Lyme Regis Eng
11C3 Lynchburg USA
107D2 Lyndhurst Aust
15D2 Lynn USA
12G3 Lynn Canal Sd USA
17A1 Lynn Haven USA
5H4 Lynn Lake Can
5H3 Lynx L Can
49C2 Lyon France
12G3 Lyon Canal Sd USA
17B1 Lyons Georgia, USA
106A3 Lyons R Aust
47B2 Lys R Italy
61J2 Lys'va Russian Fed
111B2 Lyttelton NZ
13C2 Lytton Can
22A1 Lytton USA
58D2 Lyubashov Ukraine
60E2 Lyublino Russian Fed

M

76C1 Ma R Viet
94B2 Ma'agan Jordan
94B2 Ma'alot Tarshiha Israel
94B2 Ma'an Jordan
73D3 Ma'anshan China
92C2 Ma'arrat an Nu'mān Syria
46C1 Maas R Neth
46C1 Maaseik Belg
79B3 Maasin Phil
57B2 Maastricht Belg
101C2 Mabalane Mozam
33F2 Mabaruma Guyana
42E3 Mablethorpe Eng
101C3 Mabote Mozam
58C2 Mabrita Belorussia
58D2 M'adel Belorussia

35C2 Macaé Brazil	109C4 Macquarie Harbour B Aust	7A3 Maguse River Can	96C1 Makthar Tunisia
903 McAlester USA	109D2 Macquarie,L Aust	76B1 Magwe Burma	93D2 Mākū Iran
9D4 McAllen USA	17B1 McRae USA	90A2 Mahābād Iran	98C3 Makumbi Zaire
101C2 Macalogo Mozam	112B11 Mac. Robertson Land Region, Ant	86B1 Mahabharat Range Mts Nepal	74C4 Makurazaki Japan
33G3 Macapá Brazil	45B3 Macroom Irish Rep	87A1 Mahad India	97C4 Makurdi Nig
3281 Macarani Brazil	96C1 M'Sila Alg	85D4 Mahadeo Hills India	79B4 Malabang Phil
3284 Macas Ecuador	4G3 McTavish Arm B Can	101D2 Mahajanga Madag	87A2 Malabar Coast India
31D3 Macau Brazil	108A1 Macumba R Aust	100B3 Mahalapye Botswana	89E7 Malabo Bioko
73C5 Macau Dependency, China	47C2 Macunaga Italy	86A2 Mahānadi R India	77C5 Malacca,Str of S E Asia
98C2 M'Bari R CAR	4F3 McVicar Arm R Can	101D2 Mahanoro Madag	32C2 Málaga Colombia
13C2 McBride Can	59B3 M'yarôvâr Hung	16A2 Mahanoy City USA	50B2 Málaga Spain
12F2 McCarthy USA	9483 Mádabā Jordan	87A1 Maharashtra State, India	101D3 Malaimbandy Madag
13A2 McCauley I Can	95A3 Madadi Well Chad	86A2 Māhāsamund India	107F1 Malaita I Solomon Is
42C3 Macclesfield Eng	89J10 Madagascar I Indian O	76C2 Maha Sarakham Thai	99D2 Malakal Sudan
6B1 McClintock B Can		101D2 Mahavavy R Madag	84C2 Malakand Pak
4H2 McClintock Chan Can	95A2 Madama Niger	87B1 Mahbübnagar India	78C4 Malang Indon
16A2 McClure USA	71F4 Madang PNG	96D1 Mahdia Tunisia	98B3 Malange Angola
22B2 McClure,L Can	97C3 Madaoua Niger	87B2 Mahe India	97C3 Malanville Benin
4G2 McClure Str Can	86C2 Madaripur Bang	85D4 Mahekar India	41H7 Mälaren L Sweden
19B3 McComb USA	90B2 Madau Turkmenistan	101D2 Mahéli I Comoros	34B3 Malargüe Arg
8C2 McCook USA	16C2 Madawaska R Can	86A2 Mahendragarh India	12F3 Malaspina Gl USA
13C1 Macculloch,C Can	96A1 Madeira I Atlantic O	99D3 Mahenge Tanz	73A2 Malatya Turk
13C1 McCusker,Mt Can	33E5 Madeira R Brazil	85C4 Mahesana India	101C2 Malawi Republic, Africa
4F4 McDame Can	7D5 Madeleine, Isle de la Can	110C1 Mahia Pen NZ	Malawi,L = Nyasa,L
20C2 McDermitt USA	24B2 Madera Mexico	85D3 Mahoba India	79C4 Malaybalay Phil
13E2 Macdonald R Can	21A2 Madera USA	51C2 Mahón Spain	90A3 Malâyer Iran
106C3 Macdonnell Ranges Mts Aust	87A1 Madgaon India	12J1 Mahony L Can	70B3 Malaysia Federation, S E Asia
50A1 Macedo de Cavaleiros Port	86B1 Madhubani India	96D1 Mahrès Tunisia	93D2 Malazgirt Turk
55B2 Macedonia Republic, Europe	86A2 Madhya Pradesh State, India	85C4 Mahuva India	58B2 Malbork Pol
31D3 Maceió Brazil	87B2 Madikeri India	32C1 Maicao Colombia	56C2 Malchin Germany
97B4 Macenta Guinea	98B3 Madimba Zaire	47B1 Maiche France	18C2 Malden USA
5282 Macerata Italy	98B3 Madingo Kayes Congo	43E4 Maidstone Eng	83B5 Maldives Is Indian O
108A2 Macfarlane,L Aust	98B3 Madingou Congo	98B1 Maiduguri Nig	104B4 Maldives Ridge Indian O
19B3 McGehee USA	10B3 Madison Indiana, USA	86A2 Maihar India	29F2 Maldonado Urug
45B3 MacGillycuddys Reeks Mts Irish Rep	8D2 Madison Wisconsin, USA	86C2 Maijdi Bang	47D1 Male Italy
4C3 McGrath USA	18C2 Madisonville Kentucky, USA	76B3 Mail Kyun I Burma	85C4 Malegaon India
35B2 Machado Brazil	19A3 Madisonville Texas, USA	84A1 Maimana Afghan	59B3 Malé Karpaty Upland Slovakia
101C3 Machaila Mozam	78C4 Madiun Indon	14B1 Main Chan Can	101C2 Malema Mozam
99D3 Machakos Kenya	47D1 Madonna Di Campóldo Italy	98B3 Mai-Ndombe L Zaire	84B1 Malestan Afghan
3284 Machala Ecuador	20B2 Madras USA	10D2 Maine State, USA	38H5 Malgomaj L Sweden
101C3 Machaze Mozam	28A2 Madras USA	48B2 Maine Region France	95B3 Malha Well Sudan
87B1 Mācherla India	29A6 Madre de Dios I Chile	32D1 Maiquetia Ven	20C2 Malheur L USA
94B2 Machgharab Leb	32D6 Madre de Dios R Bol	47B2 Maira R Italy	97B3 Mali Republic, Africa
87C1 Machilipatnam India	50B2 Madrid Spain	86C1 Mairābāri India	78D1 Malinau Indon
32C1 Machiques Ven	50B2 Madridejos Spain	86C2 Maiskhal I India	99E3 Malindi Kenya
23C2 Machu-Picchu Hist Site Peru	78C4 Madura I Indon	107E4 Maitland New South Wales, Aust	Malines = Mechelen
101C3 Macia Mozam	87B3 Madurai India	108A2 Maitland S Australia, Aust	40B2 Malin Head Pt Irish Rep
109C1 MacIntyre R Aust	7581 Maebashi Japan	112C12 Maitri Base Ant	84D2 Malkāla Range Mts India
107G3 Mackay Aust	76B3 Mae Khlong R Thai	74D3 Maizuru Japan	55C2 Malkara Turk
106B3 Mackay,L Aust	77B4 Mae Nam Lunang R Thai	70C4 Majene Indon	54C2 Malko Türnovo Bulg
14C2 McKeesport USA	76C2 Mae Nam Mun R Thai	30B2 Majes R Peru	44B3 Mallaig Scot
13C1 Mackenzie Can	76B2 Mae Nam Ping R Thai	99D2 Maji Eth	95C2 Mallawi Egypt
4E3 Mackenzie R Can	101D2 Maevatanana Madag	72D2 Majia He R China	47D1 Málles Venosta Italy
4E3 Mackenzie B Can	101G1 Mafeteng Lesotho	Majunga = Mahajanga	51C2 Mallorca I Spain
4G2 Mackenzie King I Can	109C3 Maffra Aust	70C4 Makale Indon	45B2 Mallow Irish Rep
4E3 Mackenzie Mts Can	99D3 Mafia I Tanz	86B1 Makalu Mt China/Nepal	38G6 Malm Nor
14B1 Mackinac,Str of USA	101G1 Mafikeng S Africa	98B2 Makanza Zaire	38J5 Malmberget Sweden
14B1 Mackinaw City USA	30G4 Mafra Brazil	52C2 Makarska Croatia	46D1 Malmédy Germany
12D2 McKinley,Mt USA	92C3 Mafraq Jordan	61F2 Makaryev Russian Fed	100A4 Malmesbury S Africa
19A3 McKinney USA	32C2 Magangué Colombia	Makassar = Ujung Pandang	39G7 Malmö Sweden
6C2 Mackinson Inlet B Can	34D3 Magdalena Arg	78D3 Makassar Str Indon	61G2 Malmyzh Russian Fed
109D2 Macksville Aust	24A1 Magdalena Mexico	61H4 Makat Kazakhstan	79B3 Malolos Phil
20B2 Mclaoughlin,Mt USA	26C4 Magdalena R Colombia	97A4 Makeni Sierra Leone	15D2 Malone USA
109D1 Maclean Aust	78D1 Magdalena,Mt Malay	60E4 Makeyevka Ukraine	101G1 Maloti Mts Lesotho
108A4 Maclear S Africa	56C2 Magdeburg Germany	100B3 Makgadikgadi Salt Pan Botswana	38F6 Måløy Nor
5G4 McLennan Can	31C6 Magé Brazil	61G5 Makhachkala Russian Fed	28A2 Malpelo I Colombia
13D2 McLeod R Can	78C4 Magelang Indon	99D3 Makindu Kenya	34A2 Malpo R Chile
4G3 McLeod B Can	47C1 Maggia R Switz	88H5 Makkah S Arabia	85D3 Malpura India
106A3 McLeod,L Aust	92B4 Maghâgha Egypt	7E4 Makkovik Can	8C2 Malta Montana, USA
13C1 McLeod Lake Can	45C1 Magherafelt N Ire	59C3 Makó Hung	53B3 Malta Chan Malta/Italy
4E3 Macmillan R Can	55A2 Maglie Italy	99B2 Makokou Gabon	53B3 Malta I Medit S
12H2 Macmillan P Can	61J3 Magnitogorsk Russian Fed	110C1 Makorako,Mt NZ	100A3 Maltahöhe Namibia
20B1 McMinnville Oregon, USA	19B3 Magnólia USA	98A3 Makoua Congo	42D2 Malton Eng
112B7 McMurdo Base Ant	101C2 Magoé Mozam	85C3 Makrāna India	39G6 Malung Sweden
13D2 McNaughton L Can	15D1 Magog Can	85A3 Makran Coast Range Mts Pak	87A1 Malvan India
18B1 Macomb USA	23B1 Magosal Mexico		19B3 Malvern USA
53A2 Macomer Sardegna	13E2 Magrath Can		85D4 Malwa Plat India
101C2 Macomia Mozam			61G4 Malyy Uzen' R Kazakhstan
49C2 Mâcon France			63D2 Mama Russian Fed
11B3 Macon Georgia, USA			61H2 Mamadysh Russian Fed
18B2 Macon Missouri, USA			99C2 Mambasa Zaire
100B2 Macondo Angola			
18A2 McPherson USA			
104F6 Macquarie Is Aust			
109C2 Macquarie Aust			

71E4 Mamberamo *R*
   Indon
98B2 **Mambéré** *R* CAR
98A2 Mamfé Cam
33D6 Mamoré *R* Bol
97A3 Mamou Guinea
101D2 Mampikony Madag
97B4 Mampong Ghana
94B3 Mamshit *Hist Site*
   Israel
100B3 Mamuno Botswana
97B4 Man Ivory Coast
21C4 Mana Hawaiian Is
101D3 Manabo Madag
33E4 Manacapuru Brazil
51C2 Manacor Spain
71D3 Manado Indon
25D3 Managua Nic
101D3 Manakara Madag
101D2 Mananara Madag
101D2 Mananjary Madag
111A3 Manapouri NZ
111A3 Manapouri,L NZ
86C1 Manas Bhutan
65X5 Manas Hu *L* China
86A1 Manaslu *Mt* Nepal
16B2 Manasquan USA
33F4 Manaus Brazil
92B2 Manavgat Turk
93C2 Manbij Syria
42B2 Man,Calf of *I* Eng
87B1 Mancheral India
15D2 **Manchester**
   Connecticut, USA
42C3 **Manchester** Eng
10C2 **Manchester** New
   Hampshire, USA
16A2 **Manchester**
   Pennsylvania, USA
69E2 **Manchuria** *Hist*
   Region, China
91B4 **Mand** *R* Iran
101C2 Manda Tanz
35A2 Mandaguari Brazil
39F7 Mandal Nor
76B1 Mandalay Burma
68C2 **Mandalgovi**
   Mongolia
8C2 Mandan USA
14A2 Mandeladena USA
99E2 Mandera Eth
16B3 Mandeville Jamaica
101C2 Mandimba Mozam
86A2 Mandla India
101C2 **Mandritsara** Madag
85D4 Mandsaur India
53C2 Manduria Italy
85B4 Mandvi India
87B2 Mandya India
58D2 Manevichi Ukraine
42D3 Manfield Eng
53C2 Manfredonia Italy
98B1 **Manga** *Desert*
   Region Niger
110C1 Mangakino NZ
54C2 Mangalia Rom
98B1 Mangalmé Chad
87A2 Mangalore India
78B3 Mangaon India
68B3 Mangnia China
101C2 Mangoche Malawi
101D3 Mangoky *R* Madag
71D4 Mangole *I* Indon
85B4 Mangral India
63E2 Mangui China
8D3 Manhattan USA
21C4 Manhuacu Brazil
101D2 **Mania** *R* Madag
101C2 Manica Mozam
7D5 Manicouagan *R* Can
91A4 Manifah S Arabia
79B3 Manila Phil
100D2 **Manilla** Aust
97B3 Maninian Ivory Coast
86C2 **Manipur** State, India
86C2 Manipur *R* Burma
92A2 Manisa Turk
41C3 **Man,Isle of** *I* Irish S
14A2 Manistee USA
14A2 Manistee *R* USA
14A1 Manistique USA
5H4 **Manitoba** Province,
   Can
5J4 Manitoba,L Can

13F2 Manito *L* Can
14A1 Manitou Is USA
7B5 Manitoulin *I* Can
14A2 Manitowoc USA
15C1 Maniwaki Can
32B2 Manizales Colombia
101D3 Manja Madag
106A4 Manjimup Aust
87B1 Mânjra *R* India
10A2 Mankato USA
97B4 Mankono Ivory Coast
12D2 Manley Hot Springs
   USA
110B1 Manly NZ
85C4 Manmad India
78A3 Manna Indon
108A2 Mannahill Aust
87B3 Mannar Sri Lanka
87A3 Mannar,G of India
87B2 Mannârgudi India
57B3 Mannheim Germany
13D1 Manning Can
17B1 Manning USA
108A2 Mannum Aust
97A4 Mano Sierra Leone
71E4 Manokwari Indon
98C3 Manono Zaire
76B3 Manoron Burma
75B1 Mano-wan *B* Japan
74B2 Mano'o *R* N Korea
84D3 Mânsa India
100B2 Mansa Zambia
6B3 Mansel I Can
19D2 Mansfield Arkansas,
   USA
108C3 Mansfield Aust
19B3 Mansfield Louisiana,
   USA
16D1 **Mansfield**
   Massachusetts, USA
10B2 Mansfield Ohio, USA
15C2 **Mansfield**
   Pennsylvania, USA
71E2 **Mansyu Deep**
   Pacific O
32A4 Manta Ecuador
79A4 **Mantalingajan,Mt**
   Phil
32B6 Mantaro *R* Peru
22B2 Manteca USA
48C2 Mantes France
52B1 Mantova Italy
38J6 Mantta Fin
61F2 **Mantyrovo**
   Russian Fed
35A2 Manuel Ribas Brazil
79B4 Manukan Phil
110B1 Manukau NZ
71A4 Manus *I* Pacific O
50B2 Manzanares Spain
25E2 Manzanillo Cuba
24B3 Manzanillo Mexico
63D3 Manzhouli China
94C3 Manzil Jordan
101C3 Manzini Swaziland
98B1 Mao Chad
72A2 **Maomao Shan** *Mt*
   China
73C5 Maoming China
101C3 Mapai Mozam
71E3 Mapia *Is* Pacific O
79A4 Mapin *I* Phil
5H5 **Maple Creek** Can
101H1 Maputo Mozam
101H1 Maputo *R* Mozam
   Ma Qu = Huange He
72A3 Maqu China
86B1 Maquan He *R* China
98B3 Maquela do Zombo
   Angola
29C4 Maquinchao Arg
31B3 Maraba Brazil
32C1 Maracaibo Ven
32D1 Maracaibo Ven
95A2 Marâdah Libya
97C3 Maradi Niger
90A2 Marâgheh Iran
99D2 Maralal Kenya
107F1 Maramasike *I*
   Solomon Is
100B2 Maramba Zambia
90A2 Marand Iran
31B2 **Maranhão** State,
   Brazil
109C1 Maranoa *R* Aust

32B4 Marañón *R* Peru
7B5 Marathon Can
17B2 **Marathon** Florida,
   USA
78D2 Maratua *I* Indon
23A2 Maravatío Mexico
79B4 Marawi Phil
34B2 Marayes Arg
50B2 Marbella Spain
106A3 Marble Bar Aust
100B3 Marblehall S Africa
16D1 Marblehead USA
57B2 Marburg Germany
49B2 Marche Belg
50A2 Marchena Spain
46C1 **Marche-en-Famenne**
   Belg
32J7 Marchena *I* Ecuador
17B2 Marco USA
34C2 Marcos Juárez Arg
12E2 **Marcus Baker,Mt**
   USA
15D2 Marcy,Mt USA
84C2 Mardan Pak
29E3 Mar del Plata Arg
93D2 Mardin Turk
87B1 Marg *R* Eth
16B1 Margaretville USA
43E4 Margate Eng
54B1 Marghita Rom
109C4 Maria *I* Aust
43C3 Mariana *Is* Pacific O
13E1 Mariana Lake Can
104F3 **Marianas Trench**
   Pacific O
86C1 Mariani India
19B3 Marianna Arkansas,
   USA
17A1 Marianna Florida,
   USA
7G4 **Maria Van Diemen,C**
   NZ
59B3 Mariazell Austria
52C1 Maribor Slovenia
99C2 Maridi Sudan
112B5 **Marie Byrd Land**
   Region, Ant
27E3 **Marie Galante** *I*
   Caribbean S
39H6 Mariehamn Fin
46C1 Mariembourg Belg
33G2 Marienburg Surinam
100A3 Mariental Namibia
39G7 Mariestad Sweden
17B1 Marietta Georgia,
   USA
14B3 Marietta Ohio, USA
19A3 Marietta Oklahoma,
   USA
27Q2 Marigot Dominica
60B3 **Marijampole**
   Lithuania
31B6 Marília Brazil
98B3 Marimba Angola
79B3 Marinduque *I* Phil
10B2 Marinette USA
30B3 Maringá Brazil
98C2 Maringa *R* Zaïre
18B2 Marion Arkansas,
   USA
18C2 Marion Illinois, USA
10B2 Marion Indiana, USA
10B2 Marion Ohio, USA
17C1 Marion S Carolina,
   USA
11B3 Marion,L USA
107E2 Marion Reef Aust
21B2 Mariposa USA
22B2 Mariposa *R* USA
60C5 Marista *R* Bulg
60E4 Mariupol' Ukraine
61G2 **Mariyskaya**
   Respublika,
   Russian Fed
94B2 Marjayoun Leb
58D2 Marjina Gorki
   Belorussia
94B3 Marka Jordan
99E2 Marka Somalia
56C1 Markaryd Sweden
43C3 Market Drayton Eng
43D3 Market Harborough
   Eng
112A Markham,Mt Ant

22C1 Markleeville USA
16D1 **Marlboro**
   Massachusetts, USA
107D3 Marlborough Aust
46B2 Marle France
19A3 Marlin USA
48C3 Marmande France
55C2 Marmara Adi *I* Turk
92A1 Marmara,S of Turk
55C3 Marmaris Turk
14B3 Marmet USA
12D3 Marmot B USA
47A1 Marnay France
46B2 Marne Department,
   France
46B2 Marne *R* France
98B2 Maro Chad
101D2 **Maroantsetra** Madag
101C2 Marondera Zim
33G3 Maroni *R* French
   Guiana
109D1 Maroochydore Aust
98B1 Maroua Cam
101D2 Marovoay Madag
11B4 **Marquesas Keys** *Is*
   USA
10B2 Marquette USA
46A1 Marquise France
21A2 Marra *R* Aust
101H1 Marracuene Mozam
96B1 Marrakech Mor
106C3 Marree Aust
19B4 Marrero USA
101H1 Marromeu Mozam
101C2 Marrupa Mozam
95C2 Marsa Alam Egypt
99D2 Marsabit Kenya
53B3 Marsala Italy
49D3 Marseille France
17B2 Marshall Alaska, USA
14A3 Marshall Illinois, USA
14B2 Marshall Michigan,
   USA
18B2 **Marshall** Missouri,
   USA
11A3 **Marshall** Texas, USA
105G3 **Marshall Is** Pacific O
18B2 **Marshfield** Missouri,
   USA
26B1 **Marsh Harbour**
   The Bahamas
19B4 Marsh I USA
12H2 Marsh L Can
76B2 **Martaban,G of**
   Burma
78A3 Martapura Indon
78C3 Martapura Indon
15D2 **Martha's Vineyard** *I*
   USA
49D2 Martigny Switz
59B3 Martin Slovakia
111C2 **Martinborough** NZ
34B3 Martín de Loyola Arg
23B1 **Martinez de la Torre**
   Mexico
27E4 **Martinique** *I*
   Caribbean S
17A1 Martin,L USA
15C3 **Martinsburg** USA
14B2 Martins Ferry USA
103G6 Martin Vaz *I*
   Atlantic O
49D3 Martiques France
110C2 Marton NZ
50B2 Martos Spain
78D1 Marudi Malay
84B2 Maruf Afghan
75A2 Marugame Japan
85C3 Mârwâr India
65H6 Mary Turkmenistan
107E3 **Maryborough**
   Queensland, Aust
108B3 **Maryborough**
   Victoria, Aust
5F4 Mary Henry,Mt Can
10C3 Maryland State, USA
42C2 Maryport Eng
21A2 **Marysville** California,
   USA
18A2 **Marysville** Kansas,
   USA
20B1 **Marysville**
   Washington, USA
10A2 Maryville Iowa, USA

18B1 Maryville Missouri, USA
95A2 Marzuq Libya
Masada = Mezada
94B2 Mas'adah Syria
99D3 Masai Steppe *Upland* Tanz
99D3 Masaka Uganda
93E2 Masally Azerbaijan
74B3 Masan S Korea
101C2 Masasi Tanz
76D3 Masaya Nic
79B3 Masbate Phil
79B3 Masbate *i* Phil
96C1 Mascara Alg
25D1 Mascota Brazil
35D1 Mascote Brazil
101G1 Maseru Lesotho
66C3 Mashad Iran
84B2 Mashaki Afghan
90C2 Mashhad Iran
98B3 Masi-Manimba Zaire
99D2 Masindi Uganda
99C3 Masisi Zaire
90A3 Masjed Soleyman Iran
101E2 Masoala *C* Madag
10A2 Mason City USA
91C5 Masqat Oman
52B2 Massa Italy
10C2 Massachusetts State, USA
15D2 Massachusetts B USA
98B1 Massakori Chad
101C3 Massangena Mozam
Massawa = Mits'iwa
15D2 Massena USA
53C2 Massénya Chad
14B1 Massey Can
49C2 Massif Central *Mts* France
98B2 Massif de la Amaoua *Mts* Cam
26C3 Massif de la Hotte *Mts* Haiti
101D3 Massif de l'Isalo *Upland* Madag
98C2 Massif des Bongo *Upland* CAR
49D2 Massif du Pelvoux *Mts* France
101D2 Massif du Tsaratanana *Mt* Madag
14B2 Massillon USA *
97B3 Massina Region, Mali
101C3 Massinga Mozam
101C3 Massingir Mozam
61H4 Masteksay Kazakhstan
111C2 Masterton NZ
74C4 Masuda Japan
98B3 Masuku Gabon
100C3 Masvingo Zim
92C2 Masyaf Syria
98B3 Matadi Zaire
25D3 Matagalpa Nic
7C4 Matagami Can
9D4 Matagorda B USA
110C1 Matakana NZ
100A2 Matala Angola
87C3 Matale Sri Lanka
97A3 Matam Sen
97C3 Matameye Niger
24C2 Matamoros Mexico
95B2 Ma'tan as Sarra *Well* Libya
7D5 Matane Can
25D2 Matanzas Cuba
34A2 Mataquito *R* Chile
87C3 Matara Sri Lanka
106A1 Mataram Indon
30B2 Matarani Peru
51C1 Mataró Spain
111A3 Mataura NZ
24B2 Matehuala Mexico
27L1 Matelot Trinidad
53C2 Matera Italy
59C3 Mátészalka Hung
85C3 Mathura India
79C4 Mati Phil
78D3 Matisiri *i* Indon
43D3 Matlock Eng

33F6 Mato Grosso Brazil
33F6 Mato Grosso State, Brazil
30E2 Mato Grosso do Sul State, Brazil
101H1 Matola Mozam
92A3 Matrûh Egypt
74C3 Matsue Japan
74E2 Matsumae Japan
74D3 Matsumoto Japan
74D4 Matsusaka Japan
74C4 Matsuyama Japan
7B5 Mattagami *R* Can
15C1 Mattawa Can
52A1 Matterhorn *Mt* Italy/Switz
26C2 Matthew Town The Bahamas
16C2 Mattituck USA
18C2 Mattoon USA
27L1 Matura & Trinidad
33E2 Maturín Ven
86A1 Mau India
72C3 Maúa Mozam
49C1 Maubeuge France
100B2 Maude Aust
103J8 Maud Seamount Atlantic O
21C4 Maui *i* Hawaiian Is
34A3 Maule *R* Chile
14B2 Maumee USA
14B2 Maumee *R* USA
21C4 Mauna Kea *Mt* Hawaiian Is
21C4 Mauna Loa *Mt* Hawaiian Is
4F3 Maunoir *L* Can
4F3 Maunoir *L* Can
48C2 Mauriac France
96A2 Mauritania Republic, Africa
100E3 Mauritius *i* Indian O
100B2 Mavinga Angola
86C2 Mawlaik Burma
Mawlamyine = Moulmein
112C10 Mawson *Base* Ant
78B3 Maya *i* Indon
63F2 Maya *R* Russian Fed
93D2 Mayādīn Syria
11C4 Mayaguana *i* The Bahamas
27D3 Mayagüez Puerto Rico
97C3 Mayahi Niger
98B3 Mayama Congo
90C2 Mayamey Iran
42B2 Maybole Scot
10C3 May,C USA
109C4 Maydena Aust
46D1 Mayen Germany
48B2 Mayenne France
13D2 Mayerthorpe Can
18C2 Mayfield USA
61E5 Maykop Russian Fed
65H6 Maymaneh Afghan
76B1 Maymyo Burma
4E3 Mayo Can
45B2 Mayo County, Irish Rep
16A3 Mayo USA
45B1 Mayo,Is *R* Irish Rep
79B3 Mayon *Mt* Phil
51C2 Mayor *R* Spain
34C3 Mayor Buratovich Arg
110C1 Mayor I NZ
30D2 Mayor P Lagerenza Par
101D2 Mayotte *i* Indian O
27H2 May Pen Jamaica
16B3 May Point,C USA
47D1 Mayrhofen Austria
16B3 Mays Landing USA
14B3 Maysville USA
98B3 Mayumba Gabon
100B2 Mazabuka Zambia
84D1 Mazar China
94B3 Mazär Jordan
53B3 Mazara del Vallo Italy

84B1 Mazar-i-Sharif Afghan
24B2 Mazatlán Mexico
60B2 Mazeikiai Lithuania
94B3 Mazra Jordan
101C3 Mbabane Swaziland
98B2 Mbaïki CAR
99D3 Mbala Zambia
100B3 Mbalabala Zim
98B2 Mbale Uganda
98B2 Mbalmayo Cam
98B2 Mbam *R* Cam
101C2 Mbamba Bay Tanz
98B2 Mbandaka Zaire
98B3 Mbanza Congo Angola
98B3 Mbanza-Ngungu Zaire
99D3 Mbarara Uganda
98B2 Mbenza Congo
98B2 Mbéré *R* Cam
99D3 Mbeya Tanz
98B3 Mbinda Congo
97A3 Mbout Maur
98C3 Mbuji-Mayi Zaire
99D3 Mbulu Tanz
96B2 Mcherrah Region, Alg
101C2 Mchinji Malawi
76D3 Mdrak Viet
9B3 Mead,L USA
5H4 Meadow Lake Can
14B2 Meadville USA
7E4 Mealy Mts Can
109C1 Meandarra Aust
5G4 Meander River Can
45C2 Meath County, Irish Rep
49C2 Meaux France
16C1 Mechanicville USA
46C1 Mechelen Belg
96B1 Mecheria Alg
56C2 Mecklenburg-Vorpommern *State* Germany
56C2 Mecklenburger Bucht *B* Germany
101C2 Meconta Mozam
101C2 Mecubúri Mozam
101C2 Mecufi Mozam
101C2 Mecula Mozam
70A3 Medan Indon
34C3 Medanos Arg
34D2 Medanos Arg
13E2 Medecine Hat Can
32B2 Medellín Colombia
96D1 Medenine Tunisia
8A2 Medford USA
54C2 Medgidia Rom
34B2 Media Agua Arg
54B1 Medias Rom
20C1 Medical Lake USA
5G4 Medicine Hat Can
35C1 Medina Brazil
80B3 Medina S Arabia
50B1 Medinaceli Spain
50B1 Medina del Campo Spain
50A1 Medina de Rio Seco Spain
86B2 Medinipur India
88E4 Mediterranean S Europe
13F2 Medley USA
61J3 Mednogorsk Russian Fed
86D1 Médog China
98B2 Médouneu Gabon
61F3 Medvedista *R* Russian Fed
64E3 Medvezh'yegorsk Russian Fed
106A3 Meekatharra Aust
84D3 Meerut India
99D2 Méga Eth
102G5 Megalópolis Greece
55B3 Mégara Greece
86C1 Meghālaya State, India
86C2 Meghna *R* Bang
94B2 Megiddo *Hist Site* Israel
91B4 Mehran *R* Iran
90B3 Mehriz Iran
35B1 Meia Ponte *R* Brazil

98B2 Meiganga Cam
76B1 Meiktila Burma
47C1 Meiringen Switz
73A4 Meishan China
57C2 Meissen Germany
73D5 Mei Xian China
73D5 Meizhou China
30B3 Mejillones Chile
98B2 Mekambo Gabon
99D3 Mekong *R* Camb
96B1 Mek'elè Eth
96B1 Meknès Mor
73D3 Mekong *R* Camb
97C3 Mekrou *R* Benin
77C5 Melaka Malay
104F4 Melanesia *Region* Pacific O
78C3 Melawi *R* Indon
107D4 Melbourne Aust
11B4 Melbourne USA
9C4 Melchor Muzuiqc Mexico
61J3 Meleuz Russian Fed
98B1 Melfi Chad
5H4 Melfort Can
96B1 Melilla N W Africa
29B4 Melimoyu *Mt* Chile
34C2 Melincué Arg
34A2 Melipilla Chile
60E4 Melitopol' Ukraine
6D2 Melville Bugt *B* Greenland
100A3 Melka Guba Eth
101H1 Melmoth S Africa
34C2 Melo Arg
29F2 Melo Urug
22B2 Melones Res USA
12D1 Melozitna *R* USA
47C1 Mels Switz
43C3 Melton Mowbry Eng
49C2 Melun France
5H4 Melville Can
27Q2 Melville,C Dominica
4F3 Melville Hills *Mts* Can
106C2 Melville I Aust
4G2 Melville I Can
7E4 Melville,L Can
6B3 Melville Pen Can
45B1 Melvin,L Irish Rep
101C2 Memba Mozam
106A1 Memboro Indon
57C3 Memmingen Germany
78B2 Mempawan Indon
11B3 Memphis Tennessee, USA
20B2 Mendocino,C USA
105J2 Mendocino Seascarp Pacific O
22B2 Mendota California, USA
29C2 Mendoza Arg
29C2 Mendoza State, Arg
55C3 Menemen Turk
46B1 Menen Belg
72D3 Mengcheng China
78B3 Menggala Indon
73B4 Menghai China
73A5 Mengla China
73A5 Mengzi China
107D4 Menindee Aust
108B2 Menindee L Aust
108A3 Meningie Aust
14A1 Menominee USA
14A2 Menomonee Falls USA
100A2 Menongue Angola
51C1 Menorca *i* Spain
12F2 Mentasta Mts USA
78B3 Mentok Indon
14B2 Mentor USA
72A2 Menyuan China
61H2 Menzelinsk Russian Fed

56B2 Meppen Germany
78D2 Merah Indon
18D2 Meramec R USA
52B1 Merano Italy
71F4 Merauke Indon
8A3 Merced USA
22B2 Merced R USA
29B2 Mercedario Mt Chile
29C2 Mercedes Arg
29E2 Mercedes
 Buenos Aires, Arg
30E4 Mercedes Corrientes, Arg
29E2 Mercedes Urug
110C1 Mercury B NZ
4F2 Mercy B Can
6D3 Mercy,C Can
99E2 Meregh Somalia
76B3 Mergui Burma
76B3 Mergui Arch Burma
25D2 Mérida Mexico
50A2 Mérida Spain
32C2 Mérida Ven
1183 Meridian USA
109C3 Merimbula Aust
108B2 Meringur Aust
95C3 Merowe Sudan
106A4 Merredin Aust
42B2 Merrick Mt Scot
14A2 Merrillville USA
13C2 Merritt Island USA
17B2 Merritt Island USA
42C3 Merriwa Aust
99E1 Mersa Fatma Eth
51B2 Mers el Kebir Alg
42C3 Mersey R Eng
42C3 Merseyside
 Metropolitan County, Eng
92B2 Mersin Turk
77C5 Mersing Malay
35C3 Merta India
43C4 Merthyr Tydfil Wales
50A2 Mertola Port
99D3 Meru Mt Tanz
60E5 Merzifon Turk
46D2 Merzig Germany
9B3 Mesa USA
46E1 Meschede Germany
93D1 Mescit Dağ Mt Turk
12C3 Meshik USA
99C2 Meshra Er Req Sudan
47C1 Mesocco Switz
55B3 Mesolóngion Greece
19A3 Mesquite Texas, USA
101C2 Messalo R Mozam
53C3 Messina Italy
100B3 Messina S Africa
55B3 Messini Greece
55B3 Messiniakós Kólpos G Greece
54B2 Mesta R Bulg
52B1 Mestre Italy
32C3 Meta R Colombia
60D2 Meta R Russian Fed
32D2 Meta R Ven
6C3 Meta Incognito Pen Can
19B4 Metairie USA
20C1 Metaline Falls USA
30A4 Metán Arg
101C2 Metangula Mozam
53C2 Metaponto Italy
44C3 Methil Scot
14B2 Methuen USA
111B2 Methven NZ
12H3 Metlakatla USA
18C2 Metropolis USA
87B2 Mettur India
49D2 Metz France
78A4 Meulaboh Indon
46A2 Meulan France
46C2 Meuse Department, France
49D2 Meuse R France
19A3 Mexia USA
24A1 Mexicali Mexico
24B2 Mexico Federal Republic, Cent America
24C3 México Mexico
23A2 México State, Mexico

18B2 Mexico USA
24C2 Mexico,G of Cent America
94B3 Mezada Hist Site Israel
23B2 Mezcala Mexico
64F3 Mezen' Russian Fed
64G2 Mezhdusharskiy, Ostrov I Russian Fed
85D4 Mhow India
23B2 Miahuatlán Mexico
11B4 Miami Florida, USA
18B2 Miami Oklahoma, USA
11B4 Miami Beach USA
90A2 Miandowáb Iran
101D2 Miandrivazo Madag
90A2 Miáneh Iran
84C2 Mianwali Pak
73A3 Mianyang China
73C3 Mianyang China
73A3 Mianzhu China
72E2 Miaodao Qundao Arch China
73B4 Miao Ling Upland China
61K3 Miass Russian Fed
59C3 Michalovce Slovakia
27D3 Miches Dom Rep
10B2 Michigan State, USA
14A2 Michigan City USA
10B2 Michigan,L USA
7B5 Michipicoten I Can
23A2 Michoacan State, Mexico
54C2 Michurin Bulg
61F3 Michurinsk Russian Fed
104F3 Micronesia Region Pacific O
78B2 Midai I Indon
102F4 Mid Atlantic Ridge Atlantic O
46B1 Middelburg Neth
20B2 Middle Alkali L USA
16D2 Middleboro USA
100B4 Middleburg Cape Province, S Africa
16A2 Middleburg Pennsylvania, USA
101G1 Middleburg Transvaal, S Africa
16B1 Middleburgh USA
15D2 Middlebury USA
11B3 Middlesboro USA
42D2 Middlesbrough Eng
16C2 Middletown Connecticut, USA
16B3 Middletown Delaware, USA
15D2 Middletown New York, USA
14B3 Middletown Ohio, USA
16A2 Middletown Pennsylvania, USA
96B1 Midelt Mor
43C4 Mid Glamorgan County, Wales
104B4 Mid Indian Basin Indian O
104B4 Mid Indian Ridge Indian O
7C5 Midland Can
14B2 Midland Michigan, USA
9C3 Midland Texas, USA
101D3 Midongy Atsimo Madag
105G2 Mid Pacific Mts Pacific O
20C2 Midvale USA
105H2 Midway Is Pacific O
18A2 Midwest City USA
93D2 Midyat Turk
54B2 Midzor Mt Serbia, Yugos
59B2 Mielec Pol
54C1 Miercurea-Ciuc Rom
50A1 Mieres Spain
16C2 Mifflintown USA
75A2 Mihara Japan
72D1 Mijun Shuiku Res China
54B2 Mikhaylovgrad Bulg

61F3 Mikhaylovka Russian Fed
65J4 Mikhaylovskiy Russian Fed
38K6 Mikkeli Fin
55C3 Mikonos I Greece
59B3 Mikulov Czech Republic
99D3 Mikumi Tanz
74D3 Mikuni-sammyaku Mts Japan
75B2 Mikura-jima I Japan
32B4 Milagro Ecuador
 Milan = Milano
51C2 Milana Alg
101C2 Milange Mozam
52A1 Milano Italy
92A2 Milas Turk
107D4 Mildura Aust
73A5 Mile China
93D3 Mileh Tharthâr L Iraq
107E3 Miles Aust
8C2 Miles City USA
16C2 Milford Connecticut, USA
15C3 Milford Delaware, USA
15D2 Milford Massachusetts, USA
18A1 Milford Nebraska, USA
16B2 Milford Pennsylvania, USA
43B4 Milford Haven Wales
43B4 Milford Haven Sd Wales
18A2 Milford L USA
111A2 Milford Sd NZ
38L2 Milk River Can
49C3 Millau France
16C2 Millbrook USA
17B1 Milledgeville USA
12F2 Miller,Mt USA
61F4 Millerovo Russian Fed
16A2 Millersburg USA
108A1 Millers Creek Aust
16C1 Millers Falls USA
16C2 Millerton USA
22C2 Millerton L USA
108B3 Millicent Aust
109D1 Millmerran Aust
45D3 Milltown Malbay Irish Rep
22A2 Mill Valley USA
15D3 Millville USA
6H2 Milne Land I Greenland
21C4 Milolii Hawaiian Is
55B3 Milos I Greece
107D3 Milparinka Aust
16A2 Milroy USA
11A3 Milton NZ
16A2 Milton Pennsylvania, USA
10B2 Milwaukee USA
51C2 Mina R Alg
93E4 Minā' al Ahmadī Kuwait
74B4 Minamata Japan
78A2 Minas Indon
29E2 Minas Urug
31B5 Minas Gerais State, Brazil
35C1 Minas Novas Brazil
25C3 Minatitlan Mexico
76A1 Minbu Burma
76A1 Minbya Burma
72A2 Mincha Chile
44A3 Minch,Little Sd Scot
44A2 Minch,North Sd Scot
40B2 Minch,The Sd Scot
12D2 Minchumina,L USA
47D2 Mincio R Italy
79B4 Mindanao I Phil
19B3 Minden Louisiana, USA
56B2 Minden Germany
108B2 Mindona L Aust
79B3 Mindoro I Phil
79B3 Mindoro Str Phil
45C3 Mine Hd C Irish Rep

43C4 Minehead Eng
30F2 Mineiros Brazil
19A3 Mineola USA
23B1 Mineral de Monte Mexico
16A2 Minersville USA
108B2 Mingary Aust
72B3 Minhe China
87A3 Minicoy I India
73D4 Min Jiang R Fujian, China
73A4 Min Jiang R Sichuan, China
22C2 Minkler USA
108A2 Minlaton Aust
97C4 Minna Nig
10A2 Minneapolis USA
5J4 Minnedosa Can
10A2 Minnesota State, USA
50A1 Miño R Spain
8C2 Minot USA
72A2 Minqin China
72A3 Min Shan Upland China
60C6 Minsk Belorussia
58C2 Minsk Mazowiecki Pol
12E2 Minto USA
4G2 Minto Inlet B Can
7C4 Minto,L Can
63B2 Minusinsk Russian Fed
72A3 Min Xian China
7E5 Miquelon I Can
22D3 Mirage L USA
87A1 Miraj India
29A2 Miramar Arg
84B2 Miram Shah Pak
50B1 Miranda de Ebro Spain
47D2 Mirandola Italy
84B2 Mir Bachchen Küt Afghan
78D1 Miri Malay
96A3 Mirik,C Maur
61J4 Mirnoye Russian Fed
63D1 Mirnyy Russian Fed
112C9 Mirnyy Base Ant
84C2 Mirpur Pak
85B3 Mirpur Khas Pak
52B3 Mirtóan S Greece
74B3 Miryang S Korea
86A1 Mirzâpur India
23B2 Misantla Mexico
44C1 Misgar Pak
14A2 Mishawaka USA
12B1 Misheguk Mt USA
75A2 Mi-shima I Japan
21F9 Misima I Solomon Is
30F4 Misiones State, Arg
59C3 Miskolc Hung
94C2 Mismiyah Syria
71E4 Misoōl I Indon
95A1 Mişrātah Libya
7B5 Missinaibi R Can
20B1 Mission City Can
15C2 Mississauga Can
11A3 Mississippi State, USA
11A3 Mississippi R USA
19C3 Mississippi Delta USA
8B2 Missoula USA
96B1 Missour Mor
10A2 Missouri State, USA
10A2 Missouri R USA
10C1 Mistassini,L Can
30B2 Misti Mt Peru
109C1 Mitchell Aust
8D2 Mitchell USA
107D2 Mitchell R Aust
11B3 Mitchell,Mt USA
45B2 Mitchelstown Irish Rep
84C3 Mithankot Pak
55C3 Mitilíni Greece
23B2 Mitla Mexico
 Mitrovica Serbia, Yugos
95C3 Mits'iwa Eth
31C3 Mitú Colombia
99C3 Mitumbar Mts Zaire
98C3 Mitwaba Zaire

Mitzic

98B2	**Mitzic** Gabon
75B1	**Miura** Japan
72C3	**Mi Xian** China
69F3	**Miyake** I Japan
75B2	**Miyake-jima** I Japan
69E4	**Miyako** I Japan
74C4	**Miyakonojō** Japan
74C4	**Miyazaki** Japan
75B1	**Miyazu** Japan
74C4	**Miyoshi** Japan
72D1	**Miyun** China
99D2	**Mizan Teferi** Eth
95A1	**Mizdah** Libya
45B3	**Mizen Hd** C Irish Rep
54C1	**Mizil** Rom
86C2	**Mizo Hills** India
86C2	**Mizoram** Union Territory, India
94B3	**Mizpe Ramon** Israel
112B1	**Mizuho** Base Ant
74E3	**Mizusawa** Japan
39H7	**Mjolby** Sweden
100B2	**Mkushi** Zambia
111B1	**Mkuzi** S Africa
57C1	**Mladá Boleslav** Czech Republic
58C2	**Mława** Pol
52C2	**Mljet** I Croatia
100B3	**Mmabatho** S Africa
84D2	**Mnadi** India
97A4	**Moa** R Sierra Leone
94B3	**Moab** Region, Jordan
9C3	**Moab** USA
98B3	**Moanda** Congo
98B3	**Moanda** Gabon
99C3	**Moba** Zaire
75C1	**Mobara** Japan
98C2	**Mobaye** CAR
98C2	**Mobayi** Zaire
10A3	**Moberly** USA
11B3	**Mobile** USA
11B3	**Mobile B** USA
8C2	**Mobridge** USA
101D2	**Moçambique** Mozam
76C1	**Moc Chau** Viet
100B3	**Mochudi** Botswana
101D2	**Mocimboa da Praia** Mozam
32B3	**Mocoa** Colombia
35B2	**Mococa** Brazil
34D2	**Mocoreta** R Arg
23B1	**Moctezuma** R Mexico
101C2	**Mocuba** Mozam
47B2	**Modane** France
101G1	**Modder** R S Africa
52B2	**Modena** Italy
46D2	**Moder** R France
8A3	**Modesto** USA
22B2	**Modesto Res** USA
53B3	**Modica** Italy
59B3	**Mödling** Austria
101D4	**Moe** Aust
47C1	**Moesa** R Switz
42C2	**Moffat** Scot
84D2	**Moga** India
35B2	**Mogi das Cruzes** Brazil
60C3	**Mogilev** Belorussia
60C4	**Mogilev Podolskiy** Ukraine
35B2	**Mogi-Mirim** Brazil
101D2	**Mogincual** Mozam
47E2	**Mogliano** Italy
34B2	**Mogna** Arg
68D1	**Mogocha** Russian Fed
65K4	**Mogochin** Russian Fed
50A2	**Moguer** Spain
110C1	**Mohaka** R NZ
86C2	**Mohanganj** Bang
15D2	**Mohawk** R USA
99D3	**Mohoro** Tanz
65J5	**Mointy** Kazakhstan
38G5	**Mo i Rana** Nor
48C3	**Moissac** France
21B2	**Mojave** USA
22D3	**Mojave** R USA
9B3	**Mojave Desert** USA
78C4	**Mojokerto** Indon
86B1	**Mokama** India
110B1	**Mokau** R NZ
22B1	**Mokelumne Aqueduct** USA
22B1	**Mokelumne Hill** USA
22B1	**Mokelumne North Fork** R USA
101G1	**Mokhotlong** Lesotho
96D1	**Moknine** Tunisia
86C1	**Mokokchūng** India
98B1	**Mokolo** Cam
74B4	**Mokp'o** S Korea
61F3	**Mokrous** R Russian Fed
23B1	**Molango** Mexico
55B3	**Moláoi** Greece
60C4	**Moldavia** Republic, Europe
38F6	**Molde** Nor
	Moldova = Moldavia
54B1	**Moldoveanu** Mt Rom
100B3	**Molepolole** Botswana
53C2	**Molfetta** Italy
34A3	**Molina** Chile
30B2	**Mollendo** Peru
60C3	**Molodechno** Belorussia
112C11	**Molodezhnaya** Base Ant
21C4	**Molokai** I Hawaiian Is
61G2	**Moloma** R Russian Fed
109C2	**Molong** Aust
100B3	**Molopo** R Botswana
98B2	**Molounddu** Cam
8D1	**Molson L** Can
71D4	**Molucca S** Indon
71D4	**Moluccas** Is Indon
101C2	**Moma** Mozam
31C3	**Mombaca** Brazil
99D3	**Mombasa** Kenya
98C2	**Mompono** Zaire
56C2	**Mon** I Den
44A3	**Monach** Is Scot
49D3	**Monaco** Principality, Europe
44B3	**Monadhliath** Mts Scot
45C1	**Monaghan** County, Irish Rep
45C1	**Monaghan** Irish Rep
27D3	**Mona Pass** Caribbean S
13B2	**Monarch Mt** Can
5G4	**Monashee Mts** Can
41B3	**Monastereven** Irish Rep
47B2	**Moncalieri** Italy
31B2	**Monção** Brazil
38L5	**Moncheqorsk** Russian Fed
56B2	**Mönchen-gladbach** Germany
24B2	**Monclova** Mexico
7D5	**Moncton** Can
9C4	**Moncton** Mexico
50A1	**Mondego** R Port
52A2	**Mondovi** Italy
27H1	**Moneague** Jamaica
14C2	**Monessen** USA
18B2	**Monett** USA
52B1	**Monfalcone** Italy
50A1	**Monforte de Lemos** Spain
98C2	**Monga** Zaire
98C2	**Mongala** R Zaire
99D2	**Mongalla** Sudan
76D1	**Mong Cai** Viet
98B1	**Mongo** Chad
68B2	**Mongolia** Republic, Asia
100B2	**Mongu** Zambia
21B2	**Monitor Range** Mts USA
98C3	**Monkoto** Zaire
43C4	**Monmouth** Eng
18B1	**Monmouth** USA
13C2	**Monmouth,Mt** Can
97C4	**Mono** R Togo
21B2	**Mono L** USA
53C2	**Monopoli** Italy
51B1	**Monreal del Campo** Spain
19B3	**Monroe** Louisiana, USA
14B2	**Monroe** Michigan, USA
20B1	**Monroe** Washington, USA
18B2	**Monroe City** USA
97A4	**Monrovia** Lib
20D3	**Monrovia** USA
56A2	**Mons** Belg
47D2	**Monselice** Italy
16C1	**Monson** USA
58B1	**Mönsterås** Sweden
101D2	**Montagne d'Ambre** Mt Madag
96C1	**Montagnes des Ouled Nail** Mts Alg
12E3	**Montague I** USA
49C3	**Mont Aigoual** Mt France
48B2	**Montaigu** France
53C3	**Montallo** Mt Italy
53C3	**Montana** State, USA
50A1	**Montañas de León** Mts Spain
49C2	**Montargis** France
48C3	**Montauban** France
15D2	**Montauk** USA
15D2	**Montauk Pt** USA
48C2	**Montbéliard** France
52A1	**Mont Blanc** Mt France/Italy
49C2	**Montceau les Mines** France
51C1	**Montceny** Mt Spain
49D3	**Mont Cinto** Mt Corse
46C2	**Montcornet** France
49C3	**Mont-de-Marsan** France
48C2	**Montdidier** France
30D2	**Monteagudo** Bol
33G4	**Monte Alegre** Brazil
52B2	**Monte Amiata** Mt Italy
47D2	**Monte Baldo** Mt Italy
15C1	**Montebello** Can
106A3	**Monte Bello** Is Aust
47E2	**Montebelluna** Italy
49D3	**Monte Carlo** Monaco
35B1	**Monte Carmelo** Brazil
34D2	**Monte Caseros** Arg
52B2	**Monte Cimone** Mt Italy
52A2	**Monte Cinto** Mt Corse
34B2	**Monte Coman** Arg
52B2	**Monte Corno** Mt Italy
27C3	**Montecristi** Dom Rep
52B2	**Montecristo** I Italy
23A1	**Monte Escobedo** Mexico
53C2	**Monte Gargano** Mt Italy
26B3	**Montego Bay** Jamaica
47D2	**Monte Grappa** Mt Italy
47C2	**Monte Lesima** Mt Italy
49C3	**Montélimar** France
53B2	**Monte Miletto** Mt Italy
50A2	**Montemo-o-Novo** Port
24C2	**Montemorelos** Mexico
26B5	**Montená** Colombia
54A2	**Montenegro** Republic, Yugos
35D1	**Monte Pascoal** Mt Brazil
34A2	**Monte Patria** Chile
53C3	**Monte Pollino** Mt Italy
101C2	**Montepuez** Mozam
8A3	**Monterey** California, USA
15C3	**Monterey** Virginia, USA
8A3	**Monterey B** USA
32B2	**Montería** Colombia
30D2	**Montero** Bol
47B2	**Monte Rosa** Mt Italy/ Switz
24B2	**Monterrey** Mexico
31C5	**Montes Claros** Brazil
50B2	**Montes de Toledo** Mts Spain
29E2	**Montevideo** Urug
52A2	**Monte Viso** Mt Italy
27P2	**Mont Gimie** Mt St Lucia
11B3	**Montgomery** Alabama, USA
96C2	**Mont Gréboun** Niger
46C2	**Montherme** France
47B1	**Monthey** Switz
19B3	**Monticello** Arkansas, USA
16B2	**Monticello** New York, USA
9C3	**Monticello** Utah, USA
53A2	**Monti del Gennargentu** Mt Sardegna
47D2	**Monti Lessini** Mts Italy
53B3	**Monti Nebrodi** Mts Italy
7C5	**Mont-Laurier** Can
48C2	**Montluçon** France
7C5	**Montmagny** Can
46C2	**Montmédy** France
49C3	**Mont Mézenc** Mt France
52B2	**Montmirail** France
50B2	**Montoro** Spain
49D3	**Mont Pelat** Mt France
14B2	**Montpelier** Ohio, USA
10C2	**Montpelier** Vermont, USA
49C3	**Montpellier** France
7C5	**Montréal** Can
14C1	**Montreuil** France
25A1	**Montreux** Switz
47B1	**Mont Risoux** Mt France
8C3	**Montrose** Colorado, USA
40C2	**Montrose** Scot
48B2	**Mont-St-Michel** France
96B1	**Monts des Ksour** Mts Alg
51C3	**Monts des Ouled Neil** Mts Alg
51C2	**Monts du Hodna** Mts Alg
27E3	**Montserrat** I Caribbean S
10C1	**Monts Otish** Mts Can
12B1	**Monument Mt** USA
9B3	**Monument V** USA
98C2	**Monveda** Zaire
76B1	**Monywa** Burma
52A1	**Monza** Italy
100B2	**Monze** Zambia
101H1	**Mooi** R S Africa
101G1	**Mooi River** S Africa
108B1	**Moomba** Aust
100D2	**Moondi Range** Mts Aust
108B1	**Moonda L** Aust
109D1	**Moonie** Aust
101C4	**Moonie** R Aust
108A2	**Moonta** Aust
109A4	**Moora** Aust
106A3	**Moore,L** Aust
42C2	**Moorfoot Hills** Scot
8D2	**Moorhead** USA
22C3	**Moorpark** USA
7B4	**Moose** R Can
5H4	**Moose Jaw** Can
5H4	**Moosomin** Can
7B4	**Moosonee** Can
16D2	**Moosup** USA
101C2	**Mopeia** Mozam
97B3	**Mopti** Mali
30B2	**Moquegua** Peru
39G6	**Mora** Sweden
31D3	**Morada** Brazil
84D3	**Morādābād** India

35B1 **Morada Nova de Minas** L Brazil
101D2 **Morafenobe** Madag
101D2 **Moramanga** Madag
27J2 **Morant Bay** Jamaica
27J2 **Morant Pt** Jamaica
87B3 **Moratuwa** Sri Lanka
59B3 **Morava** R Austria/ Slovakia
54B2 **Morava** R Serbia, Yugos
92C2 **Moraveh Tappeh** Iran
40C2 **Moray Firth** Estuary Scot
47C1 **Morbegno** Italy
85C4 **Morbi** India
93D2 **Mor Daǧ** Mt Turk
5J5 **Morden** Can
61F3 **Mordovskaya Respublika**, Russian Fed
42C2 **Morecambe** Eng
42C2 **Morecambe B** Eng
107D3 **Moree** Aust
14B3 **Morehead** Eng
47C1 **Mörel** Switz
24B3 **Morelia** Mexico
23B2 **Morelos** State, Mexico
85D3 **Morena** India
5E4 **Moresby I** Can
109D1 **Moreton I** Aust
46B2 **Moreuil** France
47B1 **Morez** France
19B4 **Morgan City** USA
22B2 **Morgan Hill** USA
14C3 **Morgantown** USA
101C1 **Morgenzon** S Africa
47B1 **Morges** Switz
46D2 **Morhange** France
74E2 **Mori** Japan
23B2 **Morice L** Can
27K1 **Moriarto** Tobago
13E2 **Morinville** Can
74E3 **Morioka** Japan
109D2 **Morisset** Aust
63D1 **Morkoka** R Russian Fed
48B2 **Morlaix** France
27O2 **Morne Diablotin** Mt Dominica
106C2 **Mornington** I Aust
85B3 **Moro** Pak
96B2 **Morocco** Kingdom, Africa
79B4 **Moro G** Phil
99D3 **Morogoro** Tanz
23A1 **Moroleon** Mexico
101D3 **Morombe** Madag
26B2 **Morón** Cuba
101D3 **Morondava** Madag
50A2 **Morón de la Frontera** Spain
101D2 **Moroni** Comoros
71D3 **Morotai** I Indon
99D2 **Moroto** Uganda
61F4 **Morozovsk** Russian Fed
42D2 **Morpeth** Eng
19B2 **Morrilton** USA
35B1 **Morrinhos** Brazil
110C1 **Morrinsville** NZ
16B2 **Morristown** New Jersey, USA
15C2 **Morristown** New York, USA
16B2 **Morrisville** Pennsylvania, USA
21A2 **Morro Bay** USA
23A2 **Morro de Papanoa** Mexico
23A2 **Morro de Petatlán** Mexico
101C2 **Morrumbala** Mozam
101C3 **Morrumbene** Mozam
61F3 **Morshansk** Russian Fed
47C2 **Mortara** Italy
34C2 **Morteros** Arg
33G6 **Mortes** R Mato Grosso, Brazil
35C2 **Mortes** R Minas Gerais, Brazil
108B3 **Mortlake** Aust
27L1 **Moruga** Trinidad

109D3 **Moruya** Aust
109C1 **Morven** Aust
44B3 **Morvern** Pen Scot
109C3 **Morwell** Aust
76B3 **Moscos Is** Burma
Moscow = **Moskva**
20C1 **Moscow** Idaho, USA
56B2 **Mosel** R Germany
46D2 **Moselle** Department, France
46D2 **Moselle** R France
20C1 **Moses Lake** USA
111B3 **Mosgiel** NZ
99D3 **Moshi** Tanz
39G5 **Mosjøen** Nor
63G2 **Moskal'vo** Russian Fed
64E4 **Moskva** Russian Fed
35C1 **Mosquito** R Brazil
39G7 **Moss** Nor
98B3 **Mossaka** Congo
100A4 **Mossel Bay** S Africa
98B3 **Mossendjo** Congo
108B2 **Mossgiel** Aust
31D3 **Mossoró** Brazil
57C2 **Most** Czech Republic
96C1 **Mostaganem** Alg
54A2 **Mostar** Bosnia- Herzegovina
60B2 **Mosty** Belorussia
93E2 **Mosul** = **Al Mawṣil**
39H7 **Motala** Sweden
42C2 **Motherwell** Scot
86A1 **Motihāri** India
51B2 **Motilla del Palancar** Spain
50B2 **Motril** Spain
111B2 **Motueka** NZ
111B2 **Motueka** R NZ
98B3 **Mouila** Gabon
108B2 **Moulamein** Aust
4G2 **Mould Bay** Can
49C2 **Moulins** France
76B2 **Moulmein** Burma
96B1 **Moulouya** R Mor
17B1 **Moultrie** USA
17C1 **Moultrie,L** USA
18C2 **Mound City** Illinois, USA
18A1 **Mound City** Missouri, USA
98B2 **Moundou** Chad
14B3 **Moundsville** USA
12J1 **Mountain** R Can
17A1 **Mountain Brook** USA
18B2 **Mountain Grove** USA
18B2 **Mountain Home** Arkansas, USA
22A2 **Mountain View** USA
12B2 **Mountain Village** USA
16A3 **Mount Airy** Maryland, USA
16A2 **Mount Carmel** USA
108A1 **Mount Dutton** Aust
108A2 **Mount Eba** Aust
108B1 **Mount Gambier** Aust
16B3 **Mount Holly** USA
16A2 **Mount Holly Springs** USA
108A2 **Mount Hope** Aust
106C3 **Mount Isa** Aust
108A2 **Mount Lofty Range** Aust
12D2 **Mount McKinley Nat Pk** USA
106A3 **Mount Magnet** Aust
108B2 **Mount Manara** Aust
107E3 **Mount Morgan** Aust
19B3 **Mount Pleasant** Texas, USA
20B1 **Mount Rainier Nat Pk** USA
43B4 **Mounts B** Eng
20B2 **Mount Shasta** USA
11B3 **Mount Vernon** Illinois, USA
19A3 **Mount Vernon** Kentucky, USA
20B1 **Mount Vernon** Washington, USA
45C1 **Mourne Mts** N Ire
98B1 **Moussoro** Chad

86B2 **Mouths of the Ganga** India/Bang
85B4 **Mouths of the Indus** Pak
77D4 **Mouths of the Mekong** Viet
97C4 **Mouths of the Niger** Nig
47B1 **Moûtier** Switz
47B2 **Moûtiers** France
96C2 **Mouydir** Mts Alg
98B3 **Mouyondzi** Congo
46C2 **Mouzon** France
59B3 **Móvár** Hung
23A1 **Moyahua** Mexico
99D2 **Moyale** Kenya
97A4 **Moyamba** Sierra Leone
96B1 **Moyen Atlas** Mts Mor
101B4 **Moyeni** Lesotho
99D2 **Moyo** Uganda
32B5 **Moyobamba** Peru
84D1 **Moyu** China
101C3 **Mozambique** Republic, Africa
101C3 **Mozambique Chan** Mozam/Madag
61H2 **Mozhga** Russian Fed
60C3 **Mozyr'** Belorussia
99D3 **Mpanda** Tanz
101C2 **Mpika** Zambia
99D3 **Mporokoso** Zambia
100B2 **Mposhi** Zambia
99D3 **Mpulungu** Tanz
99D3 **Mpwapwa** Tanz
60E3 **Mstensk** Russian Fed
101H1 **Mtubatuba** S Africa
101D2 **Mtwara** Tanz
76C2 **Muang Chainat** Thai
76C2 **Muang Chiang Rai** Thai
76C2 **Muang Kalasin** Thai
76C2 **Muang Khon Kaen** Thai
76B2 **Muang Lampang** Thai
76B2 **Muang Lamphun** Thai
76C2 **Muang Loei** Thai
76C2 **Muang Lom Sak** Thai
76C2 **Muang Nakhon Phanom** Thai
76B2 **Muang Nakhon Sawan** Thai
76C2 **Muang Nan** Thai
76C2 **Muang Phayao** Thai
76C2 **Muang Phetchabun** Thai
76C2 **Muang Phichit** Thai
76C2 **Muang Phitsanulok** Thai
76C2 **Muang Phrae** Thai
76C2 **Muang Roi Et** Thai
76C2 **Muang Sakon Nakhon** Thai
76C3 **Muang Samut Prakan** Thai
76C2 **Muang Uthai Thani** Thai
76C2 **Muang Yasothon** Thai
77C5 **Muar** Malay
78A4 **Muara** Brunei
78A3 **Muara** Indon
78A3 **Muaralakitan** Indon
78A3 **Muaratebo** Indon
78A3 **Muaratewah** Indon
78A4 **Muarenim** Indon
78A2 **Muaungmaya** Burma
99D2 **Mubende** Uganda
100C2 **Muchinga** Mts Zambia
44A3 **Muck** I Scot
109C1 **Muckadilla** Aust
100B2 **Muconda** Angola
35D1 **Mucuri** Brazil
31D7 **Mucuri** R Brazil
100B2 **Mucusso** Angola
69E2 **Mudanjiang** China
109C2 **Mudgee** Aust
76B2 **Mudon** Burma
101C2 **Mueda** Mozam
107F3 **Mueo** Nouvelle Calédonie

100B2 **Mufulira** Zambia
73C4 **Mufu Shan** Hills China
Mugadishu = **Muqdisho**
93C4 **Mughayra'** S Arabia
92A2 **Muğla** Turk
65G5 **Mugodzhary** Mts Kazakhstan
74J3 **Muguaping** China
93D3 **Muḥaywir** Iraq
57C3 **Mühldorf** Germany
57C2 **Mühlhausen** Germany
38K6 **Muhos** Fin
77C4 **Mui Bai Bung** C Camb
45C2 **Muine Bheag** Irish Rep
100B2 **Mujimbeji** Zambia
59C3 **Mukachevo** Ukraine
78C2 **Mukah** Malay
69G4 **Muko-jima** I Japan
86A1 **Muktinath** Nepal
84B2 **Mukur** Afghan
18B2 **Mulberry** USA
12C2 **Mulchatna** R USA
34A3 **Mulchén** Chile
56C2 **Mulde** R Germany
71F5 **Mulgrave** I Aust
50B2 **Mulhacén** Mt Spain
46D1 **Mülheim** Germany
47D2 **Mulhouse** France
73A4 **Muli** China
44B3 **Mull** I Scot
87C3 **Mullaitvu** Sri Lanka
109C2 **Mullaley** Aust
16B3 **Mullica** R USA
16B3 **Mullica** R USA
45C2 **Mullingar** Irish Rep
42B2 **Mull of Kintyre** Pt Scot
45C1 **Mull of Oa** C Scot
109D1 **Mullumbimby** Aust
100B2 **Mulobezi** Zambia
84C2 **Multan** Pak
Mumbai = **Bombay**
61G4 **Mumra** Russian Fed
71D4 **Muna** I Indon
57C3 **München** Germany
14A2 **Muncie** USA
15C2 **Muncy** USA
56B2 **Münden** Germany
109C1 **Mundubbera** Aust
109C1 **Mungallala** Aust
109C1 **Mungallala** R Aust
99C2 **Mungbere** Zaire
86A2 **Mungeli** India
86B1 **Munger** India
109C1 **Mungindi** Aust
Munich = **München**
14A1 **Munising** USA
29B6 **Muñoz Gomero,Pen** Chile
45B2 **Munster** Region, Irish Rep
47C1 **Münster** Switz
56B2 **Münster** Germany
54B1 **Muntii Apuseni** Mts Rom
54B1 **Muntii Carpatii Meridionali** Mts Rom
54B1 **Muntii Rodnei** Mts Rom
54B1 **Muntii Zarandului** Mts Rom
100B2 **Munyati** R Zim
93C2 **Munzur Silsilesi** Mts Turk
64D3 **Muomio** Fin
76C1 **Muong Khoua** Laos
76D3 **Muong Man** Viet
76D2 **Muong Nong** Laos
76C1 **Muong Ou Neua** Laos
76C1 **Muong Sai** Laos
76C2 **Muong Sen** Viet
76C1 **Muong Sing** Laos
76C1 **Muong Son** Laos
38J5 **Muonio** Fin
38J5 **Muonio** R Sweden/ Fin

99E2 Muqdisho Somalia
52B1 Mur R Austria
74D3 Murakami Japan
29B5 Murallón Mt Arg/Chile
61G2 Murashi Russian Fed
93D2 Murat R Turk
53A3 Muravera Sardegna
75C1 Murayama Japan
90B3 Murcheh Khvort Iran
111B2 Murchison NZ
106A3 Murchison R Aust
51B2 Murcia Region, Spain
51B2 Murcia Spain
54B1 Mures R Rom
46E2 Murg R Germany
65H6 Murgab R Turkmenistan
84B2 Murgha Kibzai Pak
109D1 Murgon Aust
86B2 Muri India
35C2 Muriaé Brazil
98C3 Muriege Angola
64E3 Murmansk Russian Fed
61F2 Murom Russian Fed
74E2 Muroran Japan
50A1 Muros Spain
74C4 Muroto Japan
75A2 Muroto-zaki C Japan
20C2 Murphy Idaho, USA
22B1 Murphys USA
18C2 Murray Kentucky, USA
108B2 Murray R Aust
13C2 Murray R Can
108A3 Murray Bridge Aust
71F4 Murray,L PNG
17B1 Murray,L USA
105J2 Murray Seacarp Pacific O
108B2 Murrumbidgee R Aust
109C2 Murrumburrah Aust
109D2 Murrurundi Aust
47B1 Murten Switz
108B3 Murtoa Aust
110C1 Murupara NZ
86A2 Murwāra India
109D1 Murwillimbah Aust
30D3 Muş Turk
54B2 Musala Mt Bulg
74B2 Musan N Korea
91C4 Musandam Pen Oman
       Muscat = Masqat
91C5 Muscat Region, Oman
106C3 Musgrave Range Mts Aust
98B3 Mushie Zaire
14A2 Muskegon USA
14A2 Muskegon R USA
14A2 Muskegon USA
15C2 Muskoka,L Can
95C3 Musmar Sudan
99D3 Musoma Tanz
8C2 Musselshell R USA
100A2 Mussende Angola
48C2 Mussidan France
55C2 Mustafa-Kemalpasa Turk
86A1 Mustang Nepal
109D2 Muswellbrook Aust
95B2 Mut Egypt
101C2 Mutarara Mozam
101C2 Mutare Zim
101C2 Mutoko Zim
101D2 Mutsamudu Comoros
100B2 Mutshatsha Zaire
74E2 Mutsu Japan
74E2 Mutsu-wan B Japan
45B2 Mutton I Irish Rep
72B2 Mu Us Shamo Desert China
98B3 Muxima Angola
63D2 Muya Russian Fed
38L6 Muyezerskiy Russian Fed
99D3 Muyinga Burundi
98C3 Muyumba Zaire
82A1 Muyun Kum Desert Kazakhstan
84C2 Muzaffarābad Pak

84C2 Muzaffargarh Pak
84D3 Muzaffarnagar India
86B1 Muzaffarpur India
64H3 Muzhi Russian Fed
82C2 Muztag Mt China
82B2 Muztagata Mt China
100A2 Mvuma Zim
99D3 Mwanza Tanz
98C3 Mwanza Zaire
98C3 Mweka Zaire
98C3 Mwene Ditu Zaire
100C3 Mwenezi Zim
98C3 Mwenga Zaire
99C3 Mweru L Zambia
100B2 Mwinilunga Zambia
83D4 Myanaung Burma
       Myanma = Burma
86D2 Myingyan Burma
76B1 Myingyao Burma
76B3 Myinmoletkat Mt Burma
82D3 Myitkyina Burma
76B3 Myitta Burma
86C2 Mymensingh Bang
69F3 Myojin I Japan
39F6 Myrdal Nor
38B2 Myrdalsjökul Ice Cap Iceland
17C1 Myrtle Beach USA
20B2 Myrtle Creek USA
39G7 Mysen Nor
56C2 Myślborz Pol
64F3 Mys Kanin Nos C Russian Fed
59B3 Myślenice Pol
69H1 Mys Lopatka C Russian Fed
87B2 Mysore India
60D5 Mys Sarych C Ukraine
16D2 Mystic USA
61H5 Mys Tyub-Karagan Pt Kazakhstan
63G2 Mys Yelizavety C Russian Fed
64H2 Mys Zhelaniya C Russian Fed
77D3 My Tho Viet
20B2 Mytle Point USA
101C2 Mzimba Malawi
101C2 Mzuzu Malawi

N

21C4 Naalehu Hawaiian Is
39J6 Naantali Fin
45B2 Nabari Irish Rep
61H2 Naberezhnye Chelny Russian Fed
12F2 Nabesna R USA
96D1 Nabeul Tunisia
94B2 Nablus Israel
101D2 Nacala Mozam
20B1 Naches USA
101C2 Nachingwea Tanz
19B3 Nacogdoches USA
76A3 Nacondam I Indian O
24B1 Nacozari Mexico
85C4 Nadiad India
50B2 Nador Mor
90B3 Nadushan Iran
59C3 Nadvornaya Ukraine
56C2 Naestved Den
95B2 Nafurah Libya
75A2 Nagahama Japan
82D3 Naga Hills Burma
75B1 Nagai Japan
86C1 Nagaland State, India
74D3 Nagano Japan
74D3 Nagaoka Japan
86C1 Nagaon India
87B2 Nagappattinam India
85C4 Nagar Parkar Pak
74B4 Nagasaki Japan
75B2 Nagashima Japan
74D3 Nagato Japan
85C3 Nagaur India
87B3 Nagercoil India
85B3 Nagha Kalat Pak
86B3 Nagina India
74D3 Nagoya Japan
85D4 Nagpur India
82D2 Nagqu China
59B3 Nagykanizsa Hung

59B3 Nagykörös Hung
69E4 Naha Japan
8A2 Nahaimo Can
4F3 Nahanni Butte Can
94B2 Nahariya Israel
90A3 Nahāvand Iran
46D2 Nahe R Germany
72D2 Nahpu China
72E1 Naimen Qi China
7D4 Nain Can
90B3 Nā'īn Iran
84D3 Naini Tal India
44C3 Nairn Scot
99D3 Nairobi Kenya
90B3 Najafābād Iran
74C2 Najin N Korea
75A2 Nakama Japan
74E3 Nakaminato Japan
75A2 Nakamura Japan
75B1 Nakano Japan
75A1 Nakano-shima I Japan
74C4 Nakatsu Japan
75B1 Nakatsu-gawa Japan
95C3 Nak'fa Eth
93E2 Nakhichevan Azerbaijan
92B4 Nakhl Egypt
74C2 Nakhodka Russian Fed
76C3 Nakhon Pathom Thai
76C3 Nakhon Ratchasima Thai
77C4 Nakhon Si Thammarat Thai
12H3 Nakina Can
7B4 Nakina Ontario, Can
12C3 Naknek USA
12C3 Naknek L USA
4C4 Nakrek USA
39G8 Nakskov Den
99D3 Nakuru Kenya
13D2 Nakusp Can
61F5 Nal'chik Russian Fed
87B1 Nalgonda India
87B1 Nallamala Range Mts India
95A1 Nālūt Libya
101H1 Namaacha Mozam
65G6 Namak L Iran
90C3 Namakzar-e Shadad Salt Flat Iran
65J5 Namangan Uzbekistan
101C2 Namapa Mozam
100A4 Namaqualand Region, S Africa
109D1 Nambour Aust
109D2 Nambucca Heads Aust
77D4 Nam Can Viet
82D2 Nam Co L China
76D1 Nam Dinh Viet
101C2 Nametil Mozam
74C2 Namhae-do I S Korea
100A2 Namib Desert Namibia
100A2 Namibe Angola
100A3 Namibia Republic, Africa
82D3 Namjagbarwa Feng Mt China
71D4 Namlea Indon
109C2 Namoi R Aust
13D1 Nampa Can
20C2 Nampa USA
97B3 Nampala Mali
76C2 Nam Phong Thai
74B3 Namp'o N Korea
101C2 Nampula Mozam
76B1 Namton Burma
86D2 Namtu Burma
13B2 Namu Can
101C2 Namuno Mozam
46C1 Namur Belg
100A2 Namutoni Namibia
74B3 Namwön S Korea
13C3 Nanaimo Can
74B2 Nanam N Korea

75B1 Nanatsu-jima I Japan
73B3 Nanbu China
73D4 Nanchang China
73B3 Nanchong China
49D2 Nancy France
87B1 Nānded India
109D2 Nandewar Range Mts Aust
85C4 Nandurbar India
87B1 Nandyāl India
98B2 Nanga Eboko Cam
84C1 Nanga Parbat Mt Pak
78C3 Nangapinoh Indon
78C3 Nangatayap Indon
74B2 Nangnim Sanmaek Mts N Korea
86C1 Nang Xian China
67F3 Nangzhou China
82D2 Nanjangüd India
72D3 Nanjing China
       Nanking = Nanjing
75A2 Nankoku Japan
73C4 Nan Ling Region, China
76B1 Nanliu R China
73B5 Nanning China
6F3 Nanortalik Greenland
73A5 Nanpan Jiang R China
86A1 Nānpāra India
73D4 Nanping China
6A1 Nansen Sd Can
19D3 Nansio Tanz
48B2 Nantes France
12E3 Nanton Can
72E3 Nantong China
11C2 Nantucket I USA
35C1 Nanuque Brazil
73C3 Nanyang China
72D2 Nanyang Hu L China
90D2 Nanyuki Kenya
85B4 Naokot Pak
22A1 Napa USA
12B2 Napaiskak USA
15C2 Napanee Can
65K4 Napas Russian Fed
6E3 Napassoq Greenland
76D2 Nape Laos
110C1 Napier NZ
       Naples = Napoli
17B2 Naples Florida, USA
19B3 Naples Texas, USA
73B5 Napo China
32C4 Napo R Peru/Ecuador
53B2 Napoli Italy
90A2 Naqadeh Iran
92C4 Naqb Ishtar Jordan
75B2 Nara Japan
97B3 Nara Mali
107D4 Naracoorte Aust
23B1 Naranjos Mexico
87C1 Narasaraopet India
77C4 Narathiwat Thai
86C2 Narayanganj Bang
87B1 Nārāyenpet India
49C3 Narbonne France
12C1 Narendranagar India
6C2 Nares Str Can
58C2 Narew R Pol
75C1 Narita Japan
85C4 Narmada R India
84D3 Narnaul India
60E2 Naro Fominsk Russian Fed
99D3 Narok Kenya
84C2 Narowal Pak
107D4 Narrabri Aust
109C1 Narran L Aust
109C1 Narran R Aust
106A4 Narrogin Aust
109C2 Narromine Aust
85D4 Narsimhapur India
87C1 Narsipatnam India
6F3 Narssalik Greenland
6F3 Narssaq Greenland
6F3 Narssarssuaq Greenland
75C1 Narugo Japan
75A2 Naruto Japan

60C2 Narva Russian Fed
38H5 Narvik Nor
84D3 Narwāna India
64G3 Nar'yan Mar Russian Fed
08B1 Narylico Aust
66J5 Naryn Kirghizia
97C4 Nasarawa Nig
03D5 Nasca Ridge Pacific O
16D1 Nashua USA
19B3 Nashville Arkansas, USA
11B3 Nashville Tennessee, USA
54A1 Našice Croatia
85D4 Nāsik India
99D2 Nasir Sudan
13B1 Nass R Can
26B1 Nassau The Bahamas
84A2 Nassau USA
54C1 Nasser,L Egypt
39G7 Nässjö Sweden
7C4 Nastapoka Is Can
100B3 Nata Botswana
31D3 Natal Brazil
70A3 Natal Indon
101H1 Natal Province, S Africa
90B3 Natanz Iran
7D4 Natashquan Can
7D4 Natashquan R Can
19B3 Natchez USA
19B3 Natchitoches USA
108C3 Nathalia Aust
6H2 Nathorsts Land Region Greenland
13C1 Nation R Can
21B3 National City USA
75C1 Natori Japan
99D3 Natron L Tanz
106A4 Naturaliste,C Aust
47D1 Nauders Austria
56C2 Nauen Germany
56C2 Naugatuck USA
57C2 Naumburg Germany
94B3 Naur Jordan
105G4 Nauru I Pacific O
63C2 Naushki Russian Fed
23B1 Nautla Mexico
9C3 Navajo Res USA
50A2 Navalmoral de la Mata Spain
29C7 Navarino I Chile
51B1 Navarra Province, Spain
34D3 Navarro Arg
19A3 Navasota USA
19A3 Navasota R USA
50A1 Navia R Spain
34A2 Navidad Chile
85C4 Navlakhi India
60D3 Navlya Russian Fed
24B2 Navojoa Mexico
55B3 Návpaktos Greece
55B3 Návplion Greece
85C4 Navsari India
94C2 Nawá Syria
86B2 Nawāda India
84B2 Nawah Afghan
85B3 Nawabshah Pak
73B4 Náxi China
55D3 Náxos I Greece
23A1 Nayar Mexico
90C3 Nay Band Iran
90C2 Nay Band Iran
74E2 Nayoro Japan
94B2 Nazareth Israel
48B2 Nazay France
22A2 Nazca Peru
92A2 Nazilli Turk
63B2 Nazimovo Russian Fed
13C2 Nazko R Can
99D2 Nazret Eth
91C5 Nazwá Oman
65J4 Nazyvayevsk Russian Fed
98B3 Ndalatando Angola
98C2 Ndélé CAR
98B3 Ndendé Gabon
98B1 Ndjamena Chad
98B3 Ndjolé Gabon
100B2 Ndola Zambia

109C1 Neabul Aust
108A1 Neales R Aust
55B3 Neápolis Greece
43C4 Neath Wales
109C1 Nebine R Aust
65G6 Nebit Dag Turkmenistan
8C2 Nebraska State, USA
18A1 Nebraska City USA
13C2 Nechako R Can
19A3 Neches R USA
34D3 Necochea Arg
86C1 Nêdong China
9BJ3 Needles USA
14A2 Neenah USA
5J4 Neepawa Can
46C1 Neerpelt Belg
63C2 Neftelensk Russian Fed
99D2 Negele Eth
94B3 Negev Desert Israel
98B2 Negola Angola
87B3 Negombo Sri Lanka
76A2 Negrais,C Burma
32A4 Negritos Peru
33E4 Negro R Argentina/Brazil
29C4 Negro R Arg
34D2 Negro R Urug
79B4 Negros I Phil
72A1 Negru Voda Rom
90D3 Nehbandan Iran
73B4 Neijiang China
72B1 Nei Monggol Autonomous Region, China
32B3 Neiva Colombia
99D2 Nejo Eth
99D2 Nek'emté Eth
60D2 Nelidovo Russian Fed
87B2 Nellore India
69F2 Nel'ma Russian Fed
13D3 Nelson Can
111B2 Nelson NZ
7A4 Nelson R Can
108B3 Nelson,C Aust
12B2 Nelson I USA
79B3 Néma Maur
72A1 Nemagt Uul Mt Mongolia
58C1 Neman R Lithuania
54C1 Nemira Mt Rom
74F2 Nemuro Japan
63E3 Nen R China
41B3 Nenagh Irish Rep
12E2 Nenana USA
12E2 Nenana R USA
43D3 Nene R Eng
69E2 Nenjiang China
18A2 Neodesha USA
18A2 Neosho USA
63C2 Nepa Russian Fed
82C3 Nepal Kingdom, Asia
86A1 Nepalganj Nepal
45B1 Nephin Mt Irish Rep
94B3 Neqarot R Israel
34A3 Nequén State, Arg
68D1 Nerchinsk Russian Fed
54C2 Neretva R Bosnia-Herzegovina/Croatia
71F2 Nero Deep Pacific O
38C1 Neskaupstaður Iceland
48B2 Nesle France
7E5 Nesleyville Can
55B2 Néstos R Greece
94B2 Netanya Israel
16B2 Netcong USA
56B2 Netherlands Kingdom, Europe
3M7 Netherlands Antilles Is Caribbean S
86C2 Netrakona Bang
6C3 Nettilling L Can
56C2 Neubrandenburg Germany
47B1 Neuchâtel Switz
46C2 Neufchâteau Belg
48C2 Neufchâtel France
46A2 Neufchâtel-en-Bray France
56B2 Neumünster Germany

52C1 Neunkirchen Austria
46D2 Neunkirchen Germany
34B3 Neuquén Arg
29B4 Neuquén State, Arg
34B3 Neuquén R Arg
56C2 Neuruppin Germany
46D1 Neuss Germany
46E2 Neustadt Germany
56C2 Neustadt Germany
52C2 Neustrelitz Germany
46D1 Neuwied Germany
8B3 Nevada State, USA
18B2 Nevada USA
34A3 Nevada de Chillán Mts Arg/Chile
23A2 Nevada de Collima Mexico
23B2 Nevada de Toluca Mt Mexico
94B3 Nevatim Israel
60C2 Nevel' Russian Fed
49C2 Nevers France
109C2 Nevertire Aust
27E3 Nevis I Caribbean S
58D2 Nevis R Belorussia/Lithuania
92B2 Nevşehir Turk
61K2 Nev'yansk Russian Fed
99D3 Newala Tanz
14A3 New Albany Indiana, USA
19C3 New Albany Mississippi, USA
33F2 New Amsterdam Guyana
109C1 New Angledool Aust
15C3 Newark Delaware, USA
16C2 Newark New Jersey, USA
14B2 Newark Ohio, USA
43D3 Newark-upon-Trent Eng
15D2 New Bedford USA
13C2 New Bella Bella Can
20B1 Newberg USA
11C3 New Bern USA
17B1 Newberry USA
26B2 New Bight The Bahamas
14B3 New Boston USA
9D4 New Braunfels USA
16C2 New Britain USA
7D5 New Brunswick Province, Can
16B2 New Brunswick USA
16B2 Newburgh USA
43D4 Newbury Eng
16D1 Newburyport USA
16C2 New Canaan USA
109D2 Newcastle Aust
14A3 New Castle Indiana, USA
42B2 Newcastle N Ire
14B2 New Castle Pennsylvania, USA
101G1 Newcastle S Africa
8C2 Newcastle Wyoming, USA
42D2 Newcastle upon Tyne Eng
106C2 Newcastle Waters Aust
45B2 Newcastle West Irish Rep
84D3 New Delhi India
109D2 New England Range Mts Aust
12B3 Newenham,C USA
43D4 New Forest,The Eng
7D4 Newfoundland Province, Can
7E5 Newfoundland I Can
102F2 Newfoundland Basin Atlantic O
18B2 New Franklin USA
42B2 New Galloway Scot
107E1 New Georgia I Solomon Is
7D5 New Glasgow Can
71F4 New Guinea SE Asia
12D3 Newhalen USA
22C3 Newhall USA

10C2 New Hampshire State, USA
101H1 New Hanover S Africa
43E4 Newhaven Eng
15D2 New Haven USA
13B1 New Hazelton Can
19B3 New Iberia USA
10C2 New Jersey State, USA
7C5 New Liskeard Can
16C2 New London USA
106A3 Newman Aust
22B2 Newman USA
43E4 Newmarket Eng
45B2 Newmarket Irish Rep
15C3 New Market USA
9C3 New Mexico State, USA
16C2 New Milford Connecticut, USA
17B1 Newnan USA
109C4 New Norfolk Aust
11A3 New Orleans USA
16B2 New Paltz USA
14B2 New Philadelphia USA
110B1 New Plymouth NZ
18B2 Newport Arkansas, USA
43D4 Newport Eng
14B3 Newport Kentucky, USA
20B2 Newport Oregon, USA
16A2 Newport Pennsylvania, USA
15D2 Newport Rhode Island, USA
15D2 Newport Vermont, USA
43C4 Newport Wales
20C1 Newport Washington, USA
22D4 Newport Beach USA
11C3 Newport News USA
26B1 New Providence I Caribbean S
43B4 Newquay Eng
6C3 New Quebec Crater Can
45C2 New Ross Irish Rep
45C1 Newry N Ire
New Siberian Is = Novosibirskye Ostrova
17B2 New Smyrna Beach USA
107D4 New South Wales State, Aust
12C3 New Stuyahok USA
18A2 Newton Kansas, USA
16D1 Newton Massachusetts, USA
19C3 Newton Mississippi, USA
16B2 Newton New York, USA
43C4 Newton Abbot Eng
45C1 Newton Stewart N Ire
42B2 Newton Stewart Scot
43C3 Newtown Wales
42B2 Newtownards N Ire
16A2 Newville USA
5F5 New Westminster Can
10C2 New York State, USA
10C2 New York USA
110 New Zealand Dominion, SW Pacific O
105G6 New Zealand Plat Pacific O
61F2 Neya Russian Fed
91B4 Neyriz Iran
90C2 Neyshabūr Iran
62D3 Nezhin Russian Fed
98B3 Ngabé Congo
100B3 Ngami,L Botswana
110C1 Ngaruawahia NZ
110C1 Ngaruroro R NZ
110C1 Ngauruhoe,Mt NZ

98B3 Ngo Congo
76D2 Ngoc Linh Mt Viet
98B2 Ngoko R Cam
68B3 Ngong Kenya
99D3 Ngorongoro Crater Tanz
98B3 N'Gounié R Gabon
98B1 Nguigmi Niger
71E2 Ngulu I Pacific O
97D3 Nguru Nig
76D3 Nha Trang Viet
108B3 Nhill Aust
101H1 Nhlangano Swaziland
76D2 Nhommarath Laos
106C2 Nhulunbuy Aust
97B3 Niafounké Mali
14A2 Niagara USA
15C2 Niagara Falls Can
15C2 Niagara Falls USA
70C3 Niah Malay
97B4 Niakaramandougou Ivory Coast
97C3 Niamey Niger
99C2 Niangara Zaïre
98C2 Nia Nia Zaïre
70A3 Nias I Indon
25D3 Nicaragua Republic, Cent America
53C3 Nicastro Italy
49D3 Nice France
26B1 Nicholl's Town The Bahamas
83D5 Nicobar Is Indian O
92B2 Nicosia Cyprus
25D3 Nicoya,Pen de Costa Rica
58C2 Nidzica Pol
46D2 Niederbronn France
56B2 Niedersachsen State, Germany
99C3 Niemba Zaïre
56B2 Nienburg Germany
46D1 Niers R Germany
97B4 Niete,Mt Lib
33F2 Nieuw Amsterdam Surinam
33F2 Nieuw Nickerie Surinam
46B1 Nieuwpoort Belg
92B2 Niğde Turk
97C3 Niger Republic, Africa
97C4 Niger R Nig
97C4 Nigeria Federal Republic, Africa
55B2 Nigrita Greece
75C1 Nihommatsu Japan
74D3 Niigata Japan
74C4 Niihama Japan
75B2 Nii-jima I Japan
75A2 Niimi Japan
74D3 Niitsu Japan
94B3 Nijil Jordan
56B2 Nijmegen Neth
64E3 Nikel' Russian Fed
97C3 Nikki Benin
74D3 Nikko Japan
60D4 Nikolayev Ukraine
61G4 Nikolayevsk Russian Fed
63G2 Nikolayevsk-na-Amure Russian Fed
61G2 Nikol'sk Russian Fed
61G3 Nikol'sk Russian Fed
60D2 Nikopol Ukraine
92C1 Niksar Turk
91D4 Nikshahr Iran
54A2 Nikšić Montenegro, Yugos
71D4 Nila I Indon
80B3 Nile R N E Africa
14A2 Niles USA
87B3 Nilgiri Hills India
85C4 Nimach India
49C3 Nîmes France
109C3 Nimmitabel Aust
99D2 Nimule Sudan
83B5 Nine Degree Chan Indian O
104C4 Ninety-East Ridge Indian O
109C3 Ninety Mile Beach Aust
73D4 Ningde China

73D4 Ningdu China
68B3 Ningjing Shan Mts China
76D1 Ningming China
73A4 Ningnan China
72B2 Ningxia Province, China
72B2 Ning Xian China
73B5 Ninh Binh Vietnam
107D1 Ninigo Is PNG
12D1 Ninilchik USA
8D2 Niobrara USA
98B3 Nioki Zaïre
97B3 Nioro du Sahel Mali
48B2 Niort France
5H4 Nipawin Can
7B5 Nipigon Can
7B5 Nipigon,L Can
7B5 Nipissing R Can
87B1 Nirmal India
86B1 Nirmāli India
54B2 Niš Serbia, Yugos
81C4 Nisāb Yemen
69F4 Nishino-shima I Japan
75A1 Nishino-shima I Japan
75A2 Nishiwaki Japan
12G2 Nisling R Can
12H2 Nisutlin R Can
7C4 Nitchequon Can
16 Niterói Brazil
42C2 Nith R Scot
59B3 Nitra Slovakia
14B3 Nitro USA
71D2 Niut Mt Malay
46C1 Nivelles Belg
49C2 Nivernais Region, France
38L5 Nivskiy Russian Fed
87B1 Nizamābād India
87B3 Nizana Hist Site Israel
61J2 Nizhniye Sergi Russian Fed
65F4 Nizhniy Novgorod Russian Fed
61F3 Nizhniy Lomov Russian Fed
65G4 Nizhniy Tagil Russian Fed
63B1 Nizhnyaya Tunguska R Russian Fed
93C2 Nizip Turk
100B2 Njoko R Zambia
99D3 Njombe Tanz
99B2 Nkambé Cam
101C2 Nkhata Bay Malawi
99B2 Nkongsamba Cam
97C3 N'Konni Niger
86C2 Noakhali Bang
12B1 Noatak USA
12C1 Noatak R USA
74C4 Nobeoka Japan
47D1 Noce R Italy
23A1 Nochistlán Mexico
23B2 Nochixtlán Mexico
24A1 Nocona USA
9B3 Nogales Sonora, Mexico
9B3 Nogales USA
23B2 Nogales Veracruz, Mexico
47D2 Nogara Italy
75A2 Nogata Japan
63D2 Noginsk Russian Fed
34D2 Nogoyá Arg
34D2 Nogoyá R Arg
84C3 Nohar India
75B2 Nojima-zaki C Japan
98B2 Nola CAR
61G2 Nolinsk Russian Fed
16D2 Nomans Land I USA
12A2 Nome USA
46D2 Nomeny France
72B1 Nomgon Mongolia
5H3 Nonacho L Can
76C2 Nong Khai Thai
101H1 Nongoma S Africa
12B1 Noorvik USA
13B3 Nootka Sd Can
98B3 Noqui Angola
7C5 Noranda Can

46B1 Nord Department, France
64D2 Nordaustlandet / Barents S
13D2 Nordegg Can
38F6 Nordfjord Inlet Nor
39F8 Nordfriesische I Germany
56C2 Nordhausen Germany
56B2 Nordrhein Westfalen State, Germany
38J4 Nordkapp C Nor
6E3 Nordre Greenland
38H5 Nord Stronfjället Mt Sweden
189 Nordvik Russian Fed
45C2 Nore R Irish Rep
43E3 Norfolk County, Eng
8D2 Norfolk Nebraska, USA
11C3 Norfolk Virginia, USA
107F3 Norfolk I Aust
18B2 Norfolk L USA
105G5 Norfolk Ridge Pacific O
1C6 Noril'sk Russian Fed
18C1 Normal USA
19A2 Norman USA
48B2 Normandie Region, France
12J1 Normanton Aust
4B3 Norne USA
12J1 Norristown USA
39H7 Norrköping Sweden
39H6 Norrsundet Sweden
39H7 Norrtälje Sweden
106B4 Norseman Aust
63F2 Norsk Russian Fed
102J2 North S N W Europe
42D2 Northallerton Eng
106A4 Northam Aust
102E3 North American Basin Atlantic O
12J1 Northampton Aust
43D3 Northampton England
43D3 Northampton County, Eng
15D2 Northampton USA
4G3 North Arm B Can
17B1 North Augusta USA
6D4 North Aulatsivik I Can
13F2 North Battleford Can
7C5 North Bay Can
20B2 North Bend USA
44C3 North Berwick Scot
7D5 North,C Can
7G4 North C NZ
11B3 North Carolina State, USA
20B1 North Cascade Nat Pk USA
14B1 North Chan Can
42B2 North Chan Ire/Scot
8C2 North Dakota State, USA
43E4 North Downs Eng
14C2 North East USA
102H2 North East Atlantic Basin Atlantic O
48B3 Northeast C USA
40B3 Northern Ireland UK
27L1 Northern Range Mts Trinidad
106C2 Northern Territory Aust
44C3 North Esk R Scot
16C1 Northfield Massachusetts, USA
12D2 North Fork R USA
110B1 North I NZ
74B3 North Korea Republic, S E Asia
North Land = Severnaya Zemlya
19B3 North Little Rock USA
1B4 North Magnetic Pole Can
17B2 North Miami USA
17B2 North Miami Beach USA
8C2 North Platte USA

8C2 North Platte R US.
27R3 North Pt Barbados
14B1 North Pt Can
40B2 North Rona I Scot
44C2 North Ronaldsay I Scot
13F2 North Saskatchewan R Can
40D2 North Sea N W Europe
40D3 North Slope Region USA
109D1 North Stradbroke I Aust
110B1 North Taranaki Bigh B NZ
9C3 North Truchas Peak Mt USA
44A3 North Uist I Scot
42C2 Northumberland County, Eng
107E3 Northumberland Is Can
7D5 Northumberland Str Can
20B1 North Vancouver Can
14B3 North Walsham Eng
12F2 Northway USA
106A3 North West C Aust
84C2 North West Frontier Province, Pak
7D4 North West River Can
4F3 North West Territories Can
42D2 North York Moors Nat Pk Eng
12B2 Norton B USA
12B2 Norton Sd USA
11281 Norvegia,C Ant
16C2 Norwalk Connecticu USA
14B2 Norwalk Ohio, USA
39F6 Norway
5J4 Norway House Can
6A2 Norwegian B Can
102H1 Norwegian Basin Norwegian S
64A3 Norwegian S N W Europe
16C2 Norwich Connecticu USA
43E3 Norwich Eng
16D1 Norwood Massachusetts, USA
14B3 Norwood Ohio, USA
54C2 Nos Emine C Bulg
74D2 Noshiro Japan
54C2 Nos Kaliakra C Bulg
44E1 Noss I Scot
91D4 Nosratäbäd Iran
101D2 Nosy Barren I Madag
101D2 Nosy Bé I Madag
101E2 Nosy Boraha I Madag
101D3 Nosy Varika Madag
58B2 Notéc R Pol
53C2 Notikeuin Can
59F7 Notodden Nor
7E5 Notre Dams B Can
43D3 Nottingham County, Eng
43D3 Nottingham Eng
6C3 Nottingham I Can
6C3 Nottingham Island Can
96A2 Nouadhibou Maur
97A3 Nouakchott Maur
107F3 Nouméa Nouvelle Calédonie
97B3 Nouna Burkina
107F3 Nouvelle Calédonie I S W Pacific O
98B3 Nova Caipemba Angola
35A2 Nova Esperança Brazil
35C2 Nova Friburgo Brazil
100A2 Nova Gaia Angola

35B2 Nova Granada Brazil
35B2 Nova Horizonte Brazil
35C1 Nova Lima Brazil
Nova Lisboa = Huambo
35C2 Nova Londrina Brazil
101C3 Nova Mambone Mozam
47C2 Nova Scotia Province, Can
7D5 Nova Scotia Province, Can
22A1 Novato USA
35C1 Nova Venecia Brazil
60D4 Novaya Kakhovka Ukraine
64G2 Novaya Zemlya I Barents S
54C2 Nova Zagora Bulg
54C2 Nove Russas Brazil
54A1 Nové Zámky Slovakia
60D2 Novgorod Russian Fed
47C2 Novi Ligure Italy
47C2 Novi Pazar Bulg
54C2 Novi Pazar Serbia, Yugos
54A1 Novi Sad Serbia, Yugos
61J3 Novoalekseyevka Kazakhstan
61F3 Novoanninskiy Russian Fed
61E4 Novocherkassk Russian Fed
60C3 Novograd Volynskiy Ukraine
58D2 Novogrudok Russian Fed
30F4 Novo Hamburgo Brazil
65H5 Novokazalinsk Kazakhstan
65K4 Novokuznetsk Russian Fed
112B2 Novolazarevskaya Base Ant
52C1 Novo Mesto Slovenia
60E3 Novomoskovsk Russian Fed
61E4 Novorossiysk Russian Fed
65K4 Novosibirsk Russian Fed
1B8 Novosibirskiye Ostrova I Russian Fed
61J3 Novotroitsk Russian Fed
61G3 Novo Uzensk Russian Fed
59C2 Novovolynsk Ukraine
61G2 Novo Vyatsk Russian Fed
60D3 Novozybkov Russian Fed
58C2 Novy Dwór Mazowiecki Pol
61K2 Novyy Lyalya Russian Fed
61F1 Novyy Port Russian Fed
61H5 Novyy Uzen Kazakhstan
58B2 Nowa Sól Pol
18A2 Nowata USA
NWroginga = Nagaon
12D2 Nowitna R USA
90B2 Now Shahr Iran
92C3 Nowshera Pak
58C3 Nowy Sącz Pol
12H3 Noyes I USA
46B2 Noyon France
97B4 Nsawam Ghana
99D1 Nuba Mts Sudan
81B3 Nubian Desert Sudan
34A3 Nuble R Chile
9D4 Nueces R USA
5J3 Nueltin L Can
26A2 Nueva Gerona Cuba
26A2 Nueva Imperial Chile

9C4 Nueva Laredo Mexico
34D2 Nueva Palmira Urug
24B2 Nueva Rosita Mexico
26B2 Nuevitas Cuba
24B1 Nuevo Casas Grandes Mexico
24C2 Nuevo Laredo Mexico
99E2 Nugaal Region, Somalia
6E2 Nûgâtiaq Greenland
6E2 Nugssuaq Pen Greenland
6E2 Nûgussaq I Greenland
108A2 Nukey Bluff Mt Aust
93D3 Nukhayb Iraq
65G5 Nukus Uzbekistan
12C2 Nulato USA
106B4 Nullarbor Plain Aust
97D4 Numan Nig
75B1 Numata Japan
98C2 Numatinna R Sudan
74D3 Numazu Japan
71E4 Numfoor I Indon
108C3 Numurkah Aust
12B2 Nunapitchuk USA
84D2 Nunkun Mt India
53A2 Nuoro Sardegna
91B3 Nūrābād Iran
47C2 Nure R Italy
108A2 Nuriootpa Aust
84C1 Nuristan Upland Afghan
61H3 Nurlat Russian Fed
38K6 Nurmes Fin
57C3 Nürnberg Germany
108C2 Nurri,Mt Aust
93D2 Nusaybin Turk
12C3 Nushagak R USA
12C3 Nushagak B USA
12C3 Nushagak Pen USA
84B3 Nushki Pak
7D4 Nutak Can
12F2 Nutzotin Mts USA
86A1 Nuwakot Nepal
87C3 Nuwara-Eliya Sri Lanka
6C3 Nuyukjuak Can
16C2 Nyack USA
99C2 Nyahururu Kenya
108B3 Nyah West Aust
4C3 Nyai USA
68B3 Nyainqentanglha Shan Mts China
99D3 Nyakabindi Tanz
98C1 Nyala Sudan
86B1 Nyalam China
94B3 Nyamlell Sudan
64F3 Nyandoma Russian Fed
100C2 Nyanga Zim
98B3 Nyanga R Gabon
101C2 Nyasa L Malawi/ Mozam
76B2 Nyaunglebin Burma
61J2 Nyazepetrovsk Russian Fed
39G7 Nyborg Sweden
39H7 Nybro Sweden
64J3 Nyda Russian Fed
6D1 Nyeboes Land Region Can
99D3 Nyeri Kenya
101C2 Nyimba Zambia
82D3 Nyingchi China
59C3 Nyíregyháza Hung
99D2 Nyiru,Mt Kenya
38J6 Nykarleby Fin
39F7 Nykøbing Den
39G8 Nykøbing Den
39G7 Nyköping Sweden
100B3 Nylstroom S Africa
109C2 Nymagee Aust
39H7 Nynäshamn Sweden
109C2 Nyngan Aust
47B1 Nyon Switz
98B2 Nyong R Cam
49D3 Nyons France
52A2 Nysa Pol
20C2 Nyssa USA
63D1 Nyurba Russian Fed
99D3 Nzega Tanz

97B4 Nzérékoré Guinea
98B3 N'zeto Angola

O

6F3 Oaggsimiut Greenland
8C2 Oahe Res USA
21C4 Oahu I Hawaiian Is
108B2 Oakbank Aust
22B2 Oakdale USA
109D1 Oakey Aust
21A2 Oakland California, USA
20B2 Oakland Oregon, USA
14A3 Oakland City USA
22B2 Oakley California, USA
14C2 Oakville Can
111B3 Oamaru NZ
112B7 Oates Land Region, Ant
109C4 Oatlands Aust
23B2 Oaxaca Mexico
23B2 Oaxaca State, Mexico
65J3 Ob' R Russian Fed
75B1 Obama Japan
111A3 Oban NZ
44B3 Oban Scot
75C2 Obanazawa Japan
47D1 Oberammergau Germany
46D1 Oberhausen Germany
47D1 Oberstdorf Germany
73D3 Obi I Indon
33F4 Obidos Brazil
74E2 Obihiro Japan
98C2 Obo CAR
99E1 Obock Djibouti
60E3 Oboyan Russian Fed
20B2 O'Brien USA
61H3 Obshchiy Syrt Mts Russian Fed
64J3 Obskava Guba B Russian Fed
97B4 Obuasi Ghana
17B2 Ocala USA
32C2 Ocana Colombia
50B2 Ocaña Spain
12G3 Ocean C USA
15C3 Ocean City Maryland, USA
16B3 Ocean City New Jersey, USA
5F4 Ocean Falls Can
22D4 Oceanside USA
19C3 Ocean Springs USA
61H2 Ocher Russian Fed
44C3 Ochil Hills Scot
17B1 Ochlockonee R USA
27H1 Ocho Rios Jamaica
17B1 Ocmulgee R USA
17B1 Oconee R USA
23A1 Ocotlán Jalisco, Mexico
23B2 Ocotlán Oaxaca, Mexico
7D4 Oda Ghana
75A1 Oda Japan
38B2 Ódáðahraun Region, Iceland
74D3 Odate Japan
74D3 Odawara Japan
39F6 Odda Nor
50A2 Odemira Port
55C3 Ödemiş Turk
101G1 Odendaalsrus S Africa
39G7 Odense Den
56C2 Oder R Pol/Germany
9C3 Odessa Texas, USA
60D4 Odessa Ukraine
20C1 Odessa Washington, USA
97B4 Odienné Ivory Coast
59B2 Odra R Brazil
31C3 Oeiras Brazil
53C2 Ofanto R Italy
94B3 Ofaqim Israel

45C2 Offaly County, Irish Rep
49D1 Offenbach Germany
49D2 Offenburg Germany
74D3 Oga Japan
99E2 Ogaden Region, Eth
74D3 Ogaki Japan
8C2 Ogallala USA
69G4 Ogasawara Gunto Is
97C4 Ogbomosho Nig
8B2 Ogden Utah, USA
15C2 Ogdensburg USA
17B1 Ogeechee R USA
12G1 Ogilvie Can
4E3 Ogilvie Mts Can
17B1 Oglethorpe,Mt USA
47D2 Oglio R Italy
47B1 Ognon R France
97C4 Ogoja Nig
98A3 Ogooué R Gabon
58C1 Ogre Latvia
96B2 Oguilet Khenachich Well Mali
52C1 Ogulin Croatia
111A3 Ohai NZ
110C1 Ohakune NZ
96C2 Ohanet Alg
111A2 Ohau,L NZ
102D2 Ohio State, USA
14A3 Ohio R USA
100A2 Ohopoho Namibia
57C2 Ohre R Czech Republic
55B2 Ohrid Macedonia
55B2 Ohridsko Jezero L Macedonia/Alb
110B1 Ohura NZ
33G3 Oiapoque French Guiana
68B2 Oijiaqing China
14C2 Oil City USA
21B2 Oildale USA
48C2 Oise Department, France
49C2 Oise R France
74C4 Oita Japan
22C3 Ojai USA
24B2 Ojinaga Mexico
23B2 Ojitlan Mexico
75B1 Ojiya Japan
30C4 Ojos del Salado Mt Arg
23A1 Quéloz Mexico
60E3 Oka R Russian Fed
100A3 Okahandja Namibia
20C1 Okanagan Falls Can
13D2 Okanagan L Can
20C1 Okanogan USA
20C1 Okanogan R USA
20B1 Okanogan Range Mts Can/USA
84C2 Okara Pak
100A2 Okavango R Angola/ Namibia
100B2 Okavango Delta Marsh Botswana
74D3 Okaya Japan
74C4 Okayama Japan
75B2 Okazaki Japan
17B2 Okeechobee USA
17B2 Okeechobee,L USA
17B1 Okefenokee Swamp USA
97C4 Okene Nig
85B4 Okha India
69C1 Okha Russian Fed
86B1 Okhaldunga Nepal
62J3 Okhotsk,S of Russian Fed
69E4 Okinawa I Japan
69E4 Okinawa gunto Arch Japan
74C3 Oki-shoto Is Japan
18A2 Oklahoma State, USA
18A2 Oklahoma City USA
18A2 Okmulgee USA
98B3 Okondja Gabon
98B3 Okoyo Congo
97C4 Okpara R Nig
61J4 Oktyabr'sk Kazakhstan
61H3 Oktyabr'skiy Russian Fed

74D2 **Okushiri-tō** / Japan
38A2 **Olafsvik** Iceland
39H7 **Öland** / Sweden
108B2 **Olary** Aust
18B2 **Olathe** USA
29D3 **Olavarria** Arg
53A2 **Olbia** Sardegna
12G1 **Old Crow** Can
56B2 **Oldenburg**
　Niedersachsen,
　Germany
56C2 **Oldenburg**
　Schleswig-Holstein,
　Germany
15C2 **Old Forge** USA
42C3 **Oldham** Eng
12D3 **Old Harbor** USA
41B3 **Old Head of Kinsale**
　C Scot
16C2 **Old Lyme** USA
13E2 **Olds** Can
72B1 **Oldziyt** Mongolia
25C2 **Olean** USA
63E2 **Olekma** R
　Russian Fed
63D1 **Olekminsk**
　Russian Fed
38L5 **Olenegorsk**
　Russian Fed
58D2 **Olevsk** Ukraine
69F2 **Ol'ga** Russian Fed
100A3 **Olifants** R Namibia
55B2 **Olimbos** Mt Greece
35B2 **Olímpia** Brazil
23B2 **Olinala** Mexico
31E3 **Olinda** Brazil
34C2 **Oliva** Arg
29C2 **Olivares** Mt Arg
35C2 **Oliveira** Brazil
13D3 **Oliver** Can
30C2 **Ollagüe** Chile
30C2 **Ollagüe** Mt Bol
18C2 **Olney** USA
68E1 **Olochi** Russian Fed
37H3 **Olofstrom** Sweden
98B3 **Olombo** Congo
59B2 **Olomouc**
　Czech Republic
60D1 **Olonets** Russian Fed
79B3 **Olongapa** Phil
48B3 **Oloron Ste Marie**
　France
68D1 **Olovyannaya**
　Russian Fed
46D1 **Olpe** Germany
58C2 **Olsztyn** Pol
54B2 **Olt** R Switz
47B1 **Olten** Switz
20B1 **Olympia** USA
20B1 **Olympic Nat Pk** USA
20B1 **Olympus,Mt** USA
20B1 **Olympus** = **Ólimbos**
64E3 **Om'** R Russian Fed
75B1 **Omachi** Japan
75B2 **Omae-zaki** C Japan
45C1 **Omagh** N Ire
18A1 **Omaha** USA
20C1 **Omak** USA
91C5 **Oman** Sultanate,
　Arabian Pen
91C4 **Oman,G of** UAE
98A3 **Omboué** Gabon
99D1 **Omdurman** Sudan
23B2 **Ometepec** Mexico
13B1 **Om Hajer** Eth
13B1 **Omineca** R Can
13B1 **Omineca Mts** Can
75B1 **Omiya** Japan
12H3 **Ommaney,C** USA
4H2 **Ommanney B** Can
99D2 **Omo** R Eth
65J4 **Omsk** Russian Fed
74B4 **Omura** Japan
74C4 **Omuta** Japan
61H2 **Omutninsk**
　Russian Fed
78D3 **Onang** Indon
14B1 **Onaping L** Can
100A2 **Oncócua** Angola
100A2 **Ondangua** Namibia
59C3 **Ondava** R Slovakia
68D2 **Ondörhaan** Molgolia
83B5 **One and Half Degree**
　Chan Indian O
64E3 **Onega** Russian Fed

64E3 **Onega** R
　Russian Fed
15C2 **Oneida L** USA
8D2 **O'Neill** USA
69H2 **Onekotan** /
　Russian Fed
98C3 **Onema** Zaire
15D2 **Oneonta** USA
54C1 **Oneşti** Rom
64E3 **Onezhskoye Ozero** L
　Russian Fed
100A2 **Ongiva** Angola
74B3 **Ongjin** N Korea
72D1 **Ongniud Qi** China
87C1 **Ongole** India
15C2 **Onieda L** USA
101D3 **Onilahy** R Madag
97C4 **Onitsha** Nig
68C2 **Onjuül** Mongolia
75B1 **Ono** Japan
75B2 **Onohara-jima** /
　Japan
74C4 **Onomichi** Japan
106A3 **Onslow** Aust
17C1 **Onslow B** USA
75B1 **Ontake-san** Mt
　Japan
22D3 **Ontario** California,
　USA
20C2 **Ontario** Oregon, USA
7A4 **Ontario** Province,
　Can
15C2 **Ontario,L** Can/USA
12C2 **Onteniente** Spain
106C3 **Oodnadatta** Aust
106C4 **Ooldea** Aust
46B1 **Oologah L** USA
46B1 **Oostende** Belg
46B1 **Oosterschelde**
　Estuary Neth
87B2 **Ootacamund** India
18B2 **Ootsa L** Can
69H1 **Opala** Russian Fed
98C3 **Opala** Zaire
87C3 **Opanake** Sri Lanka
61G2 **Oparino** Russian Fed
59B3 **Opava**
　Czech Republic
17A1 **Opelika** USA
19B3 **Opelousas** USA
12C2 **Ophir** USA
21B2 **Opochka**
　Russian Fed
59B2 **Opole** Pol
110C1 **Opp** USA
17A1 **Opp** USA
38F6 **Oppdal** Nor
110B1 **Opunake** NZ
54B1 **Oradea** Rom
38B2 **Oraefajökull** Mts
　Iceland
85D3 **Orai** India
96B1 **Oran** Alg
30D3 **Orán** Arg
109C2 **Orange** Aust
22D4 **Orange** California,
　USA
49C3 **Orange** France
19B3 **Orange** Texas, USA
100A3 **Orange** R S Africa
17B1 **Orangeburg** USA
101G1 **Orange Free State**
　Province, S Africa
17B1 **Orange Park** USA
14B2 **Orangeville** Can
56C2 **Oranienburg**
　Germany
79C3 **Oras** Phil
54B1 **Orăştie** Rom
54B1 **Oraviţa** Rom
54B2 **Orbetello** Italy
109C3 **Orbost** Aust
46B1 **Orchies** France
47B2 **Orco** R Italy
106B2 **Ord** R Aust
106B2 **Ord,Mt** Aust
93C1 **Ordu** Turk
39H7 **Örebro** Sweden
8A2 **Oregon** State, USA
14B2 **Oregon** USA
20B1 **Oregon City** USA
39H6 **Oregrund** Sweden
60E2 **Orekhovo Zuyevo**
　Russian Fed

60E3 **Orel** Russian Fed
61H3 **Orenburg**
　Russian Fed
34D3 **Orense** Arg
50A1 **Orense** Spain
56C1 **Oresund** Str Den/
　Sweden
111A3 **Oreti** R NZ
55C3 **Orhaneli** R Turk
68C2 **Orhon Gol** R
　Mongolia
23B2 **Oriental** Mexico
108B1 **Orientos** Aust
51B2 **Orihuela** Spain
15C2 **Orillia** Can
32D2 **Orinoco** R Ven
86A2 **Orissa** State, India
53A3 **Oristano** Sardegna
38K6 **Orivesi** L Fin
33F4 **Oriximina** Brazil
23B2 **Orizaba** Mexico
35B1 **Orizona** Brazil
44C2 **Orkney** I Scot
35B2 **Orlândia** Brazil
17B2 **Orlando** USA
48C2 **Orléanais** Region
　France
48C2 **Orléans** France
63B2 **Orlik** Russian Fed
82A3 **Ormara** Pak
79B3 **Ormoc** Phil
17B2 **Ormond Beach** USA
46C2 **Ornain** R France
17B1 **Ornans** France
48B2 **Orne** R France
38H6 **Örnsköldsvik**
　Sweden
32C3 **Orocué** Colombia
94B3 **Oron** Israel
　Orontes = **'Āşi**
79B4 **Oroquieta** Phil
59C3 **Oroshaza** Hung
21A2 **Oroville** California,
　USA
20C1 **Oroville** Washington,
　USA
47B1 **Orsières** Switz
65G4 **Orsk** Russian Fed
38F6 **Ørsta** Nor
48B3 **Orthez** France
50A1 **Ortigueira** Spain
47B1 **Ortles** Mts Italy
27L1 **Ortoire** R Trinidad
93E2 **Orūmiyeh** Iran
30C2 **Oruro** Bol
61J2 **Osa** Russian Fed
18B2 **Osage** R USA
75B1 **Osaka** Japan
25D4 **Osa,Pen de** Costa
　Rica
18C2 **Osceola** Arkansas,
　USA
18B1 **Osceola** Iowa, USA
20C2 **Osgood Mts** USA
15C2 **Oshawa** Can
75B2 **O-shima** I Japan
108B1 **Oshkosh** USA
97C4 **Oshogbo** Nig
75B1 **Oshosh** USA
98B3 **Oshwe** Zaire
54A1 **Osijek** Croatia
65K5 **Osinniki** Russian Fed
58D2 **Osipovichi**
　Belorussia
18B1 **Oskaloosa** USA
60A2 **Oskarshamn** Sweden
39G7 **Oslo** Nor
92C2 **Osmaniye** Turk
56B2 **Osnabrück** Germany
30F4 **Osório** Brazil
29B4 **Osorno** Chile
50B1 **Osorno** Spain
20C1 **Osoyoos** Can
12C1 **Ospika** R Can
70D5 **Ossa,Mt** Aust
16C2 **Ossining** USA
60D2 **Ostashkov**
　Russian Fed
　Ostend = **Oostende**
38G6 **Østersund** V Nor
38G6 **Östersund** Sweden
56B2 **Ostfriesische Inseln**
　Is Germany
38H6 **Östhammär** Sweden
53B2 **Ostia** Italy

47D2 **Ostiglia** Italy
59B3 **Ostrava**
　Czech Republic
58B2 **Ostróda** Pol
58B2 **Ostrołeka** Pol
60C2 **Ostrov Belyy** /
　Russian Fed
64H1 **Ostrov Green Bell**
　Barents S
64F3 **Ostrov Kolguyev** /
　Russian Fed
74F2 **Ostrov Kunashir** /
　Russian Fed
64F2 **Ostrov**
　Mechdusharskiy /
　Barents S
90B2 **Ostrov Ogurchinskiy**
　/ Turkmenistan
64G1 **Ostrov Rudol'fa** /
　Barents S
64G2 **Ostrov Vaygach** /
　Russian Fed
1B7 **Ostrov Vrangelya**
　Russian Fed
58B2 **Ostrów Wlkp.** Pol
59C2 **Ostrowiec** Pol
58C2 **Ostrów Mazowiecka**
　Pol
50A2 **Osuna** Spain
15C2 **Oswego** USA
15C2 **Oswego** USA
43C3 **Oswestry** Eng
59B2 **Oświęcim** Pol
75B1 **Ota** Japan
111B3 **Otago Pen** NZ
110C2 **Otaki** NZ
74E2 **Otaru** Japan
32B3 **Otavalo** Ecuador
100A2 **Otavi** Namibia
75C1 **Otawara** Japan
20C1 **Othello** USA
55B3 **Othris** Mt Greece
16C1 **Otis** Massachusetts,
　USA
18B2 **Otisville** USA
100A3 **Otjiwarongo**
　Namibia
72B2 **Otog Qi** China
110C2 **Otorohanga** NZ
55A2 **Otranto** Italy
55A2 **Otranto,Str of** Chan
　Italy/Alb
14A2 **Otsego** USA
75B1 **Otsu** Japan
39F6 **Otta** Nor
39F7 **Otta** R Nor
15C1 **Ottawa** Can
18A2 **Ottawa** Kansas, US
15C1 **Ottawa** R Can
7B4 **Ottawa Is** Can
7B4 **Otter Rapids** Can
6B1 **Otto Fjord** Can
101G1 **Ottosdal** S Africa
18B1 **Ottumwa** USA
46D2 **Ottweiler** Germany
97C4 **Oturkpo** Nig
32B5 **Otusco** Peru
108C3 **Otway,C** Aust
14B2 **Otwock** Pol
47D1 **Ötztal** Alps Austria
76C1 **Ou** R Laos
19B3 **Ouachita** R USA
19B3 **Ouachita,L** USA
96A2 **Ouadâne** Maur
98C2 **Ouadda** CAR
98C1 **Ouaddaï** Desert
　Region Chad
97B3 **Ouagadougou** Burkin
96A3 **Ouahigouya** Burkir
98C2 **Ouaka** CAR
97C3 **Oualam** Niger
96C2 **Ouallen** Alg
97B3 **Ouanda Djallé** CAR
96A2 **Ouarane** Region,
　Maur
96C1 **Ouargla** Alg
78C3 **Ouarra** R CAR
96B1 **Ouarzazate** Mor
51C2 **Ouassel** R Alg
98B2 **Oubangui** R Congo
46B1 **Oudenaarde** Belg

100B4 Oudtshoorn S Africa
51B2 Oued Tlélat Alg
96B1 Oued Zem Mor
98B2 Ouesso Congo
96B1 Ouessane Mor
98B2 Ouham R Chad
97C4 Ouidah Benin
96B1 Oujda Mor
38J6 Oulainen Fin
38K5 Oulu Fin
38K5 Oulu R Fin
43J6 Oulujärvi L Fin
95B3 Oum Chalouba Chad
98B1 Oum Hadjer Chad
98B1 Oum Raman
  Watercourse Chad
38K5 Ounas R Fin
95B3 Ounianga Kébir
  Chad
46D1 Our R Germany
46B2 Ourcq R France
  Ourense = Orense
31C3 Ouricuri Brazil
35B2 Ourinhos Brazil
35C2 Ouro Prêto Brazil
46C1 Ourthe R Belg
42D2 Ouse R Eng
43E3 Ouse R E Eng
40B2 Outer Hebrides Is
  Scot
22C4 Outer Santa Barbara
  Chan USA
100A3 Outjo Namibia
38K6 Outokumpu Fin
108B3 Ouyen Aust
34C2 Ovada Italy
34A2 Ovalle Chile
100A2 Ovamboland Region,
  Namibia
61H5 Ova Tyuleni Is
  Kazakhstan
38J5 Overtorneå Sweden
50A1 Oviedo Spain
60C3 Ovruch Ukraine
63E2 Ovsyanka
  Russian Fed
111A3 Owaka NZ
75B2 Owase Japan
11B3 Owensboro USA
21B2 Owens L USA
14B2 Owen Sound Can
107D1 Owen Stanley Range
  Mts PNG
97C4 Owerri Nig
97C4 Owo Nig
14B2 Owosso USA
20C2 Owyhee R USA
20C2 Owyhee Mts USA
32B6 Oxapampa Peru
39H7 Oxelösund Sweden
43D4 Oxford County, Eng
43D4 Oxford Eng
16D1 Oxford
  Massachusetts, USA
19C3 Oxford Mississippi,
  USA
45B1 Ox Mts Irish Rep
22C3 Oxnard USA
74D3 Oyama Japan
13E2 Oyen Can
44B3 Oykel R Scot
39F6 Øyre Nor
109C4 Oyster B Aust
79B4 Ozamiz Phil
17A1 Ozark USA
18B2 Ozark Plat USA
52C1 Ozarks,L of the USA
59C3 Ôzd Hung
65K5 Ozero Alakol L
  Kazakhstan
65J3 Ozero Balkhash L
  Kazakhstan
63C2 Ozero Baykal L
  Kazakhstan
65J4 Ozero Chany L
  Russian Fed
69F1 Ozero
  Chukchagirskoye
  Russian Fed
69F1 Ozero Evoron
  Russian Fed
  Ozero Chudskoye =
  Peipus,L

60D2 Ozero Il'men L
  Russian Fed
38L5 Ozero Imandra L
  Russian Fed
82B1 Ozero Issyk Kul' L
  Kirghizia
69F2 Ozero Khanka L
  China/Russian Fed
38L5 Ozero Kovdozero L
  Russian Fed
38L5 Ozero Kuyto L
  Russian Fed
38L5 Ozero Pyaozero L
  Russian Fed
65H4 Ozero Tengiz L
  Kazakhstan
38L5 Ozero Topozero L
  Russian Fed
65K5 Ozero Zaysan L
  Kazakhstan
23B1 Ozuluama Mexico

P
100A4 Paarl S Africa
44A3 Pabbay I Scot
58B2 Pabianice Pol
86B2 Pabna Bang
58D2 Pabrade Lithuania
32B5 Pacasmayo Peru
23B1 Pachuca Mexico
105K6 Pacific-Antarctic
  Ridge Pacific O
22B2 Pacific Grove USA
78C4 Pacitan Indon
35C1 Pacui R Brazil
70B4 Padang Indon
56B2 Paderborn Germany
5J3 Padlei Can
86C2 Padma R Bang
47D2 Padova Italy
9D4 Padre I USA
43B4 Padstow Eng
108B3 Padthaway Aust
  Padua = Padova
14A3 Paducah Kentucky,
  USA
11B3 Paducah USA
38L5 Padunskoye More L
  Russian Fed
74A3 Paengnyŏng-do Is
  Korea
110C1 Paeroa NZ
100C3 Pafuri Mozam
52B2 Pag I Croatia
79B4 Pagadian Phil
70B4 Pagai Selatan I
  Indon
70B4 Pagai Utara I Indon
71F2 Pagan I Pacific O
78D3 Pagatan Indon
55C3 Pagondhas Greece
110C2 Pahiatua NZ
21C4 Pahoa Hawaiian Is
17B2 Pahokee USA
39K6 Päijänne L Fin
21C4 Pailola Chan
  Hawaiian Is
21C4 Painesville USA
9B3 Painted Desert USA
42B2 Paisley Scot
32A5 Paita Peru
38J5 Pajala Sweden
80E3 Pakistan Republic,
  Asia
76C2 Pak Lay Laos
86D2 Pakokku Burma
13E2 Pakowki L Can
52C1 Pakrac Croatia
54A1 Paks Hung
76C2 Pakse Laos
76D2 Paksé Laos
99D2 Pakwach Uganda
98B2 Pala Chad
52C2 Palagruža I Croatia
46B2 Palaiseau France
  Palakhat = Palghat
78C3 Palangkaraya Indon
87B2 Palani India
85C4 Palanpur India
100B3 Palapye Botswana
17B2 Palatka USA
71E3 Palau Is Pacific O
76B3 Palaw Burma
79A4 Palawan I Phil
79A4 Palawan Pass Phil

87B3 Palayankottai India
39J7 Paldiski Estonia
78B3 Palembang Indon
50B1 Palencia Spain
94A1 Paleokhorio Cyprus
53B3 Palermo Italy
94B3 Palestine Region,
  Israel
19A3 Palestine USA
86C2 Paletwa Burma
87B2 Pālghāt India
85C3 Pāli India
85C4 Pālitāna India
87B3 Palk Str India/
  Sri Lanka
61G3 Pallasovka
  Russian Fed
38J5 Pallastunturi Mt Fin
111B2 Palliser B NZ
111C2 Palliser,C NZ
101D2 Palma Mozam
51C2 Palma de Mallorca
  Spain
31B2 Palmares Brazil
26A5 Palmar Sur Costa
  Rica
97B4 Palmas,C Lib
26B2 Palma Soriano Cuba
17B2 Palm Bay USA
17B2 Palm Beach USA
22C3 Palmdale USA
31D3 Palmeira dos Indos
  Brazil
12E2 Palmer USA
112C3 Palmer Base Ant
112C3 Palmer Arch Ant
112B3 Palmer Land Region
  Ant
111B3 Palmerston NZ
110C2 Palmerston North NZ
16B2 Palmerton USA
17B2 Palmetto USA
53C3 Palmi Italy
32B3 Palmira Colombia
107D2 Palm Is Aust
21B3 Palm Springs USA
18B2 Palmyra Missouri,
  USA
16A2 Palmyra
  Pennsylvania, USA
86B2 Palmyras Pt India
22A2 Palo Alto USA
78B2 Paloh Indon
99D1 Paloich Sudan
21B3 Palomar Mt USA
70C4 Palopo Indon
93C2 Palu Turk
84D3 Palwal India
97C3 Pama Burkina
78C4 Pamekasan Indon
78B4 Pameungpeuk Indon
48C3 Pamiers France
82B2 Pamir Mt Russian Fed
11C3 Pamlico Sd USA
9C3 Pampa USA
34B2 Pampa de la Salinas
  Salt pan Arg
34B3 Pampa de la Varita
  Plain Arg
32C2 Pamplona Colombia
50B1 Pamplona Spain
54B2 Panagyurishte Bulg
87A1 Panaji India
32B2 Panamá Panama
32A2 Panama Republic,
  Cent America
26B5 Panama Canal
  Panama
17A1 Panama City USA
21B2 Panamint Range Mts
  USA
21B2 Panamint V USA
47D2 Panaro R Italy
79B3 Panay I Phil
54B2 Pancevo Serbia,
  Yugos
79B3 Pandan Phil
87B1 Pandharpur India
108B2 Pandie Pandie Aust
58C1 Panevezys Lithuania
65K5 Panfilov Kazakhstan
76B1 Pang R Burma

99D3 Pangani Tanz
99D3 Pangani R Tanz
98C3 Pangi Zaïre
78B3 Pangkalpinang Indon
6D3 Pangnirtung Can
76B1 Pangtara Burma
79B4 Pangutaran Group Is
  Phil
84D3 Panipat India
84B2 Panjao Afghan
74B3 P'anmunjóm N Korea
86A2 Panna India
35A2 Panorama Brazil
53B3 Pantelleria I Medit S
23B1 Pantepec Mexico
23B1 Pánuco Mexico
23B1 Pánuco R Mexico
73A4 Pan Xian China
53C3 Paola Italy
18A2 Paola USA
14A3 Paoli USA
59B3 Pápa Hung
23B2 Papaloapan R
  Mexico
23B2 Papaloapan R
  Mexico
28A1 Papantla Mexico
44E1 Papa Stour I Scot
110B1 Papakura NZ
44C2 Papa Westray I Scot
107D1 Papua,G of PNG
107D1 Papua New Guinea
  Republic, S E Asia
34A2 Papudo Chile
76B2 Papun Burma
33G4 Para State, Brazil
31B2 Pará R Brazil
106A3 Paraburdoo Aust
32B6 Paracas,Pen de Peru
35B1 Paracatu Brazil
35B1 Paracatu R Brazil
108A2 Parachilna Aust
84C2 Parachinar Pak
54B2 Paracin Serbia,
  Yugos
35C1 Pará de Minas Brazil
21A2 Paradise California,
  USA
18B2 Paragould USA
33E6 Paragua R Bol
33E2 Paragua R Ven
30E3 Paraguá R Brazil
30E4 Paraguari Par
30E3 Paraguay Republic,
  S America
30E3 Paraguay R Par
31D3 Paraiba State, Brazil
35B2 Paraiba R Brazil
35C2 Paraiba do Sul R
  Brazil
97C4 Parakou Benin
108A2 Parakylia Aust
87B3 Paramakkudi India
33F2 Paramaribo Surinam
69H1 Paramushir I
  Russian Fed
30E3 Paraná State, Brazil
34C2 Paraná Urug
29E2 Paraná R Arg
31B4 Paraná R Brazil
35A2 Paraná R Brazil
30G4 Paranaguá Brazil
35A1 Paranaiba Brazil
35A1 Paranaiba R Brazil
35A2 Paranapanema R
  Brazil
35A2 Paranavai Brazil
79B4 Parang Phil
35C1 Paraope R Brazil
110B2 Paraparaumu NZ
87B1 Parbhani India
94B2 Pardes Hanna Israel
34D3 Pardo Arg
35D1 Pardo R Bahia, Brazil
35A2 Pardo R Mato
  Grosso do Sul, Brazil
35B1 Pardo R Minas
  Gerais, Brazil
35B2 Pardo R Sao Paulo,
  Brazil
59B2 Pardubice
  Czech Republic
69F4 Parece Vela Reef
  Pacific O
10C2 Parent Can
70C4 Parepare Indon

Parera

34C3 Parera Arg
70B4 Pariaman Indon
33E1 Paria,Pen de Ven
48C2 Paris France
14B3 Paris Kentucky, USA
19A3 Paris Texas, USA
18B3 Parkersburg USA
109C2 Parkes Aust
16B3 Parkesburg USA
14A2 Park Forest USA
20B1 Parksville Can
87B1 Parli India
47D2 Parma Italy
14B2 Parma USA
31C2 Parnaíba R Brazil
31C2 Parnaíba R Brazil
55B3 Párnon Oros Mts Greece
60B2 Pärnu Estonia
86B1 Paro Bhutan
108B1 Paroo R Aust
108B2 Paroo Channel R Aust
55C3 Páros / Greece
47B2 Parpaillon Mts France
34A3 Parral Chile
109D2 Parramatta Aust
9C4 Parras Mexico
6B3 Parry B Can
4G2 Parry Is Can
7C5 Parry Sd Can
14B1 Parry Sound Can
52B3 Parsberg Germany
5F4 Parsnip R Can
18A2 Parsons Kansas, USA
14C3 Parsons West Virginia, USA
48B2 Parthenay France
53B3 Partinico Italy
74C2 Partizansk Russian Fed
33G4 Paru R Brazil
101G1 Parys S Africa
19A4 Pasadena Texas, USA
22C3 Pasadena California, USA
78D3 Pasangkayu Indon
76B2 Pasawing Burma
19C3 Pascagoula USA
54C1 Pașcani Rom
20C1 Pasco USA
46B1 Pas-de-Calais Department, France
39G8 Pasewalk Germany
10A2 Pashū'īyeh Iran
108B4 Pasley,C Aust
29E2 Paso de los Toros Urug
29B4 Paso Limay Arg
21A2 Paso Robles USA
45B3 Passage West Irish Rep
16B2 Passaic USA
57C3 Passau Germany
30E4 Passo de los Libres Arg
47D1 Passo di Stelvio Mt Italy
30F4 Passo Fundo Brazil
35B2 Passos Brazil
47B2 Passy France
32B4 Pastaza R Peru
5H4 Pas,The Can
32B3 Pasto Colombia
12B2 Pastol B USA
47D2 Pasubio Mt Italy
78C4 Pasuruan Indon
58C1 Pasvalys Lithuania
85C4 Pātan India
86B1 Patan Nepal
108B3 Patchewollock Aust
110B1 Patea NZ
111B2 Patea R NZ
53B3 Paterno Italy
16B2 Paterson USA
111A3 Paterson Inlet B NZ
84B2 Pathankot India
Pathein = Bassein
84D2 Patiāla India
32B6 Pativilca Peru
55C3 Pátmos / Greece
86B1 Patna India

93D2 Patnos Turk
63D2 Patomskoye Nagor'ye Upland Russian Fed
31D3 Patos Brazil
35B1 Patos de Minas Brazil
34B2 Patquia Arg
55B3 Pátrai Greece
35B1 Patrocinio Brazil
99E3 Patta / Kenya
78D4 Pattallasang Indon
77C4 Pattani Thai
22B2 Patterson California, USA
19B4 Patterson Louisiana, USA
22C2 Patterson,Mt USA
13B1 Pattullo,Mt Can
31D3 Patu Brazil
86C2 Patuakhali Bang
25D3 Patuca R Honduras
23A2 Patzcuaro Mexico
48B3 Pau France
4F3 Paulatuk Can
31C3 Paulistana Brazil
101H1 Paulpietersburg S Africa
19A3 Pauls Valley USA
76B2 Paungde Burma
84D2 Pauri India
38H5 Pauskie Nor
35C1 Pavão Brazil
47C2 Pavia Italy
65J4 Pavlodar Kazakhstan
61J2 Pavlovka Russian Fed
61F2 Pavlovo Russian Fed
61F3 Pavlovsk Russian Fed
78C3 Pawan R Indon
18A2 Pawhuska USA
16D2 Pawtucket USA
47B1 Payerne Switz
20C2 Payette USA
7C4 Payne,L Can
34D2 Paysandu Urug
46A2 Pays-de-Bray Region, France
54B2 Pazardzhik Bulg
13D1 Peace R Can
17B2 Peace R USA
13D1 Peace River Can
43D3 Peak District Nat Pk Eng
108A1 Peake R Aust
109C2 Peak Hill Aust
71E4 Peak Mandala Mt Indon
42D3 Peak,The Mt Eng
19B3 Pearl R USA
21C4 Pearl City Hawaiian Is
21C4 Pearl Harbor Hawaiian Is
4H2 Peary Chan Can
102B1 Pebane Mozam
54B2 Peć Serbia, Yugos
35C1 Peçanha Brazil
19B4 Pecan Island USA
38L5 Pechenga Russian Fed
64F3 Pechora R Russian Fed
64G3 Pechorskoye More S Russian Fed
53C3 Pecoraro Mt Italy
9C3 Pecos USA
9C3 Pecos R USA
59B3 Pécs Hung
108A1 Pedirka Aust
35C1 Pedra Azul Brazil
35B2 Pedregulho Brazil
26B3 Pedro Cays Is Caribbean S
30C3 Pedro de Valdivia Chile
30E3 Pedro Juan Caballero Par
34C3 Pedro Luro Arg
23B1 Pedro Mentova Mexico
87C3 Pedro,Pt Sri Lanka
108B2 Peebinga Aust
42C2 Peebles Scot

17C1 Pee Dee R USA
16C2 Peekskill USA
42B2 Peel Eng
12H1 Peel R Can
4J2 Peel Sd Can
108A1 Peera Peera Poolanna L Aust
13E1 Peerless L Can
71E4 Peg Arfak Mt Indon
111B2 Pegasus B NZ
83D4 Pegu Burma
78A3 Pegunungan Barisan Mts Indon
78C2 Pegunungan Iran Mts Malay/Indon
71E4 Pegunungan Maoke Mts Indon
78D3 Pegunungan Meratus Mts Indon
78C3 Pegunungan Muller Mts Indon
78C3 Pegunungan Schwaner Mts Indon
78A3 Pegunungan Tigapuluh Mts Indon
76B2 Pegu Yoma Mts Burma
34C3 Pehuajó Arg
61G3 Péipsi Järve = Peipus,L
39K7 Peipus, Lake Estonia/Russian Fed
35A2 Peixe R Sao Paulo, Brazil
72D3 Pei Xian China
78B4 Pekalongan Indon
77C5 Pekan Malay
78C2 Pekanbaru Indon
18C1 Pekin USA
Peking = Beijing
77C5 Pelabohan Kelang Malay
78C4 Pelau Dalau Kangean Is Indon
78C4 Pelau Pelau Karimunjawa Arch Indon
78D4 Pelau Pelau Postilyon Is Indon
54B1 Peleaga Mt Rom
63D2 Peleduy Russian Fed
14B2 Pelee I Can
71D4 Peleng I Indon
12G3 Pelican USA
69F1 Peliny Osipenko Russian Fed
34C3 Pellegrini Arg
12J2 Pelly R Can
6A3 Pelly Bay Can
12G2 Pelly Crossing Can
12H2 Pelly Mts Can
30F5 Pelotas Brazil
30F4 Pelotas R Brazil
47B2 Pelvoux Region, France
78B4 Pemalang Indon
78A3 Pematang Indon
101D2 Pemba Mozam
99D3 Pemba I Tanz
13C2 Pemberton Can
13C2 Pembina R Can
15C1 Pembroke Can
17B1 Pembroke USA
43B4 Pembroke Wales
34A3 Pemuco Chile
78D2 Penambo Range Mts Malay
35A2 Penápolis Brazil
50A2 Peñarroya Spain
51B1 Peñarroya Mt Spain
50A1 Peña Trevina Mt Spain
98B2 Pende R Chad
12J3 Pendelton,Mt Can
20C1 Pendleton USA
20C1 Pend Oreille R USA
31D4 Penedo Brazil
85D5 Penganga R India
73D5 P'eng-hu Lieh-tao Is Taiwan
72E2 Penglai China
73B4 Pengshui China
71E4 Pegunungan Maoke Mts Indon

26C4 Península de la Guajiri Pen Colombia
27E4 Península de Paria Pen Ven
77C5 Peninsular Malaysia Malay
10D2 Peninsule de Gaspé Pen Can
23A1 Penjamo Mexico
87B2 Penner R India
44C2 Pennine Chain Mts Eng
16B3 Penns Grove USA
10C2 Pennsylvania State USA
6D3 Penny Highlands Mts Can
108B3 Penola Aust
106C4 Penong Aust
42C2 Penrith Eng
11B3 Pensacola USA
112A Pensacola Mts Ant
78D1 Pensiangan Malay
13D3 Penticton Can
44C2 Pentland Firth Chan Scot
16B3 Pentland Hills Scot
61G3 Penza Russian Fed
43B4 Penzance Eng
10B2 Peoria USA
78A3 Perabumulih Indon
77C5 Perak R Malay
78A3 Perawang Indon
32B3 Pereira Colombia
35A2 Pereira Barreto Brazil
61F4 Perelazovskiy Russian Fed
12D3 Perenosa B USA
34C2 Pergamino Arg
7C4 Péribonca R Can
48C2 Périgueux France
25E4 Perlas Arch de Is Panama
61J2 Perm' Russian Fed
31D3 Pernambuco = Recife Brazil
31D3 Pernambuco = Recife Brazil
54B2 Pernatty Lg Aust
54B2 Pernik Bulg
46B2 Péronne France
23B2 Perote Mexico
49C3 Perpignan France
22D4 Perris USA
17B1 Perry Florida, USA
17B1 Perry Georgia, USA
18A2 Perry Oklahoma, USA
4H3 Perry River Can
14B2 Perrysburg USA
12C3 Perryville Alaska, USA
18C2 Perryville Missouri, USA
106A4 Perth Aust
15C2 Perth Can
44C3 Perth Scot
16B2 Perth Amboy USA
32C6 Peru Republic, S America
18C1 Peru USA
103E5 Peru-Chile Trench Pacific O
52B2 Perugia Italy
52C2 Perušic Croatia
93D2 Pervari Turk
61F3 Pervomaysk Russian Fed
60D4 Pervomaysk Ukraine
61J2 Pervoural'sk Russian Fed
52B2 Pésaro Italy
22A2 Pescadero USA
52B2 Pescara Italy
47D2 Peschiera Italy
84C2 Peshawar Pak
54B2 Peski Alb
14A1 Peshtigo USA
60E2 Pesočno Russian Fed
94B2 Petah Tiqwa Israel
21A2 Petaluma USA
46C2 Pétange Lux
23A2 Petatlán Mexico

101C2 Petauke Zambia
08A2 Peterborough Aust
15C2 Peterborough Can
24B2 Peterborough Eng
44D3 Peterhead Scot
81D1 Petermann Gletscher
Gl Greenland
106B3 Petermann Range
Mts Aust
29B3 Peteroa *Mt* Arg/Chile
13F1 Peter Pond L Can
12H3 Petersburg Alaska,
USA
85C4 Petläd India
23B2 Petlalcingo Mexico
25D2 Peto Mexico
63D2 Petomskoye
Nagor'ye *Upland*
Russian Fed
34A2 Petorca Chile
14B1 Petoskey USA
31C3 Petrolina Brazil
65H4 Petropavlovsk
Kazakhstan
35C2 Petrópolis Brazil
52B2 Petrovsk
Russian Fed
68C1 Petrovsk
Zabaykal'skiy
Russian Fed
64E3 Petrozavodsk
Russian Fed
21E2 Petrus S Africa
101G1 Petrusburg S Africa
11F Pevek Russian Fed
46D2 Pfälzer Wald *Region*,
Germany
57B3 Pforzheim Germany
84D3 Phagwara India
84C3 Phalodi India
46D2 Phalsbourg France
87A1 Phaltan India
77B4 Phangnga Thai
76D2 Phan Dang *Mts*
Camb
76D3 Phan Rang Viet
76D3 Phan Thiet Viet
17A1 Phenix City USA
76C3 Phet Buri Thai
76D3 Phiafay Laos
19C3 Philadelphia
Mississippi, USA
16B2 Philadelphia
Pennsylvania, USA
Philippeville = Skikda
46C1 Philippeville Belg
71D2 Philippine S Pacific O
71D2 Philippines Republic,
S E Asia
104E3 Philippine Trench
Pacific O
15C2 Philipsburg
Pennsylvania, USA
12E1 Philip Smith Mts
USA
79B2 Phillipine S Phil
6B1 Phillips B Can
16B2 Phillipsburg New
Jersey, USA
15C2 Philpots Pen Can
76C3 Phnom Penh Camb
9B3 Phoenix Arizona,
USA
16B2 Phoenixville USA
76C1 Phong Saly Laos
Phra Nakhon =
Bangkok
76C2 Phu Bia *Mt* Laos
76D3 Phu Cuong Viet
77B4 Phuket Thai
86A2 Phulbani India
76C2 Phu Miang *Mt* Thai
76D2 Phu Set *Mt* Laos
76D1 Phu Tho Viet
47C2 Phu Vinh Viet
52B2 Piacenza Italy
109C2 Pian *R* Aust
52B2 Pianosa / Italy
52C2 Pianosa / Italy
52B2 Piaseczno Pol
54C1 Piatra-Neamt Rom
31C3 Piauí State, Brazil
47E2 Piave *R* Italy
99D2 Pibor *R* Sudan
99D2 Pibor Post Sudan

46B1 Picardie *Region*,
France
19C3 Picayune USA
47B2 Pic de Rochebrune
Mt France
34A2 Pichilemu Chile
34C3 Pichi Mahuida Arg
42D2 Pickering Eng
7A4 Pickle Lake Can
46A1 Pico / Açores
47C1 Pico Bernina *Mt*
Switz
51C1 Pico de Anito *Mt*
Spain
24B3 Pico del Infiernillo *Mt*
Mexico
27C3 Pico Duarte *Mt*
Dom Rep
31C3 Picos Brazil
50B1 Picos de Europa *Mt*
Spain
109D2 Picton Aust
111B2 Picton NZ
95A2 Pic Toussidé *Mt*
Chad
35B2 Piedade Brazil
22C2 Piedra USA
22B2 Piedras Negras
Mexico
38K6 Pieksämäki Fin
38K6 Pielinen L Fin
47B2 Piemonte *Region*,
Italy
8C2 Pierre USA
59B3 Pieštany Slovakia
101H1 Pietermaritzburg
S Africa
100B3 Pietersburg S Africa
101H1 Piet Retief S Africa
60B4 Pietrosu *Mt* Rom
47E1 Pieve di Cadore Italy
13C2 Pigeon L Can
18B2 Piggott USA
34C3 Pigüe Arg
7A4 Pikangikum L Can
8C3 Pikes Peak USA
100A4 Piketberg S Africa
6F3 Pikiutdleq Greenland
62B2 Pik Kommunizma *Mt*
Tajikistan
82C1 Pik Pobedy *Mt*
China/Kirghizia
34D3 Pila Arg
58B2 Piła Pol
30E4 Pilar Par
30D3 Pilcomayo *R* Arg/Par
84D3 Pilibhit India
58B2 Pilica *R* Pol
109C4 Pillar,C Aust
55B3 Pilos Greece
12C3 Pilot Point USA
12B2 Pilot Station USA
19C3 Pilottown USA
33F4 Pimenta Brazil
77C4 Pinang / Malay
26A2 Pinar del Rio Cuba
34B2 Pinas Arg
46E1 Pinche Belg
13C1 Pincher Creek Can
31B2 Pindaré *R* Brazil
55B3 Pindhos *Mts* Greece
19B3 Pine Bluff USA
22C1 Pine Creek Aust
22C1 Pinecrest USA
22C2 Pinedale California,
USA
22C2 Pine Flat Res USA
64F3 Pinega *R*
Russian Fed
16A2 Pine Grove USA
17B2 Pine Hills USA
17B2 Pine I USA
19B3 Pineland USA
17B2 Pinellas Park USA
5G3 Pine Point Can
47B2 Pinerolo Italy
19B3 Pines,Lo the Can
19B3 Pineville USA
72C3 Pingdingshan China
73B5 Pingguo China
72B2 Pingliang China
72D2 Pingluo China
73D4 Pingtan Dao / China
73E5 P'ing tung Taiwan

72A3 Pingwu China
73B5 Pingxiang Guangxi,
China
73C4 Pingxiang Jiangxi,
China
31B2 Pinheiro Brazil
70A3 Pini / Indon
55B3 Piniós *R* Greece
106A4 Pinjarra Aust
13C1 Pink Mountain Can
108B3 Pinnaroo Aust
Pinos,I de, I = Isla de
la Juventud
21A2 Pinos,Pt USA
23B2 Pinotepa Nacional
Mexico
70C4 Pinrang Indon
60C3 Pinsk Belorussia
32J7 Pinta / Ecuador
61B2 Pinyug Russian Fed
8B3 Pioche USA
52B2 Piombino Italy
6H3 Piórsá Iceland
59B2 Piotrków
Trybunalski Pol
44E2 Piper *Oilfield*
N Sea
82A2 Piper Peak *Mt* USA
10C2 Pipmuacan Res Can
14B2 Piqua USA
35B1 Piracanjuba Brazil
35B2 Piracicaba Brazil
35B2 Piraçununga Brazil
35B2 Piraí do Sul Brazil
55B3 Piraiévs Greece
35B2 Pirajuí Brazil
35C1 Piranhas Brazil
35C1 Pirapora Brazil
35B1 Pirenópolis Brazil
35B1 Pires do Rio Brazil
55B3 Pirgos Greece
Pirineos = Pyrénées
31C2 Piripiri Brazil
46D2 Pirmasens Germany
54B2 Pirot Serbia, Yugos
84C2 Pir Panjäl Range *Mts*
Pak
71D4 Piru Indon
22C3 Piru Creek *R* USA
49E3 Pisa Italy
29B2 Pisco Peru
57C3 Pisek Czech Republic
84B2 Pishin Pak
30C4 Pissis *Mt* Arg
49E3 Pistoia Italy
50B1 Pisuerga *R* Spain
20B2 Pit *R* USA
32B3 Pitalito Colombia
105K5 Pitcairn / Pacific O
38H5 Pite *R* Sweden
38J5 Piteå Sweden
54B2 Pitești Rom
63B2 Pit Gorodok
Russian Fed
38L6 Pitkyaranta
Russian Fed
44C3 Pitlochry Scot
34A3 Pitrutquén Chile
13B2 Pitt I Can
22B1 Pittsburg California,
USA
18B2 Pittsburg Kansas,
USA
14C2 Pittsburgh USA
18B2 Pittsfield Illinois,
USA
16C1 Pittsfield
Massachusetts, USA
109D1 Pittsworth Aust
86A1 Piuthan Nepal
47D1 Pizzo Redorta *Mt*
Italy
38B2 Pjórsá Iceland
32A5 Pjura Peru
7E5 Placentia B Can
22B1 Placerville USA
46B1 Plaine des Flandres
Plain Belg/France
96C2 Plaine du Tidikelt
Desert Region
9C3 Plainview Texas,
USA
22B2 Planada USA
30F2 Planalto de Mato
Grosso *Plat* Brazil

31D3 Planalto do
Borborema *Plat*
Brazil
32A1 Planalto do Mato
Grosso *Mts* Brazil
19A3 Plano USA
17B2 Plantation USA
17B2 Plant City USA
5J4 Plasencia Spain
61K3 Plast Russian Fed
69F2 Plastun Russian Fed
96C2 Plateau du Tademait
Alg
46D2 Plateau Lorrain *Plat*
France
48C2 Plateaux de Limousin
Plat France
48C2 Plateaux du Sersou
Plat Alg
26C5 Plato Colombia
65G5 Plato Ustyurt *Plat*
Kazakhstan
8C2 Platte *R* USA
15D2 Plattsburgh USA
11A1 Plattsmouth USA
57C2 Plauen Germany
60E3 Plavsk Russian Fed
23A2 Playa Azul Mexico
32A4 Playas Ecuador
23B2 Playa Vicente Mexico
50A1 Plaza de Moro
Almanzor *Mt* Spain
22C2 Pleasanton
California, USA
16B3 Pleasantville USA
14A3 Pleasure Ridge Park
USA
76D2 Pleiku Viet
110C1 Plenty,B of NZ
58B2 Plesezw Pol
7C4 Pletipi,L Can
54B2 Pleven Bulg
54B2 Pljevlja Montenegro,
Yugos
52C2 Ploče Bosnia-
Herzegovina
58B2 Płock Pol
48B2 Ploërmel France
54C2 Ploiești Rom
60B3 Płońsk Pol
54B2 Plovdiv Bulg
20C1 Plummer USA
12C2 Plummer,Mt USA
100B3 Plumtree Zim
22B1 Plymouth California,
USA
43B4 Plymouth Eng
14A2 Plymouth Indiana,
USA
16D2 Plymouth
Massachusetts, USA
15C2 Plymouth
Pennsylvania, USA
43B4 Plymouth Sd Eng
43C3 Plynlimon *Mt* Wales
57C3 Plzeň Czech Republic
58B2 Pniewy Pol
38K6 Poysäselkä L Fin
97B3 Pô Burkina
47E2 Po *R* Italy
97C4 Pobé Benin
69G2 Pobedino
Russian Fed
8B2 Pocatello USA
15C3 Pocomoke City USA
35B2 Poços de Caldas
Brazil
54A2 Podgorica
Montenegro, Yugos
47D2 Po di Volano *R* Italy
63B1 Podkamennaya *R*
Russian Fed
60E2 Podol'sk Russian Fed
59D3 Podol'skaya
Vozvyshennost'
Upland Ukraine
60D1 Podporozh'ye
Russian Fed
61F1 Podyuga Russian Fed
100A3 Pofadder S Africa
74B3 Pohang S Korea
112C9 Poinsett,C Ant
108C2 Point Aust
27E3 Pointe-à-Pitre
Guadeloupe

48B2 **Pointe de Barfleur** *Pt* France
98B3 **Pointe Noire** Congo
98A2 **Pointe Pongara** *Pt* Gabon
108B3 **Point Fairy** Aust
27L1 **Point Fortin** Trinidad
4B3 **Point Hope** USA
4G3 **Point L** Can
12B1 **Point Lay** USA
16B2 **Point Pleasant** New Jersey, USA
14B3 **Point Pleasant** W Virginia, USA
47B2 **Point St Bernard** *Mt* France
48C2 **Poitiers** France
48B2 **Poitou** Region, France
46A2 **Poix** France
85C3 **Pokaran** India
109C1 **Pokataroo** Aust
61G3 **Pokrovsk** Russian Fed
63E1 **Pokrovsk** Russian Fed
58B2 **Poland** Republic, Europe
92B2 **Polatli** Turk
78D3 **Polewali** Indon
47A1 **Poligny** France
87B2 **Poliyiros** Greece
87B2 **Pollachi** India
79B3 **Pololis Is** Phil
59D2 **Polonnye** Ukraine
58D1 **Polotsk** Russian Fed
60D4 **Poltava** Russian Fed
52C1 **Pölten** Austria
64F3 **Poluostrov Kanin** *Pen* Russian Fed
61H5 **Poluostrov Mangyshlak** *Pen* Kazakhstan
38L5 **Poluostrov Rybachiy** *Pen* Russian Fed
64H2 **Poluostrov Yamal** *Pen* Russian Fed
38L5 **Polyarnyy** Murmansk, Russian Fed
1B8 **Polyarnyy** Yakutskaya, Russian Fed
105H3 **Polynesia** *Region* Pacific O
32B5 **Pomabamba** Peru
35C2 **Pomba** *R* Brazil
22D3 **Pomona** USA
18A2 **Pomona Res** USA
17B2 **Pompano Beach** USA
16B2 **Pompton Lakes** USA
18A2 **Ponca City** USA
27D3 **Ponce** Puerto Rico
17B2 **Ponce de Leon B** USA
8B2 **Pondicherry** India
6C2 **Pond Inlet** Can
50A1 **Ponferrada** Spain
98C2 **Pongo** *R* S Africa
101H1 **Pongola** *R* S Africa
87B2 **Ponnāni** India
86C2 **Ponnyadoung Range** *Mts* Burma
52A2 **Ponoka** Can
64F3 **Ponoy** Russian Fed
48B2 **Pons** France
36D1 **Ponta da Baleia** *Pt* Brazil
98B3 **Ponta Delgada** Açores
98B3 **Ponta do Padrão** *Pt* Angola
35C2 **Ponta dos Búzios** *Pt* Brazil
30F4 **Ponta Grossa** Brazil
35B2 **Pontal** Brazil
46D2 **Pont-à-Mousson** France
33E3 **Ponta Pora** Brazil
49D2 **Pontarlier** France
19B3 **Pontchartrain,L** USA
52B2 **Pontedera** Italy
52A2 **Ponte Leccia** Corse
50A1 **Pontevedra** Spain
18C1 **Pontiac** Illinois, USA

14B2 **Pontiac** Michigan, USA
78B3 **Pontianak** Indon
48B2 **Pontivy** France
46B2 **Pontoise** France
19C3 **Pontotoc** USA
43C4 **Pontypool** Wales
43C4 **Pontypridd** Wales
43D4 **Poole** Eng
  Poona = Pune
108B2 **Pooncarie** Aust
108B2 **Poopelloe,L** *L* Aust
12C2 **Poorman** USA
32B3 **Popayán** Colombia
46B1 **Poperinge** Belg
108B1 **Popilta L** Aust
18B2 **Poplar Bluff** USA
19C3 **Poplarville** USA
23B2 **Popocatepetl** *Mt* Mexico
98B3 **Popokabaka** Zaire
71F4 **Popondetta** PNG
54C2 **Popovo** Bulg
85B4 **Porbandar** India
13A2 **Porcher I** Can
12F1 **Porcupine** *R* Can/ USA
52B1 **Poreč** Croatia
35A2 **Porecatu** Brazil
39J6 **Pori** Fin
111B2 **Porirua** NZ
38H5 **Porjus** Sweden
69G2 **Poronaysk** Russian Fed
47B1 **Porrentruy** Switz
38K4 **Porsangen** *Inlet* Nor
39F7 **Porsgrunn** Nor
45C1 **Portadown** N Ire
52A2 **Portage la Prairie** Can
13C3 **Port Alberni** Can
50A2 **Portalegre** Port
9C3 **Portales** USA
100B4 **Port Alfred** S Africa
13B2 **Port Alice** Can
19B3 **Port Allen** USA
20B1 **Port Angeles** USA
26B3 **Port Antonio** Jamaica
45C2 **Portarlington** Irish Rep
19B4 **Port Arthur** USA
108A2 **Port Augusta** Aust
26C3 **Port-au-Prince** Haiti
14B2 **Port Austin** USA
108B3 **Port Campbell** Aust
86B2 **Port Canning** India
7D5 **Port Cartier** Can
111B3 **Port Chalmers** NZ
17B1 **Port Charlotte** USA
16C2 **Port Chester** USA
15C2 **Port Colborne** Can
15C2 **Port Credit** Can
22C3 **Port Davey** *Pt* Aust
26C3 **Port-de-Paix** Haiti
77C5 **Port Dickson** Malay
100C4 **Port Edward** S Africa
35C1 **Porteirinha** Brazil
14B2 **Port Elgin** Can
100B4 **Port Elizabeth** S Africa
27M2 **Porter Pt** St Vincent and the Grenadines
21B2 **Porterville** USA
107D4 **Port Fairy** Aust
98A3 **Port Gentil** Gabon
19B3 **Port Gibson** USA
89E7 **Port Harcourt** Nig
13B2 **Port Hardy** Can
7D5 **Port Hawkesbury** Can

109D2 **Port Kembla** Aust
14B2 **Portland** Indiana, USA
10C2 **Portland** Maine, USA
109C2 **Portland** New South Wales, Aust
20B1 **Portland** Oregon, USA
108B3 **Portland** Victoria, Aust
27H2 **Portland Bight** *B* Jamaica
43C4 **Portland Bill** *Pt* Eng
109C4 **Portland,C** Aust
13A1 **Portland Canal** Can/ USA
110C1 **Portland I** NZ
27H2 **Portland Pt** Jamaica
45C2 **Port Laoise** Irish Rep
108A2 **Port Lincoln** Aust
97A4 **Port Loko** Sierra Leone
101E3 **Port Louis** Mauritius
108B3 **Port MacDonnell** Aust
13B2 **Port McNeill** Can
109D2 **Port Macquarie** Aust
12B3 **Port Moller** USA
107D1 **Port Moresby** PNG
100A3 **Port Nolloth** S Africa
16B3 **Port Norris** USA
89E7 **Porto Novo** Benin
50A1 **Porto** Port
30F5 **Pôrto Alegre** Brazil
33F6 **Pôrto Artur** Brazil
30F3 **Pôrto E Cunha** Brazil
52B2 **Portoferraio** Italy
27E4 **Port of Spain** Trinidad
47D2 **Portomaggiore** Italy
97C4 **Porto Novo** Benin
20B1 **Port Orchard** USA
20B2 **Port Orford** USA
96A1 **Porto Santo** *I* Medeira
31D5 **Pôrto Seguro** Brazil
53A2 **Porto Torres** Sardegna
53A2 **Porto Vecchio** Corse
33E5 **Pôrto Velho** Brazil
111A3 **Port Pegasus** *B* NZ
108B3 **Port Phillip B** Aust
108A2 **Port Pirie** Aust
44A3 **Portree** Scot
20B1 **Port Renfrew** Can
27J2 **Port Royal** Jamaica
17B1 **Port Royal Sd** USA
45C1 **Portrush** N Ire
92B3 **Port Said** Egypt
17A2 **Port St Joe** USA
100B4 **Port St Johns** S Africa
7E4 **Port Saunders** Can
100C4 **Port Shepstone** S Africa
13A2 **Port Simpson** Can
27Q2 **Portsmouth** Dominica
43D4 **Portsmouth** Eng
14B3 **Portsmouth** Ohio, USA
11C3 **Portsmouth** Virginia, USA
109D2 **Port Stephens** *B* Aust
95C3 **Port Sudan** Sudan
19C3 **Port Sulphur** USA
38K5 **Porttipahan Tekojärvi** *Res* Fin
50A2 **Port-Vendres** France
14A2 **Port Washington** USA
77C5 **Port Weld** Malay
32D6 **Porvenir** Bol
39K6 **Porvoo** Fin
30E4 **Posadas** Arg
50A2 **Posadas** Spain
47D1 **Poschiavo** Switz
6B2 **Posheim Pen** Can
90C3 **Posht-e Badam** Iran
71D4 **Poso** Indon
58D1 **Postavy** Belorussia
14B2 **Port Clinton** USA

100B3 **Postmasburg** S Africa
52B1 **Postojna** Slovenia
74C2 **Pos'yet** Russian Fed
101G1 **Potchefstroom** S Africa
19B2 **Poteau** USA
53C2 **Potenza** Italy
100B3 **Potgietersrus** S Africa
97D3 **Potiskum** Nig
20C1 **Potlatch** USA
15C3 **Potomac** *R* USA
30C2 **Potosí** Bol
30C4 **Potrerillos** Chile
56C2 **Potsdam** Germany
16B2 **Pottstown** USA
16A2 **Pottsville** USA
16C2 **Poughkeepsie** USA
35B2 **Pouso Alegre** Brazil
110C1 **Poverty B** NZ
61F3 **Povorino** Russian Fed
7C4 **Povungnituk** Can
8C2 **Powder** *R* USA
106C2 **Powell Creek** Aust
13B3 **Powell,L** USA
13C3 **Powell River** Can
8C2 **Power** *R* USA
43C3 **Powys** County, Wales
73D4 **Poyang Hu** *L* China
92B2 **Pozanti** Turk
23B1 **Poza Rica** Mexico
58B2 **Poznań** Pol
30C2 **Pozo Colorado** Par
53B2 **Pozzuoli** Italy
97B4 **Pra** *R* Ghana
76C3 **Prachin Buri** Thai
76B3 **Prachuap Khiri Khan** Thai
59B2 **Praděd** *Mt* Czech Republic
49C3 **Pradelles** France
35D1 **Prado** Brazil
  Prague = Praha
57C2 **Praha** Czech Republic
97A4 **Praia** Cape Verde
33E5 **Prainha** Brazil
35B2 **Prairie Village** USA
76C3 **Prakhon Chai** Thai
35B1 **Prata** Brazil
35B1 **Prata** *R* Brazil
  Prates = Dongsha Qundao
49E3 **Prato** Italy
16B1 **Prattsville** USA
17A1 **Prattville** USA
87B2 **Prawle Pt** Eng
78D4 **Praya** Indon
47D1 **Predazzo** Italy
63B2 **Predivinsk** Russian Fed
58C2 **Pregolyu** *R* Russian Fed
76D3 **Prek Kak** Camb
56C2 **Prenzlau** Germany
76A3 **Preparis** *I* Burma
76A2 **Preparis North Chan** Burma
59B3 **Přerov** Czech Republic
23A2 **Presa del Infiernillo** Mexico
19B3 **Prescott** Arizona, USA
19B3 **Prescott** Arkansas, USA
15C2 **Prescott** Can
30D4 **Presidencia Roque Sáenz Peña** Arg
35A2 **Presidente Epitácio** Brazil
112C2 **Presidente Frei** *Base* Ant
23B2 **Presidente Miguél Aleman** *L* Mexico
35A2 **Presidente Prudente** Brazil
35A2 **Presidente Venceslau** Brazil
59C3 **Prešov** Slovakia
55B2 **Prespansko Jezero** *L* Macedonia, Yugos
10D2 **Presque Isle** USA

42C3 Preston Eng
8B2 Preston Idaho, USA
18B2 Preston Missouri, USA
42B2 Prestwick Scot
31B6 Prêto Brazil
35B1 Prêto R Brazil
101G1 Pretoria S Africa
55B3 Préveza Greece
76D3 Prey Veng Camb
8B3 Price USA
13B2 Price I Can
60D4 Prichernomorskaya Nizmennost' Lowland Ukraine
27M2 Prickly Pt Grenada
58C1 Priekule Lithuania
100B3 Prieska S Africa
20C1 Priest L USA
20C1 Priest River USA
53B2 Prilep Macedonia, Yugos
60D3 Priluki Ukraine
34C2 Primero R Arg
39K6 Primorsk Russian Fed
60E4 Primorsko-Akhtarsk Russian Fed
13F2 Primrose L Can
5H4 Prince Albert Can
4F2 Prince Albert,C Can
4G2 Prince Albert Pen Can
4G2 Prince Albert Sd Can
6D2 Prince Charles I Can
112B10 Prince Charles Mts Ant
7D5 Prince Edward I Can
13C2 Prince George Can
4H2 Prince Gustaf Adolp S Can
5E4 Prince of Wales I USA
71F5 Prince of Wales I Aust
4H2 Prince of Wales I Can
4G2 Prince of Wales Str Can
4F2 Prince Patrick I Can
6A2 Prince Regent Inlet Str Can
13A2 Prince Rupert Can
107D2 Princess Charlotte B Aust
13B2 Princess Royal I Can
27L1 Princes Town Trinidad
13C3 Princeton Can
18C2 Princeton Kentucky, USA
18B1 Princeton Missouri, USA
16B2 Princeton New Jersey, USA
12E2 Prince William USA
12E2 Prince William Sd USA
97C4 Principe / W Africa
20B2 Prineville USA
12E1 Pringle,Mt USA
6F3 Prins Christian Sund Sd Greenland
112B12 Prinsesse Astrid Kyst Region, Ant
112B12 Prinsesse Ragnhild Kyst Region, Ant
64B2 Prins Karls Forland I Barents S
25D3 Prinzapolca Nic
58D2 Pripet R Belorussia
Pripyat' = Pripet
54B3 Priština Serbia, Yugos
56C2 Privolzhskaya Vozvyshennost' Upland Russian Fed
61F3 Prizren Serbia, Yugos
78C4 Probolinggo Indon
5G5 Procatello USA
87B2 Proddatūr India
21D2 Progreso Mexico
20B2 Project City USA

61F5 Prokhladnyy Russian Fed
65K4 Prokop'yevsk Russian Fed
61F4 Proletarskaya Russian Fed
64G2 Proliv Karskiye Vorota Str Russian Fed
83D4 Prome Burma
31D4 Propriá Brazil
20B2 Prospect Oregon, USA
107D3 Prosperine Aust
59B3 Prostějov Czech Republic
6E2 Prøven Greenland
49D3 Provence Region, France
16D2 Providence USA
15D2 Provincetown USA
8B2 Provo USA
13E2 Provost Can
6B2 Prudhoe Bay USA
6D2 Prudhoe Land Greenland
58C2 Pruszkow Pol
60C4 Prut R Romania/Moldavia
60C4 Prutul R Romania
58D2 Pruzhany Belorussia
18A2 Pryor USA
59C3 Przemysl Pol
55B3 Psará I Greece
60C2 Pskov Russian Fed
58D2 Ptich R Belorussia
55B2 Ptolemais Greece
32C5 Pucallpa Peru
73D4 Pucheng China
34A3 Pucón Chile
38K5 Pudasjärvi Fin
87B2 Pudukkottai India
23B2 Puebla Mexico
23B2 Puebla State, Mexico
50A1 Puebla de Sanabria Spain
50A1 Puebla de Trives Spain
8C3 Pueblo USA
34B3 Puelches Arg
34B3 Puelén Arg
23A2 Puente Ixbapa Mexico
32A5 Puente del Inca Arg
30B2 Puerta Coles Peru
31D3 Puerta de los Llanos Arg
31D3 Puerta do Calcanhar Pr Brazil
32C1 Puerta Gallinas Colombia
23B2 Puerta Maldonado Colombia
32A2 Puerta Mariato Panama
29C5 Puerta Médanosa Pt Arg
23A2 Puerta Mongrove Mexico
25E4 Puerta San Blas Pt Panama
23A2 Puerta San Telmo Mexico
25D3 Puerto Aisén Chile
25D4 Puerto Armuelles Panama
33F6 Puerto Artur Brazil
32B3 Puerto Asis Colombia
32D2 Puerto Ayacucho Ven
25D3 Puerto Barrios Guatemala
32C2 Puerto Berrio Colombia
32D1 Puerto Cabello Ven
25D3 Puerto Cabezas Nic
32D2 Puerto Carreño Colombia
25D4 Puerto Cortes Costa Rica
25D3 Puerto Cortés Honduras

96A2 Puerto del Rosario Canary Is
30F3 Puerto E Cunha Brazil
32C1 Puerto Fijo Ven
31B3 Puerto Franco Brazil
32D6 Puerto Heath Bol
25D2 Puerto Juarez Mexico
33E1 Puerto la Cruz Ven
50B2 Puertollano Spain
32C1 Puerto Lopez Colombia
29D4 Puerto Madryn Arg
32D6 Puerto Maldonado Peru
23B2 Puerto Marquéz Mexico
29B4 Puerto Montt Chile
30E3 Puerto Murtinho Brazil
29B6 Puerto Natales Chile
24A1 Puerto Peñasco Mexico
29D4 Puerto Pirámides Arg
27C3 Puerto Plata Dom Rep
79A4 Puerto Princesa Phil
32B3 Puerto Rico Colombia
27D3 Puerto Rico Caribbean S
27D3 Puerto Rico Trench Caribbean S
23A2 Puerto San Juan de Lima Mexico
33G4 Puerto Santanga Brazil
30E2 Puerto Suárez Bol
24B2 Puerto Vallarta Mexico
29B4 Puerto Varas Chile
30D2 Puerto Villarroel Bol
61G3 Pugachev Russian Fed
84C3 Pugal India
51C1 Puigcerdá Spain
74B2 Pukch'ŏng N Korea
110B1 Pukekohe NZ
110B1 Puketeraki Range Mts NZ
52B2 Pula Croatia
14C2 Pulaski New York, USA
71E4 Pulau Kolepom I Indon
70A4 Pulau Pulau Batu Is Indon
58B2 Pulawy Pol
87C2 Pulicat,L India
84B1 Pul-i-Khumri Afghan
87B3 Puliyangudi India
20C1 Pullman USA
71E3 Pulo Anna Merir I Pacific O
79B2 Pulog,Mt Phil
38L5 Pulozero Russian Fed
58C2 Pultusk Pol
30C4 Puna de Atacama Arg
86B1 Punakha Bhutan
84C2 Punch Pak
87A1 Pune India
23A2 Punéper Mexico
98C3 Punia Zaire
34A2 Punitaqui Chile
84C2 Punjab Province, Pak
84D2 Punjab State, India
30B2 Puno Peru
24A2 Punta Abreojos Pt Mexico
34A3 Punta Alice Pt Italy
34C3 Punta Alta Arg
29B6 Punta Arenas Chile
34A2 Punta Baja Pt Mexico
34A2 Punta Curaumilla Pt Chile
100A2 Punta da Marca Pt Angola
101C3 Punta de Barra Falsa Pt Mozam
29F2 Punta del Este Urug

24A2 Punta Eugenia Pt Mexico
25D3 Punta Gorda Belize
17B2 Punta Gorda USA
34A3 Punta Lavapié Pt Chile
53B2 Punta Licosa Pt Italy
34A1 Punta Poroto Pt Chile
9B4 Punta San Antonia Pt Mexico
34A2 Punta Topocalma Chile
73C4 Puqi China
64J3 Pur R Russian Fed
19A2 Purcell USA
12C1 Purcell Mt USA
13D2 Purcell Mts Can
34A3 Purén Chile
86B2 Puri India
87B1 Pūrna India
86B1 Pūrnia India
76C3 Pursat Camb
21D2 Puruandro Mexico
33E4 Purus R Brazil
19C3 Purvis USA
78B4 Purwokerto Indon
78C4 Purworejo Indon
85D5 Pusad India
74B3 Pusan S Korea
60D2 Pushkin Russian Fed
58D1 Pustoshka Russian Fed
82D3 Puta Burma
34A2 Putaendo Chile
110C1 Putaruru NZ
73D4 Putian China
87B3 Puttalam Sri Lanka
56C2 Puttgarden Germany
32B4 Putumayo R Ecuador
78C2 Putusibau Indon
38K6 Puulavesi L Fin
20B1 Puyallup USA
49C2 Puy de Sancy Mt France
111A3 Puysegur Pt NZ
99C3 Pweto Zaire
43B3 Pwllheli Wales
76B2 Pyapon Burma
61F5 Pyatigorsk Russian Fed
Pyè = Prome
74B3 P'yŏngyang N Korea
74B3 Pyramid Hill Aust
21B1 Pyramid L USA
111A2 Pyramid,Mt NZ
48B3 Pyrénées Mts France
58D1 Pytalovo Russian Fed
76B2 Pyu Burma

Q

94B2 Qabatiya Israel
94C3 Qa'el Hafira Mud Flats Jordan
94C3 Qa'el Jinz Mud Flats Jordan
68B3 Qaidam Pendi Salt Flat China
94C2 Qa Khanna Salt Marsh Jordan
99D1 Qala'en Nahl Sudan
94B2 Qalat Afghan
94C1 Qal'at al Hisn Syria
81C3 Qal'at Bishah S Arabia
93E3 Qal'at Sālih Iraq
68B3 Qamdo China
99E1 Qandala Somalia
99E2 Qardho Somalia
95B2 Qara Egypt
90A3 Qare Shirin Iran
91A4 Qaryat al Ulyā S Arabia
94C3 Qasr el Kharana Jordan
91D4 Qasr-e-Qand Iran
95B2 Qasr Farafra Egypt
94C2 Qatana Syria
91B4 Qatar Emirate, Arabian Pen
94C3 Qatrāna Jordan

95B2 Qattāra Depression Egypt
90C3 Qäyen Iran
90A2 Qazvin Iran
95C2 Qena Egypt
90A2 Qeydar Iran
91B4 Qeys I Iran
78B5 Qezi'ot Israel
72E1 Qian Jiang R China
72E1 Qian Shan Upland China
72E3 Qidong China
73B4 Qijiang China
84B2 Qila Saifullah Pak
72A2 Qilian China
68B3 Qilian Shan China
73B4 Qin'an China
72E2 Qingdao China
72A2 Qinghai Province, China
68B3 Qinghai Hu L China
72D3 Qingjiang Jiangsu, China
73D4 Qingjiang Jiangxi, China
72B3 Qing Jiang R China
72C2 Qingshuihe China
72B3 Qingshui He R China
72B2 Qingtonxia China
72B2 Qingyang China
74B2 Qingyuan Liaoning, China
73D4 Qingyuan Zhejiang, China
82C2 Qing Zang Upland China
72D2 Qinhuangdao China
72B3 Qin Ling Mts China
73B5 Qinzhou China
76E2 Qionghai China
73A3 Qionglai Shan China
76D1 Qiongzhou Haixia Str China
69E2 Qiqihar China
94B2 Qiryat Ata Israel
94B3 Qiryat Gat Israel
94B2 Qiryat Shemona Israel
94B2 Qiryat Yam Israel
94B2 Qishon R Israel
63A3 Qitai China
73C4 Qiyang China
72B1 Qog Qi China
90B2 Qolleh-ye Damavand Mt Iran
90B3 Qom Iran
90B3 Qomisheh Iran
94C1 Qornet es Saouda Mt Leb
6E3 Qôrnoq Greenland
90A2 Qorveh Iran
91C4 Qotābad Iran
16C1 Quabbin Res USA
16B2 Quakertown USA
77C3 Quam Phu Quoc I Viet
76D2 Quang Ngai Viet
76D2 Quang Tri Viet
77D4 Quan Long Viet
73D5 Quanzhou Fujian, China
73C4 Quanzhou Guangxi, China
5H4 Qu' Appelle R Can
91C5 Quarayyāt Oman
73B3 Quatsino Sd Can
90C2 Quchan Iran
109C3 Queanbeyan Aust
15D1 Québec Can
7C4 Québec Province, Can
35B1 Quebra-Anzol R Brazil
34D2 Quebracho Urug
30F4 Quedas do Iguaçu Brazil/Arg
16A3 Queen Anne USA
13B2 Queen Bess,Mt Can
5E4 Queen Charlotte Is Can
13B2 Queen Charlotte Sd Can

13B2 Queen Charlotte Str Can
4H1 Queen Elizabeth Is Can
112B9 Queen Mary Land Region, Ant
4H3 Queen Maud G Can
112A Queen Maud Mts Ant
16C2 Queens Borough, New York, USA
108B3 Queenscliff Aust
107D3 Queensland State, Aust
109C4 Queenstown Aust
111A3 Queenstown NZ
100B4 Queenstown S Africa
16A3 Queenstown USA
98B3 Quela Angola
101C2 Quelimane Mozam
34C3 Quemu-quemu Arg
13C2 Quesnel L Can
34D3 Quequén Arg
23A1 Queretaro Mexico
23A1 Queretaro State Mexico
13C2 Quesnel Can
84B2 Quetta Pak
25C3 Quezaltenango Guatemala
79B3 Quezon City Phil
100A2 Quibala Angola
98B3 Quibaxe Angola
32B2 Quibdó Colombia
48B2 Quiberon France
98B3 Quicama Nat Pk Angola
73A4 Quijing China
34A2 Quilima Chile
34C2 Quilino Arg
32C6 Quillabamba Peru
30C2 Quillacollo Bol
48C3 Quillan France
5H4 Quill L Can
5H4 Quill Lakes Can
34A2 Quillota Chile
87B3 Quilon India
108B1 Quilpie Aust
34A2 Quilpué Chile
98B3 Quimbele Angola
48B2 Quimper France
48B2 Quimperlé France
21A2 Quincy California, USA
10A3 Quincy Illinois, USA
16D1 Quincy Massachusetts, USA
34B2 Quines Arg
12B3 Quinhagak USA
76D3 Qui Nhon Viet
50B2 Quintanar de la Orden Spain
34A2 Quintero Chile
34C2 Quinto R Arg
34A3 Quirihue Chile
100A2 Quirima Angola
95B2 Quirindi Aust
101D2 Quissanga Mozam
101C3 Quissico Mozam
32B4 Quito Ecuador
31D2 Quixadá Brazil
108A2 Quorn Aust
4G3 Qurlurtuuk Can
95B2 Quseir Egypt
6E3 Qutdligssat Greenland
Quthing = Moyeni
73B3 Qu Xian Sichuan, China
73D4 Qu Xian Zhejiang, China
76D2 Quynh Luu Viet
72C2 Quzhou China
86C1 Qüzü China

R

38J6 Raahe Fin
44A3 Raasay I Scot
44A3 Raasay,Sound of Chan Scot
99F1 Raas Caseyr C Somalia
52B2 Rab I Croatia
78D4 Raba Indon
59B3 Rába R Hung

96B1 Rabat Mor
94B3 Rabba Jordan
80B3 Rabigh S Arabia
47B2 Racconigi Italy
7E5 Race,C Can
94B2 Rachaya Leb
57C3 Rachel Mt Germany
76D3 Rach Gia Viet
14A2 Racine USA
59B3 Radauti Rom
85C4 Radhanpur India
27L1 Radix,Pt Trinidad
58C2 Radom Pol
59B2 Radomsko Pol
58C1 Radviliskis Lithuania
4G3 Rae Can
86A1 Rae Bareli India
6B3 Rae Isthmus Can
6A1 Rae L Can
110C1 Raetihi NZ
34C2 Rafaela Arg
94B3 Rafah Egypt
98C2 Rafai CAR
93D3 Rafhā al Jumaymah S Arabia
91C3 Rafsanjān Iran
98C2 Raga Sudan
2783 Ragged Pt Barbados
53B3 Ragusa Italy
99D1 Rahad R Sudan
84C3 Rahimyar Khan Pak
90B3 Rähjerd Iran
85C4 Räichur India
87B1 Räichur India
86A2 Raigarh India
108B3 Rainbow Aust
17A1 Rainbow City USA
20B1 Rainier USA
20B1 Rainier,Mt USA
10A2 Rainy L Can
12D2 Rainy P Can
10A2 Rainy River Can
86A2 Raipur India
87C1 Räjahmundry India
78C2 Rajang R Malay
84C3 Rajanpur Pak
87B3 Räjapalaiyam India
85C3 Rajasthan State, India
84D3 Räjgarh India
85D4 Räjgarh State, India
85C4 Räjkot India
86B2 Rajmahāl Hills India
86A2 Räj Nändgaon India
85C4 Räjpipla India
86B2 Räjshähi Bang
85D4 Rajur India
111B2 Rakaia R NZ
78B4 Rakata I Indon
82C3 Raka Zangbo R China
59C3 Rakhov Ukraine
100B3 Rakops Botswana
58D2 Rakov Belorussia
11C3 Raleigh USA
7A5 Ralny L Can
94B2 Rama Israel
94B3 Ramallah Israel
87B3 Rämanäthapuram India
69G3 Ramapo Deep Pacific O
94B2 Ramat Gan Israel
46A2 Rambouillet France
86B2 Rämgarh Bihar, India
85C3 Rämgarh Rajasthan, India
90A3 Rämhormoz Iran
94B3 Ramla Israel
91C5 Ramlat Al Wahibah Region, Oman
21B3 Ramona USA
84D3 Rämpur India
85D4 Rämpura India
90B2 Rämsar Iran
16B2 Ramsey Eng
43B4 Ramsey I Wales
43E4 Ramsgate Eng
94C2 Ramtha Jordan
71F4 Ramu R PNG
34A2 Rancagua Chile
86B2 Rānchi India
86A2 Ränchi Plat India
101G1 Randburg S Africa

39G7 Randers Den
101G1 Randfontein S Africa
15D2 Randolph Vermont, USA
111B3 Ranfurly NZ
86C2 Rangamati Bang
111B2 Rangiora NZ
110C1 Rangitaiki R NZ
111B2 Rangitata R NZ
110C1 Rangitikei R NZ
Rangoon = Yangon
86B1 Rangpur India
87B2 Ränibennur India
8A2 Ranier,Mt Mt USA
86B2 Räniganj India
109C2 Rankins Springs Aust
6A3 Rankin Inlet Can
85B4 Rann of Kachchh Flood Area India
77B4 Ranong Thai
70A4 Rantauprapat Indon
18C1 Rantoul USA
49D3 Rapallo Italy
34A2 Rapel R Chile
6D3 Raper,C Can
8C2 Rapid City USA
14A1 Rapid River USA
15C3 Rappahannock R USA
47C1 Rapperswil Switz
16B2 Raritan B USA
95C2 Ras Abu Shagara C Sudan
93D2 Ra's al 'Ayn Syria
91C5 Ra's al Hadd C Oman
91C4 Ras al Kaimah UAE
91C4 Ras-al-Kuh C Iran
81D4 Ra's al Madrakah C Oman
91A4 Ra's az Zawr C S Arabia
95C2 Räs Bänas C Egypt
94A3 Ras Burün C Egypt
99D1 Ras Dashan Mt Eth
90A3 Ra's-e-Barkan Pt Iran
92A3 Râs el Kenäyis C Egypt
81D4 Ra's Fartak C Yemen
95C2 Râs Ghârib C Egypt
99D1 Rashad Sudan
94B3 Rashädiya Jordan
92B3 Rashid Egypt
90A2 Rasht Iran
91C5 Ra's Jibish C Oman
99E1 Ras Khanzira C Somalia
84B3 Ras Koh Mt Pak
95C2 Râs Muhammad C Egypt
96A2 Ras Nouadhibou C Maur
69H2 Rasshua I Russian Fed
61F3 Rasskazovo Russian Fed
91A4 Ra's Tanäqib C S Arabia
91B4 Ra's Tannürah S Arabia
57B3 Rastatt Germany
9 Ras Uarc = Cabo Tres Forcas
99F1 Ras Xaafuun C Somalia
84C3 Ratangarh India
76B3 Rat Buri Thai
86B2 Rath India
56C2 Rathenow Germany
45B2 Rathkeale Irish Rep
45C1 Rathlin I N Ire
45B2 Ráth Luirc Irish Rep
85D4 Ratlām India
87A1 Ratnägiri India
87C3 Ratnapura Sri Lanka
58C2 Ratno Ukraine
8D3 Raton USA
110C1 Raukumara Range Mts NZ
35C2 Raul Soares Brazil
39J6 Rauma Fin
86A2 Raurkela India

90A3 Ravänsar Iran
90C3 Rävar Iran
59C2 Rava Russkaya Ukraine
16C1 Ravena USA
52B2 Ravenna Italy
57B3 Ravensburg Germany
107D2 Ravenshoe Aust
42E2 Ravenspurn Oilfield N Sea
84C2 Ravi R Pak
84C2 Rawalpindi Pak
93D2 Rawändiz Iraq
58B2 Rawicz Pol
106B4 Rawlinna Aust
8C2 Rawlins USA
54C2 Rawson Arg
78C3 Raya Mt Indon
87B2 Räyadurg India
94C2 Rayak Leb
7E5 Ray,C Can
22C2 Raymond California, USA
20B1 Raymond Washington, USA
109D2 Raymond Terrace Aust
12D1 Ray Mts USA
23B1 Rayon Mexico
90A2 Razan Iran
54C2 Razgrad Bulg
54C2 Razim L Rom
43D4 Reading USA
16D2 Reading USA
4G3 Readland Can
16C1 Readsboro USA
34B2 Real de Padre Arg
34C3 Realico Arg
95B2 Rebiana Well Libya
95B2 Rebiana Sand Sea Libya
38L6 Reboly Russian Fed
106B4 Recherche,Arch of the Is Aust
31E3 Recife Brazil
107F2 Récifs D'Entrecasteaux Nouvelle Calédonie
46D1 Recklinghausen Germany
30E4 Reconquista Arg
19B3 Red R USA
77C4 Redang I Malay
16B2 Red Bank New Jersey, USA
21A1 Red Bluff USA
42D2 Redcar Eng
13E2 Redcliff Can
109D1 Redcliffe Aust
108B2 Red Cliffs Aust
13E2 Red Deer Can
13E2 Red Deer R Can
20B2 Redding USA
10A2 Red L USA
7E4 Red Lake Can
22D3 Redlands USA
16A3 Red Lion USA
20B2 Redmond USA
18A1 Red Oak USA
48B2 Redon France
22C2 Redondo Beach USA
12D2 Redoubt V USA
73B5 Red River Delta Vietnam
80B3 Red Sea Africa/ Arabian Pen
13E2 Redwater Can
22A2 Redwood City USA
14C2 Reed City USA
21B2 Reedley USA
20B2 Reedsport USA
111B2 Reefton NZ
93C2 Refahiye Turk
35D1 Regência Brazil
57C3 Regensburg Germany
96C2 Reggane Alg
53C3 Reggio di Calabria Italy
47D2 Reggio Nell'Emilia Italy
54B1 Reghin Rom
5H4 Regina Can

100A3 Rehoboth Namibia
15C3 Rehoboth Beach USA
94B3 Rehovot Israel
32D1 Reícito Ven
46C2 Reigate Eng
5H4 Reindeer R Can
50B1 Reinosa Spain
16A3 Reisterstown USA
10G1 Reitz S Africa
4H3 Reliance Can
108A2 Remarkable,Mt Aust
47B2 Rembang Indon
91C4 Remeshk Iran
46D1 Remscheid Germany
18C2 Rend,L USA
56B2 Rendsburg Germany
15C1 Renfrew Can
78A3 Rengat Indon
34A2 Rengo Chile
59D3 Reni Ukraine
99D1 Renk Sudan
6H4 Renland Pen Greenland
108B2 Renmark Aust
107F2 Rennell I Solomon Is
48B2 Rennes France
21B2 Reno USA
47D2 Reno R Italy
15C2 Renovo USA
16C1 Rensselaer USA
20B1 Renton USA
70D4 Reo Indon
35B2 Reprèsa de Furnas Dam Brazil
30E3 Reprèsa Ilha Grande Dam Brazil
30E3 Reprèsa Itaipu Dam Brazil
35A2 Reprèsa Porto Primavera Dam Brazil
35B1 Reprèsa Três Marias Dam Brazil
20C1 Republic USA
41B3 Republic of Ireland NW Europe
6B3 Repulse Bay Can
10C1 Réservoir Baskatong Res Can
10C1 Réservoir de la Grande 2 Res Can
10C1 Réservoir de la Grande 3 Res Can
7C4 Réservoir de la Grande 4 Res Can
7C5 Réservoir Cabonga Res Can
7C5 Réservoir Caniapiscau Res Can
7D5 Réservoir Gouin Can
10D1 Réservoir Manicouagan Res Can
90B2 Reshteh-ye Alborz Mts Iran
72A2 Reshui China
30E4 Resistencia Arg
54B1 Resita Rom
6A2 Resolute Can
111A3 Resolution I NZ
6D3 Resolution Island Can
101H1 Ressano Garcia Mozam
34B2 Retamito Arg
46C2 Rethel France
55B3 Réthimnon Greece
89K10 Réunion I Indian O
51C1 Reus Spain
47C1 Reuss R Switz
61K3 Revda Russian Fed
13D2 Revelstoke Can
24A3 Revillagigedo Is Mexico
12H3 Revillagigedo I USA
12D3 Revin France
94B3 Revivim Israel
86A2 Rewa India
84D3 Rewari India
8B2 Rexburg USA
38A2 Reykjavik Iceland

24C2 Reynosa Mexico
48B2 Rezé France
58D1 Rezekne Latvia
61K2 Rezh Russian Fed
47C1 Rhätikon Mts Austria/Switz
91A3 Rhazir Republic, Leb
56B2 Rhein R W Europe
56B2 Rheine Germany
47B1 Rheinfielden Switz
49D2 Rheinland Pfalz Region, Germany
47C1 Rheinwaldhorn Mt Switz
    Rhine = Rhein
16C2 Rhinebeck USA
10B2 Rhinelander USA
47C2 Rho Italy
16D2 Rhode Island State, USA
16D2 Rhode Island Sd USA
    Rhodes = Ródhos
49C3 Rhône R France
43C3 Rhyl Wales
31D4 Riachão do Jacuipe Brazil
50A1 Ria de Arosa B Spain
50A1 Ria de Betanzos B Spain
50A1 Ria de Corcubion B Spain
50A1 Ria de Sta Marta B Spain
50A1 Ria de Vigo B Spain
84C2 Riãsi Pak
50A1 Ribadeo Spain
35A2 Ribas do Rio Pardo Brazil
101C2 Ribauè Mozam
42C3 Ribble R Eng
35B2 Ribeira Brazil
35B2 Ribeirão Prêto Brazil
32D6 Riberalta Bol
15C2 Rice L Can
10A2 Rice Lake USA
101H1 Richard's Bay S Africa
19A3 Richardson USA
12G1 Richardson Mts Can
8B3 Richfield USA
20C1 Richland USA
22A2 Richmond California, USA
101H1 Richmond Natal, S Africa
109D2 Richmond New South Wales, Aust
111B2 Richmond NZ
107D3 Richmond Queensland, Aust
15C3 Richmond Virginia, USA
111B2 Richmond Range Mts NZ
15C2 Rideau,L Can
17B1 Ridgeland USA
15C2 Ridgway USA
27D4 Riecito Ven
47D1 Rienza R Italy
57C2 Riesa Germany
29B6 Riesco I Chile
52B1 Rieti Italy
52B2 Rieti Italy
58C1 Rif Mtn Mor
58C1 Riga Latvia
61G2 Riga,G of Estonia/ Latvia
91C4 Rigãn Iran
20C1 Riggins USA
7E4 Rigolet Can
39J6 Riihimäki Fin
52B1 Rijeka Croatia
13E2 Rimbey Can
39H7 Rimbo Sweden
52B2 Rimini Italy
54C1 Rimnicu Sãrat Rom
54B1 Rimnicu Vilcea Rom
10D2 Rimouski Can
22B1 Rincón de Romos Mexico
39F7 Ringkøbing Den
98A2 Rio Benito Eq Guinea
32D5 Rio Branco Brazil

24B1 Rio Bravo del Norte R Mexico/USA
32C1 Riochacha Colombia
35B2 Rio Claro Brazil
27L1 Rio Claro Trinidad
31D4 Rio Colorado Arg
34C2 Rio Cuarto Arg
31D4 Rio de Jacuipe Brazil
35C2 Rio de Janeiro Brazil
35C2 Rio de Janeiro State, Brazil
29E3 Rio de la Plata Est Arg/Urug
29C6 Rio Gallegos Arg
29C6 Rio Grande Arg
30F5 Rio Grande Brazil
26A4 Rio Grande Nic
25D3 Rio Grande R Nic
23A1 Rio Grande R Mexico/USA
23A1 Rio Grande de Santiago Mexico
31D3 Rio Grande do Norte State, Brazil
30E5 Rio Grande do Sul State, Brazil
103G6 Rio Grande Rise Atlantic O
26C4 Riohacha Colombia
49C2 Riom France
32B4 Riombamba Ecuador
30C2 Rio Mulatos Bol
29C3 Rio Negro State, Arg
35A2 Rio Pardo Brazil
34C2 Rio Tercero Arg
33E6 Rio Theodoro Roosevelt R Brazil
29B6 Rio Turbio Arg
35A1 Rio Verde Brazil
23A1 Rio Verde Mexico
14B3 Ripley Ohio, USA
14B3 Ripley West Virginia, USA
42D2 Ripon Eng
29E3 Ripon Arg
94B3 Rishon le Zion Israel
16A3 Rising Sun USA
39F7 Risør Nor
6E2 Ritenberk Greenland
22C2 Ritter,Mt USA
20C1 Ritzville USA
34C1 Rivadavia Arg
34A1 Rivadavia Chile
34C3 Rivadavia Gonzalez Moreno Arg
47D2 Riva de Garda Italy
22C2 Ritter,Mt USA
29E2 Rivera Urug
57B4 River Cess Lib
16C2 Riverhead USA
108B3 Riverina Aust
111A3 Riverside NZ
22D4 Riverside USA
13B2 Rivers Inlet Can
111A3 Riverton NZ
8C2 Riverton USA
17B2 Riviera Beach USA
7C4 Rivière aux Feuilles R Can
7D4 Rivière de la Baleine Can
7D4 Rivière du Petit Mecatina R Can
46C2 Rivigny-sur-Ornain France
93D1 Rize Turk
72D2 Rizhao China
    Rizhskiy Zaliv = Riga,G of
39F7 Rjukan Nor
6B2 Roanes Pen Can
49C2 Roanne France
17A1 Roanoke Alabama, USA
11C3 Roanoke Virginia, USA
11C3 Roanoke R USA
45B3 Roaringwater B Irish Rep
38J6 Robertsförz Sweden
19B2 Robert S Kerr Res USA
97A4 Robertsport Lib
7C5 Roberval Can

30H6 Robinson Crusoe /
Chile
108B2 Robinvale Aust
13D2 Robson,Mt Can
24A3 Roca Partida /
Mexico
103G5 Rocas / Atlantic O
31E2 Rocas / Brazil
12C3 Rochdale Eng
48B2 Rochefort France
5G3 Rocher River Can
108B3 Rochester Aust
7C5 Rochester Can
43E4 Rochester Eng
10A2 Rochester
Minnesota, USA
15D2 Rochester New
Hampshire, USA
10C2 Rochester New York,
USA
10B2 Rockford USA
11B3 Rock Hill USA
10A2 Rock Island USA
108B3 Rocklands Res Aust
17B2 Rockledge USA
8C2 Rock Springs
Wyoming, USA
110B2 Rocks Pt NZ
109C3 Rock,The Aust
16C2 Rockville
Connecticut, USA
14A3 Rockville Indiana, USA
16A3 Rockville Maryland,
USA
14B1 Rocky Island L Can
13E2 Rocky Mountain
House Can
8B1 Rocky Mts Can/USA
12B2 Rocky Pt USA
56C2 Rødbyhavn Den
34B2 Rodeo Arg
49C3 Rodez France
55C3 Ródhos Greece
55C3 Ródhos / Greece
52C2 Rodi Garganico Italy
54B2 Rodópi Planina Mts
Bulg
106A3 Roebourne Aust
46C1 Roermond Neth
46B1 Roeselare Belg
6B3 Roes Welcome Sd
Can
18B2 Rogers USA
14B1 Rogers City USA
8C2 Rogue R USA
85B3 Rohn Pak
84D3 Rohtak India
58C1 Roja Latvia
35A2 Rolândia Brazil
18B2 Rolla USA
109C1 Roma Aust
52B2 Roma Italy
47C2 Romagnano Italy
17C1 Romain,C USA
54C1 Roman Rom
103H5 Romanche Gap
Atlantic O
71D4 Romang / Indon
60B4 Romania Republic,
E Europe
17B2 Romano,C USA
49D2 Romans sur Isère
France
79B3 Romblon Phil
Rome = Roma
17A1 Rome Georgia, USA
15C2 Rome USA
49C2 Romilly-sur-Seine
France
15C3 Romney USA
60D3 Romny Ukraine
56B1 Rømø / Den
47B1 Romont Switz
48C2 Romorantin France
50A2 Ronda Spain
33E6 Rondônia Brazil
24F6 Rondônia State,
Brazil
30F2 Rondonópolis Brazil
73B4 Rong'an China
73B4 Rongcheng China
72E2 Rongcheng China

73B4 Rongjiang China
73B4 Rong Jiang R China
76A1 Rongklang Range
Mts Burma
39G7 Rønne Den
39H7 Ronneby Sweden
112B2 Ronne Ice Shelf Ant
46B1 Ronse Belg
46A1 Ronthieu Region,
France
9C3 Roof Butte Mt USA
84D3 Roorkee India
46C1 Roosendaal Neth
112B6 Roosevelt I Ant
106C2 Roper R Aust
33E3 Roraima State, Brazil
33E2 Roraima Mt Ven
38G6 Røros Nor
47C1 Rorschach Switz
38G6 Rørvik Nor
27Q2 Rosalie Dominica
22C3 Rosamond L USA
43C4 Rosario Arg
31C2 Rosario Brazil
34D2 Rosario del Tala Arg
48B2 Roscoff France
45B2 Roscommon County,
Irish Rep
41B3 Roscommon
Irish Rep
45C2 Roscrea Irish Rep
27E3 Roseau Dominica
109C4 Rosebery Aust
20B2 Roseburg USA
19A4 Rosenberg USA
57C3 Rosenheim Germany
13F2 Roseneath Can
54B2 Rosiori de Vede Rom
39G7 Roskilde Den
60D3 Roslavl' Russian Fed
61E2 Roslyatino
Russian Fed
111B2 Ross NZ
12H2 Ross R Can
40B3 Rossan Pt Irish Rep
53C3 Rossano Italy
19C3 Ross Barnet Res USA
15C1 Rosseau L Can
107E2 Rossel I Solomon Is
112A Ross Ice Shelf Ant
20B1 Ross L USA
13D3 Rossland Can
45C2 Rosslare Irish Rep
97A3 Rosso Maur
43C4 Ross-on-Wye Eng
60E4 Rossosh Russian Fed
4E3 Ross River Can
112B6 Ross Sea Ant
91B4 Rostāq Iran
56C2 Rostock Germany
Rostov = Rostov-na-
Donu
61E4 Rostov-na-Donu
Russian Fed
17B1 Roswell Georgia, USA
9C3 Roswell New Mexico,
USA
71F2 Rota Pacific O
56B2 Rotenburg
Niedersachsen,
Germany
46E1 Rothaar-Geb Region
Germany
112C3 Rothera Base Ant
42D3 Rotherham Eng
42B2 Rothesay Scot
71D5 Roti / Indon
108C2 Roto Aust
110B2 Rotoiti,L NZ
110B2 Rotoroa,L NZ
110C1 Rotorua NZ
110C1 Rotorua,L NZ
56A2 Rotterdam Neth
46B1 Roubaix France
48C2 Rouen France
42E3 Rough Oilfield N Sea
Roulers = Roeselare
101E3 Round I Mauritius
109D2 Round Mt Aust
8C2 Roundup USA
44C2 Rousay / Scot
48C3 Roussillon Region,
France

10C2 Rouyn Can
38K5 Rovaniemi Fin
47D2 Rovereto Italy
47D2 Rovigo Italy
52B1 Rovinj Croatia
59D2 Rovno Ukraine
90A2 Row'an Iran
109C1 Rowena Aust
6C3 Rowley I Can
106A2 Rowley Shoals Aust
79A3 Roxas Palawan, Phil
79B3 Roxas Panay, Phil
111A3 Roxburgh NZ
45C2 Royal Canal Irish Rep
43D3 Royal Leamington
Spa Eng
14B2 Royal Oak USA
43E4 Royal Tunbridge
Wells Eng
48B2 Royan France
46B2 Roye France
43D3 Royston Eng
59C3 Rožňava Slovakia
46B2 Rozoy France
61F3 Rtishchevo
Russian Fed
99D3 Ruaha Nat Pk Tanz
110C1 Ruahine Range Mts
NZ
110C1 Ruapehu,Mt NZ
65D3 Rub al Khali Desert
S Arabia
44A3 Rubha Hunish Scot
35A2 Rubineia Brazil
65K4 Rubtsovsk
Russian Fed
12C2 Ruby USA
91C4 Rudan Iran
90A2 Rudbar Iran
69F2 Rudnaya Pristan'
Russian Fed
54B2 Rudoka Planina Mt
Macedonia
72E3 Rudong China
14B1 Rudyard USA
14B1 Rudyard USA
74E Rue France
48C2 Ruffec France
99D3 Rufiji R Tanz
34C2 Rufino Arg
97A3 Rufisque Sen
100B2 Rufunsa Zambia
43D3 Rugby Eng
39G8 Rügen / Germany
56B2 Ruhr R Germany
73D4 Ruijin China
54B2 Rujen Mt Bulg/
Macedonia
99D3 Rukwa L Tanz
44A3 Rum / Scot
54A1 Ruma Serbia, Yugos
91A4 Rumāh S Arabia
98C2 Rumbek Sudan
26C2 Rum Cay /
Caribbean S
47A2 Rumilly France
44A3 Rum Jungle Aust
100C1 Rumphi Malawi
110C1 Runanga NZ
110C1 Runaway,C NZ
100C3 Rundi R Zim
100A2 Rundu Namibia
99D3 Rungwa Tanz
99D3 Rungwa R Tanz
99D3 Rungwe Mt Tanz
82C2 Ruoqiang China
68C2 Ruo Shui R China
5C4 Rupea Rom
7C4 Rupert R Can
46D1 Rur R Germany
32D6 Rurrenabaque Bol
101C2 Rusape Zim
54C2 Ruse Bulg
18B1 Rushville Illinois,
USA
108B3 Rushworth Aust
14A3 Rusk USA
17B2 Ruskin USA
110B1 Russell NZ
18B2 Russellville Arkansas,
USA
18C2 Russellville Kentucky,
USA
21A2 Russian R USA
62C3 Russian Fed Asia/
Europe

93E1 Rustavi Georgia
101G1 Rustenburg S Africa
19B3 Ruston USA
99C3 Rutana Burundi
46E1 Rüthen Germany
23B2 Rutla Mexico
15D2 Rutland USA
84D2 Rutog China
Ruvu = Pangani
101D2 Ruvuma R Tanz/
Mozam
99D2 Ruwenzori Range
Mts Uganda/Zaïre
101C2 Ruya R Zim
59B3 Ružomberok
Slovakia
99C3 Rwanda Republic,
Africa
60E3 Ryazan' Russian Fed
61F3 Ryazhsk Russian Fed
60E2 Rybinsk Russian Fed
60E2 Rybinskoye
Vodokhranilishche
Res Russian Fed
13D1 Rycroft Can
43D4 Ryde Eng
43E4 Rye Eng
20C2 Rye Patch Res USA
60D3 Ryl'sk Russian Fed
61G4 Ryn Peski Desert
Kazakhstan
74D3 Ryōtsu Japan
59D3 Ryskany Moldavia
69E4 Ryūkyū Retto Arch
Japan
59C2 Rzeszów Pol
60D2 Rzhev Russian Fed

S

91B3 Sa'adatābād Iran
56C2 Saale R Germany
47B1 Saanen Switz
46D2 Saar R Germany
46D2 Saarbrücken
Germany
46D2 Saarburg Germany
39J7 Saaremaa / Estonia
46D2 Saarland State,
Germany
46D2 Saarlouis Germany
34C3 Šaavedra Arg
52B2 Šabac Serbia, Yugos
51C1 Sabadell Spain
75B1 Sabae Japan
78D1 Sabah State, Malay
26C4 Sabanalarga
Colombia
70A3 Sabang Indon
87C1 Sabari R India
94B2 Sabastiya Israel
32C3 Sabaya Bol
93C3 Sab'Bi'ar Syria
94C2 Sabhā Jordan
95A2 Sabhā Libya
24B2 Sabinas Mexico
24B2 Sabinas Hidalgo
Mexico
19A3 Sabine R USA
19B4 Sabine L USA
91B5 Sabkhat Maṭṭi Salt
Marsh UAE
94A3 Sabkhet El Bardawil
Lg Egypt
79B3 Sablayan Phil
7D5 Sable,C Can
17B2 Sable,C USA
7D5 Sable I Can
90C2 Sabzevar Iran
20C1 Sacajawea Peak USA
10A1 Sachigo R Can
57C2 Sachsen State,
Germany
56C2 Sachsen-Anhalt
State, Germany
4F2 Sachs Harbour Can
47C1 Säckingen Germany
22B1 Sacramento USA
22B1 Sacramento R USA
21A1 Sacramento V USA
9C3 Sacramento Mts
USA
81C4 Sa'dah Yemen
54B2 Sadanski Bulg
82D3 Sadiya India
50A2 Sado R Port

74D3	Sado-shima I Japan
85C3	Sädri India
	Safad = Zefat
84A2	Safed Koh Mts Afghan
39G7	Säffle Sweden
92C3	Safi Jordan
96B1	Safi Mor
90D3	Safidabeh Iran
94C1	Säfítä Syria
93E3	Safwan Iraq
75A2	Sagaing Burma
76B1	Sagaing Burma
75B2	Sagami-nada B Japan
85D4	Sägar India
12C2	Sag Harbor USA
14B2	Saginaw USA
14B2	Saginaw B USA
26B2	Sagua de Tánamo Cuba
26B2	Sagua la Grande Cuba
7C5	Saguenay R Can
51B2	Sagunto Spain
94C3	Sahab Jordan
50A1	Sahagún Spain
96C2	Sahara Desert N Africa
84D3	Saharanpur India
84C2	Sahiwal Pak
93D3	Sahrā al Hijārah Desert Region Iraq
23A1	Sahuayo Mexico
107D1	Saibai I Aust
96C1	Saïda Alg
94B2	Saïda Leb
91C4	Sa'idabad Iran
51B2	Saidia Mor
86B1	Saidpur India
84C2	Saidu Pak
75A1	Saigō Japan
	Saigon = Ho Chi Minh
86C2	Saiha India
68D2	Saihan Tal China
75A2	Saijo Japan
74C4	Saiki Japan
42C2	St Abb's Head Pt Scot
43D4	St Albans Eng
15D2	St Albans Vermont, USA
14B3	St Albans West Virginia, USA
43C4	St Albans Head C Eng
13E2	St Albert Can
46B1	St Amand-les-Eaux France
48C2	St Amand-Mont Rond France
17A2	St Andrew B USA
44C3	St Andrews Scot
17B1	St Andrew Sd USA
27H1	St Ann's Bay Jamaica
7E4	St Anthony Can
108B3	St Arnaud Aust
17B2	St Augustine USA
43B4	St Austell Eng
46D2	St-Avold France
42C2	St Bees Head Pt Eng
47B2	St-Bonnet France
43B4	St Brides B Wales
15C2	St Catharines Can
27M2	St Catherine,Mt Grenada
17B1	St Catherines I USA
43D4	St Catherines Pt Eng
49C2	St Chamond France
18B2	St Charles Missouri, USA
14B2	St Clair USA
14B2	St Clair,L Can/USA
14B2	St Clair Shores USA
49D2	St Claud France
10A2	St Cloud USA
47B1	Ste Croix Switz
27E3	St Croix I Caribbean S
43B4	St Davids Head Pt Wales
46B2	St Denis France
101E3	St Denis Réunion
46C2	St Dizier France
12F2	St Elias,Mt USA
12G2	St Elias Mts Can
48B2	Saintes France
49C2	St Etienne France
18B2	St Francis R USA
100B4	St Francis,C S Africa
47C1	St Gallen Switz
48C3	St-Gaudens France
109C1	St George Aust
17B1	St George South Carolina, USA
9B3	St George Utah, USA
17B2	St George,Pt Florida, USA
20B2	St George,Pt USA
15D1	St Georges Can
27E4	St George's Grenada
45C3	St George's Chan Irish Rep/Wales
46A2	St Germain-en-Laye France
47B2	St-Gervais France
47C1	St Gotthard P Switz
43B4	St Govans Head Pt Wales
22A1	St Helena I
103H5	St Helena I Atlantic O
100A4	St Helena B S Africa
17B1	St Helena Sd USA
109C4	St Helens Aust
42C3	St Helens Eng
10B1	St Helens USA
20B1	St Helens,Mt USA
48B2	St Helier Jersey
47B1	St Hippolyte France
46C1	St-Hubert Belg
7C5	St-Hyacinthe Can
14B1	St Ignace USA
43B4	St Ives Eng
18B2	St James Missouri, USA
5E4	St James,C Can
15D1	St Jean Can
48B2	St Jean-d'Angely France
47B2	St-Jean-de-Maurienne France
10C2	St Jean,L Can
15D1	St-Jérôme Can
20C1	St Joe R USA
7D5	Saint John Can
7E5	St John's Can
14B2	St Johns Michigan, USA
17B2	St Johns R USA
15D2	St Johnsbury USA
15D1	St-Joseph Can
19B3	St Joseph Louisiana, USA
14A2	St Joseph Michigan, USA
18B2	St Joseph Missouri, USA
27L1	St Joseph Trinidad
14B2	St Joseph R USA
14B1	St Joseph,L Can
7A4	St Joseph,L Can
48C2	St Julien France
46B2	St-Junien France
46B2	St-Just-en-Chaussée France
4B2	St Kilda I Scot
27E3	St Kitts-Nevis Is Caribbean S
47A1	St-Laurent France
7D5	St Lawrence R Can
7D5	Saint Lawrence,G of Can
4A3	St Lawrence I USA
15C2	St Lawrence Seaway Can/USA
48B2	St Lô France
97A3	St Louis Sen
11A3	St Louis USA
27E4	St Lucia I Caribbean S
17B1	St Lucia,L S Africa
44E1	St Magnus I Scot
48B2	St Malo France
20C1	St Maries USA
27E3	St Martin I Caribbean S
108A2	St Mary Peak Mt Aust
109C4	St Marys Aust
15C2	St Marys Aust
17B1	St Marys USA
46C2	Ste-Menehould France
12B2	St Michael USA
16A3	St Michaels USA
47B2	St-Mihiel France
47C1	St Moritz Switz
48B2	St-Nazaire France
46C1	St-Niklaas Belg
46B1	St-Omer France
13E2	St Paul Can
10A2	St Paul Minnesota, USA
97A4	St Paul R Lib
17B2	St Petersburg USA
7E5	St Pierre Can
15D1	St Pierre,L Can
46B1	St-Pol-Sur-Ternoise France
59B3	St Pölten Austria
59B2	St Raphaël France
49D3	St Raphaël France
101D2	St Sébastien C Madag
17B1	St Simons I USA
17B1	St Stephen USA
14B2	St Thomas Can
49D3	St-Tropez France
46C1	St Truiden Belg
46A1	St-Valery-sur-Somme France
27E4	St Vincent and the Grenadines Is Caribbean S
108A2	St Vincent,G Aust
46D1	St-Vith Germany
46D2	St Wendel Germany
71F2	Saipan I Pacific O
84B2	Saiydabad Afghan
30C2	Sajama Mt Bol
75A2	Sakai Japan
75A2	Sakaide Japan
93D4	Sakakah S Arabia
10C1	Sakami,L Can
100B2	Sakania Zaire
101D3	Sakaraha Madag
60B3	Sakarya R Turk
58C1	Sakasleja Latvia
74D3	Sakata Japan
97C4	Sakété Benin
69G1	Sakhalin I Russian Fed
69E4	Sakishima gunto Is Japan
97A4	Sal I Cape Verde
61F4	Sal R Russian Fed
39H7	Sala Sweden
34D3	Saladillo Arg
34C2	Saladillo R Arg
34D3	Salado R Buenos Aires, Arg
34C3	Salado R Mendoza/San Luis, Arg
30D4	Salado R Sante Fe, Arg
97B4	Salaga Ghana
76C3	Sala Hintoun Camb
98B1	Salal Chad
81D4	Şalālah Oman
34A2	Salamanca Chile
23A1	Salamanca Mexico
50A1	Salamanca Spain
15C2	Salamanca USA
98B2	Salamat R Chad
71F4	Salamaua PNG
15C2	Salamonica USA
78D1	Salang Indon
38H5	Salangen Nor
30C3	Salar de Arizaro Arg
30C2	Salar de Atacama Salt Pan Chile
30C2	Salar de Coipasa Salt Pan Bol
30C3	Salar de Uyuni Salt Pan Bol
47C2	Salasomaggiore Italy
61J3	Salavat Russian Fed
70D4	Salayar Indon
105L5	Sala y Gomez I Pacific O
34C3	Salazar Arg
48C2	Salbris France
12E2	Salcha R USA
100A4	Saldanha S Africa
94C2	Saldhad Syria
34C3	Saldungaray Arg
58C1	Saldus Latvia
109C3	Sale Aust
18C2	Salem Illinois, USA
87B2	Salem India
16D1	Salem Massachusetts, USA
16B3	Salem New Jersey, USA
20B2	Salem Oregon, USA
78C4	Salembu Besar I Indon
39G6	Salen Sweden
53B2	Salerno Italy
42C3	Salford Eng
54A1	Salgót Hung
59B3	Salgótarján Hung
31D3	Salgueiro Brazil
55C3	Salihli Turk
101C2	Salima Malawi
39K6	Salimaa L Fin
18A2	Salina Kansas, USA
53B3	Salina I Italy
23B2	Salina Cruz Mexico
30C3	Salina de Arizato Arg
34B3	Salina Grande Salt pan Arg
34B3	Salina La Antigua Salt pan Arg
34C2	Salinas Brazil
22B2	Salinas USA
22B2	Salinas R USA
34B3	Salinas de Llancaneb Salt Pan Arg
34B3	Salinas Grandes Salt Pan Arg
19B3	Saline R Arkansas, USA
27M2	Salines,Pt Grenada
31B2	Salinópolis Brazil
47A1	Salins France
	Salisbury = Harare
15C3	Salisbury Maryland, USA
6C3	Salisbury I Can
43D4	Salisbury Plain Eng
38E5	Salla Fin
47B2	Sallanches France
43D4	Salisaw USA
6C3	Salluit Can
86A1	Salyana Nepal
93D2	Salmas Iran
38L6	Salmi Russian Fed
20C1	Salmo Can
8C2	Salmon USA
13D2	Salmon Arm Can
8B2	Salmon River Mts USA
39J6	Salo Fin
47D2	Salo Italy
49D3	Salon-de-Provence France
	Salonica = Thessaloniki
54B1	Salonta Rom
38K6	Salpausselka Region, Fin
34B2	Salsacate Arg
61F4	Sal'sk Russian Fed
94B2	Salt Jordan
30C3	Salta Arg
24B2	Saltillo Mexico
8B2	Salt Lake City USA
34C2	Salto Urug
34D2	Salto Arg
32C3	Salto Angostura Waterfall Colombia
35D1	Salto da Divisa Brazil
33E2	Salto del Angel Waterfall Ven
30E3	Salto del Guaira Waterfall Brazil
32C4	Salto Grande Waterfall Colombia
84C2	Salt Range Mts Pak
27H2	Salt River Jamaica

Saluda

17B1 **Saluda** USA	79B2 **San Carlos** Phil	34A3 **San Javier** Chile
47B2 **Saluzzo** Italy	29B4 **San Carlos de**	34D2 **San Javier** Sante Fe,
31D4 **Salvador** Brazil	**Bariloche** Arg	Arg
19B4 **Salvador,L** USA	69E4 **San-chung** Taiwan	74D3 **Sanjō** / Japan
23A1 **Salvatierra** Mexico	61G2 **Sanchursk**	31C6 **San João do Rei**
91B5 **Salwah** Qatar	**Russian Fed**	Brazil
76B1 **Salween** Burma	34A3 **San Clemente** Chile	22B2 **San Joaquin** R USA
93E2 **Sal'yany** Azerbaijan	22D4 **San Clemente** USA	22B2 **San Joaquin Valley**
57C3 **Salzburg** Austria	21B3 **San Clemente I** USA	USA
56C2 **Salzgitter** Germany	34C2 **San Cristóbal** Arg	32A1 **San José** Costa Rica
56C2 **Salzwedel** Germany	25C3 **San Cristóbal** Mexico	25C3 **San José** Guatemala
68B1 **Samagaltay**	32C2 **San Cristóbal** Ven	79B2 **San Jose** Luzon, Phil
Russian Fed	32J7 **San Cristóbal** /	79B3 **San Jose** Mindoro,
79B4 **Samales Group** Is	Ecuador	Phil
Phil	107F2 **San Cristóbal** /	22B2 **San Jose** USA
27D3 **Samaná** Dom Rep	Solomon Is	9B4 **San José** / Mexico
92C2 **Samandagi** Italy	25E2 **Sancti Spíritus** Cuba	30D2 **San Jose de**
84B1 **Samangan** Afghan	78C3 **Sandai** Indon	**Chiquitos** Bol
79C3 **Samar** / Phil	70C3 **Sandakan** Malay	34D2 **San José de Feliciano**
65G4 **Samara** Russian Fed	44C2 **Sanday** I Scot	Arg
107E2 **Samarai** PNG	9C3 **Sanderson** USA	34B2 **San José de Jachal**
78D3 **Samarinda** Indon	13F1 **Sandfly L** Can	Arg
80E2 **Samarkand**	21B3 **San Diego** USA	34C2 **San José de la**
Uzbekistan	92B2 **Sandikli** Turk	**Dormida** Arg
93D3 **Sāmarrā'** Iraq	86A1 **Sandila** India	31B6 **San José do Rio**
79B3 **Samar S** Phil	39F7 **Sandnes** Nor	**Prêto** Brazil
86A2 **Sambalpur** India	38G5 **Sandnessjøen** Nor	24B2 **San Jose del Cabo**
78B2 **Sambas** Indon	98C3 **Sandoa** Zaïre	Mexico
101E2 **Sambava** Madag	59C2 **Sandomierz** Pol	34B2 **San Juan** Arg
84D3 **Sambhal** India	20C1 **Sandoy** Faroyar	27D3 **San Juan** Puerto Rico
78D3 **Samboja** Indon	20B1 **Sandpoint** USA	34B2 **San Juan** State, Arg
59C3 **Sambor** Ukraine	49D2 **Sandray** USA	27L1 **San Juan** Trinidad
46B1 **Sambre** R France	18A2 **Sand Springs** USA	32D2 **San Juan** Ven
74B3 **Samch'ŏk** S Korea	106A3 **Sandstone** Aust	26B2 **San Juan** Mt Cuba
99D3 **Same** Tanz	73C4 **Sandu** China	8C3 **San Juan** Mts USA
47C1 **Samedan** Switz	14B2 **Sandusky** USA	34B2 **San Juan** R Arg
46A1 **Samer** France	39H6 **Sandviken** Sweden	23B2 **San Juan** R Mexico
100B2 **Samfya** Zambia	7A4 **Sandy L** Can	25D3 **San Juan** R Nic/
76B1 **Samka** Burma	34C2 **San Elcano** Arg	Costa Rica
76C1 **Sam Neua** Laos	9B3 **San Felipe** Baja Cal,	23B2 **San Juan Bautista**
55C3 **Sámos** / Greece	Mexico	Mexico
55C2 **Samothráki** / Greece	34A2 **San Felipe** Chile	30E4 **San Juan Bautista**
34C2 **Sampacho** Arg	23A1 **San Felipe**	Par
78D3 **Sampaga** Indon	**Guanajuato, Mexico**	22B2 **San Juan Bautista**
78C3 **Sampit** Indon	27D4 **San Felipe** Ven	USA
78C3 **Sampit** R Indon	51C1 **San Feliu de Guixols**	25D3 **San Juan del Norte**
19B3 **Sam Rayburn Res**	Spain	Nic
USA	28A5 **San Felix** / Pacific O	27D4 **San Juan de los**
76C3 **Samrong** Camb	34A2 **San Fernando** Chile	**Cayos** Ven
56C1 **Samsø** / Den	79B2 **San Fernando** Phil	23A1 **San Juan de loz**
92C1 **Samsun** Turk	79B2 **San Fernando** Phil	**Lagoz** Mexico
97B3 **San** Mali	50A2 **San Fernando** Spain	23A1 **San Juan del Rio**
34C2 **San** R Camb	27E4 **San Fernando**	Mexico
59C2 **San** R Pol	Trinidad	25D3 **San Juan del Sur** Nic
81C4 **San'ā'** Yemen	22C3 **San Fernando** USA	20B1 **San Juan Is** USA
98B2 **Sanaga** R Cam	32D2 **San Fernando** Ven	23B2 **San Juan Tepozcolula**
29C2 **San Agustin** Arg	17B2 **Sanford** Florida, USA	Mexico
90A2 **Sanandaj** Iran	12F2 **Sanford,Mt** USA	29C5 **San Julián** Arg
22B1 **San Andreas** USA	34C2 **San Francisco** Arg	34C2 **San Justo** Arg
25C3 **San Andrés Tuxtla**	27C3 **San Francisco** Dom	60D2 **Sankt-Peterburg**
Mexico	Rep	**Russian Fed**
9C3 **San Angelo** USA	22A2 **San Francisco** USA	98C3 **Sankuru** R Zaïre
53A3 **San Antioco**	22A2 **San Francisco B** USA	22A2 **San Leandro** USA
Sardegna	24B2 **San Francisco del Oro**	93C2 **Sanlurfa** Turk
53A3 **San Antioco** / Medit	Mexico	32B3 **San Lorenzo** Ecuador
S	23A1 **San Francisco del**	34C2 **San Lorenzo** Arg
34A2 **San Antonio** Chile	**Rincon** Mexico	22B2 **San Lucas** USA
9C3 **San Antonio** New	22D3 **San Gabriel Mts** USA	34B2 **San Luis** Arg
Mexico, USA	85C5 **Sangamner** India	34B2 **San Luis** State, Arg
79B2 **San Antonio** Phil	18C2 **Sangamon** R USA	23A1 **San Luis de la Paz**
9D4 **San Antonio** R	71F2 **Sangan** / Pacific O	Mexico
Texas, USA	87B1 **Sangareddi** India	21A2 **San Luis Obispo** USA
51C2 **San Antonio Abad**	78D4 **Sangeang** / Indon	23A1 **San Luis Potosi**
Spain	22C2 **Sanger** USA	Mexico
25D2 **San Antonio,C** Cuba	72C2 **Sanggan He** R China	22B2 **San Luis Res** USA
26A2 **San Antonio de los**	78C2 **Sanggau** Indon	53A3 **Sanluri** Sardegna
Banos Cuba	98B2 **Sangha** R Congo	33D2 **San Maigualida** Mts
22D3 **San Antonio,Mt** USA	85B3 **Sanghar** Pak	Ven
29C4 **San Antonio Oeste**	76B2 **Sangkhla Buri** Thai	34D3 **San Manuel** Arg
Arg	78D3 **Sangkulirang** Indon	34A2 **San Marcos** Chile
34D3 **San Augustín** Arg	87A1 **Sangli** India	23B2 **San Marcos** Mexico
34B2 **San Augustín de**	98B2 **Sangmélima** Cam	52B2 **San Marino**
Valle Féril Arg	9B3 **San Gorgonio Mt**	**Republic, Europe**
85D4 **Sanawad** India	USA	34B2 **San Martin** Mendoza,
23A1 **San Bartolo** Mexico	9C3 **Sangre de Cristo** Mts	Arg
24A3 **San Benedicto** /	USA	112C3 **San Martin** Base Ant
Mexico	34C2 **San Gregorio** Arg	47D1 **San Martino di**
22B2 **San Benito** R USA	22A2 **San Gregorio** USA	**Castroza** Italy
22B2 **San Benito Mt** USA	84D2 **Sangrūr** India	23B2 **San Martin**
22D3 **San Bernardino** USA	30E4 **San Ignacio** Arg	**Tuxmelucan** Mexico
34A2 **San Bernardo** Chile	79B3 **San Isidro** Phil	22A2 **San Mateo** USA
17A2 **San Blas,C** USA	32B2 **San Jacinto**	30E2 **San Matias** Bol
34A3 **San Carlos** Chile	Colombia	72C3 **Sanmenxia** China
32A1 **San Carlos** Nic	21B3 **San Jacinto Peak** Mt	25D3 **San Miguel** El
	USA	Salvador

22B3 **San Miguel** / USA		
23A1 **San Miguel del**		
Allende Mexico		
34D3 **San Miguel del**		
Monte Arg		
30C4 **San Miguel de**		
Tucumán Arg		
73D4 **Sanming** China		
9B3 **San Nicolas** I USA		
34C2 **San Nicolas de los**		
Arroyos Arg		
101G1 **Sanninneshof** S Africa		
97B4 **Sanniquellie** Lib		
59C3 **Sanok** Pol		
26B5 **San Onofore**		
Colombia		
22D4 **San Onofre** USA		
79B3 **San Pablo** Phil		
22A1 **San Pablo B** USA		
34D2 **San Pedro**		
Buenos Aires, Arg		
97B4 **San Pedro** Ivory		
Coast		
30D3 **San Pedro** Jujuy, Arg		
30E3 **San Pedro** Par		
22C4 **San Pedro Chan** USA		
9C4 **San Pedro de los**		
Colonias Mexico		
25D3 **San Pedro Sula**		
Honduras		
53A3 **San Pietro** / Medit S		
24A1 **San Quintin** Mexico		
34B2 **San Rafael** Arg		
22A2 **San Rafael** USA		
22C3 **San Rafael Mts** USA		
49D3 **San Remo** Italy		
34D2 **San Salvador** Arg		
26C2 **San Salvador** /		
Caribbean S		
32J7 **San Salvador** /		
Ecuador		
30C3 **San Salvador de**		
Jujuy Arg		
51B1 **San Sebastian** Spain		
53C2 **San Severo** Italy		
30C2 **Santa Ana** Bol		
25C3 **Santa Ana**		
Guatemala		
22D4 **Santa Ana** USA		
22D4 **Santa Ana Mts** USA		
34A3 **Santa Bárbara** Chile		
24B2 **Santa Barbara**		
Mexico		
22C3 **Santa Barbara** USA		
22C4 **Santa Barbara** / USA		
22B3 **Santa Barbara Chan**		
USA		
22C3 **Santa Barbara Res**		
USA		
22C4 **Santa Catalina** /		
USA		
22C4 **Santa Catalina,G of**		
USA		
30F4 **Santa Catarina** State,		
Brazil		
26B2 **Santa Clara** Cuba		
22B2 **Santa Clara** USA		
22C3 **Santa Clara** R USA		
29C6 **Santa Cruz** Arg		
30D2 **Santa Cruz** Bol		
34A2 **Santa Cruz** Chile		
79B3 **Santa Cruz** Phil		
29B5 **Santa Cruz** State,		
Arg		
22A2 **Santa Cruz** USA		
22C4 **Santa Cruz** / USA		
35D1 **Santa Cruz Cabrália**		
Brazil		
22C3 **Santa Cruz Chan**		
USA		
96A2 **Santa Cruz de la**		
Palma Canary Is		
26B2 **Santa Cruz del Sur**		
Cuba		
96A2 **Santa Cruz de**		
Tenerife Canary Is		
100B2 **Santa Cruz do**		
Cuando Angola		
100B2 **Santa Cruz do Rio**		
Pardo Brazil		
22A2 **Santa Cruz Mts** USA		
34D2 **Santa Elena** Arg		
33E3 **Santa Elena** Ven		
34C2 **Santa Fe** Arg		
34C2 **Santa Fe** State, Arg		

9C3 Santa Fe USA
35A1 Santa Helena de Goiás Brazil
73B3 Santai China
29B6 Santa Inés I Chile
34B3 Santa Isabel La Pampa, Arg
34C2 Santa Isabel Sante Fe, Arg
107E1 Santa Isabel I Solomon Is
21A2 Santa Lucia Ra USA
21A2 Santa Lucia Range Mts USA
97A4 Santa Luzia I Cape Verde
9B4 Santa Margarita I Mexico
22D4 Santa Margarita R USA
30F4 Santa Maria Brazil
26C4 Santa Maria Colombia
21A3 Santa Maria I Açores
96A1 Santa Maria I Açores
23B1 Santa Maria R Queretaro, Mexico
23A1 Santa Maria del Rio Mexico
32C1 Santa Marta Colombia
22C3 Santa Monica USA
22C4 Santa Monica B USA
29E2 Santana do Livramento Brazil
32B3 Santander Colombia
50B1 Santander Spain
51C2 Santañy Spain
22C3 Santa Paula USA
31C2 Santa Quitéria Brazil
33G4 Santarém Brazil
50A2 Santarém Port
22A1 Santa Rosa California, USA
25D3 Santa Rosa Honduras
34C3 Santa Rosa La Pampa, Arg
34B2 Santa Rosa Mendoza, Arg
34B2 Santa Rosa San Luis, Arg
22B3 Santa Rosa I USA
24A2 Santa Rosalia Mexico
20C2 Santa Rosa Range Mts USA
31D3 Santa Talhada Brazil
35C1 Santa Teresa Brazil
53A2 Santa Teresa di Gallura Sardegna
22B3 Santa Ynez R USA
22B3 Santa Ynez Mts USA
17C1 Santee R USA
47C2 Santhia Italy
34A2 Santiago Chile
27C3 Santiago Dom Rep
32A2 Santiago Panama
79B2 Santiago Phil
32B4 Santiago R Peru
50A1 Santiago de Compostela Spain
26B2 Santiago de Cuba Cuba
30D4 Santiago del Estero Arg
30D4 Santiago del Estero State, Arg
22D4 Santiago Peak Mt USA
31C5 Santo State, Brazil
35A2 Santo Anastácio Brazil
30F4 Santo Angelo Brazil
97A4 Santo Antão I Cape Verde
35A2 Santo Antonio da Platina Brazil
27D3 Santo Domingo Dom Rep
35B2 Santos Brazil
35B2 Santos Dumont Brazil
30E4 Santo Tomé Arg

29B5 San Valentin Mt Chile
34A2 San Vicente Chile
98B3 Sanza Pomba Angola
30E4 São Borja Brazil
35B2 São Carlos Brazil
33G5 São Félix Mato Grosso, Brazil
35C2 São Fidélis Brazil
35C1 São Francisco Brazil
31D3 São Francisco R Brazil
30G4 São Francisco do Sul Brazil
35B1 São Gotardo Brazil
99D3 São Hill Tanz
35C2 São João da Barra Brazil
35B2 São João da Boa Vista Brazil
35C1 São João da Ponte Brazil
35C2 São João del Rei Brazil
35B2 São Joaquim da Barra Brazil
96A1 São Jorge I Açores
35B2 São José do Rio Prêto Brazil
35B2 São José dos Campos Brazil
31C2 São Luis Brazil
35C1 São Marcos R Brazil
35C1 São Maria do Suaçuí Brazil
35D1 São Mateus Brazil
35C1 São Mateus R Brazil
96A1 São Miguel I Açores
49C2 Saône R France
97A4 São Nicolau I Cape Verde
35B2 São Paulo Brazil
35A2 São Paulo State, Brazil
31C3 São Raimundo Nonato Brazil
35B1 São Román Brazil
35B2 São Sebastia do Paraiso Brazil
35A1 São Simão Goias, Brazil
35B2 São Simão Sao Paulo, Brazil
97A4 São Tiago I Cape Verde
97C4 São Tomé I W Africa
97C4 São Tomé and Principe Republic, W Africa
96B2 Saoura Watercourse Alg
35B2 São Vicente Brazil
97A4 São Vincente I Cape Verde
55C2 Sápai Greece
78D4 Sape Indon
97C4 Sapele Nig
74E2 Sapporo Japan
18A2 Sapulpa USA
90A2 Saqqez Iran
10C2 Saquenay R Can
90A2 Sarab Iran
54A2 Sarajevo Bosnia-Herzegovina
90D2 Sarakhs Iran
61J3 Saraktash Russian Fed
63A2 Sarana Russian Fed
15D2 Saranac L USA
15D2 Saranac Lake USA
55B3 Sarandë Alb
79C4 Sarangani Is Phil
61G3 Saransk Russian Fed
61H2 Sarapul Russian Fed
17B2 Sarasota USA
54C1 Sarata Ukraine
15D2 Saratoga Springs USA
78C2 Saratok Malay
61G3 Saratov Russian Fed
61G3 Saratovskoye Vodokhranilishche Res Russian Fed

67F4 Sarawak State, Malay
92A2 Sarayköy Turk
90C3 Sarbisheh Iran
47D1 Sarca R Italy
95A2 Sardalas Libya
90A2 Sar Dasht Iran
52A2 Sardegna I Medit S
 Sardinia = Sardegna
38H5 Sarektjåkkå Mt Sweden
92D3 Sargodha Pak
98B2 Sarh Chad
90B2 Sári Iran
94B2 Sari R Isreal
93D1 Sarikamiş Turk
107D3 Sarina Aust
47B1 Sarine R Switz
90B2 Sar-i-Pul Afghan
95B2 Sarīr Libya
95A2 Sarir Tibesti Desert Libya
74B3 Sariwŏn N Korea
48B2 Sark I UK
92C2 Sarkišla Turk
71E4 Sarmi Indon
29C5 Sarmiento Arg
96B2 Särna Sweden
47C1 Sarnen Switz
14B2 Sarnia Can
58D2 Sarny Ukraine
6E2 Saroaq Greenland
84B2 Sarobi Afghan
78A3 Sarolangun Indon
55B3 Saronikós Kólpos G Greece
47C2 Saronno Italy
55C2 Saros Körfezi B Turk
39G7 Sarpsborg Nor
46D2 Sarralbe France
46D2 Sarrebourg France
46D2 Sarreguemines France
46D2 Sarre-Union France
51B1 Sarrion Spain
85B3 Sarstang Pak
53A2 Sartène Corse
48B2 Sarthe R France
61H4 Sarykamys Kazakhstan
65H5 Sarysu R Kazakhstan
86A2 Sasaram India
74B4 Sasebo Japan
5H4 Saskatchewan Province, Can
5H4 Saskatchewan R Can
13F2 Saskatoon Can
101G1 Sasolburg S Africa
61F3 Sasovo Russian Fed
97B4 Sassandra Ivory Coast
97B4 Sassandra R Ivory Coast
53A2 Sassari Sardegna
56C2 Sassnitz Germany
47D2 Sassuolo Italy
34C2 Sastre Arg
87A1 Sātāra India
4G2 Satellite B Can
78D4 Satengar Is Indon
39H6 Säter Sweden
61J2 Satka Russian Fed
85D2 Satluj R India
86A2 Satna India
85C4 Sātpura Range Mts India
54B1 Satu Mare Rom
34D2 Sauce Arg
39F7 Sauda Nor
80C3 Saudi Arabia Kingdom, Arabian Pen
46D2 Sauer R Germany/Lux
46D1 Sauerland Region, Germany
38B1 Sauðárkrókur Iceland
14A2 Saugatuck USA
16C1 Saugerties USA
13B2 Saugstad,Mt Can
7B5 Sault Sainte Marie Can
14B1 Sault Ste Marie Can

14B1 Sault Ste Marie Can
71E4 Saumlaki Indon
48B2 Saumur France
98C3 Saurimo Angola
27M2 Sauteurs Grenada
54A2 Sava R Serbia, Yugos
97C4 Savalou Benin
14A1 Savannah Georgia, USA
17B1 Savannah R USA
76C2 Savannakhet Laos
26B3 Savanna la Mar Jamaica
7A4 Savant Lake Can
76D2 Savarane Laos
97C4 Savé Benin
101C3 Save R Mozam
90B3 Säveh Iran
46D2 Saverne France
47B2 Savigliano Italy
46B2 Savigny France
49D2 Savoie Region France
49D3 Savona Italy
38K6 Savonlinna Fin
4A3 Savoonga USA
38K5 Savukoski Fin
71D4 Savu S Indon
76A1 Saw Burma
85D3 Sawai Mādhopur India
78A2 Sawang Indon
76B2 Sawankhalok Thai
75C1 Sawara Japan
12E1 Sawtooth Mt USA
106B2 Sawu I Indon
97C3 Say Niger
84B1 Sayghan Afghan
91B5 Sayhut Yemen
61G4 Saykhin Kazakhstan
68D2 Saynshand Mongolia
61H5 Say-Utes Kazakhstan
16C2 Sayville USA
13B2 Sayward Can
57C3 Sázava R Czech Republic
61J2 Sbisseb R Alg
42C2 Scafell Pike Mt Eng
44E1 Scalloway Scot
44C2 Scapa Flow Sd Scot
15C2 Scarborough Can
42D2 Scarborough Eng
27E4 Scarborough Tobago
44A2 Scarp I Scot
45B2 Scarriff Irish Rep
52A1 Schaffhausen Switz
57C3 Scharding Austria
46D1 Scharteberg Mt Germany
7D4 Schefferville Can
46B1 Schelde R Belg
10C2 Schenectady USA
47D2 Schio Italy
46D1 Schleiden Germany
56B2 Schleswig Germany
56B2 Schleswig Holstein State, Germany
16B1 Schoharie USA
71F4 Schouten Is PNG
7B5 Schreiber Can
21B2 Schurz USA
16A2 Schuylkill Haven USA
16B2 Schuylkill R USA
57B3 Schwabische Alb Upland Germany
57B3 Schwarzwald Upland Germany
12C1 Schwatka Mts USA
57C1 Schwei Austria
57C2 Schweinfurt Germany
101G1 Schweizer Reneke S Africa
56C2 Schwerin Germany
47C1 Schwyz Switz
53B3 Sciacca Italy
14B3 Scioto R USA
109D2 Scone Aust
6H2 Scoresby Sd Greenland
103F7 Scotia Ridge Atlantic O
103F7 Scotia S Atlantic O

44B3 Scotland Country,
107D3 Selwyn Aust
4E3 Selwyn Mts Can
78C4 Semarang Indon
61E2 Semenov
Russian Fed
112B7 Scott Base Ant
13B2 Scott,C Can
9C2 Scott City USA
112C6 Scott I Ant
6C2 Scott Inlet B Can
20B2 Scott,Mt USA
106B2 Scott Reef Timor S
8C2 Scottsbluff USA
17A1 Scottsboro USA
109C4 Scottsdale Aust
10C2 Scranton USA
47D1 Scuol Switz
Scutari = Shkodër
5C2 Seal R Can
108B3 Sea Lake Aust
18B2 Searcy USA
22B2 Seaside California,
USA
20B1 Seaside Oregon,
USA
16B3 Seaside Park USA
20B1 Seattle USA
22A1 Sebastopol USA
58D1 Sebez Russian Fed
17B2 Sebring USA
111A3 Secretary I NZ
87A3 Sedalia USA
46C2 Sedan France
111B2 Seddonville NZ
94B3 Sede Boqer Israel
94B3 Sederot Israel
97A3 Sédhiou Sen
84B3 Sedom Israel
100A3 Seeheim Namibia
111B2 Sefton,Mt NZ
77C5 Segamat Malay
51B2 Segorbe Spain
97B3 Ségou Mali
Segovia = Coco
50B1 Segovia Spain
51C1 Segre R Spain
97B4 Séguéla Ivory Coast
96A2 Seguia el Hamra
Watercourse Mor
34C2 Segundo R Arg
78D2 Segundu Indon
50D2 Segura R Spain
85B3 Sehwan Pak
46D2 Seille R France
38J6 Seinäjoki Fin
48C2 Seine R France
46B2 Seine-et-Marne
Department, France
99D3 Sekenke Tanz
99D1 Sek'ot'a Eth
71E4 Selaru I Indon
78D4 Selat Alas Str Indon
78B3 Selat Bangka Str
Indon
78A3 Selat Berhala B
Indon
71E4 Selat Dampier Str
78B3 Selat Gaspar Str
Indon
78D4 Selat Lombok Str
Indon
78D4 Selat Sape Str Indon
78B4 Selat Sunda Str
Indon
71D4 Selat Wetar Chan
Indon
12B1 Selawik USA
12C1 Selawik R USA
12B1 Selawik L USA
42D3 Selby Eng
54C1 Selçuk Turk
12D3 Seldovia USA
100B3 Selebi Pikwe
Botswana
6H3 Selfoss Iceland
95B2 Selima Oasis Sudan
5J4 Selkirk Can
42C2 Selkirk Scot
13D2 Selkirk Mts Can
22C2 Selma California,
USA
50B2 Selouane Mor
12H2 Selous,Mt Can
78B3 Selta Karimata Str
Indon
32C5 Selvas Region, Brazil

12C3 Semidi Is USA
60E3 Seminlalik Russian Fed
19A2 Seminole Oklahoma,
USA
17B1 Seminole,L USA
65K4 Sempalatinsk
Kazakhstan
79B3 Semirara Is Phil
90B3 Semirom Iran
78C2 Semitau Indon
90B2 Semnan Iran
46C2 Semois R Belg
23B2 Sempoala Hist Site,
Mexico
32D5 Sena Madureira
Brazil
100B2 Senanga Zambia
19C3 Senatobia USA
74E3 Sendai Honshū,
Japan
74C4 Sendai Kyūshū,
Japan
85D4 Sendwha India
15C2 Seneca Falls USA
97A3 Senegal Republic,
Africa
97A3 Sénégal R Maur Sen
101G1 Senekal S Africa
31D4 Senhor do Bonfim
Brazil
52B2 Senigallia Italy
52C2 Senj Croatia
69E4 Senkaku Gunto Is
Japan
46B2 Senlis France
97D3 Sennar Sudan
7C5 Sennetere Can
49C2 Sens France
54A1 Senta Serbia, Yugos
98C3 Sentery Zaire
13C2 Sentinel Peak Mt
Can
85D4 Seoni India
110B2 Seoul = Soul
76D2 Separation Pt NZ
7D4 Sepone Laos
95A2 Sept-Iles Can
72C4 Séquédine Niger
71D4 Sequoia Nat Pk, USA
71B4 Serang Indon
78B4 Serang Indon
78B2 Serasan I Indon
54A2 Serbia Republic,
Yugos
61F3 Serdobsk
Russian Fed
77C5 Seremban Malay
99D3 Serengeti Nat Pk
Tanz
100C2 Serenje Zambia
59D3 Seret R Ukraine
61G2 Sergach Russian Fed
31D4 Sergipe State, Brazil
60E2 Segiyev Posad
Russian Fed
78C2 Seria Brunei
78C2 Serian Malay
55B3 Sérifos I Greece
47C2 Serio R Italy
95B2 Serir Calanscio
Desert Libya
46C2 Sermaize-les-Bains
France
71D4 Sermata I Indon
61H3 Sernovodsk
Russian Fed
65H4 Serov Russian Fed
100B3 Serowe Botswana
50A2 Serpa Port
60E3 Serpukhov
Russian Fed
35B2 Serra da Canastra
Mts Brazil
50A1 Serra da Estrela Mts
Port
35B2 Serra da Mantiqueira
Mts Brazil
35A1 Serra da Mombuca
Brazil

35C1 Serra do Cabral Mt
Brazil
33F5 Serra do Cachimbo
Mts Brazil
35A1 Serra do Caiapó Mts
Brazil
35A2 Serra do Cantu Mts
Brazil
35C2 Serra do Caparaó
Mts Brazil
31C5 Serra do Chifre Brazil
35C1 Serra do Espinhaço
Mts Brazil
35B2 Serra do Mar Mts
Brazil
35A2 Serra do Mirante Mts
Brazil
33G3 Serra do Navio Brazil
35B2 Serra do
Paranapiacaba Mts
Brazil
33F6 Serra dos Caiabis
Mts Brazil
35A2 Serra dos Dourados
Mts Brazil
33E6 Serra dos Parecis
Mts Brazil
35B1 Serra dos Pilões Mts
Brazil
35A1 Serra Dourada Mts
Brazil
33F6 Serra Formosa Mts
Brazil
55B2 Sérrai Greece
25D3 Serrana Bank Is
Caribbean S
51B1 Serrana de Cuenca
Mts Spain
35A1 Serranópolis Brazil
33E3 Serra Pararaima Mts
Brazil/Ven
33E3 Serra Parima Mts
Brazil
33G3 Serra Tumucumaque
Brazil
54A2 Serre R France
34B2 Serrezuela Arg
31D4 Serrinha Brazil
6G3 Serrmilik Greenland
35C1 Serro Brazil
35A2 Sertanópolis Brazil
72A3 Sertar China
78C3 Seruyan R Indon
100A2 Sesfontein Namibia
100B2 Sesheke Zambia
74D2 Setana Japan
49C3 Sète France
35C1 Sete Lagoas Brazil
96C1 Sétif Alg
75B1 Seto Japan
75A2 Seto Naikai S Japan
96B1 Settat Mor
42C2 Settle Eng
5G4 Settler Can
50A2 Sétubal Port
93E1 Sevan,Oz L Armenia
60D5 Sevastopol' Ukraine
7B4 Severn R Can
43C3 Severn R Eng
1B9 Severnaya Zemlya I
Russian Fed
63C2 Severo-Baykalskoye
Nagorye Mts
Russian Fed
60E4 Severo Donets
Ukraine
64E3 Severodvinsk
Russian Fed
64H3 Severo Sos'va R
Russian Fed
8B3 Sevier R USA
8B3 Sevier L USA
50A2 Sevilla Spain
Seville = Sevilla
54C2 Sevlievo Bulg
97A4 Sewa R Sierra Leone
12E2 Seward Alaska, USA
18A1 Seward Nebraska,
USA
12A1 Seward Pen USA
13D1 Sexsmith Can
89K8 Seychelles Is
Indian O
38C1 Seyðisfjörður Iceland

92C2 Seyhan Turk
60E3 Seym R Russian Fed
108C3 Seymour Aust
16C2 Seymour
Connecticut, USA
14A3 Seymour Indiana,
USA
46B2 Sézanne France
96D1 Sfax Tunisia
54C1 Sfinto Gheorghe
Rom
56A2 's-Gravenhage Neth
72B3 Shaanxi Province,
China
98C3 Shabunda Zaire
82B2 Shache China
112C9 Shackleton Ice Shelf
Ant
85B3 Shadadkot Pak
91B3 Shādhām R Iran
43C4 Shaftesbury Eng
29G8 Shag Rocks Is
South Georgia
90A3 Shāhābād Iran
91C3 Shahbad Iran
86A2 Shahdol India
90A2 Shāhīn Dezh Iran
90C3 Shāh Kūh Iran
91C3 Shahr-e Bābak Iran
Shahresa = Qomisheh
90B3 Shahr Kord Iran
87B1 Shājābād India
84D3 Shājahanpur India
85D4 Shājapur India
61F4 Shakhty Russian Fed
61G2 Shakhun'ya
Russian Fed
97C4 Shaki Nig
12B2 Shaktoolik USA
61J2 Shamary
Russian Fed
99D2 Shambe Sudan
16A2 Shamokin USA
16B1 Shandaken USA
72D2 Shandong Province,
China
73C5 Shangchuan Dao I
China
72C1 Shangdu China
73E3 Shanghai China
73C3 Shangnan China
100B2 Shangombo Zambia
73D4 Shangrao China
73B5 Shangsi China
73C3 Shang Xian China
41B3 Shannon R Irish Rep
72D3 Shanqiu China
74B2 Shansonggang China
63F2 Shantarskiye Ostrova
I Russian Fed
73D5 Shantou China
72C2 Shanxi Province,
China
73C3 Shan Xian China
73C5 Shaoguan China
73E4 Shaoxing China
73D4 Shaoyang China
44C2 Shapinsay I Scot
75C2 Shaqqā Syria
72A1 Sharhulsan Mongolia
90C2 Sharīfābād Iran
91C4 Sharjah UAE
106A3 Shark B Aust
90C2 Sharlauk
Turkmenistan
94B2 Sharon,Plain of Israel
61G2 Sharya Russian Fed
99D2 Shashemenē Eth
73C3 Shashi China
20B2 Shasta L USA
20B2 Shasta,Mt USA
93E3 Shatt al Gharraf R
Iraq
94B3 Shaubak Jordan
13F3 Shaunavon Can
22C2 Shaver L USA
16B2 Shawangunk Mt
USA
15D1 Shawinigan Can
19A2 Shawnee Oklahoma,
USA
73D4 Sha Xian China
106B3 Shay Gap Aust
94C2 Shaykh Miskin Syria

99E1 Shaykh 'Uthmān Yemen
60E3 Shchekino Russian Fed
60E3 Shchigry Russian Fed
60D3 Shchors Ukraine
65J4 Shchuchinsk Kazakhstan
99E2 Shebele R Eth
14A2 Sheboygan USA
98B2 Shebshi Mts Nig
12F1 Sheenjek R USA
45C1 Sheep Haven Estuary Irish Rep
43E4 Sheerness Eng
94B2 Shefar'am Israel
42D3 Sheffield Eng
84C2 Shekhupura Pak
13B1 Shelagyote Peak Mt Can
16C1 Shelburne Falls USA
14A2 Shelby Michigan, USA
8B2 Shelby Montana, USA
14A3 Shelbyville Indiana, USA
12H2 Sheldon,Mt Can
12D3 Shelikof Str USA
109D2 Shellharbour Aust
111A3 Shelter Pt NZ
20B1 Shelton USA
93E1 Shemakha Azerbaijan
18A1 Shenandoah USA
15C3 Shenandoah R USA
15C3 Shenandoah Nat Pk USA
97C4 Shendam Nig
95C2 Shendi Sudan
72C2 Shenmu China
72E1 Shenyang China
73C5 Shenzhen China
85D3 Sheopur India
59D2 Shepetovka Ukraine
108C3 Shepparton Aust
6B2 Sherard,C Can
43C4 Sherborne Eng
97A4 Sherbro I Sierra Leone
15D1 Sherbrooke Can
85C3 Shergarh India
19B3 Sheridan Arkansas, USA
8C2 Sheridan Wyoming, USA
19A3 Sherman USA
56B2 s-Hertogenbosch Neth
12H3 Sheslay Can
40C1 Shetland Is Scot
91B4 Sheyk Sho'eyb I Iran
69H2 Shiashkotan I Russian Fed
84B1 Shibarghan Afghan
74D3 Shibata Japan
95C1 Shibīn el Kom Egypt
75B1 Shibukawa Japan
72C2 Shijiazhuang China
84B3 Shikarpur Pak
67G3 Shikoku I Japan
75A2 Shikoku-sanchi Mts Japan
86B1 Shiliguri India
68D1 Shilka Russian Fed
68D1 Shilka R Russian Fed
16B2 Shillington USA
97C4 Shillong India
61F3 Shilovo Russian Fed
75A2 Shimabara Japan
75B2 Shimada Japan
69E1 Shimanovsk Russian Fed
74D3 Shimizu Japan
84D2 Shimla India
75B2 Shimoda Japan
74C4 Shimonoseki Japan
75B1 Shinano R Japan
91C5 Shinās Oman
75C1 Shingū Japan
74D3 Shinjo Japan
74D3 Shinminato Japan
94C1 Shinshār Syria

99D3 Shinyanga Tanz
74E3 Shiogama Japan
75B2 Shiono-misaki C Japan
73A5 Shiping China
16A2 Shippensburg USA
72B3 Shiquan China
75C1 Shirakawa Japan
75B1 Shirane-san Mt Japan
75B1 Shirani-san Mt Japan
91B4 Shiraz Iran
90B3 Shīr Kūh Iran
75B1 Shirotori Japan
90C2 Shirvan Iran
12A1 Shishmaref USA
12A1 Shishmaref Inlet USA
84B3 Shishmaret China
72B2 Shitanjing China
14A3 Shively USA
85D3 Shivpuri India
94B3 Shivta Hist Site Israel
101C2 Shiwa Ngandu Zambia
72C3 Shiyan China
72B2 Shizuishan China
75B1 Shizuoka Japan
54A2 Shkodër Alb
109D2 Shoalhaven R Aust
75A2 Shobara Japan
87B2 Shoranūr India
87B1 Shorāpur India
21B2 Shoshone Mts USA
60D3 Shostka Ukraine
19B3 Shreveport USA
43C3 Shrewsbury Eng
43C3 Shropshire County, Eng
72E1 Shuanglia China
69F2 Shuangyashan China
61J4 Shubar-Kuduk Kazakhstan
72D2 Shu He R China
73A4 Shucheng China
74C3 Shujaabad Pak
85D4 Shujālpur India
68B2 Shule He China
54C2 Shumen Bulg
61G2 Shumerlya Russian Fed
73D4 Shuncheng China
12C1 Shungnak USA
72C2 Shuo Xian China
91C4 Shūr Gaz Iran
100B2 Shurugwi Zim
13D2 Shuswap L Can
61F2 Shuya Russian Fed
12D3 Shuyak I USA
82D3 Shwebo Burma
76B2 Shwegyin Burma
84A2 Siah Koh Mts Afghan
84C2 Sialkot Pak
Sian = Xi'an
79C4 Siarao I Phil
79B4 Siaton Phil
58C1 Šiauliai Lithuania
65G4 Šibay Russian Fed
101H1 Sibayi L S Africa
52C2 Šibenik Croatia
54C4 Siberut I Indon
84B3 Sibi Pak
68C1 Sibirskoye Russian Fed
98B3 Sibiti Congo
99D3 Sibiti R Tanz
54B1 Sibiu Rom
70A3 Sibolga Indon
86C1 Sibsagar India
78C2 Sibu Malay
79B4 Sibuguey B Phil
98B2 Sibut CAR
79B3 Sibuyan I Phil
79B3 Sibuyan S Phil
73A3 Sichuan Province, China
53B3 Sicilia / Medit S
53B3 Sicilian Chan Italy/ Tunisia
Sicily = Sicilia
32C6 Sicuani Peru
85C4 Siddhapur India

87B1 Siddipet India
86A2 Sidhi India
95B1 Sidi Barrani Egypt
96B1 Sidi Bel Abbès Alg
96B1 Sidi Kacem Mor
44C3 Sidlaw Hills Scot
112B5 Sidley,Mt Ant
20B1 Sidney Can
8C2 Sidney Nebraska, USA
15C2 Sidney New York, USA
14B2 Sidney Ohio, USA
17B1 Sidney Lanier,L USA
Sidon = Säida
52C3 Siedlce Pol
46D1 Sieg R Germany
46D1 Siegburg Germany
46D1 Siegen Germany
76C3 Siem Reap Camb
52B2 Siena Italy
58B2 Sierpc Pol
23B2 Sierra Andrés Tuxtla Mexico
34B3 Sierra Auca Mahuida Mts Arg
9C3 Sierra Blanca USA
51B1 Sierra de Albarracin Mts Spain
50B2 Sierra de Alcaraz Mts Spain
34B2 Sierra de Cordoba Mts Arg
50A2 Sierra de Gredos Mts Spain
50A2 Sierra de Guadalupe Mts Spain
50B1 Sierra de Guadarrama Mts Spain
51B1 Sierra de Guara Mts Spain
51B1 Sierra de Gudar Mts Spain
23B2 Sierra de Juárez Mexico
34C3 Sierra de la Ventana Mts Arg
51B1 Sierra del Codi Mts Spain
34B2 Sierra del Morro Mt Arg
34B3 Sierra del Nevado Mts Arg
24B2 Sierra de los Alamitos Mts Mexico
50B2 Sierra de los Filabres Spain
23A1 Sierra de los Huicholes Mexico
23B2 Sierra de Miahuatlán Mexico
23A1 Sierra de Morones Mts Mexico
50A2 Sierra de Ronda Mts Spain
34B2 Sierra de San Luis Mts Arg
50B2 Sierra de Segura Mts Spain
50B1 Sierra de Urbion Mts Spain
34B2 Sierra de Uspallata Mts Arg
34B2 Sierra de Valle Fértil Mts Arg
23B2 Sierra de Zongolica Mexico
34C2 Sierra Grande Mts Arg
97A4 Sierra Leone Republic, Africa
97A4 Sierra Leone,C Sierra Leone
79B2 Sierra Madre Mts Phil
23A2 Sierra Madre del Sur Mts Mexico
24B2 Sierra Madre Occidental Mts Mexico
24C2 Sierra Madre Oriental Mts Mexico

34B2 Sierra Malanzan Mts Arg
9C4 Sierra Mojada Mexico
50A2 Sierra Morena Mts Spain
50B2 Sierra Nevada Mts Spain
21A2 Sierra Nevada Mts USA
32C1 Sierra Nevada de Santa Marta Mts Colombia
34B2 Sierra Pié de Palo Mts Arg
47B1 Sierre Switz
55B3 Sifnos I Greece
59C3 Sighetu Marmaţiei Rom
54B1 Sighişoara Rom
38B1 Siglufjörður Iceland
18C2 Sikeston USA
55C3 Síkinos I Greece
55B3 Sikionía Greece
86B1 Sikkim State, India
50A1 Sil R Spain
47D1 Silandro Italy
23A1 Silao Mexico
79B3 Silay Phil
86C2 Silchar India
96C2 Silet Alg
86A1 Silgarhi Nepal
92B2 Silifke Turk
82C2 Siling Co L China
54A2 Silistra Bulg
39F7 Silkeborg Den
47E1 Sillian Austria
18B2 Siloam Springs USA
19B3 Silsbee USA
95A3 Silsu Well Chad
58C1 Šilute Lithuania
93D2 Silvan Turk
35B1 Silvania Brazil
85C4 Silvassa India
21B2 Silver City Nevada, USA
9C3 Silver City New Mexico, USA
20B2 Silver Lake USA
16A3 Silver Spring USA
13B2 Silverthrone Mt Can
108B2 Silverton Aust
47C1 Silvretta Mts Austria/Switz
78C2 Simanggang Malay
76C1 Simao China
90A3 Simareh R Iran
92A2 Simav Turk
55C3 Simav R Turk
61G3 Simbirsk Russian Fed
12C1 Simcoe,L Can
70A3 Simeulue I Indon
60D5 Simferopol' Ukraine
55C3 Sími I Greece
46D1 Simmern Germany
13B2 Simoon Sound Can
49D2 Simplon Mt Switz
47C1 Simplon P Switz
4C2 Simpson,C USA
106C3 Simpson Desert Aust
6B3 Simpson Pen Can
39G7 Simrishamn Sweden
69H2 Simushir I Russian Fed
99E2 Sina Dhaqa Somalia
92B4 Sinai Pen Egypt
32B2 Sincelejo Colombia
17B1 Sinclair,L USA
85D3 Sind R India
85B3 Sindh Region, Pak
86B2 Sindri India
92A2 Sines Port
99D1 Singa Sudan

77C5 Singapore Republic,
S E Asia
77C5 Singapore,Str of
S E Asia
78D4 Sinagraja Indon
99D3 Singida Tanz
78B2 Singkawang Indon
109D2 Singleton Aust
78A3 Singtep I Indon
76B1 Singu Burma
53A2 Siniscola Sardgena
93D2 Sinjar Iraq
84B2 Sinkai Hills Mts
Afghan
95C3 Sinkat Sudan
82C1 Sinkiang
Autonomous Region,
China
33G2 Sinnamary French
Guiana
92C1 Sinop Turk
54B1 Sintana Rom
78C2 Sintang Indon
50A2 Sintra Port
32B2 Sinú R Colombia
74A2 Sinüiju N Korea
51C6 Siofok Hung
47B1 Sion Switz
8D2 Sioux City USA
8D2 Sioux Falls USA
10A2 Sioux Lookout Can
79B4 Sipalay Phil
27L1 Siparia Trinidad
69E2 Siping China
112B3 Siple Base Ant
112B5 Siple I Ant
79B3 Sipocot Phil
70A4 Sipora Indon
79B4 Siquijor I Phil
13E1 Siracusa Italy
86B2 Sirajganj Bang
13C2 Sir Alexander,Mt Can
91B5 Sir Bani Yás I UAE
106C2 Sir Edward Pellew
Group Is Aust
54C1 Siret R Rom
12J2 Sir James
McBrien,Mt Can
87B2 Sir Kälahasti India
13D2 Sir Laurier,Mt Can
93D2 Sirnak Turk
85C4 Sirohi India
87B1 Sironcha India
85D4 Sironj India
55B3 Siros I Greece
91B4 Sirri I Iran
44D3 Sirsa India
13D2 Sir Sandford,Mt Can
87A2 Sirsi India
95A1 Sirte Desert Libya
95A1 Sirte,G of Libya
52C1 Sisak Croatia
76C2 Sisaket Thai
76C3 Sisophon Camb
46B2 Sissonne France
90D3 Sistan Region, Iran/
Afghan
49D3 Sisteron France
63B2 Sistig Khem
Russian Fed
86A1 Sitapur India
55C3 Sitia Greece
4E4 Sitka USA
12D3 Sitkalidak I USA
12D3 Sitkinak I USA
76B2 Sittang R Burma
46C1 Sittard Neth
86C2 Sittwe Burma
78C4 Situbondo Indon
92C2 Sivas Turk
93C2 Siverek Turk
92B2 Sivrihisar Turk
95B2 Siwa Egypt
84D2 Siwalik Range Mts
India
86A1 Siwalik Range Mts
Nepal
72D3 Siyang China
56C1 Sjaelland I Den
39G7 Skagen Den
39F7 Skagerrak Str Nor/
Den
20B1 Skagit R Can
20B1 Skagit Mt Can

4E4 Skagway USA
39G7 Skara Sweden
59C2 Skarzysko-Kamlenna
Pol
5F4 Skeena R Can
13B1 Skeena Mts Can
4D3 Skeenjek R USA
42E3 Skegness Eng
38H5 Skellefte R Sweden
38H6 Skelleftea Sweden
55B3 Skiathos I Greece
45B3 Skibbereen Irish Rep
5E4 Skidegate Can
58C2 Skiemiewice Pol
39F7 Skien Nor
96C1 Skikda Alg
74C4 Skikoku I Japan
42D3 Skipton Eng
55B3 Skiros I Greece
39F7 Skive Den
56B1 Skjern Den
6F3 Skjoldungen
Greenland
14A2 Skokie USA
55B3 Skópelos I Greece
54B2 Skopje Macedonia,
Yugos
39G7 Skovde Sweden
63E2 Skovorodino
Russian Fed
4E3 Skwentna USA
78B2 Skwierzyna Pol
40B2 Skye I Scot
39G7 Slagelse Den
45C2 Slaney R Irish Rep
54B2 Slatina Rom
78C4 Slaung Indon
5G3 Slave R Can
13E1 Slave Lake Can
65J4 Slavgorod
Russian Fed
59D2 Slavuta Ukraine
60E4 Slavyansk Ukraine
44B3 Sleat,Sound of Chan
Scot
12C2 Sleetmute USA
45C2 Sleeve Bloom Mts
Irish Rep
19C3 Slidell USA
16B2 Slide Mt USA
45B1 Sligo County,
Irish Rep
41B3 Sligo Irish Rep
41B3 Sligo B Irish Rep
54C2 Sliven Bulg
54C2 Slobozia Rom
13D3 Slocan Can
58D2 Slonim Belorussia
43D4 Slough Eng
22B2 Slough R USA
59B3 Slovakia Republic,
Europe
52B1 Slovenia Republic,
Europe
56C2 Slubice Pol
59D2 Sluch' R Ukraine
58B2 Slupsk Pol
58D2 Slutsk Belorussia
58D2 Slutsk R Belorussia
41A3 Slyne Head Pt
Irish Rep
63C2 Slyudyanka
Russian Fed
7D4 Smallwood Res Can
54B2 Smederevo Serbia,
Yugos
54B2 Smederevska Palanka
Serbia, Yugos
60D4 Smela Ukraine
15C2 Smethport USA
13E1 Smith Arm B Can
4F3 Smith Arm B Can
13B2 Smithers Can
7C3 Smith I Can
Smith Sd Can
15C2 Smiths Falls Can
109C4 Smithton Aust
13D1 Smoky R Can
109D2 Smoky C Aust
13E2 Smoky Lake Can
38F6 Smola I Nor
60D3 Smolensk
Russian Fed
55B2 Smólikas Mt Greece
54B2 Smolyan Bulg

58D2 Smorgon' Belorussia
16B3 Smyrna Delaware,
USA
17B1 Smyrna Georgia,
USA
42B2 Snaefell Mt Eng
38B2 Snafell Mt Iceland
8B2 Snake R USA
8B2 Snake River Canyon
USA
56B2 Sneek Neth
45B3 Sneem Irish Rep
22B2 Snelling USA
59B2 Snêžka Mt Pol/
Czech Republic
38F6 Snohetta Mt Nor
20B1 Snohomish USA
20B1 Snoqualmie P USA
76D3 Snoul Camb
43B3 Snowdon Mt Wales
43B3 Snowdonia Nat Pk
Wales
4G3 Snowdrift Can
5H4 Snow Lake Can
108A2 Snowtown Aust
109C3 Snowy Mts Aust
5J3 Snyder USA
74B4 Soan-kundo I S
Korea
99D2 Sobat R Sudan
31C2 Sobral Brazil
58C2 Sochaczew Pol
61E5 Sochi Russian Fed
9C3 Socorro USA
24A3 Socorro I Mexico
34A2 Socos Chile
81C4 Socotra I Yemen
38K5 Sodankyla Fin
39H6 Soderham Sweden
39H7 Södertälje Sweden
99C1 Sodiri Sudan
99D2 Sodo Eth
46E1 Soest Germany
101C2 Sofala Mozam
Sofia = Sofiya
39G6 Sofiya Bulg
69G4 Sofu Gan I Japan
32C2 Sogamoso Colombia
39F6 Sognefjorden Inlet
Nor
68D2 Sog Xian China
95C2 Sohâg Egypt
84D3 Sohipat India
46B1 Soignies Belg
46B2 Soissons France
45C2 Sojat India
74A3 Sŏjosŏn-man B
N Korea
92A2 Sŏke Turk
97C4 Sokodé Togo
61E2 Sokol Russian Fed
58C2 Sokolka Pol
97B3 Sokolo Mali
6H3 Sokongens Øy I
Greenland
99D1 Sokota Eth
97C3 Sokoto Nig
97C3 Sokoto R Nig
111A3 Solander I NZ
79B2 Solano Phil
87B1 Solapur India
47D1 Solbad Hall Austria
47D1 Sölden Austria
12D2 Soldotna USA
26C4 Soledad Colombia
43D4 Solent Sd Eng
46B1 Solesmes France
53E2 Soligorsk Belorussia
61J2 Solikamsk
Russian Fed
32C4 Solimões R Peru
38H6 Solingen Germany
38H6 Solleftea Sweden
61H3 Sol'Iletsk
Russian Fed
70B4 Solok Indon
105G4 Solomon Is Pacific O
47B1 Solothurn Switz
39F8 Soltau Germany
22B3 Solvang USA
42C2 Solway Firth Estuary
Eng/Scot
100B2 Solwezi Zambia
75C1 Sōma Japan
55C3 Soma Turk

81C5 Somalia Republic, E
Africa
54A1 Sombor Serbia,
Yugos
107D2 Somerset Aust
43C4 Somerset County,
Eng
16D2 Somerset
Massachusetts, USA
15C2 Somerset
Pennsylvania, USA
100B4 Somerset East
S Africa
6A2 Somerset I Can
16B3 Somers Point USA
16B3 Somerville USA
19A3 Somerville Res USA
54B1 Somes R Rom
46B2 Somme Department,
France
46B2 Somme R France
46C2 Sommesous France
86A2 Son R India
74A3 Sonch'ŏn N Korea
39F8 Sønderborg Den
6E3 Søndre Stromfjord
Greenland
47C1 Sondrio Italy
76D3 Song Ba R Viet
76D3 Song Cau Viet
101C2 Songea Tanz
73A3 Songjiang China
77C4 Songkhla Thai
74B3 Songnim N Korea
77C5 Song Pahang R
Malay
72A3 Songpan China
72C1 Sonid Youqi China
76C1 Son La Viet
85B3 Sonmiani Pak
85B3 Sonmiani Bay Pak
22A1 Sonoma USA
22B2 Sonora California,
USA
24A2 Sonora R Mexico
9B3 Sonoran Desert USA
22C1 Sonora P USA
25D3 Sonsonate El
Salvador
71E3 Sonsorol I Pacific O
10B2 Soo Canals Can/USA
13C2 Sooke Can
58B2 Sopot Pol
59B3 Sopron Hung
22B2 Soquel USA
52B2 Sora Italy
94B3 Sored R Israel
15D1 Sorel Can
109C4 Sorell Aust
92C2 Sorgun Turk
50B1 Soria Spain
38J5 Sørkjosen Nor
64C2 Serksop I Barents S
61H4 Sor Mertvyy Kultuk
Plain Kazakhstan
35B2 Sorocaba Brazil
61H3 Sorochinsk
Russian Fed
71F3 Soroi I Pacific O
60C4 Soroki Moldavia
71E4 Sorong Indon
71E4 Sorong Province,
Indon
99D2 Soroti Uganda
38J4 Sorøya I Nor
53B2 Sorrento Italy
38K5 Sorsatunturi Mt Fin
38H5 Sorsele Sweden
79B3 Sorsogon Phil
48C3 Sortavala
Russian Fed
74B3 Sŏsan S Korea
59B2 Sosnowiec Pol
65H4 Sos'va Russian Fed
98B2 Souanké Congo
97B4 Soubré Ivory Coast
16B2 Souderton USA
27P2 Soufrière St Lucia
27N2 Soufrière Mt
St Vincent and the
Grenadines
48C3 Souillac France
96C1 Souk Ahras Alg
51C2 Souk el Arba du
Rharb Mor
74B3 Soul S Korea
51C2 Soummam R Alg

Sour = Tyr
101G1 Sources,Mt aux
Lesotho
31D3 Sousa Brazil
96D1 Sousse Tunisia
100B4 South Africa
Republic, Africa
16B2 South Amboy USA
14B2 Southampton Can
43D4 Southampton Eng
16C2 Southampton USA
6B3 Southampton I Can
28F6 South Atlantic O
7D4 South Aulatsivik I
Can
106C3 South Australia
State, Aust
104E5 South Australian
Basin Indian O
19C3 Southaven USA
17B2 South Bay USA
14B1 South Baymouth
Can
14A2 South Bend Indiana,
USA
20B1 South Bend
Washington, USA
16D1 Southbridge USA
South Cape = Ka Lae
17B2 South Carolina State,
USA
70C2 South China S
S E Asia
8C2 South Dakota State,
USA
16C1 South Deerfield USA
43D4 South Downs Eng
19C4 South East C Aust
111A2 Southen Alps Mts
NZ
5H4 Southend Can
43E4 Southend-on-Sea
Eng
111A2 Southern Alps Mts
NZ
106A4 Southern Cross Aust
5J4 Southern Indian L
Can
27H2 Southfield Jamaica
105G5 South Fiji Basin
Pacific O
12D2 South Fork R Alaska,
USA
22B1 South Fork R
California, USA
28F8 South Georgia I
S Atlantic O
43C4 South Glamorgan
County, Wales
14A2 South Haven USA
5J3 South Henik L Can
104F3 South Honshu Ridge
Pacific O
111A2 South I NZ
74B3 South Korea
Republic, S E Asia
21A2 South Lake Tahoe
USA
112C8 South Magnetic Pole
Ant
17B2 South Miami USA
16A3 South Mt USA
4F3 South Nahanni R
Can
27B3 South Negril Pt
Jamaica
103F8 South Orkney Is
Atlantic O
8C2 South Platte R USA
80E South Pole Ant
42C3 Southport Eng
27R3 South Pt Barbados
16B2 South River USA
44C2 South Ronaldsay I
Scot
103G7 South Sandwich
Trench Atlantic O
22A2 South San Francisco
USA
5H4 South Saskatchewan
R Can
42D2 South Shields Eng
110B1 South Taranaki Bight
B NZ

44A3 South Uist I Scot
South West Africa =
Namibia
107D5 South West C Aust
105J5 South West Pacific
Basin Pacific O
103D5 South West Peru
Ridge Pacific O
43D3 South Yorkshire
County, Eng
58C1 Sovetsk Russian Fed
61G2 Sovetsk Russian Fed
101G1 Soweto S Africa
98B3 Soyo Congo Angola
60D3 Sozh R Belorussia
46C1 Spa Belg
50A1 Spain Kingdom
Spalato = Split
8J3 Spalding Eng
14B1 Spanish R Can
26B3 Spanish Town
Jamaica
21B2 Sparks USA
11B3 Spartanburg USA
55B3 Sparti Greece
69F2 Spassk Dal'niy
Russian Fed
27R3 Speightstown
Barbados
12E2 Spenard USA
14A3 Spencer Indiana,
USA
8D2 Spencer Iowa, USA
6A3 Spencer Bay Can
108A3 Spencer,C Aust
108A2 Spencer G Aust
6C3 Spencer I USA
111B2 Spenser Mts NZ
45C1 Sperrin Mts N Ire
44C3 Spey R Scot
57B3 Speyer Germany
27R1 Speyside Tobago
47B1 Spiez Switz
12F1 Spike Mt USA
20C1 Spirit Lake USA
5G4 Spirit River Can
Spitsbergen =
Svalbard
64C2 Spitsbergen I
Barents S
57C3 Spittal Austria
38F6 Spjelkavik Nor
52C2 Split Croatia
47C1 Splügen Switz
55C3 Sporádhes Is Greece
20C2 Spokane USA
22C2 Spray USA
56C2 Spree R Germany
100A3 Springbok S Africa
18B2 Springdale USA
10B3 Springfield Illinois,
USA
16C1 Springfield
Massachusetts, USA
18B2 Springfield Missouri,
USA
10B3 Springfield Ohio,
USA
20B2 Springfield Oregon,
USA
15D2 Springfield Vermont,
USA
100B4 Springfontein
S Africa
101G1 Springs S Africa
41D3 Spurn Head Pt Eng
13C3 Squamish Can
60E3 Sredne-Russkaya
Vozvyshennost
Upland Russian Fed
63B1 Sredne Sibirskaya
Ploskogor've
Tableland
Russian Fed
61J2 Sredniy Ural Mts
Russian Fed
76D3 Srepok R Camb
68D1 Sretensk
Russian Fed
76C3 Sre Umbell Camb
83C5 Sri Lanka Republic, S
Asia
84C2 Srinagar Pak
87A1 Srivardhan India
58B2 Sroda Wlk. Pol

30H6 Sta Clara I Chile
22J7 Sta Cruz I Ecuador
56B2 Stade Germany
44A3 Staffa I Scot
43C3 Stafford County, Eng
43C3 Stafford Eng
16C2 Stafford Springs
USA
Stalingrad =
Volgograd
6A1 Stallworthy,C Can
59C2 Stalowa Wola Pol
32J7 Sta Maria I Ecuador
16B1 Stamford
Connecticut, USA
16B1 Stamford New York,
USA
100A3 Stampriet Namibia
101G1 Standerton S Africa
14B2 Standish USA
101H1 Stanger S Africa
22B2 Stanislaus R USA
54B2 Stanke Dimitrov
Bulg
109C4 Stanley Aust
29E6 Stanley Falkland Is
87B2 Stanley Res India
Stanleyville =
Kisangani
25D3 Stann Creek Belize
63E2 Stanovoy Khrebet
Mts Russian Fed
47C1 Stans Switz
109D1 Stanthorpe Aust
59C2 Starachowice Pol
54B2 Stara Planina Mts
Bulg
60D2 Staraya Russa
Russian Fed
54C2 Stara Zagora Bulg
58B2 Stargard Szczecinski
Pol
19C3 Starkville USA
57C3 Starnberg Germany
58B2 Starogard Gdanski
Pol
59D3 Starokonstantinov
Ukraine
43C4 Start Pt Eng
60E3 Staryy Oskol
Russian Fed
15C2 State College USA
16B2 Staten I USA
17B1 Statesboro USA
15C3 Staunton USA
39F7 Stavanger Nor
46C1 Stavelot Belg
61F4 Stavropol'
Russian Fed
108B3 Stawell Aust
58B2 Stawno Pol
20B2 Stayton USA
12B2 Stebbins USA
16A2 Steele,Mt Can
16A2 Steelton USA
20C2 Steens Mt USA
6E2 Steenstrups
Gletscher Gl
Greenland
4H2 Stefansson I Can
101H1 Stegi Swaziland
47D1 Steinach Austria
8D2 Steinbach Can
38G6 Steinkjer Nor
13C2 Stein Mt Can
23B2 Stemaco Mexico
54B2 Stenay France
56C2 Stendal Germany
110B2 Stephens,C NZ
108B2 Stephens Creek Aust
14A1 Stephenson USA
13C3 Stephens Pass USA
7E5 Stephenville Can
100B4 Sterkstroom S Africa
8C2 Sterling Colorado,
USA
14B2 Sterling Heights USA
61J3 Sterlitamak
Russian Fed
13E2 Stettler Can
14B2 Steubenville USA
4D3 Stevens Village USA
13B1 Stewart Can
21B2 Stewart USA
12G2 Stewart R Can

12G2 Stewart Crossing
Can
111A3 Stewart I NZ
107F1 Stewart Is
Solomon Is
4E3 Stewart River Can
16A3 Stewartstown USA
101G1 Steyn S Africa
57C3 Steyr Austria
12G3 Stika USA
12H3 Stikine R Can
12H3 Stikine Ranges Mts
Can
18A2 Stillwater Oklahoma,
USA
21B2 Stillwater Range Mts
USA
108A2 Stirling Aust
44C3 Stirling Scot
59B3 Stockerau Austria
39H7 Stockholm Sweden
42C3 Stockport Eng
22G2 Stockton California,
USA
42D2 Stockton Eng
18B2 Stockton L USA
43C3 Stoke-on-Trent Eng
38A2 Stokkseyri Iceland
38G5 Stokmarknes Nor
39K8 Stolbtsy Belorussia
58D2 Stolin Belorussia
16B3 Stone Harbor USA
44C3 Stonehaven Scot
19A3 Stonewall USA
12D2 Stony R USA
38H6 Storavan L Sweden
38G6 Støren Nor
109C4 Storm B Aust
44A2 Stornoway Scot
59D3 Storozhinets Ukraine
16C2 Storrs USA
38G6 Stors168jon L
Sweden
38H5 Storuman Sweden
16D1 Stoughton USA
43E3 Stowmarket Eng
45C1 Strabane N Ire
109C4 Strahan Aust
56C2 Stralsund Germany
38F6 Stranda Nor
39H7 Strängnäs Sweden
42B2 Stranraer Scot
49D2 Strasbourg France
15C3 Strasburg USA
14B2 Stratford USA
16C2 Stratford
Connecticut, USA
110B1 Stratford NZ
43D3 Stratford-on-Avon
Eng
108A3 Strathalbyn Aust
42B2 Strathclyde Region,
Scot
13E2 Strathmore Can
18C1 Streator USA
47C2 Stresa Italy
53C3 Stretto de Messina
Str Italy/Sicily
38D3 Streymoy Føroyar
53C3 Stroboli I Italy
6E3 Strømfjord
Greenland
24C2 Stromness Scot
18A1 Stromsburg USA
38H6 Stromsund Sweden
38G6 Ströms Vattudal L
Sweden
42B2 Stronsay I Scot
43C4 Stroud Eng
54B2 Struga R Bulg
43B3 Strumble Head Pt
Wales
55B2 Strumica Macedonia
59C3 Stryy Ukraine
59C3 Stryy R Ukraine
108B1 Strzelecki Creek R
Aust
17B2 Stuart Florida, USA
13C2 Stuart R Can
12B2 Stuart I USA
13C2 Stuart L Can
47D1 Stubaier Alpen Mts
Austria

76D3 Stung Sen Camb
76D3 Stung Treng Camb
52A2 Stura R Italy
112C7 Sturge I Ant
14A2 Sturgeon Bay USA
14C1 Sturgeon Falls Can
18C2 Sturgis Kentucky,
USA
14A2 Sturgis Michigan,
USA
106B2 Sturt Creek R Aust
108B1 Sturt Desert Aust
100B4 Sturtemeim S America
19B3 Stuttgart Germany
57B3 Stuttgart Germany
38A1 Stykkishólmur
Iceland
59D2 Styr' R Ukraine
35C1 Suaçui Grande R
Brazil
81B4 Suakin Sudan
73E5 Su-ao Taiwan
34C2 Suardi Arg
78B2 Subi I Indon
54A1 Subotica Serbia,
Yugos
60C4 Suceava Rom
45B2 Suck R Irish Rep
30C2 Sucre Bol
35A1 Sucuriú R Brazil
98C1 Sudan Republic,
Africa
14B1 Sudbury Can
43E3 Sudbury Eng
99C2 Sudd Swamp Sudan
33F2 Suddie Guyana
99C2 Sue R Sudan
4H2 Suemburgh Is Can
92B4 Suez Egypt
92B3 Suez Egypt
16B2 Suez,G of Egypt
43E3 Suffolk County, Eng
109D2 Sugarloaf Pt Aust
91C5 Suhār Oman
68C1 Sühbaatar Mongolia
84B3 Sui Pak
72C2 Suide China
69E2 Suihua China
73B3 Suining China
46C2 Suippes France
41B3 Suir R Irish Rep
73C3 Sui Xian China
72E1 Suizhong China
85C3 Sujāngarh India
78B4 Sukabumi Indon
78C3 Sukadana Borneo,
Indon
78B4 Sukadana Sumatra,
Indon
74E3 Sukagawa Japan
78C3 Sukaraja Indon
60E3 Sukhinichi
Russian Fed
61F2 Sukhona R
Russian Fed
61F5 Sukhumi Georgia
6E3 Sukkertoppen
Greenland
6E3 Sukkertoppen L
Greenland
38L6 Sukkozero
Russian Fed
85B3 Sukkur Pak
87C1 Sukma India
95A2 Süknah Libya
100A3 Sukses Namibia
75A2 Sukumo Japan
13C1 Sukunka R Can
60E3 Sula R Russian Fed
84B3 Sulaiman Range Mts
Pak
70C4 Sulawesi I Indon
54C1 Sulina Rom
38H5 Sulitjelma Nor
32A4 Sullana Peru
18B2 Sullivan USA
13B2 Sullivan Bay Can
13E2 Sullivan L Can
52B2 Sulmona Italy
19B3 Sulphur Louisiana,
USA
19A3 Sulphur Oklahoma,
USA
19A3 Sulphur Springs USA

86A1 Sultānpur India
70C3 Sulu S Philip
30D4 Sumampa Arg
70B4 Sumatra I Indon
70C4 Sumba I Indon
78D4 Sumbawa I Indon
78D4 Sumbawa Besar
Indon
99D3 Sumbawanga Tanz
100A2 Sumbe Angola
44E2 Sumburgh Head Pt
Scot
78C4 Sumenep Indon
69G3 Sumisu I Japan
13D3 Summerland Can
54C4 Summit Lake Can
21B2 Summit Mt USA
111B2 Summer,L NZ
75A2 Sumoto Japan
17B1 Sumter USA
60D3 Sumy Ukraine
16A2 Sunbury USA
34C2 Sunchales Arg
74B3 Sunch'ŏn S Korea
74B4 Sunch'ŏn S Korea
86A2 Sundargarh India
86B2 Sunderbans Swamp
India
42D2 Sunderland Eng
13E2 Sundre Can
15C1 Sundridge Can
38H6 Sundsvall Sweden
38D3 Sudurøy Føroyar
78D3 Sungaianyar Indon
78A3 Sungaisalak Indon
20C1 Sunnyside USA
21A2 Sunnyvale USA
63D1 Suntar Russian Fed
97B4 Sunyani Ghana
75A2 Suŏ-nada B Japan
38K6 Suonejoki Fin
86B1 Supaul India
18A1 Superior Nebraska,
USA
10A2 Superior Wisconsin,
USA
10B2 Superior,L Can USA
76C3 Suphan Buri Thai
93D2 Süphan Dağı Turk
71E4 Supiori I Indon
93E3 Suq ash Suyukh Iraq
72D3 Suqian China
Suqutra = Socotra
91C5 Sür Oman
61G3 Sura R Russian Fed
78C4 Surabaya Indon
78C4 Surakarta Indon
109C1 Surat Aust
84C3 Surat India
77B4 Surat Thani Thai
85C4 Surendranagar India
15D2 Surf City USA
64J3 Surgut Russian Fed
87B1 Suriāpet India
79C4 Surigao Phil
76C3 Surin Thai
33F3 Surinam Republic,
S America
43D4 Surrey County, Eng
47C1 Sursee Switz
95A1 Surt Libya
38A2 Surtsey I Iceland
78A3 Surulangun Indon
47B2 Susa Italy
75A2 Susa Japan
75A2 Susaki Japan
21A1 Susanville USA
47D1 Süsch Switz
12E2 Susitna R USA
16A3 Susquehanna R USA
16B2 Sussex USA
43D4 Sussex West Eng
13B1 Sustut Peak Mt Can
100B4 Sutherland S Africa
84C2 Sutlej R Pak
21A2 Sutter Creek USA
12C3 Sutwik I USA
74D3 Suwa Japan
58C2 Suwałki Pol
17B2 Suwannee R USA

94B2 Suweilih Jordan
74B3 Suwŏn S Korea
72D2 Su Xian China
75B1 Suzaka Japan
73E3 Suzhou China
74D3 Suzu Japan
75B2 Suzuka Japan
75B1 Suzu-misaki C
Japan
64C2 Svalbard Is
Barents S
59C3 Svalyava Ukraine
38G5 Svartisen Mt Nor
76D3 Svay Rieng Camb
38G6 Sveg Sweden
39G7 Svendborg Den
Sverdlovsk =
Yekaterinburg
6A1 Sverdrup Chan Can
69F2 Svetlaya Russian Fed
58C2 Svetlogorsk
Russian Fed
39K6 Svetogorsk
Russian Fed
54B2 Svetozarevo Serbia,
Yugos
54C2 Svilengrad Bulg
58D2 Svir' Belorussia
59B3 Svitavy
Czech Republic
69E1 Svobodnyy
Russian Fed
38G5 Svolvaer Nor
107E3 Swain Reefs Aust
17B1 Swainsboro USA
100A3 Swakopmund
Namibia
42D2 Swale R Eng
70C3 Swallow Reef I
S E Asia
87B2 Swāmihalli India
25D3 Swan I Honduras
107B3 Swan Hill Aust
13D2 Swan Hills Can
13D2 Swan Hills Mts Can
26A3 Swan I Caribbean S
5H4 Swan River Can
43C4 Swansea Wales
43C4 Swansea B Wales
100G1 Swartruggens
S Africa
Swatow = Shantou
101H1 Swaziland Kingdom,
S Africa
39G7 Sweden Kingdom,
N Europe
20B2 Sweet Home USA
9C3 Sweetwater USA
100B4 Swellendam S Africa
59B2 Świdnica Pol
58B2 Świdwin Pol
58B2 Świebodzin Pol
58B2 Świecie Pol
5H4 Swift Current Can
43C4 Swindon Eng
45B2 Swinford Irish Rep
56C2 Świnoujście Pol
49D2 Switzerland Federal
Republic, Europe
45C2 Swords Irish Rep
109D2 Sydney Aust
7D5 Sydney USA
64G3 Syktyvkar
Russian Fed
17A1 Sylacauga USA
38G6 Sylarna Mt Sweden
86C2 Sylhet Bang
56B1 Sylt I Germany
14B2 Sylvania USA
112C11 Syowa Base Ant
Syracuse = Siracusa
15C2 Syracuse USA
5N Syr Darya R
Kazakhstan
93C2 Syria Republic, S W
Asia
61J2 Sysert' Russian Fed
61G3 Syzran' Russian Fed
56C2 Szczecin Pol
58B2 Szczecinek Pol
59C3 Szczytno Pol
59B3 Szekésfehérvár Hung
59B3 Szekszard Hung

59B3 Szolnok Hung
59B3 Szombathely Hung
58B2 Szprotawa Pol

T

90C3 Tabas Iran
23A1 Tabasco Mexico
32D4 Tabatinga Brazil
96B2 Tabelbala Alg
76C3 Tabeng Camb
13E2 Taber Can
79B3 Tablas I Phil
100A4 Table Mt S Africa
12F1 Table Mt USA
18B2 Table Rock Res USA
78B3 Tabooli Indon
57C3 Tábor
Czech Republic
99D3 Tabora Tanz
97B4 Tabou Ivory Coast
90A2 Tabrīz Iran
92C4 Tabūk S Arabia
23A2 Tacámbaro Mexico
82C1 Tacheng China
79C3 Tacloban Phil
30B2 Tacna Peru
8B2 Tacoma USA
99E1 Tadjoura Djibouti
87B2 Tādpatri India
74B3 Taebaek Sanmaek
Mts S Korea
74B3 Taegu S Korea
74B4 Taehoksan I S Korea
74B3 Taejŏn S Korea
51B1 Tafalla Spain
96C2 Tafasaset
Watercourse Alg
43C4 Taff R Wales
94B3 Tafila Jordan
97A3 Taganrog Ukraine
97A3 Tagant Region, Maur
79B4 Tagbilaran Phil
96B2 Taguenout
Hagguerete Well
Maur
107E2 Tagula I Solomon Is
79C4 Tagum Phil
Tagus = Tejo
96C2 Tahat Mt Alg
105J4 Tahiti I Pacific O
18A2 Tahlequah USA
21A2 Tahoe City USA
21A2 Tahoe,L USA
97C3 Tahoua Niger
71D3 Tahuna Indon
72D2 Tai'an China
72B3 Taibai Shan Mt
China
72D1 Taibus Qi China
73E5 T'ai-chung Taiwan
111B3 Taieri R NZ
72C2 Taihang Shan China
110C1 Taihape NZ
72E3 Tai Hu L China
108A3 Tailem Bend Aust
44B3 Tain Scot
73E5 T'ai-nan Taiwan
35C1 Taiobeiras Brazil
73E5 T'ai pei Taiwan
77C5 Taiping Malay
75A2 Taira Japan
78A3 Tais Indon
75A1 Taisha Japan
29B5 Taitao,Pen de Chile
73E5 T'ai-tung Taiwan
38K5 Taivelkoski Fin
69E4 Taiwan Republic,
China
Taiwan Haixia =
Formosa Str
72C2 Taiyuan China
72D3 Taizhou China
81C4 Ta'izz Yemen
82A2 Tajikistan Republic,
Asia
50B1 Tajo R Spain
76B2 Tak Thai
74D3 Takada Japan
74C2 Takahashi Japan
110B2 Takaka NZ
74C4 Takamatsu Japan
74D3 Takaoka Japan
110B1 Takapuna NZ
74D3 Takasaki Japan
75B1 Takayama Japan

74D3 Takefu Japan
70A3 Takengon Indon
76C3 Takeo Camb
75C3 Takeo Japan
   Take-shima = Tok-do
90A2 Takestān Iran
75A2 Taketa Japan
4G3 Takjvak L Can
99D1 Takkaze R Eth
*13B1 Takla L Can
13B1 Takla Landing Can
12B2 Takslesluk L USA
12H2 Taku Arm R Can
23A1 Tala México
59B3 Talabanya Hung
84C2 Talagang Pak
34A2 Talagante Chile
87B3 Talaimannar
   Sri Lanka
97C3 Talak Desert Region,
   Niger
78A3 Talangbetutu Indon
32A4 Talara Peru
50B2 Talavera de la Reina
   Spain
34A3 Talca Chile
34A3 Talcahuano Chile
86B2 Tālcher India
72C1 Taldy Kurgan
   Kazakhstan
71D4 Taliabu Indon
84B1 Taligan Afghan
99D2 Tali Post Sudan
75A4 Taliwang Indon
12D2 Talkeetna USA
12E2 Talkeetna Mts USA
17A1 Talladega USA
93D2 Tall 'Afar Iraq
17B1 Tallahassee USA
94C1 Tall Bīsah Syria
60B2 Tallinn Estonia
92C3 Tall Kalakh Syria
19B3 Tallulah USA
60D4 Tal'noye Ukraine
92C3 Talpaki Russian Fed
30B4 Taltal Chile
109C1 Talwood Aust
70D1 Tamabo Range Mts
   Malay
97A3 Tamale Ghana
96C2 Tamanrasset Alg
96C2 Tamanrasset
   Watercourse Alg
16B2 Tamaqua USA
   Tamatave =
   Toamasina
23A2 Tamazula Jalisco,
   México
23B2 Tamazulápan México
23B1 Tamazunchale
   México
97A3 Tambacounda Sen
61F3 Tambov Russian Fed
50A1 Tambre R Spain
98C2 Tambura Sudan
50A1 Tamchaket Maur
50A1 Tamega R Port
23B1 Tamiahua México
82B1 Tamil Nādu State,
   India
76D2 Tam Ky Viet
17B2 Tampa USA
17B2 Tampa B USA
39J6 Tampere Fin
23B1 Tampico México
68D2 Tamsagbulag
   Mongolia
86C2 Tamu Burma
23A1 Tamuis México
*109D2 Tamworth Aust
43D3 Tamworth Eng
38K4 Tana Nor
99D1 Tana L Eth
99E3 Tana R Kenya
38K5 Tana R Nor/Fin
72A3 Tanabe Japan
38K4 Tanafjord Inlet Nor
74D3 Tanahgrogot Indon
71E4 Tanahmerah Indon
12D1 Tanana USA
12E2 Tanana R USA
   Tananarive =
   Antananarivo
47C2 Tanaro R Italy
74B2 Tanch'ŏn N Korea

34D3 Tandil Arg
78B2 Tandjong Datu Pt
   Indon
71E4 Tandjong d'Urville C
   Indon
78D3 Tandjung Layar C
   Indon
78B3 Tandjung Lumut C
   Indon
78D2 Tandjung
   Mangkalihet C Indon
78D3 Tandjung Sambar C
   Indon
78C2 Tandjung Sirik C
   Malay
71E4 Tandjung Vals C
   Indon
85B3 Tando Adam Pak
85B3 Tando Muhammad
   Khan Pak
108B2 Tandou L Aust
87B1 Tāndūr India
110C1 Taneatua NZ
76B2 Tanen Range Mts
   Burma/Thai
96B2 Tanezrouft Desert
   Region Alg
91C4 Tang Iran
99D3 Tanga Tanz
60E4 Tanganrog
   Russian Fed
99C3 Tanganyika,L Tanz/
   Zaire
96B1 Tanger Mor
82C2 Tanggula Shan Mts
   China
   Tangier = Tanger
78A2 Tangjungpinang
   Indon
82C2 Tangra Yumco L
   China
72D2 Tangshan China
75A4 Tangub Phil
63C2 Tanguy Russian Fed
18B1 Tantaubry USA
79B4 Tanjay Phil
101D3 Tanjona Ankaboa C
   Madag
101D2 Tanjona Babaomby C
   Madag
101D2 Tanjona Vilanandro
   C Madag
101D3 Tanjona Vohimena C
   Madag
78C4 Tanjong Bugel C
   Indon
78B4 Tanjong Cangkuang
   C Indon
78C3 Tanjong Puting C
   Indon
78C3 Tanjong Selatan C
   Indon
78D3 Tanjung Indon
70A3 Tanjungbalai Indon
78A3 Tanjung Jabung Pt
   Indon
78B2 Tanjungpandan
   Indon
78B4 Tanjung Priok Indon
78D2 Tanjungredeb Indon
78D2 Tanjungselor Indon
84C2 Tank Pak
68B1 Tannu Ola Mts
   Russian Fed
97A4 Tano R Ghana
73E4 Tan-shui Taiwan
86A1 Tansing Nepal
95C1 Tanta Egypt
96A2 Tan-Tan Mor
4B3 Tanunak USA
99D3 Tanzania Republic,
   Africa
72A3 Tao He R China
72B2 Taole China
96B1 Taourirt Mor
60C2 Tapa Estonia
25C3 Tapachula México
33F4 Tapajós R Brazil
34C3 Tapalquén Arg
70B4 Tapan Indon
111A3 Tapanui NZ
32D5 Tapauá R Brazil

85D4 Tapi R India
86B1 Taplejung Nepal
111B2 Tapuaeniku Mt NZ
35B2 Tapuaritinga Brazil
79B3 Tapul Group Is Phil
33E4 Tapurucuara Brazil
109D1 Tara Aust
65J4 Tara Russian Fed
65J4 Tara R Russian Fed
54A2 Tara R Bosnia-
   Herzegovina/
   Montenegro, Yugos
97D4 Taraba R Nig
30D2 Tarabuco Bol
   Tarābulus = Tripoli
50B1 Taracón Spain
110C1 Taradale NZ
78D2 Tarakan Indon
44A3 Taransay I Scot
53C2 Taranto Italy
32B5 Tarapoto Peru
49C2 Tarare France
110C2 Tararua Range Mts
   NZ
96C2 Tarat Alg
110C1 Tarawera NZ
51B1 Tarazona Spain
44C3 Tarbat Ness Pen
   Scot
84C2 Tarbela Res Pak
42B2 Tarbert Strathclyde,
   Scot
44A3 Tarbert Western
   Isles, Scot
52B6 Tarbes France
106C4 Tarcoola Aust
109C2 Tarcoon Aust
96A2 Tarfaya Mor
95A1 Tarhūnah Libya
91B5 Tarif UAE
30D3 Tarija Bol
87B2 Tarikere India
81C4 Tarim Yemen
99D3 Tarime Tanz
82C1 Tarim He R China
82C2 Tarim Pendi Basin
   China
84B2 Tarin Kut Afghan
18A1 Tarkio USA
79B2 Tarlac Phil
32B6 Tarma Peru
49C2 Tarn R France
59C2 Tarnobrzeg Pol
59C3 Tarnów Pol
107D3 Taroom Aust
51C1 Tarragona Spain
109C4 Tarraleah Aust
51C1 Tarrasa Spain
16C2 Tarrytown USA
92B2 Tarsus Turk
44D2 Tartan Oilfield
   N Sea
47D2 Tartaro R Italy
60C2 Tartu Estonia
92C3 Tartūs Syria
35C1 Tarumirim Brazil
70A3 Tarutung Indon
52B1 Tarvisio Italy
80D1 Tashauz
   Turkmenistan
86C1 Tashigang Bhutan
82A1 Tashkent Uzbekistan
65K4 Tashtagol
63A2 Tashtyp Russian Fed
78B4 Tasikmalaya Indon
72B4 Tasil Syria
6E2 Tasiussaq Greenland
95A3 Tasker Well Niger
110B2 Tasman B NZ
71D5 Tasmania / Aust
111B2 Tasman Mts NZ
109C4 Tasman Pen Aust
107E4 Tasman S NZ Aust
92C1 Taşova Turk
96C2 Tassili du Hoggar
   Desert Region, Alg
96C2 Tassili N'jjer Desert
   Region, Alg
96B2 Tata Mor
76D1 Tataouine Tunisia
65J4 Tatarsk Russian Fed
69G2 Tatarskiy Proliv Str
   Russian Fed

61G2 Tatarstan
   Russian Fed
75B1 Tateyama Japan
5G3 Tathlina L Can
12E2 Tatitlek USA
75A2 Tatla Lake Can
59B3 Tatry Mts Pol/
   Slovakia
75A2 Tatsuno Japan
85B4 Tatta Pak
32D2 Tatui Brazil
92D2 Tatvan Turk
31C3 Tauá Brazil
35B2 Taubaté Brazil
   Taumarunui NZ
101F1 Taumaturgo Brazil
101F1 Taung S Africa
76B2 Taungdwingyi
   Burma
76B1 Taung-gyi Burma
76A2 Taungup Burma
84C2 Taunsa Pak
43C4 Taunton Eng
16D2 Taunton USA
46E1 Taunus Region,
   Germany
110C1 Taupo NZ
110C1 Taupo,L NZ
58C1 Taurage Lithuania
110C1 Tauranga NZ
110B1 Tauranga Harbour B
   NZ
110B1 Tauroa Pt NZ
7A3 Tavani Can
7A3 Tavani Can
65H4 Tavda R Russian Fed
43B4 Tavistock Eng
76B3 Tavoy Burma
76B3 Tavoy Pt Burma
92A2 Tavsanli Turk
111B2 Tawa NZ
19A3 Tawakoni,L USA
14B2 Tawas City USA
70C3 Tawau Malay
98C1 Taweisha Sudan
79B4 Tawitawi Phil
79B4 Tawitawi Group Is
   Phil
23B2 Taxco México
23B2 Taxcoco México
44C3 Tay R Scot
78C3 Tayan Indon
12E2 Taylor Alaska, USA
13C1 Taylor Can
14B2 Taylor Michigan,
   USA
19A3 Taylor Texas, USA
18C2 Taylorville USA
80B3 Taymā' S Arabia
63B1 Taymura R
   Russian Fed
76D2 Tay Ninh Viet
63B2 Tayshet Russian Fed
68B2 Tayshir Mongolia
44C3 Tayside Region, Scot
79A3 Taytay Phil
91C3 Tayyebāt Iran
96B1 Taza Mor
95B2 Tazirbu Libya
52B1 Tazlina L USA
64J3 Tazovskiy
   Russian Fed
65F5 Tbilisi Georgia
98B3 Tchibanga Gabon
95A2 Tchigaï,Plat du Niger
97D3 Tchin Tabaradene
   Niger
58B2 Tchollíré Cam
58B2 Tczew Pol
111A3 Te Anau NZ
111A3 Te Anau,L NZ
110C1 Te Aroha NZ
110C1 Te Awamutu NZ
16C1 Tébessa Alg
23A2 Teboman México
23A2 Tecaíllán México
21B3 Tecate México
61K2 Techa R Russian Fed
23A1 Tecolotlán México
23A2 Tecomán México
54C1 Tecuci Rom
18A1 Tecumseh USA
80E2 Tedzhen
   Turkmenistan
65H6 Tedzhen R
   Turkmenistan

42D2 Tees R Eng
33E4 Tefé Brazil
78B4 Tegal Indon
78B4 Tegineneng Indon
25D3 Tegucigalpa Honduras
21B3 Tehachapi Mts USA
21B2 Tehachapi P USA
4J3 Tehek L Can
90B2 Tehrān Iran
23B2 Tehuacán Mexico
23B2 Tehuantepec Mexico
23B2 Tehuitzingo Mexico
43B3 Teifi R Wales
50A2 Tejo R Port
23A2 Tejupilco Mexico
111B2 Tekapo,L NZ
82B1 Tekeli Kazakhstan
92A1 Tekirdağ Turk
55C2 Tekir Dağlari Mts Turk
86C2 Tekoa USA
110C1 Te Kuiti NZ
25D3 Tela Honduras
94B2 Tel Aviv Yafo Israel
34B3 Telén Arg
21B2 Telescope Peak Mt USA
33F5 Teles Pires R Brazil
47D1 Telfs Austria
63A2 Teli Russian Fed
94B3 Tell el Meise Mt Jordan
12A1 Teller USA
87B2 Tellicherry India
77C5 Telok Anson Malay
78C2 Teluk Darvel Malay
71E4 Teluk Flamingo B Indon
78C3 Telok Kumai B Indon
78B4 Teluk Pelabuanratu B Indon
78D4 Telok Saleh B Indon
78C3 Telok Sampit B Indon
78B3 Telok Sukadana B Indon
23B2 Teloloapán Mexico
64G3 Tel'pos-iz Mt Russian Fed
58C1 Telšiai Lithuania
78C3 Telukbatang Indon
71E4 Teluk Berau B Indon
78B4 Telukbetung Indon
70D4 Teluk Bone B Indon
71E4 Teluk Cendrawasih B Indon
78D3 Teluk Mandar B Indon
71D4 Teluk Tolo B Indon
70D3 Teluk Tomini B Indon
71D3 Teluk Weda B Indon
14B1 Temagami,L Can
23B2 Temascal Mexico
78A3 Tembesi R Indon
78A3 Tembilahan Indon
77C5 Temerloh Malay
65G5 Temir Kazakhstan
65J4 Temirtau Kazakhstan
15C1 Temiscamie R Can
109C2 Temora Aust
9B3 Tempe USA
19A3 Temple USA
45C2 Templemore Irish Rep
23B1 Tempoal Mexico
34A3 Temuco Chile
111B2 Temuka NZ
32B4 Tena Ecuador
87C1 Tenali India
23B2 Tenancingo Mexico
76B3 Tenasserim Burma
43B4 Tenby Wales
99E1 Tendaho Eth
83D5 Ten Degree Chan Indian O
98B1 Ténéré Desert Region Niger
96A2 Tenerife I Canary Is
76B1 Teng R Burma
78D3 Tenggarong Indon
72A2 Tengger Shamo Desert China

112C2 Teniente Jubany Base Ant
112C2 Teniente Rodolfo Marsh Martin Base Ant
87B3 Tenkasi India
80B2 Tenke Zaïre
97B3 Tenkodogo Burkina
106C2 Tennant Creek Aust
11B3 Tennessee State, USA
18C2 Tennessee R USA
34A2 Teno Chile
78D1 Tenom Malay
25C3 Tenosique Mexico
109D1 Tenterfield Aust
17B2 Ten Thousand Is USA
23A1 Teocaltiche Mexico
35C1 Teófilo Otôni Brazil
23B2 Teotihiuacan Hist Site, Mexico
23B2 Teotitlan Mexico
23A1 Tepatitlan Mexico
24B2 Tepehuanes Mexico
23A1 Tepeji Mexico
23A1 Tepic Mexico
57C2 Teplice Czech Republic
110C1 Te Puke NZ
23A1 Tequila Mexico
23B2 Tequistepec Mexico
51B1 Ter R Spain
97C3 Téra Niger
75B1 Teradomari Japan
52B2 Teramo Italy
96A1 Terceira I Açores
59D3 Terebovla Ukraine
31C3 Teresina Brazil
35C2 Teresópolis Brazil
92C1 Terme Turk
80E2 Termez Uzbekistan
71D3 Ternate Indon
52B2 Terni Italy
59D3 Ternopol Ukraine
53B2 Terracina Italy
100B3 Terrafirma S Africa
112C8 Terre Adélie Region, Ant
19B4 Terre Bonne B USA
14A3 Terre Haute USA
19A3 Terrell USA
56B1 Terschelling I Neth
51B1 Teruel Spain
4C2 Teshekpuk L USA
74E2 Teshio R Japan
68C2 Tesiyn Gol R Mongolia
12H2 Teslin Can
12H3 Teslin R Can
12H2 Teslin L Can
63B3 Teslyn Gol R Mongolia
96C2 Tessalit Mali
97C3 Tessaoua Niger
101C2 Tete Mozam
23A2 Tetela Mexico
96B1 Tetouan Mor
61G2 Tetyushi Russian Fed
30D3 Teuco R Arg
23A2 Teul de Gonzalez Ortega Mexico
71D4 Teun I Indon
42C2 Teviot R Scot
65J4 Tevriz Russian Fed
111A3 Te Waewae B NZ
78C3 Tewah Indon
109D1 Tewantin Aust
72A3 Têwo China
19B3 Texarkana USA
19B3 Texarkana,L USA
19A3 Texas State, USA
19B4 Texas City USA
56A2 Texel I Neth
19A3 Texoma,L USA
101G1 Teyateyaneng Lesotho
23B2 Teziutlán Mexico
86C1 Tezpur India
76C1 Tha Laos

101G1 Thabana Ntlenyana Mt Lesotho
101G1 Thaba Putsoa Mt Lesotho
76B3 Thagyettaw Burma
76D1 Thai Binh Viet
76C2 Thailand Kingdom, S E Asia
76C3 Thailand,G of Thai
76D1 Thai Nguyen Viet
76C2 Thakhek Laos
87C2 Thal Pak
77C4 Thale Luang L Thai
109C1 Thallon Aust
110C1 Thames NZ
43E4 Thames R Eng
76D2 Thanh Hoah Viet
87B2 Thanjavur India
77D4 Thanlwin = Salween
85C3 Thar Desert India
108B1 Thargomindah Aust
55B2 Thásos I Greece
76B2 Thaton Burma
76B2 Thayetmyo Burma
5F5 The Dalles USA
91B4 The Gulf S W Asia
4H3 Thelon R Can
107E3 Theodore Aust
8B3 Theodore Roosevelt L USA
55B2 Thermaïkós Kólpos G Greece
8C2 Thermopolis USA
4F2 Thesiger B Can
14B1 Thessalon Can
55B2 Thessaloníki Greece
43E3 Thetford Eng
15D1 Thetford Mines Can
101G1 Theunissen S Africa
19B4 Thibodaux USA
5J4 Thicket Portage Can
8D2 Thief River Falls USA
20B2 Thielsen,Mt USA
49C2 Thiers France
97A3 Thiès Sen
99D3 Thika Kenya
86B1 Thimphu Bhutan
49D2 Thionville France
55C3 Thira I Greece
42D2 Thirsk Eng
87B3 Thiruvananthapuram = Trivandrum
39F7 Thisted Den
55B3 Thívai Greece
48C2 Thiviers France
17B1 Thomaston Georgia, USA
45C2 Thomastown Irish Rep
17B1 Thomasville Georgia, USA
6A2 Thom Bay Can
5J4 Thompson Can
18B1 Thompson R USA
20C1 Thompson USA
13C2 Thompson R Can
16C2 Thompsonville USA
17B1 Thomson USA
107D3 Thomson R Aust
76C3 Thon Buri Thai
76B2 Thongwa Burma
49C2 Thonon-les-Bains France
42C2 Thornhill Scot
48B2 Thouars France
15C2 Thousand Is Can/USA
13E2 Three Hills Can
7G4 Three Kings Is NZ
76B2 Three Pagodas P Thai
14A2 Three Rivers Michigan, USA
20B2 Three Sisters Mt USA
6D2 Thule Greenland
47B1 Thun Switz
10B2 Thunder Bay Can
47B1 Thuner See L Switz
77B4 Thung Song Thai
47C1 Thur R Switz
57C2 Thüringen State, Germany

57C2 Thüringen Wald Upland Germany
45C2 Thurles Irish Rep
71F5 Thursday I Aust
44C2 Thurso Scot
112B4 Thurston I Ant
47C1 Thusis Switz
108B1 Thylungra Aust
73B5 Tiandong China
73B5 Tian'e China
72D2 Tianjin China
82C1 Tiān Shan Mts C Asia
72B3 Tianshui China
72A2 Tianzhu China
96C1 Tiaret Alg
35A2 Tibagi R Brazil
94B2 Tiberias Israel
94B2 Tiberias,L Israel
95A2 Tibesti Mountain Region Chad
82C2 Tibet Autonomous Region, China
108B1 Tibooburra Aust
86A1 Tibrikot Nepal
23A2 Tiburón I Mexico
97B3 Tichitt Maur
96A2 Tichla Mor
47C2 Ticino R Italy/Switz
15D2 Ticonderoga USA
25D2 Ticul Mexico
97A3 Tidjikja Maur
47C1 Tiefencastel Switz
74A2 Tieling China
46C1 Tienen Belg
65J5 Tien Shan Mts China/Kirghizia
72D2 Tientsin China
39H6 Tierp Sweden
23B2 Tierra Blanca Mexico
23B2 Tierra Colorada Mexico
29C6 Tierra del Fuego Territory, Arg
28C8 Tierra del Fuego I Arg/Chile
35A2 Tietê R Brazil
14B2 Tiffin USA
17B1 Tifton USA
32B4 Tigre R Peru
33E2 Tigre R Ven
93E3 Tigris R Iraq
23B1 Tihuatlán Mexico
21B3 Tijuana Mexico
85D4 Tikamgarh India
60D2 Tikhin Russian Fed
61F4 Tikhoretsk Russian Fed
93D3 Tikrit Iraq
1B8 Tiksi Russian Fed
46C1 Tilburg Neth
43E4 Tilbury Eng
30C3 Tilcara Arg
108B1 Tilcha Aust
78A1 Tilin Burma
97C3 Tillabéri Niger
20B1 Tillamook USA
97C3 Tillia Niger
55C3 Tílos I Greece
108B2 Tilpa Aust
32B3 Tiluá Colombia
64G3 Timanskiy Kryazh Mts Russian Fed
111B2 Timaru NZ
60E4 Timashevsk Russian Fed
55B3 Timbákion Greece
19B4 Timbalier B USA
97B3 Timbedra Maur
Timbuktu = Tombouctou
97B3 Timétrine Monts Mali
97C3 Tinia Niger
96C2 Timiş R Rom
54B1 Timişoara Rom
10B1 Timmins Can
71D4 Timor I Indon
106B2 Timor S Aust/Indon
34C3 Timote Arg
79C4 Tinaca Pt Phil

27D5 Tinaco Ven
87B2 Tindivanam India
96B2 Tindouf Alg
7F1 Tin Fouye Alg
96C2 Tin Fouye Alg
82B5 Tingmiarmiut
   Greenland
32B5 Tingo Maria Peru
87B3 Tingrela Ivory Coast
86B1 Tingri China
71F2 Tinian Pacific O
30C4 Tinogasta Arg
55C3 Tinos / Greece
43B4 Tintagel Head Pt
   Eng
96C2 Tin Tarabine
   Watercourse Alg
108B3 Tintinara Aust
72C1 Tin Zaouaten Alg
96C2 Tin Zaouaten Alg
72C2 Tioga P USA
77C5 Tioman I Malay
47D1 Tione Italy
45C2 Tipperary County,
   Irish Rep
41B3 Tipperary Irish Rep
18B2 Tipton Missouri, USA
22C2 Tiptur India
23A2 Tiquicheo Mexico
55A2 Tiranë Alb
47D1 Tirano Italy
60C4 Tiraspol Moldavia
87B2 Tirchchirappalli India
55C3 Tire Turk
93C1 Tirebolu Turk
44A3 Tiree / Scot
54C2 Tîrgovişte Rom
54B1 Tîrgu Jiu Rom
54B1 Tîrgu Mureş Rom
84C1 Tirich Mir Mt Pak
96A2 Tîris Region, Mor
61J3 Tirlyanskiy
   Russian Fed
54B1 Tîrnăveni Rom
55B3 Tírnavos Greece
85D4 Tirodi India
47D1 Tirol Province,
   Austria
53A2 Tirso R Sardegna
87B3 Tiruchendur India
87B2 Tirunelveli India
87B2 Tirupati India
87B2 Tiruppattūr India
87B2 Tiruppur India
87B2 Tiruvannamalai India
19A3 Tishomingo USA
72C1 Tisiyah Syria
59C3 Tisza R Hung
54B1 Titlagarh India
54B2 Titov Veles
   Macedonia
98C2 Titule Zaire
17B2 Titusville Eng
43C4 Tiverton Eng
52C2 Tivoli Italy
23B2 Tixtla Mexico
52B2 Tiyeglow Somalia
23B2 Tizayuca Mexico
25D2 Tizimin Mexico
96B1 Tizi Ouzou Alg
96B2 Tiznit Mor
23A1 Tizpan el Alto
   Chile
23B2 Tlacolula Mexico
23B2 Tlacotalpan Mexico
23A2 Tlalchapa Mexico
23B2 Tlalnepantla Mexico
23A2 Tlalpan Mexico
23A1 Tlaltenango Mexico
23B2 Tlancualpican
   Mexico
23B2 Tlapa Mexico
23B2 Tlapacoyan Mexico
23A1 Tlaquepaque Mexico
23B2 Tlaxcala Mexico
23B2 Tlaxcala State,
   Mexico
23B2 Tlaxiaco Mexico
96B1 Tlemcen Alg
01D2 Toamasina Madag
34C3 Toay Arg
75B2 Toba Japan
84B2 Toba and Kakar
   Ranges Mts Pak
27E4 Tobago I
   Caribbean S

13C2 Toba Inlet Sd Can
71D3 Tobelo Indon
14B1 Tobermory Can
44A3 Tobermory Scot
71E3 Tobi / Pacific O
21B1 Tobin,Mt USA
65H4 Tobol R Kazakhstan
70D4 Toboali Indon
65H4 Tobol'sk Russian Fed
31B2 Tocantins R Brazil
31B3 Tocantins State,
   Brazil
17B1 Toccoa USA
47C1 Toce R Italy
30B3 Tocopilla Chile
30C3 Tocorpuri Mt Chile
27D3 Tocuyo R Ven
85D3 Toda India
47C1 Tödi Mt Switz
75A1 Todong S Korea
9B4 Todos Santos
   Mexico
13E2 Tofield Can
13B3 Tofino Can
12B3 Togiak USA
97C4 Togo Republic, Africa
72C1 Togtoh China
12F2 Tok USA
74E2 Tokachi R Japan
75B1 Takamachi Japan
95C3 Tokar Sudan
69E4 Tokara Retto Arch
   Japan
92C1 Tokat Turk
74B3 Tökchök-kundo Arch
   S Korea
75A1 Tok-do I S Korea
82B1 Tokmak Kirghizia
110C1 Tokomaru Bay NZ
12H3 Toku R Can/USA
78C3 Tokung Indon
74C4 Tokushima Japan
75A2 Tokuyama Japan
74D3 Tōkyō Japan
110C1 Tolaga Bay NZ
10103 Tôlanaro Madag
30F3 Toledo Brazil
50B2 Toledo Spain
14B2 Toledo USA
19B3 Toledo Bend Res
   USA
10103 Toliara Madag
23B1 Toliman Mexico
32B3 Tolima Mt Colombia
29B3 Toltén Chile
23B2 Toluca Mexico
61G3 Tol'yatti Russian Fed
74C2 Tomakomai Japan
78D1 Tomani Indon
58C2 Tomaszów
   Mazowiecka Pol
11B3 Tombigbee R USA
98B3 Tomboco Angola
35C2 Tombos Brazil
97B3 Tombouctou Mali
100A2 Tombua Angola
34A3 Tomé Chile
50B2 Tomelloso Spain
50A2 Tomer Port
10683 Tomkinson Range
   Mts Aust
63E2 Tommot Russian Fed
74H Tommrit Mt Alb
65K4 Tomsk Russian Fed
16B3 Toms River USA
20C1 Tonalá Mexico
15C2 Tonawanda USA
105H4 Tonga Is Pacific O
101H1 Tongaat S Africa
73D3 Tongcheng China
72B2 Tongchuan China
72A2 Tongde China
46C1 Tongeren Belg
73A5 Tonghai China
74B2 Tonghua China
76D1 Tongking,G of China/
   Viet

72E1 Tongliao China
73D3 Tongling China
108B2 Tongo Aust
34A2 Tongoy Chile
73B4 Tongren Guizhou,
   China
72A2 Tongren Qinghai,
   China
86C1 Tongsa Bhutan
76B1 Tongta Burma
68B3 Tongtian He R China
44C2 Tongue Scot
72D2 Tong Xian China
72B2 Tongxin China
73B4 Tongzi China
9C4 Tonich Mexico
99C2 Tonj Sudan
85D3 Tonk India
18A2 Tonkawa USA
76C3 Tonle Sap L Camb
72D2 Tonopah USA
12E2 Tonsina USA
74E2 Tooele USA
109D1 Toogoolawah Aust
108B1 Toompine Aust
109D1 Toowoomba Aust
22C1 Topaz L USA
18A2 Topeka USA
9C4 Topolobampo
   Mexico
20B1 Toppenish USA
99D2 Tor Eth
55C3 Torbali Turk
90C2 Torbat-e-Heydariyeh
   Iran
-90D2 Torbat-e-Jam Iran
12D2 Torbert,Mt USA
50A1 Tordesillas Spain
56C2 Torgau Germany
46B1 Torhout Belg
49D2 Tori / Japan
47B2 Torino Italy
99D2 Torit Sudan
35A1 Torixoreu Brazil
50A1 Tormes R Spain
13E2 Tornado Mt Can
38H5 Torneträsk Sweden
7D4 Torngat Mts Can
38J5 Tornio Fin
34C3 Tornquist Arg
15C2 Toronto USA
60D2 Toropets
   Russian Fed
99D2 Tororo Uganda
92B2 Toros Dağlari Mts
   Turk
43C4 Torquay Eng
22C4 Torrance USA
50A2 Torrão Port
51C1 Torreblanca Spain
53B2 Torre del Greco Italy
50B1 Torrelavega Spain
50B2 Torremolinos Spain
108A2 Torrens,L Aust
24B2 Torreón Mexico
47B2 Torre Pellice Italy
107D2 Torres Str Aust
50A2 Torres Vedras Port
16C2 Torrington
   Connecticut, USA
8C2 Torrington
   Wyoming,USA
9C4 Torrón Mexico
38D3 Tórshavn Faroyar
47C2 Tortona Italy
53B3 Tortosa Spain
90C2 Torūd Iran
58B2 Torun Pol
40B2 Tory I Irish Rep
60D2 Torzhok Russian Fed
75A2 Tosa Japan
74C4 Tosa-shimizu Japan
75B2 To-shima / Japan
Toshkent = Tashkent
60D2 Tosno Russian Fed
75A2 Tosu Japan
92B1 Tosya Turk
61F1 Tot'ma Russian Fed
43C4 Totnes Eng
33G2 Totness Surinam
23B2 Totolapan Mexico
51B2 Totona Spain
109C2 Tottenham Aust

74C3 Tottori Japan
97B4 Touba Ivory Coast
97A3 Touba Sen
96B1 Toubkal Mt Mor
97B3 Tougan Burkina
96C1 Touggourt Alg
97A3 Tougue Guinea
46C2 Toul France
49D3 Toulon France
48C3 Toulouse France
97B4 Toumodi Ivory Coast
76B2 Toungoo Burma
46B1 Tourcoing France
96A2 Tourine Maur
46B1 Tournai Belg
48C2 Tours France
100B4 Touws River
   S Africa
74C3 Towada Japan
74C3 Towada-ko L Japan
15C2 Towanda USA
107D2 Townsville Aust
16A3 Towson USA
43C4 Towy R Wales
74D3 Toyama Japan
75B1 Toyama-wan B
   Japan
75B2 Toyohashi Japan
75B2 Toyonaka Japan
75A1 Toyooka Japan
74D3 Toyota Japan
96C1 Tozeur Tunisia
46D2 Traben-Trarbach
   Germany
93C1 Trabzon Turk
22B2 Tracy California, USA
14A3 Traiguén Chile
13D3 Trail Can
41B3 Tralee Irish Rep
45B2 Tralee B Irish Rep
45C2 Tramore Irish Rep
39G7 Tranas Sweden
76B3 Trang Thai
71E4 Trangan / Indon
109C2 Trangie Aust
12E2 Transalaskan Pipeline
   USA
100B3 Transvaal Province,
   S Africa
   Transylvanian Alps =
   Munţii Carpaţii
   Meridionali
53B3 Trapani Italy
109C3 Traralgon Aust
96A3 Trarza Region, Maur
76C3 Trat Thai
108B2 Traveller's L Aust
56C2 Travemünde
   Germany
14A2 Traverse City USA
12C1 Traverse Peak Mt
   USA
111B2 Travers,Mt NZ
47C2 Trebbia R Italy
59B3 Třebíč
   Czech Republic
54A2 Trebinje Bosnia-
   Herzegovina
57C3 Trebon
   Czech Republic
29F2 Treinta y Tres Urug
29C4 Trelew Arg
39G7 Trelleborg Sweden
43B3 Tremadog B Wales
15D1 Tremblant,Mt Can
13C2 Trembleur L Can
16A2 Tremont USA
59B3 Trenčin Slovakia
34C3 Trenque Lauquén
   Arg
43D3 Trent R Eng
47D1 Trentino Region, Italy
47D1 Trento Italy
15C2 Trenton Can
18B1 Trenton Missouri,
   USA
16B2 Trenton New Jersey,
   USA
7E5 Trepassey Can
34C3 Tres Arroyos Arg
35B2 Três Corações Brazil
30F3 Três Lagoas Brazil
34C3 Tres Lomas Arg
22B2 Tres Pinos USA
35C2 Três Rios Brazil
47C2 Treviglio Italy
47E2 Treviso Italy

Trezzo

47C2 **Trezzo** Italy
87B2 **Trichūr** India
108C2 **Trida** Aust
46D2 **Trier** Germany
52B1 **Trieste** Italy
45C2 **Trim** Irish Rep
87C3 **Trincomalee**
  Sri Lanka
33E6 **Trinidad** Bol
29E2 **Trinidad** Urug
9C3 **Trinidad** USA
34C3 **Trinidad** /
27E4 **Trinidad** /
  Caribbean S
103G6 **Trindade** / Atlantic O
27E4 **Trinidad & Tobago**
  Republic Caribbean S
19A3 **Trinity** R USA
9D3 **Trinity** R USA
7E5 **Trinity B** Can
12D3 **Trinity** B Can
17A1 **Trion** USA
94B1 **Tripoli** Leb
95A1 **Tripoli** Libya
55B3 **Tripolis** Greece
86C2 **Tripura** State, India
103H6 **Tristan da Cunha** *Is*
  Atlantic O
87B3 **Trivandrum** India
59B3 **Trnava** Slovakia
107E1 **Trobriand Is** PNG
15D1 **Trois-Rivières** Can
17A1 **Troy** Alabama, USA
16C1 **Troy** New York, USA
14B2 **Troy** Ohio, USA
54B2 **Troyan** Bulg
44B2 **Troyes** France
91B5 **Trucial Coast** Region,
  UAE
21A2 **Truckee** R USA
25D3 **Trujillo** Honduras
32B5 **Trujillo** Peru
50A2 **Trujillo** Spain
32C2 **Trujillo** Ven
109C2 **Trundle** Aust
7D5 **Truro** Can
17A1 **Truro** Eng
43B4 **Truro** Eng
68B2 **Tsagaan Nuur** L
  Mongolia
68B1 **Tsagan-Tologoy**
  Russian Fed
101D2 **Tsaratanana** Madag
100B3 **Tsau** Botswana
99D3 **Tsavo** Kenya
99D3 **Tsavo Nat Pk** Kenya
65J4 **Tselinograd**
  Kazakhstan
100A3 **Tses** Namibia
68C2 **Tsetserleg** Mongolia
97C4 **Tsévié** Togo
100B3 **Tshabong** Botswana
100B3 **Tshane** Botswana
98C3 **Tshela** Zaire
98C3 **Tshibala** Zaire
98C3 **Tshikapa** Zaire
98C3 **Tshuapa** R Zaire
101D3 **Tsihombe** Madag
61F4 **Tsimlyanskoye**
  Vodokhranilishche
  Res Russian Fed
  Tsinan = Jinan
  Tsingtao = Qingdao
101D2 **Tsiroanomandidy**
  Madag
13B2 **Tsitsutl Peak** *Mt* Can
58D2 **Tsna** R Belorussia
72B1 **Tspqt Ovoo**
  Mongolia
68C2 **Tsomog** Mongolia
55B2 **Tsu** Japan
75B1 **Tsubata** Japan
74E3 **Tsuchira** Japan

74E2 **Tsugaru-kaikyō** *Str*
  Japan
100A2 **Tsumeb** Namibia
100A3 **Tsumis** Namibia
75B1 **Tsunugi** Japan
74D3 **Tsuruga** Japan
74D3 **Tsuruoka** Japan
75B1 **Tsushima** Japan
74B4 **Tsushima** / Japan
74D3 **Tsuyama** Japan
50A1 **Tua** R Port
45B2 **Tuam** Irish Rep
60E5 **Tuapse** Russian Fed
11143 **Tuatapere** NZ
61K2 **Tubarão** Brazil
94B2 **Tubas** Israel
79A4 **Tubbataha Reefs** *Is*
  Phil
57B3 **Tübingen** Germany
95B1 **Tubruq** Libya
16B3 **Tuckerton** USA
9B3 **Tucson** USA
30C3 **Tucumán** State, Arg
34B2 **Tucunuco** Arg
33E2 **Tucupita** Ven
51B1 **Tudela** Spain
93C3 **Tudmur** Syria
101H1 **Tugela** R S Africa
109D2 **Tuggerah** L Aust
12D3 **Tugidak** / USA
79B2 **Tuguegarao** Phil
67D2 **Tugur** Russian Fed
72D2 **Tuhai He** R China
4E3 **Tuktoyaktuk** USA
58C1 **Tukums** Latvia
99D3 **Tukuyu** Tanz
84B1 **Tukzar** Afghan
60E3 **Tula** Russian Fed
23B1 **Tulancingo** Mexico
78A3 **Tulangbawang** R
  Indon
32B3 **Tulcán** Colombia
60C5 **Tulcea** Rom
100B3 **Tuli** Zim
94B2 **Tulkarm** Israel
48C2 **Tulle** France
1983 **Tullos** USA
45C2 **Tullow** Irish Rep
18A2 **Tulsa** USA
93C3 **Tulūl ash Shāmiyah**
  Desert Region Syria/
  S Arabia
63C2 **Tulun** Russian Fed
78C4 **Tulungagung** Indon
3283 **Tumaco** Colombia
109C3 **Tumbarumba** Aust
32A4 **Tumbes** Ecuador
108A2 **Tumby Bay** Aust
74B2 **Tumen** China
87B2 **Tumkūr** India
77C4 **Tumpat** Malay
85D4 **Tumsar** India
97B3 **Tumu** Ghana
109C3 **Tumut** Aust
27L1 **Tunapuna** Trinidad
93C2 **Tunceli** Turk
99D3 **Tunduma** Zambia
101C2 **Tunduru** Tanz
54C2 **Tundzha** R Bulg
87B1 **Tungabhadra** R India
68D4 **Tung-Chiang** Taiwan
38B2 **Tungnafellsjökull**
  Mts Iceland
12J2 **Tungsten** Can
63B1 **Tunguska** R
  Russian Fed
87C1 **Tuni** India
96D1 **Tunis** Tunisia
88E4 **Tunisia** Republic, N
  Africa
32C2 **Tunja** Colombia
12B2 **Tuntutuliak** USA
12B2 **Tununak** USA
34B2 **Tunuyán** Arg
34B2 **Tunuyán** R Arg
22C2 **Tuolumne Meadows**
  USA
35A2 **Tupã** Brazil
35B2 **Tupaciguara** Brazil
19C3 **Tupelo** USA
30C3 **Tupiza** Bol
15D2 **Tupper Lake** USA
34B2 **Tupungato** Arg
29C2 **Tupungato** *Mt* Arg

86C1 **Tura** India
63C1 **Tura** Russian Fed
61K2 **Tura** R Russian Fed
90C2 **Turān** Iran
82B2 **Turan** Russian Fed
93C3 **Turayf** S Arabia
80E3 **Turbat** Pak
32B2 **Turbo** Colombia
54B1 **Turda** Rom
63A3 **Turfan Depression**
  China
65H4 **Turgay** Kazakhstan
63B3 **Turgen Uul** *Mt*
  Mongolia
54C2 **Türgovishte** Bulg
92A2 **Turgutlu** Turk
92C1 **Turhal** Turk
39K7 **Türi** Estonia
51B2 **Turia** R Spain
  Turin = Torino
61K2 **Turinsk** Russian Fed
69F2 **Turiy Rog**
  Russian Fed
99D2 **Turkana,L** Kenya/Eth
80E1 **Turkestan** Region,
  C Asia
82A1 **Turkestan**
92C2 **Turkey** Republic,
  W Asia
80D1 **Turkmenistan**
  Republic, Asia
90B2 **Turkmenskiy Zaliv** *B*
  Turkmenistan
27C2 **Turks Is** Caribbean S
39J6 **Turku** Fin
97B4 **Turkwel** R Kenya
22B2 **Turlock** USA
22B2 **Turlock L** USA
110C2 **Turnagain,C** NZ
25D3 **Turneffe** *Is* Belize
16C1 **Turners Falls** USA
46C1 **Turnhout** Belg
13F1 **Turnor L** Can
54B2 **Turnu Măgurele** Rom
63A3 **Turpan** China
26B2 **Turquino** *Mt* Cuba
80E1 **Turtkul'** Uzbekistan
18A2 **Turtle Creek Res**
  USA
13F2 **Turtle L** Can
63A1 **Turukhansk**
  Russian Fed
  Tutera = Tudela
87B3 **Tuticorin** India
54C2 **Tutrakan** Bulg
57B3 **Tuttlingen** Germany
68C2 **Tuul Gol** R Mongolia
105G4 **Tuvalu** *Is* Pacific O
63B2 **Tuvinskaya**
  Respublika,
  Russian Fed
23A2 **Tuxpan** Jalisco,
  Mexico
24B2 **Tuxpan** Nayarit,
  Mexico
23B1 **Tuxpan** Veracruz,
  Mexico
23B2 **Tuxtepec** Mexico
25C3 **Tuxtla Gutiérrez**
  Mexico
50A1 **Túy** Spain
76D3 **Tuy Hoa** Viet
92B2 **Tuz Gölü** *Salt L* Turk
93D3 **Tuz Khurmātū** Iraq
54A2 **Tuzla** Bosnia-
  Herzegovina
60E2 **Tver'** Russian Fed
42C2 **Tweed** R Eng/Scot
109D1 **Tweed Heads** Aust
42C2 **Tweedsmuir Hills**
  Scot
7E5 **Twillingate** Can
22D2 **Twin Falls** USA
111B2 **Twins,The** *Mt* NZ
14A2 **Two Rivers** USA

63E2 **Tygda** Russian Fed
19A3 **Tyler** USA
65R3 **Tym** R Russian Fed
69G1 **Tymovskoye**
  Russian Fed
42D2 **Tyne** R Eng
42D2 **Tyne and Wear**
  Metropolitan County
  Eng
42D2 **Tynemouth** Eng
38G6 **Tynset** Nor
12D3 **Tyonek** USA
94B2 **Tyr** Leb
  Tyre = Tyr
45C1 **Tyrone** County, N Ire
108B3 **Tyrrell,L** Aust
53B2 **Tyrrhenian S** Italy
65H4 **Tyumen'**
  Russian Fed
43B3 **Tywyn** Wales
55B3 **Tzoumérka** *Mt*
  Greece

U

99E2 **Uarsciek** Somalia
35C2 **Ubá** Brazil
35C1 **Ubaí** Brazil
98B2 **Ubangi** R CAR
47B2 **Ubaye** R France
75A2 **Ube** Japan
50B2 **Úbeda** Spain
6E2 **Ubekendt Ejland** /
  Greenland
35B1 **Uberaba** Brazil
35B1 **Uberlândia** Brazil
76C2 **Ubon Ratchathani**
  Thai
58D2 **Ubort** R Belorussia
98C3 **Ubundi** Zaire
32C5 **Ucayali** R Peru
84C3 **Uch** Pak
63F2 **Uchar** R Russian Fed
74E2 **Uchiura-wan** *B*
  Japan
63B2 **Uda** R Russian Fed
85C4 **Udaipur** India
86B1 **Udaipur Garhi** Nepal
34D3 **Udaquoila** Arg
39G7 **Uddevalla** Sweden
38H5 **Uddjaur** L Sweden
87B1 **Udgir** India
52C1 **Udine** Italy
84D2 **Udhampur** India
61H2 **Udmurtskaya**
  Respublika,
  Russian Fed
76C2 **Udon Thani** Thai
63F2 **Udskaya Guba** *B*
  Russian Fed
87A2 **Udupi** India
75B1 **Ueda** Japan
99C2 **Uele** R Zaire
56C2 **Uelzen** Germany
98C2 **Uere** R Zaire
61J3 **Ufa** Russian Fed
61J2 **Ufa** R Russian Fed
100A3 **Ugab** R Namibia
99D3 **Ugalla** R Tanz
99D2 **Uganda** Republic,
  Africa
12C3 **Ugashik B** USA
12C3 **Ugashik L** USA
47B2 **Ugine** France
69G2 **Uglegorsk**
  Russian Fed
60E2 **Uglich** Russian Fed
60E3 **Ugra** R Russian Fed
44B3 **Uig** Scot
98B3 **Uige** Angola
61H4 **Uil** Kazakhstan
88E2 **Uinta Mts** USA
100B4 **Uitenhage** S Africa
75B2 **Uji** Japan
99C3 **Ujiji** Tanz
30C3 **Ujina** Chile
85D4 **Ujjain** India
76C4 **Ujung Pandang**
  Indon
99D3 **Ukerewe** I Tanz
86C1 **Ukhrul** India
21A2 **Ukiah** California,
  USA
20C1 **Ukiah** Oregon, USA
58C1 **Ukmerge** Lithuania

60C4 Ukraine Republic, Europe
68C2 Ulaanbaatar Mongolia
68B2 Ulaangom Mongolia
72C1 Ulaan Uul Mongolia
82C1 Ulangar Hu L China
68C1 Ulan Ude Russian Fed
68B3 Ulan Ul Hu L China
34B2 Ulapes Arg
74B3 Ulchin S Korea
54A2 Ulcinj Montenegro, Yugos
68D2 Uldz Mongolia
68B2 Uliastay Mongolia
58D1 Ulla Lithuania
109D3 Ulladulla Aust
44B3 Ullapool Scot
38H5 Ullsfjorden Inlet Nor
42C2 Ullswater L Eng
74C3 Ullung-do I S Korea
57C3 Ulm Germany
108A1 Ulooowaranie,L Aust
74B3 Ulsan S Korea
45C1 Ulster Region, N Ire
65K5 Ulungur He L China
65K5 Ulungur Hu L China
44A3 Ulva I Scot
109C4 Ulverstone Aust
63G2 Ulya R Russian Fed
60D4 Uman Ukraine
6E2 Umanak Greenland
86A2 Umaria India
86B3 Umarkot Pak
108A1 Umaroona,L Aust
20C1 Umatilla USA
38L5 Umba Russian Fed
99D3 Umba R Tanz
38H6 Ume R Sweden
38J6 Umea Sweden
101H1 Umfolozi R S Africa
4C3 Umiat USA
91C4 Umm al Qaiwain UAE
91C5 Umm as Samim Salt Marsh Oman
99C1 Umm Bell Sudan
98C1 Umm Keddada Sudan
99D1 Umm Ruwaba Sudan
91B5 Umm Sa'id Qatar
20B2 Umpqua R USA
85D4 Umred India
100B4 Umtata S Africa
35A2 Umuarama Brazil
52C1 Una R Bosnia-Herzegovina/Croatia
35B1 Unai Brazil
12B2 Unalakleet USA
80C3 Unayzah S Arabia
16C2 Uncasville USA
101G1 Underberg S Africa
60D3 Unecha Russian Fed
94B3 Uneisa Jordan
7D4 Ungava B Can
30F4 União de Vitória Brazil
34B3 Unión Arg
18B2 Union Missouri, USA
17B1 Union S Carolina, USA
14C2 Union City Pennsylvania, USA
17A1 Union Springs USA
15C3 Uniontown USA
91B5 United Arab Emirates Arabian Pen
36C3 United Kingdom Kingdom, W Europe
2H4 United States of America
6B1 United States Range Mts Can
13F2 Unity Can
20C2 Unity R USA
46D1 Unna Germany
86A1 Unnao India
44E1 Unst I Scot
13A1 Unuk R USA
92C1 Unye Turk
61J2 Unzha R Russian Fed
33E2 Upata Ven

98C3 Upemba Nat Pk Zaire
6E2 Upernavik Greenland
22D3 Upington S Africa
100B3 Uplington S Africa
14B2 Upper Arlington USA
21D2 Upper Arrow L Can
111C2 Upper Hutt NZ
20B2 Upper Klamath L USA
20B2 Upper L USA
45C1 Upper Lough Erne L N Ire
27L1 Upper Manzanilla Trinidad
39H7 Uppsala Sweden
72B1 Urad Qianqi China
91A4 Urairah S Arabia
61H3 Ural R Kazakhstan
109D2 Uralla Aust
61H3 Ural'sk Kazakhstan
65G4 Uralskiy Khrebet Mts Russian Fed
5H4 Uranium City Can
75B1 Urava Japan
18C1 Urbana Illinois, USA
14B2 Urbana Ohio, USA
52B2 Urbino Italy
42C2 Ure R Eng
61G2 Uren' Russian Fed
80E1 Urgench Uzbekistan
84B2 Urgun Afghan
55C3 Urla Turk
54B2 Uroševac Serbia, Yugos
31B4 Uruaçu Brazil
23A2 Uruapan Mexico
35B1 Urucuia R Brazil
29E2 Uruguaiana Brazil
29E2 Uruguay R, Urug
29E2 Uruguay Republic, S America
84B2 Urumqi China
69H2 Urup I Russian Fed
84B2 Uruzgan Afghan
61F3 Uryupinsk Russian Fed
61H2 Urzhum Russian Fed
54C2 Urziceni Rom
82C1 Usa Japan
75A2 Usa Japan
64G3 Usa R Russian Fed
92A2 Uşak Turk
100A3 Usakos Namibia
99D3 Ushashi Tanz
65J2 Us Tobe Kazakhstan
29C6 Ushuaia Arg
63E2 Ushumun Russian Fed
43C4 Usk R Wales
92A1 Üsküdar Turk
63C2 Usolye Sibirskoye Russian Fed
34B2 Uspallata Arg
69F2 Ussuriysk Russian Fed
47C1 Uster Switz
53B3 Ustica I Italy
57C2 Usti nad Labem Czech Republic
65J4 Ust'Ishim Kazakhstan
58B2 Ustka Pol
65K5 Ust'-Kamenogorsk Kazakhstan
63B2 Ust Karabula Russian Fed
61J2 Ust'Katav Russian Fed
63C2 Ust'-Kut Russian Fed
61E4 Ust Labinsk Russian Fed
63F1 Ust'Maya Russian Fed
1C8 Ust'Nera Russian Fed
63E2 Ust'Nyukzha Russian Fed
63C2 Ust'Ordynskiy Russian Fed
64G3 Ust'Tsil'ma Russian Fed
63F2 Ust'Umal'ta Russian Fed
75A2 Usuki Japan

25C3 Usumacinta R Guatemala/Mexico
101H1 Usutu R Swaziland
8B3 Utah State, USA
8B2 Utah L USA
23N1 Utena Russian Fed
18C2 Utica USA
51B2 Utiel Spain
14B2 Utikuma L Can
56B2 Utrecht Neth
101H1 Utrecht S Africa
50A2 Utrera Spain
38K5 Utsjoki Fin
74D3 Utsunomiya Japan
76C2 Uttaradit Thai
86A1 Uttar Pradesh State, India
65H4 Uval Russian Fed
107F3 Uvéa I Nouvelle Calédonie
99D3 Uvinza Tanz
99C3 Uvira Tanz
6E2 Uvkusigssat Greenland
39J6 Uvsikaupunki Fin
68B1 Uvs Nuur L China
74C4 Uwajima Japan
72B2 Uxin Qi China
63B2 Uyar Russian Fed
30C3 Uyuni Bol
80E1 Uzbekistan Republic, Asia
48C2 Uzerche France
59C3 Uzhgorod Ukraine
54A2 Užice Serbia, Yugos
60E3 Uzlovaya Russian Fed
92A1 Uzunköprü Turk

V

101F1 Vaal R S Africa
101G1 Vaal Dam Res S Africa
100B3 Vaalwater S Africa
59B3 Vác Hung
30F4 Vacaria Brazil
35C1 Vacaria R Minas Gerais, Brazil
21A2 Vacaville USA
85C4 Vadodara India
38K4 Vadsø Nor
47C1 Vaduz Leichtenstein
38D3 Vágar Føroyar
29E3 Va Gesell Arg
59B3 Váh R Slovakia
87B2 Vaigai R India
65K3 Vakh R Russian Fed
60B4 Válcea Rom
29C4 Valcheta Arg
47D2 Valdagno Italy
60D2 Valdaj Russian Fed
60D2 Valdayskaya Vozvyshennost' Upland Russian Fed
32D2 Val de la Pascua Ven
50B1 Valdepeñas Spain
12E2 Valdez USA
29B3 Valdivia Chile
46B2 Val d'Oise Department France
17B1 Valdosta USA
20C2 Vale USA
13D2 Valemount Can
31D4 Valença Bahia, Brazil
35C2 Valença Rio de Janeiro, Brazil
49C3 Valence France
51B2 Valencia Region, Spain
51B2 Valencia Spain
32D1 Valencia Ven
45A3 Valencia I Irish Rep
50A2 Valencia de Alcántara Spain
48B1 Valenciennes France
47C2 Valenza Italy
32C2 Valera Ven
39K7 Valga Estonia
54A2 Valjevo Serbia, Yugos
Valka = Valga
39J6 Valkeakoski Fin
25D2 Valladolid Mexico

50B1 Valladolid Spain
47B2 Valle d'Aosta Region, Italy
27D5 Valle de la Pascua Ven
23A1 Valle de Santiago Mexico
47B2 Valle d'Isère France
32C1 Valledupar Colombia
97C3 Vallée de l'Azaouak R Niger
97C3 Vallée Tilemsi V Mali
30D2 Vallée Grande Bol
22A1 Vallejo USA
30B4 Vallenar Chile
53B3 Valletta Malta
53B3 Valley City USA
20B2 Valley Falls USA
15D1 Valleyfield Can
13D1 Valleyview Can
47E2 Valli di Comacchio Lg Italy
51C1 Valls Spain
58D1 Valmiera Latvia
35A2 Valparaíso Brazil
34A2 Valparaíso Chile
23A1 Valparaíso Mexico
101G1 Vals R S Africa
85C4 Valsād India
60E3 Valuyki Russian Fed
50A2 Valverde del Camino Spain
38J6 Vammala Fin
93D2 Van Turk
63C1 Vanavara Russian Fed
18B2 Van Buren Arkansas, USA
13C3 Vancouver Can
20B1 Vancouver USA
5F5 Vancouver I Can
12G2 Vancouver,Mt Can
18C2 Vandalia Illinois, USA
14B3 Vandalia Ohio, USA
13C2 Vanderhoof Can
106C2 Van Diemen G Gulf Aust
39G7 Vänern L Sweden
39G7 Vänersborg Sweden
101D3 Vangaindrano Madag
92H Van Gölü Salt L Turk
76C2 Vang Vieng Laos
9C3 Van Horn USA
15C1 Vanier Can
1C6 Vankarem Russian Fed
38H6 Vännäs Sweden
48B2 Vannes France
47B2 Vanoise Mts France
100A4 Vanrhynsdorp S Africa
6B3 Vansittart I Can
105G4 Vanuatu Is Pacific O
14B2 Van Wert USA
72C3 Varallo Italy
90B2 Varāmin Iran
86A1 Vārānasi India
38K4 Varangerfjord Inlet Nor
38K4 Varangerhalvøya Pen Nor
52C1 Varazdin Croatia
39G7 Varberg Sweden
39H7 Varde Den
38L4 Varde Nor
58C2 Varéna Lithuania
47C2 Varenna Italy
35B2 Vargínha Brazil
38K6 Varkaus Fin
54C2 Varna Bulg
39G7 Värnamo Sweden
17B1 Varnville USA
35C1 Várzea da Palma Brazil
47C2 Varzi Italy
50B1 Vascongadas Region, Spain
60D3 Vasil'kov Ukraine
14B2 Vassar USA
39H7 Västerås Sweden
39H7 Västervik Sweden

52B2 **Vasto** Italy	13D2 **Vernon** Can	53C2 **Vieste** Italy	14A3 **Vincennes** USA
65J4 **Vasyugan** R Russian Fed	46A2 **Vernon** France	70B2 **Vietnam** Republic, S E Asia	38H5 **Vindel** R Sweden
38B2 **Vatnajökull** Mts	9D3 **Vernon** USA	76D1 **Vietri** Viet	85D4 **Vindhya Range** Mts India
38A1 **Vatneyri** Iceland	17B2 **Vero Beach** USA	27P2 **Vieux Fort** St Lucia	16B3 **Vineland** USA
54C1 **Vatra Dornei** Rom	54B2 **Veroia** Greece	79B2 **Vigan** Phil	16D2 **Vineyard Haven** USA
39G7 **Vättern** L Sweden	47D2 **Verolanuova** Italy	47C2 **Vigevano** Italy	76D2 **Vinh** Viet
9C3 **Vaughn** USA	47D2 **Verona** Italy	48B3 **Vignemale** Mt France	76D3 **Vinh Cam Ranh** B Viet
32C3 **Vaupés** R Colombia	46B2 **Versailles** France	50A1 **Vigo** Spain	77D4 **Vinh Loi** Viet
13E2 **Vauxhall** Can	101H1 **Verulam** S Africa	87D3 **Vijayawada** India	77D3 **Vinh Long** Viet
87C3 **Vavunija** Sri Lanka	46B2 **Verviers** Belg	55A2 **Vijosë** R Alb	18A2 **Vinita** USA
39G7 **Växjö** Sweden	46C2 **Vesle** R France	38B2 **Vik** Iceland	54A1 **Vinkovci** Croatia
64G2 **Vaygach, Ostrov** I Russian Fed	49D2 **Vesoul** France	54B2 **Vikhren** Mt Bulg	60C4 **Vinnitsa** Ukraine
34C2 **Vedia** Arg	38G5 **Vesterålen** Is Nor	13E2 **Viking** Can	112B3 **Vinson Massif** Upland Ant
38G5 **Vega** I Nor	38G5 **Vestfjorden** Inlet Nor	38G6 **Vikna** I Nor	100A3 **Vioolsdrift** S Africa
13E2 **Vegreville** Can	38B2 **Vestmannaeyjar** Iceland	101C2 **Vila da Maganja** Mozam	47D1 **Vipiteno** Italy
50A2 **Vejer de la Frontera** Spain	53B2 **Vesuvio** Mt Italy		79B3 **Virac** Phil
39F7 **Vejle** Den	59B3 **Veszprém** Hung	101C3 **Vila Machado** Mozam	87B2 **Virddhåchalam** India
52C2 **Velebit** Mts Croatia	39H7 **Vetlanda** Sweden	101C3 **Vilanculos** Mozam	97A3 **Virei** Angola
52C1 **Velenje** Slovenia	61F2 **Vetluga** R Russian Fed	**Vilanova i la Geltrú** = **Villanueva-y-Geltrú**	35C1 **Virgem da Lapa** Brazil
35C1 **Velhas** R Brazil	46B1 **Veurne** Belg	50A1 **Vila Real** Port	101G1 **Virginia** S Africa
39K7 **Velikaya** R Russian Fed	47B1 **Vevey** Switz	101C2 **Vila Vasco da Gama** Mozam	10C3 **Virginia** State, USA
60D2 **Velikiye Luki** Russian Fed	46A2 **Vexin** Region, France	35C2 **Vila Velha** Brazil	10A2 **Virginia** USA
61G1 **Velikiy Ustyug** Russian Fed	47A2 **Veynes** France	58D2 **Vileyka** Belorussia	21B2 **Virginia City** USA
54C2 **Veliko Türnovo** Bulg	50A1 **Viana do Castelo** Port	38H6 **Vilhelmina** Sweden	27E3 **Virgin Is** Caribbean S
97A3 **Vélingara** Sen	**Viangchan** = **Vientiane**	33E6 **Vilhena** Brazil	52C2 **Virovitica** Croatia
87B2 **Veliore** India	49E3 **Viareggio** Italy	60C2 **Viljandi** Estonia	46C2 **Virton** Belg
61F1 **Vel'sk** Russian Fed	39F7 **Viborg** Den	101G1 **Viljoenskroon** S Africa	87B3 **Virudunagar** India
87B3 **Vembanad** L India	53C3 **Vibo Valentia** Italy	9C3 **Villa Ahumada** Mexico	52C2 **Vis** I Croatia
34C2 **Venado Tuerto** Arg	**Vic** = **Vich**	34B2 **Villa Atuel** Arg	21B2 **Visalia** USA
35B2 **Venceslau Braz** Brazil	112C2 **Vicecomodoro Marambio** Base Ant	50A1 **Villaba** Spain	79B3 **Visayan S** Phil
49C2 **Vendôme** France	52B1 **Vicenza** Italy	23A2 **Villa Carranza** Mexico	39H7 **Visby** Sweden
12E1 **Venetie** USA	51C1 **Vich** Spain	52B1 **Villach** Austria	4H2 **Viscount Melville Sd** Can
47D2 **Veneto** Region, Italy	32D3 **Vichada** R Colombia	34B2 **Villa Colon** Arg	54A2 **Višegrad** Bosnia-Herzegovina
47E2 **Venezia** Italy	61F2 **Vichuga** Russian Fed	34C2 **Villa Constitución** Arg	50A1 **Viseu** Port
32D2 **Venezuela** Republic, S America	49C2 **Vichy** France	34C1 **Villa de Maria** Arg	83C4 **Vishakhapatnam** India
87A1 **Vengurla** India	19B3 **Vicksburg** USA	23A2 **Villa de Reyes** Mexico	47B1 **Visp** Switz
12C3 **Veniaminof V** USA	35C2 **Viçosa** Brazil	34B2 **Villa Dolores** Arg	49C1 **Vissingen** Neth
Venice = **Venezia**	106C4 **Victor Harbour** Aust	47D2 **Villafranca di Verona** Italy	21B3 **Vista** USA
87B2 **Venkatagiri** India	34C2 **Victoria** Arg	34C2 **Villa General Mitre** Arg	**Vistula** = **Wisla**
56B2 **Venlo** Neth	13C3 **Victoria** Can	34B2 **Villa General Roca** Arg	57C3 **Vltava** R Czech Republic
56B1 **Venta** R Latvia	34A3 **Victoria** Chile	34D2 **Villaguay** Arg	87A1 **Vite** India
101G1 **Ventersborg** S Africa	78D1 **Victoria** Malay	25C3 **Villahermosa** Mexico	60D2 **Vitebsk** Belorussia
58C1 **Ventspils** Latvia	108B3 **Victoria** State, Aust	23A1 **Villa Hidalgo** Mexico	52B2 **Viterbo** Italy
32D3 **Ventuari** R Ven	9D4 **Victoria** USA	34C2 **Villa Huidobro** Arg	63D2 **Vitim** R Russian Fed
22C3 **Ventura** USA	27D4 **Victoria** R Aust	34C3 **Villa Iris** Arg	50B1 **Vitora** Spain
60D1 **Vepsovskaya Vozvyshennost'** Upland Russian Fed	26B2 **Victoria de las Tunas** Cuba	34C2 **Villa Maria** Arg	31C6 **Vitória** Brazil
30D4 **Vera** Arg	100B2 **Victoria Falls** Zambia/Zim	30D3 **Villa Montes** Bol	31C4 **Vitoria da Conquista** Brazil
51B2 **Vera** Spain	4G2 **Victoria I** Can	23A1 **Villanueva** Mexico	48B2 **Vitré** France
23B2 **Veracruz** Mexico	108B2 **Victoria,L** Aust	50A1 **Villa Nova de Gaia** Port	46C2 **Vitry-le-Francois** France
23B1 **Veracruz** State, Mexico	99D3 **Victoria,L** C Africa	50A2 **Villanueva de la Serena** Spain	38J5 **Vittangi** Sweden
85C4 **Veräval** India	112B7 **Victoria Land** Region, Ant	51C1 **Villanueva-y-Geltrú** Spain	53B3 **Vittoria** Italy
47C2 **Verbania** Italy	86C2 **Victoria,Mt** Burma	34B3 **Villa Regina** Arg	47E2 **Vittorio Veneto** Italy
47C2 **Vercelli** Italy	99D2 **Victoria Nile** R Uganda	51B2 **Villarreal** Spain	69H2 **Vityaz Depth** Pacific O
35A1 **Verde** R Goias, Brazil	111B2 **Victoria Range** Mts NZ	29B3 **Villarrica** Chile	50A1 **Vivero** Spain
23A1 **Verde** R Jalisco, Mexico	106C2 **Victoria River Downs** Aust	30E4 **Villarrica** Par	63B1 **Vivi** R Russian Fed
35A1 **Verde** R Mato Grosso do Sul, Brazil	4H3 **Victoria Str** Can	50B2 **Villarrobledo** Spain	34D3 **Vivorata** Arg
23B2 **Verde** R Oaxaca, Mexico	15D1 **Victoriaville** Can	34D2 **Villa San José** Arg	63C2 **Vizhne-Angarsk** Russian Fed
35C1 **Verde Grande** R Brazil	100B4 **Victoria West** S Africa	34C2 **Villa Valeria** Arg	83C4 **Vizianagaram** India
35A1 **Verde,Pen** Arg	21B3 **Victorville** USA	32C3 **Villavicencio** Colombia	54B1 **Vlädeasa** Mt Rom
49D2 **Verdon** R France	34A2 **Vicuña** Chile	49C2 **Villefranche** France	61F5 **Vladikavkaz** Russian Fed
46C2 **Verdun** France	34C2 **Vicuña Mackenna** Arg	7C5 **Ville-Marie** Can	65F4 **Vladimir** Russian Fed
101G1 **Vereeniging** S Africa	17B1 **Vidalia** USA	51B2 **Villena** Spain	59C2 **Vladimir Volynskiy** Ukraine
61H2 **Vereshchagino** Russian Fed	54C2 **Videle** Rom	46B2 **Villeneuve-St-Georges** France	74C2 **Vladivostok** Russian Fed
97A3 **Verga,C** Guinea	54B2 **Vidin** Bulg	48C3 **Villeneuve-sur-Lot** France	56A2 **Vlieland** I Neth
34D3 **Vergara** Arg	85D4 **Vidisha** India	19B3 **Ville Platte** USA	46B1 **Vlissingen** Neth
50A1 **Verin** Spain	58D1 **Vidzy** Belorussia	46B2 **Villers-Cotterêts** France	55A2 **Vlorë** Alb
63D2 **Verkh Angara** R Russian Fed	29D4 **Viedma** Arg	49C2 **Villeurbanne** France	57C3 **Vöcklabruck** Austria
61J3 **Verkhnedvinsk** Belorussia	26A4 **Viejo** Costa Rica	101G1 **Villiers** S Africa	76D3 **Voeune Sai** Camb
63E1 **Verkhnevilyuysk** Russian Fed	**Vielha** = **Viella**	87B2 **Villupuram** India	47C2 **Voghera** Italy
1C8 **Verkhoyansk** Russian Fed	51C1 **Viella** Spain	58D2 **Vilnius** Lithuania	101D2 **Vohibinany** Madag
35A1 **Vermelho** R Brazil	**Vienna** = **Wien**	63D1 **Vilyuy** R Russian Fed	101E2 **Vohimarina** Madag
13E2 **Vermilion** Can	18C2 **Vienna** Illinois, USA	63E1 **Vilyuysk** Russian Fed	99D3 **Voi** Kenya
10C2 **Vermont** State, USA	14B3 **Vienna** W Virginia, USA	34A2 **Viña del Mar** Chile	97B4 **Voinjama** Lib
22B2 **Vernalis** USA	49C2 **Vienne** France	51C1 **Vinaroz** Spain	49D2 **Voiron** France
	48C2 **Vienne** R France		54A1 **Vojvodina** Aut Republic Serbia, Yugos
	76C2 **Vientiane** Laos		26A5 **Volcán Barú** Mt Panama
	47C1 **Vierwaldstätter See** L Switz		
	48C2 **Vierzon** France		

23B2 Volcán Citlaltepetl
 Mt Mexico
30C3 Volcán Lullaillaco Mt
 Chile
34A3 Volcáno Copahue Mt
 Chile
34A3 Volcáno Domuyo Mt
 Chile
 Volcano Is = Kazan
 Retto
29B3 Volcáno Lanin Mt
 Arg
30C3 Volcán Ollagüe Mt
 Chile
34A3 Volcáno Llaima Mt
 Chile
34B2 Volcáno Maipo Mt
 Chile
34B2 Volcáno Peteroa Mt
 Chile
34B3 Volcáno Tromen Mt
 Arg
23A2 Volcán Paracutin Mt
 Mexico
32B3 Volcán Puracé Mt
 Colombia
34A3 Volcán Tinguiririca
 Mt Arg/Chile
61J2 Volchansk
 Russian Fed
61G4 Volga R Russian Fed
61G4 Volgodonsk
 Russian Fed
61F4 Volgograd
 Russian Fed
61G3 Volgogradskoye
 Vodokhranilishche
 Res Russian Fed
60D2 Volkhov Russian Fed
60D2 Volkhov R
 Russian Fed
58C2 Volkovysk Belorussia
101G1 Volksrust S Africa
61F2 Vologda Russian Fed
48B2 Vologanes France
55B3 Vólos Greece
61G3 Vol'sk Russian Fed
22B2 Volta USA
97B3 Volta Blanche R
 Burkina
97B4 Volta,L Ghana
97B3 Volta Noire R
 Burkina
35C2 Volta Redonda Brazil
97B3 Volta Rouge R
 Burkina
61F4 Volzhskiy
 Russian Fed
12D2 Von Frank Mt USA
6J3 Vopnafjördur Iceland
47C1 Voralberg Province,
 Austria
47C1 Vorder Rhein R
 Switz
56C1 Vordingborg Den
64H3 Vorkuta Russian Fed
39G6 Vorma R Nor
60E3 Voronezh
 Russian Fed
38M5 Voron'ya R
 Russian Fed
39K7 Vóru Estonia
49D2 Vosges Mt France
39F6 Voss Nor
63B2 Vostochnyy Sayan
 Mts Russian Fed
112B9 Vostok Base Ant
61H2 Votkinsk
 Russian Fed
46C2 Vouziers France
60D4 Voznesensk Ukraine
54B2 Vranje Serbia, Yugos
54B2 Vratsa Bulg
52C2 Vrbas R Serbia,
 Yugos
52B1 Vrbovsko Bosnia-
 Herzegovina
51B1 Vrede S Africa
33F2 Vreed en Hoop
 Guyana
54B1 Vršac Serbia, Yugos
52C2 Vrtoče Bosnia-
 Herzegovina
100B3 Vryburg S Africa

101H1 Vryheid S Africa
54A1 Vukovar Croatia
13E2 Vulcan Can
53B3 Vulcano / Italy
77D3 Vung Tau Viet
38J5 Vuollerim Sweden
38L6 Vyartsilya
 Russian Fed
61H2 Vyatka R
 Russian Fed
69F2 Vyazemskiy
 Russian Fed
60D2 Vyaz'ma Russian Fed
61F2 Vyazniki Russian Fed
60C1 Vyborg Russian Fed
64G3 Vym' R Russian Fed
43C3 Vyrnwy R Wales
60D2 Vyshiy Volochek
 Russian Fed
59B3 Výškov
 Czech Republic
60E1 Vytegra Russian Fed

W

78B3 Wa China
54B1 Wabasca Can
5G4 Wabasca R Can
13E1 Wabasca L Can
14A2 Wabash USA
14A3 Wabash R USA
5J4 Wabowden Can
70A Wabush Can
17B2 Waccasassa B USA
16D1 Wachusett Res USA
19A3 Waco USA
85B3 Wad Pak
95A2 Waddán Libya
5F4 Waddington,Mt Can
93E4 Wadi al Batin
 Watercourse Iraq
93D3 Wadi al Ghudāf
 Watercourse Iraq
94C2 Wadi al Harir V Syria
93D3 Wadi al Mirah
 Watercourse Iraq/
 S Arabia
93D3 Wadi al Ubayyid
 Watercourse Iraq
93D3 Wadi Ar'ar
 Watercourse
 S Arabia
91A5 Wadi as Hsabá'
 Watercourse
 S Arabia
92C3 Wadi as Sirhan V
 Jordan/S Arabia
94C2 Wadi az Zaydi V
 Syria
94C3 Wadi edh Dhab'i V
 Jordan
94A3 Wadi el 'Arish V
 Egypt
94C3 Wadi el Ghadaf V
 Jordan
94B3 Wadi el Hasa V
 Jordan
94C3 Wadi el Janab V
 Jordan
94B3 Wadi el Jeib V Israel/
 Jordan
95B3 Wadi el Milk
 Watercourse Sudan
92A3 Wadi el Natrun
 Watercourse Egypt
94B3 Wadi es Sir Jordan
94B3 Wadi Fidan V Jordan
94B3 Wadi Hareidin V
 Egypt
93D3 Wadi Hawrān R Iraq
95B3 Wadi Howa
 Watercourse Sudan
98C1 Wadi Ibra
 Watercourse Sudan
94C2 Wadi Luhfi
 Watercourse Jordan
94B3 Wadi Mujib V
 Jordan
94B3 Wadi Qitaiya V
 Egypt
80B3 Wadi Sha'it
 Watercourse Egypt
99D1 Wad Medani Sudan
80B3 Wafra Kuwait
6B3 Wager B Can
6A3 Wager Bay Can

109C3 Wagga Wagga Aust
106A4 Wagin Aust
95A2 Wäha Libya
21C4 Wahaiwa Hawaiian Is
18A1 Wahoo USA
8D2 Wahpeton USA
87A1 Wai India
118B2 Waiau NZ
111A3 Waiau R NZ
111B2 Waiau R NZ
71E3 Waigeo / Indon
110C1 Waihi NZ
110C1 Waikaremoana,L NZ
110C1 Waikato R NZ
108A2 Waikerie Aust
111B3 Waikouaiti NZ
21C4 Wailuku Hawaiian Is
111B2 Waimakariri R NZ
111B2 Waimate NZ
21C4 Waimea Hawaiian Is
106B1 Waingapu Indon
13E2 Wainwright Can
4B2 Wainwright USA
111B2 Waipara NZ
110C2 Waipukurau NZ
111A3 Wairarapa,L NZ
111B2 Wairau R NZ
110C1 Wairoa NZ
111B2 Wairoa R NZ
110B1 Waitara NZ
110C1 Waitomo NZ
111B2 Waitotara NZ
75B1 Wajima Japan
99E2 Wajir Kenya
75B1 Wakasa-wan B
 Japan
111A3 Wakatipu,L NZ
74D4 Wakayama Japan
42D3 Wakefield Eng
27H1 Wakefield Jamaica
16D2 Wakefield Rhode
 Island, USA
76B2 Wakema Burma
69G2 Wakkanai Japan
108B3 Wakool R Aust
59B2 Walbrzych Pol
109D2 Walcha Aust
58B2 Walcz Pol
46D1 Waldbröl Germany
16C1 Walden USA
43C3 Wales Country, UK
12A1 Wales USA
63B1 Wales / Can
109C2 Walgett Aust
108B3 Walgreen Coast
 Region, Ant
99C3 Walikale Zaire
21B2 Walker L USA
14B2 Walkerton Can
108A2 Wallaroo Aust
109C3 Walla Walla Aust
20C1 Walla Walla USA
16C2 Wallingford USA
105H4 Wallis and Futuna Is
 Pacific O
20C1 Wallowa USA
20C1 Wallowa Mts Mts
 USA
109C1 Wallumbilla Aust
16B2 Walnut Ridge USA
110C1 Walouru NZ
20C1 Walsall Eng
9C3 Walsenburg USA
9C3 Walsenburgh USA
17B1 Walterboro USA
17A1 Walter F George Res
 USA
16D1 Waltham USA
100A3 Walvis Bay S Africa
103J6 Walvis Ridge
 Atlantic O
97C4 Wamba Nig
98B3 Wamba R Zaire
18A2 Wamego USA
18A2 Wana Pak
108B1 Wanaaring Aust
111A2 Wanaka NZ
111A2 Wanaka,L NZ
14B1 Wanapitei L Can
100A3 Wandoan Aust
110C1 Wanganui Aust
110C1 Wanganui R NZ

109C3 Wangaratta Aust
99E2 Wanie Weyne
 Somalia
62E2 Wanning China
87B1 Wanparti India
73B3 Wanxian China
73B3 Wanyuan China
13D2 Wapiti R Can
18B2 Wappapello,L USA
16C2 Wappingers Falls
 USA
87B1 Warangal India
109C4 Waratah Aust
108C3 Waratah B Aust
103H3 Warburton Aust
108A1 Warburton R Aust
109C1 Ward R Aust
101G1 Warden S Africa
85D3 Wardha India
85D4 Wardha R India
111A3 Ward,Mt NZ
5F4 Ware Can
16C1 Ware USA
16D2 Wareham USA
109D1 Warialda Aust
76C2 Warin Chamrap Thai
100B3 Warmbad S Africa
16B2 Warminster USA
21B2 Warm Springs USA
26D2 Warnemünde
 Germany
58C2 Warner Mts USA
17B1 Warner Robins USA
108B3 Warracknabeal Aust
108A1 Warrandirinna,L Aust
107D3 Warrego R Aust
19B3 Warren Arkansas,
 USA
109C2 Warren Aust
16D1 Warren
 Massachusetts, USA
14B2 Warren Ohio, USA
15C2 Warren
 Pennsylvania, USA
45C1 Warrenpoint N Ire
18B2 Warrensburg USA
101F1 Warrenton S Africa
15C3 Warrenton USA
97C4 Warri Nig
108A1 Warrina Aust
42C3 Warrington Eng
108B3 Warrnambool Aust
 Warsaw = Warszawa
58C2 Warszawa Pol
59B2 Warta R Pol
109D1 Warwick Aust
43D3 Warwick County,
 Eng
43B3 Warwick Eng
16B2 Warwick New York,
 USA
16D2 Warwick Rhode
 Island, USA
8B3 Wasatch Range Mts
 USA
101H1 Wasbank S Africa
21B2 Wasco USA
4H2 Washburn L Can
85D4 Washim India
10C3 Washington District
 of Columbia, USA
17B1 Washington Georgia,
 USA
14A3 Washington Indiana,
 USA
18B2 Washington
 Missouri, USA
16B2 Washington New
 Jersey, USA
14B2 Washington
 Pennsylvania, USA
8A2 Washington State,
 USA
14B3 Washington Court
 House USA
6D1 Washington Land
 Can
15D2 Washington,Mt USA
43E3 Wash,The Eng
85A3 Washuk Pak
13E2 Wasian USA
7C4 Waskaganish Can
26A4 Waspán Nic
70D4 Watampone Indon
16C2 Waterbury USA

45C2 Waterford County, Irish Rep
41B3 Waterford Irish Rep
45C2 Waterford Harbour Irish Rep
46C1 Waterloo Belg
54G2 Waterloo USA
15C2 Watertown New York, USA
101H1 Waterval-Boven S Africa
10D2 Waterville Maine, USA
16C1 Watervliet USA
5G4 Waterways Can
43D4 Watford Eng
15C2 Watkins Glen USA
8C1 Watrous Can
99C2 Watsa Zaire
12J2 Watson Lake Can
22B2 Watsonville USA
71F4 Wau PNG
99C2 Wau Sudan
7B5 Waua USA
70D2 Wauchope Aust
17B2 Wauchula USA
14A2 Waukegan USA
10B2 Wausau USA
14A2 Wauwatosa USA
106C2 Wave Hill Aust
43E3 Waveney R Eng
14B3 Waverly Ohio, USA
46C1 Wavre Belg
10B2 Wawa USA
95A2 Wāw Al Kabir Libya
95A2 Wāw an Nāmūs Well Libya
22C2 Wawona USA
19A3 Waxahachie USA
17B1 Waycross Georgia, USA
17B1 Waynesboro Georgia, USA
19C3 Waynesboro Mississippi, USA
16A3 Waynesboro Pennsylvania, USA
15C3 Waynesboro Virginia, USA
18B2 Waynesville Missouri, USA
84B2 Wazi Khwa Afghan
33E4 Weald,The Upland Eng
42C2 Wear R Eng
19A3 Weatherford Texas, USA
20B2 Weaverville USA
14B1 Webbwood Can
16D1 Webster USA
18B2 Webster Groves USA
29D6 Weddell I Falkland Is
112C2 Weddell S Ant
13C2 Wedge Mt Can
20B2 Weed USA
10H1 Weenen S Africa
109C2 Wee Waa Aust
72D1 Weichang China
57C3 Weiden Germany
72E2 Weifang China
72E2 Weihai China
72C3 Wei He R Henan, China
72C2 Wei He R Shaanxi, China
109C1 Weilmoringle Aust
73A4 Weining China
107D2 Weipa Aust
14B2 Weirton USA
20C2 Weiser USA
72D3 Weishan Hu L China
57C2 Weissenfels Germany
17A1 Weiss L USA
99D1 Weldiya Eth
101G1 Welkom S Africa
15C2 Welland Can
43D3 Welland R Eng
106C2 Wellesley Is Can
12G2 Wellesley L Can
43D3 Wellingborough Eng
109C2 Wellington Aust
18A2 Wellington Kansas, USA
111B2 Wellington NZ
6A2 Wellington Chan Can

13C2 Wells Can
43C4 Wells Eng
110B1 Wells,L Aust
106B3 Wells,L Aust
57C3 Wels Aust
43C3 Welshpool Wales
13D1 Wembley Can
7C4 Wemindji Can
20B1 Wenatchee USA
20C1 Wenatchee R USA
97B4 Wenchi Ghana
72E2 Wenden China
73E4 Wenling China
32J7 Wenman I Ecuador
73A5 Wenshan China
107D4 Wenthaggi Aust
108B2 Wentworth Aust
72A3 Wen Xian China
73E4 Wenzhou China
73C4 Wenzhu China
12G1 Wepener S Africa
57C2 Werra R Germany
109D2 Werris Creek Aust
56B2 Wesel Germany
56B2 Weser R Germany
106C2 Wessel Is Aust
14A2 West Allis USA
104C4 West Australian Basin Indian O
104C5 West Australian Ridge Indian O
19C3 West B USA
86B2 West Bengal State, India
43D3 West Bromwich Eng
16B3 West Chester USA
46D1 Westerburg Germany
56B2 Westerland Germany
16D2 Westerly USA
106A3 Western Australia State, Aust
87A1 Western Ghats Mts India
44A3 Western Isles Scot
96A2 Western Sahara Region, Mor
105H4 Western Samoa Is Pacific O
46B1 Westerschelde Estuary Neth
46D1 Westerwald Region, Germany
49D1 Westfalen Region, Germany
29D6 West Falkland I Falkland Is
16C1 Westfield Massachusetts, USA
15C2 Westfield New York, USA
18C2 West Frankfort USA
109C1 Westgate Aust
43C4 West Glamorgan County, Wales
102E3 West Indies Is Caribbean S
13E2 Westlock Can
14B2 West Lorne Can
45C2 Westmeath County, Irish Rep
18B2 West Memphis USA
43D3 West Midlands County, Eng
43D4 Westminster Eng
16A3 Westminster Maryland, USA
17B1 Westminster S Carolina, USA
100B3 West Nicholson Zim
78D1 Weston Malay
14B3 Weston USA
43C4 Weston-super-Mare Eng
17B2 West Palm Beach USA
18B2 West Plains USA
22B1 West Point California, USA
19C3 West Point Mississippi, USA
16C2 West Point New York, USA
12F2 West Point Mt USA

45B2 Westport Irish Rep
111B2 Westport NZ
40C2 Westray I Scot
13C2 West Road R Can
42E3 West Sole Oilfield N Sea
11B3 West Virginia State, USA
22C1 West Walker R USA
109D2 West Wyalong Aust
42D3 West Yorkshire County, Eng
71D4 Wetar I Indon
13E2 Wetaskiwin Can
99D3 Wete Tanz
46E1 Wetzlar Germany
Wevok = Cape Lisburne
71F4 Wewak PNG
19A2 Wewoka USA
45C2 Wexford County, Irish Rep
45C2 Wexford Irish Rep
5H5 Weyburn Can
43C4 Weymouth Eng
16D1 Weymouth USA
110C1 Whakatane NZ
110C1 Whakatane R NZ
44E1 Whalsay I Scot
110B1 Whangarei NZ
42D3 Wharfe R Eng
19A4 Wharton USA
111B2 Whataroa NZ
16A3 Wheaton Maryland, USA
8B3 Wheeler Peak Mt Nevada, USA
9C3 Wheeler Peak Mt New Mexico, USA
14B2 Wheeling USA
13C3 Whistler Can
15C2 Whitby Can
42D2 Whitby Eng
18B2 White R Arkansas, USA
12F2 White R Can
14A3 White R Indiana, USA
8C2 White R S Dakota, USA
7E4 White B Can
108B2 White Cliffs Aust
40C2 White Coomb Mt Scot
13D2 Whitecourt Can
14A1 Whitefish Pt USA
7D4 Whitegull L Can
15D2 Whitehall New York, USA
16B2 Whitehall Pennsylvania, USA
42C2 Whitehaven Eng
12G2 Whitehorse Can
110C1 White I NZ
19B4 White L USA
109C4 Whitemark Aust
21B2 White Mountain Peak Mt USA
12E1 White Mts Alaska, USA
15D2 White Mts New Hampshire, USA
99D1 White Nile R Sudan
7B5 White Plains USA
13D2 White River Can
15D2 White River Junction USA
White S = Beloye More
14B2 Whitesail L Can
20B1 White Salmon USA
17C1 Whiteville USA
97B4 White Volta R Ghana
42B2 Whithorn Scot
17B1 Whitmire USA
21B2 Whitney,Mt USA
12E2 Whittier Alaska, USA
22C4 Whittier California, USA
5H3 Wholdia L Can
108A2 Whyalla Aust
14B2 Wiarton Can
18A2 Wichita USA
9D3 Wichita Falls USA

44C2 Wick Scot
45C2 Wicklow County, Irish Rep
45C2 Wicklow Irish Rep
45C2 Wicklow Mts Irish Rep
109C1 Widgeegoara R Aust
46D1 Wied R Germany
59B2 Wielun Pol
59B3 Wien Austria
59B3 Wiener Neustadt Austria
58C2 Wieprz R Pol
42C3 Wiesbaden Germany
42C3 Wigan Eng
19C3 Wiggins USA
42C2 Wigtown Scot
42C2 Wigtown B Scot
47C1 Wil Switz
20C1 Wilbur USA
108B2 Wilcannia Aust
21B2 Wildcat Peak Mt USA
47B1 Wildhorn Mt Switz
13E2 Wild Horse Can
47D1 Wildspitze Mt Austria
17B2 Wildwood Florida, USA
16B3 Wildwood New Jersey, USA
101G1 Wilge R S Africa
56B2 Wilhelmshaven Germany
15C2 Wilkes-Barre USA
112B8 Wilkes Land Ant
13F2 Wilkie Can
20D2 Willamette R USA
108B2 Willandra R Aust
20B1 Willapa B USA
9C3 Willcox USA
27D4 Willemstad Curaçao
108A1 William Creek Aust
108B3 William,Mt Aust
21A2 Williams California, USA
13C2 Williams Lake Can
15C3 Williamsport USA
16C1 Williamstown Massachusetts, USA
14B3 Williamstown W Virginia, USA
16C2 Willimantic USA
16B2 Willingboro USA
13D2 Willingdon,Mt Can
17C2 Willis Group Is Aust
17B2 Williston Florida, USA
100B4 Williston S Africa
13C1 Williston L Can
8D2 Willmar USA
108A3 Willoughby,C Aust
13C2 Willow R Can
20B2 Willow Ranch USA
21A2 Willows USA
18A2 Willow Springs USA
108A2 Wilmington Aust
16B3 Wilmington Delaware, USA
17C1 Wilmington N Carolina, USA
11C3 Wilson USA
108B1 Wilson R Aust
6B3 Wilson,C Can
22C3 Wilson,Mt California, USA
20B1 Wilson,Mt Oregon, USA
109C3 Wilsons Promontory Pen Aust
43D4 Wiltshire County, Eng
46C2 Wiltz Lux
14A2 Winamac USA
101G1 Winburg S Africa
16C1 Winchendon USA
15C3 Winchester Can
43D4 Winchester Eng
15C3 Winchester New Hampshire, USA
15C3 Winchester Virginia, USA
42C2 Windermere Eng

100A3 Windhoek Namibia
107D3 Windorah Aust
8C2 Wind River Range
Mts USA
109D2 Windsor Aust
16C2 Windsor Connecticut,
USA
43D4 Windsor Eng
7D5 Windsor Nova
Scotia, Can
14B2 Windsor Ontario, Can
15D1 Windsor Quebec,
Can
17B1 Windsor USA
16C2 Windsor Locks USA
27E4 Windward Is
Caribbean S
26C3 Windward Pass
Caribbean S
13E1 Winfield L Can
18A2 Winfield Kansas,
USA
109D2 Wingham Aust
34C3 Winifreda Arg
7B4 Winisk R Can
7B4 Winisk L Can
76B2 Winkana Burma
20B1 Winisk USA
97B4 Winneba Ghana
14A2 Winnebago,L USA
20C2 Winnemucca USA
19B3 Winnfield USA
5J4 Winnipeg Can
5J4 Winnipeg,L Can
5J4 Winnipegosis Can
4J4 Winnipegosis,L Can
15D2 Winnipesaukee,L
USA
10A2 Winona Minnesota,
USA
19C3 Winona Mississippi,
USA
15D2 Winooski USA
9B3 Winslow USA
16C2 Winsted USA
11B3 Winston-Salem USA
46E1 Winterberg Germany
17B2 Winter Garden USA
17B2 Winter Park USA
22B1 Winters USA
47C1 Winterthur Switz
107D3 Winton Aust
111A3 Winton NZ
43E3 Wisbech Eng
10B2 Wisconsin State,
USA
7B5 Wisconsin Rapids
USA
12D1 Wiseman USA
58B2 Wisła R Pol
56C2 Wismar Germany
33F2 Witagron Surinam
101G1 Witbank S Africa
9D3 Witchita Falls USA
43D3 Witham R Eng
42E3 Withernsea Eng
43A4 Witney Eng
46D1 Witten Germany
56C2 Wittenberg Germany
106A3 Wittenoom Aust
46D1 Wittlich Germany
58B2 Władysławowo Pol
58B2 Wocławek Pol
58C2 Włodawa Pol
109C3 Wodonga Aust
47C1 Wohlen Switz
71E4 Wokam Indon
43D4 Woking Eng
71F3 Woleai I Pacific O
20B2 Wolf Creek USA
8C2 Wolf Point USA
57C3 Wolfsberg Austria
56C2 Wolfsburg Germany
5H4 Wollaston L Can
5H4 Wollaston Lake Can
4G3 Wollaston Pen Can
109D2 Wollongong Aust
101G1 Wolmaransstad
S Africa
59B2 Wolow Pol
108B3 Wolseley Aust
43C3 Wolverhampton Eng
16A2 Womelsdorf USA
109D1 Wondai Aust
74B3 Wŏnju S Korea

108B2 Wonominta R Aust
13C1 Wonowon Can
74B3 Wŏnsan N Korea
108C3 Worthagal Aust
108A2 Woocalla Aust
16B3 Woodbine USA
15C3 Woodbridge USA
5G4 Wood Buffalo Nat Pk
Can
109D1 Woodburn Aust
20B1 Woodburn USA
18B3 Woodbury USA
12F1 Woodchopper USA
21A2 Woodland California,
USA
20B1 Woodland
Washington, USA
107E1 Woodlark I PNG
106C4 Woodmera Aust
106C3 Woodroffe,Mt Aust
14B2 Woodstock Ontario,
Can
16B3 Woodstown USA
110C2 Woodville NZ
109A2 Woodville USA
108A2 Woomera Aust
15D2 Woonsocket USA
14B2 Wooster USA
43C3 Worcester Eng
100A4 Worcester S Africa
16D1 Worcester USA
47E1 Wörgl Austria
42C2 Workington Eng
42D2 Worland USA
46E2 Worms Germany
43B4 Worms Head Pt
Wales
43D4 Worthing Eng
8D2 Worthington USA
71D4 Wowoni I Indon
12H3 Wrangell USA
12H3 Wrangell I USA
12F2 Wrangell Mts USA
40B2 Wrath,C Scot
43C3 Wrexham Wales
17B1 Wrightsville USA
22D3 Wrightwood USA
4F3 Wrigley Can
59B2 Wrocław Pol
58B2 Września Pol
69E2 Wuchang China
76E1 Wuchuan China
72E2 Wuda China
72C2 Wuding He R China
72A3 Wudu China
73C4 Wugang China
73C3 Wuhai China
73D3 Wuhan China
73D5 Wuhua China
72B1 Wujia He R China
73B4 Wu Jiang R China
97C4 Wukari Nig
73B4 Wuling Shan _Mts_
China
97D4 Wum Can
73A4 Wumeng Shan
Upland China
73C4 Wun Jiang R China
73D5 Wunnu China
73C4 Wupu China
76E1 Wurren USA
72C2 Wutai Shan _Mt_
China
71F4 Wuvulu I Pacific O
72A2 Wuwei China
73C3 Wuxi China
73E3 Wuxing China
72C2 Wuyang China
73D4 Wuyi Shan _Mts_
China
72B1 Wuyuan China
76D2 Wuzhi Shan _Mts_
China
72B2 Wuzhong China
73C5 Wuzhou China
14B2 Wyandotte USA
109C1 Wyandra Aust
43C4 Wye Eng
43C4 Wylye R Eng
43E3 Wymondham Eng
108B2 Wyndham Aust
18B2 Wynne USA

4G2 Wynniatt B Can
109C4 Wynyard Aust
8C2 Wyoming State, USA
14A2 Wyoming USA
109D2 Wyong Aust

X

84D1 Xaidulla China
72D1 Xai Moron He R
China
101C3 Xai Xai Mozam
23B2 Xaltinguis Mexico
100A2 Xangongo Angola
46D1 Xanten Germany
55B2 Xánthi Greece
100B3 Xau,L Botswana
14B3 Xenia USA
72A2 Xiahe China
73C5 Xiamen China
72B3 Xi'an China
73B4 Xianfeng China
73C4 Xiangfan China
73C4 Xiang Jiang R China
73C4 Xiangtan Province,
China
73C4 Xianning China
72B3 Xianyang China
73A4 Xiao Shui R China
73D4 Xiapu China
73A4 Xichang China
23B1 Xicotepec Mexico
76C2 Xieng Khouang Laos
73B4 Xifeng China
86B1 Xigazê China
72A1 Xi He R China
72B2 Xiji China
73C4 Xi Jiang R China
72E1 Xiliao He R China
73B5 Xilin China
23B1 Xilitla Mexico
73D4 Xinfeng China
72C1 Xinghe China
73D5 Xingning China
73B4 Xingren China
72C2 Xingtai China
33G4 Xingu R Brazil
73B4 Xingxingxia China
73A4 Xingyi China
72A2 Xining China
72E2 Xinjin Liaoning,
China
73A3 Xinjin Sichuan, China
72D2 Xinwen China
72C2 Xin Xian China
72C2 Xinxiang China
73C3 Xinyang China
73C5 Xinyi Guangdong,
China
72D3 Xinyi Jiangsu, China
72D1 Xi Ujimqin Qi China
74A2 Xiuyan China
23B2 Xochimilco Mexico
73D3 Xuancheng China
73B3 Xuanhan China
72D1 Xuanhua China
73A4 Xuanwei China
72C3 Xuchang China
99E2 Xuddur Somalia
72A2 Xunhua China
73C5 Xun Jiang R China
69E2 Xunke China
73D5 Xunwu China
73C4 Xupu China
76E1 Xuwen China
73B4 Xuyong China
72D3 Xuzhou China

Y

73A4 Ya'an China
108B3 Yaapeet Aust
98B2 Yabassi Cam
68C1 Yablonovyy Khrebet
Mts Russian Fed
94C2 Yabrūd Syria
20B2 Yachats USA
30D3 Yacuiba Bol
87B1 Yādgir India
95A1 Yafran Libya
23A1 Yahualica Mexico
98C2 Yahuma Zaire
75B1 Yaita Japan
73A4 Yajiang China
20B1 Yakima USA
20B1 Yakima R USA

97B3 Yashkul'
97B3 Yako Burkina
98C2 Yakoma Zaire
74E2 Yakovlevka
12G3 Yakutat USA
12G3 Yakutat B USA
63E1 Yakutsk Russian Fed
77C4 Yala Thai
23B2 Yalalag Mexico
98C2 Yalinga CAR
109C3 Yallourn Aust
68B3 Yalong R China
73A4 Yalong Jiang R
China
54C2 Yalova Turk
60D5 Yalta Ukraine
74B2 Yalu Jiang R China
74D3 Yamagata Japan
74C4 Yamaguchi Japan
68D1 Yamarovka
Russian Fed
109D1 Yamba New S Wales,
Aust
108B2 Yamba S Australia,
Aust
99C2 Yambio Sudan
54C2 Yambol Bulg
71E4 Yamdena I Indon
Yam Kinneret =
Tiberias,L
108B1 Yamma Yamma,L
Aust
97B4 Yamoussoukro Ivory
Coast
85D3 Yamuna R India
86C1 Yamzho Yumco L
China
63F1 Yana R Russian Fed
108B3 Yanac Aust
75A2 Yanagawa Japan
87C1 Yanam India
72B2 Yan'an China
80B3 Yanbu'al Bahr
S Arabia
108B2 Yancannia Aust
72B3 Yancheng China
72B2 Yanchi China
108B1 Yandama R Aust
98C2 Yangambi Zaire
72C1 Yang He R China
73C5 Yangjiang China
76B2 Yangon Burma
72C2 Yangquan China
73C5 Yangshan China
73C3 Yangtze Gorges
China
72E3 Yangtze,Mouths of
the China
72D3 Yangzhou China
73B4 Yanhe China
74B2 Yanji China
108C3 Yanko R Aust
8D2 Yankton USA
72D1 Yan Shan _Hills_
108B1 Yantabulla Aust
72E2 Yantai China
72D2 Yanzhou China
98B2 Yaoundé Cam
71E4 Yapen I Indon
71E3 Yap Is Pacific O
24B2 Yaqui R Mexico
61G2 Yaransk Russian Fed
32C3 Yari R Colombia
74D3 Yariga-dake _Mt_
Japan
82B2 Yarkant He R China
86C1 Yarlung Zangbo
Jiang R China
7D5 Yarmouth Can
94B2 Yarmūk R Syria/
Jordan
61E2 Yaroslavl'
Russian Fed
94B2 Yarqon R Israel
109C3 Yarram Aust
109D1 Yarraman Aust
109C3 Yarrawonga Aust
60D2 Yartsevo
Russian Fed
63B1 Yartsevo
Russian Fed
32B2 Yarumal Colombia
97C3 Yashi Nig
97C4 Yashikera Nig
61F4 Yashkul' Russian Fed

84C1 Yasin Pak
59C3 Yasinya Ukraine
109C2 Yass Aust
109C2 Yass Aust
75A1 Yasugi Japan
18A2 Yass Center USA
98C2 Yatolema Zaire
74C4 Yatsushiro Japan
94B3 Yatta Israel
32C4 Yauri Peru
85D4 Yavatmāl India
74C4 Yawatahama Japan
76D2 Ya Xian China
9083 Yazd Iran
9083 Yazd-e Khvāst Iran
19B3 Yazoo R USA
19B3 Yazoo City USA
19B3 Yazoo City USA
59D3 Yedintsy Moldavia
108A2 Yeelanna Aust
60E3 Yefremov
Russian Fed
61F4 Yegorlyk R
Russian Fed
99D2 Yei Sudan
65H4 Yekaterinburg
Russian Fed
60E3 Yelets Russian Fed
44E1 Yell I Scot
87C1 Yellandu India
Yellow = Huang He
8B1 Yellowhead P Can
4G3 Yellowknife Can
5G4 Yellowmore R Aust
109C2 Yellow Mt Aust
69E3 Yellow Sea China/
Korea
8C2 Yellowstone R USA
8B2 Yellowstone L USA
6B1 Yelverton B Can
97C3 Yelwa Nig
81C4 Yemen Republic,
Arabian Pen
76C1 Yen Bai Viet
97B4 Yendi Ghana
76B1 Yengan Burma
63B2 Yeniseysk
Russian Fed
63B1 Yeniseyskiy Kryazh
Ridge Russian Fed
64J2 Yeniseyskiy Zal B
Russian Fed
12D2 Yentna R USA
43C4 Yeo R Eng
109C2 Yeoval Aust
43C4 Yeovil Eng
63C1 Yerbogachen
Russian Fed
65F5 Yerevan Armenia
21B2 Yerington USA
21B3 Yermo USA
69E1 Yerofey-Pavlovich
Russian Fed
94B3 Yeroham Israel
61G3 Yershov Russian Fed
Yerushalayim =
Jerusalem
92C1 Yeşil R Turk
94B2 Yesud Hama'ala
Israel
22A1 Yountville USA
73B4 Youyang China
92B2 Yozgat Turk
20B2 Yreka USA
39G7 Ystad Sweden
43C3 Ystwyth R Wales
44C3 Ythan R Scot
73C4 Yuan Jiang R
Hunan, China
73A5 Yuan Jiang R
Yunnan, China
73A4 Yuanmu China
72C2 Yuanping China
21A2 Yuba City USA
74E2 Yūbari Japan
25D3 Yucatán Pen Mexico
25D2 Yucatan Chan
Mexico/Cuba
72C2 Yuci China
63F2 Yudoma R
Russian Fed
73D4 Yudu China
73C4 Yueyang China
54A2 Yugoslavia
Republic, Europe
73B5 Yu Jiang R China

72B1 Yin Shan Upland
China
99D2 Yirga Alem Eth
99D2 Yirol Sudan
63D3 Yirshi China
73B5 Yishan China
72D2 Yishui China
55B3 Yíthion Greece
38J6 Yivieska Fin
73C4 Yiyang China
38J6 Yli-Kitka L Fin
38J5 Yli-Kitka L Fin
38J5 Yllorno Sweden
19A4 Yoakum USA
23B2 Yogope Mexico
78C4 Yogyakarta Indon
13D2 Yoho Nat Pk Can
98B2 Yokadouma Cam
75B2 Yokkaichi Japan
75B1 Yokohama Japan
75B1 Yokosuka Japan
74C3 Yonago Japan
74E3 Yonezawa Japan
73D4 Yong'an China
72A2 Yongchang China
74B3 Yŏngch'ŏn S Korea
73B4 Yongchuan China
72A2 Yongdeng China
73D5 Yongding China
72D2 Yongding He R
China
74B3 Yŏngdok S Korea
74B3 Yŏnghŭng N Korea
74B3 Yongju S Korea
72B2 Yongning China
16C2 Yonkers USA
49C2 Yonne R France
42D3 York Eng
18A1 York Nebraska, USA
16A3 York Pennsylvania,
USA
107D2 York,C Aust
108A2 Yorke Pen Aust
108A2 Yorketown Aust
7A4 York Factory Can
41C3 Yorkshire Moors
Moorland Eng
42D2 Yorkshire Wolds
Eng
5H4 Yorkton Can
22B2 Yosemite L USA
22C1 Yosemite Nat Pk
USA
75A2 Yoshii R Japan
75A2 Yoshino R Japan
61G2 Yoshkar Ola
Russian Fed
74B4 Yōsu S Korea
41B3 Youghal Irish Rep
45C3 Youghal Harb
Irish Rep
73B5 You Jiang R China
109C2 Young Aust
34D2 Young Urug
111A2 Young Range Mts
NZ
13E2 Youngstown Can
14B2 Youngstown Ohio,
USA

12C2 Yukon R Can/USA
4E3 Yukon Territory Can
76E1 Yulin Guangdong,
China
73C5 Yulin Guangxi, China
72B2 Yulin Shaanxi, China
9B3 Yuma USA
80D3 Yumen China
72D2 Yunan China
34A3 Yungay Chile
73C5 Yunkai Dashan Hills
China
108A2 Yunta Aust
72C3 Yunxi China
72C3 Yun Xian China
73B3 Yunyang China
33E5 Yu Shan Mt Taiwan
38L6 Yushkozero
Russian Fed
73D5 Yushu Tibet, China
73A5 Yuxi China
74F2 Yuzhno-Kuril'sk
Russian Fed
69G2 Yuzhno-Sakhalinsk
Russian Fed
61J3 Yuzh Ural Mts
Russian Fed
46A2 Yvelines Department,
France
47B1 Yverdon Switz

Z

56A2 Zaandam Neth
93D2 Zāb al Babir R Iraq
93D2 Zāb as Şaghir R Iraq
68D2 Zabaykal'sk
Russian Fed
59B3 Zabreh
Czech Republic
59B2 Zabrze Pol
23A2 Zacapu Mexico
24B2 Zacatecas Mexico
23B2 Zacatepec Morelos,
Mexico
23B2 Zacatepec Oaxaca,
Mexico
23B2 Zacatlan Mexico
23A1 Zacoalco Mexico
23B1 Zacualtipan Mexico
52C2 Zadar Croatia
76B3 Zadetkyi I Burma
50B2 Zafra Spain
59C1 Żagań Pol
95C1 Zagazig Egypt
98B1 Zagora Mor
52C1 Zagreb Croatia
91D4 Zāhedān Iran
94B2 Zahle Leb
51C2 Zahrez Chergui
Marshland Alg
61H2 Zainsk Russian Fed
98B3 Zaire Republic, Africa
98B3 Zaïre R Zaïre/Congo
54B2 Zaječar Yugos
68C1 Zakamensk
Russian Fed
93D2 Zakho Iraq
55B3 Zákinthos I Greece
59B3 Zakopane Pol
59B3 Zalaegerszeg Hung
59B3 Zalău Rom
59C1 Zalew Szczeciński Lg
Pol
98C1 Zalingei Sudan
63F2 Zaliv Akademii B
65G5 Zaliv Kara-Bogaz Gol
B Turkmenistan
74C2 Zaliv Petra Velikogo
B Russian Fed
69G2 Zaliv Turpeniya B
Russian Fed
95A2 Zaltan Libya
89H9 Zambesi R Mozam
100B2 Zambezi Zambia
100B2 Zambezi R Zambia
100B2 Zambia Republic,
Africa
79B4 Zamboanga Phil
79B4 Zamboanga Pen
Phil
58C2 Zambrów Pol
32B4 Zamora Ecuador
23A2 Zamora Mexico
50A1 Zamora Spain

59C2 Zamość Pol
72A3 Zamtang China
98B3 Zanaga Congo
50B2 Záncara R Spain
84D2 Zanda China
14B3 Zanesville USA
84B2 Zangla India
90A2 Zanjān Iran
73B5 Zanjitas Arg
34B2 Zanjon R Arg
99D3 Zanzibar Tanz
99D3 Zanzibar I Tanz
96C2 Zaouatallaz Alg
25B2 Zaozhuang China
93D2 Zap R Turk
39K7 Zapadnaja Dvina R
Russian Fed
65H3 Zapadno-Sibirskaya
Nizmennost'
Lowland Russian Fed
63B2 Zapadnyy Sayan Mts
Russian Fed
34A3 Zapala Arg
60E4 Zaporozh'ye Ukraine
93C2 Zara Turk
23A1 Zaragoza Mexico
50B1 Zaragoza Spain
90B2 Zarand Iran
90C3 Zarand Iran
80E2 Zaranj Afghan
33D2 Zarara Ven
72A5 Zarasai Lithuania
34D2 Zárate Arg
90B3 Zard Kuh Mt Iran
12H3 Zarembo I USA
84B2 Zarghun Shahr
Afghan
84B2 Zargun Mt Pak
97C3 Zaria Nig
92C3 Zarqa Jordan
32B4 Zaruma Ecuador
58B2 Zary Pol
96D1 Zarzis Tunisia
84D2 Zāskār Mts India
84D2 Zāskār R India
94C2 Zatara R Jordan
Zatoka Gdańska =
Gdańsk,G of
69E1 Zavitinsk
Russian Fed
59B2 Zawiercie Pol
63C2 Zayarsk Russian Fed
65K5 Zaysan Kazakhstan
82D3 Zayü China
68B4 Zayü Mt China
58B2 Zduńska Wola Pol
46B1 Zeebrugge Belg
94B3 Zeelim Israel
101G1 Zeerust S Africa
94B2 Zefat Israel
97C3 Zegueren
Watercourse Mali
99E1 Zeila Somalia
57C2 Zeitz Germany
72A2 Zêkog China
61G2 Zelenodol'sk
Russian Fed
39K6 Zelenogorsk
Russian Fed
47D1 Zell Austria
98C2 Zemio CAR
64F1 Zemlya Aleksandry I
Barents S
64F1 Zemlya Frantsa Iosifa
Is Barents S
64F1 Zemlya Georga I
Barents S
64H1 Zemlya Vil'cheka I
Barents S
73B4 Zenning China
47B1 Zermatt Switz
63E2 Zeya Russian Fed
63E2 Zeya Res
50A1 Zézere R Port
94B1 Zghorta Leb
58B2 Zgierz Pol
72D1 Zhangjiakou China
73D4 Zhangping China
72D2 Zhangwei He R
China
72E1 Zhangwu China
72A2 Zhangye China
73D5 Zhangzhou China

73C5 **Zhanjiang** China
73A4 **Zhanyi** China
73C5 **Zhaoqing** China
73A4 **Zhaotong** China
72D2 **Zhaoyang Hu** *L* China
61J4 **Zharkamys** Russian Fed
63E1 **Zhatay** Russian Fed
73D4 **Zhejiang** Province, China
67F3 **Zhengou** China
72C3 **Zhengzhou** China
72D3 **Zhenjiang** China
73A4 **Zhenxiong** China
73B4 **Zhenyuan** China
61F3 **Zherdevka** Russian Fed
73C3 **Zhicheng** China
68C1 **Zhigalovo** Russian Fed
73B4 **Zhijin** China
58D2 **Zhitkovichi** Belorussia
60C3 **Zhitomir** Ukraine
60D3 **Zhlobin** Belorussia
60C4 **Zhmerinka** Ukraine
84B2 **Zhob** Pak
58D2 **Zhodino** Latvia
72B2 **Zhongning** China

112C10 **Zhongshan** *Base* Ant
73C5 **Zhongshan** China
72B2 **Zhongwei** China
68B4 **Zhougdian** China
73E3 **Zhoushan Quandao** *Arch* China
72E2 **Zhuanghe** China
72A3 **Zhugqu** China
73C3 **Zhushan** China
73C4 **Zhuzhou** China
72D2 **Zibo** China
106C3 **Ziel,Mt** Aust
58B2 **Zielona Góra** Pol
76A1 **Zigaing** Burma
73A4 **Zigong** China
97A3 **Ziguinchor** Sen
23A2 **Zihuatanejo** Mexico
94B2 **Zikhron Ya'aqov** Israel
59B3 **Zilina** Slovakia
95A2 **Zillah** Libya
47D1 **Ziller** *R* Austria
47D1 **Zillertaler Alpen** *Mts* Austria
58D1 **Zilupe** Russian Fed
63C2 **Zima** Russian Fed
23B1 **Zimapan** Mexico
23B2 **Zimatlan** Mexico
100B2 **Zimbabwe** Republic, Africa

94B3 **Zin** *R* Israel
23B2 **Zinacatepec** Mexico
23A2 **Zinapécuaro** Mexico
97C3 **Zinder** Niger
73C4 **Zi Shui** China
23A2 **Zitácuaro** Mexico
57C2 **Zittau** Germany
72D2 **Ziya He** *R* China
72A3 **Ziyang** China
61J2 **Zlatoust** Russian Fed
59B3 **Zlin** Czech Republic
65K4 **Zmeinogorsk** Russian Fed
58B2 **Znin** Pol
59B3 **Znoimo** Czech Republic
100B3 **Zoekmekaar** S Africa
47B1 **Zofinger** Switz
72A3 **Zoigê** China
59D3 **Zolochev** Ukraine
101C2 **Zomba** Malawi
98B2 **Zongo** Zaire
92B1 **Zonguldak** Turk
97B4 **Zorzor** Lib
96A2 **Zouerate** Maur
54B1 **Zrenjanin** Serbia, Yugos
47C1 **Zug** Switz

47D1 **Zugspitze** *Mt* Germany
50A2 **Zujar** *R* Spain
100C2 **Zumbo** Mozam
23B2 **Zumpango** Mexico
97C4 **Zungeru** Nig
73B4 **Zunyi** China
76D1 **Zuo** *R* China
73B5 **Zuo Jiang** *R* China
47C1 **Zürich** Switz
47C1 **Zürichsee** *L* Switz
95A1 **Zuwärah** Libya
95A2 **Zuwaylah** Libya
61H2 **Zuyevka** Russian Fed
100B4 **Zvishavane** Zim
59B3 **Zvolen** Slovakia
54A2 **Zvornik** Bosnia-Herzegovina
97B4 **Zwedru** Lib
46D2 **Zweibrücken** Germany
47B1 **Zweisimmen** Switz
57C2 **Zwickau** Germany
56B2 **Zwolle** Neth
58C2 **Zyrardów** Pol
65K5 **Zyryanovsk** Kazakhstan
59B3 **Żywiec** Pol
94A1 **Zyyi** Cyprus